The 1987 MediaGuide

The 1987 MediaGuide

A Critical Review of the News Media's Recent Coverage Of the World Political Economy

Jude Wanniski
Editor

Peter A. Signorelli
Managing Editor
Patricia Koyce
Associate Editor

PERENNIAL LIBRARY

Harper & Row, Publishers, New York
Cambridge, Philadelphia, San Francisco, Washington
London, Mexico City, Sao Paulo, Singapore, Sydney

TV News and the Dominant Culture © 1986. Reprinted with permission of The Media Institute, 3017 M St., NW, Washington, D.C. 20007.

THE 1987 MEDIAGUIDE. Copyright © 1986, 1987 by Polyconomics, Inc. All rights reserved. Printed in the United States of America. No part of this book may be used or reproduced in any manner whatsoever without written permission except in the case of brief quotations embodied in critical articles and reviews. For information address Harper & Row, Publishers, Inc., 10 East 53rd Street, New York, N.Y. 10022. Published simultaneously in Canada by Fitzhenry & Whiteside Limited, Toronto.

First PERENNIAL LIBRARY edition published 1987.

LIBRARY OF CONGRESS CATALOG CARD NUMBER: 86-45706

ISBN: 0-06-055048-1
87 88 89 90 91 10 9 8 7 6 5 4 3 2 1

ISBN: 0-06-096124-4 (pbk.)
87 88 89 90 91 10 9 8 7 6 5 4 3 2 1

CONTENTS

INTRODUCTION 1

AN OVERVIEW OF THE PRINT MEDIA IN 1986
   1986 Press Developments 7
      Oberfeld and the *Insight* Kids 7
      Exit Abe, Enter Max 8
      Joseph Kraft's Empty Chair 9
      Musical Chairs: *Newsweek, TNR, USN&WR* 11
      Marshall Loeb's Good *Fortune* 13

   The Great Byline Inflation 14

   Major News Stories of 1986 19
      Challenger and Chernobyl 19
      Turmoil in South Africa and the Philippines 22
      The Global Economy 26
      Tripoli and Teheran 28
      Strategic Defense Initiative 32

   The Best Stories & Columns of 1986 35
      General Reporting 35
      Business/Financial Reporting 36
      Political Reporting 38
      Foreign Correspondence 39
      Commentary 40

A CRITIQUE OF TELEVISION NEWS
   A Picture Headline Service 42
   TV News and the Dominant Culture 45

PUBLICATIONS
   The Pacesetters
      The New York Times 61
      The Wall Street Journal 69
      The Washington Post 76

Major Publications
- *The American Spectator* 81
- *The Atlantic Monthly* 82
- *Aviation Week & Space Technology* 83
- *Barron's* 83
- *BusinessWeek* 85
- *Commentary* 86
- *Financial Times* 87
- *Forbes* 89
- *Foreign Affairs* 90
- *Foreign Policy* 92
- *Fortune* 93
- *Harper's* 95
- *Human Events* 96
- *Investor's Daily* 97
- *The Journal of Commerce* 99
- *The National Interest* 100
- *National Journal* 100
- *National Review* 102
- *The New Republic* 102
- *Newsweek* 103
- *Time* 106
- *USA Today* 108
- *U.S. News & World Report* 109
- *The Washington Times* 111

RATING GUIDE 113

HIGHEST RATED JOURNALISTS OF 1986 114

JOURNALISTS
- Financial Reporters & Columnists 117
- Foreign Correspondents 164
- National Security/Diplomatic Correspondents 220
- Political Columnists 231
- Social/Political Reporters 241
- Social/Political Commentators 262

BIOGRAPHICS 279

INDEX 365

The 1987 MediaGuide

INTRODUCTION

When we published the first *MediaGuide* in 1986, we knew what Orville and Wilbur Wright must have felt like at Kittyhawk, watching their gawky, heavier-than-air prototype lift off the ground for a few dozen yards. The fact that the *MediaGuide* got off the ground at all was so gratifying that we faced the complaints about its imperfections with serenity. "It's too ideological." "It's too subjective." "It's loaded with factual errors." "It isn't comprehensive." "It isn't fair." We could agree with all of this, certain that we could do better on the second flight. At least we knew it could be done.

What we had set out to do was produce a kind of *Michelin Guide* to the national print media, evaluating the work of the top reporters and columnists and rating them the way Michelin rates the restaurants of Europe. That was the easy part. The hard part would be to at least begin to win the acceptance of the news media itself, in the way the chefs and hoteliers of France accept as authoritative the observations of Michelin.

It may take several editions of the *MediaGuide* before we feel comfortable on that point. But at least the first edition was tentatively received as being plausible. Typical was the observation of *The Journal of Commerce*: "Mr. Wanniski and his crew at Polyconomics have opened a Pandora's Box with their guide. Rebuttals from wounded reporters and columnists will certainly be forthcoming. Many will ask why Mr. Wanniski should be ordained the high priest of journalistic criticism. It's a fair question, but with few other guides of this type in existence, why shouldn't Mr. Wanniski and his crew at Polyconomics be the ones to publish one? Mr. Wanniski has a strong background in journalism, and the guide is well researched."

Why have a *MediaGuide* at all? For the same reason that restaurant guides are indispensable to the culinary arts. Criticism is essential for excellence in any endeavor, including journalism. The only press criticism around has been internal and unsystematic — an "ombudsman" gingerly questioning his newspaper's play of one story or another, or citing reportorial flaws of some sort. External criticism is left to the letters columns of a newspaper or organizations like Accuracy In Media (a conservative watchdog for liberal biases) or the Media Institute (pondering broad themes and media issues). There was nothing to serve serious consumers of news — news gourmets — by identifying the various levels of quality throughout the top of the profession. Individual journalists have no systematic yardstick of achievement, and for recognition can only aspire to the big prizes, the Pulitzer and Loeb awards, for example. It has been my thought for many years that such a standard, applied to journalists rather than to their publications, would serve the interests of communication generally.

Consumers of news are forever complaining that there is too much to read, but that's like saying there's too much to eat in Paris, with its thousands of restaurants. As the *Michelin Guide* identifies the top few hundred, reducing the problem of choice for those who want only the best, so we can help identify those journalistic bylines that we think are worth special attention.

The guide is limited to the "national press," newspapers and periodicals that are readily available to national policymakers in Washington, D.C. and New York City, the political, financial, and communication centers of the nation. The major newspaper chains — Knight-Ridder, Gannett, Newhouse, Scripps-Howard, Hearst, etc. — may think of themselves as being national. But without outlets in the opinion centers, they must be considered clusters of regional papers. The *New York Post* and *Daily News* are considered local because their audience is local. They have negligible impact on Wall Street or national policymaking in Washington. "It's true," says the national political correspondent for one of the big chains. "It's like a tree falling in the forest when you don't appear in Washington. Nobody hears it."

Several of the big-circulation dailies that act as if they were national — with big Washington bureaus and a foreign corps — must still be considered regional. The *Chicago Tribune*, the *Philadelphia Inquirer*, the *Denver Post*, for example, "think regional," as they should. The *Los Angeles Times* more than any other regional paper strains to radiate a national attitude, with an excellent far-flung foreign service and a beefy Washington bureau. It goes to great expense to airlift copies from L.A. to Washington, putting them in sidewalk coinboxes in hopes of being bought by a mover or shaker. And in 1986 it bought the Baltimore Sunpapers for an incredible $700 million view of the nation's capital. But the *L.A. Times* just isn't part of the information grapevine of people who do national business from the two power centers.

Where staff people from these newspapers appear in the *MediaGuide* — and there are quite a few from the *L.A. Times* — it's because they have managed to come to our attention through irregular channels, producing material of interest that surmounted the regional obstacle. Most of these are in the excellent *LAT* foreign service, which is competitive with the national press. We added *The Christian Science Monitor* to our subscription list in 1986, on the argument that it clearly thinks national and in fact styles itself as "An International Newspaper." The *Financial Times* of London, now printed in the United States for same-day delivery into the power centers, has become indispensable at Polyconomics, as it has to Wall Street, and thus qualifies as national by our definition.

There are several thousand journalists who work for the national newspapers and periodicals, but we consider only those whose work bears on national matters. Of these, we select those whose work stands out on a regular basis, either because of excellence or prominence or both. Unlike the *Michelin Guide*, which only rewards excellence, the *MediaGuide* takes note of those prominent journalists who have had unsatisfactory years. As a rule, we focus on the 1986 product of individual journalists, and there is no reason why a rating can't leap from unsatisfactory to extraordinary, or *vice versa*, year over year.

Our criteria are described in detail in the ratings section, but generally we are looking first for objective reporters and subjective commentators. We also want depth of information or analysis, accuracy, compactness and lively writing. Because there are so many variables involved, the rating process is as intangible as that which goes into a dining guide. We'll take a degree of bias in a reporter, for example, if he or she is exceptional on other counts. "Objective" reporting in and of itself means as little to a news gourmet as the caloric count means to a food gourmet. For columnists, objectivity is as much a negative as blandness is in a dessert; we read columnists and commentators for sharp, even pungent, well-shaped points of view, "liberal" or "conservative."

The *MediaGuide* can't pretend to be comprehensive because it isn't possible for the crew at Polyconomics and our part-time news gourmets — about forty people in all — to read everything. In a reaction to the *1986 Guide*, one journalist who got a lower rating than he thought he deserved wrote to complain that we obviously hadn't seen better pieces he'd written than the ones we cited, including one that his magazine hadn't run. We are in the same boat with the *Michelin Guide* on this: We can't review the meals served on nights we weren't around. To protect against hasty judgements, though, we sample throughout the year, and get multiple confirmations from our reviewers.

Of roughly 900 journalists nominated at midyear, half were winnowed out during the final selection process, usually because of a lack of prominence. Reporters assigned to a quiet newsbeat or foreign correspondents buried in the boondocks aren't under sufficient pressure to test their level of excellence. The luck of the assignment is a factor. The sudden crisis in the Philippines in 1986 brought reporters to our attention who normally would be taken for granted.

We also take the wire services for granted. The wires are accurate and objective in their dispatches and accounts, but have little flavor because they must satisfy many tastes in many editors; they are not for news gourmets. Reporters who have the freedom to step out of these bounds, but for some reason or another don't, wind up getting culled in our nominating process.

Many of the journalists who "didn't make the cut" this year for the rating section, are included in the separate biographical section — a kind of "who's who" in the print media. We think this section will be especially useful to people in the news and to public-relations people who work for newsmakers. To a businessman about to be interviewed by a reporter from *BusinessWeek* or *The Wall Street Journal*, or a political candidate about to be interviewed by the reporter for the *Times* or *Post*, it's always useful to have a bit of background on the interviewer, if only for opening small talk to break the ice. We also believe the biographical section will be used by journalists to help identify each other, for career or social purposes. We've already heard from editors who have used the first *MediaGuide* as a source of information on the talent pool; the biographical data will be a further aid. A common trait of journalists is that they rarely ask biographical questions of each other; members of the Washington press corps will know each other for years without realizing they're from the same town or college. We expect this section will expand in subsequent years as journalists increase participation in the *MediaGuide*. If nothing else, they'll know their obituary writers will get the facts right.

In the introduction to the first *MediaGuide*, we observed that many of those applauded for excellence may resent being judged at all, and those not applauded may resent it even more. And there were all variety of complaints, some furious, some wounded. But the most common reaction was: "Why didn't anyone ever think of this before? It's a great idea!" The truth is that it has been thought of before, but the work involved is so daunting — if it's to be done right — that it could only be a labor of love. Indeed, the nicest thing said about the first effort came from Malcolm Forbes, Jr., who observed: "Wanniski...former editorial writer for *The Wall Street Journal*, is not one of those cranks waging war against the press. Quite the opposite. He's a voracious reader who loves the print media."

We also noted a year ago that we hoped those journalists who "slipped in '85 can recoup in '86....the aim is to make the press corps more conscious of a standard, including their own, to push toward, to heighten performance and excellence." Again and again in preparing this *1987 Guide*, we found ourselves pleased to be able to upgrade journalists — especially many we had rated unsatisfactory last year, and we took no pleasure in subtracting from others. Overall, we found more improvement than not in the performance of the print media. We hope readers of this *MediaGuide* can say the same of it.

HOW TO USE THE GUIDE

People don't usually curl up by the fire with a restaurant guide for an evening of reading. But the *MediaGuide* is designed to be entertaining reading as well as a reference work. In this information age, millions of Americans *must* stay on top of business and political news to stay competitive in their jobs. It helps to have a reliable framework for absorbing the news as it comes hurtling at us without a letup, from all the news media. At the front of the book are short essays on major developments in the print media during 1986, commentary on the "dominant culture" and television news, a review of the big stories of the year and who covered them best, and discussions of the major national newspapers and periodicals. This material is designed to sharpen the reader's

MediaGuide

sense of the news flow, the process of news communication, how it is being altered to adapt to the fast-changing national and global political economy.

The average reader will prefer to start by skipping about and finding familiar journalists, the columnists who more and more appear on television. Few readers will recognize more than a few dozen names here. Because there never has been a *MediaGuide* such as this, only a small number of news junkies have taken the time and trouble to find out who is consistently good, or bad, as a way of efficiently getting on top of the news. The entries are written to the journalists themselves, few of whom we know personally, with the idea that the reader can look over our shoulder, and perhaps become familiar enough with their bylines to make use of the evaluations.

It's best, then, as readers of our pilot edition informed us last year, to go from "cover to cover" after the initial sampling. Then, when the reader gets to the several hundred critical entries, even though the names are not familiar, the commentaries on their work will fit against the previous fabric.

One of our aims at Polyconomics is to make our clients in the financial and industrial world more efficient communication terminals, "receivers" of news. We believe readers of our *1987 MediaGuide* will benefit in the same way, and hope you do.

ABOUT POLYCONOMICS

Polyconomics, Inc., was founded in 1978 by Jude Wanniski, formerly Associate Editor of *The Wall Street Journal*, to advise corporate and financial clients on the emerging "Supply-side economics," a phrase he coined in *Journal* editorials of the mid-70s. The company now advises more than a hundred of the nation's biggest institutional investors and industrial corporations on the financial markets and the impact of political decisions on the unfolding world political economy. Much of the staff time of Polyconomics, Inc., in Morristown, N.J., is spent reading the world press.

Wanniski's book, *The Way the World Works*, was published in 1978 to critical acclaim. Irving Kristol called it "The best economic primer since Adam Smith"; Arthur Laffer called it "the best book on economics ever written," and Representative Jack Kemp cited it as "The original manifesto of the modern supply-side movement." Wanniski is generally credited with discovering, in 1977, the triggering cause of the 1929 Wall Street Crash, a finding central to the revival of supply-side economic theory. The *1987 MediaGuide*, though, does not revolve around economics, although it is an important element in the continuing news flow.

As an editorial writer for the *Journal* from 1972 to 1978, Wanniski concentrated on domestic and global political economics and energy, an early leader in debunking "the energy crisis." He was named "Petroleum Writer of the Year" in 1976 for his energy editorials. Wanniski joined Dow Jones & Co. in 1965 as Washington columnist for *The National Observer*, and earlier worked for newspapers in Alaska, California and Nevada.

With Alan Reynolds as chief economist, Polyconomics has been cited by *Barron's, Bond Week*, and *The Wall Street Journal* for the accuracy of its forecasts. Reynolds had previously been chief international economist for the First National Bank of Chicago, and earlier had been economics editor of *National Review*.

Managing Editor of the *MediaGuide* is Peter A. Signorelli. Patricia M. Koyce is Associate Editor. Ronald deLaRosa, general manager of Polyconomics, was publisher of the *MediaGuide*. They were assisted by Alan Reynolds, John Passacantando, Barbara Haslam, Donna White and Michael George of the Polyconomics staff. About 45 friends, associates and volunteers — the *MediaGuide's* "news gourmets" — who wish to remain anonymous, contributed to the project.

MediaGuide

AN OVERVIEW OF THE PRINT MEDIA IN 1986

1986 PRESS DEVELOPMENTS

Oberfeld and the *Insight* Kids

The Washington Times Company began publishing its weekly *Insight* magazine in September 1985. The first several issues seemed so sophomoric, the concept behind it so implausible, that we did not even mention the publication in the *1986 MediaGuide*. The Unification Church of Rev. Sun Myung Moon had blown several million dollars on a national weekly version of the *Times* before closing it down. *Insight* also looked like a sure loser.

One of the major press developments of 1986 was the dazzling critical success of the newsweekly, although it is surely costing its backers a mint. Because it isn't for sale or paid subscription, but is given away without charge to qualified, upscale readers who request it, the entire cost of the handsomely glossy, big-staff periodical must be borne by advertising. At year's end there seem precious few advertisements in *Insight*, yet the "subscription" list is said to be about 1 million. We run into it in executive offices, government bureaus, dentists' offices, barbershops, and on coffee tables everywhere, so we do not doubt the circulation claim. The expectation at the Times Company is that it will eventually catch on with Madison Avenue and ad revenues will make it a moneymaker, even to the extent of offsetting a significant piece of the giant subsidy the church provides the publishing company. The big unexpected drawback: anonymous callers complaining to corporate officers about their ads in a "Moonie" paper, which of course spooks some.

Because of the high quality of *Insight*'s editorial content, clearly it has a lot of its gratis readers rooting for its success. Instead of trying to emulate the big three newsweeklies by trying to digest the news to capsulize the world, *Insight* is more nearly like the now defunct *National Observer*, the Dow Jones newsweekly that concentrated on features "off the news," on the assumption that the upscale audience it was trying to reach had gotten a good look at the breaking news on radio, TV or in the local paper.

Insight got off to its feeble start in 1985 by trying to get by without any staff-written material. It would simply repackage the newsfeatures of the daily *Washington Times* and save a lot of money! This was the original thought at the *National Observer*, which also proved impractical. This was clearly the biggest reason why *Insight* seemed to improve dramatically in the spring of '86. Managing Editor Kirk E. Oberfeld, 41, had originally argued for resident staff, and after the first several issues the publishers agreed the magazine was stale.

He hired two dozen reporters, with an average age of about 26, neither cubs nor veterans (or deadwood). By guiding them away from breaking news toward imaginative ideas and angles ahead of the news or just behind it, Oberfeld and the other "senior editors" (in their 20s and 30s) quickly produced an astonishingly lively, readable and informative weekly. In January we were still throwing it out with a glance. By April we were forced to allot time to read it thoroughly. By September we were reading it with pleasure.

In this era of byline inflation and collective journalism, Oberfeld went in precisely the opposite direction. Like the *National Observer*, the staff covers the world from headquarters, with no regional or foreign bureaus. Instead of eight bylines on a single cover story actually written by yet another editor, which is routine at *Time, Newsweek* and *U.S. News*, the *Insight* covers are often divided into three separate stories — an umbrella piece and two long sidebars — each written by the same reporter! We first noticed this innovation in the May 12 edition, with a cover on "Booming Asia at the Crossroads," with one reporter, Adam Platt, delivering juicy takeouts on Hong Kong, South Korea, Singapore and Taiwan, and a separate interview with Asian expert Richard Holbrook. What a meal! Beautifully prepared by a 27-year-old we'd never seen before.

Throughout the year the practice was repeated, with tripart cover stories on the Israeli economy, 3-24; Nicaragua, 4-28; professional sports, 8-25; Iraq, 9-22; the space shuttle, 10-20; the drug hype, 10-27; and Japanese high-fashion, 11-3, to name some of the best of many. Inexperience, inconsistency and error appear, of course, but these drawbacks are swamped by the joy of having single storytellers master their subjects and spin them out with precise word shadings in unified themes. The Oberfeld whiz kids, growing in this hothouse atmosphere, are not only producing a sparkling magazine. They're also participating in a reform that we believe will have far-reaching effects on American journalism, toward greater development of individual talent and stardom, away from collective efforts. For the moment, at least as long as Oberfeld can maintain this high energy level and the Unification angels maintain the cash, *Insight* is one of the most interesting happenings in print news in years.

Exit Abe, Enter Max

On October 19 a long-awaited puff of smoke went up on the front page of *The New York Times*, announcing an event in a way as important to American journalism as the naming of a new pope is to the Roman Catholic Church: the report of A.M. (Abe) Rosenthal's successor as executive editor of the *Times*. Rosenthal, bumping into the 65-retirement rule, gave way to Max Frankel, 56, who had been editor of the editorial page for 10 years and was considered the front-runner for the job.

MediaGuide

This is big stuff, very big stuff. The editor of the *Times*, like the sovereign pontiff, doesn't have actual firepower. But for those of us who believe the pen is mightier than the sword, the fellow at the top of the most important newspaper in the world is a big cheese indeed. Especially when the publisher, Arthur Ochs (Punch) Sulzberger, generally stands aside, granting his executive editor czar-like powers. Ben Bradlee has similar powers at *The Washington Post*, Katharine and son Donald Graham watching from aloft. Arnaud de Borchgrave is the Top Gun at the smaller-caliber *Washington Times*, the Rev. Moon at an even loftier perch. But that's it. The top editors elsewhere tend to be gray-flannel types, controlled by owners and boards of directors and their own concentric (as opposed to eccentric) views of how newspapers should be run.

The position at the *NYT* is so important that it was news that Abe would turn 65 in May 1987, and would probably retire sooner. *The Washington Post* celebrated the event as soon as it was decently possible, with a gleeful three-part series in the "Style" section (January 7-9) by Eleanor Randolph, who covers the press for the *Post*. The headlines tell a story: "The Rich and Troubled Times," 1-7; "Abe Rosenthal, Letting Go," 1-8; "Grasping for the Keys to the Kingdom," 1-9. It seemed as if the entire intellectual, social, cultural, political firmament over the New York-Washington power corridor was trembling in anticipation. And it was! The whole point of the *Post* exercise was to remind the liberal establishment that Abe had let them down by moving the *Times* to the center, and it was time to line up for the power struggle ahead. At all costs, it was clear, John Vinocur, the neoconservative's candidate, one of Abe's proteges, had to be kept from the throne. Manhattan's Upper West Side could not stand the shock. (Vinocur heads back to Paris for a turn at the helm of the *International Herald Tribune*, a rather large solace.)

Will Max Frankel get the *Times* off center, back to port? Perhaps, unconsciously. But just a touch, just enough so the smart set will notice, but it will take years, through the effects of Frankel's participation in the personnel process. The more interesting question is whether Frankel can maintain the quality of the *Times*, which is at its highest level in more than a generation. The probability is that he will not, only because Abe's is such a hard act to follow, a hedgehog to Frankel's fox. But just by a touch, the paper notching down just enough for the news gourmets to notice, but it will take years to show up. And maybe it won't. Maybe it will get even better, we hope.

Joseph Kraft's Empty Chair

One of the most important print media events of 1986, although we did not quite realize it at the time, was the death of syndicated columnist Joe Kraft on January 9. Our entry in the *1986 MediaGuide* read as follows: "Kraft, Joseph. *Los Angeles Times*. (★★) Like Reston of the *NY Times*, Kraft's a spokesman for Old Establishment thinking, recirculated as 'moderate pragmatism.' Worth watching because signals of change in elite opinion often appear in his columns. Important pipeline to the latest in Establishment strategies on arms control, detente, even Volcker's mindset. But bad health catches him in '85, he ruminates more, reports less, and gets by with 'one source' columns. Two of his '85 best: 'Power Blueprint,' on emergence of Shultz/McFarlane combination, 4-18; 'A Near Miss,' on the Bonn economic summit, re monetary reform, 5-9.''

We appended the following line: "(Joe Kraft died on 1-9-86. We leave this item as typeset earlier. A friend and colleague, he will be difficult to replace.)"

In fact, we didn't realize until late in 1986 how dependent we had become on Joseph Kraft's syndicated column, which appeared regularly in *The Washington Post*, for all the reasons we cited. For at least 35 years there has been some one journalist in the symbolic chair Kraft occupied — the columnist "in the know" when it came to Establishment thinking. Reston of the *NY Times* was the dominant figure in the 1950s and '60s in fulfilling this function, but Kraft began taking over in the Nixon years, perhaps because he had a better feel for the GOP wing of the Establishment, but also because Reston began to wind down and was not able to get up to speed on the new global economic issues. Kraft was still young enough to study up, to learn at least enough about global money and trade to stay "in the know."

Where is the new Reston-Kraft? When we first consciously became aware of the vacuum we also realized we were not getting from all sources the distinctive notes being struck by the one individual. Reston, of course, still writes his column, but he should have retired it years ago to work on his memoirs. Hobart Rowen of *The Washington Post* and Leonard Silk of the *NY Times* give us a piece of the pie, relating to the political economy, and Rowen especially seemed to stretch in 1986 to fill the gap left by Kraft. But they are both nearing 70, really too old to "study up" on strategic arms and other non-economic power concerns of the Establishment, learning the networks of people involved, even if they wanted to.

Michael Kinsley, editor of *The New Republic*, seems a possible candidate for the chair. But as good as he is at what he does, he would have to spend several years living cheek by jowel with Establishmentarians to get the rhythms, at the same time learning the reporter's craft. Kinsley, lawyer and former "Nader Raider," is young enough, but it is hard to imagine him developing sources, rubbing elbows, going to all the right dinner parties, etc., which is what it's all about.

Peter T. Kilborn of the *NY Times* has the youth, 47, and the lofty arrogance required to learn the position, the best reporter around on global political finance. But Kilborn, like Rowen and Silk, may be too weak on power politics and the strategic issues to train for the assignment anytime soon. He could do it, but he wouldn't be ready for a half dozen years at least. R.W. (Johnny)

MediaGuide 11

Apple has the credentials on paper, with tours in Saigon and Africa, and as national political correspondent and London Bureau Chief — as if the *Times* was training him for the chair. But his decade in London was too uneventful. Like, zip. No, not Apple.

The Washington Post has a cadre of youngsters who could go into training now, to compete for the assignment down the line: Sidney Blumenthal, Paul Taylor, David Hoffman. But they don't seem quite right either, even as raw material. They seem to like what they're doing. *The Wall Street Journal* isn't the right place for the chair, although there are plenty of liberal establishment types at the paper.

While the profession composes itself, contemplating the problem, it could be that the chair may be occupied for a few years by the gentlemen who has just bowed out at the *NY Times* in a puff of smoke: Abe Rosenthal, 65. Now listed on the masthead as Associate Editor, Rosenthal is not going out to pasture, but will have space twice weekly for a column on whatever. This man, one of the Great Reporters and Newsmen of Our Time, could surely fill the Reston-Kraft chair for five, even ten years. At the top of the heap for 20 years, Abe is Mr. Lofty himself, with mainline ties to all elements of the Establishment. In 1987, if he's willing to exert himself that much, Rosenthal could amply fill the Kraft Chair. We'll see.

Musical Chairs: *Newsweek, TNR, USN&WR*

The newsweeklies didn't have a very good 1986. They're all more or less losing revenues on a slight decline. They still have multi-million circulations and represent an important supplement to television news and the local newspapers for Main Street America. But as the U.S. population has become more educated in the last 20 years, the function served by *Time, Newsweek,* and *U.S. News & World Report* has been largely taken over by the increase in the quality of the other print media, especially the major national newspapers. The newsweeklies no longer seem as vital as they were even through the 1960s, when they were still read by the upper tier of opinion leaders and policymakers, and so were integral to the national discourse.

It isn't possible to say that there is something intrinsically wrong with the newsweekly concept "in this day and age," only that the big three have not changed in the ways that could have kept them in the play. As *The Wall Street Journal* became reliably available from coast to coast on its day of publication, created a foreign service at least on a par with the newsweeklies, and expanded coverage in all the "departments" that had been the purview of the weeklies — science, education, law, medicine, leisure and arts — as well as national politics, the relative attraction of the newsweeklies declined. The upgrading of national distribution of the *NY Times*, which also added special sections on sports, science and "living," took another bite. The newsweekly circulations are impressive, but they are smaller percentages of the highly educated. And in order to keep the numbers high, the magazines have made their news coverage more "entertaining" and marginally less reliable. We were harsh last year in our observation on *Time*'s Gorbachev cover. This year, *Newsweek*'s Philippine coverage was the deplorable standout, although its South Africa and Libya material was plain awful.

We'd thought in 1985 that Morton Kondracke's move from *The New Republic* to be *Newsweek*'s Washington bureau chief might crack through the "regimentation, homogenization and incrementalism" that afflicts the newsmags generally. But Kondracke did not last through '86, returning to *TNR* in late summer after demonstrating an inability to "wag the dog," i.e., New York. The consensus, we gather, is that Kondracke wasn't the right fellow to lead some kind of reform, and wasn't up to running the bureau. Trying to act as intermediary between his staff writers and the New York editors, he fought with both and lost on both ends — several of his better hands were recruited away during the year, to *U.S. News*, the *WSJ*, and the *Los Angeles Times*. The new bureau chief, Evan Thomas, 35, out of *Time*'s Washington Bureau, was hired by another former *Time* newsman, Stephen Smith, who had been hired early in 1986 as executive editor of *Newsweek*.

A widely-read article in the *Washington Journalism Review* by Barbara Matusow in the November 1986 issue ("Trauma at *Newsweek*: The Struggle to Reverse the Slide") gives all the grisly details. But there is one especially interesting report: "The morale problem in (the) Washington (bureau) and throughout *Newsweek* generally goes beyond personalities. Editors are seeking to 'reinvent the magazine,' as they like to say, in the hopes of becoming the kind of 'hot book' *Newsweek* was in the late 1960s and early 1970s. In the process, they are finding that the journalistic skills they once valued are changing. 'We're looking for more individualistic writers who can do big stories,' says Steve Smith. 'We need people who can not only report, but who can write, think and conceptualize. The competition tries to speak with one voice. We try to speak with many. We are encouraging our younger writers to use their own voice and make what they say more surprising to readers.'"

To be sure, the magazine has to change, and the kind of transformation Smith talks about sounds good, but it will take a lot longer to pull off than he imagines (and is probably finding out). And there is no way of knowing, once they get to where they think they want to be, if it will be profitable.

Another important lateral move among the weeklies in 1986 was Mike Ruby's jump from *Newsweek* in New York, where he'd been the No. 3 man, to *U.S. News* in Washington as No. 2 to David R. Gergen. Gergen, though, is not a journalist, having come to the magazine as an associate editor from the Reagan Administration where he was Director of Communications — and previously

MediaGuide 13

a speechwriter in the Nixon and Ford administrations. When Shelby Coffey III quit as *USN&WR* editor early in 1986 for an easier job at the *Dallas Times Herald,* which he left shortly thereafter, the real estate tycoon who owns *U.S. News,* Mortimer Zuckerman, elevated Gergen to prove the Peter Principle.

A year ago we said: "It has been a sad sight to watch *U.S. News & World Report* dying by inches, year after year sinking into the ooze, irrelevant in the power centers and a factor only in Junction City, if that....What would (Zuckerman) do to pull this old warhorse out of the quicksand?....Let's give him '86." As it turns out, '86 was spent figuring out that he and Gergen needed somebody like Mike Ruby to run the magazine. Ruby arrived just in time for the Soviet snatching of Nicholas Daniloff, the *U.S. News* Moscow correspondent, a great piece of luck for Zuckerman in that it reminded the nation that there *was* an old warhorse under all that quicksand. It also gave Gergen and Zuckerman the opportunity to go on all the talk shows and tell how their magazine was getting exclusive interviews with Nick Daniloff.

Let's give them '87.

Marshall Loeb's Good *Fortune*

There was no publication we were more critical of in the *1986 MediaGuide* than *Fortune*. We had been great admirers of this flagship of business periodicals, founded by Henry Luce at the dawn of the Great Depression. It had been the "hot" publication of the 1960s, its monthly issue awaited eagerly by up-and-comers who wanted to know what they should be thinking about big business and more modern, stylish Republican politics. The magazine soured in the early 1970s, going out of sync with newer modes and creaking with the weight of deadwood on its staff. The decision to go biweekly a decade ago gave it a new lease on life as a score of younger writers were inhaled to fill all that new space. The magazine didn't make it back to its earlier eminence, but at least was back in the thick of things by the late 1970s.

As we put it last year, "A steady decline began with the arrival of William S. Rukeyser as managing editor, one of the great disappointments in the current era of American journalism. Brother of 'Wall Street Week's' Louis, William S. came from a successful tenure as editor of *Money*, with a winning personality and a reputation as a can-do kind of guy." But over the Rukeyser years we found ourselves spending less and less time with *Fortune*. What was wrong? Writers who had fled told us the layers of bureaucracy were smothering spontaneity, the editorial bottlenecks were approaching gridlock, and the top brass at Time, Inc. hover and intervene — the net result being a hopelessly impacted mediocrity. Rukeyser either lacked the authority to break through these crusts or was not the strategic thinker we'd been led to believe. We were told he made it a point to read every word of every *Fortune* before it went into the book. A *Fortune* editor might have managed that when it was a monthly. But the top strategist should be reading material published by others, especially the dailies, and mixing and mingling at political and business gatherings to catch a feel for the future.

These observations had barely been out for three weeks and a change was made at *Fortune*. Rukeyser's departure for a Time, Inc. post in Europe was announced, and his successor at *Money*, Marshall Loeb, 56, was named the new editor at *Fortune*. Loeb's good fortune is that where he had a tough Rukeyser act to follow at *Money*, he now has an easy Rukeyser act to follow. And he can bring the magazine up to a certain degree simply by showing up and puffing his pipe in a knowing way. When a team has been losing it tends to quit on its manager, and it can improve its scoring just by a change at the helm, for awhile.

We did not expect we'd see improvement in 1986, given the fact that Loeb did not take the reins until midyear. But there is no question there is now more than a pulsebeat at *Fortune*. Our serious readers report that by November they were spending 45 minutes on an issue against their recollection of 15 early in the year. Loeb got himself started by reading old, old copies of *Fortune*, to get a feel for the magic in the magazine's golden era, which is a good sign. He's also spending less time copyediting the magazine and more time talking to people outside *Fortune* trying to pick up the throb of the political economy. The issue of October 27, with Digital Equipment's Ken Olsen on the cover, was the best in years, with a liveliness and easy reading reminiscent of the *Fortune* of yore.

It's much too soon to say Loeb has revived the magazine. The team may quit on him sooner or later if the fundamental problems that bedeviled the Rukeyser years, whatever they are, can't be corrected. But so far, so good.

THE GREAT BYLINE INFLATION

In 1960, or thereabouts, Bernard Kilgore, then the visionary editor of *The Wall Street Journal*, issued a directive to all hands outlawing the use of double bylines. "By John Doe and Mary Roe" was no longer allowed at the top of *Journal* stories. It had to be one or the other or none at all. Other editors of the newspaper objected to the Kilgore edict, thinking it unfair to deny one reporter or another byline recognition when they had worked on a story. But Kilgore had the power of a czar at the time and out went the double bylines.

Vermont Royster recalls another famous Kilgore "ukase," as he terms the edicts: that no front-page leader (the day's main story offerings in columns one and six) be allowed to continue to an inside page. It had to be self-contained, to spare the busy businessman the need to slog through lengthy treatises that

MediaGuide   15

the reporter should be able to cover if he followed another Kilgore ukase: two facts per line!

If he were still around, the legendary Kilgore would not be pleased with developments at the *Journal*. Not only do all the leaders jump to the inside, often filling entire pages. But the center column, called an A-hed, also usually jumps inside. A-heds were traditionally designed to give the *Journal* readers a quick dose of cheer by musing on some quirky, upbeat feature that was related to the business world. They are still quirky, but rarely quick, and seldom related to business. We doubt the busy businessman stops very often for their cheer. As they've lengthened, they've become limp.

The front page is still anchored by the paper's best read columns, the "What's News" digest. But very often this is the only place in the *Journal* where the two-facts-per-line rule is observed. In Kilgore's day, bright, young reporters were assigned the news digest, at first spending hours boiling an earth-shaking event into a paragraph. Where you see skintight writing in the *Journal* today, it's usually a veteran like Alan Otten or William Carley, who learned their craft in the Kilgore era. The size of the staff has at least tripled in 25 years and the young recruits no longer get this kind of institutional training.

Kilgore's idea was not to save space, but to get to the essence of communication. Time is money; it's also a non-renewable resource. If the 4 million readers of the *Journal* could save 10 seconds a day by tighter writing, they'd save 11,000 man-hours daily. The readers know when they're making good use of their time, and will spend more time with a newspaper that is communicating with them efficiently.

Skintight writing can only do so much. Reporters have to have the raw material, the stuff and substance of news, before communication can really be efficient. Skimpy material is unsatisfying no matter how tightly written. This is why Kilgore, we think, banned the double byline. Collective journalism, like collective farming, is inherently inefficient. Most reporters get into the business because of their youthful byline fantasies (By Clark Kent, By Lois Lane). Those who know they are wholly accountable for the material under their byline are sensitive to its quality in every nuance. The pressure of time, of deadlines, forces all reporters to "go with what they have," to end the telephoning, interviewing, reporting, and assemble the material. On a big story that counts, on a major publication that counts, a reporter facing a deadline of hours or even a fraction of an hour sometimes passes through a psychological threshold of fear and panic that releases mental reserves. Time stretches. Fingers fly. The effort that seemed impossible ends in a quiet exultation of achievement, a journalistic "high." This addictive high is one reason newspaper people get into and stay in the business, and it's where the byline counts the most — both to the writer and the reader.

Editors who put two, three or more reporters to work on the same piece make it easier to get the reporting done. On business "roundups" this is unavoidable: sampling coast-to-coast grass roots reaction to a presidential economic initiative, for example. But then, the practice has been to identify the article as a roundup, and display no byline at all. Here, for example, is the tag on a *BusinessWeek* "item" of June 30, 1986, on the coast-to-coast popularity of Dove ice-cream bars: "By Paul B. Brown in New York, with Kenneth Drayfack in Chicago, Alex Beam in Boston, Mary J. Pitzer in Minneapolis, Kimberly Carpenter in Philadelphia, and Joan O'C. Hamilton in San Francisco." Bylines on such stories mean little or nothing to veteran reporters. (The magazine could fit a small ad into that space and split the profits with the editorial staff.) When more than one reporter works on a discrete news development, as opposed to a roundup, it is unavoidable that the level of psychological commitment to the story will be lower on all sides — a sense that the partner will take up the slack.

Excellent material still can be produced under these circumstances. Journalists who work as a team year after year — Evans & Novak, Germond & Witcover — don't run into the efficiency problems that are endemic to double and multiple bylines. Almost always, one or the other is producing the entire column. They are also accountable to each other, to keep their joint effort competitive in the syndication market. They can't slack off. But when individuals are thrown together on an assignment, the unavoidable loss of communication efficiency builds up in many ways (the individual versus the collective). The psychic waves get snarled over who should be doing what and who will get credit for what's accomplished. At best, the work behind a story loses its edge.

Those who read many newspapers and periodicals to track developments in the global political economy, as we do at Polyconomics, have become sharply aware of the debilitating effects of multiple bylines. Probably the worst offender in the national press is *U.S. News & World Report*, which usually tags its cover stories and major efforts with multiple bylines, as many as eight. A September 15 piece on "The KGB's New Muscle," is "by Peter Ross Range, with Miriam Horn, Charles Fenivesi, Steven Emerson, David Whitman, Dennis Mullin and James M. Hildreth in Washington and reports from the magazine's foreign bureaus." It reads as if it were written by the Chicago Bears and then run through a Veg-o-matic. Over the years, the process surely smothers intrinsic talent.

This may be what's been happening at *The Wall Street Journal*, where the double and triple bylines have been growing like noxious weeds. Those of us who place as much importance on the byline of a story as on the headline become especially frustrated when we see "odd-couple" double bylines. In 1985, we read with surprise an inflation leader "By Lindley Clark, Jr. and Laurie McGinley," he a devoted monetarist, she not. The piece read like a Clark-McGinley wrestling match to those of us who know; *Journal* readers would only experience an unconscious "static." In February of 1986, in following the *Journal*'s coverage of the Philippine election campaign, we noticed early on

MediaGuide   17

that June Kronholz could not conceal her fondness for Cory Aquino, but Anthony Spaeth remained consistently neutral. We'd skip Kronholz and read Spaeth's dispatches from Manila. Lo, on the critical front-page report of the election itself, we found: "By June Kronholz and Anthony Spaeth." Alternate paragraphs of bias and neutrality?

As a result of this frustration, a complaint went to Peter R. Kann, associate publisher of the *Journal*, who responded in part in a February 28 letter:

"I agree with you that double byline pieces can wind up weaker than solos because no single thinker/reporter/writer is going to have to bear full responsibility. Or, because committee journalism of any sort can wind up leading to a lower common denominator of thinking and writing, of substance and style.

"At other times, I think all this can work in reverse. There are occasions when two minds can work better than one. When two sets of expertise mesh. When two colleagues can help each other think through a story and write it.

"Here at the *Journal* I think the trend toward more double bylines partly reflects the effort to make the paper more timely and topical. If some shared bylines are a price to be paid for moving faster on stories, for cutting across turf lines, or for getting reporters to cooperate on big, breaking stories then the price seems worth paying.

"Double bylines in the *Journal* may also be an alternative to the practice at the *Times, Washington Post* or some other papers where, particularly on a big event, each reporter gets his or her own story. Six or eight separate overlapping stories on an event, each with one byline, may not serve the reader as well as one story with two bylines that makes some sense of the event.

"Still, the worst fate of all would be to wind up producing the kind of collective journalistic mush spooned out by the news magazines. I don't think we're in much danger of that. But I guess, all things considered, I personally think we may be using too many double bylines."

Unhappily, there was an increase in the use of multiple bylines during the *Journal*'s following months. The most noted *Journal* piece of the year, its embarrassing August 25 "disinformation" story about "New Signs That Libya is Plotting Terrorism," was under the double byline of two of its best reporters, John Walcott and Gerald F. Seib. We suspect Walcott was suckered, not Seib, because he subsequently wrote a silly, "analytical" tirade about the Reagan Administration's loss of credibility for having suckered the press (him). If he and Seib had not been meshed on this big story, would one or the other have double and triple checked, knowing their single neck was on the line?

David Graulich, a San Francisco management consultant (with Waterman & Co. — of "In Search of Excellence" fame) and former *Wall Street Journal* reporter, observes that "the way to encourage teamwork and cooperation is by assigning *individual* bylines. For all of its good intentions, the gang-bang byline syndrome creates exactly the opposite effect: poor teamwork, suspicion, resentment and communications breakdowns. Like most commonalizing ideas, shared bylines start with a charitable, plausible premise and lead to destruction of wealth — in this case, talented reportorial wealth."

It works like this, says Graulich: "When you have individual responsibility for an article, you stake your reputation and your job on it coming out well. Therefore you set up an informal bartering system of trust with your reporter colleagues, especially on big breaking stories when the pressure is greatest: help me out on this one, give me stuff that makes me look good, and I'll owe you one. Next time around when it's your rear end on the line, it's up to me to return the favor. Those who don't play the game and aren't deserving of trust get known very quickly throughout the circuit; either they change or they leave.

"The very crux of cooperation is the sense of individual risk and reward. When you water that down with multiple bylines the system starts to collapse. To make matters worse, there are those irritating little italicized boxes that aren't even primary multiple bylines, but *secondary* multiple bylines: 'Additional reporting for this article was done by Tom Thumb in New York, Peter Piper in Los Angeles, and Granny Goose in Bangkok.' Do tertiary bylines lie ahead? The fact is that multiple bylines are symbolic of a slide toward mediocrity and sloppy management that can easily overtake a newspaper."

The New York Times avoids double bylines as a rule, tacking the names of contributing "helpers" to the end of stories where they pitched in. (This is also the practice at the *Post*). But the *Times* also succumbs to the practice now and then. It was also suckered by a State Department manipulative ploy in February, when it ran an election-eve, front-page "expose" of Ferdinand Marcos' war record. The story helped bring down Marcos, who the State Department decided had become a liability. But it was 95 percent distortion, a rare blot on the *Times* record in 1986, written "By Joel Brinkley and Jeff Gerth." One wonders if either Brinkley or Gerth would have addressed the information they were handed with greater circumspection if they knew it was a "solo." We suspect they would have, human nature being what it is. Teams share blame as well as credit.

We simply don't agree with Peter Kann that double bylines are sometimes "the price that has to be paid" for getting reporters to work together on big stories. Nor do we agree that readers are well served by merging several natural stories into one collective effort. (That is the fast-food role of the news magazines.) And editors shouldn't even think of bylines as if they were wages or gratuities, to be handed out for hours worked. Very few journalists would mind if half the meat-and-potatoes stories they file didn't carry a byline at all, as long as they know everyone else is treated the same for purposes of promotion and pay. This is how it worked until the profession ran into the great byline inflation of the 1970s. As reporters' real incomes declined in the monetary

MediaGuide 19

inflation of the period, the established standards on bylines fell as they in fact were used by editors to supplement the psychic incomes of their staffs. In the Soviet Union, the practice of rewarding workers with medals instead of pay boosts loses its effectiveness when everyone is a "hero" of the labor force.

The *Journal* would be better off with a smaller staff, bigger salaries and fewer bylines. The same is true of the news magazines, which abound in unrealized talents, smothered in their formative years by collective journalism. It is the younger reporters who lose out when journalism is collective, those who are denied the excruciating trials of flying solo on big stories, whose limits aren't really tested, and who never do reach journalistic stardom. This is surely the reason why there are so many more stars at *The New York Times* — especially on the business side. Ironically, the supposedly more "socialist" newspaper, the *Times*, puts greater stress on individual initiative than does the *Journal*, at least on the news side.

Ultimately, the biggest beneficiary of an end to the great byline inflation is the reading public. It will get more stars, greater excellence, better communication. That's what Bernie Kilgore had in mind back in 1960.

MAJOR NEWS STORIES OF 1986

Challenger and Chernobyl

Two disasters occurred in 1986 that were widely and deeply covered by the press — the explosion of the space shuttle Challenger on January 28 and the explosion of the Chernobyl nuclear reactor no. 4 on April 26.

The New York Times provided superior coverage of the Challenger disaster, deploying its host of science reporters. Thorough in their efforts, comprehensive and well-organized in reporting the known information, it was the *Times*men who were digging hardest to find and report what had caused the explosion. David E. Sanger provided an informed treatment in "Cold and Vibration in Rocket Studied," 2-5, of leads in the initial investigation, with William J. Broad reporting on past shuttle servicing problems, 2-4, and what was different about Challenger's liftoff, 2-5.

Philip M. Boffey produced the investigative scoop of the year, pursuing a lead he reported 2-7, that a pre-launch discussion had taken place between Morton Thiokol (manufacturer of the booster rockets) personnel in Utah and space officials in Alabama and Florida regarding the effect of cold temperatures on the synthetic rubber booster seals. Others also reported this, Boyce Rensberger of *The Washington Post* alert and leading with it in "Prelaunch Chill Was

Discounted," 2-7. But it was Boffey who found his way to the O-rings, the defective rocket seals, and the sensational report that "NASA Had Warning of a Disaster Risk Posed by Booster," 2-9, that changed the entire nature of the story from what went wrong to who screwed up. Under his byline, the *Times*, using NASA's own documents, reported the many earlier warnings of a disaster risk posed by the booster seals. The next day, the Rogers Commission requested all NASA's records on problems involving the safety seals and its investigation confirmed what Boffey had reported as to the cause of the Challenger explosion.

The newsbeat goes to Boffey and the *Times*, but solid reporting came from others. Craig Covault of *Aviation Week & Space Technology* produced one of the must-read reports at the time, "Ruptured Solid Rocket Motor Caused Challenger Accident," 2-10. And *AW&ST*'s editor, Donald E. Fink, added a new dimension to the Challenger accident investigation with "U.S. Launcher Crisis," 4-28, in the wake of Titan 34D's failed launch. Throughout the early stages, *The Orlando Sentinel* opened many leads that the national reporters picked up.

The Washington Post stayed close, Boyce Rensberger's series of reports backed up by work from Kevin Klose, but without the instinct for relentless pursuit of leads that distinguished the *Times*.

The Wall Street Journal stayed far behind. Adequate coverage from Laurie McGinley, an enterprising financial reporter in 1985 who'd been reassigned away from her strength, but the *Journal* seemed to hold back on throwing resources into the story. Most coverage was a roundup of bureau reports, the information less rigorously treated than by the *Times* or *Post,* perhaps assuming it was simply a disaster story outside their central interest.

* * *

With the secrecy lid imposed on the Chernobyl disaster by the Soviet government compounded by their own confusion and clogged information channels, the Western media had to display remarkable resourcefulness to get out the story of what had occurred just north of Kiev April 26. And the press was up to the task, going after and reporting every aspect of the disaster. It was *The Wall Street Journal*, however, that took the lead on Chernobyl reporting.

Ironically, the *Journal* seemed most disadvantaged, lacking at the time even a Moscow bureau. *The New York Times* had the big advantage, solid professionals in its Moscow and European bureaus, a host of science writers, fresh with an aggressiveness carrying over from their superb Challenger coverage, and the top-down commitment of the paper to getting the whole story. (Arthur Gelb even considered a report re fall-out on the gourmet food industry). A similar advantage existed for *The Washington Post*, and even the newsweeklies were one up on the *Journal; Newsweek*, for example, organized a team of 25 correspondents to piece together the story.

MediaGuide

What we found in the *Journal* coverage was the best-organized reporting of complex issues in an concise, understandable manner; Jerry E. Bishop and Michael Waldholz were outstanding on the medical consequences, 5-1; John J. Fialka and Robert E. Taylor the most informative on the possible loss of control over the other Chernobyl reactors, 5-1; Bishop again, 5-2, on the experimental breeder reactor no. 2, in the wake of discussions over nuclear safety. And the *Journal* was more quickly focused on the political and economic consequences, Frederick Kempe in front, 4-30. Bernard Gwertzman of the *Times* scored with "Reactor Still Afire," 5-1, also early in reporting there may have been damage to a second reactor. Whereas the competition was running six to seven articles a day at times, the *Journal* provided the same information, with a more organized focus on essential news, in much less space.

Journal managing editor Norman Pearlstine, explaining the *Journal*'s fast start, acknowledged an awareness that the paper had been swamped by the competition on the Challenger, and quickly moved after Chernobyl to pull together the basic team under veteran editor Barney Calame. The *Times*, with its far greater depth of science writers and space to devote to the issue, soon overtook the *Journal* and by mid-May was in command, Stuart Diamond excellent in a score of news and analytical reports over this longer distance. But on this kind of story the earlier material was critical in finding the *Journal* superior.

The *Times* was better than *The Washington Post* on coverage from the USSR. Serge Schmemann, pushed harder for information beyond the official government communiques and releases, although the *Post*'s Celestine Bohlen was first with the best truly informative human interest feature, "Kiev, Its Playgrounds Vacant, Scrubs On," 6-9. Both Bohlen and Schmemann continued to follow through on the disaster, with solid reports on the Soviets' disclosures of what had gone wrong, 7-20 and 7-21 respectively; notable also was the *Times*' Felicity Barringer who showed a determination to go after information the Soviets were still not disclosing.

The most astonishing headline of the breaking story was the *New York Post*'s: "2,000 Buried in Mass Grave," 4-30, which was muted by the *Times* to: "U.P.I. Says Toll May Pass 2000." The false dope was passed to U.P.I.'s foreign editor, Sylvana Foa, by an unidentified Kiev informer.

With the Soviets providing almost no information from official sources until much later, the Chernobyl coverage was an outstanding testimony to the U.S. press corps in 1986.

Turmoil in South Africa and the Philippines

The two major stories on the foreign scene in 1986 were the year-long struggle within South Africa and the Philippine electoral crisis.

Pressures mounted for a dismantling of *apartheid* in 1985, with significant changes taking place. As 1986 opened, the question was whether the South African government would move deep enough and fast enough to avert a tragedy of serious proportions.

As a whole, the press on South Africa was very good in 1986. On coverage of the Botha reforms, Ned Temko of *The Christian Science Monitor* was superior, providing detailed accounts of their content and reception: "End to SA Pass Laws Tests Climate for Black-White Dialogue," 4-24, and "Africa's Black Leaders Near Showdown on How to Win Control," 5-5, two examples. And for day-to-day coverage, with attention to the economy, shifts and turns among the various political and racial factions, the pace of change or resistance within various insitutions, etc., *CSM* was thorough, consistently reliable, informative, and indispensable in following South Africa in 1986.

The collision between the new pass law reforms and influx control was handled best by Anthony Robinson of the *Financial Times*, "The Tragedy at Crossroads," a comprehensive picture of the dilemma. Robinson was outstanding with broad overviews of what has changed in South Africa for better and for worse, and with deep analysis of the new contours emerging, as with "In Memory of Soweto."

Allister Sparks, special correspondent for *The Washington Post*, filled gaps in our knowledge with reports that provided the background and context for events in South Africa. His January dispatches on the surprising outbreak of violence in the Moutsie Reserves were unmatched.

Peter Younghusband, a Capetown correspondent hired away from *Newsweek* by *The Washington Times*, also impressed us. He provided informed readings on the sanctions issue within the country, reported Japan and Taiwan ready to swoop into the vacuum, 9-9, and revealed Nobel Peace Prize winner Tutu's other side in a report on his "the West can go to hell" outburst, 7-24. *The Washington Times* was particularly solid on following the "Year of the Spear" offensive outlined by ANC's Oliver Tambo early in the year and, along with the *Monitor* and *Post*, had to be read to fill out the picture on South Africa.

Most disappointing was the coverage provided by *The New York Times*. An important Sunday Magazine feature by South African anti-*apartheid* spokeswoman Helen Suzman, notwithstanding, the *Times* failed to provide reliable information. Alan Cowell's dispatches were inadequate, with bias handicapping his reporting: body-counts a heavy focus, with a late acknowledgement of the black-on-black aspect of the violence, editorializing and criticism in accounts of the government's every new reform, and a questionable selection of what to report and not report, with a too frequent use of "many say" formulations. A sample, a report on the opposition to the school boycotts by Zulu Chief Buthelezi, who "critics say is a fascist." Also lagging was the coverage of *The Wall Street Journal*, handled by Steve Mufson earlier in the year prior to retirement. His efforts always seemed less than thorough, writing about the ANC without ever examining the Communist Party component in its leadership, for example.

We seriously missed the high-quality features that used to appear in *The Economist* under the byline of former political editor Simon Jenkins. And *The Economist*'s coverage of South Africa was far too preachy, several articles more appropriate as editorials instead. Yet, its editorials this year lacked the resolute insight and strategic focus that Simon's direction used to give them.

No one was "neutral" on South Africa, but the print media as a whole mustered the mettle to cover the story in a professional way in 1986.

* * *

Less rigorous standards were applied to the coverage of the Philippine electoral crisis. News reports from 1985 had already shown a disposition to mix in a bit of editorializing, citing President Marcos as a liability for stability in the country. By early 1986, the election was almost unnecessary for some journalists who'd already concluded that Corazon Aquino would sweep the polls. The only news to cover was whether Marcos could successfully steal the election or not. Because of this awareness, we devoted more resources to tracking press coverage of this story than any other. Ultimately, we decided that Marcos probably got more votes than Mrs. Aquino, did not steal the election, and was the victim of forces centered in the U.S. State Department that viewed the corruption and fatigue of the Marcos regime contrary to U.S. interests. This may have been true, but our sole interest was in determining the quality of the press coverage of a critical sequence of events in a Third World ally, that had parallels to South Vietnam in the early 1960s. A 10,000-word report and analysis for Polyconomics' clients, "The Philippine Election and Constitutional Crisis: A Media Report," 2-24, ran in its entirety in *The Washington Times*, 3-7, under the inaccurate front-page headline "How the American Media Pushed Marcos Out of Malacanang Palace."

The single most important story leading up to the February 9 election appeared on the front page of *The New York Times* of January 23: "Marcos Wartime Record Discredited in U.S. Files." The story essentially stripped Marcos of his heroic WWII record as a guerrilla fighter and was based on inconclusive and contradictory fragments of postwar files, which was clear on a very careful reading of the long dispatch by Jeff Gerth and Joel Brinkley. The rest of the press corps did not read the story carefully. From that point the press *knew* that Marcos had been a fraud all along and there was little to restrain it from reverting to an advocacy journalism (typical of the 1960s) to prevent him from stealing the election.

By far the worst excesses were committed by *Newsweek*, with senior writer Harry Anderson producing outrageous copy week after week, especially "The Maharlika Papers," 2-3, that pumped up the *Times'* story of 1-23 to Pumpkin Paper proportions, and "Reagan's Double Take," 2-24: "While Ferdinand Marcos was stealing the election last week, Ronald Reagan was looking the other way."

Our broadest conclusion was that given the voting procedures established for the election, and the intense concentration of the Philippine people on the process, the margin of victory reported by the National Assembly for Marcos, 10,807,179 to 9,291,716 — more than 1.5 million — was simply too many to have been stolen with the precincts being watched like hawks by both the official government poll workers and an organization established by the Aquino people with government sanction. In its pre-election editorial, 2-5, the *NY Times* noted "Wholesale fraud cannot be kept from his own people," and in fact there were no serious signs of popular discontent with the voting outcome, as *The Washington Post's* William Branigan reported 2-17.

American public opinion, especially as reflected in the U.S. Congress, turned decidedly against Marcos when during the vote counting at the Manila electoral center, three dozen computer operators dramatically walked off their jobs, complaining the numbers being chalked on the tally board were not those being supplied by election officials. Meanwhile, the officials denied any wrongdoing and asserted the event was staged. The videotape of these tearful ladies, shown repeatedly on U.S. television with no critical examination of what was going on, was the "smoking gun" that aroused Washington and that led to demands for Marcos' removal. In television interviews, Marcos treated the incident as a tempest in a teapot and pointed out that all the tallies could be checked and verified.

The *Post's* William Branigan reported a week later that the head of the computer section that led the walkout was the wife of a leading reformist colonel of the anti-Marcos faction, an item buried by the *Post* editors on page A-34 ("Probe of Philippine Vote Set by Reformist Officers," 2-17). Weeks later, Paul Quinn-Judge of *The Christian Science Monitor* reported that the reformist colonel in question was chief of intelligence in the Defense Ministry and "was the moving force behind the revolt" ("Marcos's Fall: How it Happened," 3-4). By this time, though, Marcos was long gone.

In the *1986 MediaGuide* we were especially critical of the *Post*'s foreign service and praiseworthy of *The Times'*. In this instance, the *Post* was the best of the bunch, with John Burgess contributing a few important additions to the Branigan reports. The *Times* was awful, almost uniformly, with Seth Mydans, the Manila bureau chief, a conveyor belt for Marcos' opposition and the U.S. Embassy. The *Times'* biggest failing was in reporting no detail on the mechanics of the election process, which would have made it difficult for the fraud analysis to be sustained. Best here was *The Los Angeles Times'* reports of Mark Fineman, 2-11 and 2-16, and a graphic in *USA Today*, "Steps in the Philippine Election," 2-11, that provided the only such details. The *LA Times* also ran a provocative column by its chief pollster, I.A. Lewis, 2-6, on how in 1978 he was hired to poll for the Aquino faction in advance of the assembly. He was hustled onto a departing airplane as soon as he advised them his polls indicated a Marcos landslide: "In the morning, I read in the Tokyo newspapers that the underground had conducted a poll showing the opposition winning by a large majority....Most observers at the time reported widespread election fraud (but) if Marcos was going to win the election anyway, why did he bother to rig the result?"

The Wall Street Journal had two reporters on the scene, June Kronholz and Anthony Spaeth, with Spaeth the most professional of the entire press contingent in his balance, lacking a bit in the depth of experience it would have taken to get on top of the story. Kronholz was obviously rooting for Aquino throughout and we discounted her dispatches. But her report the day after the election (with Spaeth's byline in tow) advanced a theory on how Marcos might have caused 1.4 million voters to be dropped from the rolls, stealing the election through "disenfranchisement." The theory came from Jose Conception, head of the Aquino polling organization, with nothing in the story to suggest the reporters had done the slightest checking to see if 20% of the Manila election rolls had been purged. But this "disenfranchisement" theory now was conventional wisdom, *The Economist* of London reporting that "By the reckoning of *The Wall Street Journal*, that could have deprived Mrs. Aquino of 1.4 million votes, more than enough to have swung a close election."

In the wake of all these "smoking guns" came the coup. Evans & Novak reported in *The Washington Post*, 2-21, that an anti-Marcos faction in the State Department, including two holdovers from the Carter administration, were arguing that the "U.S. could save its interest...only by shoving Marcos from power." To signal the anti-Marcos elements in Manila that it was behind a shove, the State Department on February 13 released its annual human rights report, which the *Post*'s John Goshko led with: "The State Department said yesterday that Philippine government security forces engaged in murder and other serious human rights violations during 1985."

On February 17, Leslie H. Gelb of *The New York Times*, also a Carter assistant secretary of state, had a front-page story on unnamed high authoritative Reagan officials predicting resignations from the Marcos cabinet that will weaken him, although these sources "insisted they were not promoting desertions from the Marcos camp." On February 18, Frederick Kempe of *The Wall Street Journal* joined in the State Department campaign to promote the desertions it insisted it was not promoting: "U.S. officials and members of Congress now agree that U.S. interests in the Philippines would be best served if President Ferdinand Marcos leaves office through an orderly transition." All sources in the story are anonymous.

After Marcos' departure, the victorious Aquino government dissolved the assembly, dismissed hundreds of local elected officials on the grounds they had been Marcos' supporters, suspended the constitution, and instituted what amounted to a military junta with Mrs. Aquino as commander in chief. These events were reported on inside pages of the *Times*, with headlines such as "Now Mrs. Aquino is Taking Aim at City Halls," 3-1, a light-hearted account of all those mayors being dismissed.

Mrs. Aquino has survived so far, but her November dismissal of her entire cabinet, her "fresh start," after a public struggle with her defense minister, might actually leave her in an even weaker position, judging by the terms of her "truce" with Communist insurgents. The press corps for the most part hailed these developments as if her hand was now firm on the tiller. But it's more likely Mrs. Aquino will have a very difficult 1987. The U.S. news media may yet have to answer for its rather relaxed coverage of the Philippines in 1986.

The Global Economy

Several historic events and developments in the global economy added up to another demanding year for the print media — the U.S. tax reform, an economic summit in Tokyo, changes at the Federal Reserve, movement on monetary reform, Treasury's third world debt initiatives, and the Japan-U.S. accord on exchange rates. The insider-trading scandal on Wall Street provided a fascinating drama related to the continuing restructuring of U.S. industry.

The press generally improved its coverage of tax reform progress, but it was *The New York Times* that proved to be the indispensable reading on the issue. David E. Rosenbaum doggedly pursued it, hanging in when *The Wall Street Journal* seemed to give up. He had the precise bead on Sen. Packwood long before anyone else and his reports from mid-April through mid-May were outstanding. Anyone reading the *Times* was not surprised by Packwood's turnaround or his forceful movement of the bill toward passage. *BusinessWeek*'s Howard Gleckman stumbled briefly, but was also exceptional.

The *Times* also excelled in its attention and coverage on the Tokyo summit, Peter T. Kilborn providing the best overall picture in "The Economic Summit," 5-7. Kilborn was also very quick to report the new implications for global monetary strategy in "Monetary Plan Urged by Baker," 4-10, being the first to identify the significance of the Treasury Secretary's call for "automaticity."

It was less successful in adequately reporting on budget matters, though Kilborn's "Economists Now Detect Falling Trend in Deficit," 3-20, reporting on how $200 billion had just been "saved" in one year, helped make up for Jonathan Fuerbringer's lapse in "Fears Rise as Deficit Estimates Drop," 3-5.

On the budget, *National Journal* was very useful in 1986. A feature by Jonathan Rauch on Sen. Domenici at the center of the storm, 2-1, was a fine overview. *National Journal* also was must-reading for comprehensive reporting on the content of the tax bill proposals.

The significance of the court rulings on the budget-balancing law was best handled by *The Wall Street Journal*, Stephen Wermeil particularly far-sighted in a 2-10 article. The *Journal* also was indispensable for news of the U.S. tax reform's impact on Europe, an update on stirrings in Austria done by William McGurn, 7-16, a good example. Journal editorials on the range of economic issues were always the most informed, focused and pertinent. A little weaker on his tax reform coverage than in '85, Jeffrey Birnbaum couldn't seem to see that Packwood, a Republican, could save a tax reform Birnbaum regarded "Democratic." But Birnbaum's technical superiority counted.

Good reporting on the changes at the Fed and aspects of U.S. monetary policy came from *BusinessWeek,* Blanca Riemer super with her 3-3 and 7-28 reports. And *Newsweek*'s Rich Thomas scooped the dailies on the missing U.S. dollars in "Perils of the Green Plague," 3-10. But it was syndicated columnists Rowland Evans and Robert Novak who, in "Secret Fed Vote Shows Volcker's Power Waning," 3-17, had the year's biggest newsbeat. The two also were outstanding with best reporting Reagan's anti-tax determination, 1-13, and their treatment of the tax-stagger issue, 8-6. Singularly outstanding was Warren Brookes in 1986, his "More Balanced Economic Growth," 7-31, debunking the "bi-coastal recovery" myth, a particularly important report.

Hobart Rowen of *The Washington Post* did the best job covering the Baker debt initiative during the year. Rowen also had the best report on the G-2 exchange-rate agreement between the U.S. and Japan, 11-9. Rowen's attention to these issues helped keep the *Post* in competition all year. Rowen did fumble in his March writings insisting that Volcker hadn't lost power, as Evans & Novak correctly perceived.

An impressive effort at a global overview came from Robert Kuttner of *The New Republic*, "James Baker Remakes the World," 4-21. Both the *Financial Times* and *Journal of Commerce* filled in gaps on the global scene. *FT*'s Jurek Martin was early with Japan's tax cut plans, 2-5, and *JofC*'s A.E. Cullison reported the developments with Japan's monetary policy.

Notably lacking was adequate coverage of the Mexican debt crisis, a shortcoming that hadn't improved over the previous year. The best economic reporting came from William A. Orme, Jr., whose articles appeared in the

Journal of Commerce and occasionally *The Washington Post*, with no one doing as thorough a job — though Anatole Kaletsky of the *Financial Times* was better with analytics on the IMF rescue plan, as in "Crying Wolf in Mexico," 7-1. Notable, however, were the reports by *The Wall Street Journal* team, Mary Williams Walsh and S. Karene Witcher, on the rapid dissolution of the social fabric there.

The Ivan Boesky scandal and its aftermath will extend beyond 1986, of course, but the best continuing coverage of the arbitrage, merger & acquisition scene was clearly from *The Wall Street Journal*'s James B. Stewart.

Tripoli and Teheran

The Achille Lauro hijacking had barely receded from the front pages when 19 people were murdered and 110 wounded by terrorists at the Rome and Vienna airports December 27, 1985, with the bloody trail of the atrocity appearing to lead back to Tripoli. The new year opened with Colonel Qaddafi making headlines everywhere. Issuing a call for the unleashing of terror against "Americans in their own streets" should the U.S. retaliate against Libya for the recent atrocities, the Libyan command was unrepentent. This was confirmed by Celestine Bohlen of *The Washington Post*'s Moscow bureau who reported 1-10 on the high-level Libyan official who called the attacks totally justified while on a visit to the USSR.

The New York Times put out an informed roundup of the views on Libyan involvement in the terrorist deployments, "Trail of Mideast Terror: Exploring the links to Qaddafi," by David Shipler, *et al.*, and "do something" commentaries, op-eds and editorials sprouted up everywhere in the media. The Administration announced a trade embargo against Libya, 1-7, called upon its allies to institute sanctions, and told Americans working in Libya to vacate the country. It was Bernard Weinraub of *The New York Times* who got out the story of the President's singular role in setting the course of action, "Response to Terrorism: How the President Decided," 1-12.

The Washington Post ran with a different angle on Reagan's determination, with an incredible 1-9 front-pager, "Qaddafi's Love-Hate View of U.S." David Ottaway, a former Middle East correspondent reassigned to national security issues, and author of the article, wrote: "President Reagan seems to have his own fixation on Qaddafi and to have singled him out as a prime example of irresponsible leadership and state-sponsored terrorism that the West must crush." However, Qaddafi, added Ottaway, "has repeatedly sent messages...of his desire to restore normal relations and regain respectability....You've got to understand," Ottaway quoted one analyst, "Qaddafi loves America. He's stung by our rejection."

From the field, the press as a whole provided informative and useful readings on the tensions within Libya, background and updates on factional struggles, divisions within the high command, grumbling by the armed forces over Qaddafi's elevation of the "armed masses," etc. Judith Miller of the *NYT*, Christopher Dickey of *The Washington Post*, and John Borrell of *Time* each got out good information on the sorry condition of Libya's economy. Miller in particular was resourceful, digging a little deeper to come up with more than official communiques and press conferences. The exception was *The Wall Street Journal*, where coverage was sparse, little appearing outside its "What's News" column.

The March 24 action in the Gulf of Sidra received editorial endorsement in most media, but it was bypassed with a flurry of articles "reporting" the adverse consequences of Reagan having crossed the Colonel's line of bluff. Official communiques of condemnation by Arab and other governments were simply retailed without much effort to lift any veils. Frederick Kempe of *The Wall Street Journal*, however, reported that despite Peking's condemnation of the U.S. action, Chinese citizens were publicly congratulating Americans on the street for swacking Qaddafi. Michael Kramer of *New York* magazine stepped out of the conventional mold to draw a broader perspective, discerning the mosaic of a strategic design, and anticipating the forthcoming Tripoli strike, "Reagan Crosses the Line of Bluff," 4-7.

Some of the best reporting involved what the Sidra and subsequent Tripoli-Benghazi engagements demonstrated militarily. "Moscow routinely sells its schlock arms to its allies" was Michael Kramer's reading on the poor performance of Soviet SAM-5 missiles. Commitment to hi-tech weapons has been strengthened, reported Tim Carrington of *The Wall Street Journal* in "Attack Analysis," 4-21. Michael Gordon of *The New York Times*, approached the subject from the other end, reporting on the technical problems that showed U.S. aircraft vulnerable to malfunction, in "7 American Planes Aborted in Mission," 4-18.

Analytical reporting was still thin, however. From the *Times*, R.W. Apple, "Experts Say Attack on Libya Will Do Major Damage to U.S. in Arab World," 4-21, and David Shipler "Where Will Reagan's Battle Plan Lead?" 4-20, couldn't get beyond a roundup of opinion and cataloging of pluses and minuses. A little better was Frederick Kempe's 4-21 effort, though it also couldn't quite step out of the consensus on Reagan's action: an opening for the Soviets, undermines moderates, strengthens Qaddafi, damages Britain, etc.

Notable were reports by Edward Schumacher, 4-21, and Charles Mohr, 4-17, of the *Times*, both attempting to determine how non-military targets were hit. Morbid, however, was *Newsweek*'s gory color-photo display of bloodied corpses splashed across the pages of its Tripoli story. Exceptionally clear-sighted was the *Times* editorial "The Terrorist and His Sentence," 4-15, in backing the

President's action. "The Response to Terror" editorial, 5-5, in *The New Republic* was a well-done geopolitical analysis. The best editorial came later from *The Washington Times*, "So Much for Trepidation," 7-28, locating the historic Hassan-Peres meeting and the call for peaceful negotiations with Israel by the anti-Arafat leader of Fatah, as consequences of Reagan having clipped Qaddafi's claws.

On his own track, Bob Woodward of *The Washington Post* had claimed in late 1985 that the Administration was preparing covert actions against Colonel Qaddafi. There was a tendency at times in the *Post*'s '86 coverage to come close to suggesting that Qaddafi was merely a convenient "scapegoat," someone the Administration could bash so as to appear it had a strategy for dealing with terrorism. Christopher Dickey treaded close to this; "In Tripoli, Revolutionary Fervor Is Only Diversion," 1-19, and his accounts of unidentified Americans attesting to Qaddafi's hospitality, 1-8 and 1-9, are examples. Woodward later reported the disinformation campaign against Libya being conducted by the Administration through the press, leaving the *WSJ* chagrined at having been taken in. (However, it's worth recalling the Tripoli-filed dispatches of various journalists months earlier were reporting aspects of the same news from the field, as for example, "Qaddafi Is Also Facing Homegrown Opposition," 4-20, by Judith Miller).

* * *

On November 3, a pro-Syrian Lebanese weekly, *Al Shiraa*, reported that the U.S. had been engaged in secret negotiations with Iran, the U.S. mission to Teheran headed by former NSC chief Robert McFarlane. The U.S., *Al Shiraa* reported, had been sending spare parts and ammunition for jet fighters to Iran.

The Iran gambit quickly became the major news story for the rest of the year. The President in his first press conference on the issue announced, "The responsibility for the decision is mine and mine alone." But the wisdom and morality of the policy came under immediate barrage, the follow-up questions addressed to him by reporters heavy with a tone of skepticism and even hostility.

Almost alone in addressing the motives of the policy from a geopolitical perspective was the *The Wall Street Journal*. Its editorial "Arms and the Imam," 11-17, found it a close call, but on the margin gave critical support to the President's geostrategic gamble. Political columnist William Safire of *The New York Times* instead wrote, "Mr. Reagan plays the hypocrite" in "Tar Baby Strikes Again," 11-13, adding in "The Secret Agent," 11-17, that in addition to being shown up as a liar, the President may also be a "softy and dupe" as well. Of course, that was political commentary, but that tone sometimes intruded into press reporting as well.

MediaGuide 31

The Washington Post was particularly aggressive in its coverage. David Hoffman in "Reagan Denies Paying 'Ransom' To Iran for Release of Hostages," 11-14, reporting on the President's press conference, found it unsatisfactory in answering questions, citing a number that had been omitted or sidestepped. Walter Pincus in "Reagan Told Deal Key to Iran's Help," 11-14, provided a history of how the eighteen-month covert diplomacy had emerged and evolved, based on information from unidentified State Department and Administration sources. But the use of "sources say" left us unsatisfied with some of his assertions; for example, "Although Reagan had agreed in January that the United States would shun arms-for-hostages bargaining, the president was 'unhappy' with that position largely because he was under pressure from the hostages' families to take action, sources said."

Similarly, a front-page article by Bob Woodward, "CIA Operation Still Kept in Place by President," 11-23, reported that the President was keeping intact a covert operation against Iran. Again, not a single identifiable source was cited, which was irritating. But what was unsatisfying with Woodward's account, who has a reputation for investigative skills, is that it showed no effort to go further in order to come up with confirmation or verification of what his sources were telling him. We just had to hold in abeyance any sense of whether there was a real story there or not.

The *Post* did produce one of the major stories, however, with its 11-23 front-pager by David Hoffman and Lou Cannon, "White House Shake-Up Plotted," a report on a group of long-time California supporters of President Reagan, who with Nancy Reagan, were urging wide-sweeping personnel changes in the top levels of the Administration.

The most satisfying reporting came from *The New York Times*. Bernard Gwertzman's coverage was the best in that regard. Gwertzman's "All Eyes On Shultz," 11-18, for example, also used "sources say" formulations, but with him we always had the sense that it was he who was using the sources, not *vice versa*, the latter a skill that all journalists have to have in order to remain credible and reliable. We found his reports the most informative on the issue. Also exemplary of thoughtful and informed reporting from the *Times* was R.W. Apple, Jr. With the 'contra' connection on the Iran arms deal under scrutiny, the already circulating themes of a lame-duck president at the nadir of his career facing a Democratic Congress flushed with victory intruded even moreso into the press's reporting. Apple's "Risks for the Democrats," 11-27, however, reported the real substance of the Democrats' divided strategy at this point.

The Wall Street Journal, we thought, lagged the *Post* and *Times*, "Deepening Crisis," 11-26, by Robert S. Greenberger and Jane Mayer, adequate as a "roundup," but lacking anything new. A disturbing piece was "This Iran Policy Makes Carter's Look Good," 11-13, by foreign editor Karen Elliott House. Lacking was her usual insight, the sense of having thought through on the issue, and the tone was almost hysterical. It was simply an inappropriate kind of article for a foreign editor to produce.

Press coverage so far has been mixed, some satisfying, informed, useful; other confused, misfocused and unsatisfying. But with the issue likely to continue into 1987 as a major story, we have a sense of who will best cover it by their '86 efforts.

Strategic Defense Initiative

The Strategic Defense Initiative was again a major story in 1986, ongoing, with two overlapping aspects. The first and most important revolved around President Reagan's radical vision — the idea that defenses can render nuclear weapons "impotent and obsolete" and the determination of the Soviet Union to resist that idea insofar as the U.S. is concerned.

The second part of the story during the year concerned general advances in technology that have made it possible to actually deploy some SDI systems now. Mixed in with both was coverage of the bureaucratic war involving SDI: who stood where in the administration, in Congress, and the fierce and subtle efforts of proponents and opponents to advance or kill SDI.

It was still very difficult in 1986 to find consistently good reporting on the most relevant aspects of these struggles, but there were singular efforts that were outstanding. Elizabeth Drew of *The New Yorker* had the most thorough and professional report on the arms control-SDI debate prior to the Reykjavik meeting in her "Letter From Washington" column, 7-28. It provided, among other things, a roadmap for identifying the various bureaucratic factions involved, which still will be a standard reference as the issue moves into 1987. Importantly, Drew described with depth and objectivity the rise of the "third side" in the SDI debate, those who step outside the "for or against" SDI research and development debate to argue limited deployment is now a viable option.

Commentary magazine, which ran the pathbreaking "Case for Star Wars" by Robert Jastrow in December, 1984, produced "How SDI Is Being Undone," by Angelo Codevilla, 5-86, the author describing how the Administration's focus on never-ending research was undermining the Reagan vision of a deployable defense that would spur arms control.

The other singularly important item was the post-Reykjavik Max Lerner column in *The Washington Times*, "A Vision With Consequences," 10-28. Lerner identified what Reagan had been moving toward before and during the summit: "shifting the discourse of deterrence from a rivalry in destructive technology to a rivalry in defensive technology" and suggesting that this will inevitably shift the center of moral gravity between the two superpowers, with global moral perspectives to follow.

MediaGuide

The print media was not as taken in as the networks with the idea that SDI would be traded away at Reykjavik, but the President's assertions to the contrary were still getting tertiary coverage, as "arms control" took the lead instead.

Post-Reykjavik, the press in general immediately focused on Secretary of State George Shultz's downbeat summit assessment, with "setback for arms control" a running theme. But there were notable exceptions to that poor reporting job. Bernard Weinraub of *The New York Times* had one of the best accounts of what Reagan said, thought and did there, "How Grim Ending in Iceland Followed Hard-Won Gains," 10-14. And Fred Barnes found what much of the press missed in Reagan's upbeat speech at the Keflavik airport just before departure from Iceland. Reagan is eager to eliminate nuclear weapons, but he's also the hardest hard-liner on developing "Star Wars." Iceland demonstrated that "he'll always take Star Wars over weapons reductions," Barnes wrote in "Beaming Legacy," *The New Republic*, 11-17.

The Washington Times also provided important coverage on this with an article by syndicated columnist Gregory A. Fossedal, "Is SDI Now Moving on a Faster Track?" 10-10. Fossedal, surely the leading advocate of SDI in the press, which makes his column essential for tracking the debate, noted importantly that Reagan had actually requested a speedup of various ongoing studies of deployment options. And *The Washington Times* was the only paper that followed up the clear signals in Reagan's speech to the U.N., "U.S. Speeds SDI as Arm Pact Insurance," 10-29, by Warren Strobel and Richard Beeston.

Reporting on SDI technology improved somewhat in 1986. Philip Boffey and William Broad at *The New York Times* and Walter Pincus of *The Washington Post* were attuned, at least, to the new advances in the state of SDI art. Pincus seemed to rely on a narrow White House source for his technology leads, and thus seemed to have only a piece of the picture. The *Times* produced the important material. "Star Wars Traced to Eisenhower Era," 10-28, by William Broad, was a superb historical account of how technical difficulties at each stage of SDI had been overcome from the late '40s to the present. Phil Boffey's "Software Gap Seen As Obstacle In Developing 'Star Wars'," 9-16, on the issue of computer systems was a singularly well-organized explanation of what is and isn't a problem, with Boffey clear on the "third side" position. In other ways, the *Times*' SDI coverage seemed improved in 1986: Charles Mohr, for example, reported on high-level Administration "early deployment" discussions, " 'Option' Sought to Deploy Space Shield Soon," 3-26. And John Cushman reported on the new group of strategists and scientists put together by Reps. Jim Courter and Jack Kemp and Sen. Malcolm Wallop who urged rapid SDI deployment to the President in a pre-Reykjavik letter, "Conservatives Ask Quick Action by President on Missile Defenses," 10-3.

The Wall Street Journal coverage was sporadic, with much of the best reporting done on the editorial page. Its "King Caucus" editorial of 10-28 had stunning political detail not seen elsewhere in the entire press on the anti-SDI maneuvers of congressional liberals to smother the program. From Washington, Frederick Kempe was focused and sure-footed with his report on the politics of "Star Wars," in "Divisions Slow Reagan Decision on Arms," 7-21. Tim Carrington's "Shaky Launch," 7-22, though, was wobbly and confused, reporting Reagan's "lofty promise" ("Astrodome America") was being "abandoned" or "undercut." But the *Journal* improved with John Walcott describing Reagan's arms control vision, "Approach to Arms Control Combines Missile Reductions, Work on Defense," 10-20, although he failed to note that the "middle-of-the-road" case advanced for modest deployments and arms reduction was identical to the case SDI proponents on the "third side" had made all along. Surprisingly, the *Journal* left the entire field of commercial impact to the *Times*, perhaps with New York considering all this a "Washington issue," and Washington considering it exclusively a "political issue."

In its editorial "Star Wars' Bastard Brother," 7-10, the *Times* was soured on Reagan's "idiosyncratic" vision of SDI, declaring "Star Wars has lived off glitz for long enough. It's time to restore it to what it was before Mr. Reagan's 1983 speech: a vigorous research program permitted by the antiballistic missile treaty of 1972 and designed to insure against any technical advance made by a comparable Soviet program." So we were struck by a shift in tone of the *Times*' editorial, "In the Reagan World, With No Missiles" 10-19: "Mr. Reagan's vision may deserve more serious consideration. If so, let him begin to make a more serious case." This was no endorsement of SDI, but an acknowledgment of the potential shift in the discourse of deterrence that could be effected by the President's vision.

Similarly, *The Washington Post*'s lead editorial of 10-15, "Beyond Reykjavik," read: "The Soviets insist that all these positions [for offensive cuts] are part of a package that must include further American concessions on SDI, but surely it is in the Soviet interest...to consummate agreement on these issues. That is necessarily the main American objective now." Also, a very much different tone.

But inviting the President to "present it clearly," is only a change of tone, albeit a welcome one to those of us frustrated with a press corps that should not wait for clear presentations, but should be clarifying for us. With 1986 drawing to a close, the future of Reagan's SDI vision was folded into the broader question of the future of his administration.

MediaGuide

THE BEST STORIES & COLUMNS OF 1986

For the first time in 1986, we decided to highlight individual efforts by print journalists in five categories, the 10 best in each: General, Business/Financial, Political, Foreign and Commentary. (Listed in alphabetical order.) Unlike the many established awards and citations for specific articles or commentaries, the *MediaGuide* did not solicit nominations from the publications and choose among those submitted. This method serves the Pulitzer and Loeb committees, but the ingredient it misses on is timing, which so often elevates material at its time of publication, but is lost when reviewed by a panel of judges several months later.

Our selections may thus seem unusual, but we explain why our selection panel chose as it did in each category. The selections were made in December after *MediaGuide* readers and editors first nominated more than 250 items to be narrowed to the final 50. One criterion was that we *had to remember* reading the material at the time of its publication and its impact on us. There are several stories that seem simple, even flawed, with hindsight, but were exciting and enriching in the context of their time. We assume there were marvelous pieces we did not see that would have crowded some of the entries off these lists, had we seen them. This is not the definitive list of the 50 best pieces of print journalism in 1986, but a parallel of what the critics of the Michelin dining guide would come up with if they were asked to describe the 50 best meals they had in a year.

General Reporting

1. **Bishop, Jerry** and **Waldholz, Michael.** "Soviets Biggest Health Problem Could Take Weeks to Develop," *The Wall Street Journal*, 5-1. The most comprehensive *early* report on the medical/health aspects of the Chernobyl catastrophe, written with lucidity and authority, precisely when we wanted such a piece.

2. **Boffey, Philip M.** "NASA Had Warning of a Disaster Risk Posed by Booster," *The New York Times*, 2-9. The biggest newsbeat of the year, his report that NASA had been warned in 1985 that the "O-ring" seals on the space shuttle's booster rockets might break and cause a catastrophic accident. This shifted the inquiry of the Challenger disaster from what went wrong to who went wrong.

3. **Dionne, E.J., Jr.** "For Jet-Age Pope: Angels, Devils, Indulgences," *The New York Times*, 7-18. What's this? The Pontiff is actually going about talking about angels and devils and the Holy Spirit in this modern day and age. Maybe he's right. Dionne's feature is a marvelous, uh, revelation.

4. **Fields, Suzanne.** "She Who Hesitates..." *The Washington Times*, 2-27. Remember the *Newsweek* and *People* magazine covers on a Yale report on how the female of our species in the USA has a dramatically declining chance of matrimony as she turns 25, 30, 35 and 40? Fields, who looks for such material, had it first.

5. **Getschow, George.** "A Widow's Fortune, Left to Benefit Poor, Instead Sets Off Scandal," *The Wall Street Journal*, 10-8 and 10-9. Santiago. In the highest tradition of investigative journalism, superb reporting, he tells of huge, international skullduggery from back-country Texas to the Vatican. As good as it gets.

6. **Grenier, Richard.** "If 'Evita' Could be a Hit, Just Think of 'Imelda!'," *The Washington Times*, 9-19. The gifted "Point Man" feeds us political analysis painlessly in this darkly whimsical report on his visit to Manila, anticipating the Enrile-Aquino conflict and giving us an amusing Peron/Marcos parallel.

7. **Irish, Jeffrey S.** "A Yankee Learns to Bow," *The New York Times*, 6-8. After Irish gets a history degree from Yale in 1982, with Japanese studies, he goes to work as the only American among 5,000 Japanese in a Tokyo construction firm. In this absorbing, novel piece, he describes one typical day as he experienced it.

8. **Mansfield, Stephanie.** "Steamy Sex! Shop Talk! Judith Krantz!," *The Washington Post*, 5-20. A Style section sizzler on novelist Krantz that moves at breathless, hilarious speed in a magic caricature of *Style* section pieces, establishing Mansfield with us as the best feature writer in the business, for now.

9. **Sanger, David E.** "Doubt Computers Could Detect Fire," *The New York Times*, 2-2. At this very early date, this was the best authoritative report on the possible causes of the space shuttle explosion, Sanger establishing a foothold here that led to a superb news analysis column, "Challenger Inquiry," 2-17.

10. **Sellers, Valita.** "As Black Women Rise in Professional Ranks, Marriage Gets Chancy," *The Wall Street Journal*, 5-16. Sellers, a junior intern at the *Journal*, illuminates with this report on the unique "bubble" of educated black women, aging and unmarried, because of so few *older* black professional men. A great insight.

Business/Financial Reporting

1. **Bianco, Anthony.** "Power on Wall Street," *BusinessWeek*, 7-7. Bianco's December 8, 1985 cover on Salomon Brothers was one of the best of the year. With this deep, dramatic, concise and yet almost lyrical piece on

MediaGuide 37

Michael Malkin of Drexel Burnham Lambert, he established himself as the best at this in the profession.

2. **Bianco, Anthony.** "The Man Behind a $5 Billion Dynasty," *BusinessWeek*, 10-20. An audacious Bianco gets behind the Bass Brothers of Texas into a fourth dimension of power dealmaking with an unknown Richard Rainwater. We begin to understand not only what is happening out there, but how these Titans think.

3. **Kwitny, Jonathan.** "Two Lorimar Officials Have Had Ties to Men of Underworld Repute," *The Wall Street Journal*, 9-15. The *Journal*'s ace investigative reporter disappeared for most of 1986 then dropped this H-bomb on Lorimar-Telepictures Corp., Merv Adelson and Irwin Molasky. But there wasn't even an echo. Why?

4. **Lee, Susan.** "What's With the Casino Society?," *Forbes*, 9-22. In reaction to the *BusinessWeek* plugging of a "Casino Society," with irrational markets that might need regulating, Lee strikes back for *Forbes* with everything you always wanted to know about program trading, etc., teaching *BW* a lesson on markets. Classic.

5. **Petre, Peter.** "America's Most Successful Entrepreneur," *Fortune*, 10-27. A wonderful cover on Digital Equipment's Ken Olsen that gets us as close to knowing Olsen as we can simply by reading about him. In the process we are left with useful pictures of this continually unfolding computer business world.

6. **Rosenbaum, David.** "Voting On Tax Bill Delayed in Senate," etc. *The New York Times*, 4-19, 4-24, 4-25, 4-28, 5-3, 5-8. A critical string of reports feeding back to Capitol Hill and Wall Street on the unfolding tax reform in the Senate Finance Committee, Rosenbaum plowing ahead decisively as the *WSJ* hesitates.

7. **Sloan, Allan.** "Understanding Murdoch: The Numbers Aren't What Really Matters," *Forbes*, 3-10. Outstanding on Rupert's magic, breathtaking numbers and an exciting story that captures both the sweep of what Murdoch is doing as well as the kind of tri-continent dealmaking that is the wave of the future.

8. **Symonds, William C.** "Big Trouble at Allegheny," *BusinessWeek*, 8-11. A three-month probe into why Allegheny International has been sagging turns up such conclusive evidence of misfeasance, or worse: lavish spending on perks, conflicts of interest, etc., that the CEO resigned soon after publication. Great journalism.

9. **Valery, Nicholas.** "High Technology: Clash of the Titans," *The Economist*, 8-23. Virtuoso, effortless journalism on the U.S. versus Japan in the high-tech markets. Deeply factual, objective, written with style and grace, a piece worth filing for quick reference by other journalists as it is state-of-the-art.

10. **Williams, Winston.** "Carl Icahn's Wild Ride at TWA," *The New York Times*, 6-22. An extraordinary angle on the corporate raider now having to actually manage his takeover target, timed just as we looked for it, organized and written with such efficiency that its pleasurable length was behind us much too soon.

Political Reporting

1. **Apple, R.W., Jr.** "Risks for the Democrats," *The New York Times*, 11-27. The Iran-Contra connection is too good to be true for the Democratic party fortunes, and Apple does exactly the kind of piece one expects from the Chief National Correspondent, the Dems worried they will squander the advantage by playing Torquemada.

2. **Barnes, Fred.** "Designated Scapegoat," *The New Republic*, 1-27. At exactly the moment when the political wolf pack is chewing up White House Chief of Staff Donald Regan, Barnes bravely cuts entirely against the grain and the pack dissipates soon thereafter, reminding us of David Broder's Nixon defense of 1969.

3. **Blumenthal, Sidney.** "Forget Centrist Democrats, Watch Kennedy Forces," *The Washington Post*, 2-9. The conventional wisdom is that Teddy's dropout opens the way for a centrist to grab the Democratic party, and the Gephardts and Babbitts try it. This is alone and correct in stating the opposite. Witness Cuomo and Hart.

4. **Broder, David.** "The Right Signals," *The Washington Post*, 9-2. The wolf pack had decided that Rep. Jack Kemp had flamed out somewhere over Michigan re 1988 and presidential politics. Broder knows better and stops the pack with this, recounting Kemp's lead role in moving the GOP congressional pack for RR's tax reform.

5. **Brownstein, Ron.** "The Big Sweep," *National Journal*, 11-8. Brownstein's second post-election story of the issue, with 1991 reapportionment implications, is even better than the first, "The End of the Road." Together they present the most acute, insightful and thorough review of the 1986 elections.

6. **Donohoe, Cathryn.** "Cuomo: Is the Democratic Prospect a Terrible Tease?," *The Washington Times*, 9-11. Every political writer on the East Coast tried to get Mario on paper, but Donohoe turns him into a Gingerbread Man, "Catch me if you can," and it somehow works to yield the best political profile of the season.

7. **Drew, Elizabeth.** "Letter From Washington," *The New Yorker*, 7-28. Drew has become the best pure reporter on arms control, SDI and the players

involved. This pre-summit report on the power alignments is written with such icy detachment and fine detail we have a sure sense she's left nothing out that we should know.

8. **Edsall, Thomas B.** "Massachusetts: A Model for Democrats?," *The Washington Post*, 10-5. You can't write this kind of political piece unless you're willing to spin the world on its axis, seeing a cut wherein upper-incomes in Mass. move to the Democrats, low-incomes to Republicans, with the latter not motivated to vote.

9. **Evans & Novak.** "Secret Vote Shows Volcker's Power Waning," *Chicago Sun Times*, 3-17. A blockbuster scoop for the dynamic duo, Novak on this one, finding Tall Paul outvoted 4-to-3 on the 2-24 discount-rate Fed tally. Reverberations from this were felt around the planet, and the boys got there first.

10. **Hoffman, David.** "Bush: Loyal Soldier Maneuvers in Private," *The Washington Post*, 10-28. Of all the attempts to capture the Vice President on paper, Hoffman's is easily the best. A sharp focus on the *shadows* Bush casts over the major issues debated inside — deficits, taxes, arms talks — leaves little doubt.

Foreign Correspondence

1. **Burns, John F.** "Why Investors Are Sour on China," *The New York Times*, 6-8. The premiere foreign correspondent beams his flash at Beijing bureaucrats, blocking foreign business development with red tape and bullheadedness just as China seeks more hard currency. Reforms followed, but Burns was heaved from the country.

2. **Hieronymous, Bill.** "Reinventing Brazil: Inflation Doesn't Live There Any More," *Barron's*, 6-16. Amazing, so many reporters on the big dailies and magazines bumping into each other in Rio and Sao Paulo and *Barron's* gets this comprehensive report over the transom from a free-lancer. This should be standard. It isn't.

3. **Kestin, Hesh.** "Terror's Bottom Line," *Forbes*, 6-2. Revelations of the PLO's secret $5 billion investment empire was a major investigative news scoop in 1986. But Kestin shows how to really do investigative reporting on a foreign beat to get the real story: Yasir's fortunes are sinking — the PLO's going broke.

4. **Mackenzie, Richard.** "A Nation Stares Into a Dark Abyss," *Insight*, 9-22. The Iran-Iraq war mostly goes unreported because of diplomatic disinterest in who wins or loses. Mackenzie's six weeks in Iraq, reporting on the war's human impact (one soldier in 10 killed on the battlefield), wrenches our conscience.

5. **Martin, Richard.** "Telling the Tale of Mass Exodus," *Insight*, 4-28. A powerfully done three-part cover story on the refugees of Nicaragua: The Ladinos, the Creoles, the Miskitos. With this kind of space and commitment, the magazine should be able to tell this kind of story to our complete satisfaction; Martin was up to it.

6. **Platt, Adam.** "Booming Asia at the Crossroads," *Insight*, 5-12. Platt immerses himself in the region for this four-part cover story on Hong Kong, Singapore, South Korea and Taiwan. The length intimidates until you're drawn into it, demonstrating the power of *Insight*s' innovation, the single-writer multiple story.

7. **Robinson, Anthony.** "In Memory of Soweto," *Financial Times*, 6-14. On the 10th anniversary of the black revolt that shook South Africa, Robinson organizes a decade's worth of history to lay open the clearest focus of what lies ahead. If you had but one item to read for understanding South Africa, this was it.

8. **Rupert, James.** Afghanistan series: "Depopulation Campaign Brutally Changes Villages," 1-16, etc. *The Washington Post*. With news slim from this front, Rupert's travels with the resistance filled the void. The Soviet strategy revealed with all its horror — "Destroy the fish by emptying the water." Powerful then and even a year later.

9. **Seib, Gerald M.** "Dangerous Split: Religious Discord Rises Among Israeli Jews," *The Wall Street Journal*, 6-18. When you have a "religious state," as Israel, a political clash between fundamentalists and reformists has uncomfortable overtones that are redolent of South Africa. A powerful, startling report.

10. **Spaeth, Anthony.** "The Marcos Vote Machine is Put to Test As the Philippines Goes to Polls Today," *The Wall Street Journal*, 2-7. A simple election-day wrap-up that looks so ordinary now, but was sublime at the moment because of its strict adherance to the most basic standards of journalism: fairness, accuracy, balance.

Commentary

1. **Blumenthal, Sidney.** "Once Upon a Time in America," *The New Republic*, 1-13. A sulfuric review of Geraldine Ferraro's book by this fierce liberal presents the known record of Ferraro/Zaccaro mob connections so starkly that its effect is stunning. A stake in the heart, then cremation. She was not heard from again.

2. **Cockburn, Alexander.** "Mainstream Democrats Swept Along by the Current," *The Wall Street Journal*, 10-23. Cockburn, a fierce leftist, is the first to notice Democratic candidates, with "a certain craven edge" to their

voices, are "wallowing in the mainstream" instead of challenging GOP policies. Delicious.

3. **Cohen, Richard.** "Making Trends Meet," *The Washington Post Magazine*, 9-28. A hugely entertaining spoof of newsmag "trend" covers, which practically summarizes 1986: "*People*...reported that everyone who was not already doing crack or shopping at the new Ralph Lauren store was having an affair." And much more.

4. **Fossedal, Gregory A.** "A Morality Test for South Africa Opposition," *The New York Times*, 2-4. Fossedal argues against a floating standard for moral and other commitments in foreign policy, but proposes a higher one for right and left regimes that boils down to this: "Will You Hold Free Elections?"

5. **Kinsley, Michael.** "We Wuz Robbed," *The New Republic*, 6-9. In his TRB column, Kinsley lashes at the Democratic Leadership Council for trying to rebuild the party around themes the GOP has swiped and developed, exhorting it to forthrightly present the party to the left of the Republicans or fold its tent.

6. **Kristol, Irving.** "Schools Can Do This Much," *The Wall Street Journal*, 9-8. This is just about as delicious a social commentary as you can find anywhere. Professor Kristol in a delightful passion writes about the parlous state of American education as we might imagine coming from G.B. Shaw's Professor Henry Higgins.

7. **Lerner, Max.** "A Vision With Consequences," *The Washington Times*, 10-22. Post-Reykjavik, Lerner sees Reagan, in shifting the discourse of deterrence from destructive to defensive technology, has also shifted "the center of moral gravity between the two superpowers," and political perspectives *must* follow. Inspired.

8. **Lewis, Anthony.** "The Stupidity Factor," *The New York Times*, 9-18. Lewis originally railed at the Kremlin for the Daniloff snatch, but then, seeing the Soviet side and U.S. stupidity, makes a lawyer-like case — the best we saw — for the deal to get him back. Norman Podhoretz fumed at it, but not lawyer-like.

9. **Pipes, Richard.** "Team B: The Reality Behind the Myth," *Commentary*, October. In 1975, the CIA's annual report on Soviet strategic strength was challenged from the right and a "B" team of outsiders appointed to do a parallel study. Pipes chaired it. These are his recollections, a vital addition to current debate.

10. **Raspberry, William.** "Would Elections Really Help Haiti?," *The Washington Post*, 2-5. Raspberry questions George Shultz' cure for Haiti, democratic elections, and wonders, with so much concern about leftist takeovers in the Third World, "we make virtually no effort to export the American economic system." Ah, yes.

A CRITIQUE OF TELEVISION NEWS

A Picture Headline Service

Sometime in the mid-1970s, when the petroleum industry was being accused of having concocted the global energy crisis and the U.S. auto industry was being accused of causing an imaginary environmental crisis, yet another corporate executive told us he was getting ulcers watching the network evening news. It didn't matter which, since ABC, CBS and NBC were all fanning these conspiracy theories. Our advice was to stop watching. Actually, we had stopped regular viewing of television news years earlier, having determined that the cost of taking in a half or whole hour of network news each evening far exceeded the benefits. At best television provides "a picture headline service," to use Walter Cronkite's term. At worst it provides ulcers. In between, it is simple-minded and "disinformative." That is, over time network news imparts so much "slightly inaccurate" information that the effort required to live one's life as an informed person with it is far too great.

It would not matter if the dominant culture of TV newsland were "conservative" or "liberal." Because it is a mass medium that requires the visual as well as the auditory attention of the viewer, TV newspeople can't use the parts of their brains that deal with complexities. When at work, they are forced to be simple-minded, refusing to listen to nuance, rejecting the unconventional, blocking out subtleties, all of which complicate the task of conveying a picture headline and no more. Print media people have a difficult time conversing with TV newspeople for more than 60 Minutes. Radio news, though, is relatively pure and informative, an audio headline service written by wire service print reporters who are not required to entertain.

A captain of industry once observed that "If you have to read a newspaper to know what's going on, you don't know what's going on." Which is another way of saying that the truly informed are those who have the essential news imparted to them by telephone and in person, by those who are close to the news or are actually on the inside making the news. Many people think the President knows what's happening before "the news" hits the street, while there is still time to "do something about it."

In fact, newspapers are indispensable to all policymakers, including the President and the captains of industry. The biggest reason is that by the time individuals become policymakers they know how to extract the information they need more rapidly from newspapers than from all other sources. They are used to reading papers, "skimming" pages in "fast forward" and "rapid rewind" several times faster than they could ever glean comparable information from televised news programs — even if video news could pack in as much information as a newspaper. The print media are indispensable to TV news programmers.

MediaGuide 43

The personal computer will eventually be able to replace printed newspapers with electronic news for a significant portion of policymakers. Much of Wall Street now gets most of its spot news by scanning computer terminals for headlines of news that may be impacting the financial markets. But it will be decades before electronic news improves and a new generation of policymakers is comfortable enough with it to seriously challenge the national print media. Not so network television news, which is already in serious decline as a primary source of information to the public at large — about 20% from its peak — and we suspect is watched by policymakers only for specific events. We would not be surprised if this decline continued to the point where the format we've come to know as "the network evening news" is itself challenged in the 1990s.

In Britain, for purposes of comparison, the people who read the news off teleprompters on television news are known as simply that, "news readers," as opposed to the highly and speciously glamorized personnages known in America as "anchor men." When, for example, the Marxist-Leninist leader of Mozambique was killed in a plane crash in October 1986, Peter Jennings of ABC announced to America, before the news of the crash had even been reported to the public in President Machel's own country, that a sense of "enormous loss" was being felt throughout Mozambique. This intriguing piece of misinformation had been written for him by his news staff, under the direction of his executive producer, and had simply been read by him, to a degree without even thinking.

Not all public affairs broadcasting is this mechanical. The print media can't match television in communicating information that is most easily absorbed visually. Footage of natural disasters, space shots, civil spectacles and confrontations are obviously in this category. But the kind of debate formats provided on the MacNeil-Lehrer evening hour of public television, with pros and cons around a timely issue of public policy, conveys information more effectively than the print media can: We see the body language and hear the voice inflections of the protagonists, which add value to the verbal content. There is the added bonus in knowing there is no print reporter letting personal bias intervene. The morning "wake-up programs" provided by the networks are useful in providing a quick headline news service followed by a mini-debate of some sort and an interview that is news related. Politicians are "telegenic" when the viewers size them up favorably by observing and interpreting their facial expressions, body language and voice intonations for added signs of wit, wisdom and integrity.

We were asked many times after publication of the first *MediaGuide* in 1986 if we planned to rate television journalists in future editions. No. We can't imagine doing so any more than we can imagine the *Michelin Guide* rating hamburger stands. We eat the occasional Big Mac and Whopper and Wendyburger, but the standard of excellence applied to fine restaurants can't be applied to these. To rate Dan Rather of CBS, Peter Jennings of ABC, and

Tom Brokaw of NBC, let alone the field reporters, would be just as meaningless, and we'd have to start them with letters of "F" and below if we threw them in the same pot with the print media. As the collective performance of the network "news readers" made plain at the October mini-summit at Reykjavik, their grasp of the complexities of serious matters such as arms control is limited to the ABCs. There was a touching naivete to the breathless, seemingly mindless accounts of impending history, followed by crestfallen meanderings about dashed hopes. These were completely out of sync with the broad national audience, which collectively seemed perfectly pleased with the President's handling of things as well as the outcome.

Behind the apparent mindlessness, of course, lies a value system, a framework of interpretation, the same that allowed Jennings to read the piece of imaginative fancy about the death of Mozambique's president — the "enormous loss" that swept the uninformed nation — with the sense that it felt "right."

We don't suggest that network news would be any better if all suspected "liberals" were replaced with suspected "conservatives," who would put a different spin on the evening news. Quite the contrary, we don't think it would matter, except that the viewing public would have to get used to discounting a new set of biases. We're perfectly happy with Brokaw, Jennings and Rather at their respective hamburger stands, can think of no others better suited for the posts, and believe the only way to bring noticeable improvement to the network news is to improve the performance of the print media — from which television news takes its cues. The improvement in the print media, particularly the steady strengthening of *The New York Times* in recent years, has already had this kind of calming effect on the network news, and few of our acquaintances complain of television ulcers.

John Corry, television critic of *The New York Times*, has made a deeply significant contribution to understanding "news" as it appears on television by analyzing what he calls the "dominant culture" which shapes and forms the world view of Jennings, Rather, Brokaw, and the other great "opinion molders" of America.

Corry, who has had a vast experience in almost every branch of print journalism, including 22 years on *The New York Times*, was given a newly created job in 1984 as his newspaper's public affairs television critic. The aim was to establish a wide, informed, balanced frame of reference and to apply the highest standards of print journalism to television news, documentaries, and all other programs which touch on public affairs. Following is an abridged version of a most thoughtful, provocative essay that he wrote in 1986 as a Media Institute monograph, which we believe is the finest treatment of the subject we've ever encountered. The abridgement of "TV News and the Dominant Culture" is published here with the permission of the author and the Media Institute.

TV News and the Dominant Culture

By John Corry

The argument now arises frequently, usually in the interstices where journalism and ideology meet. Is television somewhere on the left, reflecting a liberal bias? Does it report the news according to journalistic principles or the political beliefs of the journalists? It will be argued in this paper that television does not consciously pursue a liberal or left agenda, although it does reflect a liberal to left point of view. This is because the point of view is fixed and in place, a part of the natural order. The television journalist's personal beliefs (and print journalist's, too) are incidental. What determines much of what a journalist calls news and how he approaches it is not so much his faith in a political creed as it is the intellectual and artistic culture that shapes his assumptions. The culture determines the point of view; it focuses the journalist's attention. Most importantly, it supplies the moral dimensions to his thinking, allowing him to identify goodness and just causes.

This intellectual and artistic culture, also argued here, is rooted firmly in the political left, where it finds its own closed frame of reference. Little dissent is tolerated, and very little is found. Boundaries and beliefs are clear, even when reality must be altered. A new reality then blossoms.

The culture, as will also be argued, does not have the slightest difficulty in identifying political virtue and vice, or in establishing degrees of wickedness. Mislabeling, an accompaniment to the artistic and intellectual culture, is injurious to proper journalism. Distinctions are blurred. Conclusions are arrived at too easily.

In this sense, artists and intellectuals have come to dominate the culture, distributing ideas and fixing the signposts that journalists follow. This does not mean that journalism is dishonest, but rather that it becomes selective. Almost to a person, however, television journalists deny their coverage is influenced by ideology. Print journalists, in general, uphold them on this. Meanwhile, conservative critics make extravagant accusations.

It seems vain to argue that journalism is divorced from the most prominent intellectual and artistic influences of its time — the dominant culture — or that the journalist's point of view is not affected. Intellectuals and artists articulate passions, impulses, and ideas. They traffic in causes. Increasingly in 20th-century America they resemble a secular priesthood. Their power is in the strength of their beliefs, and the way they are able to voice them. Causes are popularized this way. Liberal to leftist political attitudes are, too. But foreign affairs, wars, revolutions, race relations, domestic legislation, questions about the national psyche, and other matters leave room for maneuver. Where does the journalist's eye fall? Why is the story being covered? There are fewer rules of pure journalism here than journalists pretend, even to themselves. Journalists, especially big-time journalists, deal in attitudes and ideas as much as events, and when they indicate otherwise they show an imperfect understanding of how they earn their livings.

Consider the charge most often brought, and most easily documented, against television journalism: It is overly negative, too easily dismissing what is healthy and productive, too often telling us what is sick and wasteful. Television news most often implies that things don't work, and that if they do work, they don't work very well.

Certainly there are non-ideological factors. In part, the negativism in television news is only a corollary of American journalism, which, not always to our sorrow, sees itself in an adversarial role, criticizing authority and front-runners. And, in part, the negativism is something that simply goes with the territory of television. Adversity, crisis, and malfeasance play better than peace, prosperity, and piety. Television is a dramatic medium, unhappy with vacuums, and conflict is more dramatic than calm.

But negativism has a political background, and ideological factors are also at work. It is part of the political history of our times. Once there was something like ideological parity between the two parties. George Wallace said there wasn't a dime's worth of difference between either one. Republicans had a right wing; Democrats had a left wing, but in the broad middle they were alike. Consensus existed, and bipartisan policies were forged. Each party had some separate constituencies — big business and small towns favored the Republicans, while organized labor and civil-rights groups stood with the Democrats — but the constituencies had realizable goals. They could be negotiated. The legislative process functioned as a matter of give and take. Certainly there were competing interests, but there were no special interests. Differences could be reconciled.

The '60s changed this, and changed our political symbols as well. Counterculture politics introduced the notion of victims, a category wide enough to include everyone except middle-aged white males. Blacks were victims; women were victims; young people were victims; so were homosexuals, lesbians, Latins, and native Americans. Each was a special interest, due specific rights and reparations. America was Balkanized. At the same time, the causes of all victims were joined. The gay-rights movement embraced the women's movement; the women's movement embraced the civil-rights movement; everyone joined to oppose the war in Vietnam. Oppression had to be fought simultaneously on many fronts, and there was no give and take. Righteousness and high moral purpose, divorced from any test of experience, spread through the dominant culture.

And, as it turned out, the '60s were made for television — conflict and strife, much of it wonderfully visual. See the United States senators parading behind a Vietnamese flag. Watch the Alabama policemen beating up black marchers. It is instructive, meanwhile, to recall Richard Nixon's "last press conference," when he told reporters, "You won't have Nixon to kick around anymore." That was when he lost the election for governor of California in 1962. At the same news conference, he also compared print and television journalism. "I think," he said, "that it's time our great newspapers have at least the same objectivity, the same fullness of coverage, that television has. And I can only thank God for television and radio for keeping the newspapers a little more honest."

Two years later, delegates to the Republican National Convention in San Francisco wore buttons that said, "Stamp out Huntley-Brinkley." When former President Eisenhower, in his address to the convention, spoke about "sensation-seeking" news men who were trying to discredit Barry Goldwater, the delegates roared in anger and shook their fists at the network anchormen above the convention floor. In the two years since Nixon had thanked God for television, the evening news programs had doubled in length to 30 minutes, and television had begun to find its new formats. In 1963, Reuven Frank, the president of NBC News, sent this memo to his staff: "Every news story should, without any sacrifice of probity or responsibility, display the attributes of fiction, of drama. It should have structure and conflict, problem and denouement, rising action and falling action, a beginning, a middle and an end."

It was terrific, really; so much was happening at once. The year Mr. Frank wrote his memo was also the year the Roper organization, which had been conducting a similar survey since 1959, once again asked people "where (do) you usually get most of your news about what's going on in the world today — from the newspapers or radio or television or talking to people or where?" In 1963, for the first time, more people said they were getting their news from television than from newspapers. Meanwhile, radical politics was beginning to coalesce: Students for a Democratic Society issued its Port Huron manifesto in 1962; the Berkeley demonstrations would erupt in 1964. A perfect match was being born. Print journalism was burdened with old strictures about who, what, when, and where, told right at the top of the story. Television was onto something new: structure and conflict, problem and denouement, rising and falling action.

TV and the New Politics

Thus television became a wonderful vehicle for the new politics, which was just like the old Manichaeism. Light and darkness clashed, and any issue could be reduced to two minutes. Besides, the visuals were wonderful. The tactics of confrontation and demonstration saw to that. The country seemed to be falling apart.

And it was falling apart, although on television this was never quite what it seemed. When television journalists argue (and believe) that they are nonpartisan and objective, they mean they have gotten their facts right, and given each party in a dispute a chance to respond to accusations. Grant that they do this, but it is beside the point. The real question is what television journalists see when they report. In the '60s, they seemed to see television images and draw their truths from them. There was some fine television reporting out of Vietnam, but the single, best-known, most celebrated (and most damned) piece of work was Morley Safer's 1965 CBS story about the razing of Cam Ne village by Marines. Put aside now questions about the story's factual accuracy. The moral intonations were clear. There was no doubt about oppressed and oppressor.

And that, of course, was what radical politics was also about. There were no issues there, only sides. An ironclad, constantly reappearing practice in mainstream journalism, meanwhile, is to reject the worst excesses of the left, but to allow some residue to linger. This is why out-right lies, grotesque distortions, and slippery half-truths are effective as political weapons. Journalism tries to ameliorate them. It operates on the theory that where there is smoke there is fire. It may not be as large a conflagration as charged, but certainly there must be flames. When radical politics charged that America was racist and imperialistic, it colored television's thinking. America might not be absolutely racist and imperialistic, but there were things for which it must answer, and clearly Vietnam was one. Protests and demonstrations, as seen on television, confirmed this. Americans were ashamed of themselves.

Television, accommodating itself to the radical political vision, changed our perception. Therefore the reality itself changed. In American politics, the perception of an event is more important than the event. That is why the media in general and television in particular are fought over so fiercely by both left and right. If perception is controlled, the political and social environment is controlled.

Obviously, this wasn't all television's doing, but certainly television helped. Television news, even at its least objective, its least "journalistic," does not necessarily tell us what to think, but it does tell us what to think about. In the '60s, we were meant to think about a society that was breaking down and a system that had to be restructured. This was a message from the left, and to the extent that television allowed the message to capture its news agenda, television was a captive of the left.

In *The Good News Is the Bad News Is Wrong*, Ben Wattenberg argues that the news media "are missing the biggest stories of our era...and missing them regularly, consistently, structurally, and probably unwittingly." Wattenberg cites any number of statistics that indicate we are living better than ever before, particularly those of us who are most often thought of as disenfranchised. Progress has been made. Wattenberg says this is not the kind of thing you hear much about on television and he is right. It does not play as well as bad news; but, more importantly, it does not fit in the framework of the dominant intellectual and artistic culture. As it did in the '60s, the culture favors the idea of victims.

There is confusion about this in the 1980s. An article in the *New York Times Sunday Magazine*, for example, tells us that "the prevailing ideology among New York intellectuals today is neo-conservative." And: "Whether the neo-conservatives are more influential than their (liberal) ancestors is open to question; that they're now the dominant voice in American cultural life isn't." The left is supposed to be in tatters, inoperative as a social and political force.

What is inoperative, however, is the assumption about the left's decline. Whatever the recent literary gains of neoconservatives, the dominant culture still favors the left. The truth is that the right may have passions and impulses, but the left controls ideas.

Television, meanwhile, does not exist in a vacuum, and journalists are not hermetically sealed. Ideas and attitudes travel. Journalists go to plays, read books, see movies, visit galleries, and talk to people outside the newsroom. Perhaps they send their children to the better Eastern schools. The broad theme they encounter in the dominant culture is alienation — a feeling of separation from institutions, a feeling that American life is rotten.

As a political and social force, the arts are liberal to left, a condition so firmly entrenched it seems to be part of the natural order. In serious theater and elsewhere in the arts, there is a feeling that something is wrong.

Obviously, not all the arts at all times and in all places are this way — but when artists and writers act collectively to make their views known, the views are left of center. No one joins to support the government of Jose Napoleon Duarte in El Salvador, or to protest the murder and kidnapping of elected mayors by guerrillas. Here and there a few individuals—the novelist Saul Bellow, say, or the playwright Tom Stoppard — take different positions, but they do so individually and never as members of a group. At the same time, the support for political candidates by artists, writers, and intellectuals is generally proportionate with the distance a candidate is thought to have traveled from the center to the left. Candidates who have moved to the right get no support at all. In the last election, Ronald Reagan and George Bush may have had Clint Eastwood and some country-and-western singers, but Walter Mondale and Geraldine Ferraro had everyone else.

Labels and Attitudes

What is most striking is how little diversity there is, and how moralistically positions are held. In the 20th century, redemptive politics has replaced redemptive religion, a situation foreseen by Nietzsche when he said that "God is dead." Since the 1930s, it has been assumed that intellectuals as a group stood somewhere on the left; since the '60s, whole communities of creative people have joined them. At the same time, it is virtually impossible for any political or cultural figure to be identified as a leftist save on the pages of *Human Events*, or, if William Buckley and his staff are impassioned, in *National Review*. On respectable television news broadcasts, the word leftist is applied only to foreigners — Daniel Ortega of Nicaragua, or Asian or African revolutionaries. Jane Fonda, who once said, "If you only understood Communism, you'd be down on your knees begging for it," is a liberal; so is Norman Mailer, who voices his "protest, disgust, and rebellion" toward American society. So, for that matter, is the Rev. Jesse Jackson when he says that Yasir Arafat and Fidel Castro are only misunderstood. Good manners and cultural conventions preclude their being called leftist.

Right wingers, on the other hand, are clearly identified. Television correspondents found them in abundance, for example, at the 1984 Republican National Convention, although they found no left wingers at the Democratic National Convention. This is not just a matter of semantics. The dominant culture, which journalism reflects, is clear about the right. It is racist, imperialistic, and cruel. It wants no accommodation with the Soviet Union; it favors an ever-escalating arms race; it is in league with forces that pollute the air and water; it opposes the legitimate rights of women and all minorities; it takes the side of the rich over the poor; it is contemptuous of the arts and humanities. This last is a more profound indictment than it may seem. The arts and humanities are battlegrounds of redemptive politics; they are also where many leftist members of the new class make their livings.

The right wing is isolated this way; no moral person could possibly support the things it favors. This is a political mentality that does not sort out issues, but instead treats them as all of a piece. If one supports the women's movement, then support is expected for environmental causes and the nuclear freeze as well. We know what we are for because we know what our enemies are against. Myth-making goes on here: The right is thought of as a single entity, with a single position on issues. In real life — in the halls of Congress, for instance — there is more political diversity among conservatives than liberals. A congressman may support freedom of choice for women, regard school prayer as less than monumental, oppose protective tariffs, champion the First Amendment, call for sanctions against South Africa, and still be regarded as a conservative. The culture demands a greater degree of uniformity among liberals.

In theory, journalism's role is to define issues, without taking sides. To do this, it presumably stands in the center, applying neutral, non-judgmental standards to both right and left. The question, however, when journalism supposedly stands in, or hovers above, the center, is, the center of what? What defines the center? When reporters and commentators identify a right wing and right-wing thinking, but decline to recognize a left wing and left-wing thinking, they are saying the left does not exist. At the same time, it is the left that makes up the moral and intellectual framework of the dominant culture. The right, morally discredited, barely contributes. The center does not contribute ideas; it only absorbs them. The left becomes the only game in town this way, shaping the culture that tells journalism what news is and how it must be regarded.

Television claims print journalism's theology, but doesn't accept its responsibilities. It says it is practicing journalism, but as a practical matter it does this mostly on fast-breaking stories. When it fails, it fails on the Big Pictures; the outline is blurred. The culture gives television a starting point, an attitude, ordinates on which to box its moral compass. Issues and causes favored by conservatives are suspect, while probity clings to the other side. At the same time, the old consensus morality has disappeared. Once it was understood that the United States was generally right and its enemies generally wrong. This is no longer true, and it has become the critical battleground for television news — indeed, the only really important one. By definition, objective journalism is supposed to be neutral and not take sides, and in its way television is extraordinarily objective. It declines to take sides on the most important issues of our time.

The problem is that there are issues on which we cannot afford to be neutral. Totalitarianism is a fact. The Soviet Union is an expansionist empire. A democracy is a more moral form of government than a dictatorship. No reputable television correspondent is likely to disagree with any of these as abstract notions, but there is a problem in concretizing the abstractions. The value system determines the point of view. The values do not make television journalists anti-democratic, anti-Western forces. This becomes increasingly apparent as the networks increasingly become supranational organizations — roaming the world, negotiating with foreign governments, allowing anchormen and prominent correspondents to become surrogate secretaries of state. They represent not their country's interests, but their own, *i.e.*, television's. This does not mean they are unpatriotic; one supposes that most of them would go to war or wave a flag as quickly as anyone else. But it does mean their own imperatives come first.

Television was responding to the moral dimensions the culture had imposed on journalism. Until, say, 20 years ago, the dimensions were different. Anchormen and prominent correspondents could even narrate documentaries produced by the Pentagon. Flags waved; martial music was heard. The assumption was that the United States and its allies were morally sound in their behavior. Whether it was proper for the anchormen and correspondents to have associated themselves with documentaries is debatable. The cultural assumption that allowed the association, however, is preferable to the assumption in force today.

Supranational Networks

Thus television is now expected to rise above national interest and exercise neutrality on the great questions of our time. There are apparent anomalies in this. Dan Rather grew teary while he watched the marching bands during Ronald Reagan's second inauguration. This was permissible behavior. Television critics and other sophisticates may have responded unfavorably, but viewers and network executives, presumably, found it endearing. Certainly it proved that Mr. Rather was as susceptible to patriotic blandishments as his most conservative critics. Nonetheless, on the eve of the Geneva summit conference between Reagan and Mikhail S. Gorbachev, Mr. Rather could also tell his huge audience that the "central point" of the summit conference would be Mr. Reagan's position on "Star Wars" — the Strategic Defense Initiative. Would the President say, "No, I'm not giving at all," or would he be "flexible?" Actually, this was Gorbachev's position, too. World peace could be achieved only if the United States decided not to build a defense against incoming intercontinental ballistic missiles.

This gives us what may seem like a contradiction: The CBS anchorman, who is the most-watched television journalist in America, is emotionally touched by American symbols; but he also agrees with the world's foremost representative of the forces that oppose these symbols. There is no contradiction. In the first instance, Mr. Rather responds viscerally; in the second, he responds according to the rules of the dominant culture. In international matters, the burden is on the United States. American power is suspect. Arms control, a complex technical question, can be reduced to a few moral certainties: Nuclear weapons are threatening; it is better to disarm than to arm; the United States and the Soviet Union are equally menacing. On this last, the dominant culture and television's increasing supranationalism comes neatly together. It is not that television journalists consciously pursue a policy of moral equivalence; it is just as much that television in the 1980s knows no geographic or symbolic boundaries. Satellites and earth stations instantly connect our living rooms to the world's farthest places. Time and distance are obliterated. Jesse Jackson can campaign for the presidency in Syria as easily, and probably more effectively, than in Chicago.

At the same time, television networks negotiate with foreign governments rather as one sovereign state to another. A newspaper moves a reporter into a foreign country; a network moves a presence. The newspaper reporter files a story that will appear along with many other stories in the newspaper. Thus even the most benighted, inaccurate and misleading story is given some context. It coexists with other reports about the state of the world, and must compete for attention. As one of many stories in the newspaper, meanwhile, it is less likely to be regarded as carrying any special imprimatur. Television journalism, of course, is a wildly different operation.

MediaGuide 53

For one thing, the logistics have no similarities. Newspaper reporting is a solitary pursuit; a ballpoint pen and notebook are the essential pieces of equipment. A television correspondent travels in a group — correspondent, cameraman, soundman, and field producer — along with mounds of equipment. A portable machine for editing videocassette material may weigh half a ton. The *Times* covered most of the 1980 Iranian hostage crisis with a single reporter in Teheran. ABC had five correspondents, five producers, five two-man camera crews, seven assistants, and a business manager. Transportation, housing, and technical facilities must be found, usually through the assistance of the host government. At the same time, the host government is likely to regard the products of print and television journalism in markedly different ways. The print story, reaching a limited number of readers, is an inconvenience. The television story, broadcast to a mass audience, is an opportunity. There was never any real news during the Iranian hostage crisis; each day was very much like another. The network presence, however, was a positive boon to the Ayatollah. His aide, Sadegh Ghotbzadeh, made deals. Feed interviews and other film to ABC, CBS, and NBC; then get it on EuroVision. If EuroVision uses the film, Japan will pick it up. Then it goes out to the rest of Asia. The world would get the Ayatollah's message.

The *sine qua non* of television coverage, meanwhile, is what it has always been; it can't be boring or tedious. As Reuven Frank told his staffers in 1963, it must "display the attributes of fiction, of drama," with "structure and conflict, problem and denouement, rising action and falling action." It's not what the coverage says; it's how it says it.

How dominant is the artistic and intellectual culture? It is pervasive; orthodoxy is strictly defined. Heresy is noticed. It is as if a departure from the norm, real or imagined, threatens the established order. The *Washington Post*, for example, ran a fulsome three-part series on the retirement of the executive editor of the *New York Times*. As news pegs go, the retirement wasn't much; it was still a year and a half away. On the other hand, there were the rumors, explored by the *Post*, that the executive editor of the *Times*, A. M. Rosenthal, was moving the paper to the "right." That was the real subject of the series. In fact, no serious observer had said that Rosenthal tampered with news stories, bent the rules of journalism, or distorted the *Times'* coverage. No serious observer had to; it was enough that there was a perception of a rightward drift. The drift did not have to exist (in truth, it did not exist at the *Times*); but the fiercesome possibilities the culture attaches to the right moved the *Post* to carry the series. It was as if deviancy had to be sniffed out. Indeed, deviancy was sniffed out. Who had Rosenthal promoted? Which reporter harbored conservative views? What had been overheard at cocktail parties? It was like reading the entrails of a goat.

The PBS Citadel

Nowhere, however, is orthodoxy enforced more strictly, or protected more zealously, than in public broadcasting. It is worth noting here that one Rothman-Lichter study found that members of the public-broadcasting community were more liberal in their attitudes than their counterparts at the three commercial networks. They were also more liberal than staff members at the *New York Times* and *Washington Post*. The clearest expression of this is not in PBS programming, however; it is in the way the public-broadcasting community regards itself. It is wrapped in its own pieties. There was a wonderfully clear expression of this when PBS showed "Television's Vietnam: The Real Story," a documentary produced by Accuracy in Media, or AIM, the conservative watchdog group that looks for liberalism in the press. Its documentary, "Television's Vietnam," was a rebuttal to "Vietnam: A Television History," a 13-part series that public television presented two years before.

The salient point here, however, is not AIM's rebuttal, or even the original series. It is the dispute that embroiled the public-broadcasting community and much of the nation's news media. Why was AIM, clearly a right-wing organization, being allowed air time? Worse, it had been given $35,000 by the National Endowment for the Humanities to help finance the production. This seemed to be a clear sign that the conservative Reagan Administration was trying to force its views on public television. Federal dollars were being used to spread an alien philosophy. When PBS entertained television critics and reporters on its annual "press tour," the AIM documentary dominated their questions. Was the Reagan Administration trying to intimidate public television? Would PBS succumb to right-wing pressures? And if it did not, would the Administration then move to cut off its funding? Already there had been an ominous sign. A White House official had arranged a showing of the AIM documentary while PBS was still deliberating whether to include it on its schedule. A tremor ran through public television then, and battle lines were drawn.

As real battles go, however, it was pretty much one-sided. The dominant artistic and intellectual culture, perceiving a threat, rallied unto itself. One must remember the moral ordinates imposed on journalism. The right wing is the enemy of all good things, and no negotiation is possible. Few stories about the dispute mentioned that "Vietnam: A Television History," the series that AIM wanted to challenge, had received almost $1 million from the Corporation for Public Broadcasting, which disburses taxpayers' dollars. Even fewer stories noted that the Administration already had authorized a higher level of funding for public broadcasting than anyone had expected. No news story recognized that when the National Endowment for the Humanities gave AIM the $35,000, it was doing what Government agencies in any Administration, Republican or Democratic, do all the time. Political constituents must be pleased, and senators and congressmen lobby the agencies. It is how the Great Republic works. The

$35,000 that the Endowment gave AIM — a pittance, incidentally, by television standards — was a bone thrown to conservative Republicans. In the real world of politics, it had nothing to do with public television.

It wasn't read that way, of course; it was seen as a foray by hostile forces onto hallowed ground. Public television not only dispenses the dominant culture; it is protected by it as well. Moreover, Vietnam, the subject of the AIM documentary, was the single subject on which the culture was most impassioned. There is no room for many points of view about Vietnam; there is room for only one. Public broadcasters' protests grew more anguished. The *New York Times*, along with other newspapers, reported the broadcasters' fears: From now on, they would be expected to promote Administration positions; their integrity was being threatened. Careful readers of the *Times*, however, may have noted that the story was based on the speculations of a single public broadcaster — the producer of the series that AIM wanted to criticize. So much for the *Times*' move to the right. The story was played on page one.

Eventually, AIM's 57-minute documentary did air, carefully sanitized by PBS. Panel discussions, interviews, and explanatory material were added to ring the documentary fore and aft. Arthur Miller of Harvard Law School, the host for the now two-hour program, said soberly that "Accuracy in Media (is) so controversial that this program, the one you are now watching, has itself become the object of intense interest in the press." It was as if PBS were showing an X-rated movie, and apologizing in advance. The paradox was that "Television's Vietnam: The Real Story" turned out to be a reasonable piece of work, with reasonable criticisms of the 13-part series: The series presented Ho Chi Minh as a nationalist rather than as a Communist; it minimized the brutal treatment of American prisoners of war; it ignored the role of the South Vietnamese Army; it paid insufficient attention to actual military operations. The criticisms may have been debatable, but certainly they weren't outrageous. In interviews on the program, however, the producers of the 13-part series declined to give an inch. Television critics and newspaper columnists agreed with them. The series had to stand as Holy Writ.

Forget the free flow of ideas and a multiplicity of view points; the dominant culture stands for no dissent. Public broadcasting is one of its citadels. It has never had the slightest difficulty in identifying the enemy. Once and forever, the enemy is the right wing. Indeed, public broadcasting interprets all criticism as an attack from the right, which is the way it stays in business. Thus it was conceived in the '60s, when the Johnson Administration was interested in setting up all good things, and the idea that broadcasting might not be a proper involvement for government was never really discussed. Why, for example, should taxpayers' dollars be used to produce news shows? No matter how carefully the money is administered, it blurs the American tradition of an independent press. It still does today. Moreover, in the '60s, television was relatively new; there wasn't that much of it around. Public television was supposed to provide an alternative to "Bonanza" and "Gomer Pyle." Art, music, and drama would flower. Children would be better educated. Their parents would be better informed. Television, used properly, would have redemptive powers. No one believes that today, not even public broadcasters, but the government funding still lingers. In the '80s, the argument that public television was necessary to provide an alternative has also disappeared. New forms of television proliferate. There are now more than 6,500 cable-television systems in operation, with others being planned, while new forms of electronic communication — low-power television, multipoint distribution service, satellite master-antenna systems, for instance — are coming up fast.

Nonetheless, public broadcasting — radio and tv — stays on, enjoying a protected status. It is a billion-dollar industry that long ago outgrew the need for federal subsidies, and long ago moved away from the idea that it was supposed to operate in the public interest. In recent years, its principal concern has been ratings, and it has behaved very much like the commercial networks in pursuing them.

Meanwhile, public broadcasting has been so strongly sanctified by the dominant culture that serious criticism of its method of operation is virtually unknown. As an institution, it has been brilliant at isolating its critics. The corollary, as always, is that in identifying the enemies, the friends are known as well. They represent the positions the enemies do not.

At its best, the thinking is frivolous. Whimsy takes over instead of facts. At its worst, the thinking surrenders to totalitarian forces. It is as if the culture must attack the prosperous, pluralistic society that allows it to exist. Journalism fails when it allows the dominant culture to determine what it sees. As it is, the news agenda is out of balance already. Cameramen and reporters do not accompany Soviet troops in Afghanistan, or North Korean, East German, and Cuban military advisers wherever they may be. A large part of the world is simply blocked from view. At the same time, we are living in a world of moral relativism. One set of values is as good as another, and words no longer mean what they did. Philosophies become blurred, and so, in a way, do objective data. We do not grasp the meaning of genocide. We do not seem to understand the idea of boat people, refugees or internment camps. Television is important here; it now seems to be our window on the world — a way, if not *the* way, in which events are made known. When television does not come to grips with 20th-century horrors as honestly as it can, it meets neither its moral nor professional responsibilities.

That there should be a moral component to television is never discussed, save when there are arguments about television, sex, and violence. The moral component of television journalism, however, is ignored. When television broadcasters congratulate themselves at awards dinners, they talk about their bravery in examining difficult subjects. Reporters and cameramen who operate under fire may indeed be brave, but that's not the kind of bravery the broadcasters mean. Almost always, they are referring to the bravery that is supposedly required to report on unpopular topics. It is self-serving. The unpopular topics usually turn out to be indictments of the existing order — toxic wastes, homeless people, unsafe products. The common denominator in the journalism here is that it will all be culturally sanctioned. Not much appears on television news programs that is not approved.

There is something like obverse proof of this when CBS presented "The Vanishing Family: Crisis in Black America," a two-hour report with Bill Moyers. Its thesis was that black family life in the United States, especially in the inner cities, had broken down. "Black teenagers have the highest pregnancy rate in the industrial world," Moyers reported, "and in the black inner city practically no teenage mother gets married." Very carefully then, Moyers and his colleagues went on to make a secondary point: The social structure erected by the state can be counter-productive; welfare assistance may destroy a recipient's sense of personal responsibility. The program was provocative and intelligent, sensitively done and widely applauded. Amid the applause, however, it was scarcely noted that the subject of the disintegrating black family had been briefly on the American agenda more than 20 years before. The Department of Labor issued the so-called Moynihan Report, whose principal author, then Assistant Secretary of Labor Daniel P. Moynihan, had argued that "the Negro family in the ghetto is crumbling." Nonetheless, while the research in the Moynihan Report was impeccable, its assertions found little favor. The Moynihan Report was widely criticized as racist, and even Martin Luther King, Jr. said that it might be used to justify an argument for "innate Negro weakness." As a subject for respectable journalistic, political, and academic discussion, the disintegration of black family life was virtually dead, ruled out by a culture that could not look beyond the idea of oppressor and oppressed. The consequence was that rational planning for any national policy of families was further delayed. When CBS resurrected the discussion, television critics and journalists hailed it for its bravery. It was possible, however, that CBS had shown not so much bravery as a sense of opportunity. The moral and political ordinates of the culture presumably had changed. There are fashions in politics, and new interests arise. The black family is now an acceptable topic.

Journalism, television or print, has never been as serious a profession as its practitioners pretend, and in a way it has always pursued fashionable interests. Often, of course, it has created them. There has always been an element of whimsy in journalism, although in the past this made less difference than it does now. Print reached a limited audience; television now reaches a mass audience. Newspapers relied, and still do rely, on reporters, whose sensibilities and grasp of factual material were strained through an editorial process. At the same time, there were always rules to follow. Who, what, when, and where exercise a disciplinary effect. A television correspondent, filmed in action, has no such restraints. There is something very solemn going on here. Perfectly ordinary men and women, most of them with only moderately good educations, none of them elected, licensed, or franchised, indeed most of them employed primarily because of their stage presence, now speak directly and self-assuredly to millions of people about some of the most important things in their lives. At the same time, these perfectly ordinary men and women are given a good deal more leeway than print reporters in expressing their opinions. Television news is immediate, one on one, with correspondent and viewer in something like a communion. This means there is an ineluctable pressure toward making the correspondent a performer. This also means there is a temptation to trivialize the news.

Trivialization of the News

Trivialization is also what happens when television allows the culture to shape its reporting. Real issues get lost then, replaced by less-substantial concerns. When television journalism is good it can be very, very good, with an immediacy that print can never hope to match. But increasingly in television now, trivialization seems to be almost in a race with itself. Which kind of trivialization will win out? Television journalism's obeisance to the dominant culture or to the performing arts? In unexpected places, the two can even merge.

Thus at the start of the Geneva summit conference, the *Washington Post* quoted Donald Regan, the White House chief of staff, as saying that women are more drawn to human-interest stories than to hard analysis about missiles and throw-weights. This was the stuff of which small embarrassments are made, even if, in a way, Regan was right; men, too, are more drawn to human-interest stories. On the second day of the summit conference, however, Sam Donaldson of ABC, acting as a pool reporter, confronted both Gorbachev and Ronald Reagan. "Do you think," he asked Gorbachev, "women are interested in missiles and throw-weights and the other topics of the summit?"

It was a fascinating, and depressing, moment in television history. Donaldson looked supremely pleased with himself; President Reagan looked grim. Gorbachev waited while the question was translated; and then made a propaganda speech. The Donaldson question and Gorbachev reply were broadcast on all three American networks and around the world as well. A print reporter who behaved as Donaldson did would be considered something of a flake. Donaldson is one of television's most esteemed correspondents.

Meanwhile, network news as we have known it is declining. The one-hour documentary is almost a thing of the past, and managements have cut back on the size of the news divisions. Grant that cable now gives us an increasing amount of news, and that local stations, relying on satellite technology, may cover the world. An older generation of television journalists, many of whom began in print, has just about disappeared, and a new generation is rising. The problem is that the generation's loyalty may not be to journalism, but to television itself.

Consider that CBS News labored to bring forth a new kind of television journalism, and the result was "West 57th." It turned out not to be journalism at all; it was video — words, music, and images, blended to tell less than compelling stories, and closer in spirit to MTV than to Edward R. Murrow. If "West 57th" had been presented by the CBS entertainment division, it might have passed unnoticed. As it was, "West 57th" was a news program by no recognizable standards, and it was rather as if the network didn't care. Many of the "West 57th" producers had been enlisted from entertainment programs, not news or public affairs. It wasn't the news topic that was important; it was how the topic was presented. Style didn't just take precedence over substance; it buried it completely. In the aftermath of the program's debut, newspaper stories said that the "old guard" at CBS News was alarmed; journalistic tradition was being flouted. The irony here was that the old guard, for the most part, seemed to be drawn from "60 Minutes," and "60 Minutes," which reportedly accounts for about one-fourth of the network's profits, pioneered in the matter of style over substance. It grew famous by giving us the hunt, the chase, the triumph of good over evil: Watch Mike Wallace and his colleagues close in on the bad guys. This is docudrama, and "60 Minutes" is a news program only by lenient definition. At CBS, however, it represented the old guard, projecting journalistic tradition.

What is new then, and who is a newsman? It is easier to say what they are not, and the answers bring us back to the dominant culture. Journalism demands a fidelity to facts, a sense of fair-mindedness and an instinct about the great issues of our time. Something was terribly wrong when the League of Women Voters sponsored a series of tv debates for the Democratic presidential candidates in 1984, and chose Phil Donahue, the talk-show host, as one of the moderators. Something was even worse when no one objected. Donahue, a perfect representative of the dominant culture, asked John Glenn about aid to El Salvador. Would he suspend it? Yes or no? Donahue demanded a one-word answer. When Glenn hesitated, Donahue mentioned death squads and corpses, and then moved on to the next candidate. It was an astonishing display of simple-mindedness.

More recently, Donahue conducted something called "A Citizens' Summit." Satellite technology allowed him to stand in a studio audience in Seattle, and exchange thoughts with a Soviet counterpart and his studio audience in Leningrad. The generic name for programs like this is spacebridge, and they seem to be coming into favor. In general, they tell us that the United States and the Soviet Union have common interests, and that the citizens of both countries are very much alike. Substantive issues are dissolved. Spacebridges do not have much to do with real journalism, although they have a good deal to do with a journalism that finds it contours in the dominant culture.

It is likely we will see many more spacebridges on television. They are perfect accessories to a journalism that has allowed its critical faculties to lapse. When President Reagan gave a televised speech on military spending in February of 1986, ABC News put a Communist functionary in Moscow on the air to rebut him. When the White House complained, ABC admitted it had "erred" in turning to the functionary, but it also said its mistake was not in allowing him to speak; it was in allowing him to speak too long. This missed the point entirely. ABC had allowed a representative of a totalitarian state to join in an American political debate, even to having him follow the House majority leader, who made the Democratic response to Mr. Reagan. One side was as good as the other; there was no distinction between East and West. The Communist functionary was given a moral and political status he simply did not deserve. Meanwhile, when Lawrence K. Grossman, the president of NBC News, was asked to comment on the ABC-White House dispute, he made it clear that NBC recognized no distinctions, either.

"It is appropriate when the President is accusing the Soviet Union of aggressive behavior," Mr. Grossman said, "to get a perspective from the people on the other side. We didn't do it ourselves, but I see nothing wrong with it. In fact, I think it was a good thing to do."

It was not a good thing to do, unless Mr. Grossman and NBC were also prepared to argue that the Soviet Union did not practice aggressive behavior. The Soviet Union does practice aggressive behavior; history testifies to that. The need for "a perspective from the people on the other side" suggests either that the aggressive behavior does not exist, or that somehow it can be explained or justified. Mr. Grossman, as well as the ABC News executives, found the framework for their journalism not through independent analysis, but in the ready-made, close-at-hand scaffolding of ideas, passions, and impulses that make up the dominant culture. Statements by a democratically elected American President, meant for domestic debate, must be tested against those of Soviet spokesmen.

Is television somewhere on the left, reflecting a liberal bias? Of course it is, but it is there more because of slovenliness than conscious choice. It is there because television journalism, for the most part, raises no independent standards. Sometimes it raises no standards at all. It would be reassuring to think that none of this matters, but it does, and in time to come it is likely it will matter more. The great issues will not go away, and neither will the need for their being examined.

PUBLICATIONS

THE PACESETTERS

The New York Times

The New York Times is the most important newspaper in the world, without challenge since the 1920's — when *The Times* of London was still astride the globe. This importance derives mainly from its location in the world's communication and capital center, New York City, which gives it the loftiest of vantage points on the global political economy. The *Times* has been growing into this role for more than a century and of course is conscious of its history and standing, its immense influence on global opinion, and its responsibility in maintaining journalistic standards. Where *The Wall Street Journal* no doubt thinks of its new bureau in New Delhi as a luxury it can finally afford, the *Times* thinks of its New Delhi bureau as an *obligation* which it must maintain whether it can afford it or not. In a sense, the newspaper has come to think of the entire apparatus in this institutional way. *The Wall Street Journal, The Washington Post* and the other national print and electronics news media are important linkages in the international communications grid. But the *Times* properly lays claim to the unique position of being at the top of the top. It is more than just the newspaper of record for the United States, it is the center of journalistic gravity for the world, the communication core of the global polity, which is something it is just beginning to realize.

By this we mean the *Times*, insofar as it has institutional thought and memory, in recent years has begun to convey a greater awareness of its importance as a medium of *exchange* as opposed to a repository of wisdom that it is obliged to broadcast for the betterment of man. We observed in the *1986 MediaGuide* that a newspaper can strive for power or for perfection, but not directly for both, and the *Times* "spent the decade of the 1970s in a schizophrenia on this point, diverted by Vietnam and Watergate into a merry chase with *The Washington Post* in a pursuit of power at perfection's expense....After more than a century in pursuit of excellence, it may have been good for the *Times* to join the party in the 1970s, have a little fun for a change, whoop-de-do. The inebriation was fun while it lasted, but there will be an institutional memory of the hangover that will probably carry it another century, more or less. It had gotten more than a trifle self-important, more than a trifle arrogant."

This probably sprang from a problem of youth. In 1945, the United States was in early adolescence as the world political leader, having inherited that responsibility from Great Britain in stages. It seems reasonable to suggest that the arrogance that developed at the *Times* in the decades that followed, reflected the kind of hubris that is particular to adolescent years. There was no doubt that the power elite of New York and Washington knew what was best for the world, with little of the questioning that comes with experience. Mature political leadership expresses doubt and hesitation when it is not quite sure of direction, asking the greater assistance of those being led. In these years the *Times* editorials read like manifestos of an empire, with no attempt at persuasiveness because there simply was no argument. Given the political and economic upheavals that followed in the wake of these manifestos, it's instructive to reel back to them on microfilm and realize how quaint they seem. It's a sign of the *Times* maturity that its editorials now grapple with issues and ideas and are more interesting to read.

We suggested last year that 1985, in many ways, was the *Times*' best year in twenty. Nineteen eighty-six was at least as good, and A.M. (Abe) Rosenthal, who retired as executive editor in September, 1986, can feel justifiably pleased with the quality of the newspaper he has turned over to Max Frankel, who at 56 will have a good nine-year run at leaving his own mark on the *Times*. Rosenthal, one of the best American reporters of the postwar era, mainly improved the reporting strengths of the paper, which of course is the foundation of any chronicle. Frankel, the editorial page editor of the *Times* since 1977, was also a reporter's reporter in his formative years — in Vienna, Moscow, the United Nations, the White House, and as chief diplomatic correspondent in the Washington bureau. It would be surprising if the paper's reporting prowess slipped under Frankel, but Rosenthal had a gift for keeping a hum in areas that would tend toward the routine. If the routine is handled with zest, all else is elevated.

The Editorial Page

The editorial columns and op-ed page were reformed in the Frankel years, giving them a feel of editorial tension and vitality missing in earlier years. Our eye goes first to the letters column, where opinions are sharpest and this vital tension is greatest. But we have come to make time also for at least the lead editorial, unquestionably liberal, but almost always without the arrogance that follows when opposing views are dismissed out of hand. There's less passion here than in *The Washington Post*'s editorials, but sharper reasoning, and our palates are divided on which we'd prefer if we had to choose one page over the other for left-of-center opinion.

Of the many *Times* editorials we noted, three are worth an observation. In "The Terrorist and His Sentence," 4-15, the smoke had barely cleared after the U.S. bombing run over Tripoli and the *Times* briskly laid out its *reasoning* for unalloyed support of the action. In "Toward a Rehnquist Court," 6-18, we see a graciousness toward the Reagan high court appointees that invites those who normally don't agree with the *Times* to give them more thought. "A Costlier

MediaGuide 63

Yen is Not Enough," 4-7, is a throwback to the imperious days, insisting that the Japanese save too much and "we could insist" they invest more in poor countries.

The op-ed page improved a bit in 1986 if only because William Safire did, after an exceptionally vacant and grouchy 1985. James Reston and Flora Lewis continue to put us to sleep with their columns, and should retire to write memoirs. Russell Baker, who used to keep us smiling, gets grouchier with age. Tom Wicker wrote the worst column of the year, "A Star is Born for the Democrats," 9-9, lavishing praise on Barbra Streisand for hosting a gala fundraiser for Democratic pols. Anthony Lewis maintained a high quality to his vigorous liberal analytics, at times admirably bold in holding to positions that other liberals have abandoned. There's not much room left for outsiders, but when there is the selection rarely arouses us. There is even less room now that A.M. Rosenthal's column will run, but we of course happily look forward to Abe's contribution. The new editpage editor is Jack Rosenthal, Frankel's assistant and no relation to Abe, who knows the domestic scene. His assistant is Leslie Gelb, a veteran national security reporter up from the Washington bureau. Gelb has worked for liberal politicians, the late Jacob Javits and the Carter administration, and is not quite trusted by defense hardliners. But he has such a command of the material compared to the fellows who have been writing the *Times*' editorials on these matters that this alone will improve the page.

The Business Pages

Business editor Fred Andrews, an emigre from *The Wall Street Journal*, and Sunday business editor Soma Golden, an economics writer who served time on the editorial page, have made the *Times* competitive with the *Journal* and in some ways superior. If we only have time for one business reading during the day, we prefer the *Journal*'s for comprehensiveness. But if we know we can read both, we'll read the *Times* first. Indeed, in 1986 for the first time we *began* our reading of the Sunday *Times* with the business section, where there often seems more interesting news about what's going on generally than in the news pages.

At least some of the dramatic improvement at the *Times* in the last two years came as a result of the big expansion of the *Journal*'s staff in 1983, which alarmed the *Times* into beefing up. Instead of hiring carloads of young reporters, which has been a disappointment so far at the *WSJ*, the *Times* added fewer, but with heavier credentials, and turned them into stars by letting them loose to write: Steven Prokesch, David E. Sanger, Andrew Pollack, Eric Berg, Winston Williams, Robert A. Bennett, Nicholas Kristof, etc.

There's room for improvement in the Sunday business section, especially the Forum commentaries on pages two and three. The section is far too reliant on establishment business figure taking predictable stands on public policy issues, the usual suspects being Felix Rohatyn, J.K. Galbraith, Robert Reich, Malcolm Baldridge and someone from the Treasury or State Dept. No imagination, and certainly no wit, daring, humor or unconventional thinking even in the pros and cons.

The Sunday section could also do more with its company and personality profiles. These improved smartly in 1986 when the stars are at work, but too many of them are formula pieces: "CEO Ed Smith Takes Helm of Jones Co. With Firm at Crossroads." Then a safe recitation of Jones Co.'s current woes, a couple of analyst appraisals ("They've got tough problems") including one counter opinion ("They're well positioned to bounce back") and a flattering consensus ("If anyone can get the job done it's Ed Smith"). Too many soft profiles of the *Fortune* 500 companies.

The Washington Bureau

Washington bureau chief Bill Kovach, 54, had been in the running to succeed Abe Rosenthal. When he didn't make it, he clearly wouldn't make it down the line; he'd be 61 at Frankel's retirement. On November 14, the *Times* announced that Kovach was leaving to be editor of the Atlanta newspapers, a great gain for Atlanta and a blow to the *Times*. Craig Whitney, the assistant managing editor for foreign news, was named bureau chief, Judith Miller, the Mideast correspondent, his deputy. In the wider reshuffling, this first of the Frankel regime, Kovach's talented deputy, Howell Raines, 43, was named London bureau chief. Raines, who had been the bureau's national political correspondent, helped Kovach establish the eminence of the bureau in recent years after a long period in the *Post's* shadow; London may round him out for even loftier positions.

The biggest move earlier in 1986 was the drafting of E.J. Dionne, Jr., 34, the Rome bureau chief, to be national political correspondent, the slot vacated by Raines in early '85. R.W. Apple, the chief Washington correspondent, shared political chores with Dionne, but was in effect relieved of full-time political duties to work the broader portfolio his title implies. This may turn out to be an inspired move. Dionne, one of the highest rated (★ ★ ★ ½) journalists in the *1986/87 MediaGuides*, hit the ground running at midyear and more or less kept up with the veterans in his first outing, the off-year congressional elections. The way he works, by 1988 he could be the star political reporter of the pack, which already has the competitive juices flowing in those Beltway circles.

The bureau in 1986 was clearly the best in covering the Challenger disaster in all its aspects, improved on 1985 in keeping ahead of the curve on tax reform, led the parade at the Tokyo economic summit, and made important

MediaGuide

contributions on the Reykjavik developments and Iranian arms/hostage controversy. The *Post*, though, hammered them on the unfolding espionage stories early in the year. The worst mistake of the year was their "expose" of Ferdinand Marcos' war record, letting themselves be manipulated by the State Department's anti-Marcos crowd. The bureau got away with the story in the general hurrah and relief when civil war was averted in the Philippine constitutional crisis. But the story did contribute to Marcos' demise.

The Sunday Magazine

Just when we thought the Sunday *New York Times Magazine* was sharing in the benefits of the paper's renaissance, it slumped on us. Either Edward Klein, the editor, could not inspire the galaxy of *Times* staffers, or outsiders, to send him better material, or he is less sensitive than he should be on what is being commissioned after a decade at the helm. The magazine is one of the most important components of the *Times* not only because Sunday subscribers are so let down when it fails them, but also because it provides a classy platform for the paper's writers and correspondents to display their best material.

On both counts the magazine suffered in 1986. Too often we felt the early morning dismay of a meager table of contents that would provide nothing for brunch. Or, a promising cover story would lead to disappointment when the material let us down. A ghastly piece previewing the Philippine elections, 2-2, as seen through the eyes of an old Barnard graduate still makes us wince. A cover on Mario Cuomo, 9-14, got our hopes up, but it seemed uninspired and bloodless, as did a cover on Mitterand, 3-2, that did not deliver the goods. A flaky "A Time Bomb is Ticking in South Korea," 11-16, by Edwin O. Reischauer seemed like he hadn't been there for years. The Tokyo bureau's Susan Chira produced a better cover story on South Korea, 12-14.

The pits, though, was a cover story on Justice William Brennan, 10-5, written by his former law clerk!!! ("He is also easily the warmest member of the Court, famous for his charm, always linking arms with his colleagues or reaching out for a hand or shoulder.") There were, though, plenty of satisfying weeks: a cover on Treasury's Darman, 2-16; a fine profile of actor Jack Nicholson by freelancer Ron Rosenbaum, 7-13; "What America Should Do About South Africa," 8-3, by Helen Suzman. Given the talent pool that the magazine has to draw upon, it is unforgivable that it produces so many disappointments.

The Cultural Pages

With Arthur Gelb now firmly in place as managing editor for the next two years, we don't expect any changes in the cultural coverage, daily or Sunday's Section II. Too bad. The first three or four pages of the Sunday Arts Section seem designed to act as an unofficial subsidy to keep a moribund Broadway going. Feature articles are generally couched as curtain raisers, filler for all the advertising from the Broadway theatres, dance and musical performances, and new movies.

Theatre critic Frank Rich has honed to a remarkably fine degree the art of writing a review that always ends on a positive note. His "sink the show" reviews are rare, and when he's forced to kill, it's always regretful, never gleeful. Negatives are carefully shaded and usually buried within reviews that begin and end positively.

Writing in Section II is on the order of drab, utilitarian blandness, reading like filler copy. Though generally accurate, the pieces are often used as source material for others who can write. Style has been rigorously suppressed since the late Seymour Peck was replaced as editor of the cultural pages by William Honan, and when Honan was moved up by Gelb to be overall culture editor, by Robert Berquist. Honan, we learned in *The Village Voice*, which has somewhat less than contempt for him, in 1986 posted a notice on the third floor bulletin board of the *Times* calling for all critics to henceforth put in 9-to-5 workdays!

The *Times* Abroad

With Craig Whitney named Washington bureau chief in Max Frankel's year-end shuffle, Foreign Editor Warren Hoge moved up as assistant managing editor, Joseph Lelyveld, the London bureau chief, was named Foreign Editor. The most important foreign bureau shift saw Serge Schmemann moving to Johannesburg from Moscow, his able deputy Philip Taubman moving up as Moscow bureau chief. We were pleased to see a new hand in Mexico City, Larry Rohter, with the economic and social crisis there making it an extremely important beat.

Among earlier '86 redeployments in the *Times*' foreign bureaus, two in particular were of significant consequence for its foreign reporting.

First, an unintended move, was caused by the expulsion of Peking bureau chief, John F. Burns, on July 27, by the Chinese. Burns, had been taken into custody July 17, questioned for 15 hours, held in detention for six days, and then charged with espionage. The Chinese claimed that he'd engaged in intelligence gathering in restricted military areas on his 1000 mile motorcycle trip into prohibited areas of central China. Both *Times* executive editor, A.M. Rosenthal and foreign editor Warren Hoge traveled to Peking to secure his release. The charges were a "misunderstanding" as Rosenthal put it — "Burns is no more a spy than my grandmother."

The espionage charges were spurious, but there was a case for his expulsion. Burns, who again is rated with four stars in this year's *MediaGuide*, is probably the best foreign correspondent around. No one quite pushes against the limits and constraints on information gathering the way he does. This was evident when he was the *Times*' Moscow bureau chief and dramatically confirmed again during his post in Peking. That's why amid all the generally adequate to very good reporting by other journalists on the mainland, his dispatches were singularly outstanding. Great changes have been taking place in China, so much so that "a new China" is an oft-used expression in the press now. Yet it was Burns who actually tested the boundries and limits of the "new China." But what probably tipped the scales in favor of the high-level decision to boot him out of the country was his unsurpassed, critical eye for key detail. On 6-8, the *Times* printed his report "Why Investors Are Sour on China," a critical examination of what was clogging up the works there. It was more than coincidental that the report was shortly followed by a round of reform in that area by the Chinese, and Burns got the boot. He'd simply become too good for a country still bound by totalitarian traditions to tolerate.

We cite Burns because he exemplifies the highest standards in professional foreign correspondence, typical of the criteria the *Times* attempts to employ. We don't know how his replacement, former Abidjan-based Africa bureau chief Edward A. Gargan will fare in Peking, but with most China reporting in the press generally satisfying, we can look at Peking's loss as Toronto's gain.

The *Times* Moscow bureau displays a similar kind of commitment. The principal challenge of newspapering in the communist bloc is resisting the fatigue that accompanies the probing, pushing, straining, sometimes daring leaps that are required to get to and even beyond the limits imposed on news reporting there. Settling for what's safe, what the censors might let slip by, ends up producing mediocrity. Bureau chief Serge Schmemann was rigorous again in 1986 in not letting any flab accumulate. We noted also a tenacity in bureau correspondent Felicity Barringer to move beyond rewriting official communiques and instead going after the news; "news" in the Soviet Union often being what isn't being reported. Likewise, Michael T. Kaufman, Warsaw bureau chief, pushed and plumbed, making his own openings where access was closed.

A second redeployment, this one calculated and intentional, and perhaps the most important in the long-run, was the decision to put Tokyo bureau correspondent Susan Chira on the economic/business beat in northeast Asia, with Tokyo bureau chief Clyde Haberman concentrating on the political/defense issues. We had noted in last year's *MediaGuide* that treatment of economic issues in this awkward period of U.S.-Japan commerce wasn't as satisfying as we'd hoped from the *Times*, wondering if the bureau could get beneath the surface in this center of global power. But with this new arrangement the *Times*'s Tokyo bureau excelled in 1986. The immediate consequence is that it's now nudging up against the *Financial Times* (where a similar arrangement exists between bureau chief Jurek Martin and Tokyo correspondent Carla Rapoport) as the premier reporting team in Tokyo.

A broader consequence we hope will come to pass is that the *Times*' application of the "Tokyo model" elsewhere. The Mexican bureau, for example, was very weak again in 1986, with the *Times* the paper of last recourse for information on the economy and debt crisis there. Its series on Mexico in November, an effort involving a number of its journalists, provided some new information, but it never got beyond the fringes on the critical question of what the country's economy is all about. Similarly, the *Times* missed several important economic developments in the Caribbean and Central America. The *Times* has bureaus in Port-au-Prince, Managua and San Salvador, yet it was the much smaller staffed *Journal of Commerce* that provided the key information on the area's economies. The *Times* missed completely key tax and trade reforms that took place in Haiti, Grenada, Jamaica, and Costa Rica, for example, and it was stingy with its economic coverage for the whole area.

This is not to say the *Times*' foreign bureaus should give us "more economic news" *per se*. As the *Times* grows deeper into its role as the most important newspaper in the world, foreign correspondence has also been growing beyond what it was when *The Times* of London dominated the scene. But there's a residue from the older focus that carries over still, with the subject of the reporting remaining "nation-states" rather than *countries*. Regimes and administrations, legislation and politics, diplomacy and foreign policy, war and revolution will continue to be the stuff of the news. So it's not to say "and add on economics, business and finance." But the dynamic of a country is missed when there isn't sense of what is intrinsic to making it tick — or not tick. Can any report on as complex a country as India, for example, be satisfying if it neglects treatment of the economic debate there, the implementation of tax and other reforms and their impact, a picture of what's new and being transformed or set back there as a consequence? Yet New Delhi bureau chief Steven Weisman avoided that, falling short on filling out the picture of what distinguished the India of 1986 from the India of 1985. It wasn't just "another aspect" to cover, but rather an intrinsic component of the whole picture. The Peking bureau operated on that understanding, and now the Tokyo bureau's in sync as well.

New bureau chiefs had come on line at the end of last year. Lelyveld in London put in a solid first year with his '86 reporting. Kifner in Cairo, decent, but not setting the pace yet on a beat the press as a whole hasn't mastered. Mydans in Manila, after a brief intoxication during the hysterical days of the Philippine electoral crisis, has recovered and improved. And this year, the *Times* beefed up its Buenos Aires bureau, a new chief there in '86, Shirley Christian, pulling Chile under her competent purview. Robert Suro moved into E.J. Dionne's slot in Rome, the former bureau chief's talents now utilized in the *Times*' U.S. political coverage.

Thomas Friedman in Jerusalem found serious competition coming from others, and may be motivated now to get back out ahead. Richard Bernstein, off the track, in fact not even at the station during the French elections, looking reoriented again at year's end. Alan Riding in Rio, okay, but the bureau needs help in getting its arms around that globally important economy. Barbara Crossette in Bangkok, sharper and more keen-eyed in 1986, good work out of that bureau for the year. As we detail elsewhere, the able performances were mixed with a few slips and regressions. The *Times* foreign correspondents were stellar as a whole for the year, with only one really bum performance.

The singular and disturbing disappointment in the *Times*' foreign correspondence was its Johannesburg bureau. We single it out because it was glaring for its failure to meet the *Times*' own standards. Because we examined and compared the South Africa coverage in all the other press during the year, we know something is seriously amiss in this bureau. It was not the only one where the *Times* was merely unsatisfying, sketchy or incomplete, but rather the only one where its coverage was *unreliable*. (See Page 22.)

Editor: Max Frankel

Circulation: Sunday 1,625,649
Weekday 1,035,426

Address: 229 West 43rd Street
New York, NY 10036

Telephone: 212-556-1234

The Wall Street Journal

With a daily circulation of 2 million, the *Journal* is the most prestigious, best-read national newspaper, easily eclipsing the readership of *The New York Times* and surpassing Gannett's *USA Today* on all counts. It no longer seems appropriate to refer to it as "the most important business publication in the world," as we did in the *1986 MediaGuide*. Neither the paper nor most of its readers think of it as a "business publication," as *Barron's* thinks of itself, for example, or the *Financial Times*. The *WSJ* aspires to the standing enjoyed by *The New York Times* as the nation's best newspaper, at least in a critical sense. Without weekend editions, it can't challenge the *Times* as a newspaper of record, and there doesn't seem to be an interest in that pursuit even over the long run. In the public affairs community, the *Journal* is already given equal standing with the *Times* and *The Washington Post* in terms of broad influence on decision making.

The *Journal*'s best material during 1986 was business related; the paper excelled in bird-dogging on the merger & acquisition beat. It can, because of the breadth and depth of its contacts, always dominate a big, breaking business story — the Texaco/Getty brouhaha for example. We also thought it excelled in covering Chernobyl in the important early phase of the story, edging out the *NY Times* (which, as expected, dominated the latter phases of the story).

The *Journal*'s Middle East coverage was best on the oil industry, and it made impressive efforts to improve its coverage of foreign economies, particularly in South America. The editorial page, the best anywhere, recovered from its 1985 slump. However, overall it was not a good year for the newspaper.

We observed in the *1986 MediaGuide* that the *Journal*'s biggest problem was growing pains. The problems persist. Dow Jones & Company, the parent of the *Journal*, has been engaged in a major expansion of production facilities in recent years to enable the printing of bigger papers that can carry more advertisements. The 1979 failure of the Dow Jones newsweekly, the *National Observer*, left management wary of new initiatives and without expansion options; the path of least resistance and risk was to double and redouble the number of *Journal* pages.

Managing editor Norman Pearlstine, who had been managing editor of both *The Asian Wall Street Journal* and the European edition after running the Tokyo bureau from 1973-76, was given the task of developing a staff that could eventually fill a multi-section newspaper running to as many as 80 pages. We stated last year that: "Reporters were hired by the carload" in 1983-84 and "What we're watching now is the equivalent of a boa constrictor swallowing a pig: We can watch the digestive process from the outside."

In early summer of 1986, Pearlstine seemed to believe the paper had already turned a corner in this digestive process, and steady improvement would be seen thereafter. But on November 16, the *NY Times* reported:

"For the last month, the *Journal* has been printing 68-page papers in some areas. 'It has been a struggle,' Norman Pearlstine, the managing editor, said in a memorandum to the staff demanding adherance to deadlines.

"'Page flow has ranged from terrible to ridiculous,' he wrote. 'We have ambitious plans for improving the paper — a corporate index, additional news space and features, more graphics and ultimately a three-section paper. We must get our act together before we can seriously consider tackling larger news holes and additional features.'

"Warren H. Phillips, chairman of Dow Jones, said the final decision on a third section had not been made. 'There are a lot of people working on prototypes, to see how such a section would look,' he said. 'But there are also projects under way to examine a reorganized second section.' But one thing is certain, he said, 'There will still be no photographs'."

In fact, we did not need to read that Pearlstine is having continuing problems of growing pains. Dow Jones & Company is flourishing financially, its stock on a crest, but in general the *Journal* lost qualitatively to its competitors in 1986. There were aspects of the paper that saw improvement. The editorial page we criticized for seeming tired and distracted in 1985, possibly because the staff

MediaGuide   71

was moving to new quarters, was rambunctious again and frequently more informative than the news pages. There were individual stellar performances throughout the year, lifting the newspaper above the run of the mill. But we became sufficiently concerned during our running evaluation of the paper — wondering if we were being too hard on it — that we cast a wider net for opinions and found only confirmation. As a rule, not as the exception, the *Journal* has become a more "loosely written" newspaper than it has been in memory. The term does not imply inattention to substance, but to the rigor of the writing process itself. There is no doubt that it took longer to get information out of a *Journal* reading in 1986 than it did in 1983, simply because the writing was looser. There is more froth in the casual leads of main events of each issue, the leaders of columns one and six, and the articles go on and on filling those news holes of the inside paper.

On reflection, it stands to reason that the pressures on the editorial staff from a management desirous of profit expansion will produce a less disciplined editing process. Unfortunately, the central idea of the *Journal* is to provide the business community throughout the nation a running start on the business day. If a tightly written 24 pages becomes a loosely written 48 pages, it takes the businessman four times as long to get a running start on the business day. To talk about 80 pages, with a staff harangued to meet deadlines in order to fill space, the *Journal* is risking the loss of its most prestigious readers, those who haven't time to swim against this tide of froth. The *Journal* is still more tightly written than, say, *The Washington Post*, but the *Journal* has a different niche and simply has to be skintight.

The most serious problem is on the front page. It may be the case of an old baseball fan believing the players of yesteryear were better than they are today, but we do believe the column one and column six "leaders" were superior not too long ago. These columns anchor the paper. The best material the editors have to offer is supposedly in these columns. So if they seem flimsy, we unconsciously assume the inside stuff is of less moment. Then when we find better material on the inside pages, it strikes us that the editors have some reason for being frothy. We would welcome an old-fashioned account of the state of the Polish economy, but instead get "How the Hairdressers in Warsaw Overcame a Scarcity of Scissors," 3-11. We'd grab at a full-blown report on the shape of India's economy, but get "Amid Social Progress, Bride-Burning Seems on the Rise in India," 8-21. Either piece makes sense in the second section, but too many like them are in the *Journal*'s lead positions.

Also discouraging is the dominant use of the soft lead on the front page. We know William M. Carley, veteran reporter, is capable of telling us a good part of his story in the opening paragraph, and he usually does when his material appears inside. Yet on page one, his May 20 leader on Robert Carlson's departure from United Technologies began thusly: "It was Sept. 21, 1984,

Robert Carlson's last day at United Technologies Corp., and a trying time for the executive. Just a few days before, he had been ousted as president of the company. In previous weeks, his home had been surreptitiously entered by persons unknown. Now, entering his office, he saw that sofas had been torn open and the lightswitch plates removed."

This is not William Carley, of course. It's the work of a phantom front-page rewriter, acting on instructions of front-page editor Glenn Mapes, who for some reason has adopted this approach from what we call the Snoopy School of Journalism, with gentle openings to big stories: "It was a dark and stormy night..."

On January 28, the newspaper's lead story on IBM office PC's: "Joseph Brody spent much of last summer on his hands and knees."

On May 19, the lead story on People Express: "It was the weekend before last Christmas at San Francisco International Airport."

On May 21, the lead on the national inflation outlook: "Behzad Touhidi always gets a good price. As an automobile 'broker,' he spends his days haggling with auto dealers to find the best possible buys for his clients."

Our assumption is that the *Journal* paid a consulting firm a fortune to conduct sensitivity sessions, to observe who reads what from behind one-way mirrors, or some such. If they would put us behind one-way mirrors at 7:30 a.m., with only one hour for both the *Journal* and the *Times*, they would find we have precious little time for Snoopy leads.

A third weakness on the front page is the so-called "A-Hed" of column four, initiated eons ago to provide light and frothy relief from the hard-nosed, rat-a-tat pieces in columns one and six. The idea, though, was that they would be 1) funny and 2) related to some aspect of the business world. Now they are almost never funny and almost never related to anything in particular. On May 19 we read four paragraphs on the common sea slug of mainland China before giving up without a smile. On May 21 we read four paragraphs about the *preparations* for a shrimping excursion in Florida before quitting, grimly. On May 27, we read about the tour of the Nelson Riddle's orchestra after Mr. Riddle's death, stopping with the quote, "It's a little macabre." These points are belabored, as well as the *Journal*'s growing penchant for multiple bylines (see "The Great Byline Inflation, page 14), because they have become so pronounced.

On its current accelerated expansion course, the *Journal* may increase earnings, but continue to decline in quality. Dow Jones chairman and CEO boss Warren Phillips is clearly on the spot, along with Peter R. Kann, the associate publisher directly responsible for the *Journal*. If the boa ever does digest the pig, they will be heroes, but the line of least resistance could swallow them instead.

MediaGuide 73

The Editorial Page

The great strength of the editorial page, unlike other editpages, is its editorial column, "Review & Outlook." On other editpages, the strength is in the columnists or the op-ed features, or even the letters. Under the stewardship of Robert L. Bartley, the editorial has evolved into a new genre, the "reported editorial." Editors and editorial writers have traditionally been hired to study the news, reflect, and voice a position appropriate to the newspaper's general philosophical framework. When an editorial is read in most newspapers, the reader is getting opinion based on news he or she has read or heard about elsewhere. This may save time and trouble.

Under Bartley, though, the *Journal* editorials combine news and editorial functions. Most *Journal* editorials are "reported" in that the writer either works from the reported news and digs to a deeper level before opining, or news is developed from scratch. This means that readers are getting more than just opinion; they are actually being informed simultaneously. Readers may feel satisfaction in reading the editorials and think it is because they "agree" with them, but there's an unconscious satisfaction in learning things in an editorial that had not appeared elsewhere. One of the best examples was "King Caucus," 10-28, on the maneuverings of the House Democrats to prevent funding for the Strategic Defense Initiative. "Mystery of the Lazy J," 4-8, was the most instructive analysis of the "J Curve," we had seen anywhere on that element of the trade effects of exchange rates.

The *Journal* editorials are also important when they lean against the wind, as in "Arms and the Imam," 11-17, on the Iran arms/hostage controversy, partly because of their rigor, but also because Bartley has built credibility during his regime. The editorials are not uniformly excellent, of course. Many are pedestrian. But the general level in 1986 was as high as it has ever been. The op-ed page was at par, no more, no less.

The one aspect of the editorial page that forces critical comment is the "Manager's Journal" column, edited by David Asman. The column was originated several years ago by Adam Meyerson, now the editor of *Policy Review*, and it then genuinely addressed topics of interest to managers. The column has deteriorated into predictably broad discussions of drugs, alcohol or AIDs in the workplace, suggesting the editor knows little about the mundane subtleties of management.

The Washington Bureau

(The response of the national print media to the initial *MediaGuide* of 1986 was overwhelmingly positive, as evidenced by the response to our survey of biographical data in this edition. The *Journal*'s Washington bureau boycotted the survey because of the animosity of its bureau chief, Albert Hunt, to Jude Wanniski, the *MediaGuide* editor and former associate editor of *The Wall Street Journal*. A personal conflict between the two extends back to Mr. Wanniski's years at the *Journal*.

Mr. Wanniski visited the bureau in 1986 in an attempt to ameliorate the differences, but as Mr. Hunt told *The Washington Post*, "I insulted him out of the office." The reader may thus wish to discount the remarks on the bureau accordingly.)

The *Journal* pays its biggest price in not having Saturday and Sunday editions in its coverage of national political affairs. Little happens in the business world on Saturday that won't wait for the Monday *Journal*. But the Sunday editions of *The New York Times* and *Washington Post* are so important to the New York-Washington political grid that the *Journal* suffers a disadvantage day in and day out in developing its source network. It's not so big that it overwhelms, but it is an obstacle. In covering, say, the Reykjavik summit, which spanned a weekend, both the news sources and the *Journal* news team would realize the paper was not in the hunt.

There is this inherent disadvantage that works against the *Journal*'s Washington coverage, especially on diplomatic news. The bureau hired *Newsweek*'s chief diplomatic reporter, John Walcott, in 1986 to try to close the gap with the *Times* and *Post*. But its embarrassment in the Libya "disinformation" episode, with Walcott himself suckered, pointed up the weakness here.

The bureau has sufficient manpower and great contacts on Capitol Hill and throughout the executive branch. So it gets its share of newsbeats and is watched closely for the meat-and-potato tidbits that it churns up constantly. The Friday front-page "Washington Wire" is one of the best-read political gossip and trend columns in the world, and the bureau takes special pride in having it look smart, which it did again in 1986 after sagging in previous years. "Did you see the 'Washington Wire' today?" is one of the most frequently asked telephone questions in New York and Washington each Friday.

An inherent advantage the *Journal* bureau has over its competitors is that its New York editors understand the significance of Washington news that impacts the business and financial world. This gives it an edge on space, placement and timing over, say, the *NY Times*, which is marginally less attentive to these kinds of stories. But the *Journal* has not had a Washington bureau chief in memory with Wall Street experience, the assignment going to a series of political reporters, currently Albert Hunt. As a result, the bureau has done well over the years on the political beat, doing so again in 1986. But it has allowed the *Times* and the *Post* to keep up with it and often surpass it, even with this natural advantage.

The *Journal* clearly excelled in its coverage of tax reform in 1985, but was matched by the *NY Times* in 1986, beaten briefly at a critical juncture in thinking the reform was dead, a thought that did not color the *Times*' coverage. The bureau badly lagged the competition on international monetary coverage, dispatching its trade reporter instead of its monetary reporter to the Tokyo summit. It was also weakened by shifting Laurie McGinley, who had developed monetary expertise in earlier years, to the space beat, where she kept her feet on the ground. The *Journal* was demolished by the *Times* on the space shuttle coverage (which led Pearlstine to pull together a Chernobyl team under veteran editor Barney Calame that did score over the *Times*).

A bright spot was the bureau's coverage of the 1986 political races, especially by David Rogers and David Shribman, keeping the *Journal* competitive here. But these were on the set-piece stories that are less demanding than the trend pieces that one expects from a political "Bigfoot," as the trade refers to the Broders and Apples. Bureau chief Hunt had this status before his promotion, and Robert W. Merry seemed headed toward it — the national political correspondent. But Merry left the bureau early in 1986 to be editor of the Capitol Hill *Roll Call*, and he was missed during the political year.

The *Journal* Abroad

The quality level of the *Journal*'s foreign correspondence in 1986 was about equal to '85's. There were individual reports that were very good, some even the best in the press at the time, and improvement on some fronts. But it came in spurts, unsystematically and inconsistently, and there seemed to us to be a relative decline because of the improvement of *The Washington Post*'s foreign service.

Some of the best work came from the *Journal*'s Mideast and Mexican coverage. Youssef Ibrahim, was much improved over the previous year, giving us good reporting on Egypt and the oil industry. Gerald Seib moved out ahead several times: a report on secular-religious tensions in Israel, 6-10, outstanding, and a gem, 3-14, on Sheik Yamani's problems with the royal family. But he also lagged at times, as in his and Barbara Rosewicz's 7-21 feature on the PLO's financial secrets. An 11-4 special report on Egypt, with a front-page leader by Seib that jumped over to the international page, was wonderfully innovative, almost all of it given over to stories on the country. But we didn't get from him and Ms. Rosewicz what we needed, the stories skimpy on the country's economic and internal debates.

Mary Williams Walsh, sometimes sharing the byline with S. Karen Witcher of the NY bureau, produced several solid reports out of Mexico. Each had fresh, critical information on the societal breakdown, with a 6-12 feature the best in the press. Yet, as good as they were, we still didn't get sufficient treatment in 1986 of the IMF's plans, internal economic debate, or regular coverage on the economy of the "need-to-know" variety. We wondered, therefore, why Peter Truell, who had done a superb job on this in 1985, hadn't been coaxed back from the London bureau in 1986.

Former Paris bureau chief Roger Ricklefs' reporting on the French elections, 3-31, had the best presentation at the time of what differentiated the various conservative contenders, superior to the *NYT*, although well behind *The*

Washington Post's overall coverage. And there were other notable, singular efforts, as we detail under the journalists' entries. However, these were the only two areas where the *Journal*'s foreign coverage was consistently sought out during the year.

The *Journal* was finally granted permission by the Soviets to open a Moscow bureau in 1986, with Mark D'Anastasio heading it up. Managing editor Norman Pearlstine forsees strengthened coverage of east-west relations and political/economic coverage from the area. With Moscow, the *Journal* now has 33 overseas bureaus, including its European and Asian editions.

Out of *The Asian Wall Street Journal* the work of Vigor Fung in China and Anthony Spaeth in Manila stood out in particular. Fung's reporting was solid all year, his byline eagerly awaited. Spaeth was less consistent; nonetheless, his election-eve Philippine wrap-up, 2-7, was outstanding, a classic piece of foreign reporting. Southeast Asia economics editor Raphael Pura and Malaysia correspondent John Berthelsen had been producing excellent investigative reporting on the economics and politics of that country. Their dispatches on the evidence of "moral rot" in Malaysia resulted in both their expulsions and a three month ban on the distribution of the *AWSJ*, rescinded late in the year. Again there were fine, singular efforts, New Delhi's Matt Miller for example, early with details on opposition to Gandhi's economic policies, 4-2. But both for India and the Asian-Pacific rim, regular and consistent reports with fresh new information and detail just weren't sufficiently frequent enough. We turned more and more to the *Financial Times* and *Journal of Commerce* to fill the information gaps and also regularly saw material in the *Asian WSJ* weekly that should have made it to the parent publication.

Editor: Robert L. Bartley   Circulation: 1,985,559

Managing Editor: Norman Pearlstine

Address: 200 Liberty Street   Telephone: 212-416-2000
           New York, NY 10281

The Washington Post

In the *1986 MediaGuide*, we cited as the most striking feature of *The Washington Post* its relentless advocacy of the Liberal Establishment's agenda. That was not merely an observation regarding its editorial policies, an area where such a disposition is appropriate, but rather the focus of what disturbed us about the *Post* in the past. Its "advocacy" tended to spill over into an area where it should have been prohibited — its reporting. In 1986, however, there was strong improvement by the *Post* in overcoming that problem.

MediaGuide

Donald Graham, *Post* publisher, selected Leonard Downie, Jr. in 1984 as managing editor. Accordingly, Downie is viewed as the likely successor to executive editor Benjamin Bradlee and apparently shares his publisher's plans to keep the paper moving away from the flamboyance of its previous years. Some of this has shown up in the paper's editorials, this year more thoughtful, less strident than in the past. Its political coverage as a whole continued to improve. The *Post* excelled in '86 on the espionage stories and trials, and its foreign reporting made impressive strides forward. Some of the *MediaGuide*'s more sensitive readers continue to find a consistent advocacy-leaning by some reporters pushing an anti-Reagan agenda of their own, but we note the improvement by how much more comfortable it has been in 1986 to read *The Washington Post*'s news columns.

Indeed, this greater balance has been noted by some who expect a liberal news tilt to the *Post*. "One of the most unpublicized ideological shifts in American journalism," a consumer advocate told a *Wall Street Journal* reporter; "The paper has gone hilariously right-wing." That hyperbole notwithstanding, 1986 was a period of shifting at the *Post*, some very positive, forceful and large-scale, some a little sluggish and less thorough. The *Post* had spent a good part of the previous year unsuccessfully attempting to get "Lameduck Reagan" scenarios to fly. But by early 1986, columnist Lou Cannon was noting the President's resiliency and durability. Not that advocacy disappeared from the national affairs reporting, but it was far more muted in '86 than previously, perhaps only held in abeyance.

The most noticeable change, however, was in the *Post*'s foreign reporting, where professionalism was the bottom-line in 1986. Assistant managing editor Michael Getler deserves credit for advancing the reporting on that front to where the *Post* foreign correspondents are now indispensable for reliable and thorough information in a number of areas.

We may still be disturbed by an unfortunate slant and indulgence of old bad habits that we can detect in the reporting of a Joanne Omang, for example, on foreign events, but she no longer produces that out of a Central American bureau, reassigned instead to the national affairs desk. While Getler has forcefully upgraded the *Post*'s foreign reporting, we couldn't say a similar change occurred in the *Post*'s national affairs reporting. Nonetheless, there was an overall, decided improvement in the *Post*'s performance in 1986.

The Political Beat

The *Post* prides itself on its coverage of national political affairs, and has the deepest bench of political reporters in Creation. With so many bodies, there should be uniforms, numbers and scorecards. Henceforth, in fact, Anne Devory, moving over from *USA Today*, will be "Political Editor" simply to direct traffic, and is the lady to court if you want your candidate covered.

Because as far as the *Post* editors are concerned David Broder's word is God's word on politics, he is still the most important political reporter in the country. When Broder in 1984 announced post-Maine that Mondale's candidacy "hangs by a thread," it did. What Broder pronounces after a primary isn't just the conventional wisdom, it is the fact. And he can turn the entire Beltway pack around on a dime, doing so in '86 with a sweeping piece on Rep. Jack Kemp's leadership potential, "The Right Signals," 9-2, the day after Labor Day when a new political season always begins in Washington. Where Broder's confreres had been writing all summer about Kemp being semi-washed up, it all stopped instantly with Broder's *obiter dictum*. And he doesn't particularly care for Kemp!

Broder continues to be an evangelist for the radical center, especially in his columns. He had an incredibly prolific year, but it does get tiring following him around, logging thousands of bonus miles on obscure airlines. Letting others take over the chores of covering campaigns in '86, Broder hunts for grand themes in odd nooks and crannies, and it wouldn't surprise us in the least if he found global significance at a convention of elected dog catchers. Actually, no grand themes were discovered by any of the political press in '86, the "themeless pudding" being the best anyone could come up with.

With all its personnel, the *Post* did not score a clear knockout of *The New York Times* in '86. A small survey of "political experts" suggests E.J. Dionne and R.W. Apple of the *Times*, and their team of reporters, were superior to Broder, Paul Taylor, Tom Edsall and their team. But our *MediaGuide* readers say the *Post* won on detail and found Tom Edsall the best of the *Post*'s political team. The best daily "political page" is *The Wall Street Journal*'s back page, easy to find, and consistently a lighthearted/nasty read. The *Times* Washington page we also appreciate, after a short hunt for it. The *Post* scatters its material throughout. A catch-all political column by Maralee Schwartz was fine once a week, but daily too skimpy.

The Editorial/Op-Ed Page

The *Post*'s unsigned editorials seemed to move more toward the "center" in 1986, balanced, thoughtful and well-written, and without the "this is what I'd believe if I were a better person" flavor to them. But there was no loss of passion in them, editorial-page editor Meg Greenfield keeping the page frothy, combative rather than strident, focused rather than scatter-shot.

The op-ed page still remains heavily dominated by conservative and neo-conservative columnists, Jeane Kirkpatrick coming aboard in 1985, to join George Will, Evans & Novak, Charles Krauthammer, William Buckley, Norman Podhoretz, R. Emmett Tyrrell, and James Kilpatrick. It is still short of sharp, unabashedly liberal commentary, although Richard Cohen was a colorful and muscular exponent of that point of view all year — among the best in all the national press. William Raspberry had a lively '86, surprising us enough that we now always have to look. And the weekly column of Steven Rosenfeld, an editorial writer otherwise, also had us back for looks in '86.

The Sunday "Outlook"

Under associate editor David Ignatius, the *Post*'s commentary and opinion section, "Outlook", continued to improve as solid reading fare for Sunday brunch, though it can still end up producing more than can be digested. An innovation, "Outposts," devotes the entire third page to a feature on the "cutting edge" of ideas being debated in research labs and on university campuses. The material seems misplaced in "Outlook," though, where we doubt readers will bother, and might be better read in the new magazine. But "Outlook" otherwise picked up a beat over the previous management of Robert G. Kaiser, who had moved up the ladder to assistant managing editor for national affairs. Ignatius has made better use of Sidney Blumenthal, who admittedly hits and misses with his higher risk political analytics, and he made plenty of room for that deep political bench, which is what the Sunday brunchers want most.

Ignatius does get a black mark in our book for leading "Outlook" with "Daniloff Forgot A Reporter Can't Do His Country A Favor," 10-12, by former *Post* Moscow bureau chief Dusko Doder, which broke the solid ranks of the press corps behind Daniloff. While Doder generously conceded that Nicholas Daniloff wasn't an American spy, he proceeded to treat the *U.S. News & World Report* correspondent as if he were a CIA dupe — "The Nicholas Daniloff case contains an important but little-noted lesson for the press: in a place like Moscow, doing a favor for the U.S. Embassy can get you in big trouble."

The Washington Post Magazine

Usually discarding the *Post*'s Sunday magazine after a quick scan of its uninteresting table of contents, we looked forward to the "new" magazine scheduled to appear Sept. 9. The effort got off to a very rough start, its cover story in the premier issue provoking outrage in D.C.'s black community. A feature by Richard Cohen, "Closing the Door on Crime," was criticized as racist, with the bewildered white liberal profusely apologizing in later articles, Ben Bradlee joining in to solicit forgiveness for any offense, Sunday "Outlook," 10-25. Despite the stormy reception — and rejection (thousands of copies were being dumped back on the *Post*'s doorsteps by angry readers every Sunday for months after the episode), the "new" magazine would still have been a dud. It's thin fare, the sense of a mind behind the operation just not there. But it's much too early to write it off.

Getler Gets It Going

The single most impressive improvement for the *Post* in 1986 was in its foreign correspondence. It was here the *Post* seemed furthest removed from advocacy and where there was least evidence of intrusion by any unacceptable bias. We credit a lot of it to Michael Getler, who took over the job of assistant managing editor for foreign affairs late in 1985. Of course, the *Post* also has a string of foreign reporters who are solid professionals and who can excel when their strengths are backed up from the home office.

Blaine Harden was unmatched in the entire press corps on sub-Saharan Africa coverage. James Rupert's Afghanistan stories were outstanding. William Branigan and John Burgess in east Asia, steady and solid on the Philippines and Japan all year. Allister Sparks careful and reliable on touchy South Africa. Celestine Bohlen in Moscow working better, although new bureau chief Gary Lee has not yet found his footing. Michael Dobbs had the best election coverage out of Paris. South and Central American reporting improved with the work of Bradley Graham and Edward Cody. There remain some holes, as we detail among the individual entries.

The Business Section

The most parochial and least satisfying section of the *Post*, the publication simply concedes business and financial reporting to *The New York Times* and *The Wall Street Journal*. To give one example of respective coverage on a major business news story, both the *NYT* and *WSJ* devoted serious coverage to the Sperry acquisition by Burroughs; the *Post* acknowledged it with an AP wire item. But we noticed some stirring there in '86, particularly in the work of Peter Behr, David A. Vise, a mortgage banker turned newsman, and Mark Potts, back from a turn on the *San Francisco Examiner*. As the Boesky affair continues to unfold and Wall Street anxious about government re-regulation, we may have to watch the *Post* more carefully in 1987 for business developments.

Executive Editor: Benjamin Bradlee   Circulation: Sunday 1,091,307
                                                 Weekday 781,371

Address: 1150 15th St., NW   Telephone: 202-334-6000
         Washington, DC 20071

MAJOR PUBLICATIONS

The American Spectator

Back in the days when neocons were playing David to liberal Goliaths as conservatives groaned about the new dark ages, this monthly periodical was among the most eagerly sought-after publications. Feisty and combative, irreverent and daring, it had a razor-sharp cutting edge that awed friend and foe alike. With a neo-Menckenesque wit and eloquence, editor-in-chief R. Emmett Tyrrell, Jr. swacked goofy liberal and stodgy conservative verities alike, ruthless with deadly-honed aim in his "The Continuing Crisis" column. It set the tone for *TAS* as a whole, the contributions from others analytically fresh, rigorously worked and entertainingly presented.

In the '80s, though, Tyrrell's attention drifted away from his magazine to his bookwriting, television appearances, a syndicated column and lengthier vacations, in perhaps unconscious emulation of William F. Buckley's wafer-thin spread. The Tyrrell column declined in quality, instead of 50 items spun out with machine-gun hilarity, a dozen per week air-pumped became the norm. Whereas the magazine's dull gray format and black and white antique woodcuts were perfect offsets to the effervescent bouyancy of the material itself, all had become leaden.

In 1986, we began to detect signs of life once again. The magazine has moved from Bloomington, Indiana, to space in the Virginia suburbs of our nation's capital. Tyrrell has shortened his vacations a bit, there was no book in the works, his magazine column showed its old compact verve, sporadically, and managing editor Wladyslaw Pleszczynski found some livelier material than we'd become used to seeing.

Among the contributions: a perspective for consolidating the ground gained from Charles Murray's *Losing Ground*, in "The Second War on Poverty," 2-86, by Gregory Fossedal; "East Bloc Ecology," 3-86, by Arch Puddington, a piece of excellent reporting on central Europe's truly serious and real environmental crisis; a muscular drubbing of the *NYT* Sunday magazine's "About Men" column "as public therapy, where the patient rises from the couch and struts and preens", "The About Men Men," 5-86, by Andrew Ferguson; "Conservatives and the Democratic 10," 9-86, by Fred Barnes, adroit sketches of who might grace or disgrace the '88 Democratic presidential ticket.

Barnes, Fossedal (who also teamed up with N.J. Rep. Jim Courter, the House GOP's emerging expert on defense, for "The Military-Industrial Complex," 6-86, a perspective for "reforming reform") and *Insight* magazine writer Malcolm Gladwell, were frequently utilized with good results by *TAS* in '86.

Most importantly, humorist P.J. O'Rourke was brought on as a regular at *TAS*, his "Crimsom Celebrations," 11-86, on Harvard's 350th anniversary yawn party a hilarious treat. O'Rourke has now become "the opener," the columnist that invites us to open the magazine when it shows up on our large pile, often inspiring us and the *Spectator*'s other readers to browse elsewhere.

Editor: R. Emmett Tyrrell   Circulation: 38,517

Address: 1101 North Highland St.   Telephone: 703-243-3733
         Arlington, VA 22210

The Atlantic Monthly

Perhaps the best way of describing *The Atlantic Monthly* these days is to note that the venerable magazine devoted its April cover to "Four Ways to Walk a Dog: Training Man's Best Friend," by Michael Lenehan and its July cover to "Pasta", a "Tribute and Guide to the World's Greatest Food" by Corby Kummer. Each article was given space and space enough for a small pamphlet. That might be forgivable if the content were only lively or sufficiently informative to merit, but the best part of each article unfortunately was in the cover illustration.

The October issue featured Margie Scarf on "Intimacy," which was carried over to November with a Part II. Potentially a reader draw because of the subject matter, the lengthy piece proved virtually unreadable with jargon-bound prose.

The liberal bias of the magazine seems set in the glory years of the '60s and early '70s. The editors seem to feel Conor Cruise O'Brien is an asset as a thinking man's reporter, but the results — such as O'Brien exclaiming about "Danny" Ortega and his soft hair blowing in the evening breeze — makes us wonder at their critical judgment.

The December issue with some great artwork by Fred Otnes features another interminable essay by Atlantic managing editor Cullen Murphy on an ambitious subject: "Who Do Men Say That I Am?". The writer tackles a vast subject that has been covered extensively by writers far more qualified than he. Indeed, Jeri Pelikan's book, *Jesus Through His Centuries*, currently in paperback, seems to have been the possible inspiration. In sum, disappointing to find such intellectually mushy work featured so proudly in what was once one of America's proudest publications.

MediaGuide 83

The bite is just not there. Editor William Whitworth and senior editor Jack Beatty seem to be personifications of what could be kindly termed the Soft Left.

Editor: William Whitworth   Circulation: 463,406

Address: 8 Arlington St.   Telephone: 617-536-9500
        Boston, MA 02116

Aviation Week and Space Technology

AW&ST continues to be one of the finest publications of its kind. It is probably read by more engineers and scientists than its circulation implies, since it's the most passed around magazine in the industry. The shuttle disaster in late January 1986, set the tone for the whole year, with coverage expanded to include problems in the entire U.S. space program and special reports on the European, Chinese, and Japanese space programs. It provided its usual on-the-margin reporting of technological advances, running the gamut from fighter planes to SDI, and in depth analysis of such events as the Libya attack and The Presidential Space Study.

The quality of the editorials has decreased dramatically since the changeover from William Gregory to Don Fink late in 1985, with many of Fink's early ones merely shilling for articles appearing in the same issue. Gregory still manages to slip some gems in under his byline from Boston, and Fink seems to have settled down producing workmanlike editorials after his shaky start. "US Launcher Crisis," 4-28, was one of his best.

Editor: Donald Fink   Circulation: 145,694

Address: 1221 Ave. of the Americas Telephone: 212-512-2000
        New York, NY 10020

Barron's

Having devised a winning formula years ago — reams of Wall Street statistics, a patented roundtable Q & A, and mostly negative stories on wayward companies — *Barron's* has had almost no serious competition. Decades ago, the late *Commercial and Financial Chronicle* might have given it a run for its money, but no other publication has really tried. The intense competition among the slick business journals — especially the shootout between *Forbes* and *BusinessWeek* — is eating into *Barron*'s niche on the company negatives.

Investor's Daily is hitting them in another corner of their niche, superior graphics providing a faster review of the week's markets. All this is worrisome, leaving *Barron's* with only one secure leg of its strategic triad — the Q & A interviews with financial wizards. But then there are two important columns.

Editor Alan Abelson's front-page column sets the pace for the periodical, with an appetizer of breezy Wall Street chatter followed by a hunt for those wayward companies — not *crooked* companies, mind you — but the out-of-the-way outfits, usually traded Over the Counter, that he finds going to untoward lengths in applying cosmetics to their warts and rashes. Abelson was especially adroit in watching the generic drug companies in '86. The columns on the stock and commodity markets are well done, by Floyd Norris and Richard A. Donnelly, respectively, but the star of *Barron's* in recent years has been Randall Forsyth on the credit markets, making analytical sense in pulling together the forces working on the credit markets better than all his competitors in the dailies.

Barron's staff below the top tier of editors has had a complete turnover in the last several years, junior reporters going on to bigger things once seasoned, and the business reporting has begun to perceptibly fade in quality relative to the other business press. A staff-written report on Puerto Rico's economic comeback was a standout, 2-10, and there were pieces on John Connally's troubles in the oil patch as early as 3-24. But not much mouth-watering material is coming from the rookies of the staff.

The best piece we saw anywhere on the Brazilian economy showed up 6-16 by an outsider. And material seems to drift in over the transom to sustain a minimum level of interest. But the third leg of the winning formula, the roundtable (or individual) Q & A interviews are the most discussed material among investors, the most important staple. What makes this work is an abhorrence for the usual hack economists that are recycled in the daily financial press and the "Nightly Business Report." In a Q & A about oil pricing, 8-11, they go to First Boston's Tom Petrie in Denver, one of the keenest of the energy specialists. On whither the bull market, they regularly pull in Barton Biggs of Morgan Stanley, Alan Shaw of Smith Barney, or Robert Nurock, the technician. On the Boesky scandal, the Q & A with Bob Wilson was a stroke of editorial genius, going to a respected money manager who has no ax to grind in the junk-bond debate because he now only manages his own personal fortune. It crackled with clarity and wisdom, and was "the talk" of the Street for a bit.

For all intents and purposes, Publisher Bob Bleiberg has no editorial responsibilities, doing semi-retirement chores on the business side and writing a fact-filled, too-long weekly column. Abelson is still energetic enough to write his column, put out the sheet, and do television commentary and even

MediaGuide 85

promotional spots. But the winning formula is being chipped away and no new ideas, or seasoned talent, have appeared for quite a while. We reckon a start will be made in '87.

Editor: Alan Abelson

Circulation: 283,504

Address: 200 Liberty Street
New York, NY 10281

Telephone: 212-416-2000

BusinessWeek

There is no publication in American journalism that improved as much in 1986 over 1985 than *BusinessWeek*, which doesn't particularly surprise us because the magazine has had hot and cold streaks in the many years we've been following it. Nor do we have any particular theory on why it heated up so clearly in 1986. But where it had been sitting well down in the pile, suddenly we were being forced to get to it earlier because it was creating a buzz so regularly. Editor-in-chief Stephen B. Shepard moved people around to seemingly good effect, Editor Bill Wolman seemed to spend more time on the job and less on TV appearances, and the team in general came up with a steady stream of magnetic covers.

Our complaint a year ago was that *BusinessWeek* had become the fast-food magazine of corporate America, with its breathless business news tending toward the sensational, from one crisis to the next, "merger mania" in June and "selloff sprees" in July, entertaining and irritating at the same time. We cited "The Casino Society" of 9-16-85 as being typically unbalanced, pointing toward financial deregulation as meaning "our economic future is at stake." The piece was written by Anthony Bianco, a senior writer whom we tended to dismiss. In 1986 he emerged as the most important business writer around. Indeed, like a home run slugger on a so-so team, Bianco seemed to generate excitement every time he came to bat, and the enthusiasm spread throughout the team and to the fans.

Our awareness that Bianco is truly an extraordinary reporter began with his cover on Salomon Brothers, 12-9-85. Probably the best single piece written about Salomon ever, not only because it reads as if Bianco lived in the place on a cot for a year and a half, but because of the squeaky economy of his writing — a mixture of images, quotes and wordsmithing sleekly organized into an immensely satisfying, informative piece. We didn't catch up with it until the *1986 MediaGuide* was out the door, but there have been plenty more where that came from. The problem, we realized with his disappointing cover on the bull market, which he wrote with three others, is that covering "markets" is not his schtick. It's the people who make the markets that he does with such excellence, the covers on Drexel's Michael Milken, 7-17, and dealmaker Richard Rainwater, 10-20, two of the best business stories of the year.

It wasn't all Bianco, of course. William Symonds' cover on Allegheny International, 8-11; Blanca Riemer's cover on pre-Tokyo summit international money, 4-28; James Norman's on America's deflation belt, 6-9; William Hampton's on the new auto supermarkets, 6-2; and Joan O'C. Hamilton on Genentech, 4-14, were only a few of many top stories ahead of the information curve that the magazine harvested in the year. Coverage of tax reform, "undistinguished" we said a year ago, was clearly distinguished in 1986, with Howard Gleckman inspired.

The weakest part of *Busiweek* remains the kind of thinking that led Bianco in 1985 to produce "The Casino Society," a blind spot on the Markets and Investment desk that continued to produce silly cover stories in 1986 ("Those Big Swings on Wall Street," 4-7, and "ZAP!," 9-29) which boldly assert that this market is being driven by that market. The implication is that the government should do something about this.

We do remember that *BusinessWeek*'s constituency is mid-sized, middle-aged corporate America, which means it's not surprising there is a dichotomy in its support of efficient markets. Middle-aged corporate America is divided whether it's better off with deregulated markets or more government protection. The tension is interesting, and it will be interesting to see how it plays out in *Busiweek*'s pages in 1987, which will be a big year for tension on these issues. We would love to see Editor Shepard ban multiple bylines. It's so clear that the best of *Busiweek* is produced by its single stars.

Editor-in-Chief: Stephen Shepard   Circulation: 875,659

Address: 1221 Avenue of the Americas   Telephone: 212-512-2000
New York, NY 10020

Commentary

Commentary is the preeminent vehicle for neoconservative thought. Published by the American Jewish Committee, it has carried the thoughts of many eminent intellectuals from the gentile community, the most flamboyant of which were Sen. Daniel P. Moynihan, and former UN ambassador Jeane J. Kirkpatrick, who unquestionably owe their present careers to their appearances in its pages.

During the past year, *Commentary*'s editor Norman Podhoretz withdrew somewhat to parochial Jewish concerns, particularly to what he perceives as a growing tide of anti-Semitism, an issue that is of concern. This led to the

MediaGuide 87

featured article by him "The Hate That Dare Not Speak Its Name," 11-86, which wound up speaking "the poison of anti-Semitism will continue spreading through the American air, with what consequences no one can foresee."

With the December issue, Podhoretz seems to be reemerging from this preoccupation, leading the magazine with "How the Nicaraguan Resistance Can Win," by Penn Kemble and Arturo Cruz, Jr., an inadvertent piece of nice timing.

We saw in 1986 a number of important, must-read articles: "How the Constitution Disappeared," by Lino Graglia, 2-86; "How SDI Is Being Undone From Within," by Angelo M. Codevilla, 5-86; "Losing Central America," by Max Singer, 7-86; "Team B. The Reality Behind the Myth," by Richard Pipes, 10-86.

Editor: Norman Podhoretz   Circulation: 48,800

Address: 165 E. 56th Street   Telephone: 212-751-4000
         New York, NY 10022

Financial Times

Aided by satellite technology, which allows it to be printed in the United States, the famous peach paper from London has been aggressively moving into the void left by U.S. papers and news magazines, which continue to virtually ignore foreign news, particularly financial news. To take a glaring example, no U.S. paper, not even *The Wall Street Journal*, even contains a table of market interest rates or stock prices in the major countries, much less any daily or even weekly commentary on foreign markets. In a world of increasingly integrated finance, with coordinated monetary policies, international mutual funds, and ongoing trade tensions, this U.S. provincialism is truly amazing. As a result, we often read the *Financial Times* from the back forward, with "World Stock Markets" and "Money Markets" invariably enlightening, though unsigned. An irregular and hard to find table of "World Economic Indicators" is likewise worth looking for, and it saddens us that we have to dig around in a London newspaper for such material when New York City is supposed to be at the center of global capital and communications.

The *FT* is clearly the best source in the English language of general, political and economic news around the world. It is not easy to read, partly because of tiny type that smudges where the paper is folded, partly because of a lot of small entries on seemingly trivial or distinctly local topics. Some that made the front page, for example, were "Constable Painting Sold for Record," 11-22;

"Lifeboat Tamils Came from West Germany," 8-14; and "Brasilia Threatens to Force Sale of Cattle," 10-10. After the front page, the percentage of winners declines, though the best stories may be buried anywhere. Very few articles are continued on later pages, which is convenient for the reader, so perhaps they are simply placed wherever they fit. And there are page headings that help, such as "Labour" (a British obsession) or "European News."

With regularity, almost weekly, the *FT* includes a special section on a comprehensive "Survey" of a single topic or country, such as "Computer Software and Services," 9-22, "Japanese Investment in Europe," 11-13, or "The Netherlands," 10-16. The staff writers consider these special sections advertising supplements, more or less, but they manage to sustain a higher quality than similar efforts we're seeing at *The Wall Street Journal* and *New York Times*. There is nothing comparable for in depth timely information, except in the reknowned country or issue surveys of *The Economist*.

The *FT* still lags *The Journal of Commerce* in general coverage of commerce and trade in the Pacific region. While *The Asian Wall Street Journal* is a better source of geopolitical coverage in the region as a whole, the *FT*'s coverage of Japan in 1986 was a delight, with Jurek Martin doing the politics and Carla Rapoport the business and finance. We relied on Anthony Robinson's dispatches and analytical pieces from Johannesburg, and the work of *FT* bureaus in Bonn, Paris and New Delhi.

Lead editorials are often perceptive, such as "The Defence of Europe," 10-21, and "Europe's Fear of Competition," 11-13. The two editorial pages are mostly staff written, however, which is far less diverse than a U.S.-style "op-ed" page. Columnist Sam Brittan is certainly competent, but may not always be right, yet his views almost monopolize controversial economic topics. There has been virtually no debate on tax policy in Europe, for example, except Brittan's "How to Attack Eurosclerosis," 10-20, which briefly noted that German professor Herbert Giersch wants "to cut general taxes on income or on payrolls...to boost profit expectations." There has also been surprisingly little innovative editorial commentary on world trade.

From time to time in 1986, we noticed a fresh breeze blowing through the editorial columns, as in "Reforming Tax Without a Map," 6-26, a brave analysis of why U.S. tax reform bears emulation in the U.K., and "Food in the Wrong Places," 9-4, on how dumping surpluses on black Africa is undermining its agricultural economies.

Editor: Geoffrey Owen

Circulation: 235,000 (worldwide)

Address: Bracken House
        10 Cannon Street
        London, England EC4P 4BY

Telephone: 202-347-8676

MediaGuide

Forbes

Still far and away the best business magazine for investors, although James W. Michaels, one of the best editors of the modern era, knows he's had some free passes in recent years with soggy competition from *Fortune* and *BusinessWeek*. One sign of its vitality, keeping Malcolm Forbes starring on "Lifestyles of the Rich and Famous," are advertising revenues, up 158% since 1980, compared to *Fortune*'s 108% and *Busiweek*'s 30%. Now *Busiweek* has come on with a rush, and *Fortune*, the sleeping giant, has been roused by a new editor, Marshall Loeb, whom Michaels respects. We detect a new spirit of competition among them and *Forbes*, which seemed to be coasting a bit early in the year, according to some of our readers, snapped back for a fast finish that got our attention.

This was all the more surprising since in the early part of 1986, Michaels had been losing talent left and right. Raids from *Busiweek* picked off some and the bull market grabbed a fistful of hotshots who saw a chance to make big bucks with Wall Street firms. A loss of several reporters in a short period usually means an end to a bull market, those who remained behind assert.

Michaels, a hard taskmaster who is not coasting toward retirement, insists on excellence and comes down hard on mediocrity. Names disappear from the masthead with a certain regularity, as when he saw *BusinessWeek*'s cover story on Richard Rainwater, the brains behind the Bass Brothers $5 billion dynasty in Texas, 10-20. It was one of the best stories of the year and the kind *Forbes* is *supposed* to get, and soon *Forbes*' Southwestern bureau chief was gone.

Forbes is a "hard core" financial magazine because Michaels keeps it focused that way, shunning wrap-ups of breaking news stories or Washington political stuff. He "gives away" to *Busiweek* those readers who only do one business read a week and don't get their political economy from one of the dailies, not all that many. *Forbes* reporters make their mark by producing quick and dirty company profiles or longer industry looks stuffed with sharp quotes and hard numbers. The reporters are expected to have opinions and well-shaped viewpoints, doing some of the readers' work by coming to conclusions. Over time, readers can often pick up a snide, officious undertone to *Forbes*. We think this is the static they hear from those reporters who can't deliver the goods and are substituting sneers for confidence.

It's the one business magazine that has a decent shelf life. Wall Streeters can save it for the last of their periodical reading matter, knowing *Busiweek*'s output will soon be conventional and *Fortune*'s too frequently already is.

There were no great changes at *Forbes* in '86 that we noticed. Malcolm Sr. and Malcolm Jr. (Steve) still stay out of Michaels' way in the front of the book. Steve's column, which was distinguished in 1985 for its lonely battle against the Fed's deflationary monetary policies, lost some of its edge in '86 as Chairman Volcker receded in importance and Steve spent more time running around on behalf of Voice of America and Radio Free Europe. It's still as smart as paint.

Emerging as a major talent in '86 (after we rather pooh-poohed her last year) was Susan Lee, who we see explaining the stock market on "Good Morning, America" to David Hartman now and then. Ms. Lee, who once was a professor of economics at Columbia U., has learned how to write like a non-economist and produced two dazzling covers for *Forbes* in '86 (out of its total 26): A majestic overview of the world economy, "The Rising Stars," 5-5, and a brilliant debunking of *BusinessWeek*'s "Casino Society" thesis, 9-22.

If there is a weakness developing at *Forbes* it surely is the cover material, which is why Editor Michaels, who is rather small and frail, became so large and volcanic over *Busiweek*'s Rainwater cover. More often in '86, *Busiweek* succeeded in having its cover story "the talk" of business and financial America, because it wants it that way. *Forbes* had some great covers in '86, "A Crush Like You Wouldn't Believe," 1-27, on the auto glut, and "Hold the Obits," 3-10, on the steel industry, both by Jerry Flint, both "the talk." But otherwise excellent cover stories could never make it at that level (repair service, 7-14; Ralph Lauren fashion competition, 4-21; America getting fat, 11-17). But there's nothing wrong with not being "the talk" week after week, as long as the quality of the entire book stays as high as it has at *Forbes*.

Editor: James W. Michaels   Circulation: 725,000

Address: Forbes Building   Telephone: 212-620-2200
60 Fifth Avenue
New York, NY 10011

Foreign Affairs

Published by the Council on Foreign Relations five times a year, *Foreign Affairs* is the forum through which the Eastern Establishment addresses foreign policy. Still a voice for liberal neo-isolationism in foreign policy, *Foreign Affairs* opened the year with "The Luck of the President," by Michael Mandelbaum, as the lead of its "America and the World 1985" issue. Adept statecraft and political skill don't define the largely successful American foreign policy under Reagan's stewardship. Instead, Mandelbaum opined, the key is that the President is fortuitously blessed with the essence of luck — good timing.

Foreign Affairs provided critical examination of the changes in foreign policy under Reagan — the arms buildup, SDI, and the Reagan Doctrine. Charles William Maynes, editor of *Foreign Policy* authored "Lost Opportunities," in

MediaGuide 91

the same issue, the title of which sums up all he had to say of Reagan's policy. The question of SDI political desirability was taken up in "Farewell to Arms Control?" Fall '86, by Joseph H. Nye, Jr. Little fresh or new appeared in those efforts. Far better, however, was Harold Brown's "Is SDI Technically Feasible?"

The quarterly, once one of the most influential publications in the world, lost its way in the Vietnam '60s as the Establishment itself was sidetracked in its understanding of the way the world works and substituted pompous arrogance for the cool confidence it emitted in the early postwar years. But we noticed some improvement in *Foreign Affairs* in 1986 through the efforts of William Hyland, the best editor the magazine has had in decades, reflecting the influence of a younger class of geopolitical thinkers and leaders who are not frozen in the assumptions of the '40s and '50s.

"Reagan's Turnaround on Human Rights," Summer '86, by Tamar Jacoby, deputy editor of *The New York Times* op-ed page, caused some stir, neocons and conservatives divided in their reactions to it. And "The Nicaragua Debate," Winter '86/'87, by Joshua Muravchick was one of its best contributions for the year. An important article was "Nuclear Winter Reappraised," Summer '86, by Starley L. Thompson and Stephen H. Schneider. It was *Foreign Affairs* that had initially given credibility to nuclear winter when it printed Carl Sagan's "Nuclear War and Climate Catastrophe," Winter '83/'84. But in the article by the two National Center for Atmospheric Research scientists, we learned "On scientific grounds the global apocalyptic conclusions of the initial nuclear winter hypothesis can now be relegated to a vanishingly low level of probability."

Interestingly, members of the print media had more of a share of the contributions in '86. In addition to Jacoby, there were, among others, articles by Strobe Talbott, *Time*'s Washington editor, "Reykjavik and Beyond," (with Michael Mandelbaum); Robert G. Kaiser, assistant managing editor of *The Washington Post*, "The Soviet Pretense;" Robert B. Cullen, *Newsweek*'s diplomatic correspondent, "Soviet Jewry;" and Edward Schumacher, then *NYT*'s Madrid bureau chief, "The U.S. and Libya," all in the Winter '86/'87 issue.

After years of letting the quarterly gather dust, our dutiful subscription unopened, we began to look at it again in 1986.

Editor: William G. Hyland

Circulation: 91,175

Address: 58 East 68th Street
New York, New York, 10021

Telephone: 212-734-0400

Foreign Policy

Published quarterly by the Carnegie Endowment for International Peace, the journal is the principal forum for the viewpoints of "responsible internationalism," what *FP* calls "realism." Old themes of detente or advancing global social democracy could still be found in the contributions to the journal in '86, but for the most part they were passively presented. *FP* was aggressive, though, in its efforts to change the terms of discourse on U.S. foreign policy. Viewing the Reagan Doctrine as the head of an emergent "new nationalism," the journal intervened against it all year.

The Winter '85/'86 issue contained "The Twilight of Internationalism," by Thomas L. Hughes, president of the Carnegie Endowment, "The Real National Interest," by associate editor Alan Tonelson, and "The Real Conservative Agenda," by Christopher Layne, a NATO/Western Europe analyst with the U.S. Army's Arroyo Center think tank in 1984. "The internationalist mindset animates next to nothing these days in the mainstream of American political discourse," Hughes lamented as the Reagan regime "has proudly asserted a high-handed nationalistic role." Layne argued that "vital American interests are not engaged in Afghanistan, Angola, Cambodia, and similar Third World hot spots....There is no Third World region or country, whose loss would decisively tip the superpower balance against America — including the Persian Gulf..." Tonelson also advanced the neo-isolationist theme; he opposed the vision of the Reagan Doctrine with his perspective for cutting loose from the Third World (lacking worthiness for the American taxpayer) and committing significant resources to the defense of Western Europe and Japan.

That critique and perspective was advanced all year in *Foreign Policy*. "A Trap in Angola," Spring '86, by Wayne S. Smith, the State Department's Cuba man until 1982, attacked the Reagan Doctrine's support for Jonas Savimbi; it prevents a "compromise" and ensures Cuban troops and Soviet advisers will remain. And the old theme: "The Soviets were pursuing a policy of detente with the United States" and "Havana too, was interested in improving relations with Washington." Challenging the Brezhnev Doctrine apparently was a tragic mistake.

The "reason over ideology" theme appeared frequently. "Why Is Reagan Strong?" Spring '86, by Terry L. Deibel, resident associate of the Endowment, asked "Why is a president with so few concrete achievements in foreign relations considered so successful?" Not so much luck, but will, ideological commitment and willingness to use force. The issue of "proper balance" between the use of military force and "sensible" conduct of military policy was addressed. Similarly folded in were contributions on cutting regional deals, "South Asia:

Avoiding Disaster," Spring '86; on stategic defense, "Pork Bellies and SDI," Summer '86, and on arms control, "America Is Cheating Itself," Fall '86.

Editor: Charles William Maynes   Circulation: 23,000

Address: 11 Dupont Circle, NW   Telephone: 202-797-6420
Washington, DC 20036

Fortune

If *BusinessWeek* is the Burger King of business journals, *Fortune*'s dining room is at the Harvard Business School. *Busiweek* is at home with middle-aged corporations, George Bush, midwestern country clubs, and the Senate Budget Committee. *Fortune*'s home is with General Motors, the older entries in the Fortune 500, Chase Manhattan Bank, George Shultz and George Ball, Connecticut country clubs, and the New York Fed.

Fortune was the brainchild of the legendary Henry Luce, who brought out the first issue at the onset of the Great Depression, at the staggering price of $1 per monthly issue. It thought big thoughts, not only about the business world, but about business's place in the world at large, and while there wasn't quite the equivalent of Hefner's *Playboy* philosophy, *Fortune*'s sense of business *noblesse oblige* became part of the fabric of the Eastern Establishment. Its tone was knowing and confident, as befitting the premiere business journal of the mightiest industrial nation the world had ever seen. The world, though, moved slowly, giving *Fortune* time to think deeply. By the mid 1950s and well into the 1960s, *Fortune* was not only eagerly awaited by its business readers each month, but also by other business editors and writers, wishing to know immediately where the Great Helmsman was steering.

Fortune's slide paralleled the slide of the Eastern Establishment's grip on public affairs, as its wisdom on matters of foreign policy crashed in Southeast Asia and its confidence on matters of economics bled away in the great stagflations of the 1970s. The world sped up, *Fortune* did not have time to think deeply, and it began to fall behind the information curve. *The Wall Street Journal* picked up speed and influence, *BusinessWeek* made enough adjustment to take over as the "hot" business journal of the '70s, *Forbes* crowded in too, and *Fortune*'s response a decade ago was to become a biweekly.

This alleviated the problems associated with the deadwood on its masthead, the slowthinkers of the earlier age. Young blood rushed in to help get 26 issues published annually instead of 12. But it did not change the magazine's perspective, and its confident tone was replaced by an arrogant tone, its knowing by know-it-all as it knew less and less. Next came gimmicks and graphics and indecisiveness and layers of bureaucracy as new editors tried to do something about the slide, by brute force. By the end of 1985, those who were not reading it out of habit were not reading it at all. Its forecasts were always wrong. Its corporate profiles became routine and superficial. Its story ideas came from conventional wisdom, which meant the stories were stale. An editor of a great publication has to be able to sense what lies beyond the horizon — by deep thought on top of awesome experience, by talking to the smartest unconventional people around, or by sending out scouts. This was not happening at *Fortune*. Editor William S. Rukeyser had run out of ideas.

The January 6 issue is evidence enough. The cover story, "America's Most Admired Corporations," is the results of a survey of 8,000 "senior" business people. We would rather know what corporations the editor of *Fortune* admires, and why. But this Big Survey cop-out fits the magazine's "success" formula of giving readers "lists." If the *Fortune* 500 works, why not the Most (and Least) Admired: "The Most Wanted Managers," 2-3 cover, "The 50 Top Mafia Bosses," 11-17 cover.

The first-of-the-year economic forecast piece, "Hold the Bubbly: Growth Will Slow," tells us that *Fortune*'s economic model "has been largely on the money," but typically never tells us what the model is, instead making pronouncements: "Inflation will accelerate only a bit, and since productivity will improve, the rising number of people working will enjoy more gains in real income than they have recently. But unemployment, which has been surprisingly stable in a period of such slow growth, will climb toward 8%." We get one clear assumption: "The tax reform bill won't be passed next year." Our problem is not with the accuracy of the forecast, let it be clear. It is this vestige of the glory days, when we would allow *Fortune* to make economic pronouncements without being obliged to give us the reasoning. The continued practice, after a decade of stupefying wrongness in its forecasting of anything, makes the effort seem ridiculous.

The good news is that the new editor, Marshall Loeb, who replaced Rukeyser in June, began his stewardship by sitting down in a quiet place with *Fortune* magazines of long ago, and then, as one young reporter advises us, "talking to 200 people a week who don't work for *Fortune*." Our *MediaGuide* readers agree that improvement began with the October issues, and are told the editors of the other business journals have noticed the change too. We'll see in 1987 if this Sleeping Giant awakens.

Editor: Marshall Loeb   Circulation: 745,431

Address: Time-Life Building   Telephone: 212-586-1212
         Rockefeller Building
         New York, NY 10028

MediaGuide 95

Harper's

Another proud publication brought ever lower this year is *Harper's*. The magazine gets visibly thinner each month, and power byline name contributors fewer and fewer. Editor Lewis Lapham who can still write a stylish sentence almost as a Pavlovian response at the sight of a blank piece of paper, seems to have just about lost his editorial flair. Dull roundtable after duller roundtable appear month after month. There has been virtually nothing in the last year to incite us to pick up the magazine from a newsstand to read what the cover offers us.

The exception to this reaction came in November 1986 when Editor Lapham, possibly in a desperate effort to reverse this trend, featured "AIDS and the Question of Privacy," examining Roy Cohn's medical records by Dale Van Atta of Jack Anderson's staff. Spread over two pages were reproductions of a hospital printout of comments by Mr. Cohn's attending physician, together with annotated reflections and analysis of the remarks. Under the guise of virtuously reproving the media for keeping silent on the nature of the late Roy Cohn's last malady, Van Atta — and Lewis Lapham — way overstepped the limits, not merely of journalistic decency, but the ethics of the medical profession. Printing hospital records would be reprehensible enough coming from some supermarket sheet, but is totally inadmissible for a publication of the reputation of *Harper's*.

Under the editorship of Michael Kinsley a few years back, *Harper's* was a touch uneven, feeling its way, but nonetheless every issue had several sparkling, strong articles. The coverlines promised and delivered month after month, until Kinsley and the MacArthur family had their falling out. The vivacity of *The New Republic* today under Kinsley is eloquent testimony to what the MacArthur family lost in Kinsley.

It strikes us as probable that unless something very drastic is done in 1987, this once distinguished publication may not be with us for review in another year's time.

Editor: Lewis Lapham   Circulation: 160,000

Address: 666 Broadway   Telephone: 212-614-6500
         New York, NY 10012

Human Events

Probably no one in American journalism writes more words per week than *HE*'s Capitol Hill editor Allan Ryskind, and for a generation the first several pages of *Human Events*, which never carried his byline, nourished movement conservatives with reports from the trenches. No national journal was read more closely by Ronald Reagan in the 1965-80 period than *HE*, and his pockets were always stuffed with its clippings. But during the Reagan White House years this comforting niche in the national press was allowed to become a rut. While Ryskind's torrent of words are still there, the music is not.

The most serious problem is the new kid on the block, *The Washington Times*, which has become the publication conservatives — including the President — want to see. *Human Events* never had such competition from the old *Washington Star*, which offered middle-of-the-road, commercial conservatism. By the time this new *Times* "Commentary" section, "Pruden on Politics" column, and editorial page rips through the news, there's nothing much left over for Ryskind. In a way, because the *Times* has a populist, conservative texture, *HE* has in recent years been drifting toward middle-of-the-road commercial conservatism, in search of a wider niche. It's perhaps time for Ryskind and *HE* editor Thomas S. Winter to rethink where the publication ought to be going.

In '86, it was spinning its wheels for the most part. "Good Riddance to 1985," it declared 1-4, writing off the previous year — an incredibly successful year for Reagan by everyone else's lights — as almost totally bleak. The Reagan Revolution had gained no new ground, and the liberals were more than just holding their own.

Take tax reform, for instance. It "Looks Like a Bust," 12-28-85, and *Human Events* lobbed punches all year at Treasury's Baker and Darman for urging the President to clasp "this snake [the House Ways & Means tax reform package] to his bosom." You just can't work with Democrats — and see, it's unfair to capital formation! "Senate Finance Considers Major New Taxes," 3-1, okay as a roundup of "revenue enhancement" then floating around. But *HE* saw the President cracking open the door to a net tax increase in his second term. "Tax Reform Marching Through Congress," 5-17, a *mea culpa* for having miscalled the process, acknowledges Packwood as the man of the hour, with kudos to Rep. Kemp (but next to silent on Democrat Sen. Bradley). Back to being gloomy with "Tax Reform: A Mystery Pudding," 8-30 — the tax breaks to lower income taxpayers will come out of the hide of American business! "Will Candidates 'Take the Pledge' on Tax Reform?" 10-4, sums up a lot about *HE*'s withdrawal and distance from the action in '86.

After fighting the President's tax reform all year, and then seeing it passed with Democrats sharing in the credit, the paper exclaims: "The real authors, those who inspired the measure and created the environment for its passage...[was] the band of conservative, populist and libertarian economic theorists associated with supply-side economics." Flowers intended for a funeral quickly substituted for the blessed event instead.

There was one area where *Human Events* showed vitality, its best material in the reporting and commentary on the anti-Sandinista freedom fighters issue. "The Contras *Can* Win," 3-22, was a theme they hammered away at in '86, providing at times some of the best commentary and reporting on the issue in the press. It was in *HE* where we got the story on *The Washington Post*'s "journalistic dirty tricks" — among them ignoring a White House request not to endanger the physical safety of NSC staffer Oliver North by identifying his name in a "contra" story, the *Post* running his picture also, "The President Can Win on Contra Aid," 3-15.

Human Events rarely uses bylines for the articles by its regular staff. An exception was "Myth of the Decade: Proxmire Strong on Defense," 3-8, by associate editor Joel Himmelfarb, which was an impressively organized and presented case. Himmelfarb also runs the "Conservative Forum" column, at times useful and informative with snippets of news about conservative organizations and individuals. But it, like the "Focus on the Media" column which was dropped later in the year, could be richer and more attuned to the critically important margins, if that sense of direction came from the top.

Editor: Thomas S. Winter

Circulation: 45,000

Address: 422 First St., SE
Washington, DC 20003

Telephone: 202-546-0856

Investor's Daily

Investor's Daily is the closest approximation that we know to the secret ideal of many professional editors: a newspaper without journalists, entirely written by computers. *Investor's Daily* does carry terse, factual reports of recent market action and other related news. But these are entirely overshadowed by page after page of statistics provided by the paper's parent, William O'Neil & Co., the respected Los Angeles-based chart service.

This doesn't sound like a very appetizing mix for writers or media mavens. But whether they like it or not *Investor's Daily* seems to have found a niche. The reason is highly significant: ever since Kilgore, *The Wall Street Journal* has really been more interested in Main Street than Wall Street. It has been written primarily for midwestern widget makers, and possibly for their congressmen. It has made relatively less effort to serve professional and private investors who are interested in "technical analysis," the art of predicting future stock movements from current price and volume minutiae, although their demands have been growing steadily more sophisticated. One symptom: the Dow Jones statistics bureaucracy has obstinately refused to refine the obsolescent Dow Jones Industrial Average, with the result that most professional investors have by now switched to broader-based alternatives such as the Standard & Poor's 500 or the Wilshire 5000.

Investor's Daily was the inevitable result. It is specifically designed for investors who want statistics. And these statistics are served up for them in many tasty ways. For example, *Investor's Daily* runs charts, "graphic displays" on the thirty stocks on each major exchange that either hit new highs or had the largest percentage increase in volume on the previous day, showing past history and technical measures like "Earning-Per-Share Rank," which is O'Neil's way of comparing one company's earnings record with any other, and "Group Relative Strength," which is its method of putting the price performance into context with other types of stocks.

Like we said, you have to want this sort of thing in order to want this sort of thing. *The Wall Street Journal* clearly realizes investors do want this sort of thing, because it is now carrying a few more charts. But it apparently hasn't yet sorted its data sufficiently to allow it to carry the compressed — perhaps over-compressed — comparative information that appears in *ID*.

As a national paper, *Investor's Daily* has been enormously expensive to launch, and it's still costing the eponymous William J. O'Neil heavily every day. It still seems short of "tombstones" and other institutional investor ads, which may well mean that it hasn't yet established itself as a daily habit for enough investment professionals. On the other hand, it does carry many investment letter ads. Investment letter proprietors are acutely sensitive to the efficiency of their advertising dollars, because they can immediately measure the results in terms of the number of coupons clipped and returned to them. The fact that they are continuing to favor *Investor's Daily* suggests this missile that was aimed at *The Wall Street Journal* may, in fact, have hit *Barron's*, which for several years past has been raising its rates on the assumption that investment letters were a captive clientele.

Editor: Steve Fox

Circulation: 71,000

Address: 1941 Armacost Ave.
         Los Angeles, CA 90025

Telephone: 213-820-7011

The Journal of Commerce

This relatively obscure daily offers by far the best domestic source of international economic news, particularly for countries of interest to its shipping trade audience. The Asian-Pacific news rivals even London's prestigious *Financial Times* or *The Economist*, thanks to skilled veteran reporters P.T. Bangsberg and A.E. Cullison. Coverage of Caribbean and Latin American countries improved in 1986 with William Orme's reports on Mexican politics and policies. There are occasional rewards in scanning news on smaller but critical economies, such as those of Greece or Israel. Unfortunately, this is a less thorough source for major European countries, and, like every other U.S. paper, offers relatively little solid, timely coverage of Canada.

Reading *The Journal of Commerce* is an acquired art. For those not in the shipping business, the entire second section gets discarded. The "News Summary" on the second page is so detailed that the reader might as well go directly to the convenient topic headings on each page. For our limited purposes, we find the first four pages the most useful, and those listed under International Trade, but there are specialized pages on Petroleum, Coal, Insurance, Aviation, Rail-Trucking, and Financial-Commodities. There is a new, sophisticated index of commodity prices, developed by Geoffrey Moore of Columbia University, which is explicitly designed to give early warning of shifts toward inflation or deflation — it is watched by the Federal Reserve, including its chairman.

The editorial page runs occasional pieces by staff reporters, often excellent, which helps keep their opinions out of the news sections. The publisher, Don C. Becker, is curiously protectionist (e.g., his "Trade Deficit Approach Too Passive," 11-5) — a policy that would bankrupt his paper's commercial clients — but this does not seem to infect the rest of the journal. Frequent editorials and articles pleading for tax breaks and subsidies for shippers, such as "Maritime Industry Needs Support," 8-7, are too blatant to be more than annoying.

Its specialized audience could get much the same material by reading *The Japan Economic Journal*, Canada's *Financial Post*, the Asian and European editions of *The Wall Street Journal*, the *Financial Times*, and *The Christian Science Monitor*. But *The Journal of Commerce* seems to have its arms securely around this niche.

Editor: Albert Kraus

Circulation: 72,000

Address: 110 Wall St.
New York, NY 10005

Telephone: 212-425-1616

The National Interest

With the Reagan Doctrine ascendant, the Brezhnev Doctrine full of holes, and the President's vision of SDI revolutionizing strategic defense, the old hegemonic conceptions of diplomacy and foreign policy are simply no longer hegemonic. We were pleased, therefore, when this new journal devoted to "the content, conduct, and making of foreign policy and the ideas that inform all three" appeared late in 1985. Fresh analysis and debate, we hoped, in the controversy over the course of U.S. foreign policy, with *The National Interest* making a breakthrough. But one year old now, *TNI* has made only a small dent.

Co-editor Robert Tucker carried on a running debate all year with *The New Republic*'s Charles Krauthammer over "isolationism vs. interventionism," and whether explicitly identified as such or not, the "Krauthammer Doctrine" seemed an obsessive preoccupation for so much of what was addressed by *TNI*. Co-editor Owen Harries took it up in "The Idea of a Third Force," the lead feature of the Spring '86 issue. Tucker implicitly fixated on it in "A New Foreign Policy Consensus?" Summer '86.

We had wondered last year if *TNI* would move beyond narrow Old Guard hardline boilerplate. The fact that Irving Kristol (publisher of the far more widely read and influential *The Public Interest*) was publisher and the brains behind *TNI* wasn't enough to assure us. Our fears that foreign economic policy wouldn't get more than a bare nod from *TNI* were realized in '86. More telling is the fact that among all the articles appearing in the quarterly during the year, there wasn't a single one that stood up as the "must-read" piece on a subject or issue.

Editors: Owen Harries
        Robert W. Tucker

Circulation: 5,000

Address: 1627 Connecticut Ave., NW
        Washington, DC, 20009

Telephone: 202-483-0630

National Journal

Of *NJ*'s 5,800 subscribers, 100 copies go to the White House staff, another 500 to Capitol Hill. A weekly chronicle of official Washington, it is probably never seen by the President, members of Congress, or the most senior bureaucrats. But it's must reading for a mid-management layer inside Washington that slices across Capitol Hill, the federal bureaucracy, the Administration, the lobbyists, and the heavier guns of the national press corps.

MediaGuide

With annual subscriptions running $575, the cost is justified by those offices that can make wide use of it, and the average copy is seen by six readers, each dipping into the department of his or her responsibility. *NJ* is consistently thorough, accurate, and non-partisan in its coverage of politics and government. Very strong on broad overviews, it also stays sharp with in-depth analysis, comprehensive reporting and focused perspectives. The detail of each article is far beyond the needs of even the informed citizenry. But it's at a loftier vantage point than its chief competitor in Washington, *Congressional Quarterly*, Capitol Hill's trade magazine, which is all nuts and bolts.

Professional excellence is a hallmark of the *National Journal*. It's hard to recall reading many *NJ* articles in '86 that were poor, but the relentless flow of detail produces plenty of boring ones. Not a scoop oriented publication — it doesn't try to be — it still maintains a timeliness. Often an article read one week may not have direct application, but a week or two later is recalled as a basic reference on an issue or subject, Ron Brownstein's profile of Senator Joe Biden, "The Politics of Passion," 2-2, an example. Solid with its political reporting, the national scene, Congress and the White House were always richly mined for news that affects policy.

Publisher and president John Fox Sullivan, has an array of top professionals whose reporting kept *National Journal* a reliable source of information all year on politics, budget issues and particularly tax policy. Timothy Clark always had to be read regarding the latter. We also noted the consistently fine political reporting by White House correspondent Ron Brownstein, whose material we would often see utilized by others on the political beat.

Less satisfying, its coverage on defense issues, the limited range of sources employed debilitating for much of the year. Interest group lobbyists sometimes got a bit too much space in features. Very well-handled were its interviews, no chopping up what the politicians and policymakers being interviewed had to say. "At A Glance" column, a weekly checklist of major issues, is the best in the business and is always worth reading. The publication was acquired in 1986 by the Times-Mirror Syndicate.

Editor: Richard S. Frank

Circulation: 5,800

Address: 1730 M Street, NW
        Washington, DC, 20036

Telephone: 202-857-1400

National Review

Once the most important journal of opinion in shaping the conservative agenda, the *National Review* was on the verge of becoming an anachronism, but snapped back in 1986 with its best year in several. Editor William F. Buckley had been losing interest in it in favor of the imitation early James Bond novels that he now cranks out once a year. He's still cranking, but roused himself at least to give a modicum of authority to a new articles editor, Richard Vigilante, who is actually going out and soliciting material for the bimonthly. In its heyday, *NR* was practically the only platform for movement (intellectual) conservatives. Commercial conservatives could always find space for their views in *The Wall Street Journal*. A steady river of unsolicited manuscripts flowed over the transom into Buckley's lap. But by '85, Old Man River was carrying the same old stuff from Buckley's old pals. It had become soporific.

It's still hard to imagine *NR* actually running material that Buckley and William Rusher, the publisher, basically disagree with, which is an ingredient of the magazine's counterpart on the left, *The New Republic*. But at least younger writers are appearing, and tackling issues and ideas — especially economic — that should help keep conservatism vital in the post-Reagan era. Vigilante's task in trolling the river for fresh material has been made easier by the development of *The Washington Times* and its thematic weekly magazine, *Insight*, which have yielded a breeding ground for young, more populist conservative talent.

Richard Brookhiser, the new managing editor after Priscilla Buckley stepped down in 1986, is being groomed as WFB's heir apparent, and seems able enough. The magazine benefits from the unsigned economic editorials of David Henderson, the signed economic features of Tom Bethell — who is pushing the Reaganomic framework internationally, and the revived Washington column of John McLaughlin, of "McLaughlin Group" television fame, which is once again on our reading list.

Editor: William F. Buckley, Jr.

Circulation: 115,000

Address: 150 E. 35th Street
New York, NY 10016

Telephone: 212-679-7330

The New Republic

TNR extended its reign as the country's liveliest, most important political journal with a rousing 1986. So many hands grabbed for it we had to add a second office subscription. Theoretically, the torch of at least social liberalism, the bimonthly continued to shift from left toward center. But since the terrain continued to shift for everyone in keeping with the Reagan landslides, the magazine held its leadership as the rest of the liberal press moved too.

The ferment on the masthead goes on. In December, Michael Kinsley, the incandescent editor, quit his second tour under Martin Peretz, the owner and publisher. But true to this George Steinbrenner-Bill Martin relationship, Kinsley was hired right back for more liberal wages and editorial policies. Peretz considers himself merely a neo-liberal, whatever that is, and the air occasionally turns blue between the dugout and the owner's box. We expect there will be several more Kinsley tours in years to come.

In addition, Morton Kondracke came home after a quick 18 months as *Newsweek*'s Washington bureau chief, James K. Glassman came home after a tour as publisher of *U.S. News*, while Fred Barnes stayed put, and is now the penultimate political columnist in the press corps (back of Robert Novak). Has Barnes gotten more conservative? What about Kondracke? The litmus seems to be SDI, and maybe only Kinsley hung in there with the liberal opposition.

Forget all that stuff, though, and just enjoy Kinsley's "TRB" column, whacking Armand Hammer and executive porn, 1-20, bashing Norman Podhoretz and neo-McCarthyism, 3-20, disgusted with the wimpishness of the Democratic Leadership Council, 6-9. Or Barnes, cutting way against the grain in defending Donald Regan, 1-27, sizing up Marcos in Manila, 2-10, sniffing at Jack Kemp getting nowhere fast, 3-3, or needling Senator "Hackwood," 5-5. Or see Charles Krauthammer pushing the Krauthammer Doctrine, 4-28, or Bob Kuttner putting his arms around the world economy, 4-21, or Mickey Kaus breaking ground on the Work Ethic State, 7-7, or Murray Wass on Al D'Amato, 3-10, and Paul West on Cuomo's thin-skinned petulance, 2-17, or Glassman bashing the plutocrats all year long. It's fun, fun, fun, and whatever happens between dugout and owner's box in 1987, we hope it goes on, on, on.

Editor: Michael Kinsley

Circulation: 95,000

Address: 1220 9th St., NW
Washington, DC 20036

Telephone: 202-331-7494

Newsweek

It was musical chairs, performed *con molto brio* all year, at *Newsweek*, but at least its "identity crisis" is no longer a problem. Now, merely its identity itself is the problem. Strife there still is, but the angst at the top is gone, *Newsweek* knowing very well where it wants to go.

Let *U.S. News* worry about losing the small-town bankers and shopkeepers as readers, and *Time* about its franchise on reliable news condensation for informed cocktail party chatter. (*Insight* is simply the non-other.) *Newsweek* — the magazine for Properly Progressive Persons — is cutting its niche with the free-spirited types who make up the lib-culture set. "Impact! impact! impact!" was increasingly the criterion for getting a story into print during the year.

Editor-in-chief Rick Smith was beaming with pride as *Newsweek* led the way with "impact" stories in '86. Among them: "Growing Up Gay," 1-13, with the authors finding hope for acceptance of the lifestyle. After all, "The extensive publicity about AIDS, has, at the same time raised the general consciousness of homosexuality. In the long run, the resulting public knowledge may help to overcome some public prejudices."

Also cited with pride by editor Smith was *Newsweek*'s run of features on AIDS. "Future Shock," 11-24, a cover story on the subject, acknowledges the problem as a public health crisis, but indulges arguments that it's a constitutional issue and simply dismisses the belief that homosexuality is relevant anymore to its spread.

Syndicated columnist Joseph Sobran, writing about this 11-24 issue in *The Washington Times*, "Accredited Victims Need Not Fear," 11-25, suggests that the magazine's editors really don't care that so much of this stuff is offensive to the great majority of Americans: "The article ends with an anecdote about a couple who met, quickly satisfied each other that neither had AIDS, 'and then, just like in the old days, they went to bed.' Clinch and fadeout. On the same page is a photo of a homosexual public bath, with two naked men, discreetly clad in bubbles, gazing into each other's eyes. Interesting. Such a picture is bound to offend a lot of readers — but for *Newsweek*, such readers clearly don't count. Nobody here but us liberals."

And "for better or worse, for richer or poorer," *Newsweek* also geared in on the singles market in '86, advising in "The Marriage Crunch," 6-2, "Today the poetry of the marriage vow has come to represent a practical choice."

In some ways it seemed as if it were "movement time" again at *Newsweek*, the flavor and tone of '60s and '70s journalism cropping up repeatedly, though dressed up for the '80s. Sometimes Levi's, T-shirt, and headband, *Rolling Stone* tucked in the back pocket; other times foulard bow tie, Ray-Ban wayfarers with a copy of *The Wall Street Journal* along with *GQ* and *Ms* always nearby.

Newsweek continued to lose talent all year, defense reporter John Walcott to *The Wall Street Journal*, its frustrated Washington editor Morton Kondracke back to *The New Republic*, senior editor Mel Elfin and Washington bureau reporter Gloria Borger to *U.S. News & World Report*, White House reporter Eleanor Clift to the *Los Angeles Times*, etc., etc. But it picked up new blood from its competitors. Stephen Smith came aboard from *Time* as executive editor early in the year, who with another recruit from *Time*, Evan Thomas filling Kondracke's vacated position, plans to refocus the Washington direction of the magazine. Gregg Easterbrook, a contributing editor for *The Atlantic*, was picked up to supplement the effort with special features for 1987.

Thomas may be ideally suited for *Newsweek*'s new identity. Coming from that rebellious generation that didn't trust anyone over 30, Evans is now 36, an aging "Baby Boomer." But he knows the ties that bind the generation from its 40-year-old oldtimers on one end to the 22-year-old newcomers on the other — as he put it when still at *Time*: "chiefly rock 'n' roll and the changing role of women."

There's still a wealth of talent there, and we cite elsewhere the work of those *Newsweek* journalists. However, a few we single here for special attention because of particularly good work: Jonathan Alter and Bill Powell, with the cover story, "Civil War at CBS," 9-15; Joyce Barnathan's "Inside a Mind Jail," 8-11; Rich Thomas' "The Green Plague," 3-10.

"Impact!" also was provided in its foreign reporting, deposing dictators for a start in 1986. Its Philippine coverage was the worst in all the press. Instead of news reporting, we got unrestrained senior writer Harry Anderson heading up an Oxbow version of jury duty on Marcos in Manila, as in "Reagan's Double Take," 2-24 and "The Marharlika Papers," 2-3. We would read report after report, wondering how editors could let coverage degenerate to the level of political cartooning.

We can certainly not imagine the reporters in the field were filing at the level of the finished product. New York provided the hype. In "The Exiles: There Goes the Neighborhood," 3-11: "Ferdinand Marcos, no longer master of his fate, walks around Hawaii's Hickham Air Force Base 'moaning incessantly'...General Fabian Ver...wolfs down New York steaks and looks for bodyguards.... What's a poor dictator to do?....his damsel...[was] burning up the phone lines....calling up her jet-setting ladies-in-waiting around the world, running down the tacky base accommodations. There's no exercise room...which gave the plump exile another reason to fast....Marcos and Imelda have not dared to step out, but General Fabian Ver was seen feeding at many of Honolulu's best troughs." The reporter is Nikki Finke Greenberg, but over her byline, Rod Nordland — *Newsweek*'s deputy foreign editor!

We saw impact from Nordland again with "Inside Terror, Inc.," 4-7, Ray Wilkenson sharing the byline, which let the terrorists speak for themselves; but just before they hang themselves with their own words, a reprieve — the absence of a Palestinian homeland is what drives them to commit their horrors.

If nothing else, *Newsweek* proved in '86 that the print media can compete with TV news in providing drama, in chucking serious news coverage since it might bore, in not worrying about what its coverage actually says, but more about how it says it. Photo editor Karen Mullarkey understood the "impact!" focus, providing with such zeal ghoulish color photos of the bloody maimed and dead all year: looking down on the floor of the Rome airport, 1-6, the corpses strewn about, arms and legs akimbo, in pools of blood; after the U.S. strike on Libya, a dead child being pulled from rubble, then to the Tripoli morgue for more, broken bones protruding from dead flesh, 4-28; and one of its worst, the photos by Picture Group photographer Charles Cole, showing in sequence a young Aquino supporter being beaten and kicked to death at a pro-Marcos rally, 8-11.

Is this what publisher Katharine Graham wants to be remembered for?

Editor: Richard M. Smith

Circulation: 3,727,000 (worldwide)

Address: 444 Madison Avenue
New York, NY 10002

Telephone: 212-350-4000

Time

Still the biggest of the "Big Three" newsweeklies, *Time* has a global reach that includes within its readership of 32 million, 9 million abroad. *Time* sees its responsibility to its readers as a comprehensive presentation of the week's news, so much so that it felt it necessary to almost apologize for its 6-16 issue "American Best." It was one of only seven times in the last 16 years that the magazine departed from its standard in devoting an entire issue to a single subject. That theme was, as publisher Richard B. Thomas put it, "an unabashed and (mostly) eclectic and breezy celebration of what America does best," the effort the brain child of Washington correspondent Barrett Seaman who wanted an original contribution to the 100th birthday of the Statue of Liberty.

Where *Newsweek* is no longer taken seriously as a newsmagazine by the public policy elite, *Time* has regained some of the influence it had in its heydey. Henry Anatole Grunwald, who led the magazine in hot pursuit of *Newsweek* and the flower children in the 1970s, was early in seeing diminishing returns to that gambit and reined things in. There may never again be the conditions that enabled *Time* or any other newsweekly to be the powerhouse of political and cultural influence that *Time* was *inside the United States* for half a century. In an expanding world economy of the 1990s, *Time*'s foreign editions could have the kind of influence in many parts of the world that it once enjoyed here.

At home, though, we noticed a re-orientation in its economic and business focus during the year as senior writer Charles Alexander replaced George M. Taber as business editor. Seen less frequently, thereafter, was the use of *Time*'s Board of Economists, a genuine anachronism, especially with the lineup that had accumulated like barnacles on the Board over the years.

Tired of writing, as he put it, "about abstract things like economic policy," Alexander engineered a distinct change of pace. Instead of burying himself with statistical reports, the numbing effect of which was apparent in his 1985 cover story on the budget deficit, he went into the field instead for the cover story on People Express, "Super Savings in the Skies," 1-13. Offering a heavily consumer-oriented approach, he discovered what many airline travelers already knew, though the effort to present a comprehensive picture was impressive.

In search of a "compelling" feature, Alexander tried another change of pace, supervising the "Drugs on the Job" project, 3-17, as a business and economy cover story. The magazine also hailed the tax reform of 1986 in its cover story "The Making of a Miracle," 8-25, "One of the few pieces of legislation that can be truly be called historic," even taking a poke at Charls Walker, defeated lobbyist for the Business Roundtable, for his injudicious "Wait till next year" remark.

A serious weakness continued at *Time*'s Washington bureau, not because bureau chief Strobe Talbott is incompetent. Quite the contrary, he's said to be thoroughly competent. But in one area, coverage of the Strategic Defense Initiative, Talbott's public posture as a leading opponent of strategic defense makes it hard to avoid the severe bias we continued to see in 1986. In its cover story, "Star War Games," 6-23, we found Pentagon correspondents Bruce van Voorst and Michael Duffy, a recruit from *Defense Week*, stacking the deck in their contribution, "Scientific Hurdles." First, inaccurately presenting "Star Wars" defense as a virtually leak-proof umbrella against nuclear missiles, they round up critics Sidney Drell, Ashton Carter, Harold Brown, and John Pike to shoot holes in SDI's defensive shield. "...the SDI system would have to work perfectly the first time out" they wrote, asserting what just isn't true: "Few scientific experts find it possible to put faith in the ability of such a system to operate in a nuclear showdown."

Talbott himself simply produced three pages of editorializing in his story, "Grand Compromise," the essence of which ran: "If there is a summit in November or December, Reagan the Star Warrior might be able to extract from Mikhail Gorbachev an agreement-in-principle for a trade-off between existing Soviet offensive forces and the American SDI while it is only a gleam in the President's eye. Since there are reasons to question whether SDI is scientifically feasible or strategically wise, restricting the program to research in exchange for significant reductions in the most threatening Soviet weapons could be the deal of the century."

Certainly more restrained on the Philippine electoral crisis than *Newsweek*, we found more of a commitment to news reporting in *Time*'s coverage. There were several cover stories early in the year where *Time* provided information missed or ignored by its competition, and in some cases even by the dailies; in particular, on the role of the U.S. State Dept. in orchestrating behind the scenes. "A Test for Democracy," the main story in its 11-page cover feature of 3-3, written by associate editor George Russell, with Hong Kong bureau chief Sandra Burton, Manila correspondent Nelly Sindayen and diplomatic correspondent William Stewart doing the leg work: "Behind a facade of impartiality, however, the Administration has been straining for months to shape what it feels to be the inevitable post-Marcos transition. So persistent have the U.S. efforts been that Ambassador Bosworth is referred to by some Marcos aides as 'the leader of the opposition'." In "Anatomy of a Revolution," 3-10, *Time* reported administration policymakers "breathed a sigh of relief that their plans and strategies so painstakingly worked out over the past two years, had gone so well." George Shultz had just told Marcos Labor Minister Blas Ople that only Marcos' relinquishing of the presidency could prevent civil war in the country.

Time got fatter in '86, needing more space for advertising as it began to surpass *Newsweek* in raw ad pages, a just reward for its higher level of journalism.

Editor: Henry Anatole Grunwald   Circulation: 6,045,000 (worldwide)

Address: Time & Life Building   Telephone: 212-586-1212
Rockefeller Center
New York, NY

USA Today

When the *Harvard Lampoon* set out to do this year's parody, they had an easy target with *USA Today*. The overall impression is a small town paper gone national. Typical front-page news, 11-24: "Frequent flier rules tightened," "Teddy Ruxpin: talking bear's sales hit $93 million," "On tap, a football feast," and "Some are better at writing letters." But *USA Today* does not aspire to be an intellectual force. It is frankly aimed at impatient readers who want to relax. The paper's major competition is television and *People* magazine. There seems to be a compulsion to underestimate the readers, or to remain safely in the minor leagues.

Easily the most attractive paper around, with full color sections on News, Sports, Money and even "Life" (e.g., TV and sex). "Across the USA" offers a tiny paragraph on each state, doubtless read by nobody, but sometimes has useful data comparing how state economies are doing. There is a full page on weather around the nation, useful to travelers. The "Opinion" page offers four tiny pieces plus an editorial on a single subject. This is better than printing whatever drifts in, but it is more than most people want to know about these often frivolous topics, and yet less than the authors have to say (how deep can you get in 400 words?). Since the topics are supposed to change each day, that makes it inherently difficult to do more than one a year on big issues like trade. There are also interviews, mainly with irrelevant people like Angela Davis (remember her?), "I Joined The Communists To Be A Trailblazer," 8-21.

The "Money" section is the most serious, mainly because of uniquely informative statistics and graphs in the "Market Scoreboard." There even used to be a breakdown of stock performance by industry, which for some reason has been dropped, as were some valuable charts on the price of gold. Aside from adequate, but routine, efforts to explain what happened to yesterday's stock market, and good long-run perspectives by Anne Kates, there are mainly short articles on specific companies (Doug Carroll is good on autos).

Financial reporters seem to come and go, producing at a frantic pace in the meantime. This high turnover makes it difficult to evaluate specific contributions, though some bear watching if the paper can hold onto them. Daniel Kadlec's "Do Small Investors Know Something the Pros Don't?" 8-20, and "Investors Still Hunt Treasure In Junk Bonds," 11-24, were certainly worthy of attention.

As in the rest of the paper, even the editorial page, the "Money" section contains almost no mention of national or international politics or policies, particularly if they might seem controversial. *USA Today* readers would only know there is a Federal Reserve Board after a discount rate change, if then. A major exception was the paper's outstanding treatment of tax reform, which was unusually detailed, though mainly by anonymous authors (James Cox was one). There was even a toll-free "Tax Hotline" where readers could ask what was going on. The talent is there, and probably just needs more room to move — and not just move to another paper.

Editor: John C. Quinn   Circulation: 1,459,049

Address: 1000 Wilson Blvd.   Telephone: 703-276-3400
         Arlington, VA 22209

U.S. News & World Report

The McWeekly of the newsmags, fast, fast food, almost none of which sticks to the ribs. Major revamping of the editorial staff in 1986 did not help. David Gergen went from Managing Editor to Editor, offering a vision of *U.S. News* "as a great newsweekly, one that could blaze fresh trails of insight and interpretation for a growing audience." It isn't and it doesn't, though it surely strains. The magazine enjoyed a niche in the 1960s and '70s as the "conservative" newsmag, when *Time* and *Newsweek* were frolicking among the flower children. But with the flower children now in the world of Yuppie, carrying *Wall Street Journals* under their arms, and *Time* magazine easing its way right of center, the *USN&WR* niche has narrowed to a nick.

The cover stories are often ambitious, as with "High Tech Anxiety," 5-19, which promised much on post-Challenger, Titan, Chernobyl fiascos, but there either isn't anyone around smart enough to pull these off, or they assign so many people to the cover team — which is more likely — that we get the mush of collective journalism at its worst. Eight bylines on a story, routine at *U.S. News*, signals a dearth of confidence at the top.

The business section has improved to a noticeable degree. It isn't competing with the business weeklies, after all, but there were occasional business vignettes that showed life, a few bylines we would find ourselves reaching at the their stories' end. Economics editor Edward Mervosh, hired from *BusinessWeek* a year earlier, increased average levels of competence at both magazines in the process. The political coverage did not show up on our screen. Most of the foreign reports are bare and mere summaries of what has appeared in the dailies. At its worst, which happens on occasion, the magazine seems only to summarize what has appeared in the other weeklies.

Oddly, the biggest break *U.S. News* got was to be handed, literally, an exclusive story by the Russians. The seizure, detention and subsequent release of Nicholas Daniloff, its Moscow correspondent, gave the publication more good publicity than all Editor-in-Chief Mort Zuckerman's real estate millions could buy. For the space of several weeks last fall, *U.S. News* was a constant part of the news, both television and printed, with both Gergen and Zuckerman interviewed and press conferenced to death. Of course, they were understandably up in arms, fighting for Daniloff's freedom, but it didn't hurt the journal to have its correspondent so elevated.

Surprisingly, Editor Zuckerman, a novice at all this, turned out to be a credible reporter, his pieces on the Philippine elections — where he was a member of the official observer team — well-written, superior to much of what appeared elsewhere.

At midyear, with Zuckerman perhaps realizing that neither he nor Gergen knew how to ride this horse, another body was hired as jockey from *Newsweek*, but Mike Ruby is probably not the strategist to bring the nag back into the race.

It still looks as if Zuckerman needs a man of the world (or a woman of the world) to run things — and a political correspondent who will break some news — and a foreign editor who knows what's going on out there.

Editor: David R. Gergen   Circulation: 2,255,943

Address: 2400 N Street, NW   Telephone: 202-955-2111
        Washington, DC 20037

The Washington Times

The most important development in the national print media cited by the *1986 MediaGuide* was the naming of Arnaud de Borchgrave, a former *Newsweek* foreign correspondent and best selling author (*The Spike*, with Robert Moss), as editor-in-chief. The *Times*, founded in 1982 by the Rev. Sun Myung Moon's Unification Church, attempted to fill the hole left by the folding of *The Washington Star*, which had given *The Washington Post* a monopoly in the most important political capital in the world. The church has poured millions into the *Times* with no end in sight, but clearly its pockets are deep enough to happily subsidize the newspaper *as long as it holds the respect of the Washington political establishment*. It had not really achieved this status until de Borchgrave arrived, stabilizing gains made by previous editors, and lifting the paper's visibility with more aggressive reporting.

Where the *Post* is consciously liberal and Democratic, the *Times* is consciously conservative and Republican, but becoming more and more identified with the younger, populist wing of the GOP, not the Republican Old Guard that *The Washington Star* represented before its demise. The editorial page, edited by William Cheshire, is in the same vein as Robert L. Bartley's *Wall Street Journal* editpage. The editorials are shorter and punchier, and *The New York Times* has correctly observed that the White House looks to them as clearer signs of conservative thinking than those of the *Journal*, which always stays in range of establishment turf. In "There He Goes Again," 4-21, Jimmy Carter is bashed for criticizing the Tripoli raid: "Few had guessed that, in the undemanding job of ex-President, Jimmy Carter would be a disaster as well." Months later in "So Much for Trepidation," 7-28, it cites payoffs from the Tripoli raid: "(which) did not, as solemnly predicted by Anthony Lewis and other apostles of the grin-and-bear-it school, cause Arab moderates to vanish like water on the sand." In "Transcending Sanctions," 8-20, it presents positive electoral ideas on the South African dilemma as sanction alternatives.

The *Times* continued its advance in 1986. Circulation is far behind the *Post*'s, 105,000 daily to 800,000, but this was a smart gain over the 88,000 circulation of a year ago. There also seems more advertising support from local merchants, who generally avoided "the Moonie paper" in earlier years. The stigma is still there to a degree, but de Borchgrave and the editorial staff seem very sensitive to any potential signs of church intervention, which suggests this problem can continue to decline as the quality of the editorial product increases.

The award-winning graphics are among the best in American newspapers. The "Commentary" section's especially lush artwork enhances the presentation of the consistently conservative columns. The section, edited by Mary Lou Forbes, is undoubtedly read by President Reagan. There's always at least one winner among seven or eight commentaries. But the steady diet of right wing viewpoints gets tedious and the section lacks the tension that puts snap into the *WSJ* and *Washington Post* opinion sections. To spice up the gruel, liberal viewpoints that the paper's regular readers (and probably owners) would find *unacceptable* would have to be brought in.

The reporting strength of the *Times* is in those areas of de Borchgrave's experience, national security and defense, and a surprisingly adept foreign coverage squeezed out of a small foreign contingent, excelling in Manila and Johannesburg. The paper's continuing great weakness is in domestic politics. It never got into the ballgame in the 1986 elections, either in covering match-up races or trend pieces. (The best single political piece it had, a profile of Mario Cuomo, was written by a feature writer.) It made a better effort in covering local politics and issues affecting the dominant black community, which has had its problems with the *Post* and is now noticing the *Times*.

The single most attractive feature of the *Times* is Richard Grenier's thrice-weekly "Point Man" column, which began in late 1985 when Grenier, 54, was hired away from the *NY Times* by de Borchgrave and converted from a culture/movie critic to a columnist. This was the journalistic equivalent of pitching coach Roger Craig rescuing Mike Scott of the Houston Astros from mediocrity by teaching him the split-finger fastball. Grenier's column — literate, erudite and sassily impudent on political and cultural events great and small — is unlike anything that has appeared in American journalism since the 1920s, when men of letters still wrote newspaper columns.

De Borchgrave, who is also a throwback to the Front Page days with his stop-the-presses eccentricities, makes news himself in Washington. In early November, his interview with French President Chirac in Paris made an international splash when Chirac denied telling de Borchgrave a sensational story involving the Israeli Mossad (secret service), terrorist plots involving Syria, and West German suspicions of double dealing. De Borchgrave produced a tape recording of the interview. Later in the month all of Washington was talking about de Borchgrave almost hiring Lally Weymouth away from the *Los Angeles Times* syndicate. But Ms. Weymouth instead negotiated a column with her mother, Katharine Graham, owner of *The Washington Post*, who apparently was unwilling to give her politically conservative daughter such a platform until de Borchgrave forced her to contemplate seeing Lally in the opposition hometown paper. The main importance is that Washington is forgetting the *Times* is a "Moonie paper," and is identifying it with de Borchgrave.

Editor: Arnaud de Borchgrave   Circulation: 104,186

Address: 3600 New York Ave., NE   Telephone: 202-636-3000
Washington, DC 20002

RATING GUIDE

In this second year of the *MediaGuide* we have slightly tightened the standards applied. The number of rated journalists has expanded by more than a third, mainly adding foreign and business reporters. A (★) was slightly harder to achieve this year, but is assured of a review in the 1988 guide while a lower rating could drop, as several did from the '86 lists. We consider all journalists listed as being at the top of the profession, the big leagues of print journalism. All ratings are based on 1986 work. Quantity of output means almost nothing; as a rule we look at at least three major pieces for each entry, usually many, many more for the upper tiers. The bulk of a reporter's work in a year is routine and could be adequately handled by thousands of other reporters not listed in this guide; as in the Michelin dining guide, caloric output doesn't count. Past reputations have some effect, we find; it's harder to lose a (★) at the top and to gain one from the bottom than to move through the middle range. Past reputations thus have this shadowing effect, which has parallels in all kinds of human experience, including team dynamics in the sporting world.

The criteria for reporters are the three basic criteria of the wire services, fairness, accuracy, and balance (objectivity), plus three additional that elevate work toward excellence: depth of reporting, writing skills, and consistency. For columnists and commentators, the basic criteria are: content reliability and a minimum level of interesting material presented on a regular basis, plus three additional: depth of insight and information, presentation, and consistency.

(−) Failing in the basic criteria on one or more counts.

(½★) Failing the secondary criteria on one or more counts.

(★) Fair. Reporters: Professional. Columnists: Worth trying.

(★½) Fair/Good inconsistently.

(★★) Good. In reporters, above average level of reporting and writing, average analytical skills. In columnists, generally interesting content and presentation.

(★★½) Good/Excellent, above average in consistency.

(★★★) Excellent. In reporters, superior reporting and writing, above average in analytical skills. In columnists, superior content and presentation, frequent important insights and information.

(★★★½) Excellent/Exceptional, approaching the very best.

(★★★★) Exceptional. In reporters, loftily objective, pacesetters for the profession in reporting and writing, penetrating analytical skills, always worth reading. In columnists, pacesetters for the profession in journalistic integrity and independence, must reading for insights and information, a consistently well-shaped point of view.

(NR) Not rated. Insufficient sampling. Material cited has promise.

HIGHEST RATED JOURNALISTS OF 1986

Bianco, Anthony	*BusinessWeek*	Financial Reports	★★★★
Brookes, Warren	*Detroit News*	Financial Reports	★★★★
Burns, John F.	*New York Times*	Foreign Dispatch	★★★★
Evans & Novak	*Chicago Sun-Times*	Political Column	★★★★
Grenier, Richard	*Washington Times*	Commentary	★★★★
Kinsley, Michael	*New Republic*	Commentary	★★★★
Mansfield, Stephanie	*Washington Post*	Domestic Reports	★★★★
Rapoport, Carla	*Financial Times*	Foreign Dispatch	★★★★
Stewart, James B.	*Wall Street Journal*	Financial Reports	★★★★
Barnes, Fred	*New Republic*	Political Column	★★★½
Bering-Jensen, Henrik	*Insight*	Foreign Dispatch	★★★½
Cohen, Richard	*Washington Post*	Commentary	★★★½
Dionne, E.J.	*New York Times*	Domestic Reports	★★★½
Gwertzman, Bernard	*New York Times*	Diplomatic Reports	★★★½
Kilborn, Peter T.	*New York Times*	Financial Reports	★★★½
Lewis, Anthony	*New York Times*	Political Column	★★★½
Martin, Richard	*Insight*	Domestic Reports	★★★½
Prokesch, Steven	*New York Times*	Financial Reports	★★★½
Robinson, Anthony	*Financial Times*	Foreign Dispatch	★★★½
Rosenbaum, David	*New York Times*	Financial Reports	★★★½
Rupert, James	*Washington Post*	Foreign Dispatch	★★★½
Sanger, David E.	*New York Times*	Financial Reports	★★★½
Seib, Gerald M.	*Wall Street Journal*	Foreign Dispatch	★★★½
Temko, Ned	*Christian Sci. Monitor*	Foreign Dispatch	★★★½
Valery, Nicholas	*Economist*	Financial Reports	★★★½
Bailey, Jeff	*Wall Street Journal*	Financial Reports	★★★
Bangsberg, P.T.	*Journal of Commerce*	Foreign Dispatch	★★★
Baum, Julian	*Christian Sci. Monitor*	Foreign Dispatch	★★★
Bennett, Robert A.	*New York Times*	Financial Reports	★★★
Berthelsen, John	*Wall Street Journal*	Foreign Dispatch	★★★
Blumenthal, Sidney	*Washington Post*	Domestic Reports	★★★
Boroweic, Andrew	*Washington Times*	Foreign Dispatch	★★★
Brownstein, Ronald	*National Journal*	Domestic Reports	★★★
Chira, Susan	*New York Times*	Foreign Dispatch	★★★
Christian, Shirley	*New York Times*	Foreign Dispatch	★★★
Cockburn, Alexander	*Nation*	Commentary	★★★
Cullison, A.E.	*Journal of Commerce*	Foreign Dispatch	★★★
D'Souza, Dinesh	*Policy Review*	Commentary	★★★
Dobbs, Michael	*Washington Post*	Foreign Dispatch	★★★

MediaGuide

Donohoe, Cathryn	*Washington Times*	Domestic Reports	★★★
Echikson, William	*Christian Sci. Monitor*	Foreign Dispatch	★★★
Edsall, Thomas B.	*Washington Post*	Domestic Reports	★★★
Einfrank, Aaron	*Washington Times*	Foreign Dispatch	★★★
Fields, Suzanne	*Washington Times*	Commentary	★★★
Flint, Jerry	*Forbes*	Financial Reports	★★★
Forsyth, Randall	*Barron's*	Financial Reports	★★★
Fossedal, Gregory	*Copley News Service*	Commentary	★★★
Friedman, Thomas	*New York Times*	Foreign Dispatch	★★★
Fung, Vigor	*Wall Street Journal*	Foreign Dispatch	★★★
Glassman, James K.	*New Republic*	Financial Reports	★★★
Harden, Blaine	*Washington Post*	Foreign Dispatch	★★★
Kristof, Nicholas D.	*New York Times*	Foreign Dispatch	★★★
Kristol, Irving	*Wall Street Journal*	Commentary	★★★
Lee, Susan	*Forbes*	Financial Reports	★★★
Martin, Jurek	*Financial Times*	Foreign Dispatch	★★★
Norman, James R.	*BusinessWeek*	Financial Reports	★★★
Petre, Peter	*Fortune*	Financial Reports	★★★
Platt, Adam	*Insight*	Domestic Reports	★★★
Quinn-Judge, Paul	*Christian Sci. Monitor*	Foreign Dispatch	★★★
Riemer, Blanca	*BusinessWeek*	Financial Reports	★★★
Rowen, Hobart	*Washington Post*	Financial Reports	★★★
Schmemann, Serge	*New York Times*	Foreign Dispatch	★★★
Seligman, Daniel	*Fortune*	Commentary	★★★
Sherman, Stratford P.	*Fortune*	Financial Reports	★★★
Shields, Mark	*Washington Post*	Political Column	★★★
Sieff, Martin	*Washington Times*	Foreign Dispatch	★★★
Sloan, Allan	*Forbes*	Financial Reports	★★★
Thomas, Rich	*Newsweek*	Financial Reports	★★★
Truell, Peter	*Wall Street Journal*	Foreign Dispatch	★★★
Walsh, Mary Williams	*Wall Street Journal*	Foreign Dispatch	★★★

MediaGuide

FINANCIAL REPORTERS & COLUMNISTS

Abelson, Alan
Barron's. (★ ★ ½)

Editor. The front-page "Up & Down Wall Street" is really two columns, the opening section a wise-guy review of the week's happenings read avidly by one audience. After a record daily drop in stocks, 9-15, Abelson reports that "The technicians to a man agreed that we should have sold on Wednesday. The academic economists assured us the market couldn't have gone down 86 points in a single session because it's too efficient...But stocks, we think, jumped without a parachute last week because they were simply out of gas." A second audience of investors skips the funny stuff and goes straight to the second half of the column, where Abelson continues to do serious work, mainly slogging through 10-Ks, insider trading reports and company press releases to ferret out company weaknesses. He jumps on Memory Metals, 9-29, with this sideswipe: "The rather staunch showing of the stock is all the more heartening since the shares have had to contend with persistent and heavy insider selling." The stock slides. He sniffs at the finances of Carrington, a drug company, 5-12, and it bucks the bull market. His best of '86, a persistent probe of Zenith Labs and its problems with the FDA, 7-14, 9-1, that led the stock's slide.

Anders, George
The Wall Street Journal. (★ ½)

Wall Street stocks and bonds. A reliable reporter who covers the ground ahead of him. His "Boom Time Bond Rally is Bonanza for Big Corporations, Wall Street Traders," 3-11, well done, but ending weakly, hemming and hawing on whether rally will continue. A very competent description of the makeup of Boesky's fund and the problems that will be encountered in dismantling it, "Boesky's Major Fund, etc.," 11-18. In "Contrarian Walks Lonely Path, Puts Faith in Oil Service Stocks," 3-24, wastes our time telling us about an investor who has been right in the past on contrarian picks, but does not tell us "why" oil prices will rise as the stock market wilts. Which is the only reason to read the article.

Auerbach, Stuart
The Washington Post. (★)

A veteran bread-and-butter government/business reporter a cut above the ordinary. Best we saw: "Trade, Security Links Worry Officials," 3-30, on Third Worlders asking for more U.S. trade in exchange for basing rights.

Bailey, Jeff
The Wall Street Journal. (★ ★ ★)

Sparkling management pieces with lovely writing surprises all year. Good detail, early '86 alarm with "Deferred Loan Losses At Thrifts and Banks Snowball Across U.S.," 1-8. A marvelous touch with "Fuji Bank Perseveres At Heller International," a zany $1 billion gamble, but: " 'Banks are farmers,' Mr. Uemura says. 'They take care of the land for 100 years. Finance companies are more like hunters.' " He has us hooked after an excellent "Where the Action Is: Executives in Staff Jobs Seek Line Positions," 8-12. Best line: "After decades of bulking up on consultants and layers of corporate staff, American businesses were waddling around festooned with people who liaised, facilitated, coordinated, analyzed, advised and planned, but who never managed anything."

Banks, Howard
Forbes. (★ ★)

"What's Ahead for Business" is often quite conventional, columns that worry about losing "Keynesian stimulus" and that "the dollar, inevitably, will have to go down...a good deal more," 10-6. But there are occasional sparks of brilliance, particularly in digging out little-noticed facts. In "Manufacturing Is Not All That Sick," 4-28, we learned that "manufacturing output in 1985 was 11% greater (in 1982 dollars) than in 1979, the last major peak." On 4-7, he reminds us that "two-thirds of federal farm payments now go to the 14% of farms with sales over $100,000 (and average household incomes over $55,000 a year)" and "net dollar incomes were records in 1984 and 1985" (thanks to subsidies). In "Voodoo Tax Economics, But It Works," 5-19, he reports that the "topmost 1% or so of taxpayers, with an adjusted taxable income over $92,000, paid no less than 15% more tax than in 1983." Nuggets.

Barnard, Bruce
The Journal of Commerce. (★ ½)

Looks beyond the obvious, such as "Coal Market Turmoil Seen: So. African Ban Could Spur More Upheaval," 8-6, where sanctions benefit Colombia and Australia, but lay off a third of the black South African workers. In a possibly premature piece, "OPEC Restraint Confounds Cynics," 10-1, the UAE, Venezuela and Libya are cheating, but the Saudis are cutting enough production to keep total OPEC oil supplies down.

Barry, John M.
Dun's Business Monthly. (★ ★)

Barry's superior 1985 fell off sharply as he misfired on topic and timing too often. But as we said, it's tough, tough to plan a dozen pieces a year with the lead times he has, and it's a surprise he can do it at all. His January entry,

"CEO's Make the Best Lobbyists," stood out because it could stand anytime, an "evergreen," but gets lost in "The Turmoil in Natural Gas," February, and in the blah, blah, blah maze of liability insurance, June. A March look at the November Senate races is much too early, especially written in January for the pub date. He's good at lofty material like "The Cracks in the GOP," September, analysis of how the Reagan coalition of born-agains, supply-siders and mainstreeters could fall apart before '88. His best, though, was a profile of Rep. Jim Wright of Texas, the Speaker of the House in the 100th Congress, for *The NYT Sunday Magazine*, 11-23, starting as slow as quicksand, but with easy reading at the jump.

Bartlett, Sarah
BusinessWeek. (★ ★)

Money and Banking editor. A relative youngster to hold this lofty a pinstripe slot, her fresh eye doesn't disappoint us when she tackles a big story on her own, but we were dismayed in 1986 to see her byline too often blended in with three or four others on pieces that read like quilted patterns. A satisfying exception was her cover on "John Reed's Citicorp," 12-8, the first reports we've seen that Walter Wriston's successor is surfacing in public after two years submerged studying Walter's bad loans. She doesn't do a puff piece either: The cover appeared as New York and Washington banking and political circles seethed over Citibank's blocking of loan concessions to the Aquino Philippines. "Reed personally refused to go along, despite the threat of further destabilizing Aquino's government...'He doesn't look beyond the numbers,' complains one banker. 'He doesn't see the political complexities.' " But she can't quite figure whether Reed is planning for boom or bust, and the piece doesn't tell us why customers will want to do business with Reed's Citibank rather than Morgan or Manny Hanny or Chemical or Sumitomo.

Behar, Richard
Forbes. (★ ★)

A standout among the magazine's crew of in-and-out business reporters. "The Cutter Gets Clipped," 3-24, an archetype of the genre, problems of a haircutting chain. His 4-21 "SCF's Little Secret" tweaks the Save the Children Foundation; its Paul Newman-Joanne Woodward appeals for funds still pretend to sponsor poor kids abroad, but are spent for other, less appealing community projects. Great stuff.

Behr, Peter
The Washington Post. (★ ★ ½)

One of the few *Post* business writers competitive with the New York crowd. Steady meat-and-potatoes, but with carefulness and depth. A 2-12 takeout on the restructuring of the deflated oil industry impressed. He covers the government-business link with the best and often better, certainly livelier. On an FTC ruling, "Antitrust 7-Upmanship," 6-26: "Maybe most things do go better with Coke, but Dr. Pepper isn't one of them." A well-told account of an SEC probe into Blinder Robinson & Co., "Uneasy Rests the Crown of the Penny Stock King," 10-19. And new angles we hadn't seen on SEC regulators trying to cope with insider trading on the "international electronic highway," "Trade Link Promises Regulatory Headaches," 10-26. Behr is in position to make the *Post* business page a must for Wall Street in '87.

Bennett, Amanda
The Wall Street Journal. (★ ½)

New York, management beat. Capable young reporter with experience in Detroit and Beijing (where she was ★ ★ ★ in '85), she's struggling a bit in her new slot, producing pieces that are dutiful, balanced, dull and yet prominently displayed, as "Airline's Ills Point Out Weaknesses of Unorthodox Management Style," 8-11. Others of genre, "After the Merger: More CEO's in Uneasy Spot, Looking For Work," 8-27, and "Laid-Off Managers of Big Firms Increasingly Move to Small Ones," 7-25. We're rooting.

Bennett, Robert A.
The New York Times. (★ ★ ★)

A banking pro on the Sunday business section who seems to triple-check facts on his beefy features. "Sizing Up the World From a Banking Perspective," 3-30, a deft approach to the Fed/farm crisis. Good quotes in interview with Goldman's J.L. Weinberg, 4-13, and an impressive piece on "John Reed's Calming of Citibank," although Reed wouldn't be interviewed. He captures Columbia's Robert Mundell in "Supply-Side's Intellectual Guru," 1-12, and Dean Witter's credit-card marital problems with Sears, 10-5. His profile of Dutch Finance Minister Onno Ruding, 9-28, helped alert Treasury to his drawbacks as potential IMF chief. "Economists Warn Inflation Isn't Dead," 3-4, way off stride. But always crystal clear.

Berg, Eric
The New York Times. (★ ★ ½)

Banking. One of the muscular young heavyweights the *Times* has brought in to play rough with the *WSJ*. A Stanford MBA, aggressive, ambitious, hard to fool. "U.S. Banks Swap Latin Debt," 9-11, opens with a compelling example. Nissan buys $60 million in shaky Mexican debt for $40 million, resells to Mexican central bank for $54 million in pesos, and reinvests in a Mexican subsidiary. "The result: Some $60 million of Mexican debt was wiped out; Nissan had more equity in its Mexican operation, and Citicorp, Nissan's investment banker, pocketed a fat fee." Berg can make the complex comprehensible, even exciting, as again in "Loan Sales Market Swelling," 1-20, how and why big banks are selling-off good, new loans to smaller banks for a collection fee and a share of the interest. "Guilty Plea in Morgan Case Is Seen," 10-9, neatly unravels a mystery about "Byzantine relationships that often exist between bankers and [foreign] flight capitalists." In "Bank One Stretches Borders," 7-7, an innovative bank gobbles smaller banks in four Midwestern states "at the rate of one every eight weeks."

Berger, Joan
BusinessWeek. (★)

Articles ostensibly on "Economics" are invariably sensational and amateurish, often relying on the old crutch of creating a phantom consensus of unnamed economists ("most economists agree..."). "Why Hardly Anybody's Worried About A Wage-Price Spiral," 5-19, thinks the idea that lower unemployment causes inflation "goes back to the 1960s...[and] Milton Friedman." Actually, it goes back to 1958, and A.W. Phillips, and has been discredited for years. In "Breadwinners Are Still Running to Stay in Place," 6-23, her problem is bad figures: Average wage rates include a rising percentage of part-time workers, exclude lower tax rates, and do not even pretend to measure "breadwinners' " " salaries, much less their net worth. "America's $250 Billion IOU Will Be Hell To Pay," 10-27, can't even distinguish between foreign-owned equity and "debt," but does quote a live economist, Robert Barro, to the effect that her whole story is wrong and backwards. "The False Paradise of a Service Economy," 3-3, fails on perspective — there are *always* more low-paid jobs than high-paid, but average real incomes have been rising. Better: "Good Riddance to Tax Breaks — They Haven't Done Much for Business," 9-1, showed more research effort.

Berry, John
The Washington Post. (★)

A skilled veteran on the Fed/banking beat having trouble weaning himself from Fed spokesmen, including Tall Paul. He has the stock market rallying, 3-30, when assured Volcker won't leave Fed (in an otherwise useful advance of an important Fed meeting). "U.S. to Weigh Currency Talks," 2-5, okay on Reagan State of the Union. Good reporting 5-18 on likely Fed policy changes, with thumbnail sketches of Fed governors. Best of year, 9-28, "Volcker Engineers Shift of Focus to Rates," but still no mention of the commodity watch.

Bianco, Anthony
BusinessWeek. (★ ★ ★ ★)

Suddenly, *Busiweek*'s Big Star, hitting home runs the past year with deep, thoughtful cover stories, an epic on Salomon Brothers (12-9-85) that dazzled with its colorful authority and writing skill. Best of the year: "Power on Wall Street," on Drexel Burnham's junk-bond superstar Mike Milken, 7-17, beating

Forbes to the punch; "The Man Behind a $5 Billion Dynasty," 10-20, a profile of Richard Rainwater, the brains behind the Bass Brothers of Fort Worth. (True, *Forbes* beat *BW* to the punch on a Bass Bros. cover, but Bianco's music, drama and dimension far excelled.) Superb in his coverage of financial services, investment bankers, and some of the great deals in this era of dealmaking, he's fun to read, entertaining, with insights galore into the thinking of world-class investors. Off-stride once, 3-17, with a meandering cover on the bull market (with four bylines). But he did not disappoint with his wrapup on "How the Boesky Bombshell is Rocking Wall Street," 12-1, with Christopher Farrell. His byline should run on the cover!

Birnbaum, Jeffrey
The Wall Street Journal. (★ ★ ½)

Ace on tax reform in '85, he stumbles near the finish line in '86 with a spate of "tax reform is doomed" pieces, then puzzling determination to heap excessive credit on Jersey's Bill Bradley — who deserves plenty — when it succeeds. But always a must read, technically superior. "Radical Tax Overhaul Now Seems Probable," 5-8, catches up. "High Stakes Game," 6-25, is an interesting curtain-raiser on the Senate-House tax conference. An almost topnotch profile of Senator Packwood, 3-19, misses the finance chairman's new respect for the President. At his best, 3-17, on fate of investment tax credit and 4-22 negotiations in Senate Finance.

Bladen, Ashby
Forbes. (−)

Read one Bladen column and you have read them all: "The Wolf Is At The Door," 8-25, says it is "1929 all over again." "Market Madness," 5-5, says the stock and bond markets are both crazy, and we're in for a "Mexican-style inflation" (like 1930?). A reader in the November 17 issue notes that "when he does finally come around, admits he was wrong and states that the stock market is on its way up, we will know it is time to bail out." The hook!

Bleiberg, Robert M.
Barron's. (★ ½)

A *Barron's* editor since 1954, Bleiberg writes his full-page "Editorial Commentary" in a high dudgeon. His hard-right conservative rumblings on the perilous state of the Republic have mellowed out in the recent Reagan years *cum* Bull Market, and with few editorial chores now, he devotes his column to business analytics, with some hard, old-fashioned research. An inherent weakness is the space he has to fill, which invites *too much* detail, slowing the reader. A one-third cut would also force snappier leads and pull in more readers. His "Florida Makes Waves," 6-16, on tort reform, is an exception that sustains with impressive detail and angles. "U.S. Steel to USX," 7-14, no particularly new insight, but a useful review of the industry. In "Wisdom of Salomon?" he warns against Salomon Brothers short-term bullish forecast, catching the slide. His best for prescience, though, was "What Price Glory?," 1-13, bashing Oxy's Armand Hammer for sinking megabucks into natural gas deals on the assumption that oil and gas prices will firm at $25 and rise: "Those who bet on higher oil prices are likely to lose."

Blustein, Paul
The Wall Street Journal. (★★)

We expected a bigger bang out of this big gun of the Washington bureau, the Fed reporter, but accurate preconceptions often stale by the time he's written. A fine profile from Kansas of Fed Gov. Wayne Angell, 4-24, who Blustein earlier spotted as a potential problem for Volcker. But a major effort, 10-6, "Over Course of Year, Fed Puts More Stress on Avoiding Slump," should have run earlier, but at least makes plain the Reaganite Fed won't worry about "overheating" simply because of growth. On 10-3, he cites supply-side absence of inflation concern, out of date as gold price climbs. A sharp 3-11 ridicule of White House economist Beryl Sprinkel is on target, but makes us wince. The potential is clearly there, however.

Bornstein, Paul
Forbes.

(See Stern, Richard L.)

Brimelow, Peter
Forbes. (★★)

A talented reporter and author who moved to *Forbes* from *Barron's* late in the year, and spent most of the last few years working on books, on investment letters and Canada, from whence he hails. His *Barron's* contributions were confined to high calibre profiles of investment advisors, such as "Zadeh Knows the Score," 7-28. A rare and perceptive report from Canada, "The Northern Peso," 4-28, linked a new tax surcharge to the emerging weakness of the Canadian dollar, despite much higher interest rates than in the U.S. "Since government is a cost of doing business...Canadian dollars have been heading south." A deep-dyed conservative, he argues against U.S. responsibility for reform of South Africa, 6-9.

Brittan, Samuel
Financial Times. (★ ½)

His "Economic Viewpoint" columns came off the ground in '86 as he finally ditched monetarism as a guide to fine-tuning the world. He now favors stable exchange rates for the U.K., 10-9, since a falling pound inflates import prices.

Yet in "The Anatomy of Black Friday," 5-22, he argues that low global inflation figures "reflect non-recurring gains from the fall in import prices, itself due mainly to the drop in oil and commodities." He should then argue (but did not) that the global inflation of 1978-80 was irrelevant because it was "due mainly" to a *rise* in prices of oil and commodities. Much better in "The Yen-Dollar and Bank Lending," 11-6, where he argues cogently against "the dread of bank lending" as "unhelpful puritanism." A good survey of the international monetary issues in "Washington Gets Tired of Excuses," 7-24. But by 9-18, in "When Even Good News Causes Jitters," he only thinks "German and Japanese demand management is too cautious. But this...has almost nothing to do with U.S. trade anxieties." Bad arithmetic. How could the U.S. reduce its trade deficit unless some other countries reduce their trade surpluses (e.g., buy their own products)?

Brookes, Warren
The Detroit News, Heritage Features Syndicate. (★★★★)

A nonpareil at what he does, digging into the economic themes that are constantly floating to the surface of the conventional wisdom; challenging assumptions, facts, numbers and logic; hard-headed debunking that every business editor and columnist should follow to stay with the state-of-the-art. In our rating system, he had one four-bagger (★★★★), an interview with the CEO of the most integrated enterprise in South Africa (7-21, *Insight*), but led the entire press corps with triples. A few: "Tracing High Interest Rates," 1-2, with Columbia's Fred Mishkin; "Beware of Oil Tax Soothsayers," 1-30, pointing out this could push Mexico into bankruptcy; "Gross National Guesswork," 4-1, untangling statistical confusion; "The Rich Get Richer, and Pay More," 5-5, arguing "Tax the rich, there are so many more of them now!"; "Bye, Bye Voodoo," 6-12, an interview with the Veep; "Why U.S. Booms and Europe Stagnates," 9-1, because it still fights inflation with unemployment; and "Farmbelt, Doing Better Than You Think," 5-26, on the fast income growth in Nebraska, Georgia and Minnesota. He could only improve with restraint, his exuberance making him seem tendentious. He's an umpire!

Bulkeley, William M.
The Wall Street Journal. (★★½)

Boston. Computer beat. Among the best in catching business trends in software, geared to the investor. "Many Software Prices Rising Despite Birth of Cheap Clones," 10-23, is an excellent report from stem to stern, explaining recent burst of share prices for Lotus, Microsoft, Ashton-Tate, etc. His lead feature on Digital Equipment, 4-3, was not as colorful or absorbing as the *Fortune* cover of 10-27, but it had most of the detail six months earlier. Another good update in the Technology column, where we stop for his byline: "Teaching Computers

MediaGuide

to Read," 7-25, because they are "rotten at reading" and those that do still cost $40,000 or so.

Buss, Dale D.
The Wall Street Journal. (★ ½)

Detroit. A good year on the auto beat, with a big splashy front-pager on Ford Motor Co.: "On A Roll," 10-7, is probably his biggest effort of the year, an unalloyed puff, but worth a careful read. But he bases one of its themes, that only Ford has a "strategy," on the say-so of one obscure analyst, thereby detracting from the whole. His "GM Slows Big Drive for Saturn," 10-30, (with Melinda Grenier Guiles) is much too easy on Roger Smith. With Doron Levin 12-1, he annihilates *The New York Times* with a huge scoop on the GM/EDS story. His follow-up on the GM-Perot split, 12-2, (with Amal Kumar Naj) tails with an anonymous quote, "This is one of the dumbest things that Roger (Smith) has ever done," which we wished he'd developed earlier. A good reporter who needs seasoning.

Bylinsky, Gene
Fortune. (★ ★ ½)

A 20-year business science writer at *Fortune*, we remember his "Hot Rocket to Nowhere," NASA's nuclear-rocket boondoggle of the early '60s. Not as prominent these days with so much competition, but he can still turn on the afterburner. The cover special: "The High Tech Race," who's ahead and where the U.S. stands, is chiefly his, the lead in *Fortune*'s best single issue in years. But it's still a notch behind the incomparable *Economist* survey of global high tech of August 23. (See Valery, Nicholas.)

Carley, William M.
The Wall Street Journal. (★ ★ ½)

A *WSJ* veteran on the airline beat who jampacks his business reports with facts. Can you beat this, "USX Might Face TWA-Style Shake-Up," 10-10: "If Carl Icahn gains control of USX Corp., he will probably fire most top executives, slash wages of unionized workers, close unprofitable facilities, mortgage the remaining facilities to raise cash, and then go hunting for a takeover or merger candidate to create a stronger company." His piece on People Express shifting strategy to attract businessmen, 4-29, could have been much tougher on the People zoo. He doesn't always beat the competition when he goes head to head, but he did with "Pan Am and Eastern Gird for Battle Over Shuttle at La Guardia," 9-30, simply getting more than we wanted to know in his story. And he was on top with "Flight Attendants Unions are Losing Strength," 4-8.

Cieply, Michael
The Wall Street Journal. (★★)

Los Angeles. Seasoned business writer covering entertainment industry with a flair for fresh angles, rich detail attractively presented. A nifty piece, 10-14, on Hollywood tapping student screenwriters ("Since 90% of the movies are about kids trying to lose their virginity, the studios think they can get more realism by using a writer who's still trying to lose his.") His 10-16 article on the threat to phono records by CDs was so vivid it became part of the danger. Should have been front page. Cieply won the Overseas Press Club Award for best business news reporting from abroad in 1984 for work he'd done while at *Forbes*.

Clark, Lindley, Jr.
The Wall Street Journal. (−)

The "Speaking of Business" columnist on the editorial page, lingering past his retirement, clinging to monetarism day in and day out although there is now almost unanimous agreement that the Planet Earth does not revolve around the money supply. Lin, play golf.

Clark, Timothy B.
National Journal. (★★)

Tax reform beat in '86, with several solid wrap-ups. Frequent double bylines, but his individual efforts were substantial. A good picture of restrictions on municipal revenue bonds in the House bill, 1-25, found few Capitol Hill allies for the bond industry. "A Tough Year," 2-15, was timely with good profiles of key Packwood aides, followed by a sharp examination of the Senate GOP perspectives on the reform, 2-22. Also well-organized and focused, a report on the regional terms of the tax reform debate, 3-22. On perspectives, his profile of new assistant Secretary of the Treasury, J. Roger Mentz, 6-7, was very sharp, noting the hovering presence of Richard Darman at every critical juncture for the bill. On content, "Bill's Biggest Boon Is to Working Poor," 7-12, a bit off-focus, but informative. Occasional treatment of subjects outside of tax reform, were well-done, as his focus on Mexico as the test of Baker's Third World debt initiative, 8-9. Skimpier than usual: "The Next Chapter," 10-4, an overview projecting congress may revisit tax reform next year under the weight of the budget deficit and economic effect of the new tax bill.

Cole, Robert J.
The New York Times. (★½)

The "Business Day" veteran on mergers, acquisitions, LBOs, got out front in '85 beyond the day-to-day news, where he is always competent, but in '86 could not match the pace set by the *Journal*'s J.B. Stewart and Daniel Hertzberg, who were everywhere. When the big Boesky story broke, James Sterngold was hurled into the breech. Cole was thoroughly proficient in handling backup, as "Drexel-Boesky Tie For Some Investors," 11-19, but he may not have the knack of handling deep sources from a hot-seat.

Cook, James
Forbes. (★★)

Specializes in enlivening mundane subjects like nonferrous metals, the economy of Dubuque, Iowa, American Indians. An older breed of thoughtful, gentlemanly *Forbes* writer who can take on big issues in a non-obvious way. Noteworthy piece, 3-24, on the amazing pace of job creation in the U.S., jam packed with facts, although he doesn't quite address Europe's lag.

Cooper, James. C.
BusinessWeek. (★ ½)

Co-author of "The Business Outlook" (see Franklin, William B.), he also writes some features, such as "The Expansion Looks Unstoppable: Almost Every Sign Points to Stronger-Than-Expected Growth in 1986," 2-24. That one is easy to criticize in retrospect, mainly due to weakness in prices and inventories, but it was more useful than the usual wishy-washy, inconclusive confusion. The problem, as with the column, was circularity: consumers will spend because businessmen will hire, and businessmen will hire because consumers will spend. There was no mention of trouble in the rest of the world, and how that could affect profitable production opportunities.

Debes, Cheryl
BusinessWeek. (★ ½)

Singapore. Prolific, all over the region from week to week, often lost in multiple bylines, but the reporting strength shows through. From Jakarta: "Japan's Investment Binge in Southeast Asia," 11-3, on Tokyo replacing U.S. as main source of capital in area, nicely informative. From Singapore, same issue: "How Michael Hatcher Turns Sunken Treasure Into Good Business," a clever feature that held us all the way.

Dowd, Anne Reilly
Fortune. (★)

Washington bureau. Still struggling to get ahead of the news. In "The Oil Tax Urge," 3-3, she has most oddsmakers predicting Reagan will have to boost energy taxes. She sees "Gramm-Rudman is Starting to Work," 4-14, wrong again, not mentioning fall in bloated defense projections. Better with "Your Coming State Tax Hike," 10-13, an old story on the state impact of federal reforms, jumping ahead with the best state by state graphs on combined marginal rates. A cover on "What Managers Can Learn From Ronald Reagan," 9-15, was someone's tricky idea, but RR lives in a fishbowl, and there's nothing she could stick in her piece that we all don't see day in, every day.

Dunn, Donald H.
BusinessWeek. (★)

Editor of "Personal Business," a collection of tips on everything from travel in Tokyo, 5-12, to moving an IRA, 2-17. Usually confined to two pages, the column can scarcely compete with *Money* magazine, *Consumer Reports*, and the travel section of *The New York Times*, but does find things the others don't. Although much of the advice is useful to only a few readers (e.g., how to insure fine wines, 11-3), it makes entertaining and sometimes profitable reading. One of the earliest to notice that "Falling Rates Are Making Savings Bonds Look Good," 5-5. The column expanded in '86, probably for advertising reasons, or we'd drop it for more serious work.

Ehrbar, Aloysius
Fortune. (−)

An unreconstructed, diehard monetarist, mercantilist who we hear has been assigned editing chores, where he can do double damage by ruining the material of the younger reporters. His "The Super Yen Won't Save the Day," 2-3, reports the yen has grown 20% stronger but Japanese prices are only inching upward, but "Eventually" the strong yen will bring a decline in the U.S. trade deficit with Japan. Mossback.

England, Robert
Insight. (★ ½)

An earnest young plodder who tried and just missed with several financial pieces early in the year. But he scored with the best piece on the fiasco in the Canadian economy, 4-7, with conservatives following liberals down the deficit trail. Good detail on West Germany's economy, policy prospects, 12-8. His wrap-up of the Sperry-Burroughs merge, 6-23, was a cut above the *WSJ* and other newsmagazines, suggesting his talent is on the business beat. Plenty of potential.

Fabrikant, Geraldine
The New York Times. (★)

New York. Entertainment industry. Steady, reliable on movieland. Best of year: "Ted Turner's Screen Test," 3-30, a breezy account of Ted's debt situation after buying MGM.

MediaGuide

Farnsworth, Clyde
The New York Times. (★★)

A veteran on the IMF/World Bank beat, slipped a notch in '86 after a sterling '85. Still old reliable day in and day out, but we didn't see much out in front where there are controversies galore. Best we saw: "The Ex-Im Bank's Tricky Tactic," 2-2, its "mixed credit" maneuver, information rich. A so-so "U.S. to Spur Licensing of Exports," 6-18, misses the "Gold Card" metaphor the *WSJ*'s Lachica spotted. On the spot with "U.S. Studying Export Spurs," 11-6, a post-election interview with Special Trade Rep Yeutter.

Fisher, Anne B.
Fortune. (★)

She tackles big stories, but in '86 at least, bit off more than we could chew. "Who Prospers Next in Health Care," 2-17, is a good summary/analysis of the big players who've taken a beating and the new entrants who plan on making it big in this market, and how. Her conclusion seems to ride on one assumption, that we'll see "a lot more non-health care companies making health care acquisitions," without persuading us why, especially after quoting the Boston Consulting Group's thinking that total medical spending in the U.S. could shrink by as much as one-third in the next decade. Also, in "GM is Tougher Than You Think," 10-10, her optimism leaves us unpersuaded. She may be right that GM has finally begun to conquer its bloated bureaucracy, but her supporting material doesn't quite do it. Is Roger Smith the right guy? She never even asks and left us unprepared for the Ross Perot imbroglio in December.

Flint, Jerry
Forbes. (★★★)

A designated hitter at *Forbes* for years, snappy business reporting from the old slam-the-keyboard-squawk-on-the-phone school of newspaper reporting (a former *NYT* auto reporter). An editor for most of '85, he's back reporting, and had three splashy cover stories in '86 (11.5% of *Forbes* total). Two of them were "the talk" of business and Wall Street, "A Crush Like You Wouldn't Believe," 1-27, on the glut of autos being churned out by Detroit, a remarkable call especially since he had the story to himself. And a unorthodox piece on the coming good times in the steel industry, "Hold the Obits," 3-10, on which the jury is still out. Also scoring with a little less heat, "Here Come the Truckbusters," 6-30, on railroads, a new growth industry? Keep your eye on Flint.

Fly, Richard
BusinessWeek. (★ ½)

Washington. Politics. A welcome addition to the bureau, a seasoned political reporter off *The Dallas Times Herald* who will move up as he shakes the mud from his shoes. He can handle other material too, starting with a Gramm-Rudman piece, "Jim Miller's Trial by Fire," 2-10, more balance and depth than we expected. An old scam story, "Think Tanks for Presidential Hopefuls," 5-12, leaves us with "so what." Better use of him with "Jesse Jackson: Even More of a Force to Reckon With in '88," 4-7, "trying to put some new colors in his rainbow...family farmers...independent oil producers." And he can do the set-piece political match-up, as in his 11-3 no-frills effort on the Louisiana Senate race.

Foldessy, Edward P. and **Herman, Tom**
The Wall Street Journal. (★ ½)

The "Credit Markets" column broadened its horizons and sources a bit, at times even observing the deflationary international forces behind falling world interest rates. Disappointing only in a relative sense, failing to anticipate rather than react. There's no sense of direction in the column, no tides coming in or going out over periods of days, if not weeks, but a day-to-day choppiness that probably results from the dual responsibility and double byline. Michael Quint, the *Times* bond columnist, is more comfortable to read for that reason alone.

Forbes, Malcolm S., Jr.
Forbes. (★ ★ ½)

Deputy editor in chief. Malcolm's son Steve, who wins the "golden owl" award almost every year for the best forecasting record among financial journalists. An early devotee of supply-side economics. His free-wheeling column covers everything imaginable, with wit and wisdom. In "Central Bankers of the World — Get Off Your Duffs," 4-21, *Forbes* was one of the first to notice that "the Bank of Japan and the Bundesbank are out-Volckering Volcker in keeping too tight a grip on money." In "Good Times Ahead," 6-2, he writes that "People run companies, investment tax credits don't...If people are not punished for getting ahead, the economy will do well." His column slipped in consistency in '86, perhaps his other duties catching up.

Forsyth, Randall W.
Barron's. (★ ★ ★)

The "Current Yield" column is simply the best on interest rates in the public prints. He also reports relevant economic news and political developments, providing better "Outlook" columns than others who use that title. Unusually well-educated and informed, Forsyth can and does put more of his own ideas

MediaGuide 131

into print, and always gives the reasons behind the forecasts of Wall Street analysts, rather than just the forecasts themselves. "If Tax Rates Fall, Interest Rates Should Follow," 5-12, was quick to spot that implication of tax reform. In "How Low Can You Go?," 9-1, he uncovers that almost half of the growth of the "M2" money supply consisted of a rush into passbook savings accounts, because their 5.5% yield was looking relatively high. On August 18, he noted that "tying U.S. policy to a currency [the German mark] whose exchange rate is being pushed up by high real interest rates in the midst of deflation is hard to justify. The Fed has begun to move away from that stance. As it's done so, gold had advanced, the stock market resumed its uptrend and bonds even gained ground."

Francis, David R.
The Christian Science Monitor. (★ ½)

Ottawa. Competent, informative, uneventful columns, he's best on explaining statistics, such as "Canadian, U.S. Deficits Compared," 3-14, where only two of the the seven major countries has a smaller budget deficit than the U.S. (as a percent of GNP). Also prompt and detailed reports on Canada, as in "Mulroney Government Bites the Bullet and Calls for Tax Increase," 2-28. Like other somewhat disillusioned Friedmanites, Francis is most ambiguous where economic theory is involved. In "Economists' Debate: Will Cutting Deficit Choke or Spur Growth?," 2-11, though, he notes that "If such monetarists as [Jerry] Jordan are wrong again this year [about "inflationary pressure and higher interest rates"], they will have to offer some good excuses to save their economic theory from disrespect." The question posed by the headline is an intriguing one, inherently embarrassing to Keynesians, but Francis does not ask it of them.

Frank, Allan Dodds
Forbes. (★ ★)

Smuggling, gun-running, money-laundering, all that business is Frank's beat and he knows his stuff. His "Shopping the Great Satan," 1-27, now seems a trifle quaint: "Guess who is helping resupply Iran's battered army and its bloodthirsty terrorists? The U.S.— even if unwittingly," the best piece of its kind all year. Want to know the best place to launder your cocaine cash? "New Hub for an Old Web," 4-7, fingers the Netherlands Antilles, whose businessmen are sick of their new image as a no-questions-asked money laundry, but see no reason to ask questions. "See No Evil," 10-6, traces the flow of dope money out of the U.S. to Panama and back to Miami for deposit at the Federal Reserve. "Illegal out, legal in." Maybe somebody should do a TV series on this hotshot reporter.

Franklin, William B.
BusinessWeek. (★ ★)

"The Business Outlook" column, written with James C. Cooper, has usually been the best available review of near-term developments in the U.S. economy, though it was less informative in '86. Looks behind the publicized statistics to see what makes them move, finding that oil drilling was holding down industrial production, 11-3, or that a flaw in the way the U.S. treats falling prices of imports (especially oil) understates real economic growth, 10-6. Too much emphasis on what consumers spend, rather than why producers produce. Typical Keynesian confusion attributes contradictory effects to government borrowing, as in "deficit spending gave a massive dose of stimulus to growth," 8-25, but "a very expansive fiscal policy is fanning inflationary expectations," 9-22. Weak on international influences.

Fuerbringer, Jonathan
The New York Times. (★)

A competent, talented reporter chained to the budget beat, his perspective warped by those mountainous deficits. The headline writer plumbed his soul, 3-5, with "Fears Rise as Deficit Estimates Drop"!!! Less grating in '86, perhaps with Stockman gone. A good report on Gramm-Rudman Circuit Court ruling, 2-8. Best we saw in '86: Budget report on military cuts, 5-16, good analytics that clarifies the budget struggle. Perhaps he needs a change of scenery after looking at Senator Domenici all these years.

Gall, Norman
Forbes. (½ ★)

The magazine's global business "philosopher," Gall does a couple major cover stories a year pushing austerity and mercantilism, but with such a high gloss that we sometimes doubt the Forbes's realize what's up. A highly touted cover on "The Four Horsemen Ride Again," 7-28, (socialism, civil disorder, urbanization, corruption) are ravaging the underdeveloped Third World. This is pure Malthus analysis, with the solution, "less consumption at home...unfortunately...even lower standards of living." His cover story "Can the U.S. Still Profit By Its Own Technology," 12-15, is a straightforward protectionist pitch, totally one-sided arguments on why the U.S. better wake up or all those poor countries he worried about in "The Four Horsemen" will be stealing our technology. His rigid Keynesian mercantilism does help him turn up a nugget now and then, "A Yen to Spend," 5-19, was persuasive in suggesting Japan's national debt, 69.4% of GNP, is the reason it resists expansion. But Gall, we're afraid, is one of the horsemen.

Gelman, Eric
Newsweek. (★ ½)

A General Editor at *Newsweek*, Gelman writes on varied economic topics. Never stale, but sometimes inconsistent in the quality of writing and reporting. There's a humorous streak to his work (he christened September's 86.6 point loss in the DJIA "a three martini drop," 9-22). A recent interesting piece: "Grave Dancing on Lost Homes," 10-20.

Gladwell, Malcolm
Insight. (★ ½)

Member of the new magazine's kiddie corps, 23-year-old British-born Malcolm popped up in our paper flow with regularity. A look at how the Caribbean Basin Initiative is doing, 9-29, finds it floundering on protectionism and bureaucracy. A dandy business grabber on Hallmark Cards, Inc., sued by competitors for copycatting, with artwork as evidence, "The Look, the Style, the Litigation," 10-13. A fresh reprise on the AT&T breakup is a Gladwell cover story, 9-15.

Glassman, James K.
The New Republic. (★ ★ ★)

A free-lance *bon vivant* in the Washington press corps who pops up in *Washingtonian, U.S. News, Vanity Fair, Roll Call*, but saves his best for his occasional column in *TNR*, "The Money Culture." Wry observations on the new greed chic, deliciously written, but with the authority of a man who knows Wall Street, money and banking. In "A Waste of 'Time'," 4-21, he skewers the free-spending extravagances at Time, Inc. "Pushing Buttons," 5-5, "defends" Mike Deaver as a "piker" compared to the big bucks rolling in at Kissinger Associates for genteel influence peddling and zaps "the champion moralizer of Wall Street, Felix Rohatyn...one of the dozen or so guys you're supposed to call if you want to take over Exxon or the State of Idaho in a leveraged buy-out." His "Apres Ivan," 12-15, on the pre-Boesky misfeasance at Goodyear is flawless commentary: "Some would call (Sir James) Goldsmith's $93 million profit on the Goodyear deal 'greenmail.' I'd call it a very generous consulting fee." Somebody should give this fellow a magazine of his own that he could call home.

Gleckman, Howard
BusinessWeek. (★ ★)

Washington. Budget and taxes. If he didn't flinch a few days before Senator Packwood began rolling on tax reform, "Tax Reform: Mission Impossible," 3-17, he would have had a super year. Still solid, with a comeback that was early, "The 25% Solution Might Save Tax Reform," 5-12 with Ronald Grover, written well before the pub date, and "Suddenly, Tax Reform Looks Like a Survivor," 5-19. On top of the story from then on: "Winners and Losers — If Your Load is Heavy Now, You'll Love This Bill," 5-26 with Joan Berger, *et al*; "Collision on the Hill," 6-30 sees "legislators of both parties are eager to campaign as champions of lower taxes for 'average Americans.' Business tax breaks are likely to be trampled in the rush;" a jubilant "Tax Reform at Last!" 9-1 cover, is well-focused, a good wrap-up that has the politics right as far as we can tell. And he didn't get roped into the "inevitable" tax hike cover of 2-3.

Gray, Pat Bellew
The Wall Street Journal. (★)

Law beat. She surfaced a few times above the vast herd of *Journal* business reporters. Informative feature, clear on technology and legal ins and outs, on the CopyIIPC and its "Software Lockpicker," 2-7. An eye-popper on the sky-high starting lawyer salaries in New York, 6-19, but without a real stab at why it's happening.

Greenhouse, Steven
The New York Times. (★ ½)

Chicago. A stalwart business reporter who excels in company/industry pieces and stumbles at times when he gets into the national economy. "The Rise and Rise of Big Mac," 6-8, is a hamburger hummer, leading the Sunday business section, as is "Can the Cow Make a Comeback," on "designer beef," 9-28. But "The Average Guy Takes It On the Chin," 7-13, is awful, "proving" Joe Sixpack hasn't benefitted in the expansion (using pre-tax income, ignoring decline in interest rates, using statistical illusions.) He's still touting the Sidlinger Poll mythical "31-state recession" on 9-28, a month after it was punctured. But "Few Benefits Yet of Dollar Drop," 4-5, is a tidy effort, even suggesting the benefits may never arrive.

Hall, Trish
The Wall Street Journal. (NR)

Good news for *WSJ*'s management beat in the creative, funny, "When Budding MBA's Try to Save Kool-Aid, Original Ideas Are Scarce," 11-25. Hall sat in while six business-school teams presented their ideas about Kool-Aid to General Foods and a panel of judges. Best line: "In what seemed like a throwback to the time when women were all but invisible in business, the men [on the U. of Michigan team] presented the team's solution while the woman operated a projector."

MediaGuide   135

Hall, William
Financial Times. (★)

New York. Mostly conventional cliches on the markets, with the customary, vague "form letter" quotations from Henry Kaufman and David Jones. Hall gets some shots at bigger stories, such as "Wall Street Gets Greedy," 11-17 (with Roderick Oram), which was a routinely moralistic rehash of the Ivan Boesky "scandal."

Hamilton, Joan O'C.
BusinessWeek. (★★)

San Francisco. A high-tech writer whose lucid, carefully organized material has our appreciation. She first impressed us in '86 with "How Bob Fildes Engineers Growth at Cetus," 3-17, an engaging three-dimensional profile of the CEO, never mind the OTC shares have coasted south. She can dine out all year on her cover "Biotech's First Superstar," 4-14, of course Genentech, which told us all we wanted to know and were afraid to ask, also bullish while observing its PE ratio of 360! In this case, the bulls came through for her.

Hampton, William J.
BusinessWeek. (★ ½)

Detroit. We're not always sure we agree with his assessments of whither autos, but he's daring, putting ideas into play with regularity. "Why Auto Stocks Only Look Like Bargains," 4-14, relies on an economic downturn, and Ford and Chrysler advanced smartly thereafter, GM dipping; yet in same issue, "GM's Price Hike: Foresight or Folly," while unusually informative, suggests method in GM's "madness." Yet another 4-14 "Downsizing Detroit" posits the Big 3 becoming auto intermediaries. Hmmmm. By autumn, GM clearly needs revitalizing, "Ross Perot's Crusade," 10-6, tells us how, maybe. His clear big win of '86: "The New Super Dealers," 6-2 cover, a nifty scoop for a weekly on the new auto supermarkets that are chewing into the mom and pop dealerships, but also improving service. The kind of piece *Forbes* does best, but not this time.

Harris, Anthony
Financial Times. (★ ½)

His Saturday ruminations from London on various aspects of the world economy are unusually pleasant for an economist, less arrogant than most. We usually stop for a look. "Why Europe Can Envy U.S. Tax Reform," 6-28, lists his reasons, alas, why balkanized Europe can't emulate Reaganomics!: "it is likely to prove a major international economic event, and a source of enduring envy in other countries...steeped in sour grapes." The "War of Words as Friends Fall Out," 7-26, reflects on the U.S., German, Japan argument over world growth: "The truth is that although nearly everything that is said about distortions and incentives contains a lot of important truth, that does not mean that the Americans are not right too." But his "Fever Abates and Good Riddance," 5-31, on takeovers and bull markets, is particularly muddled.

Hector, Gary
Fortune. (★★)

West Coast bureau. Financial services and banking. A sound, dependable talent of the kind *Fortune* will need to encourage if it's going to make a comeback. A modest improvement over '85, when we scolded him for under-performance. Still, "A Longer Fuse for Mexico's Debt Bomb," 7-7, was stale, perhaps laying around for a month: it quotes Finance Minister Herzog, who quit 6-17. But his "Dubious Act II at BankAmerica," 11-10, was a dazzler, his best in years, almost savage in working over A.W. Clausen (who refers to short employes as dwarfs).

Herman, Tom
The Wall Street Journal. (★½)

Co-author of the "Credit Markets" column (see Foldessy, Edward P.), Herman also wrote several front page "Tax Report" columns this year, which are evaluated here. The tax report is a unique idea that so far lacks focus, leading to frivolous filler. We learn that "a Nevada couple donated 442 African art objects," 1-29, or "President Reagan got a letter from a Tenneseean suggesting a deduction for pets," 2-5. A "Tax Report" column could tell what is going on in the 50 states, as well as other countries, and what accountants and economists are discovering about tax reform. Given time and encouragement to develop more sources, and a clearer mandate, Herman is probably up to the job.

Hershey, Robert D., Jr.
The New York Times. (★★)

A journeyman in the Washington bureau, reliable on government economics beat, but nothing flashy or lasting. He misses with "Spending Up in Reagan Revolution," 2-2, a muddy effort. He's beaten by Evans & Novak, 3-17, on the pivotal 2-24 Fed vote after writing "A Tough Time for Fed Watchers," 3-9. Much better 4-3 with front-pager on oil price decline. Best we noticed of dozens, 10-14, "High, but Stable, U.S. Unemployment Is Gaining Acceptance," with fresh quotes and angles.

Hertzberg, Daniel
The Wall Street Journal. (NR)
Working the mergers, acquisition, leveraged-buyout beat after a tour on banking. No entry because his name appears almost exclusively with others,

MediaGuide 137

usually James B. Stewart's, but he is clearly more than a legman, with a reputation as being a very bright and dogged reporter, but short on color in his writing skills. The Boesky-related story, "SEC is Probing Drexel on Junk Bonds," 11-18, carries his byline atop Stewart's on this sensational story, evidence of his reporting skills. (See Stewart, James B.)

Hieronymous, William
Freelance. (NR)

His "Reinventing Brazil" in *Barron's*, 6-16, the best report we've seen anywhere on what's happening in the Brazilian economy. "Inflation doesn't live there anymore." But it's all we saw of him in '86.

Holusha, John
The New York Times. (★)

Detroit. Plugging along on the auto beat, rarely a mistake, nothing fancy, no gaudy overviews, but straightforward reporting that doesn't strain in search of a Pulitzer. "Speedometer at Eye Level," 4-3, was a tricky technology item that caught our fancy — a digital readout on the hood! A good account of the big breaking story, "Perot is Removed From G.M. Board after Long Feud," 12-2, but *The Wall Street Journal* embarrassed him and the *Times* with a major scoop on this story the day before — the *Times* played Holusha's story on top of the front page anyway, a bit of bravado.

Horowitz, Rose A.
The Journal of Commerce. (★ ★)

Two major pieces use facts and logic to debunk the bogey of Japanese capital spontaneously pulling out of the U.S. in "Japanese Love U.S. Bonds," and "Japanese Bet on US Stock Market," 5-13 and 5-14. "Group Urges Reform of U.S. Monetary Policy," 5-2, where the Business Roundtable backs right policy for wrong reason ("sustainable" trade balance).

Huey, John
The Wall Street Journal. (★ ★)

Dallas. A breezy, colorful business writer who had a wealth of material in the suddenly tattered oil patch. A three-part series on "The Empire Builders," (3-24,27,28) looked at the giant developers (Trammell Crow Co., Lincoln Property Co., Vantage Cos.) and the end of their party. A great lead on the second piece: "Back around 1975, when Trammell Crow faced several hundred million dollars in unpayable debt, he would rise each morning at 4:30 to start 'psyching himself up' for the day's meetings, a close friend recalls." What next? An old-fashioned informative A-hed on "Tennessee Caviar," 5-7, is pungent in describing the hunt for hackleback sturgeon roe in a "filthy, stinking johnboat."

Ibrahim, Youssef
The Wall Street Journal. (★ ★ ½)

New York oil writer. Marked improvement in '86, generally on top of Saudi-led price plunge. Early on mark with "Global Oil Price War Is Expected to Affect the Industry For Years," 2-11. A very good 5-13 leader on Saudi options, prestige decline on Capitol Hill. Nicely on October OPEC palaver, "OPEC Ministers Patch Up Pact, Oil Markets Show Little Faith," 10-23, quoting a Wall Streeter: "The fact that some people get together to increase the price of oil by boosting production is not very good economics." But he's still not connecting the global monetary/exchange rate policies and the oil markets. Egyptian-born, his year's best effort was an op-ed commentary, 3-13, "The Center Holds in Egypt," a good feel on the situation after the riots.

Kaletsky, Anatole
Financial Times. (★ ★)

Often novel, unpredictably opinionated. Not his best year, but better than '85. In "Anxieties Behind the Euphoria," 5-12, "euphoria has reigned" since India's *reduction* of tax and tariff rates and perhaps "Mr. Gandhi has grossly underestimated the energising effects of his reform programme on the supply side of the Indian economy." But there's only unsupported opinion, in "Not So Rich Uncle Sam," 5-22, saying U.S. economic growth will almost certainly be below the rates in other industrial countries, and a "European-style industrial colossus may be preferable to a horde of small businessmen who make all their money by suing each other or even underwriting junk bonds." Hmmmm. But in "Labour's Plans For Jobs," 6-19, he finds no jobs in Labour support for Maggie's high surtaxes. "Crying Wolf in Mexico," 7-1, can't imagine U.S. punishing Mexico, prescient. Best of the year: The first perceptive criticisms of "Misguided Austerity" in Germany and Japan, 6-10, and "Last Bastion of Deflation," 8-1, West Germany's readiness to accept permanent high unemployment. Weak and wordy explaining, the global stock market setback on 9-13, "The Paradoxes Amid the Panic," from "nothing really has changed" to "the markets have been panicked by the fear that there is no recession on the horizon."

Karmin, Monroe
U.S. News & World Report. (−)

Senior Editor for Economics. Consistent miscalls on the economy, in '86 as previously, his only utility that he provides us a public record of the consistent miscalls of the sources he always uses: Alan Greenspan, Lacy Hunt, David Jones, Larry Kudlow, Allan Meltzer, Alan Sinai, *et al*. For example, "Reagan's 'Gang of Four' Moves In On The Fed," 1-27: "We're entering a new round of inflation stimulated by super high money growth." Another — bad marks for Treasury Secretary Baker: tax reform stalled, likelihood of passage dim, 5-5.

Kestin, Hesh
Forbes. (★ ★ ½)

An emerging star, not afraid to discard preconceptions in the middle of an assignment, takes chances and comes up with the unconventional. A startlingly original on the Palestine Liberation Organization's troubled finances and implications, "Terror's Bottom Line," 6-2, complete with balance sheet, probably new to the CIA! He went to Israel looking for efficiency in its defense industry and found colossal waste in the Lavi jetfighter program, a U.S. subsidy of Israeli national pride, "A $640 Hammer is a Bargain," 6-30. A 1-27 look at USSR hard-currency problems is insightful on Gorbachev.

Kilborn, Peter T.
The New York Times. (★ ★ ★ ½)

Washington bureau's big hitter on global economy. Another great year tracking exchange-rate manipulations, Baker Plan, economic summit: "Baker Effort on Rates is Seen," 1-16, and "Baker Calls Currencies Too Volatile," 1-25, way out front, leading to "U.S. Seeks Global Economic Plan," 3-3, and "Monetary Plan Urged by Baker," 4-10, reviving concept of "automaticity." A front-page summation on "The Economic Summit," 5-7, was gloriously lofty. Also remarkable: "Economists Detect Falling Deficit Trend," 2-20, with a stunning chart showing $200 billion "saving" in one year; "Monetarism Falls From Grace," 7-3, done gracefully. But he still slumps now and then, as in 7-27, "The Sudden Wilting of Reagan's Rosy Economy," narrow and crabby, a sudden, temporary wilting of Kilborn. His Keynesian bias doesn't get in the way except with an unquestioning faith that currency devaluations improve trade deficits. And he doesn't worry enough about Mexico. Still, a must read for Wall Streeters.

Kirkland, Richard I., Jr.
Fortune. (★ ½)

European editor. We knocked him last year for getting tangled in exchange rates, and in '86 he shies away instead of mastering them. "A Dose of Capitalism Turns Italy Around," 4-14, heightens expectations. Yes, the stock market is up and capitalism is being committed, but no hint of domestic policy moves at the bottom of all this. There must be more specific reasons for the Italian stock market to be skyrocketing and their firms being more profitable than they have been in years. There must be more to this than the waning influence of the Communist Party. His "Growth Takes Hold in Europe," 2-3, offers a good overview of the European growth prospects, but at a time when the U.S. is urging monetary ease in Bonn, there's no mention of monetary policy. In "Banks Seek

Life Beyond Lending," 3-3, competition between investment and commercial bankers heats up as investment bankers take on lending business by using the securities markets. Good piece — not too judgmental — points out that this is an irreversible global trend. He enticed with "U.S. Tax Cuts Now Go Global," 11-24, but not much new, no Third World, perhaps chopped by editors.

Klott, Gary
The New York Times. (★ ★)

Washington bureau, a backup to David Rosenbaum on taxes, a big improvement over his rookie year. He cashed in on drudge work of '85, learning details of tax code, keeping competitive with and pressure on *The Wall Street Journal*, beginning with a 12-part series on '85 tax returns and another 12-parter on the new tax law beginning 10-26. "Regan Asks Shift in Senate Tax Plan," 3-17, confidently done. "The IRS Loses Its Muscle," 4-6, leads the Sunday business section on the billions in revenues lost because of David Stockman's thriftiness on the IRS budget. In a notable report, 9-5, he caught nuances of Ways & Means Chairman Rostenkowski proposing future income-tax boost, but making clear this slammed the door on the consumption-tax crowd. DJIA up 38 that day.

Kneale, Dennis
The Wall Street Journal. (★ ★)

If you read David Sanger of *The New York Times* and Kneale of the *WSJ* you will have a blanket over Big Blue. "New IBM PC Gives Clues to Firms' Course," 4-18, tells us more about where IBM is headed than the previous weeks' special IBM section. The front-page editors put a sappy lead on his front page "U.S. Firms Operating in South Africa Debate Whether to Stay or Go," 7-11, but the body of the article probably helped grease the exodus. We read "IBM Maps New Steps to Hold Back PC Clones," 7-21, to the end.

Koepp, Stephen
Time. (★ ½)

One of the staples at the weekly, Koepp's reports are well-balanced and well written. Notables include cover story "Selling a Dream of Elegance and the Good Life," 9-1, on Ralph Lauren and "And Now, the Age of Light," 10-6, on the future of fiberoptics. One to watch.

Koretz, Gene
BusinessWeek. (★ ½)

"Economic Diary" abandoned the illusion of daily dating early in 1986, and is now even more clearly just a collection of what economists say about this or that. Many were obviously self-serving and wide of the mark, such as "Why Monetarism's Star May Start Rising Again," 2-24, and there was too much filler,

MediaGuide 141

so informed readers had to fish for the prizes. A random sample: A 6-16 entry attributes unusually rapid R & D spending in 1984-86 to pressure from international competition; a 1-27 entry shows that measuring real GNP in 1982 dollars (when oil was $32) exaggerates the importance of the energy industry; a 4-14 entry finds that since top tax rates were cut from 70% to 50%, tax payments by the most affluent 1% of all taxpayers rose by 33%; a 6-2 entry notes that "the greatest demand for U.S. bonds...has come not from across the Pacific but from bond mutual funds in the U.S."; a 5-12 entry notes that manufacturing productivity from 1982 to 1985 grew at a 4.7% rate, "faster than in any prior postwar recovery."

Koselka, Rita
Forbes. (NR)

An eye-catching gem, "How to Build a Terrific Little Business," 7-28, is *Forbes* at its best. "An Up and Comers" piece about Ken Boudrie, a corporate executive — handicapped by a disabling accident as a youth — who dropped out to start The Bartlet Collection, an outfit selling assemble-them-yourself Chippendale and Queen Anne furniture, now thinking about a venture capital fund for handicapped entrepreneurs. Great job, Rita, clearly an up-and-comer too.

Koten, John
The Wall Street Journal. (★ ½)

Chicago, airline reporter we elevated last year for earlier work, but not much to speak of in '86. He had the makings of a handsome piece with "United Airlines Has Yet to Capitalize on Advantages of Size," 6-9, but leads with a catalog of dereg trivia, and seems hesitant in criticizing United for not using its size to grow as fast as, say Texas Air, simply portraying it as arrogant and hesitant. A piece on "Increased Fares, Fewer Flights are Likely Results of Airline Mergers," 9-17, is okay, but the headline tells it all. No mention of whether these increased fares he sees will still be lower than pre-dereg.

Kraar, Louis
Fortune. (★)

Asian Editor. A *Fortune* veteran who can do okay business stories, "Pepsi's Pitch to Quench Chinese Thirsts," 3-17. But we don't see him handling political economies and delivering the goods. We sat up for "India Bids for Business," 1-6, Rajiv Gandhi pushing Reaganomics to get the country going, and Kraar reports he must fight the bureaucracy first. But there's not much information *about* the bureaucracy or how difficult it will be to beat, so we're left without a clue as to which way the economy will go.

Labich, Kenneth
Fortune. (½ ★)

We can't warm up to Labich, sensing an irritating tone drifting up from his work. In "America's Most Arrogant Union," 11-10, he has some interesting angles on the Airline Pilots Assn, who are getting pay cuts, but we winced at his sniffy ha-ha that where they used to date movie stars they're now reduced to dating stewardesses. In "Stocks: Looking Beyond the Double Dow," 1-20, the Dow still has room to go higher, but he heavily qualifies this position, then tosses up a buffet of technicals, but zip on the global picture.

Laderman, Jeffrey M.
BusinessWeek. (½ ★)

Markets and Investments, department editor. Plenty to do in 1986, most of it poor to fair because he doesn't seem to understand markets. In "Those Big Swings on Wall Street," 4-7 cover, he insists that program trading moves the market, but is it moving it toward where it should be or from where it should be? "Program trading is funneling billions of dollars into stocks, helping drive the market up nearly 500 points in 6 months," by which reasoning so does the telephone system. At least a Harvard economist is quoted saying program trading increases efficiency, but also breeds volatility. Much worse is "ZAP!," 9-29 cover on "How Chicago Drives Wall Street," based on the *assumption* that the Dow falls because futures prices fall and program trading is the culprit. No proof presented, nor do they ask: Why did the futures market fall? Incredibly, in a sidebar by Norman Jonas and Christopher Farrell, Yale's Burton Malkiel is asked if program trading caused the decline: "Absolutely not." They simply increased market efficiency by "speeding the adjustment of prices to new information." The *BW* editors still seem proud of "ZAP!," an irresponsible story. They should read Susan Lee's "What's With the Casino Society?," *Forbes* 9-22.

Lawrence, Richard
The Journal of Commerce. (★ ½)

Consistently solid, careful explanation of difficult trade issues. We learn, in a 9-4 op-ed piece, that the Senate bill for sanctions against South Africa also permits subsidized farm sales to South Africa. "The Shake and Shingle Tax Fillip," 6-5, quickly caught the Canadian retaliation in reaction to U.S. protectionism. Enlightened clarification of the Administration's position in "Baker Pledges Help on Trade Legislation," 5-14. Even small tidbits, like "Latin Commodity Earnings on Rise," 7-15, give the reader something novel. Confines personal opinions to the editorial page, where his articles are surprisingly superficial — like speeches from the National Association of Manufacturers — such as "Improving U.S. Competitiveness," 10-20, and "Tax Reformers Ignore Trade Woes," 8-7.

MediaGuide

Lee, Susan
Forbes. (★ ★ ★)

Senior editor, Wall Street columnist, PhD. in economics, and the lady who explains arbitrage and such on ABC-TV's "Good Morning, America." She really found her footing in '86, tackling bigger stories than the stockpicking of '85 and doing remarkably well. Her "What's With the Casino Society," 9-22, a lucid, enterprising treatise on the high-tech, high-speed markets, frenetic trading, programmed buying and selling that should be required reading at every business school, brokerage firm, and in Congress. Her best of '86, though, was the immensely ambitious, "The Rising Stars," (5-5 with Tatiana Pouschine), nothing less than an assessment of global economics and which nations will come out ahead. Parts read as if they were edited at the wire by an ax, but even with its flaws, the piece is worth going back to for those who missed it. It makes a big, big topic understandable, quotes some articulate and thoughtful people who were new to us as well as the usual suspects. It is quite witty in spots, as ABC's morning viewers will agree about Dr. Lee (who performed a great service on the 11-17 show by gushing about how deliriously happy Wall Streeters were that Boesky finally got caught)!

Levin, Doron P.
The Wall Street Journal. (★ ½)

One piece that caught our attention, "In a High-Tech Drive, GM Falls Below Rivals in Auto Profit Margins," 7-22, a fine analytical study of current problems facing General Motors and how it's wrestling with them, but perhaps because all of Detroit loves Roger Smith, respected, decent, good fellow, he doesn't get a hard look here either. Levin had the big auto newsbeat of '86 with "GM Plans Offer to Pay $700 Million to Buy Out Its Critic H. Ross Perot," 12-1, with Dale D. Buss.

Lewis, Paul
The New York Times. (★ ½)

Paris. Over the years, one of the most dependable bylines out of Europe, he's probably winding down. But not bad with "Denationalization for France," 3-12, pre-election, close detail. "France in New Waters," 3-17, is better than *WSJ* on analysis, "normalization," and Chirac's "capitalism with a human face." Sloggy with "Mitterrand and Right," 3-19, though, okay analysis as far as it goes, but zip on policy implications of the Mitterrand/Chirac divided house. Still, day in, day out, a byline we appreciate.

Loomis, Carol J.
Fortune. (★ ½)

Over the years, a big byline at *Fortune*, but lately distracted? "The Comeuppance of Carl Ichan," 2-17, though, has juicy quotes — a bit dramatized, but exciting.

Among *Fortune*'s best of 1986, certainly the longest, "The Rockefellers: The End of a Dynasty?," 8-4, an excellent article — the great Rockefeller fortune of a few billion is split among 83 heirs with scant interest in business, overwhelmingly money consumers, not generators. We remember our Schumpeter!

Louis, Arthur M.
Fortune. (★ ½)

A stalwart who gets right what he gets but often leaves us thinking he didn't get enough. In "Does Gannett Pay Too Much?" on the newspaper chain, we expected more than a reference to *USA Today*, although the angles he had were informative. "America's New Economy," 6-23, was a good effort on managing in the "new economy" — no inflation to hide inefficiency, global competition, monetary stability — it all looks pretty sound and very competitive, but no mention of taxes or looming protectionist variables. Still, he gets close.

Magnet, Myron
Fortune. (★)

We've been told this fellow is an ace, but in two years haven't seen a face card. Close with: "What Merger Mania Did to Syracuse," 2-3, explains it isn't so bad when a business in your community is taken over (it won't always liquidate) but, when this is the case, the takeover company is an easy scapegoat, while global forces are really behind it. There are advantages to having the home office in your town. In "A New Crop of Farmland Gamblers," 4-14, three farmland speculators make the plunge, and Myron looks over their shoulders, but what's the point? His "Decline and Fall of Business Ethics," 12-8, extrapolates Boesky & Co. into an entire rotting empire. He grudgingly mentions that corporate restructuring may be good for the economy, but quickly points out we've passed that point. A few words on how restructuring is causing the destruction of the corporate culture suggest an entire article on this. We see the potential here and there, but he needs a rifle, not a shotgun.

Main, Jeremy
Fortune. (★ ½)

One of the magazine's most prolific writers, several pieces in '86 that we looked at. His is the most knowing know-it-all tone we encounter in *Fortune*, the pieces coming close to "findings" rather than stories, yet many seem schizophrenic. In "Brazil's Tomorrow is Finally in Sight," 9-15, he first determines that the government's new, wise technocrats have the right programs to solving the economy's headaches, then insists Brazil's tomorrow won't be reached unless the bloated government programs give way to entrepreneurial capital. Still, a thorough piece. Again, in "Who Will Clean Up by Cleaning Up?," 4-17, we're first advised of tremendous profit opportunity in this toxic dump mess for the companies who get into the field, since lots of money is being thrown around, but at the story's end reveals the high risks that suggest nobody in his right mind should want to get into this business. "Companies that Float from Owner to Owner," 4-28, offered nothing new, but we wondered why Main didn't give more reasons why these companies are such floaters?

Malabre, Alfred L. Jr.
The Wall Street Journal. (★ ½)

A senior economics writer and one of the authors of the Monday "Outlook" column. He began the year with gloomy stuff about the crash of 1929, or the "Kondratieff Wave," 1-20, suggesting "another crash may be at hand." He worried about efforts to slash the budget deficit, with "spending cuts and possible tax increases" causing another "1930s slump." On 3-10, however, "record-smashing federal deficits...cast doubt on prospects for the current upswing." By 6-30, he had switched to concern that "deep deficits" could instead "overheat the economy, straining its capacity to grow." Citing "many [anonymous] economists" and "many analysts" who supposedly believe the U.S. economy can't grow as fast as three percent a year, he decided that "deep deficits and brisk monetary growth" might be making the economy grow too fast. In short, budget deficts cause too much growth, while reducing deficits threatens a crash and collapse. A breakthrough for Malabre was co-authored with Lindley Clark on 3-7: "Economists Predict Interest Rate Decline Will Be Over Soon," perhaps the last of many columns relying entirely on opinions of monetarist economics (see, for example, 5-5-83 forecast of spiraling prices). His best "Outlook" column: "A Good Statistic Tells of Good Times," 9-8, debunks a story by *U.S. News & World Report* that claimed family incomes had fallen. He put much more into a major article, "Solid Growth: Despite Big Problems, U.S. Economy Seems Surprisingly Healthy," which was unusually rich in statistical detail.

Melcher, Richard A.
BusinessWeek. (★ ★)

London Bureau Manager. A brisk, no-nonsense correspondent who can tell us more with fewer words than most of the authors who file out of London. "An Insider Case Puts the City to a Test," 12-1, wraps up the Morgan Grenfell affair in short order. And his "Will London's Stock Market Break Into the Big Leagues?" 11-3, has the best lead of all the "Big Bang" stories: "For years now it has cost nearly four times as much to buy or sell in London as it has in New York. So it's no surprise that shares of some of Britain's most prestigious companies, such as Imperial Chemical Industries PLC, often trade far more actively across the Atlantic than they do at home." This is what it's all about, not big fees or computer breakdowns.

Mervosh, Edward
U.S. News & World Report. (★ ½)

The change of scenery (from *BusinessWeek*) and his own weekly column led to a modest improvement in '86 over his '85 meanderings (we remember how tax reform was going to be good for the stock and bond markets, but bad for the economy). But his "Economic Outlook" columns are still morose: "The Economic Forecasting Follies," 8-18; "Facing Up to a Down Economy," 9-29; "The Politics of Business Uncertainty," 10-13; "Debt, Debt and More Debt," 10-6. He rarely strays from commercial Keynesianism (Alan Greenspan's name appears regularly amidst the gloom). But he's a little better than most on international trade and capital flows. Cheer up, Ed. Things aren't so bad.

Mitchell, Cynthia F.
The Wall Street Journal. (NR)

Dallas. A rookie with an MBA in finance from Vanderbilt, '85, she caught our attention with a front-page leader, 10-14, "Some Firms Resume Manufacturing in U.S. After Foreign Fiascoes" both timely and satisfying in detail, examples, whys and wherefores.

Moffett, Matt
The Wall Street Journal. (★)

A strong business reporter who fills his notebook with detail, two facts per line. Typical is "Houston's Fiesta Stores a Success," 10-23, a chain catering to international food tastes ("We get 90% of the Romanian business in Houston."), including Russian gooseberry jam, Irish kidney pie, frozen cow heads. A look at the drug problem in small-town America (Guymon, Okla.), "Rural Scourge," is okay, but hardly persuades us that "Drugs Are Now Rife" in small towns, as the headline puts it, the effort much too soft for the front page.

Murray, Alan
The Wall Street Journal. (★ ★ ½)

Washington bureau. One of the capable utility reporters of the economic unit, always alert and accurate: a balanced account, 2-7, on CEA's Sprinkel call for tighter money; good detail on Administration budget options, excise tax possibilities, 3-17; straight news account, 4-2, "Third World Exports May be Curbed" better than the competition. His byline dropped off after Labor Day as he and colleage Jeffrey Birnbaum teamed to write the definitive history of tax reform, for Simon & Schuster, autumn 1987. Still on the rise, he could star with a regular slot in a starting lineup. Probably better than he thinks he is.

MediaGuide 147

Nasar, Sylvia
Fortune. (★)

A young professional economist who studied under Leontieff, she still hasn't learned "journalism" means communication and is still pushing her own stuff, we are doomed by budget deficits, etc. Very poor on the *Fortune* Forecast, "Business Won't Untie Its Purse Strings," 12-8, typical partial equilibrium analysis: Business taxes going up, cash flow down, ergo business investment down. No mention of possible dynamics of the new tax law. "The $2-Trillion Debt Headache," 11-10, okay as far as it goes, but also partial equilibrium, ignoring vast expansion of asset base. But there is promise at a less exalted level. "Jobs Go Begging At the Bottom," 4-17, a good overview of this problem and how it is influenced by demographics, geography and statistical problems.

Nash, Nathaniel C.
The New York Times. (★ ★)

Washington bureau regulatory beat. On the rise, young and energetic, obviously benefitting from a previous editing stint in New York. It's hard to make an SEC profile sparkle, but Nash does it, 3-30, with a stellar job on two new SEC folk, Joe Grundfest and Ed Fleishman. Best we saw, "U.S.'s 'Fix-It' Anti-Trust Policy," 9-16, the Reagan administration's new twist: letting Texas Air "fix" its Eastern deal.

Nenneman, Richard A.
The Christian Science Monitor. (−)

Highly predictable preachy column, with minimal analysis or evidence. In "Plumbing the Mystery of Why the U.S. Deficit Doubled Under Reagan," 2-10, "the deficit as a form of major fiscal stimulus made it possible for the Federal Reserve to have a tighter monetary policy." But tight money didn't contribute to the deficit? Not enough plumbing. In "U.S. Has Licked Inflation, Oil Blockage; But Who's Minding the Deficit?," 3-31, "the inflation brought on by the adjustment to the oil shocks...was solved largely by the persistence of the Federal Reserve." Monetary policy thus works in only one direction — inflation is caused by oil but cured by the Fed, and that cure (again) had no impact on the deficit.

Newton, Maxwell
New York Post. (★ ★)

Wall Street commuters read Max on the way home, and he keeps them awake with his fulminations against the twists and turns of Fed policy, blasts against Henry Kaufman and others high-priced and mighty, and spicy common sense. "Fed Not Likely to Ease Up on Money," 10-27, is better reasoned than parallel pieces in the big dailies.

Norman, James R.
BusinessWeek. (★ ★ ★)

Houston. Late in the year we noticed he'd been piling up points, with no subtractions. A cover on Hugh Liedtke, "The Scrappy Mr. Pennzoil," 1-27, started him off fast as "Liedtke embarked on a relentless crusade for retribution." Then "Casualties Start to Pile Up in the Oil Patch," 2-10, with memories of the grisly '60s, when "half the independents died." Everyone's onto Texas Air's Lorenzo, but Norman does a satisfying "Nice Going Frank, But Will it Fly?," 9-29. His best, we thought, "America's Deflation Belt," 6-9, which hits all the bases: "To be sure, much of the inflation in the 1970s was beyond the nation's control. But if oil embargoes, world crop failures and rising prices in other countries were the kindling, domestic policies clearly poured fuel on the fire with vast creation of dollars, untamed government borrowing, a tax code that skewed investment into oil and real estate, and a farm subsidy program guaranteed to produce costly surpluses."

Norman, Peter
The Wall Street Journal. (★ ★ ½)

London. Always worth reading on developments in the U.K. economy and government policy shifts. His "Britain Faces an Uncertain Economic Path," 9-24, is a quality update on the crosscurrents there. "Britain Looking Toward Full EMS Role," 10-28, is revealing on Thatcher's opposition to fixing the pound. Norman is so talented in such efforts we expected more on European monetary politics in busy '86. He's got star potential.

O'Reilly, Brian
Fortune. (★ ½)

Dallas. A mixed year. A solid, timely account of Mexico's economic crunch, "Business Makes a Run For the Border," 8-18, where we hear for the first time of the Maquiladoras — foreign owned factories. But "This Builder Wants It All — Without Risk," 5-12, tries to persuade us that through new financing schemes — of course Drexel Burnham Lambert is mentioned — this builder can build into a glut and still profit. This suggests Drexel has a pool of stupid investors, but the story doesn't explore that side of the deal. "A Man With a Screwdriver Operates on AT&T," 6-23, presents an interesting and thorough personality sketch on Chairman Olsen, who seems able to make the tough decisions, but his success or failure may depend more on the markets they choose or choose to exit than on his personal quirks. We'd rather more than the few paragraphs devoted to where Olsen thinks the company should go.

MediaGuide

Pennar, Karen
BusinessWeek. (★)

A growing economic journalist, Pennar usually gets one or two good points into essays that nonetheless miss the big picture. "Will It Take a Recession to Close the Trade Gap?" 11-3, never quite grasps how relevant and yet absurd that question is. "The Trade Medicine Isn't Working," 7-28, wonders if it is because "the dollar hasn't weakened everywhere," though it is precisely the currencies that *had* gained against the dollar (the yen and the mark) where the trade deficit got wider. A much better point was that "one-third of the increase in manufactured exports in 1983-85 was in parts and components that went into products subsequently imported into the U.S." Her 6-9 article "The '20s and the '80s: Can Deflation Turn Into Depression" was reasonably accurate, although two years later than similar analyses.

Petre, Peter
Fortune. (★ ★ ★)

A talent for profiling captains of industry. His 7-7 "What Welch Has Wrought at GE" was marginally superior to *BusinessWeek*'s entry, with a clearer picture of Welch, greater depth. A wonderful, gorgeous cover on Digital Equipment's Ken Olsen, "America's Most Successful Entrepreneur," 10-27, one of the year's best: "Olsen was shocked at the regimentation and insularity of the culture [IBM's] Thomas Watson had created. 'It was like going to a Communist state,' he says today. 'They knew nothing about the rest of the world, and the world knew nothing about what went on inside'." The *Fortune* of yore.

Pine, Art
The Wall Street Journal. (★ ½)

Washington bureau. Veteran covering IMF, World Bank, global debt. We've previously faulted him for being too close to the institutions and for deficiency in understanding international money. Still a problem, and he was swamped by *Times*man Peter Kilborn covering Tokyo summit. A front-page scare story, "Big U.S. Trade Deficit Supplants Debt Crisis as Top Economic Peril," 10-20, is completely one-sided. But he was better elsewhere, very good, 5-16, on two-step U.S. trade strategy with the EEC, "loading its guns" for a trade war but not firing. An important newsbeat on Dutch Finance Minister Onno Ruding overplaying his hand for the top IMF job, 10-3.

Platt, Gordon
The Journal of Commerce. (★)

Financial editor. Not much depth under this byline. "The Basics of Money Management," 8-19, was a bit *too* basic. "Tax Bill Could Hurt Banks," 8-29, likewise quotes a few people saying the obvious, like "the banking industry has been battered recently."

Pollack, Andrew
The New York Times. (★★)

San Francisco. Roaming Silicon Valley and wine country, another young talented *Times*man. A sharp account, newsfeature approach, 6-27, on ITT's sale of telecommunication unit to France's GTE. Good read on Gallo boys and their wine cooler, 7-6. Front page on "Video Games, Once Zapped, In Comeback," thought-provoking on software waves, 9-27.

Powell, Bill
Newsweek. (★★)

A quality second banana to Rich Thomas, whom he often teams with. Consistent in the quality of his reports, whether business or financial topics. Lively images brighten his pieces. Solid efforts: "Using the Dollar as a Weapon," 7-28, "The Case For Asbestos," 9-29. Best we saw in '86, "The New Dealmakers," 5-26: "Welcome to Wall Street chic....Dealing on Wall Street is to the 1980s what high tech was to the '70s and what advertising was to the 1950s — the profession of choice for the top graduates of the nation's elite schools."

Prokesch, Steven
The New York Times. (★★★½)

New York ace on management, combining old wire-service reporting doggedness and lively imagination. A brilliant idea, 7-6, asking six experts to recommend salvation strategies to People Express' Donald Burr. Prokesch still manages to zip, 9-25, with a reprise on the done-to-death offbeat management "Behind People Express' Fall." He finds faddish "Intrapreneurship" at Levi Strauss a flop, 7-28, and finds "McIlhenny Finally Bestirs Itself" with its new Tabasco flavors, a neat Sunday feature, 6-29. A three-part series on "The Family Business" (6-10,11,12) still worth reading.

Quinn, Jane Bryant
Newsweek. (★)

Rarely anything insightful, her advice is nothing you couldn't have thought of yourself (in "Shelters: The Great Escape," 8-4, she tells the reader to contact an accountant or attorney before investing). She's also hell bent on constantly giving people advice on how to effectively avoid paying their fair share in taxes, which gets annoying. Give her points for spitting out a full-page biweekly column.

Quint, Michael
The New York Times. (★★)

"Credit Markets" column. In recent years, Quint has been slightly more original than the rival column in *The Wall Street Journal*, partly because the *WSJ* clung too long to a "money supply" focus, slow to notice that the new Fed was instead concerned with exchange rates and commodity prices. Both fish in the same waters finally, but Quint sometimes casts a wider net, getting insights from a changing list of economists and (less often) even actual bond traders. In "More Rate Drops Seen Likely," 3-17, there were a record three or four unfamiliar analysts, who had the advantage of being right. Occasional longer pieces, such as "End of Road for Sturdy '8's," (on the ill-fated 8% bonds issued in 1976) have been thoughtful and fresh. As the bond market rallied after Gramm-Rudman was emasculated, Quint squirmed in "Bond Market Hopeful Despite Ruling," 2-8, not considering the possibility that the budget scheme might be irrelevant or harmful. But the *WSJ* bond column hasn't figured this out either.

Rasky, Susan F.
The New York Times. (½★)

One of the weaker members of the business staff, especially when she wanders into economics. Typical is a Sunday business section front-page feature, "A New Generation of Non-Savers," 11-2, that repeats the hoary Keynesian myth that the savings rate shows the U.S. is becoming a nation of profligate grasshoppers instead of frugal ants. (The measurements are hopelessly flawed.) Other *Times*men have overcome their economic preconceptions by casting a wider reporting net, which Rasky will have to do to improve.

Redburn, Tom
Los Angeles Times. (★★½)

Washington bureau. Thorough on money and taxes in '86, unappreciated because so few see his material in New York or D.C. He didn't miss or miscall much on the tax story in '86, keeping ahead of the conventional, never fading on tax reform prospects, displaying a knowledgeable reading on its progress, as in " 'Fairness' Issue Foremost in Reconciling of Tax Bills," 7-8. Other notable efforts on economic policy: "Summit to Grapple With Trade, Currency Issues," 5-4, and "Economic Growth May Rival 1960s'," 3-23. A clever lead in "Baker: Summit's Monetary Master," 5-22: "The old joke was that Treasury Secretary James A. Baker never left home without him, for Richard A. Darman was his American Express Card. But this week, Baker traveled halfway around the world without Deputy Treasury Secretary Darman, the bright, puckish strategist who has been at his side since the beginning of the Reagan Administration, and he emerged from the economic summit meeting with a stunning victory of his own."

Reed, Julia
U.S. News & World Report. (★ ½)

A very aggressive young reporter with a surprising breadth of experience in business and political reporting, bristling with ideas, colorful writing. "Hollywood's Big New Mogul," 6-23, a solid job on Coca Cola's deep pockets buying the movies. Reed had one of the cleverest lines of 1986 in the "Travel in America" cover series of 5-5, on how to plan your dining on a coast-to-coast trip: "Some travelers couldn't care less about seeing the purple mountain majesties. They are more inclined toward the fruited plain."

Reinhold, Robert
The New York Times. (★ ★)

Dallas. Kept up with oil-patch recession in imaginative ways. "In Troubled Oil Business it Matters Little if Your Name is Bush, Sons Find," 4-30, he uses two sons of George Bush to illustrate what falling oil prices have done to an entire economic sector. His biggest splash in '86 was the Sunday business lead, "John Connally's Texas-Sized Troubles," 9-14: "In many ways, the saga of John Connally is the story of Texas, a state that bet too heavily on itself, believing it could not lose." We also liked "Texans Fight For Their Land and Way of Life," 6-29, the U.S. government's trouble finding a nuclear depository, another bigger story using Texas as microcosm.

Riemer, Blanca
BusinessWeek. (★ ★ ★)

Washington bureau, covering IMF/World Bank as well as the Federal Reserve, which gives her an edge over those who divide these beats. Up from (★ ★) in *1986 MediaGuide*. Originally from Paris, her global perspective probably helps, too. Energetic, always poking around. A nice survey, 3-3: "As the Dollar Falls, Tempers Rise," Germany and Japan scream, but Treasury wants more. A solid piece on Treasury's "scheme" for non-bank banks to buy ailing thrifts, 3-17. Not quite with a skimpy "Now, a Real Global Try at Stable Currencies," 4-14. But ahead of the big dailies with "Good Luck, Mr. Conable. You'll Need It," 7-7," on the new World Bank chief's limitations. Best of year, also out front, "Forget the Money Supply, the Fed Watches Pork Bellies," 7-28.

Riley, Barry
Financial Times. (★ ★)

Financial Editor. A byline we'd like to see more often. "Why the 'Arbs' Are Under Fire," 5-21, was a spirited defense of arbitragers, including Ivan Boesky, suggesting that the interests of corporate managers are not always the same as those of the stockholders. "It is chiefly the risk aversion of U.S. investment institutions that makes it all possible." His 10-27 article on London's big bang was about all you needed to read on the event.

Riley, Karen
The Washington Times. (★)

Tax-reform reporter, a cut above the wire-service reports, she kept up with most of the twists and turns during the year, but couldn't match the competition on technical prowess. "Progress on Tax Reform," 4-10, was surprisingly upbeat when others were throwing in the towel. Out in front briefly with "Packwood Puts Tax Reform Ahead of Deficit Reduction," 3-5.

Robbins, William
The New York Times. (★ ★ ½)

Roving Midwest reporter. He caught our eye in '85 with fine reports on farmland despair. More of same in '86, a notable entry on hundreds of Midwest communities cut off from all public transport with bus service ending, 10-14. He does heavy-duty reporting too: a 6-18 account of the start of the small-crop harvest was comprehensive, packed with well-presented statistics, all we needed to know.

Rosenbaum, David
The New York Times. (★ ★ ★ ½)

Washington bureau. Lead tax reporter, sticking with the tax-reform story when others had it buried. "Voting on Tax Bill Delayed in Senate," 4-19, a bold, important account. Then, an interview with Sen. Packwood, 4-24, who says, at crisis stage, there will be a bill. By 5-8 he's on front page, "Tax Revision in '86 is Almost Assured," with details on how Packwood got his 20-0 vote by peddling "transition rules." Also notable, interview with Sen. Russell Long, 2-2, who proposes a tax-reform of his own, a clue to potential. A handsome record.

Rowan, Roy
Fortune. (★ ½)

An old hand at the magazine, almost 40 years and many of them vintage. Not '86. "America's Most Wanted Managers," 2-3, just another list to satisfy our craving to know who is the best...who are the top 30. There are several commonly-based attributes of prospective corporate stars, we are told, such as "action-oriented," able to "build a sense of shared values," able to "motivate and generate loyalty," "team builders," "willing to pay the price," "a drive, strong, ambitious." Also underweight: "How American Business Broke with Marcos," 4-17, American business saw chaos and instability coming with the election fraud and abandoned an old ally. Rowan has written about the mob on and off, and his big effort of '86 was the cover: "The Fifty Biggest Mafia Bosses," 10-19, another losing gimmick list, which we did not read, and could find no one who did. Enough of this, Marshall Loeb.

Rowen, Hobart
The Washington Post. (★ ★ ★)

Economics Editor. In 1985, Bart seemed "hopelessly trapped in the Keynesian model," as we put it in assigning (★ ★). Pushing 70, he may have outproduced everyone else in the national press in 1986. He also foraged well outside demand management, his wide sweep yielding a torrent of columns, features and news dispatches on just about everything economic — leaving his youthful competitors muttering. Two fine pieces from Zurich, back to back: "Bill Bradley to the Rescue," 7-13, on the Bradley Plan for the Third World; "Europe Needs Tax Reform Too," 7-14, on the prospect of a West German reform. He's on his toes, 3-26, with Don Regan hinting Volcker may get a third term at the Fed, but spied hints the other way later in the year.

Rublin, Lauren R.
Barron's. (★ ½)

A bright young up-and-comer who has just about mastered the business formula piece and seems to have the potential for material of greater depth. Her memorable report from San Juan on Puerto Rico's "economic about-face and its resurrection as a tourist mecca" one of *Barron's* best of '86, "Comeback in the Caribbean: Puerto Rico's Back in Business," 2-10, a piece we wouldn't normally expect to see in *Barron's*. Maybe they should do more.

Sanger, David E.
The New York Times. (★ ★ ★ ½)

New York. The *Times* 26-year-old whiz kid on the computer beat, marvelous clarity whether its the doings at IBM or analytical reports of the Challenger disaster. His 5-28 account of Burroughs/Sperry deal beat the socks off three *WSJ* reporters. His "Doubt Computers Could Detect Fire," 2-2, was at this point the best we'd seen on the cause of the shuttle disaster, clear as a bell. "Challenger Inquiry," 2-17, is news analysis, but with terrific reporting, writing wrap-up. Another front-page four-bagger, 9-23, "NASA Pressing Shuttle Changes Amid Concerns," questioning new shortcuts on redesign of spaceshuttle boosters. Sanger and Phil Boffey are the best one-two punch around on this kind of reporting, also zeroed in on the importance of SDI ("Star Wars") on software development, and vice versa.

Sapulkis, Agis
The New York Times. (★★)
Airlines. A veteran who doesn't miss very much. Standouts of '86: "Frank Borman's Troubles at Eastern," 2-27; "Some See Threat to Low Air Fares," 4-5, a thoughtful angle — mergers give discount firms enough leverage to avoid deep discounts; Texas Air buying People Express, 9-16, more thorough than *The Wall Street Journal*'s triple byline.

Schershel, Patricia
U.S. News & World Report. (★ ½)

Versatile and competent in her writing, her pieces are sometimes short on column space, but rarely on information. She's just, however, keeping up with the Joneses: it's all there, but it's not always new. Some we liked: "Bewitched, Bothered and Bewildered," 9-29, "What to do before year-end" and "Basking in the Security of Savings Certificates," 10-20.

Seabury, Jane
The Washington Post. (★ ½)

Covering national economy, utility role, Seabury had a standout '85 with important stories on the national GNP accounts, which led to their revisions. Slipped a bit in '86, taken in by phony partisan reports of Rep. David Obey's Joint Economic Committee on rich getting richer, 31 states in recession, etc. Smart, aggressive, she almost squared accounts with "Critics Say JEC Has Lost Its Influence," 9-28, but pulled her punches. Best of year: "Theorist Targets City Woes," 5-18, on Heritage Foundation's Stuart Butler, enterprise zone advocate, with nice counterpoint from liberal Jeff Faux.

Sherman, Stratford P.
Fortune. (★★★)

Brisk, authoritative, well-written reports on unfolding management plays. One of his and the magazine's best of '86, "Ted Turner: Back From the Brink," 7-7: Life on the edge, MGM/UA deal and other "crazed amoebas." On top of the new doings at CBS, 10-13, which braces itself for the Larry Tisch regime: "Tisch is as well known for the icy rationality of his investment decisions as for his warmth of personality. He shows no sign of being intimidated, much less deceived, by the costly trappings of CBS's faded preeminence." A lot of pictures with a few words.

Sherrid, Pamela
U.S. News & World Report. (★)
A steady, competent business writer whose reports have some life to them. "The Pitfalls of Investing Your Money Overseas," 6-23, was nothing fancy, but we didn't see anybody else on this angle.

Silk, Leonard
The New York Times. (★★½)

Still the most important of the economic columnists because of his experience, stature and platform. Although it's always valuable to know what's on his mind, he seemed less relevant in 1985, either his focus of attention off the mark or his analysis half-hearted. Still on the sunny side of 70, he snapped back in '86 after a slow first quarter, commanding our attention again. His "Budget's Link to the Dollar," 2-7, is fuzzy and "Shultz Takes Broad View," 2-12, a kid-gloves interview with the Secretary of State. "Pressures on the Fed Top Ease," 2-26, is late. "Stabilizing Currencies," 4-2, gets him back in a groove, tracking the general unhappiness with the float. "Even Volcker is Optimistic," 5-7, builds around the chairman's speech, "After years of turmoil there can be years of growth — a good harvest." With the *Times* reporters missing the setback to the Dutch Finance Minister's bid for the top IMF job, Silk keeps them in play with his "New Problems Loom at the IMF," 10-3. If '87 is a big year for global monetary reform, he should be ready to chronicle it.

Sloan, Allan
Forbes. (★★★)

A Wall Street reporter who writes with unusual confidence in his always well-shaped viewpoint and who does seem to get deeper into a subject than most. In "The Game is Getting Out of Hand," (3-24 with Laura R. Walbert) he asks "What the hell is going on?...We ask because there are increasingly clear signs that the mutual fund business is once again entering a period of wretched excess." His best, though, is "Understanding Murdoch, Numbers Don't Really Matter," 3-10, outstanding on Rupert's magic, with breathtaking numbers, an exciting story that captures both the sweep of what Murdoch is doing as well as the kind of tri-continent dealmaking — done in real time thanks to communications technology — that is the wave of the future. A terrific, memorable kicker line: "While much of the U.S. media has been bemused by arguments about Murdoch's personality and his editorial style, they have tended to miss the real story: That here is the quintessential late 20th-century man, a sardonic figure who understands in his gut what modern communications, modern finance and modern politics is all about."

Smith, Geoffrey
Financial World. (NR)

We don't normally see *FW*, but Smith spent most of '86 with *Forbes*, where he'd brought the "Up and Comers" column to prominence and where we saw "The Yankee Samurai," 7-14. A sharp, important piece on Cummins Engine Co., a prototypical U.S. smokestack company — how it got its cost structure under control to keep Japanese product out.

MediaGuide 157

Stern, Linda
The Journal of Commerce. (★★)

Occasional insights, such as "CPI shows weakness in economy" — a sharp contrast with other reporters who see falling prices as an unmixed blessing. Surveyed some tax specialists and provided useful information in "Minimum Tax Impact Depends on the Industry," 5-12. Also has a new column "Economic Beat," usually composed of sketchy, inconclusive Washington anecdotes. An exception, 9-5, where "some observers suspect House Democrats fought for the one-year phase-in with the intent of maintaining it into perpetuity" (she notes that the same trick with delaying tax indexing did not succeed).

Stern, Richard L.
Forbes. (★★½)

One of the *Forbes* heavy hitters, on investments and markets, always looking for new angles in the new-issues market. He teams frequently with Paul Bornstein on new issues, but he's clearly the captain. "Here We Go Again," 3-10 (with Bornstein) alerts us that "As things are shaping up, 1986 could be the biggest year for new issues in history, and watch out!" "Investors and Slow Learners," 5-19 (with Bornstein) assures us that while the new issues market is starting to boil, it is "but just starting. It is nothing like the frenetic pace it reached before the resounding crash of new issues in the fall of 1983." And he makes his case. In "Stacked Odds," 7-14 (with Bornstein) the new issues market "is boiling," and he finds your odds are better with companies that got their start with venture capital funds. He finds a security of unsecured loans concocted by Salomon Brothers and an Ohio bank in "What Will They Think of Next?" 5-19, a dandy about CARDS (Certificates for Amortizing Revolving Debts): "Any old fairy godmother can turn pumpkins into coaches or mice into footmen. But it takes a very special talent to transform unsecured loans into securities."

Stevens, Charles W.
The Wall Street Journal. (★)

A youngish bread-and-butter reporter on commodities and exchange rates, who we read for careful presentation of data. Usually adequate on splicing news into numbers, "Dollar Recovers as Volcker Says It Fell Enough," 2-20, a good example. But he's still green, we remember, when we see in a 10-29 report on the dollar weakening as traders await U.S. trade figures, quoting Peter Rogers of Banco Di Sicilia, New York: "Whether they're good, bad or indifferent should give us some clue to the dollar's future." This is a waste of our time.

Stewart, James B.
The Wall Street Journal. (★ ★ ★ ★)

The paper's ace on mergers and acquisitions, busier than ever in '86. A lawyer by training (Harvard, '76), Stewart put in three years at Cravath, Swaine and Moore before becoming executive editor of *American Lawyer* magazine ('79), moving to the *Journal* in 1983 to cover law and the legal profession. His byline, coupled frequently with the reporter whose beat includes the takeover target, is carefully watched by editors of competing papers for the earliest stirrings of a new deal. Not much time left for flashy features or lengthy front-page leaders. He'll stray from this beat occasionally, a legal background showing in a splendidly balanced report on U.S. reluctance to assist Aquino government on recovering Marcos' wealth, 3-17. He's out front with "Contingency Legal Fees for Mergers," 10-24, has takeover lawyers buzzing over $11 million paid to lawyers by Burroughs on the Sperry takeover. (See Hertzberg, Daniel.)

Swardson, Anne
The Washington Post. (★ ½)

Tax beat. She improved perceptibly over her rookie year, didn't miss much and had to be read by serious watchers of tax reform. But still in third place to the *NYT*'s Rosenbaum and *WSJ*'s Birnbaum on newsbeats. Her "'86 Is the Year of Tax-Wise Giver," 10-22, out front on extraordinary implications of tax law on charity. But she buried her lead in the last paragraph: "We believe we will collect against past, present and future pledges a record amount of cash and appreciated property," says United Jewish Appeal.

Symonds, William C.
BusinessWeek. (★ ★ ½)

Rome. Just getting his feet on Italian soil, opening the new bureau, no doubt as a reward for his sterling performance as Pittsburgh bureau manager. His cover, "TROUBLE!," 8-11, on the problems at Allegheny International was one of the year's 10 best: The charismatic chairman who has gotten away with lavish perks, abuses of corporate privileges, and seemingly stupid business decisions, primarily because his directors act less like independents and more like his soldiers. The story precipitated convulsions at Allegheny and the departure of CEO Robert Buckley. Our only problem with the piece was overkill. So much sensational evidence was presented against AI to make the argument convincing that it was not necessary to lard the barrage with unnamed sources, or drop a line like: "Three other outside directors have received money from the company beyond their normal directors' fees," without further explanation. Which three are guilty? Otherwise, *bellissimo*. We will now watch for a cover from Italy.

MediaGuide

Tagliabue, John
The New York Times. (★ ★)

Oil beat, recently out of Bonn, keeping up with the *WSJ* big hitters. "OPEC Set to Discuss News Strategies," 3-17, impressive, good, straight reporting. One of the best on Sheik Yamani we'd seen, perhaps because of his fresh eye, "Squeezing OPEC and the U.S.," 4-13. Very impressive in hitting a beat so fast, we expect a climb.

Tanner, James B.
The Wall Street Journal. (★ ½)

Dallas. The *Journal*'s peerless petroleum writer in the 1970s, Tanner left for a private newsletter. Back in '86, but second banana to Youssef Ibrahim, still a byline to watch carefully. He taught us the difference between "dry" barrels and "wet" barrels. There's a new spin on the oil price plunge, 3-17, warning of long-term shortages. Early with "Oil-Rig Count Shows Drilling in Deep Slump," 5-13. And a thorough roundup with facts and figures on how "Even $18 Oil Won't Halt Plunging U.S. Oil Output," 11-3.

Terry, Edith
BusinessWeek. (★ ½)

Toronto. A Chinese-speaking Asian specialist, somehow assigned in '83 to Canadian bureau as No. 3, floating to the top by attrition and eagerness to understand Canada. "As Free-Trade Talks Falter, So Does Mulroney," 11-3, keeps up on trade strife with U.S. and Canadian politics. A report on plight of Canadian oil industry, "This is Like Stepping Off the Edge of a Cliff," 4-14, is thorough and fresh. We're watching for her first Canada cover.

Thomas, Rich
Newsweek. (★ ★ ★)

Newsweek's "Chief Economic Correspondent," Washington bureau, Thomas is the magazine's star, somehow beating the dailies now and then on critical news. He doesn't appear often in a single byline — but when he does, it's something special, always readable and enjoyable. "Perils of the Green Plague," 3-10, on billions of dollars in the monetary base used out of the U.S., important but not seen elsewhere. His "Slouching Toward a Slump," 5-19, on the Tokyo economic summit is the only place we learn George Shultz talked the President out of pressing Germany and Japan on growth. "The Monetary Barroom Brawl," 10-13 is a delightful and accurate summary of the "mauled float," Jim Baker slugging it out with Germany's Stoltenberg: "It may not be elegant, but for now Baker's mauled float is all the international monetary reform we're going to get."

Ticer, Scott
BusinessWeek. (NR)

Atlanta bureau manager. We noted his enthusiasm for Ashton-Tate when he still worked in L.A. "The Dark Horse Who Has Ashton-Tate Galloping Again," 2-10, from Torrance, when the OTC shares were almost 20!! Then it doubled by November. We'll watch for his enthusiasm in the Southeast.

Trachtenberg, Jeffrey A.
Forbes. (★★½)

Marketing beat, writing with marketing style. "Everybody Makes Money But Kadinsky," 11-17, on how the "golden age" of restaurant design at NYC's Aurora pulls in an average $40 lunch tab. In "You Are What You Wear," he catches designer Ralph Lauren going into competition with his best customers, an imaginative cover, as was his best of the year, "Shake, Rattle and Clonk," 7-14, a cover story with cover copy, "If this is a service economy, where's the service?" An excellent blend of down-to-earth household anecdotes, elevated economic theory and good corporate reporting, especially from General Electric's revived Appliance Park division in Louisville, Ky. Outstanding work.

Urquhart, John
The Wall Street Journal. (★)

Ottawa. Twice in '86 he gave us the best spot news on tax-reform developments in Ottawa: "Canada Considers Revising Tax System," 7-21, covers Finance Minister Wilson's press conference with good quotes; "Canada Proposes Major Tax Reform," 10-24, hits the high spots, but very stingy with details considering the importance of the story.

Uttal, Bro
Fortune. (★½)

West Coast, looking over Silicon Valley, imperiously concluding that bad management is always the problem. "Who Will Survive the Microchip Shakeout?," 1-6, lists reasons for the severe shakeout (stalled computer industry and Japanese willingness to lose fortunes in exchange for market share), then concludes U.S. industry needs new management. "How to Cope When the CEO Has a Stroke," 3-3, interesting piece about Software Publishing Corp. and their CEO Gibbons who had a stroke at 36. Some useful comments about the makeup of the software market and some heroics in Gibbons' return to work. A good cover story: "Inside the Deal that Made Bill Gates $350 Million," 7-21, a step-by-step account of Microsoft's deal to go public — great quotes — the whole process is revealed as a lot less glamorous than one might believe, with painstaking attention to detail being the bulk of the work. Best work: "A

MediaGuide 161

Surprisingly Sexy Computer Marriage," 11-24, on why the Sperry-Burroughs deal seems to be working out. Could be (★ ★ ★) in '87.

Valery, Nicholas
The Economist. (★ ★ ★ ½)

The Economist doesn't believe in bylines, but every now and then awards one on a major effort. Valery's "High Technology: Clash of the Titans," 8-23, is virtuoso journalism, effortlessly superb on the battle between the U.S. and Japan in the high-tech markets. Deeply factual, objective, written with style and grace, it's worth filing for quick reference by other journalists in the field and by corporate speechwriters. State-of-the-art.

Vise, David A.
The Washington Post. (★)

A young Wall Streeter turned newsman. Energetic, looking around for an offbeat business story outside the Beltway. Caught our eye with 3-2 piece on New York's Forstmann-Little, leverage-buyout firm, "Small Firm, Big Fortunes." An ambitious, exhaustive takeout on insider trading on the CBS takeover moves, 9-28, needed better organization, tighter writing, up-front conclusions.

Watson, Ripley, Jr.
The Journal of Commerce. (★)

Comments on stock and bond markets usually take the easy way out, leaning on cliches, like "Seesawing credit market expected to continue," 9-29, or falling stock prices are "a case of money managers becoming cautious and therefore anxious to take profits," 9-9, or "the market appeared to be drifting along without direction," 10-29. Much better on foreign exchange, Watson showed initiative in quoting Sam Cross, a powerful member of the New York Fed, 9-5, and in highlighting the causes of $63 billion in *daily* foreign exchange trades in "Currency Transactions Soar," 8-20.

Welles, Chris
BusinessWeek. (★ ★ ½)

New York. Senior Writer. A breezy, veteran Wall Street journalist who loves the big story, but likes to cut corners at times for the poetry. "The Mysterious 'Coincidences' in Insider Trading Cases," 9-8 with John Templeman in Lausanne and Vicky Cahan in Washington, was intriguing and on the beam, but a bit too heavy handed in practically convicting their subjects based on hearsay, speculation, and coincidence. With a little care it could have been in the top 10, but still close. "Why the E.F. Hutton Scandal May Be Far From Over," 2-24, an excellent summary of the scandal that gives the clearest picture we've seen from one source, crammed with chewy quotes, although many from unnamed sources. He tagged along on the Boesky scandal with a superb psychosketch: "A Man Who Made a Career of Tempting Fate," 12-1, with an anonymous quote: "He made money the old fashioned way. He stole it." Welles could give colleague Bianco competition if he tried.

Wildstrom, Stephen
BusinessWeek. (★½)

Editor of the "Washington Outlook," collecting staff contributions. "Ed Zschau is putting Alan Cranston on The Endangered List," 6-16, was only slightly less foolish than "Why Bob Packwood Is No Shoo-In For Re-election." Many so-called "Washington Outlook" columns are bare-fisted editorializing, posing as news. On 5-26, we learn that Budget Director James Miller's "rigid, ideological approach to the budget alienated moderate leaders used to dealing with the more flexible David A. Stockman." Stockman could only be considered flexible, non-ideological or moderate by the authors, perhaps Wildstrom himself, the column simply hoping, rather than predicting that "the Senate may finally get up the nerve to consider a serious tax increase." Since Wildstrom takes credit for the editing, he should either use his red pen less sparingly or change the column's name to "Washington Advice."

Williams, Winston
The New York Times. (★★½)

One of the stars we watch for in the Sunday business section, writing with style and authority. We liked "Man and Myth on Wall Street," profiling Peter Dawkins of Lehman Brothers (on his way to Washington?). A startling piece, 10-5, "Business Brings Back the Lockout," rich in detail, but doesn't quite see lockouts go with deflations, strikes with inflations. Best of the year: "Carl Icahn's Wild Ride at TWA," 6-22, with the corporate raider graying in the executive suite.

Willoughby, Jack
Forbes. (★★)

A knack for coming up with pieces we don't think we'll be interested in, but turn out to win us over with angles, information and deft writing. In "More Fun Than Flogging Frosting," 11-17, we're invited to read about the world's largest privately held corporation, Cargill, Inc., the Minnesota commodity trader with 46,000 employes and $32 billion in sales, "a very patient group of 38 shareholders" earning less than if their equity was in a bank, the cash flow pouring into agricultural and energy investments because "someday they will rebound." His "A License to Steal," 9-22, is a gem on Michael Hellerman, the '70s Wall Street swindler who went under Fed protection after helping put 30 folks in prison, resurfacing now under a new name and cover to scheme again.

Witcher, S. Karene
The Wall Street Journal. (★★)

New York. Made her mark in '86 teaming up with Mary Walsh on several important stories on Mexico, its economic demise, debt problems. [See Walsh, Mary in Foreign Correspondents.] But Witcher can hold her own. "Latin Nations Seek to Reduce Debt Payments," 3-3, on the Punta del Este meetings was more than competent, and "Soviets Consider Joining IMF, World Bank," 8-15, intent on increasing ties to west and tapping new funds. "Mexico's Commercial Creditors Urge World Bank to Grant New Loans," 9-25, is better than most in satisfying detail.

Wolman, Clive
Financial Times. (★★)

London. Smart in examining comparative fiscal policies. His "Corporations to Carry a Greater Burden," 5-14, provided a good factual account of Senator Packwood's second U.S. tax reform, with some figures and details we hadn't seen. "A Clean Thrust Can Skewer the Lobbyists," 6-3, gives keen insights on U.K.'s timorous attempts at tax reform, i.e., Reagan succeeded by being open and gaining public support, Maggie failed by being secretive to counter lobbies, that knew anyway, while public did not.

Worthy, Ford S.
Fortune. (★½)

An able, journeyman business reporter. "A Phone War that Jolted Motorola," 1-20, offers a *cautious* view of Motorola's comeback in the cellular phone market while the Japanese regroup after losing a dumping verdict; can it regain competitive position once hit with eastern competition again? We get plenty of background and a thorough review of the current status of Wesray, in "Wes Threatens to Pull Out of Wesray," 7-21, with abundant speculation from unnamed sources. His cover story, "Wall Street's Spreading Scandal," 12-22, awfully late, although a good summary for first-time readers.

FOREIGN CORRESPONDENTS

Almond, Peter
The Washington Times. (★)

London Correspondent. A big slump in his U.K. reporting for '86. Coverage of the Westland affair and Heseltine's fallout lacked fresh information. Both "Bitter Helicopter War Rocks British Cabinet," 1-16, and "Thatcher Hangs On, But Nobody Cheers," 2-11, were superficial, at a wire-service level. Instead of an extended treatment or feature on proposed budget and tax reform plans and economic issues we got — "A National Furor Over Sex Crimes," 4-28. Better efforts: a report on the positive shift in Europe's attitude toward the U.S. strike at Libya, 6-9, and "Labor Rose Grows Anti-American," 10-20, a look at Kinnock's exploitation of anti-U.S. sentiment in a bid for votes, although weak on accounting for the source of the sentiment. Both were faint reminders of Almond's better '85.

Armbruster, William
The Journal of Commerce. (★★)

Taipei. Admirable attention to detail, as in "U.S. Trade Concerns Taiwanese," 10-19: Taiwanese businessmen would like to import U.S. machinery, but "are reluctant to invest in new plant and equipment because they fear protectionist measures in the United States would leave them with excess capacity." Subsidiaries of U.S. companies "account for some 25% of Taiwan's exports to the United States."

Asman, David
The Wall Street Journal. (★★)

"The Americas" Column Editor. This column sparkled in '85, but there were fewer gems in '86. In particular, features on the region's economies were less thorough. Trying to edit both the "Manager's Journal" and "The Americas" columns, Asman is probably spread too thin, with both columns suffering. His own contributions were polished nuggets: a detail-rich account of free market theories becoming public policy in Ecuador under the Febres-Cordero Administration, 4-11; and his best, "Mexico's Political Steamroller," 7-24, "The PRI faces a Catch-22": "In order to keep control, it cannot give political power to the private sector, but it needs revenue from the private sector to stay in power." Still, he has to work this lode harder to get up to the three-star category he's capable of achieving.

MediaGuide   165

Axebank, Albert
The Journal of Commerce. (★★)

Moscow correspondent who often helps us to understand and explains the Soviet view. A good example was "Disarmament: A Question of Trust," 10-17, which covered the Iceland talks with a generous sprinkling of quotes from Gorbachev. Also, competent factual reportage on events that others miss, such as "US Eases Export Bans On High-Tech to Soviets," 9-4.

Balmaseda, Liz
Newsweek. (NR)

Central America Bureau Chief. Her byline too often combined with others, it was hard to get a reading on her efforts in '86. "Miami's 'Little Managua'," 5-26, a snide feature on the Miami-based "contra" leadership, who "live in comfortable suburban homes" and "bring their wounded to be treated in Miami at cut-rate prices by exiled Cuban doctors," told us a bit about her bias, little about the anti-Sandinista leadership.

Bangsberg, P.T.
The Journal of Commerce. (★★★)

Hong Kong Bureau. Still indispensable in tracking Asian trade happenings, East Asia trade policies, reactions to U.S. protectionism, always a nugget or two in his dispatches. Early reporting on the "growth pause" in China, 1-22. Close watch on Hong Kong's economy, with good details on the slippage in exports to the U.S., 2-18, and an information-rich report on Hong Kong's new budget, 2-27. "China Favors Scrapping MFA," and "Chinese to Promote Exports," 3-3, both provided early readings on China's trade perspectives. Also attentive to Korea, "South Korea Acts to Curb Exports," 3-11. An excellent "Bill's Defeat Threatens Thai Government," 5-2, sees the links between commodity deflation, U.S. protectionism and farm policy, and political turmoil in this important ally and market. Reminds us that Thailand is the world's largest producer of rice, second in tin and third in rubber. "U.S., Asian Suppliers Seek to Sew up Textile Pact," 5-15, exposes Washington violating its own textile agreements a year before they're up, and jeopardizing its chance of new GATT talks.

Barnathan, Joyce
Newsweek. (★★)

Moscow Bureau Chief. She did some gutsy, insightful work in '86, pushing a little harder, digging for new angles, and showed the Moscow corps how to go after the broader dimensions of "routine" subjects. Barnathan transformed coverage of the "dissident" issue with "Inside a Mind Jail," 8-11, a compelling feature on the incarceration in a "psychiatric institution" of a Soviet subject for a unique crime; quoting the "dissident's" wife: "They are killing us because we....just want to leave."

Barnes, John
U.S. News & World Report. (★ ½)

Middle East Correspondent. Steady, reliable, one of a handful of *U.S. News* foreign reporters we note with regularity. No breakthroughs, but he's usually there: "Mubarak: Down But Not Out," 3-24, an organized picture of economic decline, fundamentalist advance, Nasserite noises, and the squeeze on Egypt's president; "Looking Past Khomeini," 10-20, signs of change amid rampant Islamic fervor. A little late, though, with "West Bank: No Quarter in Hostilities," 4-7. His best, "Lashing Iraq's Fighting Spirit," 2-24, an on-the-scene report of Saddam Hussein's "fight as a hero or be executed as a coward" policy in Iraq: "It is not clear how the country will react when bills come due and Hussein is forced to impose austerities. But such action is bound to affect the standing of a leader whose rule depends not so much on charisma as on ruthlessness."

Barringer, Felicity
The New York Times. (★ ★)

Moscow Correspondent. We found in a very short dispatch, "Test That Led to Chernobyl Accident Is Described," 7-25, the best demonstration of her talent. Various Moscow-beat journalists covered the official explanation presented by the Foreign Ministry, but Barringer's dispatch went beyond mere regurgitation, raising questions as informative as anything in the Soviets' statements. The same standards were evident in a feature on changing relationships between cultural activity and the State since Gorbachev's accession; " 'Unofficial' Artist's Life in Russia," 10-7, found Soviet painters still waiting for concrete changes: "They lead their creative lives in a world as distorted as any surreal canvas."

Baum, Julian
The Christian Science Monitor. (★ ★ ★)

Peking Bureau Chief. "China in Transition," a five-part series in early March, was a well-organized sweep of the scene: the hurdles confronting reform, Deng's style of leadership, reform's impact on rural areas, profiles of China's younger leaders, and the pros and cons youths face in joining the Party. Cautious, but not sluggish, Baum stayed attuned to significant nuances in China's policy shifts. He understood the "consolidation" phase of China's modernization, reporting the Party Congress would move for better control of society to maintain successful economic policies, 3-24. He steps out front frequently, as in a 6-18 report that Peking will provide economic aid to Aquino government and won't support communist insurgency, and again on 8-19, with a foreign policy twist affecting the two Koreas in his report on China's athletes in the Asian Games. Reporting from post-Marcos Manila, he caught critical issues early: a report on Marcos' former Labor Minister Blas Ople as spokesman for a loyal opposition, 3-18; on the communist insurgency as a test of Aquino's presidency, outlining the policy emerging toward the New People's Army, 3-31. A very productive year from Baum.

Bering-Jensen, Henrik
Insight. (★ ★ ★ ½)

Staff Writer. One of the most productive of *Insight*'s stable of top-notch journalists on foreign beats. He was all over Europe in '86, with sallies into Africa and Asia. Almost monthly a three-star or better feature from him, all crisply written, well-organized, meaty with facts, sharp on perspective. A small sample: searching for solid ground in the Northern Ireland quagmire after the Anglo-Irish agreement, 1-13; the tragedy of central Europe, absorbing, moving analyses of culture and fate, 2-24; from Portugal, an account of Mario Soares' amazing comeback and the tough act ahead, 3-17; Austria, West Germany, and anti-Semitism once again, 4-21; in beleaguered Mozambique, where anti-communist insurgents compound the crisis of its collapsing economy, 5-26; "How the Soviets Break News: Selectively and Dishonestly," 6-2, a sobering perspective on Chernobyl; Holland, Britain, Thailand, Japan, Poland, etc. for the rest of the year — overall excellence overwhelming a few uncharacteristic disappointments. His best: "Italy: the Chaotic Country That Works," a three-part cover story, 4-14, the best account of the country's economy we saw in '86. A stunning year for Bering-Jensen.

Bernstein, Richard
The New York Times. (★ ½)

Paris Bureau Chief. We gave Bernstein '85 to adjust to Paris, and he began to make headway near the end of '86. The French elections, one of the major stories for that beat, given a ho-hum treatment "French Campaign Abandons Staid Tradition," 2-19. Insufficient attention to critical detail, the "right's" candidates presented as undifferentiated conservatives, "Split on Right an Asset to French Socialists," 2-9. Thin on economic issues "Jacques Chirac, on the Stump, Limbers Up for '88," 3-6, a liability particularly notable in the paucity of coverage on tax debate. His big effort, "Socialism Under Siege" Sunday magazine, 3-2, disappointingly light. But a report on Chirac-Mitterrand getting along with Francois happily ceremonial, was juicy and appetizing, 4-7. He also scored with a front-pager on Chirac getting the upper hand, 11-7, and again with a report on indiscreet Chirac quotes re Israel/Syria to *The Washington Times*. Best: "The Terror: Why France? Why Now?" Sunday magazine, 10-19, a tough accounting of France's policy of accommodation toward Arab radicals, a colonial hangover paid for in blood. It made us recall his heyday at the UN bureau, when he always seemed trenchant, tough. He may be back on the beam.

Berthelsen, John
The Asian Wall Street Journal. (★ ★ ★)

Malaysia Correspondent. Berthelsen's reporting on Malaysia's New Economic Policy, was a rigorous investigative effort in '86. "Malaysia Loosens Banking Rules to Stimulate Business," 7-21, caught the backtracking there on reforms, revealing the serious weaknesses in the country's savings cooperatives. "Malaysian Premier Firms Power Base With Election Win," *WSJ*, 8-5, a perceptive assessment of the prime minister's election gamble, noted the government's favoritism toward the indigenous Malay population. "Pride and Punishment," *AWSJ*, 9-1, a report on the "moral rot" infecting some elites, was piercingly insightful. With the *Journal*'s southeast Asia economics correspondent, Raphael Pura, he co-authored a blockbuster investigative feature on Malaysia's Finance Minister, 9-29, that got him temporarily booted out of the country and a three-month ban slapped on the paper.

Betts, Paul
Financial Times. (★ ★ ½)

Paris. Shows promise. "Communists try to turn ebbing tide of support," 5-15, provided a good survey of the Party's decline in Europe: "No one talks these days anymore about Eurocommunism." Another strong article, "OECD Defends Scheme to Fight Tax Evasion," 6-3, on a scary "Orwellian scheme." "Foreign Banks Circle Over Paris," 6-30, compared privatization plans in France with Britain's earlier denationalizations, which showed imagination.

Bohlen, Celestine
The Washington Post. (★ ★)

Moscow. Strictly a feature writer. Few come close to her in reporting out a steady stream on the day-to-day functioning of Russia's subjects. Her "Kiev, Its Playgrounds Vacant, Scrubs On," 6-9, was the first really informative human interest piece we saw post-Chernobyl: "Without children the city seems strangely calm....the absence of children is one of the abnormalities of life...where...people have been trying to live up to the image of normality portrayed by the official Soviet media." She wrote a dandy feature on a Moscow party chief standing on lines to find out what it's like, 2-10. Her non-feature efforts are generally without mistakes and adequate, as in "Gorbachev Presses Changes," 3-23, but without the insightful twists. She works on a hard news beat at times, particularly on Soviet-Mideast matters, as in reporting Libyan statements in Moscow justifying the late '85 airport atrocities, 1-10, and on a warming of Soviet-PLO ties, 1-22. She showed close attention to the issue in "Soviet Cautions Libyan on Terror," 5-28.

Boroweic, Andrew
The Washington Times. (★ ★ ★)

Chief Roving Foreign Correspondent. From Rabat to Romania, from Istanbul to Iceland, Boroweic covered a wide beat in '86, and he did it well. Broad experience in various foreign bureaus before coming aboard at *The Washington Times*, it served him well for the year. "Acquittals Likely in Papal Shooting," 1-16, early with a bead on what was to occur; "KGB at Doorstep...," important data on Soviet intelligence penetrations in France not seen elsewhere, 1-13; a report on Poland's secret police from inside sources, 4-27, startling and unique. His best, 7-11, an impressive news beat, interviewing Abu Zaim, commander of the anti-Arafat Fatah faction based in Jordan: "The military option has failed; there is only the peace option....My dream is not just to be a man who fought against the Israelis but a man who knew how to make peace. Now we need constructive acts. We must no longer deceive our people... peace will not come without direct negotiations with Israel."

Bourne, Eric
The Christian Science Monitor. (★ ½)

Vienna-based, covering Central Europe. Never quite daring, but always good on basics, covering the Warsaw troop cut plan, 6-12, aimed at Western opinion, but also a challenge for the West to present its own case. Better, a report, 8-28, from Poland: "Six years ago the word was *solidarnosc* — solidarity. Today, it is *mieszkanie* — a place to live, an apartment." One of his best, on the dull but shrewd Bulgarian leader Zhikov, 3-24, with fresh information on Bulgaria's government-party reshuffling in the face of tensions between Zhikov and Gorbachev.

Boustany, Nora
Financial Times, The Washington Post. (★ ½)

Beirut. One of the least desirable beats anywhere, where the fatigue shows up in body-count dispatches. Boustany generally didn't succumb, starting the year with attention to the constantly shifting relationship of forces among the myriad players in Lebanon, as for example, "Defeated Militia Chief Flies Out of Lebanon," 1-17, the defeat of Syria's leading ally in the Christian camp, and "Moslem, Druse Leaders Urge Gemayel's Ouster," 1-19, the Syrians and allies counterattack (both *The Washington Post*). Even "Car Bomb in Beirut Kills 7...," 5-24, still kept that focus. Actually her best, though, was outside Lebanon — the result of a trip to Libya (!!) of all places, for a break — "Poorer But Still, It Seems, Loyal" (*FT*, 9-6) with an update on the country several months after the U.S. strike: "Libya's future continues to depend on Col. Gadaffi. He is a slave of a system he has institutionalized. The revolution in Libya exists because he feeds it."

Branigan, William
The Washington Post. (★ ★ ½)

South Asia Correspondent. Impressed us with a balanced effort on Philippine electoral crisis, distanced from the "lynch Marcos mob." Digging deeper than most, he's one of the few in Manila we read thoroughly, often finding critical details near the end of his dispatches that were missed, ignored or avoided by others. Occasional reports from elsewhere on the beat, as in "Varied Mandates in Thailand and Malaysia," 8-15, "...testaments to the vibrant young democracies of the two," useful and informing, and "Cambodian Opposition Split," 1-3, sorting out the messy infighting there. A strong reporter, his detail on Defense Minister Enrile's riches and ambitions, 9-14, was superb. Good on travels with New Peoples' Army (9-29, weekly), out in front with "Philippine Rebels Targeting Rights Groups, Churches," 10-18. But weak on analytics, he swallowed the "disenfranchisement" bunk, 2-27, and muffed "The Troubled Presidency of Cory Aquino," 9-14. Still, a good year.

Breen, Tom
The Washington Times. (★ ½)

Manila. Nothing special during February election crisis, but he got our attention thereafter. A sharp eye for local political news that his confreres often ignored: Pro-Marcos legislators want defunct assembly to meet, 4-1; Communist leader Sison asks protests on Weinberger visit, 4-2; Aquino learning Marcos right on rebels, 5-22; best report on military frustrations with policy of restraint, 9-17. Vietnam selling weapons to the Philippine insurgents, 10-10, the first report out on that connection. He'll improve with experience: An interview with Marcos on Honolulu, 4-17, still a mite green.

Bridges, Tyler
Freelance. (★)

Latin America. A freelance journalist we didn't see a lot of in '86, but his report on Venezuela's efforts to reschedule its debt without IMF help and to keep a rein on foreign investment showed an ability to handle economic subjects (*The Christian Science Monitor*, 2-27). New info in "EuroCommunism With a Latin Beat" (*The Wall Street Journal*'s "Americas" column, 10-17), an update on the historic truce between Columbia's government and most of the country's guerrilla groups, also impressive.

MediaGuide 171

Brooke, James B.
The New York Times. (★)

Abidjan. Reporting from Luanda and Port-au-Prince early in '86 with articles that had us watching for his byline: "Angola's Economic Struggles," 1-31, on the irony of Western bankers eagerly putting $1 billion into the country's ruinous Marxist-run economy; several sharp-sighted dispatches from Haiti during the February upheaval, among them "Once More Duvalier Lets Loose the 'Bogeymen'," 2-4, where he sniffed what was coming: "Protesters have made open appeals to the military to depose Mr. Duvalier." On the metro beat for most of '86, we were pleased when his byline appeared above dispatches from Angola again late in the year.

Bruce, James
The Journal of Commerce. (★ ★)

Sao Paulo. Frequent reports from a huge but neglected country. "Carmakers Urge Reform in Brazil," 10-28, reveals trouble behind the apparent turnaround in Brazil's economy. Price controls are causing shortages, taxes are half the price of a car, and the protected computer market is causing inefficiency in industries like autos that use computers. His 9-9 piece, "Brazil Logs $12 billion trade surplus" provides ample information. On 10-29, we learn that Brazil will run a sizable trade deficit in chemicals and petrochemicals.

Buchan, David
Financial Times. (½ ★)

Eastern Europe. Buchan doesn't seem to go after much, his reporting only a rewriting of news officially circulated by the Soviets. "Gorbachev Draws Allies Closer," 1-16, was a pedestrian outline of Soviet leader's regional policy perspectives. A bit better, his covering the inside debate on free market economy in Yugoslavia, 6-17.

Burgess, Thomas
The Washington Post. (★ ★ ½)

Tokyo. Skilled as both reporter and analyst on his NE Asia beat, his material is often useful. We'd hoped for better in his Philippine reports during the electoral crisis, but they were just okay. The best of the lot "Aquino Rally Marks Risky Shift in Tactics," 2-16, "In question is whether this intensely religious woman will have the nerve to lead her throngs of supporters in yellow T-shirts into situations that could provoke violence." Better later with: "Asian Games Open in Seoul," 9-20, and "Koreas Brace for Wars, Old and New," 9-29. Particularly solid, "Japanese See Soviet Visit as Breakthrough," 2-6, a very thorough account of Shevardnadze's visit and signs of a thaw in Japanese-Soviet relations, a report that prepared us for Gorbachev's Vladivostok initiative. He tries to get us closer to the real life, though, "Falling Dollar Upsets Life for Americans in Japan," 5-21, a $63 haircut and manicure, and "Japanese Proud of Homogenous Society," 9-28, on problems tiny black minority confront. Reports on Japan's aging population, 10-12, and the rice bowl subsidies that bleed the treasury, 10-22, piled up his points.

Burns, John F.
The New York Times. (★ ★ ★ ★)

We saw less from the *Times'* former Peking Bureau Chief in '86 than in '85, even before he was booted out by the Chinese. But the quality was still there. "Peking Happily Deals With Both Sides," 4-13, a quality Burns look at China's triangular relationship with the U.S./U.S.S.R.; followed by a nifty feature on Peking's mayor of 9.5 million, cast as a populist. "Suffering a Setback, Deng Is Free to Play His Hand," 7-15, Burns at his best, in a complex area that confused most of his competition. "Through China's Newly Opened Door," 7-20, a Sunday travel section feature from the indomitable Burns, testing the limits of the new China with a 2000 mile overland motorcycle trip. Unquestionably his *piece de resistance* for '86 — "Why Investors Are Sour on China," 6-8, — which may have led to Burns' expulsion, but also produced a round of reforms.

Butler, Steven B.
Financial Times. (★ ½)

Seoul. Appearing in both the *Financial Times* and *The Christian Science Monitor*, Butler was up and down in '86. A nice start, 1-26, reporting anti-U.S. sentiment fanned by Korean press accounts of U.S. protectionist sentiment. But we wanted to know more about the emerging political opposition, and Butler was short on detail here. "S. Korea Opposition Makes Gains in Drive to Reform Constitution," *CSM*, 3-14, too heavy on "people power" scenarios, imposing a Philippine model on Korea; a report on oppositionist Kim Young Sam was disturbingly slim on substance, 3-28. A little more data in "South Korea's 'Two Kims'," *CSM*, 5-19. One of the few full-timers in Seoul, his byline has to be watched.

Carr, Jonathon
Financial Times. (★ ½)

Frankfurt. His reports rarely stand out. One that did, "The Japanese Find it Hard to Take the Europeans Seriously," 6-4, reports on a conference, finding "the Japanese seemed unconvinced that the Europeans had much to offer which they could not get better in the U.S."

MediaGuide 173

Chavez, Lydia
The New York Times. (★)

Metro Reporter. We'd found her Central American reporting substantial and were hoping for the best in '85 when she got the Buenos Aires bureau. A slow start with feature items — "Argentina's New Caudillo," 1-2, and "Elementary for the Argentines: the Analysts," 2-9, interesting (more analysts per capita than in NYC), but still skirting the beat. An effort to get into the economic issues, "The Frustration in Argentina," 3-6, still on the shallow side, and it looked as if Buenos Aires was too much to handle. The change back to the Metro beat was a wise one for '86.

Chesnoff, Richard Z.
U.S. News & World Report. (★)

Senior Correspondent, Western Europe. With no way to determine who contributes what in features with multiple bylines, we were restricted to very few samples of Chesnoff's individual efforts in '86. Both "How Big a Defeat Faces Mitterrand?," 3-17, and "Spain Gives Nod to NATO, Europe," 3-24, were standard meat and potatoes.

Chipello, Christopher J.
The Asian Wall Street Journal. (★ ★)

Tokyo Bureau Chief. "Japanese Recycling Export Earnings Through Purchases of Foreign Stocks" was basic, but we hadn't seen that before — U.S. stocks the go-go investments. An examination of the newest fad among Japanese investors — mortgage-backed securities — found a frustrated finance ministry declaring "We have no idea what goes on in some of these companies," amid fears of fraud and calls for regulation, 6-23. Nicely done, a wrap-up on the dismissal of Japan's outspokenly nationalistic Education Minister, Masayuki Fujio, 9-15.

Chira, Susan
The New York Times. (★ ★ ★)

Tokyo Bureau. Energetic, resourceful, taking on analytics with confidence. Some penetrating, fresh reports; produces straight accounts, good detail and feel for local dynamic. Her February dispatches from Seoul, flawed a bit by anticipation of Philippine scenarios there, improved by midyear, as in a fresh round-up on "Korea's Opposition Inching Toward Its Goal," 6-8. But her real strengths came out in in a four-part Japan series beginning with "New Global Top Banker: Tokyo and Mighty Money," 4-27, a front-pager of impressive analytics and detail. Chira filled the gaps in the *Times*' economic coverage on this beat and she moved the paper's northeast Asia coverage up a big notch in '86.

Christian, Shirley
The New York Times. (★ ★ ★)

Buenos Aires Bureau Chief, replacing Lydia Chavez. The bulk of her reporting came from Chile, with timely dispatches from Argentina: "Inflationary Relapse Dismays Argentina," 9-1, sized up removal of the country's central bank president as a victory for free-market economic advisers. Christian quickly finds the margin, reporting that an opposition to Pinochet was consolidating within the Navy, Air Force, and National Police, 4-28, then a timely and focused attention to the new shifts taking place, "Pinochet In No Hurry to Quit Center Stage," 5-15. She got ahead again when the margin shifted, "The Opposition in Chile Has Trouble Closing Its Ranks," 7-20. Her depth keeps her the one to follow here.

Claiborne, William
The Washington Post. (★)

South Africa Correspondent. Jerusalem correspondent for most of '86, he and southern Africa correspondent Glenn Frankel switched respective bureaus later in the year. He kept pace with Israel news, but never really got ahead. Competently organized reports on the political scene, sticking to essentials, never inserting his point of view, though a little too conventional to fully satisfy. "Israeli Leaders Deadlocked on Land Issue," 1-13, okay coverage of divisive political issues in Israel. The same again in "Israelis Divided on Trying Aide," 5-26, though meager analysis a chronic shortcoming; similarly, "Israeli Cabinet Split on Probe," 6-30, and bare-bone details with "Israel Denies Trying to Skirt Arms Technology Ban," 7-10. Often after a new bureau assignment there's a tendency to put out human interest features before the journalist settles in. But Claiborne's South Africa dispatches have been timely, relevant, and well-done, as for example, an outstanding report on Buthelezi's angry denunciation of critics, 9-28. An impressive start on his new assignment. But how about a broader analytic once in a while?

Clines, Francis X.
The New York Times. (★ ½)

London. "Frankie," as his friends call him, moved around in '86. A veteran reporter with a light touch in his writing that buoys his features and profiles. A good Sunday magazine piece on Treasury's Richard Darman, "Reagan's Master of Compromise," 2-16, but perhaps a bit too effusive. Clines was rushed to Manila to help on the February election story, covering Marcos' side of the story for awhile, "Marcos Denies Charges of Corruption," 2-2, but he was soon swept up in revolutionary fervor too, "Marcos's Opponents Charge Aim Is Their 'Extermination'," 2-13. Transferred to London at midyear, he was soon doing what he does best, sprightly political features. One such, a feature on John Hume, 7-20, Catholic leader of Northern Ireland's Social Dem and labor party, who exudes optimism despite the contradiction of history. From Dublin, "U.S. Envoy Displays the Gift, Enchanting the Irish," 10-1, on U.S. Ambassador Margaret Heckler. A nice feature on the BBC for Sunday entertainment section, 11-9.

Cockburn, Patrick
Financial Times. (★ ★ ½)

Moscow Bureau. Competent surveys of the broad scene combined with a nice touch on the critical marginal turns. Watch for his optimistic bias, but don't be put off by it. "Moscow's New Self-Confidence," 1-16, incisively assesses the new directions in Soviet foreign policy. "An End to the Cavalry Charge," 1-18, a meaty report on the end of Siberian investment with clear policy implications. A report on Russian criticism of mock heroics, inaccuracy and sentimentality in Soviet WWII films is a revealing feature, 1-21. "Reconditioned Engine Still Lacks Power," 6-12, a midyear assessment of the insufficiency of Gorbachev's reforms; "Warmer Days in a Cold Winter," 7-9, on the intellectual thaw permitted by Gorbachev. In "Moscow Penalizes its Black Economy," 7-2, good detail on country homes built with the illegal use of state equipment and with Soviet auto plants supplying "only 40 to 45 percent" of needed spare parts, "Clearly, some people do accumulate small fortunes," filling these needs. In "Moscow to Ease Path for Private Enterprise," 11-17, "house repair, tailoring and car maintenance can only be obtained by hiring workers illegally."

Cody, Edward
The Washington Post. (★ ★ ½)

Central America. A veteran correspondent with wire-service background, he impressed us in '86 with his Haiti reporting, ahead of the field. Best early piece, "Open Political Activity Beginning in Haiti," 2-12. Then, looking a little beyond the revolutionary festivities: "A New Atmosphere in Port-Au-Prince," 2-23, and a post-Duvalier follow-up, "Cries for Change Louder in Haiti," 4-4. Early with economic discontent making Jamaicans look back fondly on Michael Manley in "Luster Off Jamaican 'Example'," 1-21. From Mexico, held back by deficiency in economics, but still worth a look: "Renewing Mexican Party," 5-11, offers a perspective on the challenge to PRI in northern states' elections. A new angle, not seen elsewhere, on the environmental losses accompanying the Mexican oil boom/bust, 5-24. On Nicaragua: "Congressmen Confirm Ideas in Nicaragua," 3-16, is a good example of Cody keeping his distance; he clearly helped upgrade the *Post*'s Central American coverage in '86.

Cohen, Roger
The Wall Street Journal. (★★)

Miami. The *Journal* still covers all of Latin America out of Miami. A fast finish boosted Cohen, his work on South America adding up as a whole. "Brazil's Latest Economic Moves Mark Start of Drive of Sustained Growth," 7-25, got on top of the country's "reimbursable taxes" plan, a diversion of spending from consumption and investment for infrastructural development. Offbeat at times, he can pop an unexpected angle on you, as in "Peru, Fearing a Coup, Sought U.S. Help," 7-29, suggesting that the new regional cooperation and support from Washington could threaten the general shift toward democracy. A front-pager on Argentina "Struggling Back," 11-12, is worth the history lesson, a sharp parallel: "At a time when much of the world is flirting with protectionism, Argentina vividly illustrates the devastating costs of trying to grow by shutting out the competition." Also sharp in "Brazil Vote Precedes Economic Overhaul," 11-13: "Brazil's emergence as an economic power hasn't been accompanied by the development of a sophisticated political process." Open the Rio bureau and send Roger!

Cohen, Sam
Freelance. (NR)

Istanbul. Another of those promising stringers we noticed in *The Christian Science Monitor*. Not much in '86, but Ozal's "trade, not aid" message to the U.S. was well-done, with new material added in, 3-26. Only here did we learn about the most popular political figure in Turkey, Istanbul's Mayor Bedrettin Dalan, the "ruthless bulldozer" who's also seen as the "redeemer," 5-1. Also new, a report that the lifestyle of Ozal's family had become an issue in Turkey's elections, 8-15.

Coone, Tim
Financial Times. (★★)

Buenos Aires. Coone had the first report we saw, 1-14, that the Sandinistas were expropriating opponents' holdings under guise of "land reform." Reassigned from Managua to Buenos Aires, he produced insightful reports on the economic clouds over Argentina, as in "IMF Challenges Argentina's Dream," 6-25: "It would be ironic indeed if President Alfonsin felt obligated to turn to the police and the military to deal with the unions as the only way to salvage an economic programme which pays off the foreign debt but fails to deliver the dream." His "Trade, Disarmament Top Agenda of Soviet-Argentine Talks," *The Christian Science Monitor*, 10-15, on hard Soviet bargaining linking continued grain purchases to more of their exports.

MediaGuide 177

Cornwell, Rupert
Financial Times. (★ ★ ½)

Bonn. Excels in recognizing subtleties on the German scene. "Bonn Achieves Record Monthly Trade Surplus," 6-5, provided good detail on the less than vigorous domestic economy, not found anywhere in the U.S. financial press. "Bonn Shows Concern at U.S. Push on Interest Rates," 8-4, nicely focused picture of the external/internal pressures on West German economic policy. "Bonn Resists pressure to boost growth," 4-25, "the real imbalance now, they believe, lies between the U.S. and Japan." One of the first reports that German officials, with prices falling, were mainly worried about inflation! Has co-authored some good pieces with David Warsh on monetary maneuvers between the Bundesbank and Bank of France.

Cowell, Alan
The New York Times. (–)

Athens Bureau Chief. Because the *Times* is the paper of record, it was painful to witness its toleration of something very amiss in what Cowell was reporting out of South Africa as Johannesburg bureau chief for most of 1986. So many, many leads on numbers of blacks or whites killed for whatever reason (with a running update in each article on how many people have died in violence since 9-84, etc.) we began to call him "The Body Counter." "South African Rebel Calls for Stepped-Up Attacks," 1-10, ostensibly a report on Oliver Tambo's call for escalation of war against white rule, instead argues a case for the ANC probably not being responsible for the bomb murder of five white civilians. "Rightist Break Up Rally in South Africa," 5-23, turns into a speculation that Botha orchestrated the confrontation to show the outside world he's "trying." Cowell was very late with the black vs black aspect of the violence and coverage of the fiery necklaces execution. "Turf Fight in the Townships," 7-8, advises the term "comrades" adopted by ANC-inspired activists is used merely to taunt authorities, whereas the anti-ANC black "vigilantes" are potentially murderous gangs intent on killing anti-apartheid activists. "Groups Oppose School Boycott in South Africa," tells us nothing about Buthelezi's reasons, but says his critics think his organization is fascist. Cowell's fact selection invited a sense that he'd slipped into partisanship so deeply that we were discouraged from reading anything by him on the subject.

Crossette, Barbara
The New York Times. (★ ★)

Bangkok Bureau Chief. More productive on this beat in '86. Starting to dig into economics, she was also super-alert on geopolitical shifts with "Soviet Seeks Larger Role in Southeast Asia," 4-8: "Taking advantage of widespread discontent in Southeast Asia caused by falling commodity prices and protectionist moves in the United States and Western Europe, Moscow has been sending high-level delegations to the region offering aid and trade.'' Updated in "Moscow Sees A Bigger Role for Itself In the Pacific," 8-10. "Vietnam Names Hard-Liner as New Party Leader," 7-15, very revealing on the consequences of the regime's back and forth attitude on economic reform — grass-roots cynicism widespread, the US$ replacing official currency as the standard of exchange. We were pleased to see her byline show up in Manila on a report of the Aquino-Enrile-Ramos struggle, 11-1.

Cullison, A. E.
The Journal of Commerce. (★ ★ ★)

Tokyo Bureau Chief. Consistently among the top two or three sources on Japan, starting the year with a flurry of fact-filled reports on its economy and following the tensions with Washington all year. Several timely dispatches on early monetary policy debates in Japan: "EC Urges Japanese to Promote Yen," 1-22; "Aides Urge Nakasone to Reverse Yen Rise," 2-21; "Dollar-Yen Rate Held About Adequate," 2-27. New information on trade perspectives and practices: "Japanese Federation Urges Freer Trade," 2-27; "Toyota to Use US Flags For 10% of Exports," 1-23; "Japanese Auto Firms Expect to Sell Quota," 2-21. Early and meaty work on the economic slowdown: "Has Growth In Japan Plateaued?" 3-3. "Japan Calls for Intervention to Stem Dollar Fall," 4-23, notes that business and the Cabinet were already upset with the yen's deflationary rise, and the Bank of Japan was spending $5 billion a day to try to prevent it without lowering interest rates. Another early update, 5-15, "Soaring Yen Worries Japan and US," has the U.S. also having second thoughts. A bit late, though, with "Japan's Economy Headed for First Slump in Three Years," 8-27. Timely on "Japanese Tax Cut Plans Cross Hurdle," 10-18.

Curtius, Mary
The Christian Science Monitor. (★)

Jerusalem. Okay on reporting "what," but passive on "how come" or "why," as, for example, her almost tautological "Morocco Talks...," 6-24: the Peres-Hassan meeting is a gain for moderates — reflecting a drop in radical influences; easy "analysis," but harder, and unaddressed by her, was how that came to be. Reports from Jordan, where she was detained, questioned and eventually released in June, similarly okay on data but reticent on forceful analysis, as in: "Jordan's Hussein Stakes Prestige on Syria-Iraq Thaw," 6-19, and "Jordan's Plan for West Bank Development Likely to Widen Jordan-PLO Rift," 6-24. Better in "Why Hussein Split With Arafat," 9-21, where she inched toward analysis: "Hussein is telling the Palestinians that their dream of retaking Palestine militarily is dead....he is also saying that the PLO leadership stands in the way of the Palestinians..."

Danguilan-Vitug, Marites
Newsday. (NR)

Correspondent. Respectable work from the Philippines early in the year for *The Christian Science Monitor*, fleshing out the emerging post-Marcos story: a curious angle on the military's new sense of a new responsibility while riding a popularity wave, 3-18. Noteworthy for holding her footing during the hysteria that afflicted a number of other journalists reporting from Manila.

Daniloff, Nicholas
U.S. News & World Report. (★)

Seeing so frequently the preface "one of the most astute journalists on the Soviet scene" to the articles on Daniloff following his arrest, we thought maybe we were wrong in believing his '86 effort was inferior to '85. But re-examining the evidence, '86 was even more sluggishly pedestrian than '85. Perhaps in anticipation of his scheduled departure from the Moscow Bureau, he allowed himself to coast for most of the year. Few dispatches appeared with his sole byline, most including one or more other journalists. But even those suggested superficial efforts, as in "America's Favorite Bolshevik" (with Michael Doan, 4-21), a profile of Dobrynin so slim that it misinformed more than informed. A better effort, "Soviet TV: New Words, Same Story," 6-9. But '86 was a thin year from Daniloff.

De Onis, Juan
Los Angeles Times. (★ ½)

Rio Bureau. A steady hand, De Onis was particularly attentive to Brazil's "life-and-death" struggle against inflation all year. "Sarney Picks New Cabinet," 2-15, provided a good look at the new president's perspectives for taking on the problem. He followed the course of the various wage-price controls and currency reforms with timely, informative dispatches, as with "Brazil Moves to Fight Inflation," 3-1, and "Low-Income Brazilians Cheered by Monetary Reforms," 3-13. "Brazil to Offer Deal on U.S. Imports, Debt," 9-9, a nicely done report on President Sarney's vision of the road ahead. Occasional reports from other countries adequate, as in "New Colombia President Vows Social Reforms," 8-8. Good sources apparently, he scooped the U.S./Bolivian anti-drug operation.

de Silva, Mervyn
The Christian Science Monitor, Newsweek. (NR)

Stringer. Colombo. A professional with wide experience in Sri Lanka, his byline's worth watching for. Two reports in *The Christian Science Monitor*, 5-14 and 6-13, fleshing out the picture on Sri Lanka's strife impressed us with their balanced, informative treatment.

DeYoung, Karen
The Washington Post. (★★)

London Bureau Chief. A good year for DeYoung, her dispatches from London valuable and informative. Very thorough and alert on Northern Ireland, "IRA Attack Gives Warning of Troubles Ahead in Ulster," 1-2, the fallout over the Anglo-Irish agreement; one of the first to report on the role of Royal Ulster Constabulary amid the reaction, "Marches Peaceful in Ulster," 7-13, an important item at the time. Her treatment of the Heseltine-Westland affair, "Defense Chief Quits Cabinet in Britain," 1-10. Thatcher's problems within her party and government, "Thatcher Relaxes Above the Fray," well done. She put in a respectable tour of duty as one of the correspondents selected for coverage of the U.S. strike on Libya, followed the El Al bomb trial with a close watch on its foreign policy implications, and occasionally came up with new angles to cover an issue. An example, "Barristers Plead Their Case," 2-23, an absorbing feature on the new level of labor action. However, pursuing the "Thatcher image problem" a little too much ("Like her friend Ronald Reagan, Margaret Thatcher's personal popularity sometimes has exceeded public support for her policies"). She remained weaker on economic issues.

Dickey, Christopher
The Washington Post, Newsweek. (★)

Cairo Bureau Chief. Not a great year from this bureau. In "Growing Pains in Egypt," 1-2, he looks at Egypt's economic sluggishness, but takes the easy way out: too many people, not enough resources. Shuttling from Cairo to Tripoli early in '86, his Libya dispatches were too frequently an uncritical reporting of the official communiques or press releases, among the examples, "Arabs Warn Against Reprisals," 1-5. "Qaddafi Seen Reining in His Army," 1-14, was more speculative than informative. And he came close to presenting Qaddafi's case that Americans shouldn't vacate the country with "Americans Not 'Hassled' in Libya," 1-8, and again 1-9, telling us the Americans in Libya were unhappy with Reagan's decision, quoting one who was "afraid to comment" but said, "There are so many other ways you can be got at other than being arrested. You know, audits and things." We keep watching though, expecting some depth, attracted by his promising leads, as in "Egypt Has An Air of Calm, But Potential Threat Looms," 5-29: "Shocking events have come with such numbing regularity to Egypt recently that every moment of calm begins to carry the menace of a silent pause in a Hitchcock movie." But he has yet to pull the curtain aside.

Diehl, Jackson
The Washington Post. (★★)

Warsaw Bureau Chief. Doing good work in Poland, he digs hard, finding new material and slants. Several January reports on the stagnating Polish economy were the best we saw from anyone on that beat. His story, 1-24, that 30% of Poland's families can't afford minimum daily necessities no doubt played a role in Jaruzelski offering to send NYC blankets for its homeless. From Belgrade, "Economic Crises Test Yugoslavia's System," 2-25, another competent economic survey. Limited in his post-Chernobyl report, 5-2, on the future of nuclear power plants in central Europe, but he makes the effort. He scores with " 'We Knew It Was Bad Here Even If No One Said So'," 5-3, on the reaction among Poles to Chernobyl fallout. He's as adept with political and intellectual issues as with economic. Two examples "Arrests Mar Polish Peace Congress," 1-17, on the failure of the government to control the opposition-dominated intellectual community, and "Polish Jails Filling Again with Political Prisoners," 5-10. A candidate for expulsion if he keeps it up.

Dobbs, Michael
The Washington Post. (★ ★ ★)

Paris. He's best at broad, analytical overviews with a subtle feel for the ideological shifts in France: "Socialist Metamorphosis," 3-16, the best we saw at this important point. Focused coverage of the French elections, the policy implications of Mitterrand's power-sharing perspective ably treated, 3-2. What initially sounds offbeat at times segues into a new angle or perspective for a heightened view, as in "Mitterrand Still Holds Key," 3-18, an analytic on Francois' turning defeat into victory. Jockeying between Chirac and Mitterrand captured well in a report on the latter's opposition to denationalization, 7-15. Best we saw: professional account, satisfying in detail, of "Trial of Century Falls Short of Billing," re the Turks/Bulgars and papal assassination attempt, 3-30. A byline we've come to respect.

Done, Kevin
Financial Times. (★ ★)

Oslo. Perceptive, analytical. In "Norwegian Economic Crisis is Worst for Years," 5-14, he outlines the perils of a fashionable "policy mix" — more taxes and a weak currency. "Many economists believe the devaluation will lead to a much bigger jump in the inflation rate." Stock prices also "fell back sharply" on news of tougher taxes on capital gains and stock trades.

Drodziak, William
The Washington Post. (★)

Foreign Editor. Formerly with *Time*'s Cairo bureau, he subsequently got the Bonn bureau after switching over to the *Post*. But more into diplomatic issues than the German scene *per se*, we didn't get as much as we'd hoped from him in '86. Yet he was solid in following and reporting on East-West tensions. "Burt, the New Model Diplomat," 2-28, an example of his top-notch feature style. "Nerve Gas Proposal Approved," 5-23, seemed a little slack, more attentive to U.S. Congressional critics then European reactions, but amply compensated for by "West Rejects E. German Demand," 5-28, a picture of allied reaction and fears over restrictions in Berlin. Within range of the Bonn beat, "Austria Confronts Its Nazi Past," 5-3, and "Netherlands Voters Reelect Pro-Nuclear Government," 5-21, were standard Drodziak, concise and informed. He left Bonn to take over the foreign desk as Michael Getler moved up the ladder.

Echikson, William
The Christian Science Monitor. (★ ★ ★)

Paris. Strong reporting in '86, he stays on top of events, displaying a mastery of background and context. We relied on his coverage of the French elections: a sharp profile of Chirac, 3-20, and well-focused coverage of the division of powers between Jacques and Francois, 3-21; offering perspective in a 6-9 look at the widening cracks of the Mitterrand-Chirac partnership: "The resulting marriage, which the French call 'cohabitation' has turned into an armed truce....[yet] 'cohabitation' answers a need for checks and balances." A solid grasp and presentation of socio-cultural features involved in a timely report on the stalled efforts of French conservatives in selling Reaganomics, 8-26. Echikson strayed from Paris to Central Europe with dispatches that rewarded: sharp analytics on the Czech Communist Party Congress, 3-31; Solidarity — down but not out, 7-14; several features on Hungary in June, "Hungarian Environmentalists Push for Nuclear Power," 6-17, impressive on what type of organized protest is permissible; Poland again, 9-22, with a picture of the economy spun out of a feature on its strawberry glut. Broad and deep workmanship in '86.

Einfrank, Aaron
The Washington Times. (★ ★ ★)

Pakistan. Stringer for *The Washington Times*, his January dispatches on Afghanistan were the best anywhere. Prescient in reporting Barbak Karmal's days were numbered, 1-8. Provided an unmatched analysis of internal conditions behind Soviet "peace" gestures there, 1-1 and 1-13, as well as new info on Soviet involvement with drug trade in region, 2-3. Displays same kind of powerful insight in his reporting from Pakistan, as a 4-23 dispatch revealed on the heady fervor, but narrow support, for Benazir Bhutto.

Elliott, John
Financial Times. (★ ★ ½)

New Delhi. A veteran reporter and former labor editor of the *FT*, Elliott is among the best sources of day-to-day news on the subcontinent, especially India. A report on new tax policy (12-20-85) was seen nowhere else. "India Seeks to Reopen Bombay Stock Exchange After Tax Raid," 10-27, was revealing, as was "India Launches Fresh Plan to Boost Exports," 10-27. Forays into Sri Lanka, 5-28, and the Punjab, 6-16, to report on civil disturbances also connect with economic developments, although we'd like more specifics.

Fineman, Mark
Los Angeles Times. (★ ½)

Manila. Comported himself well during the elections and constitutional crisis. A post-election dispatch, "Critical Final Count Begins in Legislature," 2-11, gave us critical detail we found nowhere else, that the official tally sheets were "examined by a special committee of nine legislators called the Board of Tellers — five from the Marcos party and four from the opposition — created by the Assembly Monday as an official examination board." A 5-4 split was certainly no evidence Marcos' people were stacking. How few correspondents realize the importance of reporting such minor details. Another dispatch "Grand Scale Voter Fraud," 2-16, with Doyle McManus, lays it on both sides. He has our confidence and we read "Church Takes Stronger Role as Philippine Crisis Grows," 9-3, with a little extra attention.

Fitzgerald, Mary
The Christian Science Monitor. (★)

Nairobi. Generally a little too skimpy, though she was quick in calling attention to Museveni's significantly positive differences from his predecessors in Uganda, 3-20. Useful material, as in several serious efforts on Kenya: potential vulnerability of its leadership to growing unrest, 6-17; learning a lesson and going with fiscal incentives for farmers amid a recession, 6-3; a profile of Kenya's Asian community, needed but not wanted, victims of their own success. But her "Starvation in Sudan," 8-21, is a weaker effort, lacking substantial new material.

Ford, Peter
The Christian Science Monitor. (★ ½)

Managua. His March series on Nicaragua was a mixed bag, alternately very slender: his "some say this" and "some say that" report "Hope, Disillusionment Divide Nicaraguans," 3-25; or substantial, as in "Nicaraguan Opposition Tightly Controlled," 3-26, where we learned that Ortega can legislate independently of the Assembly's approval. From Tegucigalpa, 3-28 and 3-31, okay reports on U.S.-Honduran relations and the latter's reticence on spotlighting Sandinista incursions into Honduras. "Nicaragua: A Siren to Many Foreigners," 6-12, is mildly entertaining on the "rucksack revolutionaries." Best was a four-part series on Guatemala in June, particularly "Rural Guatemala: Under Army's Forceful Thumb," 6-26: "It is in these provinces, thoroughly militarized by the anti-guerrilla war, where President Vinicio Cerezo Arevalo's bid to democratize Guatemala is likely to face its toughest challenge."

Frankel, Glenn
The Washington Post. (★ ½)

Now in Israel, but most of his '86 work was in southern Africa. The first to dig out and report on the escalation of "fiery necklace" murders in South Africa (in 1985), we'd come to rely on him and were disappointed when he seemed to slacken a bit in '86. An attempt at geopolitical analysis, "Moscow's Gains in Africa," 5-25, was below par for him, citing Somalia as a big "plus" for the West, without mentioning Ethiopia as a bigger coup on the Soviet side of the ledger. A sloppy report on the outcome of the mass protest called for in July, his lead of massive participation contradicted later in the dispatch that the union movement didn't join it, 7-15. A steady source of Mozambique news, but disappointing with "Mozambique Rethinking Its Ties to West," 5-15, too much a mere retailing of an official Samora Machel communique. Typically keen angles in "Mozambique Dam: Death of a Dream," 5-25, and "Car or No Car, Gasoline Sells in Mozambique," 5-25, were in high-Frankel form, resourcefully done illustrations of the economic malaise there.

Friedman, Thomas
The New York Times. (★ ★ ★)

Jerusalem Bureau Chief. A Pulitzer prizer in the region (1983) Friedman would be in a four-star category if he kept in front of his casual competition. Certainly one of the best Middle East correspondents, "The Three Sides of the Palestinian Side," 3-9, and 4-28, "Loose-Linked Network of Terror," were powerfully organized demonstrations of his acuity; "Armed and Dangerous," 1-5, conceptually superb: "If there is one ironclad rule of Middle Eastern politics, it is that when things are not moving forward they usually move backward. The mood of quiet hope and expectation that was in the air a few months ago...has soured....What happpened...? Nothing...and that was the problem. The positive noises that Jordan, Yasir Arafat and Israel were making...turned out to be just noises. None of the principals was ready to make a fundamental change." But he's let others beat him on a number of stories (the Lavi jetfighter boondoggle; the secular-religious tensions within Israel). He catches up, managing to treat the issue with a firm grasp of its content, policy implications, throwing in new material, as in "A Skirmish Over Israel's New Jet," 7-20, and a reprise on the controversy over religious orthodoxy. We watch for his byline (brief profile of Yitzhak Shamir, 10-21, was satisfying). But he's been beaten so frequently in '86 that it's getting noticeable.

Fung, Vigor
The Asian Wall Street Journal. (★ ★ ★)

Peking. Next to John Burns of the *NYT*, we looked for Fung's China bylines. Each dispatch filled with information, insight, critical analysis, local detail, etc., he produced some of the best reports from the mainland on China's economy and politics in '86. Among them: "Elder Statesman Applies Brakes to China's Reform," 6-9; "China's Big Boost...," 7-21; "Peking's Tight-Credit Policies...," 7-7; "A Chinese Factory Falls Prey To That Byproduct of Capitalism — Failure," 8-4; "Peking Announces Regulations Meant to Mollify Foreign Investors...," 10-13. Each, individually satisfying and solid efforts, but somehow, putting them all together we still didn't get the "gestalt" of China we could from reading John Burns.

Gardner, David
Financial Times. (★ ½)

Mexico. Nicely informative on Central American politics, such as "Outlook for Contadora Peace Treaty Still Cloudy," 5-29, or "Mexican Leaders Play Down the Challenge of Chihuahua," 7-26. Too few factual reports on economic conditions and policies, though "Mexico Pressed to Clarify its Intentions on Finance Policy," 6-20, was a notable exception. Mexico's short-term interest rates were revealed to be 81%, to "stem capital flight," and "each one point rise in base rates adds [$220 million] to the Government's domestic interest bill." So, Mexico can't handle its budget deficit without first reforming its monetary policy.

Gargan, Edward A.
The New York Times. (★)

Peking bureau chief. Sub-Sahara Africa for most of '86. Early in the year reports from West Africa, "Nigeria's Economy Faces a New Burden," 1-27, and "Moslem Fervor in Nigeria," 2-21, both substantial efforts on the economics and socio-religious complications of black Africa's largest country. Consistent reporting from this beat has been weak in the U.S. press, and we regret not having seen more out of Lagos from Gargan. In South Africa briefly, he covered the passbook reform in a report for the *Times*, 4-24, that was one of the few well-done efforts out of that bureau — concise, factual, and without editorializing or selective presentation. "Whites Who Left Zimbabwe, Fearful of Future Drift Back," 5-18, also notable. His West Africa swan song in the Sunday magazine, "In the Heart of Africa," 12-7, read like boilerplate.

Garvin, Glenn
The Washington Times. (★ ★)

Central America. Tough, thorough, relentless. He produced some of the best reports out of Managua, which earned him, and fellow *Washington Times* correspondent Sue Mullin, a night in jail and expulsion from Nicaragua. "Sandinista Regime a Threat, Neighbors Say," 3-25, an important dispatch at a time when other journalists were confusing Central American apprehensions of U.S. military intervention as toleration of the Sandinista regime. In El Salvador, 4-11, he gave us a savvy "Duarte Backers Straying, Left and Right," fresh with details on Salvador's super-harsh economic austerity program that "was greeted with cheers at the U.S. Embassy but met with almost universal disapproval at home." No sloppiness from him, Garvin is conceptually rigorous, which keeps his reports timely and useful; for example, "Sandinistas' Grip Tightens Around Nicaragua's Neck," 7-15 — not yet a totalitarian state, but that's the Sandinista goal. "Contra Political Sideshows Strain Support Inside Nicaragua" (10-10, "The Americas" column, *WSJ*), crisply informative.

Germani, Carla
The Christian Science Monitor. (★)

Caracas, Bogota. A little more rigor would be advantageous. An assessment of the waning of rebel forces in South America, 3-28, bothered us with sloppy usage of terms like "rebels" to indiscriminately include some of the most deadly terrorists in the world. " 'Contra' Leaders Seek Unity and Democratic Reform," 5-19, too much on the order of a spot-news account, with no picture of the differences presented; similarly, "Rights Abuses Rise Sharply in Colombia," 8-5, was meager on background and context.

Giradet, Edward
The Christian Science Monitor. (★ ★)

Sub-Sahara Africa. Traversing the continent from Khartoum to Capetown, Giradet provided feature stories more than news reporting on events at the time. His best were from Malawi: "At 'Eton of Africa,' the Style Is Boaters and Blazers," 4-28, on Malawi's Kamuzu Academy, ranked as black Africa's top school, illuminating on President Banda's perspectives for creating a classically trained corps of new administrators. "Mostly Rural Malawi's Emphasis on Farming Pays Rich Dividends," 5-1, absorbing presentation of this free-enterprise economic success story. "Africa: Romanticism for the Strong," 6-9, is Giradet summarizing his travels: "No matter what the system...one often hears the complaint that the leaders are out of touch...entrenched in power... shielded from everyday realities."

Graham, Bradley
The Washington Post. (★ ★)

Buenos Aires bureau chief. Heading his third foreign bureau for the *Post*, a real workhorse. Dispatches from Caracas, Santiago, Rio, Asuncion, Buenos Aires, etc., never letting the forest obscure individual trees. Alert, and apparently with good contacts, he scooped (simultaneously with De Onis of the *LA Times*) the U.S.-Bolivian anti-drug operations. From Santiago, "Public Sector Strong in Chile," 5-23, good details and perspectives on Pinochet's stalled efforts to sell off state firms. From Bogota, the best picture of Barco Vargas' tasks and perspectives as Colombia's new president, 5-26 and 5-27. From Rio, "Brazilians Take to President Sarney's Drive Against Inflation," 5-9: "Sarney's bold economic stroke has gained him a fresh start in moving the world's eighth largest economy toward a sound footing based on long-term investments and away from speculation in a fevered inflationary climate....But beneath such outbursts of economic enthusiasm — rare these days in debt-ridden Latin America — festers a range of social ills barely addressed." His best from Buenos Aires: "Argentina Is Paying Its Debts — but Falling Apart," 9-15 (weekly edition), a graphic picture of infrastructural decay, informative with telling examples. Spread wide, though, he didn't quite give the depth on Argentina we expect of him.

Graham, Robert
Financial Times. (½ ★)

Latin American editor. Perhaps it was his editorial duties, but we didn't see much of him in '86. "Guatemala Looks Beyond Its Borders," 1-16, was an interesting angle, though speculative, on changes for Central America's foreign policy. "Watershed Elections Add to Stability," 7-15, on the Dominican Republic didn't make it, just too thin on content and details.

Gupte, Pranay
Freelance. (NR)

"Embattled Sri Lanka Takes on Marxism Alone," 12-23-85, *WSJ* op-ed, a singularly informative article had us watching for his byline in '86. We didn't see it enough, though "Terror vs. the Third World," 5-11, *NYT* op-ed, and "El Salvador: Humane Development Is a Long Haul," 4-23, *International Herald Tribune*, both reaffirmed our sense that he's astute on Third World themes.

Haberman, Clyde
The New York Times. (★ ★ ½)

Tokyo bureau chief. The bureau strengthened in '86 with Haberman turning over most of the business/economic reporting to Susan Chira, concentrating on the political/security issues himself. His most prominent effort was the Sunday magazine cover, "Challenge in the Pacific," 9-7, an impressive overview. We also noted: "Japan and Soviets Testing Waters," 1-14, astute, alert and early on the Soviet's Pacific fishing expedition; "Aquino Challenge Seems to Be Wary," 2-17 and "Filipinos and U.S. Differ on Strife," 3-24, both straight reporting that stood out, no unnecessary spin tacked on; "Nakasone's Fate Rests on Vote today," 7-6, appreciated for its important details on factional differences over taxes, fiscal austerity, military budget; "Nakasone Calls Party Victory the 'Voice of Heaven'," 7-8, with insight into the socialists' sharp decline. Good on covering basics of Korean problems all year, as in "Radical

Surge on Campuses Shakes Seoul," 5-15, but "Seoul Lets Currency Inch Up," 10-3, was very sharp work, reporting the U.S. embassy disagreed with Treasury's leaning on Korea to appreciate, and said so.

Harden, Blaine
The Washington Post. (★ ★ ★)

Nairobi-based Africa correspondent. Nigeria, Uganda, Ethiopia, Sudan, etc. The young man (34) is all over Africa, and no one did quite as well as he did in telling of the continent's story for '86. January reports out of Uganda had us watching his travels all year: "Ugandan Peace Accords Falter," 1-11; "Ugandans Learn to Live With Tribal War," 1-20; "Few Starving in Ugandan War," 1-21, etc. He handled Nigerian debt problems, 1-5, produced a powerfully compelling feature on "Africa's Children," a four-part series mid-July, enthralled us with a Sunday Outlook section on life in the bush in the Sudanese civil war, 9-21, and did the finest critique of the controversial PBS television series, "The World of 'The Africans'," 10-7, blending sober criticism of the series with his own review of Africa today. "In crucial ways, Mazrui's biases are out of control. They prevent him from leavening his legitimate criticisms of the legacy of colonialism, his sound analysis of unfair western trade policies, with the plain fact that African governments themselves are primarily responsible for the catastrophic decline of post-independence Africa."

Hijazi, Ishan
The New York Times. (★)

Beirut. It was hard wading through his '86 dispatches, too frequently not enough information contained in them different from the body count headline. And for a while this was all that seemed to be coming from the Beirut bureau. But he came through more often than not, as in "Arafat and Aides Differ Over Responses to Hussein," 3-8, and "Palestinian Resurgence Seen in Southern Lebanon," 9-25, both fresh reports on shifting relationships there. Also among his better reports, "Hostage's Release Is Linked to Shift in Iranian Policy," 11-4.

Homan, Richard
The Washington Post. (★ ½)

Middle East. Decent reporting on the bloody change of regimes in South Yemen early in the year. A little inaccurate in getting the focus right at first, "Heavy Fighting Reported in Marxist South Yemen," 1-15, and "Evacuation and Fighting Continue in S Yemen," 1-19, but caught it and overcame the problem, "Rebels Say They Hold Southern Yemen," 1-21. Showed an ability to organize on the spot and find the margin in a complex and very disorganized situation.

MediaGuide

Housego, David
Financial Times. (★ ★ ½)

Paris. Always sprightly and able dispatches on the range of political, business, social events of France. We seemed to see less of him in '86, but always found him dependable and entertaining. "Cohabitation Not Easy to Live With," 6-27, on Mitterrand-Chirac: "Mr. Jacques Chirac, the French Prime Minister, has been celebrating his first 100 days in office this week with all the damp bravado that goes with a first night that has misfired. Notwithstanding, there is a noticeable confident bounce to his stride" and "the advantage of Mr. Chirac's high-pressure legislative tactics is that most of his program will have been pushed through parliament by the end of the summer, thus reducing Mr. Mitterrand's ability to lay snares across his path." A perceptive profile in "Free Market Faith Guides French Finance Minister," 9-15, and "Balladur Planning Further Cuts in French Taxation," 9-11 — important material not seen elsewhere.

Iyer, Pico
Time. (★ ½)

World affairs staff writer. One of *Time*'s most versatile foreign writers, we know he's talented. A crisp writer, he pops out an occasional essay or review as well. Thoroughly in control of his pieces, but he may be sacrificing insight and investigation to prudence and discretion, perhaps because he moves around so much. "Locking Out the 20th Century," 1-20, an engaging report from Burma on the country's autarkic socialism, one indication of solid individual effort. Other substantial work includes: "Storybook Rise, Uncertain Future," 5-26; "How Paradise is Lost — And Found," 6-9; "Dead Men Don't Pay Up," 6-23; "Adding Fuel to the Fire," 8-18, (with Robert Slater); and "War is Better Than A Bad Peace," 9-22, (with James Wilde). Please, *Time*, single byline or none.

James, Canute
The Journal of Commerce. (★)

Kingston. He caught the frustrations of Jamaica's prime minister with destructive IMF conditions, giving us the details in "Jamaica Holds IMF Payments," 9-3. He was good on that all year, but the country's tax reform, which took income tax rates down from 57.5% to 35%, was the big story he shouldn't have missed.

Jameson, Sam
Los Angeles Times. (★ ★)

Tokyo. Covering northeast Asia in '86, with alternating satisfaction. "Toshiba Expects Profit Dip, Gears for Upturn," 2-4, a good inside reading on the sales-slumping electronics giant's plans to recoup export earnings loss with higher prices overseas. But "Japan Urged to Reform Economy," 2-21, on Ambassador Mansfield's criticism of Nakasone's buy-foreign program, too thin, the complaints merely reported without background, context or analysis. Similarly watery serving with "Nakasone Backs Economic Reform Plan," 4-8. "For Host Nakasone, Conference May Mark End of Career," 5-5, a better mix of info and analysis, as also "In Wake of Major Victory, Nakasone May Have Tenure Extended by Rules Change," 7-8. "South Korea Shifts Gears," 6-22, meaty with details on the country's shift from chronic deficits to surplus. "S. Korea Angered by U.S. Demands to Open Market," 6-23, reviewing the tensions in U.S.-Korea trade relations, with details and analysis of anti-American sentiments being exploited there.

Jenkins, Loren
The Washington Post. (★)

Rome. Way behind the competition. A weak bureau, producing very little in '86. Jenkins bounced back and forth to Libya and Iran, and produced a few decent pieces outside his beat. "Iran-Iraq War May Hinge on Economics," 3-6, okay, but reports from Italy and the Vatican very stingy on fresh information. "Unity Provides Divisive Issue in Italy," 1-8, typically trivial. The Italian economy? Zip. He was leading on nothing, often lagged the wires. He did get into Vatical politics with " 'The Pope's Enforcer'," 11-13, a profile of the Vatican's "guardian of doctrinal purity," Cardinal Ratzinger. But why so late from him? He's unhappy with the Italy assignment, preferring Mexico, we know, where he sees a role for educating the public about problems. This talented pro of yesteryear coasted for most of '86.

Jones, Clayton
The Christian Science Monitor. (★ ½)

Manila. Didn't see his byline during the electoral crisis, but he was ahead of the competition with a report on a new tax code in the Philippines, 6-19. "The Philippines Other Insurgency," 6-24, okay on the Muslim south. "We're Safe Without Bases," 6-25, an interview with Aquino, adequate, though it could have been worked harder. "Filipino Communists Go Public," 8-29, there quickly with the story on the new legal front for the party's political activity. "Aquino Gets New Charter," 10-15, critical details on the new Philippine constitution, with foresight on the 1-87 plebiscite, "a referendum on Aquino herself" after "14 months with virtual dictatorial powers." Alert to the China complications in Soviet-Vietnamese relations, "Vietnam: Trying Ping-Pong Diplomacy?" 10-25.

Kamm, Henry
The New York Times. (★ ★)

Budapest. Athens in '86. A veteran professional on the foreign beat, with steady workmanship again this year. Kamm in earlier years kept global attention on the "boat people" of Southeast Asia. In '86 he was moving between Greece, Turkey, Israel, etc., on the news but also projecting ahead, as in "Israelis Expect Effort by Hussein To Woo West Bank Palestinians," 2-25, an example of a skill he displays from time to time. But we'd like to see some broader efforts if he could rouse himself for an analytic piece or two. "Greek Socialist Austerity Prompts a Leftist Rebuff," 10-26, had the beginnings.

Kaufman, Michael T.
The New York Times. (★ ★)

Warsaw bureau chief. Like Diehl of *The Washington Post*, pushing always against the limits imposed on Central European-based journalists. An innovative style with a knack for illustrating the general through a telling particular; "Buying a Polish Washing machine: Start by Being Young," 2-27, was a clever and revealing economic feature. "The Message In Warsaw," 7-2, with promises of no more Solidarities by Gorbachev, a top report on the Polish party congress. We particularly liked "Charge Against Walesa Is Dropped," 2-12: "Walesa wouldn't budge from his stand. It was poker and he was standing pat."

Kaylor, Robert
U.S. News & World Report. (★ ½)

East Asia. Doing decent work in the region, he supplied meat-and-potato reports from Manila, "Manila's Troubled Outlook," 2-17, and "Aquino Begins the Tough Calls," 3-17, that didn't have the glazed-eye look of *Newsweek*'s Philippine coverage. Especially well done, "Vietnam: Firmly on Course but Losing the Peace," 6-30: "Human sweat is the currency in a land where money is too scarce for anything but essentials."

Kifner, John
The New York Times. (★ ★)

Cairo bureau chief. On a wide swing through the region in '86 (Aden, Baghdad, Cairo), he covered the bases. "Massacre With Tea: Southern Yemen at War," 2-9, very useful in sorting out the complicated situation there. "Iraqis Stalled by Tenacious Enemy," 2-28, good assessment of why sharp-looking, well-equipped Iraqis aren't producing results in the war with Iran — their grunts just aren't steadfast in action. We waited all year for some depth on Egypt's economic problems. "Egypt's Army Praised in Quelling Riots, but for Mubarak, Crisis Is Not Over," 3-9, acknowledged the subject, but Kifner skirted it for the rest of the year, deciding it must be an overpopulation problem, "Cairo's Flood of People Destroys Nile Farmlands," 11-6. Better with "Syrian President Reported to Face Harsh Challenges," 5-18, with the focused assembly of facts and competent analysis typical of him.

Kinzer, Stephen
The New York Times. (★★)

Managua. A tough beat, but Kinzer stayed on top of it, though never really getting ahead of the curve. But we always follow his byline, trusting his work. Noted in '86, "Nicaragua Assembly to Form Charter," 1-2, good on opposition charges that it was a masquerade: "We're tired of helping the Sandinista front convince the world there's political pluralism here." Likewise, "Nicaragua Businessmen Express Fear of Attacks by the Sandinistas," 3-6, an important dispatch reporting the criticisms from the private-sector federation; "In One Nicaraguan Town, Silent Sunday Mornings," 7-17, solid on background for the expulsion of Bishop Vega. Though "Nicaragua Finds C.I.A. Behind Every Mishap," 9-7, despite intriguing headline and lead was skimpier than usual for Kinzer.

Knight, Robin
U.S. News & World Report. (★)

Generally straight reporting from South Africa: as in "A Roll of the Political Dice by Botha," 5-5, on the hurdles for reform; "Missing in South Africa: Black Unity," 5-12, late on the issue, but at least addressing the complexities; "Change Is Sure, Issue Is How," 5-26, more of the same, though only a thin gloss; " 'No' From the Right in South Africa," 6-9, covering the noise in Botha's right ear. All of it okay, but just too thin, with no value added to compensate for following after the dailies. *U.S. News*' editors aren't very demanding though, and so from another beat: "There's No End of Woe in Troubled Ulster," 11-17, which could have been written in an airport lounge awaiting a connecting flight.

Krauss, Clifford
The Wall Street Journal. (½ ★)

Miami. Covering the Caribbean and Central America with reporting that left us cold in '86. A spongy analysis "Nicaragua's Push Into Honduras Shows Its Indifference to Congress," 3-26, was remote, a problem that showed up again in "El Salvador Kidnap-Ring Investigation Is an Opportunity to Tame the Military," 5-9: "And, at a time when President Duarte's economic-austerity policies are undermining his labor base, the appearance that the government is making a serious effort on human rights gives him new credibility among liberals." Ringing up Carter's ambassador to El Salvador, Robert White, an academic "expert" and a CFR fellow, wasn't very serious resourcefulness. From Cuba, "Blacks Praise Cuban Revolution Benefits," 7-9, reports black Cubans are poor, but happy. "Cross Purposes," 9-26, examines economic and political instability in the region with a one-dimensional focus on U.S. sugar protectionism, the failure of Salvador's land reform to boost economic performance too simplistically attributed to that.

Kristof, Nicholas D.
The New York Times. (★ ★ ★)

Hong Kong. Kristof spent most of '86 in the Los Angeles bureau. One of the whiz kids of the business staff, he hit the ground running with his choice assignment in early '86 and by year's end was sent further west, a very fast track indeed. His "Polaroid Bets on a New Camera," 4-3, sends the stock down 3½ points. Timely, well done analysis, 4-8, on "Cheap Oil: Boon or Bane?" has $15 a barrel okay, under $10 disaster. He showed initiative in interviewing Arthur Laffer, the supply-side economist turned Senate candidate, and had new angles, 2-2. Early with lively profile of First Interstate's Joe Pinola, "BankAmerica's Audacious Pursuer," 6-8. Manages an absorbing "X-Rated Industry in a Slump," 10-5, without a smirk. We're expecting Kristof to push the *WSJ* Pacific crew.

Kronholz, June
The Wall Street Journal. (★)

Hong Kong bureau chief. A *Journal* star, she soured us very early with "In the Filipino Election Game, Marcos Holds the Aces," 1-29, which was an important contribution to the "Marcos-is-guilty-of-stealing-the-election" wisdom that preceded the election. Badly tilted throughout this breaking story. An interview with Finance Minister Jaime Ongpin, 3-5, struck us as shallow, breathlessly reported. Better with "Despite Some Success, Aquino Beset By Problems," 4-3, which Marcos may have read, leading to his Manila radio swansong, 4-5. Ranging out, "Political Change Inches Ahead in Taiwan," 6-18, tells us President Chiang is encouraging Kuomintang to meet with all segments, but the piece starts "sooo" slowly (editors?). We can see her stellar attraction in her Singapore feature, 6-19, an excellent cut above all the other Singapore features appearing in this period.

Lee, Gary
The Washington Post. (★)

Moscow bureau chief. A new beat early in '86, but even after allowances for settling in, still disappointing. He's not the patsy for the Kremlin line that his predecessor was, but we'd almost prefer Dusko Doder to Lee's routine dispatches: "Party Congress Shows Gorbachev's New Style," 2-28, an enticing headline, but wire service content; "Arms Offer Shift Seen," 2-7, again unaccountably thin, an item that begged for some critical treatment; "Soviets Seek Wider Acceptance for Afghan Regime," 1-16 — the headline said it all. Pale stuff for the first part of the year. A little more color in his Chernobyl coverage — "Soviet Lid on News of Chernobyl Reflects Cost, Security, Image Concerns," 5-2, and "Soviet Confusion Seen" with the first mention that Ukrainian Party boss Shcherbitsky was under fire for his tardy notification of Moscow — but still without much initiative shown for going beyond the official news being put out by the Soviets. Attempts at analytics also weak, as in "Daniloff Case Reflects U.S.-Soviet Strains," 9-12, "an example of the Soviet tit-for-tat policy gone amok...[in] the continuing quest by the Soviet leadership to be judged and treated as an equal superpower by the United States."

Lelyveld, Joseph
The New York Times. (★★)

London bureau chief, named Foreign editor, 12-6. A *Times*man to his toes, copy boy on up, Harvard, Columbia J-school. Changed beats to London from Johannesburg in '85, and was fine when he stuck to the U. K. scene, i.e., good coverage of Heseltine-Westland affair, "Crisis for Thatcher Winds Down As Helicopter Dispute Is Settled," 2-13, and the pressures and tensions within the Thatcher government, "Troubles Mount at 10 Downing Street," 2-4; again on Heseltine in "Fluctuating Fortune of the Tories' Heir Apparent," 7-22. "Britain Heads for Nuclear War at the Polls," 10-5, getting out ahead on Kinnock's bid for 10 Downing Street. But when he wanders over into assessing moods or sentiments regarding European attitudes toward U.S. foreign policy, he's careless, asserting what isn't there, as in "Europeans Grumbling About U.S. Handling of Daniloff Affair," 9-21.

LeMoyne, James
The New York Times. (★★½)

San Salvador bureau chief. A stickler for verification who checks and rechecks the evidence. That standard there in "US Is Said to Aid Contras Via Salvador," 2-12; "C.I.A. Accused of Tolerating Killing in Honduras," 2-14; and the 2-2 report on civilians in guerrilla-held territory being bombed by the Salvadoran Air Force. He whetted our appetite with "Duarte's Critics on the Rise at Home," 2-9, and we watched, without satisfaction, for further coverage on the country's deteriorating economy. "In Salvador, an Uneasy Peace Between Duarte and the Army," 9-23, almost delivered but only almost. A major feature on the Salvadoran guerrillas, 4-6, Sunday magazine, was totally exasperating — a stale rehash of info he and others provided a year earlier. "Rivalry Threatening to Split 'Contras'," 5-16, was standard LeMoyne, alert and out in front, though short on details of the policy disputes. Similarly, "Contras Prepare for Combat," 7-6, fresh and informative; "U.S. Prisoner in Nicaragua Says CIA Ran Contra Supply," 10-10, clear, comprehensive treatment on the Hasenfus case. Still, he left us frustrated with his efforts in '86.

Lewis, Flora
The New York Times. (½★)

Paris. "Foreign Affairs" column. She never fears treading into new issues, which is commendable. But in the last few years she's rushing into print with half-baked, uninformed commentary: "A 'Star Wars' Coverup," 12-3-85, was sad indeed. In '86, she seemed even more confused on issues of strategic defense:

"The Scientific Gag Rule," 1-14, and "The Peace War," 1-17. With a venture into monetary policy, "The Gold Standard," 1-28, she left us gasping. At her usual stand she's still worth a look: "The Serenity Vote," 2-6, on the French elections, and "The Next Steps," 2-13, prescriptions for policy toward Haiti and the Philippines. But with little snap or pungency. Tendentious on arms control, but unlike Tony Lewis, rarely at the margin of the debate: "Soviet S.D.I. Fears," 3-6, and "A Hidden Nuclear Quarrel," 7-20, are out of sync. Perhaps as a result of this innocence, she was almost alone in seeing "Faint Soviet Signals," 7-31. She does best in columns where her subject speaks at length: "Canada's Friendly Advice," 4-13, an interview with Brian Mulroney, was at least interesting.

Liu, Melinda
Newsweek. (★)

Based in Hong Kong, covering the Southeast Asia beat. *Newsweek*'s Philippine coverage during the heat of the electoral crisis didn't make it, a problem not so much of the field journalists on that beat, as the senior writer assigned. Some of Liu's individual work, we noted, reflected balance and a steady, straight effort, as in "The Philippines: Can Cory Handle Dissent?" 8-11.

Lohr, Steve
The New York Times. (★ ½)

London. The City beat, covering the November "Big Bang" of market deregulation well enough, with heavy focus on the changes it will mean to people (up-and-comers making big money, maybe too much, brokers working longer hours, earlier trains scheduled, etc.), but we didn't see any really big picture stuff from him. His "Japan's Challenge in the Euromarkets," 2-13, was indeed mid-lofty and appreciated. We noted, "Push on Hiring Bias in Ulster," 9-3, and "The Commonwealth Leans Hard, and Thatcher Is Feeling It," 8-3, as superior, informative. A Sunday feature on the problems at Guinness, 12-8, opens with a nice anecdote, but again suggests Lohr may be a bit class conscious. He could get deeper into the economic debate, the players and politics.

Long, William
Los Angeles Times. (★ ★)

Impressive reporting from Caribbean America, with substantial material, a sense for critical new developments, as in "Marxist Rebel Group Competes in Colombian Election," 3-10, a landmark in Colombia's peace efforts and political development. His best, a report on Fidel's exasperation with signs of capitalist remnants in Cuba where "there's not enough revolutionary fervor to suit the revolutionary leader," 8-18. Quoting a horrified Castro: "We have to wash the dirty linen...There are thousands of small farmers...[and] truck drivers who have become rich....There are tens of thousands of rich people in this country."

Lopez, Laura
Time. (★ ½)

Managua. "A Cardinal Under Fire," 5-2, very solid reporting on the Sandinista offensive against the Church in Nicaragua, as good as any in the U.S. daily press. A impressive indication of her ability. But also disconcerting, because she's another of the newsweeklies' foreign correspondents whose shared bylines handicaps judgment of their '86 work.

MacDougall, Colina
Financial Times. (★ ½)

Peking. About the best on offbeat PRC business stories, tailored to the *FT*. Early (12-4-85) with "The Doubts Start to Grow" on China's economic reforms. The most striking was on the realization of foreign industry that PRC Chinese aren't Hong Kongers or Taiwanese and have low skill levels; the Japanese treat them as junior partners. See: "General Realism Dawns Over China's Problems," 6-23.

MacLeod, Scott
Freelance. (NR)

Middle East. Occasional dispatches from Cairo and elsewhere in the Middle East from him in '86, but it wasn't until "How Assad Won," 5-8, *New York Review of Books*, appeared that we had something substantial enough to note. Impressive with a regional geopolitical analysis, penetrating in its examination of the Mideast gamemaster: "Greater Syria is less a living ideology than an expresssion of Assad's ambitions....Assad has become the state itself...."

Mann, Jim
Los Angeles Times. (★ ★)

Peking bureau chief. It's not easy for us to see his stuff, but it bubbles up through channels and we're always informed in some way. His "Chinese Aides Under New Scrutiny," 2-15, was the best update we'd seen in three months on the tensions between the Party and reformers, finding "a temporary ideological truce prevails in the semipublic skirmishing between reformers within the party who advocate further economic liberalism and the traditionalists who fear the party may be drifting from its moorings." His news dispatch of 9-3, "China to End Lifetime Jobs for Workers," was the first we'd seen of this blow to the "Iron Rice Bowl": all new workers in the state-owned enterprises will be hired under labor contracts and will be assured of work for a fixed period, afterwards they can quit or be let go. Still, he could push deeper analytically.

MediaGuide

Manning, Richard
Newsweek. (★)

Ejected from his post in Johannesburg mid-summer in the midst of Botha's crackdown on the press, Manning's best work came immediately before and after his expulsion: "Soweto: The Spirit of '76," 6-23, and "Farewell, South Africa," 7-7. He tends to be one-sided in his reports though, and this holds him back.

Markham, James
The New York Times. (★ ★)

Bonn. A seasoned, respected correspondent now running his fourth foreign bureau (Saigon, Beirut, Madrid), but shy on economics on a pivotal economic beat. Still, we liked his innovative, "Who Owns the Past?" 4-27, on East Germany rewriting history with a Marxist slant. His election-eve notes on Kurt Waldheim, from Vienna, "Silence Louder Than Oom-Pah-Pah," 6-8, were unusual. "The Cold War of Letters Raging in Gunter Grass," 2-15, a prickly interlocution with the country's thin-skinned premier political activist; "West Europe Cool to Removal of U.S. Medium-Range Missiles," 2-25, timely on West Germany's fears of de-coupling; "Europe Keeps Up Pressure on Libya," 6-1, a trenchant Markham analysis: "In the seven weeks since American bombers struck at Tripoli and Benghazi, an ambiguous calm has settled over the debate about terrorism...between the U.S. and its European allies. In this breathing space, President Reagan is getting something like the benefit of strategic doubt...this halcyon moment owes much to....the shifting of the discussion from Libya to Syria..." From Vienna, 11-23, a fine sketch of U.S. Ambassador Ronald Lauder, of the cosmetics family.

Marsh, David
Financial Times (★)

Bonn. Added here and there to our watch on the German government's economic doldrums. "West Germany Urged to Speed Cuts in Taxes," 10-21, reported internal pressure for change from "the country's five leading economic research institutes."

Martin, Jurek
Financial Times. (★ ★ ★)

Tokyo. Impressive credentials [see bio] and his work is just as good. He leaves most of the business/finance beat to Carla Rapoport, handling politics and culture. (The team edges out Haberman & Chira of *The New York Times*, but not by much.) His "Tokyo Plans to Reduce Top Rate of Income Tax," 2-6, was very early and not fully confirmed until September. There's no journalist writing in English who covers "local" politics in Japan as well as Martin. His "Party

Fixers Defy the Omens," 6-4, is rich in local detail on the Japan elections. The post-election "Voice of Japan," 7-8, was a gem, opening with this: "Visible displays of hubris do not become Japanese politicians. Humility is the preferred demeanour in victory as in defeat. But yesterday Mr. Yasuhiro Nakasone was finding it hard to stop the corners of his mouth twitching with pleasure as he sought to explain how it was that he had presided over the biggest electoral triumph in post-war Japanese political history."

McCartney, Robert J.
The Washington Post. (★★)

Bonn, after bureau chief in Mexico for most of '86. Decent reporting from Central America, an improvement over his previous year. A very good start with report, 1-10, on Mexican electoral contest, detailed with a decent stab at analysis; followed by an insightful and focused "Guatemala Inaugurates Civilian President," 1-15. "Shift in Honduras...on Contra Aid," 1-21, a tricky issue, but he handled it well. Not quite as well done, "Latin Mood Shifts Against Washington," 3-12, where he seemed a little too eager to accept official pronouncements without assessing or testing. A switch from Mexico bureau chief to Bonn in '86, with mixed production. From Vienna, 7-9, a report on Waldheim's inauguration, not much beyond the wire services, but better in "Terrorist Group Kills Executive Near Munich," 7-10, with some new material on the Red Army Faction. He was in Reykjavik in preparation for summit coverage, uncharacteristically vacuous — Madame President as the first woman's libber, a haunted house as the site for the summit, the novelty of Thursday TV in Iceland.

Meisels, Andrew
The Washington Times. (★½)

Israel-based correspondent. We didn't see as much as we'd hoped from this astute correspondent in '86. "Israel Works for Alternative to PLO," 1-24, was one of the best accounts in the press of Israel's perspective for building an alternative leadership among West Bank Arabs to the PLO; the experiment in Nablus was reported just right, not overdone nor the Jordanian reaction ignored. Also notable, "Peres Revives Dayan's Autonomy for West Bank, Gaza," 2-11, on the mark analytically, with Meisels catching the Dayanesque perspective of Peres: "We must distinguish between the rhetoric of the West Bank Palestinians and their real political views. I want established political dialogue based on practical realities."

Miller, Judith
The New York Times. (★★)

Washington bureau, deputy bureau chief in 1987, but Paris bureau in '86. We've often wondered why so many outfits assign distaff reporters to Tripoli. Miller,

38, spilled the beans, 6-14, with a zinger on Qaddafi's obsessive passes at female journalists (and now she is *persona non grata* in his tent). Her reporting from France was at best undistinguished, with one clap for her interview "President Yves Montand? Not Everybody Scoffs," 5-23. She couldn't seem to fathom the country as she does the Arab world. She scored with "Hussein Questions Who Should Speak for Palestinians," 2-23. But she was at her best on the Libya beat. Not into chasing down Qaddafi on his tractor, she instead camped outside Muammar's tent, dogged him for an interview — and got it! Resourceful, persistent, gutsy, with compact assessments of economic life under Qaddafi: "Oil Ample, Food Short for Libya," 1-13, an inside picture on empty shelves, toilet paper shortages, and food riots; "Libyan Military Termed Restive Under Qaddafi," 1-14, on using economic shortages to replace professional control over the army with "armed masses."

Miller, Matt
The Asian Wall Street Journal. (★★)

New Delhi. Dow Jones opened this New Delhi bureau in '86 with this youngster, who started fast. "Calcutta's Marxist Government Extends The Red-Carpet Treatment to Capitalists," 2-28, caught our eye. But his best score was "Economic Policy Spurs Gandhi Opposition," (reprinted in the 4-2 *WSJ*) jam-packed with detail on Old Guard opposition to Rajiv's capitalism, plus "a strong, pro-Soviet lobby interprets the government's continuing admiration of Western technology as detrimental to India's alliances with socialist and communist countries." Also brings us along with "Dissidents in Disarray," 8-25, from Karachi, on swirling unrest kicked up by Benazir Bhutto. But we still need more on domestic economic policies throughout the subcontinent.

Montalbano, William D.
Los Angeles Times. (★★)

Buenos Aires. All newsmen on this beat had problems getting inside the story of Argentina's economy in '86. Montalbano didn't crack it, but we usually found new material in his attempts. "Argentina Facing Summer of Discontent Over Costs of Austerity," 1-22, was timely and detailed on Alfonsin's perspectives, and hurdles he faced. "Disenchantment Grows Over Argentina's Inflation Fight," 6-16, examined what had and hadn't been accomplished after one year of the Austral Plan, and noting plans to cut taxes on agricultural exports, also reported plans to pay for the cut with tax hikes on farm land. From Quito, "Scrappy Ecuador Leader Facing Oil Price Crisis," 3-9, a meaty report on Febres Cordero's attempts to keep economic reform rolling despite an oil price pinch. From Lima, "Honeymoon Comes to Halt for Peru's Garcia as Crisis Escalates," 6-26, a fine example of Montalbano's overall performance, analytically rich, buttressed by new information.

Morgan, Jeremy
The Journal of Commerce. (★ ½)

Watching the grain trade, commodities in the Southern Cone, and we watch especially for fresh information on Argentina, such as "Alfonsin Pledges Cut in Farm Export Taxes," 5-2, where we learn that although Argentina's grain and oil-seed exports rose 94% from 1980 to '85, the value rose only 40% due to falling prices. He also reports Soviet trade tensions with Argentina, on 10-26, with the USSR threatening to cut grain purchases unless Argentina narrows its trade surplus.

Mydans, Seth
The New York Times. (½ ★)

Manila bureau chief. New to Manila when the electoral crisis hit, transferred in late '85 after an undistinguished stint in Moscow. His best piece, with his big bosses visiting from NYC and looking on, "Aquino Says If She Is Elected Marcos Faces Murder Trial" (12-16-85). But it was disappointingly downhill after that. The Philippine electoral crisis was one of the year's major events in which the press's ability to provide unbiased news and analysis was tested. Mydans scored poorly. A Sunday magazine feature, 2-2, on the middle-class turn against Marcos, was flimsy, with a silly focus. "Marcos Victory May Be Costly for His Country," 2-16, was tilted, replete with "many observers say" formulations, obviously feeding at the Embassy trough. Here and there, okay analysis, "Aquino's Uphill Path," 3-4, and straightforward reporting, as in "Marcos on Radio Asks Support for Aquino," 4-6. But the vague, unfocused reports are too frequent, as in "Filipinos Grumbling: Can Aquino Govern Nation?" 4-21, or "Is Aquino Falling Behind In Political Posturing?" 10-26. But there was so little meat on the bones, we sensed he really was thrown in over his head, and we can't expect '87 will improve.

Neilan, Ed
The Washington Times. (★ ★)

Tokyo. Northeast Asia correspondent. A veteran Asian hand with vast experience, giving up his foreign policy column in Washington for another Japan tour in '86. He can see a big picture as well as almost anyone, and we loved, "Japanese Politics May Hit Page One," 5-26 — "articles on Japanese domestic politics in the American media are almost as rare as the whooping crane," extremely perceptive on why economic integration, exchange-rate, trade tensions will force a change in this regard. "China Plans Slowdown on Reforms," 4-4, and Shanghai Adopts a Capitalist Aura," 4-28, uncharacteristically slender on detail. Better with "China and Japan Detect No Sign That Soviets Are Softening Policy," 11-13, three months after Gorby's Vladivostok speech. At least:

"Japanese were pleasantly surprised when Mr. Gorbachev dispatched an ambassador — Nikolai Solovjev — who speaks Japanese and who is a professional diplomat rather than a party functionary." We expect a big '87 from him now that he's finished settling in.

Nordland, Rod
Newsweek. (−)

Consistently biased, inflammatory and dramatic — everything you don't need in a journalist or a diplomat. His writing is always colorful, but often at the expense of accuracy and/or fairness. Typical: "Inside Terror, Inc.," 4-7 (with Ray Wilkinson), a unique and chilling look at terrorist groups from the inside that gave the bottom line for terrorism as the absence of a Palestinian state.

Norton, Christopher
The Christian Science Monitor. (★)

San Salvador. His reports from El Salvador sometimes catch details not reported elsewhere, but usually just keep pace. "Duarte's Call for Peace Talks Sparks Some Skepticism," 6-3 and "Little Progress Expected at Talks Between Duarte, Rebels," 6-17, okay on basics, all the various players quoted on the issue. The best we saw, with Norton on his toes, "Duarte Resists U.S. Pressure to Devalue Currency," 9-5.

O'Boyle, Thomas F.
The Wall Street Journal. (★ ½)

Bonn. Snappy, no-nonsense analyst of the German political scene. "White House Has Shot Itself in Foot...," 7-29, one of the best features on the West German nerve gas accord — explains binary chemical weapons, why accord is a setback militarily, why Germans aren't happy. A brisk summary of Helmut Kohl's "Goebbel's" goof, "West German Chancellor's Clumsiness Unlikely to Harm Reelection Chances," 11-10: "If Ronald Reagan is the Teflon President, then Helmut Kohl is the Flypaper Chancellor. Everything sticks to him."

O'Brien, Conor Cruise
The Atlantic. (−)

Sophisticated espousal of "Third World" revolutionary views, but this is not journalism. Disinformation, misinformation, pronounced biases characterize his work. Very bad job on Nicaragua and the Church, weak attempt to "understand" the "legitimate" basis of terrorism, unobjective blathering on South Africa. *Atlantic* made a mistake in confusing him with a journalist. Perhaps acceptable as a columnist, but no need for Christo-like features. If you don't believe us, check out, "What Can Become of South Africa?" 3-86, or

"God and Man in Nicaragua," 8-86, on the "God of the Rich" vs. the "God of the Poor," with the Catholic Church on the wrong side of his ax: "John Paul II is getting to look more and more like an international Canute, magisterially perambulating all the strands of the world, before huge and admiring audiences, without the slightest effect on the tides."

O'Leary, Timothy
The Washington Times. (★)

A quiet year from him in South America, but "No American Apples on the Shelves in Brazil," 5-28, had us taking notice: the state protected computer industry ends up with low efficiency, 80,000 units produced in a year by 250 companies.

Orme, William. A., Jr.
The Journal of Commerce. (★ ★ ½)

Mexico. One of the best reporting out of Mexico. Good sources. Informative, perceptive, steady attempts to keep on top of economic policy, coming the closest of anyone in mastering it. Occasionally appears in the *Financial Times* and *The Washington Post*, with frequent reports in the *JofC*, as "Mayor Challenges Mexico's Ruling Party," 5-11, a capably presented profile of Chihuahua's PAN candidate. Way ahead with "Mexico Hears Call for Tax Reform In Order to Check Massive Tax Evasion," 8-26: "Inflation...has pushed most regular taxpayers into...the 42 percent bracket...[Yet] personal income tax collections last year amounted to just 2% of GDP [!]" Equally astute on politics, as in "Mexico's Presidential Sweepstakes," 10-21, where neither leading "successor" appears democratic, but Manuel Bartlett looks better on economic issues.

Parks, Michael
Los Angeles Times. (★ ★ ½)

Johannesburg. Adept at getting inside complex issues. He was refreshingly sharp with feature-style reports, avoiding their use for moralizing, working them instead to broaden the picture of what was going on inside the country in '86. An example, "S. African Blacks Face Rent Strike Dilemma," 8-28. "Civilian deaths were 'tragic', ...but virtually unavoidable," he reports ANC military chief of staff and Communist Party chairman Joe Slovo declaring, in "S. African Crackdown Sparks Rebel Offensive," 7-14. A wide and detailed examination of the ANC's escalation of terrorist attacks against civilian targets, this was one of his best. Other notable reports, "South Africa Court Curbs Police Powers in State of Emergency," 7-29, and "Hamstrung Civil Rights Lawyers, Courts Both Show Courage in S. Africa," 8-16, on the "judicial" revolution; "S. Africa Black Mayor Quits in Blow to Hopes for Moderate Leadership," 4-23, on the collapsing local self-government option; " 'Banning':

MediaGuide 203

Kafkaesque Punishment," 5-6, an interview with an old S. African radical who was made a non-person for 33 years, requiring ministerial dispensation to speak even with his wife. Parks' work permit renewal was denied by S. Africa at year's end.

Perry, James M.
The Wall Street Journal. (★)

London. One of the best U.S. political reporters of the late '60s, Perry has been in the U.K. covering the queen, "Queen Elizabeth at 60," 4-21, waiting for the 1988 presidential contest to begin in earnest; he'll return home in July '87. He seemed a fish out of water in London, producing little competitive political news or analysis. The closest, "British Labor Party Tries Purge of Revolutionary Infiltrators," 6-11, but doesn't tell us why these radicals flourish at all; what are the issues? A front-page leader on Maggie's poor image, 9-30, tells us what the man-in-the-street is saying. A look at Labor's Neil Kinnock, 11-24, is sparse, two-dimensional. A scattering of features on British movies and roof thatchers suggests he's ready to come home, which we'll welcome.

Pond, Elizabeth
The Christian Science Monitor. (★ ½)

Bonn. Not that much from her on the German economy and the debates over tax and monetary reforms, a big hole in her reporting. She focused frequently on defense issues instead. "US and Germany Finally Come to Terms on 'Star Wars'," 3-28, an analysis of the agreement covered the basics well and noted the agreement covered only current phase research, development an issue that NATO would have to take up. "Europe and Star Wars Jr." 4-23, examined the military, organizational and political issues involved within Germany's push for a European missile defense. Innovative at times, she catches shifting political nuances on the cultural scene, as in "W. German Film Irks Both Right and Left."

Powers, Charles
Los Angeles Times. (★ ½)

Former Nairobi bureau chief, Powers' reports on the East African rethinking about socialist economic models were timely and detailed. The best on that, a broad and informing picture of Tanzania's economic destitution, that appeared in *Human Events*, "Tanzania: Another Proven Failure of Socialism," 2-22. Also well done, "Uganda No Longer Africa's Killing Field," 6-8, with information about the emerging economic perspectives of the Museveni government, the Ugandan leader anxious to institute pro-growth reforms, but hostile to IMF austerity and currency devaluation prescriptions.

Pura, Raphael
The Asian Wall Street Journal. (★★)

Southeast Asia economics correspondent. His reports from Malaysia resulted in his expulsion from the country (along with Malaysia correspondent John Berthelsen) and a three-month ban there on *The Asian Wall Street Journal*, all later rescinded. "Disappearing Records," 7-14, on the unusual transactions between the $9.55b Employees Provident Fund and the state-created Mukuwasa Securities syndicate, was serious investigative work, going right up to the offices of the Finance Minister. "Malaysia's Tin Scheme Stuns the Industry," *WSJ*, 9-25, on the Malaysian government's disastrous attempts in 1981-82 to corner the tin market, another blockbuster. "Malaysian Minister to Sell Big Bank Stake," 9-29, (with John Berthelsen) reported the Malaysia Finance Minister was selling his shares in a bank, at a hefty profit, to a government agency he controlled. At that point, his investigative reporting was abruptly ended, Malaysia rescinding his journalist work permit.

Quinn-Judge, Paul
The Christian Science Monitor. (★★★)

Moscow bureau chief. Moscow's his beat, but he keeps East Asia within his purview, his reporting on both very satisfying all year. An extremely valuable analytic: "Marcos Fall: How it Happened," 3-4. Another from early post-Marcos Manila, "Power Struggle in Aquino Ranks," 3-10, out ahead on the maneuvering within Cory's coalition over plans for a "revolutionary government." In "Soviets Count on Summit," 7-2, he has a nice quote from a Russian who views Reagan as "a senior citizen with very clear-cut ideas." "Loss of Vietnam Leader May Trigger Power Struggle," 7-11, was where we first learned the late Le Duan had initiated supply-side economic reforms in North Vietnam. In "Gorbachev's Counselors," 10-27, he catches the unexpectedly important role of Armed Forces Chief of Staff Sergei at Reykjavik, maybe "Gorbachev's standing with the military is better than many observers had thought." In "Kremlin Is Satisfied With Results So Far," 11-13, (*FarEastern Economic Review*), very informative material assessing the progress of Gorbachev's Vladivostok initiative.

Randal, Jonathan
The Washington Post. (★ ½)

Covering the Middle East, from the Maghreb to the Levant. From North Africa, some coverage on the economic squeeze there provided information not much reported elsewhere. "Tunisia Seen Vulnerable to Move by Qaddafi," 5-4, with details on the economic problems faced by Bourguiba. "Algeria Braces for Drastic Austerity Measures," 5-11, covered the pull-back on economic liberalization under the pinch of falling oil prices. Into Syria for an interview with Assad (with Jim Hoagland), Randal reported in "Syrian Changes Hinted," 5-29, signs

MediaGuide 205

of a breach in its alliance with Iran. "Sudan Slow in Coming to Grips With Problems," 7-7, a good organization of details and information for a picture of that country's weighty problems. Terrible, however, the post Peres-Hassan meeting analytic, "Moroccan Has Long Encouraged Contacts Between Arabs, Israelis," 7-23, his biases coming through; the king has "turned to Moroccan Jews abroad to improve relations with Israel, the U.S. and western powers," delighting among others the "influential rump community of 16,000" Moroccan Jews, and "the powerful Israeli lobby in the United States has never flexed its muscles in Congress to oppose aid to Morocco."

Rapoport, Carla
Financial Times. (★ ★ ★ ★) Tokyo.

The most consistently rewarding byline out of Japan, in the lead with fresh, concise stories about technological innovation, economic policy shifts, and a thorough grasp of what it all means. She explains, 10-31, why Bank of Japan finally cut the discount rate, why cutting 20 points from income tax is better politics and economics than a new tax on savings (VAT): "they may simply save more in order to cover the tax". Great quote in "Tactics in the New TV Contest," 6-2: "The Japanese can't be stopped from thinking up products a lot of us want to buy." In "The Pressures That Led To A Switch in Semiconductor Strategy," 10-29, we learn why Fujitsu acquired Fairchild, how deflated Japanese industry dropped computer chip prices, and that "Fujitsu is likely to end up paying IBM between $100 million and $1 billion [!] for the latest alleged violation" of IBM copyrights. In "Rising Yen, the Mother of Invention," 7-25, she sees technology shifts responding to currencies. "Japanese Press the Pause Button," 7-14, finds purposeful delay of a new compact disc a sign of maturity. She notes on 9-2 the Tokyo stock market "is now standing on a breathtaking 50+ price-earnings ratio," seeing a downturn for unconventional reasons. Brava, Carla! Encore!

Revzin, Philip
The Wall Street Journal. (★ ★)

Paris bureau chief. New to Paris late in '86, but the work he did elsewhere in the year suggests the *WSJ* may have the right man. A slow start with "Greeks Complain as Austerity Plan Bites," 1-29, with little idea what "austerity" he's talking about. Much better, also from Athens, with "Greek Drama," etc., 3-28, on socialists wooing the capitalists, with the kind of fine detail we like: "Foreign investors, who can take no more than 12% of their profits out of Greece, have stopped coming. Foreign manufacturers invested only $11 million in Greece in 1984." From Ankara, a solid dispatch on Turgot Ozal's bid for entry to the European Community, 4-22, "2000 is a nice round number." Best from Paris, a profile of "Sir James Goldsmith, As Enigmatic as Ever, Bails Out of Goodyear," 11-21, with James B. Stewart in NYC.

Richburg, Keith
The Washington Post. (★1/2)

Manila. We saw him first, briefly, in the *Post*'s foreign service, reporting out of Port-au-Prince early in '86. Slim pickings in "Baby Doc's Lost Land," the cover story in the *Post*'s Sunday magazine, 3-30, and his 2-16 peek at Haiti's economic morass. But "Our Haiti Meddling Worked," 2-23, informed on the behind the scenes activity of U.S. State Department not reported elsewhere. In Manila, arriving after the electoral crisis, he seemed uniformly professional, "Aquino's Aides Undercut Policies in Her Absence," 9-23, on the escalation of the Enrile-Ramos-Aquino rift, an impressive treatment of the issue; followed by "Philippine Rebels Say Peace Is Distant," 10-12, an inside report on New People's Army leaders' (Ocampo and Zumel) dampened prospects for a peaceful end to their armed struggle, the Pol Pot-like nature of the NPA revealed. Quoting Ocampo: "about 60 suspected government infiltrators — called 'zombies' in the movement — were executed by overzealous NPA comrades," and peasants and businesses who refuse to pay the NPA's "progressive taxation" find their livelihood destroyed. Richburg's coverage of the November ceasefire was also well above the average, and we increasingly look to the *Post* on this beat.

Ricklefs, Roger
The Wall Street Journal. (★1/2)

Paris. Competent in keeping up with French political scene, better on feature material. "French Worry That Parliamentary Vote Could Lead to Government Stalemate," 3-10, typically steady. A good analysis, 3-17, on the impact of the narrow vote, wondering if Mitterrand will name Chirac. "Mitterrand Riding High in French Polls," 3-31, another satisfying account of situation. Ricklefs shifted back to New York late in '86, excellent news feature on employers hiring and training retarded to do unskilled work, "Faced With Shortage of Unskilled Labor, Employers Hire More Retarded Workers," 10-21. Arresting lead: "The older man can print his name only if you print it first. The younger man can do nothing more demanding intellectually than tell time. But together they have made a once-filthy shopping mall in Jersey City, N.J. spotless."

Riding, Alan
The New York Times. (★ ★)

Rio bureau chief. His shortcoming in '85 was an inability to get deeply into the economics of the region. Like Graham of *The Washington Post*, he also traverses the continent, encompassing even Mexico, but being spread thin isn't the reason for meager or poor reporting on economic issues. He just doesn't have a clue as to what it's all about, as in "Brazil Gets Back on the Fast Track," 10-12: "Paradoxically, an immediate general price rise is probably necessary to ease inflationary pressures, in part by cooling the current consumer boom." Despite features on Brazilian shamans or kayaking the Amazon, we still got a lot out of him in '86. "Uruguay's New Freedoms...," 1-6, a report the Tupumaros want back into the democratic process; from Asuncion, 1-14, the end of Paraguay's economic boom, dissent astir; from Rio, 3-2, one of his best, a profile of Brazilian Finance Minister Funaro, full of details on his "shock treatment" plans for the economy; Bogota, 5-18, on Colombia's largest guerrilla movement taking steps to end its 30-year insurgency; Lima, 8-31, on Peru's Garcia, squeezed by the military and an IMF bill; Mexico City, 10-24, the waning of Mexico's foreign policy offensive in Central America. But he could cover the big hole in his work if he'd take a cue from his counterpart in the *Times*' Tokyo bureau, Clyde Haberman.

Robbins, Carla Anne
U.S. News & World Report. (1/2★)

Latin America correspondent. A weak year from her. She hasn't found the way yet to present fresh material, with new information, a different angle or perspective, or a tightly organized sweep of the essentials on a subject. "Time Runs Out for 'Baby Doc', 2-17, was very stale. "Has Mexico Hit Bottom?" 4-7, a better effort as a summary, but still lagging on anything fresh; likewise "Tugging at the Rug Under a Wily General," 5-5, meat-and-potatoes fare, but undercooked and unpeeled. Marginal for '86, but maybe her weakness was a consequence of the inadequacy higher up at *U.S. News*.

Robinson, Anthony
Financial Times. (★ ★ ★ 1/2)

Johannesburg. Superior work on South Africa, Robinson provided pure information combined with penetrating insights and fresh analyses all year. He can simultaneously get into the heart of any complex subject and yet step back from it to present a coherent picture. Meticulously free of any taint of bias, he's must-read on this beat. Among his best, "Conflict at the Crossroads," 5-31, an incisive account of the government's attempt to pursue "orderly urbanization" after abolishing influx control and pass laws: "What has been destroyed at Crossroads is faith that the Government has indeed changed its heart and is prepared to approach black urbanization in a humane way in consultation with the communities affected." "In Memory of Soweto," 6-14, a detail-rich account of the breakdown of tribal affiliations of parents and grandparents in the extended family, the rise of the "youth factor," the dark side of the radicalism and optimism of the young. "Twenty-six Years of Siege," 7-11, on South Africa's mastery of the economics of the laager, "whether the siege economy is best handled by letting market forces or direct government control dictate the future pattern." No one packs more into dispatches, despite government censorship, than he does. Our only complaint — we don't see enough of him.

Rohter, Larry
The New York Times. (NR)

Mexico City bureau chief. Transferred from the Metro section in late '86, where he'd worked since coming to the *Times* in 1984. In late October, the *Times* ran a seven-part front-page series on the economic and social crisis afflicting Mexico, each by a different writer, and Rohter's "Mexico's New Type of Emigrant: Well-to-Do, Skilled, Disillusioned," 10-21, was head-and-shoulders above the other six, the only one that got far enough beneath the facts and figures that have become standard fare from Mexico to touch on the sources of the problem, the reasons for the flight of human capital, the business class that would otherwise be employing the working class. Quoting one executive who fled and now works in Dallas: " 'When I went to work one day, there were soldiers with machine guns there and they wouldn't let us in,' he said. 'When I was finally able to return to work, I found that I was working in a totally different environment, as a government bureaucrat with no future.' Other factors in his decision to leave Mexico, he said, included constant currency devaluations and a high income tax rate. He also says he was embittered by an experience as a poll watcher in which 'I delivered one set of figures, which when they were published weeks later were totally rigged....' "

Ross, Michael
Los Angeles Times. (★)

Was the Administration peddling misinformation in its disinformation ploy with Libya? Ross's Tripoli-filed "Libya Hit Hard by Oil Price Collapse," 4-6, found an economy in disarray, admissions that Qaddafi's "Green Revolution" doesn't work, and reports that "the unrest has become evident — in the streets, on university campuses and, more significant, in the ranks of the armed forces." We didn't see a lot by him in '86, but what we did was useful. Also noted, "Egypt, Israel: Neither Can Afford Genuinely 'New Era' Ties Right Now," 9-13, a sober analysis of why the "dawn of a new era" in Israeli-Egyptian relations has produced so little in the way of specific achievement.

Rule, Sheila
The New York Times. (★)

Nairobi bureau chief in '86 after the Metro desk, and a good start. On the East Africa shuttle from Mogadishu to Harare, displaying a talent for assessing the capacity and capability of the area's political leaders, as for example, "Nkomo Says Sole Ambition Now Is Peace," 3-2, one of her best for the year. Again with "Somalia Braces for Transition Politics," 7-20, on Said Barre and potential successor Gen. Samantar, a beat not much covered by others. In "Crisis Roils Government In Uganda," 10-19, we get a timely update on Museveni's political crisis. In "Master of Mozambique," 11-4, she gave us the first quickie look at Machel's successor, Joaquim Alberto Chissano, relative to the late President

Machel: " 'Chissano is less fiery,' a friend said today, 'but I've seen him address rallies that are three hours long and people pay attention to him. He is more democratic than Samora people. People talk back to him and he lets them. He is a warm and pleasant man'." In '87 we begin to look for deeper analytics.

Rupert, James
The Washington Post. (★ ★ ★ 1/2)

Over the Pakistani border and into Afghanistan, Rupert travelled with the resistance in October, '85, emerging 1-86 with a ★ ★ ★ ★ series (Jan. 12-16) on the country, each feature totally absorbing, gripping, detailed material on the battle for Afghan culture, the Sovietization of the country, raids on Soviet strongholds, the pattern of the brutal destruction, the Soviet depopulation campaign clearly revealed: "kill the fish by emptying the water." A brief stint in the Philippines, where he produced straight reports, fresh information and detail during the waning days of Marcos, "Marcos Denounces Modern-Day Imperialists," 2-22, and "Associates of Marcos Resurfacing," 2-27. From Peshwar again in May, solid analyses of new events in Afghanistan: "Afghan Party Chief Babrak 'Ill,' Is Replaced," 5-4, and "Afghan Rebel Forces Regroup," 5-12, both sharp on identfying the new tactical and strategic shifts underway there. Back over the border, hooking up with the Afghani resistance in July and September, chronicling his travels in an October series (beginning 10-5). Unequivocally the must-read journalist on Afghanistan.

Ryan, Leo
The Journal of Commerce. (NR)

Canadian bureau chief. Provides remarkably little information on Canada, particularly anything remotely critical of the Mulroney government. An op-ed piece on 8-6, "Canada's African Influence Strong," praises the government for appointing a "brilliant" socialist to the U.N. ("giving Canada an enviable image among African delegations"), famine assistance, and pushing Britain to impose sanctions against Pretoria.

Schmemann, Serge
The New York Times. (★ ★ ★)

Johannesburg in 1987, but Moscow bureau chief in '86, maintaining the outstanding pace he set the year before with superior reports on the Soviet Party Congress. He followed day-to-day personnel shifts as well as drawing back with analytical overviews of the latest "new reality" by measuring it against real events. "Gorbachev on the Soviet Economy: A Flock of Innovative Ideas," 2-27, and "Gorbachev's Fast Start Puts New Team in Charge," 2-24, identified the new margin — Gorby's personnel changes was the easy stuff, pressing change in the economy is the harder reality. "Afghan War, After Six Years, Becomes a Soviet Fact of Life," 2-18, was the best of anyone on this, revealing the brooding anger of the vets coming back home. His Chernobyl coverage was more than competent, straining to go beyond the imposed limits. A follow-up, "Chernobyl Fallout: Apocalyptic Tale and Fear," 7-26, impressive. From one of his year's best, in advance of Reykjavik, "Gorbachev Puts Russia's Best Face Forward," 10-12: "The Iceland meeting gives him a chance to elude the ideologues in Mr. Reagan's entourage, to appeal directly to the pragmatist in the President, and to do so without pressure for an immediate, tangible result."

Schumacher, Edward
The New York Times. (★)

Madrid. A mixed year, with a weakness on economy handicapping his reporting on Spain and Portugal. "Spain's New Face," 6-22, Sunday magazine, a timely, focused profile of Felipe Gonzalez: "he has abandoned the ideology of the old Spanish left and replaced it with large doses of pragmatism and moderation." — though it left too many stones unturned. Far inferior, "Back on Top in Portugal," 2-18, a profile of Mario Soares that offered no clue as to how Soares went from last place to victory in four months. "Power to the Provinces, To a Point," 9-21, on decentralization in Spain, the ironic contradictions illuminated. In and around Libya also during '86, "Dissatisfaction with Qaddafi Reported Rising in Libya," 9-7, the best of the genre during that period. Moved to New York, December '86.

Seib, Gerald R.
The Wall Street Journal. (★ ★ ★ ½)

Among the best foreign correspondents in the U.S. press, sometimes so far ahead of the curve that later accounts of the same material still seem fresh. "Yamani Gets His Wings Clipped," 3-14, a dazzler, with great quotes on the Sheik's backyard problems we remembered in November when he got fired. "Why the Saudis Won't Back Down Soon," 4-8, connects the U.S. bull market with enhanced Saudi assets, political relief. In "Unity Rule Brings Stability to Israel," 5-1, we can sense Seib groping to understand why such a lack of burning issues divides the two elitist parties. "Religious Discord Rises Among Israeli Jews," 6-18, a front-page pathbreaker on the passionate conflicts between the secular-religious factions, with political implications for the entire region. Friedman of the *NYT* follows up a month later.

Serrill, Michael
Time. (★)

Staff writer. Tends to take a lot for granted in his writing in the way he manipulates words. In "Moscow Takes A Hostage," 9-15, he reports "The ruse [Daniloff's arrest and subsequent detention] was such a ham-handed throwback, so lacking in artful subtlety." He's done a professional job though, and we'll continue to watch in '87.

Sherwell, Chris
Financial Times. (★)

Manila. A cut above wire services in getting beneath an economy. Good on laying out the challenges facing the Aquino reqime, in "A Hundred Days, A Hundred Dangers," 5-22, but rather late. Also lagging with "Six Months Will Tell," 7-19, a disappointingly glossy treatment of Cory Aquino. Did Sherwell catch the only known IMF-sanctioned tax reform in the world, in June? We didn't see anything. He misses any explanation of *why* the economy "remains in its worst shape since the devaluation," except that "tariffs protecting domestic industries have to be lowered," and socialist enterprises are losers. But this was all true before.

Sieff, Martin
The Washington Times. (★ ★ ★)

Soviet Union & Middle East. Assistant foreign desk editor. A *Times* stringer in '85, Sieff's reporting from Northern Ireland was impressive. Brought onto the foreign desk as assistant editor and as editor for Soviet and Middle East news, his '86 efforts were characterized by solid craftsmanship, broad and deep knowledge, and incisive reporting. Out ahead on several fronts with new information and insights beyond the conventional, he's helped to significantly upgrade *The Washington Times*' foreign reporting. Notable on the USSR, "Soviet Navy Can Tie Up 16 Sea Gates," 2-19, reported elsewhere, but no one provided analysis as did Sieff; likewise "Christian Refusniks Plead to West for Help," 2-24, and "Orgakov's Return Casts Doubts on Theories of Disgrace," 3-18. From the Middle East, "Mubarak Uneasy About Right Hand Man's Popularity," 4-29, much fuller treatment of Egypt's Defense Minister Abu Ghazala than anyone else; and " 'Return to Islam,' Poor Economy Put Mubarak on the Spot," 5-5, a profile of Sheik Omar Abdel-Rahman's fundamentalist offensive. The first foreign byline we look for in *The Washington Times*, he's a standout in the foreign press corps.

Simon, Bernard
Financial Times. (★)

Canada. A sophisticated analysis, "Canada Waits for a Signal from U.S. Democrats," 11-13, shows how U.S. protectionism helped the opponents of free-trade agreements, though more Canadians than ever back such agreements with the U.S. "Canadian Dollar Falls to Fresh Low," 2-4, failed to come up with reasons, like capital escaping Canada's new tax surcharge.

Smith, William
Time. (★ ½)

Senior writer. He gives a real sense of what he reports on, even though he works out of the States using dispatches from primarily South African correspondents. Two good pieces: "Carnage Once Again," 9-15, a comprehensive overview of the Karachi skyjacking, and "Life Behind the Walls," 7-14, a haunting portrait of division in South Africa.

Southerland, Daniel
The Washington Post. (★ ★)

Peking bureau. A bright reporter, abreast of the China dynamic. A particularly close watch on Sino-Soviet relations, starting with "China Hardens View on Ties to Moscow," 1-17, and "Chinese to Try Soviet in Hijacking," 2-21, reporting at the time that despite Russia's overtures, Peking remained an unimpressed suitor. Equally attentive to the '86 policy shifts on the mainland, as in "China Warns on Economic Crime," 1-20. Cautious, he doesn't muff much, but sometimes lags in advancing a perspective of where it's all going. That's illustrated in one of his year's best, an interview with Hu Yaobang that had us hungering for some analytical follow-up. "Party Leader Says China to Extend Economic Reform," 9-24, quoting Hu's answer why Chinese youth were losing faith in the party: "I think it's not only in China, but also a worldwide phenomenon....The image [of socialism] is not too good, because...first economic development has not been very fast. Second, there have been problems politically speaking, in the field of democracy and in the field of human rights."

Spaeth, Anthony
The Wall Street Journal. (★ ★)

Manila (*Asian WSJ*). Spaeth's election-eve wrap-up, 2-7, on Marcos/Aquino election was the best produced in that hothouse atmosphere — detached, detailed, complete, the only account that noted signs of Marcos' strength on election eve. He's a bit clumsy, though, in handling economic issues: "Philippines Laying Foundation for Economic Reform" (6-9, Asian edition), is only fair on detail, lacking opposition views. An interview with Central Banker Jose Fernandez is also light on issues facing him, 6-16. He's still trying, though. Better on straight politics, as in "Enrile Criticism of Aquino Upsets Philippine Politics," 10-23, with colorful detail on the defense minister, Juan Ponce Enrile, "His weekly schedule includes regular stops at certain coffee shops and hotel lounges, where he holds court." A feature on the new bigshots in the Aquino government casually selling off state properties is memorable as Spaeth mentions one "drinking a midmorning Scotch." Marvelous touch.

MediaGuide

Sparks, Allister
The Washington Post. (★ ★ ½)

Johannesburg. Impressive with hard work in serving up both context and background, with a sense for what the reader needs to understand, not just the event being reported but its placement in the broader scope of South Africa's story in '86. Several outstanding reports at the beginning of the year alerted us to the value of his work. When the Moutsie reserve exploded with violence, it wasn't until we saw his series of reports (among them, "Tribes Battle Over Homelands Merger," 1-3) that we could understand why that historically peaceful area was thrown into the maelstrom. Sparks makes efforts to tell the story, without letting any personal bias intrude, as for example in "Botha Calls Raids 'First Installment'," 5-22, and "Rightists Defy S. African Vow to Hold Banned Rally," 5-24. With William Claiborne now reporting also from South Africa, we anticipate an even better year from this bureau in '87. His best, [first runner-up in 10-best foreign stories of '86] "Jackson Scores Points in South Africa," 9-1, a splendid account of the Rev. Jesse's tour.

Sterba, James P.
The Wall Street Journal. (★)

Assistant foreign editor. The paper had him running around the globe for a good part of the year, getting "looks" at this and that. His reports were of the quality of the travel section of *The New York Times*, not bad, but hardly worth the front-page treatment. We got a look at Vanuatu, a Pacific island chain "where they drink kava," 1-10. We caught him again in Auckland, N.Z., 3-5 ("Think of the South Pacific. Paradise usually springs to mind.") Okay with "Peking's Streets Teem With Merchants Again," 6-16, but it was teeming with merchants when we were there in September 1983. Another front-page leader, "Foreign Firms Tired of Meager Payoffs in China," 7-21, lagged John F. Burns' better *NYT* account of 6-8. We wonder if his news judgment is up to his important foreign-desk slot.

Stockton, William
The New York Times. (★)

Mexico City bureau chief in '86. Moved to New York, 12-86, Stockton simply cannot handle economic issues. This was also painfully apparent in '85, but the economy was the heart of Mexico's '86 story, shaping the context of all else. So even his reports on political developments, foreign relations, sociocultural issues, were routine at best, and distortedly misinformed often. He accepts the IMF assumptions without question, "A Delicate Balance in Mexico," 6-13. "Mexico Tries An Open-Door Policy," 2-16, tells it all in the headline. A cut above the wires with "Significant Vote Looms for Mexico," 6-8, as National Action Party challenges one-party rule. Better with "An Economy Struggles to Break its Fall," 6-8, with "Dead men don't pay debts." In his contribution to the *Times*' October series on Mexico, "Hard-Hit Mexico Tries to Cope," 10-23, he offered a feeble overview via an assessment of President de la Madrid of what had gone on there all year. His worst of '86, "A Subway Jolt for the Mexicans," 8-1, weeping over a boost in the subway fare to three cents, not mentioning it had been eight cents pre-inflation.

Suro, Robert
The New York Times. (★ ½)

Rome. With former Rome bureau chief E.J. Dionne moving back to the U.S., we'll probably see more from this correspondent. Some early year reports on the Mafia trials in Sicily 2-9 and 2-21 were well-done, their historic importance located. From Venice, "A Volcker Trade Gap Warning," 9-1, alert, reporting the Fed Chairman's warnings against seeking a weaker dollar. "Pope Reinforcing Clerics in Dispute with Sandinistas," 9-4, tight, solid material on the Pontiff-Managua wrangle, not a church-state dispute, but a matter of human rights. Not making it, however, "John Paul's Economic Compassion," 9-7; noting the Pontiff's "pro-labor stance has led him to sharp criticism of free markets," Suro overdoes it.

Tamayo, Juan
The Miami Herald. (NR)

Jerusalem bureau. Among the regional press, the *Herald* caught our notice with its solid Central American coverage and focused editorials. We singled out for special acknowledgement, Tamayo's Managua dispatches, "World Leftists Find a Haven in Nicaragua," and "Sandinistas Attract a Who's Who of Terrorists," 3-3, gutsy, detailed, four-star investigative reporting on Nicaragua's nest of international terrorists that left the national press in the dust.

Taubman, Philip
The New York Times. (★ ★)

Moscow. No. 2 man, he skyrocketed in '85 with features galore and a ★ ★ ★ rating. Come the New Year and he fell off the table, at least relatively. We searched for his byline and when it did appear, it was over merely good material. "Classless Soviet Far Off, Paper Says," 1-27, and "Reagan's Speech Gets Scathing Review in Soviet," 2-6, covered the basics of both issues, but without the broader scope of detail and analysis of his previous political reporting. "Oil's Decline Seen Curbing Soviet Plans," 3-10, was late, however, *CSM*'s David Francis there a month earlier, though some new info was folded in. Better, "Soviet Announces Decision To Trim Its Afghan Force," 7-28, and "Soviet Diplomacy Given a New Look Under Gorbachev," 8-10. Slack in '86, but with a little more rigor for details and analytical scope, we think he'll snap back.

MediaGuide 215

Taylor, Walter A.
U.S. News & World Report. (★ ★ ½)

Singapore bureau chief. One of the best bylines in the magazine's foreign section, with good material on Pakistan, "Pakistan's Violent Turn," 9-1; the Philippines, "Aquino Comes Calling With Eye on U.S. Help," 9-22 and "In Aquino's New Charter, a Problem for the U.S.," 10-27. Best we saw in '86, "Democratic Drumbeat is Heard in Seoul," 4-14, thorough, accurate, holding up extremely well against later accounts of his competitors. On-target reporting and interpretations, maybe he's the guy to run the foreign desk.

Temko, Ned
The Christian Science Monitor. (★ ★ ★ ½)

Johannesburg. We found him to be the most consistently reliable source of information on South Africa in 1986. His dispatches appearing almost daily all year, he was everywhere — in the townships, the homelands, on the veld, at the mines, etc. Among the many fine reports, we cite: "End to S. Africa 'Pass Laws' Tests Climate for Black-White Dialogue," 4-24; "Educating S. African Blacks," 4-25; "Mandela: Focus of S. African Political Debate," 5-8; "Cracks in Apartheid's Foundation," 6-12; each the best in the press on the issue. Always on his toes, as with "Pretoria Hopes Rise of Gold Price Will Quell Unrest," 9-2, there was very little he missed. Rigorously free from any hint of partisanship, he was the unmatched journalist on the beat. His only shortcoming, the failure to produce a piece that "gestalted" the country's story for 1986, the way Anthony Robinson of the *Financial Times* did. An effort along those lines, "Building Apartheid's Pillars," 6-11, from his series "Afrikaners: The Trek Continues," didn't make it.

Tenorio, Vyvyan
The Christian Science Monitor. (★)

New Delhi. Working the sub-continent, so-so on Pakistan and India coverage. "India's Punjab Quieter, But Tensions Deepen," 4-4, for example, gives some details behind the upheavals there, but not enough to satisfy. Better, her work from Sri Lanka, "Gulf Widens Between Sri Lankan Government and Rebel Tamils," 4-16, and "Aura of Prosperity Masks Sri Lanka's Economic Decline," 9-30.

Thomson, Robert
Financial Times. (★ ½)

Peking. A workmanlike year, no more, no less, our entries on his material ranging from fair to good at the extremes. "The Revolution That Shamed China," 7-26, grabs us with the headline, and we're let down with the meager analysis. Bread and butter stuff okay: "China Plans to Reduce Imports This

Year," 3-27, and "China's Tough Import Curbs Add to Tension With Japan," 6-24. "China Pays the Price for Year of Rapid Expansion," 4-30, (with Colina McDougall in London) carried a misleading headline. It was a solid survey of the results of a deliberate policy shift, involving import restrictions and inflation (devaluation): "Attempts to slow economic growth...have backfired and there is now a danger of economic stagnation." Increases in industrial production slowed from 18% to 4% a year. Also good on Hu Yaobang prepping for his trip to London, the Communist Party General Secretary apologizing for being "weak on economics," in "The Long March in the Shadow of Deng," 6-7.

Thurow, Roger
The Wall Street Journal. (★★)

Johannesburg. Early in the year covering central Europe, "Poland Finds Economic 'Reforms' Don't Necessarily Produce Results," 2-27, well-done, with good details and analysis. But we'll have to wait for '87, to see if his South Africa reporting gets beyond the wading-in stage. In '86, it was shallow and thin. "Sanctions Force South Africa to Rely On Itself to Achieve Economic Growth," 9-18, reported differing perspectives and debate over "inward industrialization," okay as a quick roundup, but inadequate depth. "Despite Cocky Pose, South African Firms Admit Concern About U.S. Sanctions," 10-7, not much deeper, nor any fresh new info. "South African Town's Apartheid Vote Became More Than It Bargained For," 10-2, was trivial and very stale: "In South Africa, even the sporadic local efforts to clear away petty apartheid — the segregated beaches, buses and other facilities — often meet strong citizen opposition."

Treaster, Joseph
The New York Times. (½★)

Port-au-Prince. Chance of a reporter's career, a major revolution going off around him, but he's barely a step above wire-services, perhaps overwhelmed. Likewise, developments in the Caribbean escape his notice; Grenada's part of his beat, but he hasn't found a story worth note yet. Barely able to provide useful material on post-Duvalier Haiti. "Protests in Haiti Said to Continue," 2-2, could have been a press release, and we learned more from Gwertzman's piece from D.C. "Haiti Looks to U.S. For Aid and Comfort," 2-16, a bit better, but still two-dimensional. Covering the Grenada murder trial of 17 accused of killing PM Maurice Bishop in '83 comes out, "To Ordeal in Grenada, Add a Trial," 7-28, lackluster writing and information. What does he need? Okay with "Grenada Now Sunnier, With Calypso on Its Mind," 8-11.

Truell, Peter
The Wall Street Journal. (★ ★ ★)

London. Truell's 10-1-85 account, "Mexico is Likely to Get Longer-Term Lending if It Accepts Austerity," wasn't matched in '86 by anyone in conceptual thoroughness, and we're dismayed that this talent is wasted on the relatively minor, micro City beat. He's sterling at what he does, "British Central Bank Used Borrowing To Disapprove of Banks in China Offer," 10-18, and "U.K.'s Regulatory Rush Vexes 'Big Bang'," 10-7, two examples of what he can do in low gear. But he's *probably* the only talent Dow Jones has to match Peter T. Kilborn of *The New York Times* or Bart Rowen of *The Washington Post* on the geopolitical banking beat.

Walsh, Mary Williams
The Wall Street Journal. (★ ★ ★)

Mexico City. The disintegration of the Mexican economy, fraying of the social fabric and human exodus was one of the biggest stories of the year, handled abysmally and antiseptically by most of the press. Walsh was an exception, finding ways to tell us the country has reached its limit. "Ailing Mexico Tries to Placate Its Creditors and Working Class," 2-12, and "Political Tide," 2-20, catch the brewing desperation, the hope that maybe democracy can bring economic answers. The almost complete erosion of a once great institution in "Hard Times Hit Mexico's State University," 10-31, is almost hard to believe. "As Debt Turmoil Ebbs and Flows in Mexico, Human Misery Persists," 6-12, with S. Karene Witcher, was the most important single article to appear on Mexico during the year, an incredible picture of the horror stalking the country, widely read on the *Journal*'s front page by the relevant policymakers. "A whole region is being pushed backward, so that what was once the middle class now plunges toward poverty, and what was once the poorer class now lives hand to mouth...Nearly half of those in the working class have now cut back on meat — and that much of what they do serve is viscera... Those squeezed hardest in the coils of austerity are beginning to show their feelings...."

Weisman, Steven
The New York Times. (★)

New Delhi. From the White House to the subcontinent in 1985, he started fast and we expected big things from one of Abe Rosenthal's fair-haired lads. But he simply missed too much in '86, shying away from India's economy, the big story along with Rajiv's problems with the Old Guard. Instead, we got, "A Festival of Classical India Dancing," 3-17, and (no kidding) "A Hospital for Fighting Nightingales," 4-3. He's not flipped out entirely. Okay, with a pre-election wrapup, albeit thin on issues, in "Bangladesh Regime's Resolve Tested," 5-7, and "Struggle in Pakistan," 9-21, the return of Benazir Bhutto, plus "The 'Islamization' of Pakistan," 8-10. But we didn't expect rinky-dink from this hitter. His big outing "The Rajiv Generation," 4-20, Sunday magazine, fizzled.

Whitaker, Mark
Newsweek. (★)

A senior writer assigned to the foreign arena, mostly to South Africa and related stories. He's showed some improvement over the year restraining his use of outrageous language and including more and more interesting tidbits. We noted particularly "South Africa's '1984'," 6-30, "South Africa: Shifting Tactics," 7-14, and "Super Power Hardball," 8-18.

Whitley, Andrew
Financial Times. (★)

Tel Aviv. Better than most on non-economic issues. In "War Talk Grows in Syria and Israel," 5-13, Israel expects Syrian attempt to grab Golan Heights; Syria expects an Israeli attack on Syrian missiles. But superficial reports on the Israeli economy: "Israeli Economy Healthier But Not Cured," 7-7, or "Peres Tames Inflation but Growth Pains Linger," 10-8. Not enough to quote an anonymous government economist saying "Israel has got used to no growth in recent years....and the government does not know how to start the engines." Why not ask Michael Bordo, head of Israel's central bank or Don Patinkin, a famous economist at Hebrew University? Why not ask a few shopkeepers and workers "how to start the engines?" The criticism is generic, and applies with at least as much force to most other foreign correspondents, who merely keep a scorecard on official statistics.

Williams, Dan B.
Los Angeles Times. (½ ★)

Mexico. No *ole*! for the *LA Times*' Mexico coverage. Williams did not dig very deeply in '86, the information provided generally stale news, meager on details, thin on analysis. "Mexican Crisis May Shift Focus to Private Sector," 3-31, a not fully accurate or perceptive historical analysis of Mexico's road to crisis, was very sparse with details on the debate over economic "structural reform." "Mexico Returns to Coping With Economic Woes," was an update on the worsening crisis, but the pictures of both the Baker Plan and the IMF's were skimpy. No new information in "Mexico Woes Reflected in U.S. Border Towns," 6-30: "For the poor, it's almost tradition to go north," a story that's been told over and over in the press. "Ruling Mexican Party Faces Tough Battle in Chihuahua State Balloting," 7-5, covering the most hotly-contested election in 60 years, gave us zip on the program of the opposition National Action Party.

MediaGuide

Wysocki, Bernard Jr.
The Wall Street Journal. (★ ★)

Tokyo bureau. Grappling with the yen rise and trade flows, Wysocki tried to get inside the issue in '86. "Trade Cloud," 3-21, quotes a Japanese estimate that "even a 30% to 40% rise in the yen's value would pare Japan's export volume only 4% to 5%," and in examining why the yen appreciation wouldn't impact trade flows as some expected, stays clear of suggesting the Japanese had to do more. It was good to see the *Journal* running that as its front-page news leader. On other subjects: "Reaching Out," 1-7, comprehensive and detailed on sensitive aspects of Korean-Japanese relations, as the latter grows wary of Korea's strategy to go high-tech. "Getting Oriented," 3-24, on the new fad in Japanese corporations — hiring a token westerner, intriguing with its picture of how the new hires adjust to a new way of life. And "Barren Ground," 7-9, on Christian missionaries competing with Buddhism and Shintoism, offered some illumination on Japan's cultural grip. A very timely piece with new information, "Japan's Nakasone Picks New Cabinet, Appoints Rival to be Finance Minister," 7-23, a report that Minister Miyazawa's perspective of stimulating the economy via public-works programs, financed by tax hikes, could throw a clinker into proposed tax reforms.

Younghusband, Peter
The Washington Times. (★ ★ ½)

South Africa correspondent. Replacing Michael Sullivan as *The Washington Times*' South Africa reporter early in '86, Younghusband had already attracted out attention in 1985, with reporting that stood out when he was *Newsweek*'s Capetown correspondent. Alert, and providing information or new angles missed elsewhere, he kept *The Washington Times* an important source of fresh information on South Africa in 1986. A series of reports in June covered that convulsive period well: "Pretoria Bans Gatherings to Avoid Violence," 6-5, reported the escalation of terrorism and targetting of black moderates by radical forces prior to Botha's crackdown; "ANC Tempts S. Africa to Reapply Martial Law," 6-9, very timely reporting on ANC's strategy to cut off any progress for reform options. "Tutu Outburst Stuns Diplomats, Churchmen," 7-24, on the "The West can go to hell" advice, revealed another side of the Bishop not much covered elsewhere. "Sanctions? Insiders Hint They'll Be Broken," 9-9, dug deep, coming up with news of Japan and Taiwan ready to swoop into any sanctions vacuum. We rely on his material, so we hope his 10-9 analysis of South African reactions to the U.S. sanctions, was an isolated aberration; angry and preachy, his emotions intruded.

NATIONAL SECURITY/DIPLOMATIC CORRESPONDENTS

Andrews, Walter "Bud"
The Washington Times. (★ ★ ½)

Defense. Producing tight, informed pieces that complement the *Times'* overall effort to bolster national security coverage in areas ignored by the *Post*. Standout pieces include "Military-Recruit Pool Dries Up, But Metcalf Says Navy Can Cope," 6-26. The interview with Deputy CNO serves as a backdrop for cogent analysis of demographic problems facing military, with implications for the future of AVF (return of the draft a subtheme). Also, "Gorbachev Apparently Needs Nuclear Accord, Colby Says," 7-18, says more about the predilection among some experts (Colby and Walter Slocombe are mentioned) for Wishful Kremlinology than it does about Gorbachev's "needs."

Brinkley, Joel
The New York Times. (−)

State Department. We cited Brinkley in the *1986 MediaGuide* as one of the up-and-coming new crop of aggressive *Times*men, but were troubled by his 4-84 piece alleging top to bottom CIA control of Costa Rica and his 6-85 front-pagers warning of an imminent U.S. invasion of Nicaragua. Neither was responsible journalism, certainly not worthy of a Pulitzer winner (1980 for international reporting). Our worst fears were realized with his report, "Marcos' War Record Discredited in U.S. Files," 1-23, with Jeff Gerth. A twisted, heavily massaged EXPOSE! of selected postwar records that slandered Marcos, who, whatever he did later, was a genuine WWII hero who received the Distinguished Service Cross, America's second highest military decoration for "extraordinary heroism" in 1942, which the Brinkley "expose" never mentioned. Appearing two weeks before the election, the front page piece did more to poison the climate in the U.S. against Marcos than anything else that had appeared, laying the foundation for the post-election charges that Marcos had stolen the election. Luckily, the crisis ended without full-scale bloodshed or civil war.

Broad, William
The New York Times. (★ ★ ½)

Science, Technology, with a new focus on SDI/ASAT/"militarization" of space Embodies the current labor pains in *The New York Times* over SDI, since Broad's pieces are becoming more even-handed on the technology involved and its spinoffs. One can still see old traces in pieces such as "CIA Disputes White House on Soviet Anti-Missile Gain," 5-29, which makes much policy ado over minor bureaucratic flaps. And he was behind the curve on "NASA Official Advised Against Liftoff," 11-5, since Rogers' report and other stories already covered the intrigues and finger-pointing surrounding the shuttle. But he was on a steep upward curve in 1986. Two of his best we saw in '86: "Newest Titan

Groomed as Rival for Shuttle," 5-20, a carefully reported, comprehensive development widely read in the aerospace industry; "Star Wars Traced to Eisenhower Era," 10-28, digs back into the history of strategic defense and writes the book for us — an automatic must reference for every term paper on the subject!

Carrington, Tim
The Wall Street Journal. (★ ½)

Pentagon reporter with feet fully wet now, makes up in hustle and style what he lacks in defense expertise. *WSJ* emphasizes defense stories underreported elsewhere, as illustrated by Carrington's leader, with Bill Richards, "Controversy Grows Over Pentagon's Work On Biological Agents," 9-17, an issue that will soon be much discussed. Also good on dovetailing with the budget, "All Agree Gramm-Rudman-Hollings Will Increase Costs, Harm Efficiency," 12-26-85, was the best of the kind. His front page "U.S. Raid on Libya Called Military Success," 4-21, was among his best of the year. He disappointed on SDI issues, shy on homework perhaps. With "Star Wars Scientists Aren't as Hopeful," 3-31, he should have done more than rewrite the press release on this report to three Democratic senators. A young, aggressive up and comer.

Corddry, Charles
Baltimore Sun. (★ ½)

With the *de facto* retirement of Drew Middleton, Corddry assumes the mantle of dean of the Washington Pentagon press corps. May be a regular on "Washington Week," but generally he is the most sensible Conventional Wisdom-giver. A sound piece on Star Wars I (population defense) vs. Star Wars II (missile sites), "Senate Panel Urges Shift in SDI goals," 6-29, outlining confused and contentious positions within the Administration without trashing the idea of defense. Also good on the Pelton case ramifications, 6-11, and pre-Reykjavik maneuverings, 8-4. But weak on Soviet arms control violations, 7-20, relying on only one source (Michael Drepon) from outside government. Sometimes he *is* his own best source.

Cushman, John H., Jr.
The New York Times. (★)

Pentagon. Moving over to the *Times* from *Defense Week*, the excellent industry trade magazine, we expected a lot from Cushman. He seemed to bring with him a predilection for trendy issues. "One Whom the Revolving Door Hit," 7-25. There seemed a little too much following on the trail of press releases issued by anti-defense Congressmen, not as much hard digging as we thought there would be. "Research on Bio Warfare Is Challenged," 9-3, was well-written and balanced, albeit on the trendy path. His piece on the budget pressures hitting the Israeli jetfighter, the Lavi, with mind-numbing cost overruns, 6-18, one of his best in '86, concurrent with *Forbes*' Hesh Kestin, 6-30, pub date.

Davidson, Ian
Financial Times. (★ ★)

London. Perhaps it's his vantage point, but he does seem to develop clever angles in pondering global diplomacy. "Questions for Mr. Gorbachev," 3-24, offers fresh insights on the Euromissile gambit and suggests Soviets perhaps have second thoughts on SDI. He posits a possible European arms verification role in "Who Will Police the Policeman," 6-2, scalds Maggie for a weak anti-SA sanctions stance, "No Tactics, No Strategy, No Doubts," 6-23, and adds good Commonwealth statistics in other sanctions commentary, "Sir Geoffrey Steers Clear of the Rocks," 7-21. His post-Reykjavik punditry, "At the Headland of History," 10-27, could be zippier, but makes the case that French Chauvinism and British Atlanticism "have both been serious obstacles to the evolution of viable European policies, and have helped perpetuate Europe's dependence on the superpowers," which the fresh winds from Iceland may change. "Illusions of the Left," 9-15, calms anxieties about European defense, so long as "the U.S. administration keeps reasonable control of its anti-communist instincts."

Engleberg, Steven
The New York Times. (★ ★ ½)

Very young for a *Times* reporter with a major beat (intelligence) picking up experience fast. Fair, accurate and balanced, just needs depth. A nice job on "Slow Pace Seen for Revamping Security Policies," 7-28, examining the depth of the espionage problem and citing $80 billion a year as prohibitive cost of rechecking all clearances. "State Department Opposed U.S. Efforts to Cut Soviet Presence, Aides Say," 10-7, explaining why left and right hands don't know what's up during expulsion of Soviet UN employes. His peripheral work on the Iranian arms/hostage controversy was noteworthy for its cool, which we appreciated, especially "Iranian Named as Key Intermediary," 11-14, very professional communique. We'll watch for his efforts on upcoming Iran/Intelligence hearings, where he should become a star. Skeptical of old boys, but respectful of knowledgeable intelligence sources, Engelberg was shining with the Pelton trial, 5-25, 29 & 6-3. A scoop on "Contra" radio, 11-5, shows some bias, some investigatory zeal.

Fialka, John
The Wall Street Journal. (★ ½)

A careful, seasoned pro who moved over to the *Journal* after *The Washington Star* folded up shop, Fialka covered a variety of subjects in 1986. A 3-20 effort, "White House Claims of Soviet Test Ban Cheating Are Challenged by New Bomb Detection System," assessing test ban verifications, wasn't his standard form, too narrow in the range of sources employed, the architects of the Administration's policy ignored. Much better, "Army Engineer's Anti-Tank Missile Idea Proves Cheap, Reliable — and Tough to Sell at Pentagon," 4-30,

MediaGuide

an insightful angle on the consequences of bureaucratic mindsets. One of his best, a feature outside his usual beat "Sisters in Need," 5-19: "The nation's Roman Catholic bishops, who for two years have been deliberating how to improve the moral quality of the U.S. economy, are facing a large moral problem in their own economic house: the looming poverty of increasing numbers of Catholic nuns." A two-part series, "Mexico: Drugs and Corruption," 11-19 and 11-20, comprehensive, well-organized, absorbing on the grid of graft and lure of the U.S. market.

Fink, Donald E.
Aviation Week & Space Technology. (★★)

Editor. The replacement for retired editor William Gregory, Fink hasn't quite mastered the "reported-editorial" format that made *AW&ST*'s editorial page the always-must-read item for the industry. The quality slipped some in '86, particularly earlier in the year, as in "The ATC Crisis," 3-31, and "Resolve With Restraint," 4-14 (post Libya-raid assessment), both flat, no new information. He scored later in the year, though. Among them: "U.S. Launcher Crisis," 4-28, tough on NASA and DOD, incisive, to the point — "the U.S. is grounded on both coasts now;" "Space Business Challenge," 6-30, one such, trying to get U.S. competitive juices off dead center and flowing again; "NASA After Challenger," 6-9, tight, on-focus synopsis of shuttle report, identifying still existing pitfalls; "Who's In Charge?" 7-28, one of the best summaries in all the press of tasks and perspectives of U.S. space program.

Fontaine, Roger
The Washington Times. (½ ★)

Former NSC staffer, former American Enterprise Institute scholar, bright and hard worker, still needs seasoning as journalist. Former colleagues haven't become the great inside sources he (and his editors) might have thought. A look at Radio Marti, "Builds Audiences, Wins Critics," 5-20, an okay op-ed column. Best we saw, his account of "O'Neill Defends His Mission," 4-11, on Tip's Argentina trip and the clash with Ambassador Frank Ortiz, Jr.

Gelb, Leslie
The New York Times. (★★½)

Now assistant editorial page editor, Gelb was national security correspondent in 1986 with unsurpassed sources, knowledge and style. He got his start in all this as a staff aide to Jacob Javits in the '60s. A former Assistant Secretary of State in the Jimmy years, he has his own slant, with subtextual offerings closer to Zbig Brzezinski than to former boss Cy Vance. In "Reagan's Maneuvers," 3-27, he sees Reagan freer to act in believing Soviets are on the run. In "Daniloff and the Summit: A New Test for Reagan," 9-17, he sees RR in a no-win position, smart analysis, although RR somehow won. Also smart, "Resurgent Shultz: How a Comeback is Made," 7-21, on George inching his way back into control, which Reykjavik showed wasn't quite the case either. In "U.S. Sees Marcos Losing High Aides," 2-17, Gelb was proven right, but he had been played like a violin by his national security sources, who wanted to signal the anti-Marcos military faction to begin its move against him.

Gerstenzang, James
Los Angeles Times. (½ ★)

National security correspondent. Prolific, though he sometimes spreads himself too thin. Good sources, so-so instincts. Behind it on "Israel and US Sign Agreement on Star Wars," 5-7, and relied heavily on SDI critic John Pike for "Star Wars Leads All Defense Costs," 7-13.

Gerth, Jeff
The New York Times. (½ ★)

An erratic investigative reporter in national security/diplomatic matters, he can be objective or subjective from day to day, tempted by the big story. He co-authored with Joel Brinkley the sensational "Marcos' Wartime Role Discredited in U.S. Files," 1-23, a trumped up scandal that helped bring Marcos down. He also contributed to the Marcos-the-billionaire story with "Manila Has Data on Marcos Holdings," 3-9, leaning on Marcos' rival Steven Psinakis. But he is then flawlessly objective with "Marcos Wealth: Long Fight Expected," 4-1. He scored heavily later in the year with newsbeats linking the Saudis to the Iranian/Contra Arms Deals, first 11-23, then 11-30. It will take awhile before he gets us back, but he's pointed in the right direction.

Gertz, William
The Washington Times. (★ ★ ½)

The yeoman of Arnaud's guard, Gertz is a tireless reporter who can cover the waterfront. He may not have the style of Walter Lippmann, but he has common sense, good instincts, and a decent Rolodex. One of the reasons people who don't like the *Times* read it, with second-order newsbeats on security issues about once a week. Two pieces on the Pelton affair, a report, 5-26, and analysis, 6-2, ranks with some of his best pieces on Soviet arms control violations in '86, as in "Further Cheating By Soviets on Arms Control," 2-19.

Gordon, Michael
The New York Times. (★)

Strategic defense, formerly defense beat of the *National Journal*, with a subtle bias that has carried over to the *Times*, showing now on strategic matters. He's a devoted arms controller who feeds off the same old experts, as in "Experts Criticize Reagan Proposal for Weapons Cuts," 7-13. He's also quick with unbalanced accounts of all anti-Reagan reports issued by the arms-control community: "ABM Pact Tied to Fund Pledge for Star Wars," 5-19. In "Arms Goals: Flexibility and Firmness," 9-3, he rings up three advocates of the sign-any-treaty school — Alton Frye, Jack Mendelsohn and Walt Slocombe — and that's that. Throughout June and July he was hitting the front page with regularity on potential U.S. violations of SALT II, scarcely noting the Soviet cribs, and he surely must have learned by now that SDI isn't a leak-proof shield. His "A Bureaucrats War on Star Wars," 5-14, outlining Paul Nitze's last stand, and "A Gathering in Moscow That Proved Irresistible," 8-11, did demonstrate stylistic flair. But Gordon, hired as backup to Les Gelb, is now the lead man for the *Times* with Gelb moved to the editorial page. It won't do to keep grinding one side of the ax on this critical beat.

Greenberger, Robert S.
The Wall Street Journal. (★ ½)

Third string behind Walcott, Kempe at State, but he seems to have the talent for a starting slot. A back-pager 1-15 on Secretary Shultz's problems with the right, and his testiness, had those circles buzzing. "Liberals and Conservatives Seek a Foreign Policy Consensus," 3-31, is a few days behind Paul Taylor of *The Washington Post*, but with value-added. Most impressive we saw, buried inside, "Reagan Administration Gets Nervous As Soviet Union Woos Latin America," 11-17, with an interesting twist: "The wave of democracy that has swept across Latin America has brought with it new diplomatic opportunities for the Soviet Union and problems for the U.S. in its own backyard," i.e., democracies have replaced right wing dictatorships, and if they now falter, Soviets could be in position for left wing dictatorships. Should have been expanded for the front page.

Gregory, William
Aviation Week & Space Technology. (★ ★)

Boston bureau. Former editor of *AW&ST*, who made the magazine's editorial page the must-read-and-clip page for the industry, was retired to the Boston bureau. We didn't, therefore, see as much from him in '86, though he was still producing timely, informative reports during the year. Among them: "Medical X-Ray Measuring Device Finds Use in Explosive Detection," 4-28, on technology for protecting against terrorism; "Aerospace Firms' Financial Reports Underscore Industry Stability," 5-12, other press accounts dry on this; His crisp, "Government Weighs Value of Second-Source Procurement," 7-14, clear on motivation for cost-cutting via competition.

Gwertzman, Bernard
The New York Times. (★ ★ ★ ½)

Chief diplomatic correspondent and the best of what he does. We said a year ago that somehow he'd managed to stay out of the Secretary of State's hip pocket and continue to marvel at his professionalism, with the exquisite balance of a top wire service reporter and a depth we suspect gives him a subterranean view of the State Department. He's just shy of ★ ★ ★ ★ because he is so careful; we wish he'd push the analytical envelope, even if he misses at times. He practically covered the Haiti revolution from Washington, "Frustration Boils," 2-2, concise backgrounder, and after poking around charges of Marcos stealing zillions, 3-8, quotes a U.S. official: "There doesn't seem to be a smoking gun." His Reykjavik reporting was icily correct. We read every word of all of his dispatches in the Iranian controversy, "All Eyes on Shultz," 11-18, reinforcing our confidence that he has stayed at a proper distance from George's hip. As long as he's at State, the competition at Foggy Bottom is for second place.

Halloran, Richard
The New York Times. (★ ★)

Pentagon. The classic Pentagon reporter, sticking to weapons systems, defense reorganization and procurement issues. Minimal spin on his stories. He took a sabbatical to write a book, *To Arm a Nation: Rebuilding America's Endangered Defense*, Macmillan, 1986, not startling or original, but reliably thorough. Former paratrooper with the 82nd Airborne, Halloran is no-nonsense, but occasionally colorful, "Hyperbole and Grins," 4-18, on gleeful Pentagon briefers after the Tripoli raid was one such gem. Plenty of beef in "U.S. May Establish Afghan Rebel Ties," 6-18. In "U.S. Moving to Expand Unconventional Forces," 11-26, we get the latest in a long line of first class reportage and analysis on low-intensity conflict and special ops, sure 1987 buzzwords for other reporters on the defense beat.

Hiatt, Fred
The Washington Post. (½ ★)

Tokyo correspondent, but spent most of 1986 at the Pentagon. Energetic, he learned the proper lingo along with the art of backgrounding disgruntled losers in inter-agency quarrels, but blatantly slanted in his coverage of SDI, as "U.S. Resumes Program on Space Reactor," 4-14 and "Official Seeks Like Minds on 'Star Wars'," 5-13, attest. Both pieces fit the acceptable criteria at the *Post* for SDI exposes: the first deals with the "nuclear" bogeyman, second with the imposed groupthink on SDI contractors and scientists from "officials" in SDI. In "6,500 College Scientists Take Anti-SDI Pledge," 5-14, he swallowed a Rep. Brown press release without examining the numbers involved. Elsewhere we find many colleges couldn't get even half of their science departments to sign the pledge. Also, buried suspiciously deep in the piece is an acknowledgement of a *pro*-SDI scientist group. The *Post* chooses not to be serious on defense.

MediaGuide

House, Karen Elliott
The Wall Street Journal. (★ ★)

Foreign editor. The focus of her articles in 1986 was predominantly on the Middle East, intervening with timely analytical pieces on U.S. policy there during the year. Not prolific in '86, but so incisive that her articles were all widely read and discussed in policy circles. "The Gravest Show on Earth," 4-29, was a marvelous analytic, "The U.S. ought to try to play the role of ringmaster to the Mideast Circus," with reverberations long after it appeared. "Don't Expect Too Much From Efforts by Assad to Free Hostages," 5-16, another such, a sharp challenge to the White House's misreading of Assad's powers. But whereas those were hard and tough, more importantly they were thought-out. Not so "This Iran Policy Makes Carter's Look Good," 11-13. Shrill, hysterical almost, we see her venting immediate gut-feelings of outrage. But it is a mistake for a foreign editor to set that kind of a tone.

Kempe, Frederick
The Wall Street Journal. (★ ★)

Young diplomatic correspondent, his first year in Washington after covering Moscow very well from Vienna, a smooth stylist with a comprehensive approach. But the first big splash we saw, "U.S. Officials Want Marcos to Step Down," 2-18, with a string of anonymous quotes, played into the State Department manipulations of Manila via the press. A 4-22 report on "Reagan to Seek Marshall Plan for Middle East," was wire-service level, not the Kempe of Vienna. He didn't quite hit paydirt with "Reagan's Move on SALT II Could Lead to Effort to Loosen ABM Treaty," 6-2, but was right on target with "Divisions Slow Reagan Decision on Arms," 7-21, presaging the mishmash at Iceland. With his feet now planted, we expect the Kempe of yore.

Morrison, David
National Journal. (★)

Defense. A former staffer of the very partisan Center for Defense Information, the replacement for Michael Gordon is a hard worker. For example, the cover story "The Weekend Warriors," 2-1, examining the consequences of Total Force policy and the U.S. capacity to meet its military commitments in time of war. "The Pentagon's 'Black Budget'," 3-1, another cover, also showed hard work. But his hard work seems at times to be only on one side of the street. Are John Pike and William Arkin the only people in Washington who know anything about defense? His sources are so predictable that he invites suspicion that a bias is at work here. "ASAT Questions," 1-18, "Nuclear Bureaucracy Flunks a Test," 1-25, (on nuclear testing), "Nuclear Winter," 6-21, didn't cut it as balanced efforts. Improving though, with "Shooting Down Star Wars," 10-25, presenting some of the case being made for limited deployment.

Pincus, Walter
The Washington Post. (½ ★)

Strategic nuclear beat, plus an extra load while diplomatic correspondent Don Oberdorfer sabbaticals, Pincus moved up from "F" to "D" by marginal improvement in coverage of nuclear technology matters in 1986. But he's still part of the outmoded anti-defense zeitgeist at the *Post*, with favorite demons (the Pentagon's Richard Perle), clowns (Arms Control agency's Ken Adelman), and heroes (John Pike of anti-Star Wars Federation of American Scientists). But his material preaches to the diminishing converted. While some SDI technologies he played straight, a 4-18 piece on the Free Electron Laser, an important and promising SDI component, reads like a press release from the Union of Concerned Scientists, so narrow is its reach. The Soviet 'threat' always in quotes to Pincus, as in "Officials Debate Threat of New Soviet Missile, SS-24," 8-12. He frequently teams up with Lou Cannon, as in "Star Wars Compromise Discussed," 7-10, with a palpable hype for those wanting to trade SDI. A smart, smart fellow with great reporting skills. Because these issues are so crucial, the national debate so important, we'd read every word if he could only squeeze out the tilt. As it is he's wasted.

Sciolino, Elaine
The New York Times. (★ ½)

United Nations bureau chief. A skilled foreign correspondent with wide experience in Europe, she also produced high-quality reporting from the Middle East when she was the Rome bureau chief for *Newsweek*. And she stuck with it in 1986; "South Lebanon Is Called Explosive," 2-18, an example of her skill for taking on complex areas and coming up with fresh, new information. She also made some enemies there — Assad's security forces pulling her out of her hotel room and throwing her out of Syria earlier in the year. But her big effort in '86, a feature on Nicaragua's U.N. ambassador, Nora Astorga, 9-28, Sunday magazine, was incredibly out of character for Sciolino. Almost sycophantic, it was heavy on the PR charms of the lady and very soft on all else, perhaps merely reflecting a feminist bent.

Shenon, Philip
The New York Times. (★ ½)

Washington bureau. A young utility reporter who scores off and on, clearly on the way up as he learns the ropes, including basic skills of presentation. In "FBI Unit Tracing Some Disclosures to Press," 10-2, about the search for who are leaking classified information to the press, he has the bones of a good story, but doesn't seem to know how to present it. In "Doubts Cling to Pacific Assassination Verdict," 11-27, on the murder of Palau's first elected president, it takes a while for him to get rolling in an otherwise excellent report. Best we saw in '86, a story on "U.S. Officials [Against City Corruption]," 3-30, on how NYC Democratic officials back GOP prosecutors in fighting city corruption.

Summers, Col. H.G.
U.S. News & World Report. (★)

Senior military analyst with outstanding credentials for the job (see bio). Articulate, intelligent and informative, his best piece, "Military Reforms Hit at the Wrong Targets," on the attempts to reform the Joint Chiefs of Staff, appeared in the *Los Angeles Times*, 6-18: "those concerned with America's future security shouldn't kid themselves that such changes will produce anything close to a system [so perfect] where 'no one will have to be good.' Indeed, the Joint Chiefs of Staff had *better* be good if they're going to continue to make that still-flawed system work."

Talbott, Strobe
Time. (½ ★)

Washington bureau chief. Walter Mondale's favorite strategic expert, graduate of Eastern Establishment schools, Hotchkiss and Yale, excellent Russian translator, apparently solid bureau manager. His occasional pieces on arms control and US-Soviet relations, however, are usually predictable. Excessive attachment to background leaks from self-interested parties, his "America Plays Black," 8-4, is anti-Reagan sophistry that pales with the thoughtful critique of Reagan arms control policies by Lars-Erik Nelson. His "Grand Compromise," 6-23, proposal (trade SDI for an arms control agreement with the Soviets) not original, but well-presented. Talbott is so thoroughly identified as an SDI foe, he should quit as bureau chief and write a column, where his material could get very high marks.

Walcott, John
The Wall Street Journal. (★ ½)

State Department. He of the Libyan "disinformation" ploy, the article, "Collision Course," 8-26, (with Frederick Kempe) actually contained sufficient qualifiers and explanation of "psywar" elements in keeping Qaddafi off-balance. But burned on it, he went off course the rest of the year, his anger at the administration evident and coloring much of his work. Prior to the flap, Walcott, an '86 recruit from *Newsweek* looked sharp. A critical scoop, "US Analysts Find New Soviet Radars, Possibly Complicating Arms Pact Effort," 8-22, on legal periphery phased array radars just as dangerous as Krasnoyarsk violation, getting a great quote from violations apologist Michael Krepon, "It certainly helps worst-case thinking along." "Approach to Arms Control Combines Missile Reductions, Work on Defense," 10-20, a good job describing Reagan's SDI "vision," unaccountably fogs out on the "third side" of the debate. "Reagan Distrust of the Establishment Helped Create His Troubles Over Iran," 11-24, should never have slipped by his editors, Walcott's angry emotions all over it — Reagan couldn't count on the "mainstream" professionals at State, etc., so he sought to hornswoggle and manipulate the public. He'll be okay when he cools down.

Woodward, Bob
The Washington Post. (★)

Ben Bradlee's "snoop for a scoop" ace reporter, who has no apparent ideological bent, but agnostic on some journalistic standards. An 11-86 expose frightened the Egyptians away from a U.S. proposal for joint action against Libya. "U.S. Unable to Persuade Egypt to Back Plan for Joint Anti-Qaddafi Move," 4-2, bared the conflicting details of the eight-month secret efforts. A major scoop, the Administration's "disinformation" operation against Libya, "Gaddafi Target of Secret U.S. Deception Plan," 10-2, though overly harsh and unfair with the *Journal* for getting sucked in. A follow-up, "State Department Urged Libya Coup," 10-5, reveals his connections with top-level sources, unidentified, but all the relevant memos from State, NSC, etc. quoted. "Reagan Ordered Casey to Keep Iran Mission From Congress," 11-15, mostly stirring of already troubled waters, reporting the secret presidential order authorizing covert operations, 1-17. "Tale of Two White House Aides," 11-30, very sharp, perceiving through the Iran/Contra flap the battle over the Reagan agenda: "Poindexter's critics and friends seem to agree that some of the major policies have come out confused...also in shambles....the Middle East, arms control, South Africa and U.S.-Soviet relations."

MediaGuide

POLITICAL COLUMNISTS

Barnes, Fred
The New Republic. (★ ★ ★ ½)

Disparagingly referred to as "the conservative senior editor" of *TNR* by *The Washington Post*'s liberal columnist, Richard Cohen. Barnes' weekly column is not that easy to pigeonhole, but because he is 90% reporter and 10% commentator, his less-than-liberal ideological bent isn't obtrusive. His "Designated Scapegoat," 1-27, on the Beltway savaging of White House chief-of-staff Donald Regan was superb. A 2-10 "The Shaking of a President" was the best analytical curtain-raiser on the Philippine elections we saw (with Barnes in Manila). His "Running in Place," 3-3, was the first to observe Jack Kemp going nowhere fast in early '88 heats. "Senator Hackwood," 5-5, stung Senator Packwood and may have helped break the logjam on tax reform. "Flying Nunn," 4-28, misfired with Senator Sam getting too much halo. "Run, Bill, Run," 8-11 and 8-18, sounds a boomlet for Senator Bradley. "Conservatives and the Democratic 10," (*The American Spectator*, 9-86), offers 10 very sharp thumbnail sketches of the '88 Democratic contenders.

Barone, Michael
The Washington Post. (★ ★)

He's best when focused on the campaign trails, even when it's an "issueless" campaign, but we didn't see as much of him as we'd like in '86. Always early in spotting trends, and still at it, 10-12, on the vanishing of personal campaigning from statewide races, with added perspective on the liabilities of avoiding risks in the short-run, "Unfamiliar Waters Beyond the Campaign," 10-28. Solid with insight, "A Small Uptick for the Outparty," 11-6, on reelected Dem governors who were "asked for an encore because they've been singing some Republican tunes."

Broder, David
The Washington Post. (★ ★)

Dean of the political press corps, Broder slumped in '85, a non-election year, but his 1986 file was a pleasant, steadily productive surprise: more news bylines than we'd seen from him in years, plus his usual column output. His strength has always been his love of the political process — he enjoys being a combination cheerleader, talent scout and umpire. He got back to this mode after anguishing over the budget in '85. "The Post-Kennedy Dilemma," 12-24-85, covered the implications of Teddy's decision to stay out of '88. He led off a seven-part *Post* series on "Dixie Rising," 5-18, with an impressive front page effort. An interview with George Bush, 3-25, has the Veep saying he has differences with Reagan, but he won't say which! "The Dishonor of David Stockman," 4-16, is vintage

Broder, the Beltway referee calling a foul. "Reagan's Spring Slump," 3-26, is a handwringer over the absence of a budget. He gives Pierre DuPont a pat on the back for running for President, 9-21, chiding his colleagues for not taking a former successful governor seriously. His analysis of Jack Kemp's leadership on the tax bill, "The Right Signals," 9-2, saw subtleties that others missed. A typical Broder weakness: Every two years since 1963 he's been predicting that the election of moderate GOP governors will stop the party's rightward drift. It never happens. But there it is again, "Governors May Pull GOP to Middle," 10-26.

Broyles, William, Jr.
U.S. News & World Report. (★)

Eloquent contributing editor who seems to be trapped by his memories of Vietnam. He's written countless essays and a book on the subject, but still hasn't gotten it out of his system, and it colors every piece he writes. His writing itself though is wonderful: "These best and brightest young Americans appear not to want to add anything to their country, only to take. One imagines a world in which Imelda Marcos's hundreds of pairs of shoes are seen as success, not shame...What brings men and women to betray their country? The answer was as ordinary and predictable as on Wall Street: The petty, human emotions of lust, greed and revenge" ("At Last, Loyalty Makes the Headlines," 6-30). Again, in an essay describing the Vietnam Veterans Memorial ("A Ritual for Saying Goodbye," 11-10), "We left so much in Vietnam — so much innocence, so many dreams, so many good men and women...To lose those people and those dreams was like a death in the family, without a funeral to give focus to the grief and the emotions, without the ritual of saying goodbye. The Wall changed all that; it is about the dead, but not for them. It is for the living."

Cannon, Lou
The Washington Post. (★)

White House correspondent and "Reagan columnist" who we drubbed in last year's review for unacceptable bias *in reporting*, Cannon came back in '86 with acceptable bias. But Cannon, a veteran who knows how to cultivate sources, has had much better years. We flagged as useful a 4-9 story on Bush advisers' distress on the VP's oil-price remarks. A shrewd piece on "Senator Laxalt's...no known passion to be President," 3-3, citing the Nevada problem. Insightful "Success in Small Bites," 3-17, as Reagan chips away for Contras, tax reform. Good field report, "Reagan Disappoints Gorton Campaign," 11-1, as RR won't reconsider nuclear-dump site.

MediaGuide 233

Crozier, Brian
National Review. (★ ½)

Columnist and Contributing Editor. "A Britisher normally aghast at the feebleness of Western foreign policies," Crozier's "The Protracted Conflict" biweekly column gauges how close or how distant the U.S. comes in adopting "sensible foreign policy designed to ensure its own survival" against the advances of totalitarianism. A worried watch in '86, almost everywhere he looked, so much so that a tendency to come across as predictable shadowed his better efforts. But he's not hide-bound, and admits it when he's been off track, as in his reassessment of Mitterrand, "a leader [who] will go down in history as the man who broke the back of the Communist party, against the prognostications of the pundits, this one included," 5-21. And because he focuses on "what next?", there's always an edge to be gained from his work. His best, "South Africa: A Way Out," 8-1, pointing to federalism as the democratic alternative to "the trap of universal suffrage and the facile snare of majority rule," with the column widely discussed in U.S. foreign policy circles.

Evans, Rowland & Novak, Robert
Chicago Sun-Times. (★ ★ ★ ★)

The gold standard for political columnists, still the most influential in the world. At one time or another everyone in Washington is mad at the dynamic duo, especially Bob Novak, the Prince of Darkness, who never pulls a punch. A team for 25 years, their sources are the best because they're always mining among the up-and-comers left, right and center, never squeal on a leak, work inhuman hours, and intimidate with their excellence. Their biggest scoop of '86, "Backstage at the Fed," 3-17, on a secret 4-to-3 vote against Volcker, revealed the far-reaching realignment at the Fed and left the entire financial press eating dust. They're also ahead on the Strategic Defense Initiative, 7-7; Reagan and taxes, 1-13; GOP farm problems, 4-7; the rise of the evangelicals; conversion from center to right of Bob Dole and implications of the Senate elections. Accused at times of being cheerleaders for Rep. Jack Kemp, they seemed almost gleeful in reporting his '86 setbacks. Their syndicated column appears in both Washington and New York, the *Post* of each, and is *always* must reading.

Germond, Jack & Witcover, Jules
The Washingtonian. (★ ½)

Their *Baltimore Sun* five-a-week national political column is unique in that regard, but it isn't seen where it counts. They improved some in '86 where we saw them, these political horseplayers actually circling *ideas*. "Kennedy, You SOB!," 2-86, a quickly produced replacement for an intended "Why Kennedy's Running," was long on details of how political experts have been crossed by "candidates" in the past, but short on locating the meaning of Teddy's bowing out. "Hard Hitter," 3-86, acknowledges as a Cuomo asset his ability to bring old ideas alive, but quickly shifts from ideas to ponder the Mafia, religious and ethnic background, and the political mechanics of going from the state house to the White House. Their insight, "One of the lessons of Gary Hart's success was that going through the mechanical motions was far less important than catching the fancy of the TV networks." They didn't have a clue as to why Mikulski might win in Maryland in "Want to Fight?," 7-86. But they moved out front in "Kemporisms Grab 'Em," (*Baltimore Sun*, 3-31) and "Going out After Bush," 10-24, scenting some issues, pooh-poohing the polls, and ruminating on issues for a change. We detect some vitality here.

Harsch, Joseph
The Christian Science Monitor. (★)

The usual focus is on diplomatic issues, striving to discern patterns, but he was too laid-back and conventional to invite more than passing notice in '86. "Next Step?," 4-22, a shallow assessment of the U.S. Libya strike, citing an academic "expert" that it strengthened Qaddafi and failed to deter further acts of terrorism. "Why 'Star Wars' Bothers the Russians," 8-19, a bit better, on the potential neutralization of the Soviet's land- and sea-based deterrent, but when he says Reagan doesn't recognize SDI's prime purpose as "defense of America's capacity to retaliate" we wonder where he's been. He does get close at times, as in "The Most Perplexing Thing," 8-12, raising alarums about protectionism, and citing the failure of dollar devaluation to affect the U.S. trade imbalance, but then he writes: "The whole purpose of the massive devaluing of the dollar, which has been one of the more spectacular successes of the Reagan Administration, was to dampen down foreign imports and boost United States exports." Nope.

Hempstone, Smith
The Washington Times, The Hempstone Syndicate. (★)

A grizzled veteran of the foreign press corps, the old *Washington Star*, briefly editor-in-chief of the *Times*, Hempstone turns out a fair column we always start and often finish. A good writing stylist, but grouchy in most political pieces: "But Did We Go Far Enough?," 4-2, thinks it's "high time" we got tougher on Qaddafi; "The Trashing of Monosexual Diversity," 5-22, is alarmed at Goucher College going co-ed. A very nice bye-bye in "George Wallace's Amazing Grace," 4-9. He's happiest alone: "A Quiet Time By the Sea," 10-29, is lyrical on an isolated retreat in October Maine.

Hitchens, Christopher
The Nation. (−)

Author of the "Minority Report" column, upfront with scathing invective for the nemesis of the leftist agenda: Reagan "the village idiot," "the klutz," the "ignoramus," who "is not a hapless blooper merchant" but "a conscious,

MediaGuide   235

habitual liar,'' 9-20. Ideologically hidebound, he too often comes across as foolish, as for example his concession to the USSR for not being "indiscriminate" in its support of anti-imperialist movements, while lambasting the Reagan Doctrine for supporting "riffraff or rabble" like UNITA, the Afghani resistance and the Contras. A primitive slash-and-burn approach that may please *The Nation* faithful, but he's more restrained as the London *Spectator*'s Washington columnist. From his most widely-read effort in '86, sophistry on the use of the word terrorist: "It disguises reality and impoverishes language and makes a banality out of the discussion of war and revolution and politics....the perfect instrument for the cheapening of public opinion and for the intimidation of dissent," *Harper's*, 9-86.

Hughes, John
Los Angeles Times Syndicate. (★ ½)

A regular in *The Christian Science Monitor*, he often succeeds in coming up with some piece of info or new angle we don't see elsewhere. "Libya: Why the US Moved," 4-16, challenged the convention that the U.S. strike made a hero of Qaddafi, but more importantly, presented a good case that the Soviets had signaled beforehand they'd rant and rave but essentially look the other way. "Soviet Offensive," 4-4, also impressive with a reading on the Russians' single-minded public relations push for an arms control agreement, and Reagan's determination not to give away the store to get it.

Kondracke, Morton
The New Republic. (NR)

Back at *The New Republic* late in '86 after a sojourn as *Newsweek*'s Washington Bureau Chief, we can only say "welcome back" to Kondracke. One of the top attractions of *TNR* in '85, we expect '87 will be a repeat, with him on the foreign policy beat. "The Democrats' 'Yes, But' Foreign Policy," 10-20, was a good start.

Lewis, Anthony
New York Times. (★ ★ ★ ½)

The best liberal political columnist around. Conservatives cringe when they approach Tony's column because they know he asks no quarter and gives none, and he scored in '86 with so little competition in contesting the Reagan Agenda. His "Rhetoric and Reality," 1-27, makes the best case we saw against Angola's Savimbi. "Words and Action," 2-17, has good detail on the South African debate (where he has knowledge) not seen in news columns. His legal expertise shows in "The Court: Scalia," 6-26, analyzing legal opinions with subtlety and insight, no knee-jerk this time. "A Divided Society," 6-5, details 13% unemployment in Thatcher's U.K. Best of '86: "The Stupidity Factor," 9-18, making a reasonable case for a deal on Nick Daniloff based on fresh analysis, after Lewis earlier condemned the Kremlin. "Before he entered the White House, for 20 years, Mr. Reagan tried to make it hard for American Presidents to do any business with the Soviet Union. He and his people, in the right-wing backlash fostered by their ineptitude, are getting a taste of their own old medicine." If Lewis did not exist, a Devil's Advocate would have to be hired.

McLaughlin, John
National Review. (★ ½)

Fine polish, tight organization, showing some improvement over last year, but late, late, late for most of '86. Inconsistent as well, with good filling looks at Cuomo, 3-14; Kemp, 4-11; Jackson, 6-6; and Bush, 8-1; but with not so good looks at Hart, 9-12; Iacocca, 8-15; and Senator Paul Simon, 9-26, all of which left us feeling hungry. His terminally consistent use of "unnamed" sources is maddening, and not just to us: one reader complained in a letter to the editor published 12-5, "He didn't quote any real people....I know journalists have to protect their sources, but I would like to know once in a while who Mr. McLaughlin was actually having lunch with." So would we.

Meyer, Cord
News America Syndicate. (★ ★)

A nationally syndicated columnist who focuses on foreign affairs, Meyer's columns regularly appear in *The Washington Times*. There's usually an angle or perspective in them that can broaden the perceptions into an issue. He was critically supportive of Reagan for a high-risk gamble in the Tripoli action, a little too ready to chronicle adverse consequences, but insightful on George Shultz's Libyan game-plan, 4-25. "Chernobyl Details...," 6-20, was one of the best accounts of reporting by the Soviet press of horror stories about dangerous conditions at its nuclear plants — pre-Chernobyl, with the info tied to a perspective on Gorbachev's economic reform plans. Timely amid the rash of arrests and convictions of American citizens for espionage against the U.S., "Defectors Damage the KGB," 7-7, on the conditions behind the increasing number of Soviet defections. Strategically focused and probing, "Gorbachev's Back-up Strategies," 10-17, on the European targets of their Reykjavik PR offensive. His best, "Why the Dog Did Not Bark," 8-29, calling attention to the strategic implications of the still unlaunched though constantly promised MPLA-Cuban-Soviet offensive against UNITA in Angola.

Pruden, Wesley
The Washington Times. (★ ★)

The *Times* managing editor unburdens himself of opinion on the breaking news as well as how it's being handled by his competitors in the 4th Estate. A great improvement over '85, when he produced it in his meager spare time. With a promotion to M.E., drudge work turned over to Tom Diaz, he writes instant

MediaGuide 237

analysis with a hot word processor "off the news." Still erratic, as one might expect with the riskiness of the format, but so passionate and informed it's compelling. He chews on the ASNE (newspaper editors) with "Crime Won't Pay Unless You Print It," 5-5, for its absolutist position on the 1st amendment. Chews on RR with "Words Won't Do in This Crusade," 9-12, for being as soft on drug dealers as on Gorby re Daniloff. Chews on Rehnquist opponents on the eve of the Senate vote, well done quotes, 9-17. Chews on Associated Press the day after Reykjavik, 10-13, for its lead that the summit broke down because *the U.S.* rejected Gorby's SDI deal. Best chew of all, "The Class Hellion Throws a Tantrum," 7-27, on Senator Biden's outburst on South Africa.

Reeves, Richard
Universal Press Syndicate. (½ ★)

Poor George Shultz, "mad as hell" but "caught in the middle" because the "leading exponent of our newest version of isolationism: Ronald Reagan," made him the "sixth man" on the bench when funding for State's budget came up, "Reagan's 'Gunboat Isolationism' Burns Shultz," 5-19. Reeves can be novel, but was out in left field for most of '86, knocking the stuffing out of straw men of his own creation. Another example, "Baker Leading a Retreat from Laissez-faire," 4-25, "Reaganomics is dead in the world."

Reston, James
The New York Times. (−)

We thought for sure the once great, now way-over-the-hill Scotty Reston would hang it up to write his memoirs in '86, after a contemporary, *The Wall Street Journal*'s Vermont Royster, retired his column. But he hangs in there, filing his snoozers, which we still read because he was once our hero. But there's nothing to chew on. "Where Are We Going?" he asked, 2-2, at Challenger's wake: "We need to ponder the meaning of the shuttle tragedy." He can still get an hour and a half with world leaders, as in "A Conversation With Mitterrand" (9-7 in Paris). But there's so little to show for it. At least in '86 he suspended his weekly theme of 1980-85, on Reagan's dumb luck. And we will be annoyed if he gets hit by a truck without writing his memoirs, which we've been waiting for.

Rosenfeld, Stephen F.
The Washington Post. (★ ★ ½)

Deputy Editorial Page Editor and weekly columnist. He tried hard in '85, but couldn't quite get down the court to score. Rosenfeld was much improved in '86. His best, "Year of the Insurgencies," 2-7, 80 feet out, but right through the hoop locating Reagan's delinking of regional disputes from arms control summits, not as a retreat, but a sharpening of great power competition in the Third World. All the right questions in "Castro, Fair Game," 8-6, on the disclosures of Cuba's Solzhenitsyn, Armando Valladares, powerfully done. Singular insight, one of the best in the press on a "not-hot item on our national agenda," African development aid, in "Crumbs for Africa," 10-31, hitting the Administration and Congress for a joint policy collaboration that produced a mean result.

Rutherford, Malcolm
Financial Times. (★ ½)

"Politics Today." A fine analytical mind when he's interested, but too often prefers to explain why subjects that fascinate the reader are really boring, if not irrelevant. In "Walking Back to Happiness," 6-30, the politics of Ireland are "even more of a mess than usual," though "uncertain," and "it may not matter that much any more either way." In "How the Fire Went Out of the Parties," 6-27, "It does not matter whether the left or the right is in power...the policies are broadly the same." In "A Confident Gamble," 7-4, "a truly self-confident white South Africa would simply tell the outside world to buzz off.... [And] the point about Britain taking the lead [in imposing sanctions] is that, if it does not, somebody else will." But smashing with "The Man Who Went Too Far," 1-10, on the departure of Michael Heseltine.

Safire, William
New York Times. (★ ★)

Back from his 1985 "vacation," which he spent pulling the wings off USIA's Charlie Wick and anyone who wouldn't return his phone calls. A former Nixon speechwriter, Safire is best thought of as an "anti-Reagan Republican" who — like Nixon and Ford — can't get used to RR's success. In "The Speech That Failed," 2-7, he thinks RR's State of the Union speech was poorly written. In a series of columns, he tries to pump the Mike Deaver molehill of common venality into DeaverGate proportions: "The Age of Access," 2-17; "The Secret Mandate," 5-9; "Toadying to Deaver," 6-13. He likes a good scoop and sometimes scores: "Vive le Pinprick," 4-18, on a French/Libya proposal that had jaws wagging. But mostly he's out to pull down RR, one way or another. "Reagan's Other Cheek," 10-2, on Cold War wheeling/dealing over Daniloff ("It's going to be a long fourth quarter.") His columns on the Iran arms/hostages controversy seethed: "Tar Baby Strikes Again," 11-13; "The Secret Agent," 11-17. He loves George Shultz, an old pal from the Nixon years. Common complaint about him: Sometimes so cutesy, insidey, you can't figure out what he's writing about. See "Spilling the NID," 5-12, an exercise in self-glorification. For the most part, he's back in form and a must read again.

Shields, Mark
The Washington Post. (★★★)

A street-smart Boston, Irish pol with Capitol Hill in his Democratic past, his good humor bubbles up through everything he writes, looking more like Tip O'Neill as he eats and ages, but with RR's laid-back easiness. "What Iacocca Started," 2-27, a nice touch on the Statue of Liberty controversy. Insightful on Reagan's "emotional security index," 2-9. "A Master in the House," 3-17, friendly to Tip. "One Man's Destiny," 9-10, friendly to Ohio's Jim Rhodes. Shields has the most memorable paragraph of the year in "Some Memorable Moments in a Mediocre Year," 11-2: "Democrats' Least Effective Argument for 1986. First prize: 'The Strategic Defense Initiative Won't Work.' On Nov. 21, 1963, in San Antonio, Democrat John Kennedy spoke these words: 'Frank O'Connor, the Irish writer, tells us in one of his books about how as a boy, he and his friends would make their way across the countryside, and when they came to an orchard wall that seemed too high and too doubtful to permit their voyage to continue, they took off their caps and tossed them over the wall. And then they had no choice but to follow them.' The President concluded: 'This nation has tossed its cap over the wall of space, and we have no choice but to follow it.' " A lot of Democrats read the column.

Sidey, Hugh
Time. (★★½)

A good year for the writer of the weekly "Presidency" column. His pieces have generally been rich, quirky and almost poignant at times, always original, though not always pivotal in terms of topic or issue, providing intriguing glimpses into history made 200 years ago or yesterday. His writing is oddly lyrical, making for rather a nice change of pace from the hard-nosed style of other writers. "Cries of the Heart," 8-11, "The Wit and Wisdom," 9-22, and "Colliding with Realities," 9-1, are typical. His Iran/Contras interview with the President, 12-8, was the talk of the town, the first time RR let himself be seen in a boil: "I have to say that there is a bitter bile in my throat these days. I've never seen the sharks circling like they are now with blood in the water." Sidey's column the same issue was also vivid: "Washington is in its full Watergate crouch. This time it took about two minutes following the Iran-*contra* money-deal revelation."

Sperling, Godfrey, Jr.
The Christian Science Monitor. (★½)

Senior Washington Correspondent. A Beltway institution, with his Wednesday VIP breakfasts. He swam against the conventional current that often overwhelms other inside veterans. Early, "Reagan's Goals," 1-28, has the President "confounding the critics who were certain he'd be a lame duck by this time" but who "will be a formidable force right up to the very end." One of his best,

"Jesse Jackson and the Morality Issue," 4-22, "Jackson may well find his 'family values' issue unique and...appealing...Reagan and the Republican party should no longer enjoy the political edge of holding a monopoly on [the]...issue." And " 'I'm Fond of Ron,' " 8-19, a reprise on the failure of lame-duck scenarios to take hold: "His influence is continuing long after critics have said it was beginning to fade...What really irks many of these critics is Reagan's continuous optimism." With all his standing, though, he never makes waves.

Wicker, Tom
The New York Times. (★ ½)

A Southern, Kennedy liberal who came north to the *Times* at Camelot's dawn, 1960, and remains impressed with the Kennedy tax cuts of the time. He continues to warn Democrats against a tax hike because "(a) it isn't necessary and (b) it could be disastrous for the economy" in "The Deficit Strawman," 2-4, and "The Mondale Trap," 2-7. But still scarred from Camelot's Vietnam adventure, Wicker rejects "A False Parallel," 3-4, in equating the "Glorious Revolution" in Manila with the Contra "minor guerrilla war" in Nicaragua. We've always liked him and his willingness to examine the other side of the coin, but he can't seem to escape the past in order to renew his material. The Democratic Party is looking for "new ideas," and so should Wicker, too often stale. His worst, perhaps his career worst, was "A Star is Born For the Democrats," 9-9, awarding Barbra Streisand his column for her gala $1.5 million fundraiser for California Democrats. ("Do I hear $2 million?")

Yoder, Edwin
Washington Post Writers Group. (★)

Still useful for representing the views of the old GOP, but leaden in '86, he's starting to sink. For example, "It is indeed 'the illusion of American omnipotence' in D.W. Brogan's phrase to think that American presidents have the leverage to manipulate revolutionary situations everywhere. It is unhistorical to insinuate that Carter bore responsibility for the fall of the Shah, or to give Ronald Reagan credit for more favorable turns of events in the Philippines and Argentina", in "Only Revisionists Call Reagan Democracy's Hero," 7-17.

SOCIAL/POLITICAL REPORTERS

Alter, Jonathan
Newsweek. (★ ★ ½)

Consistent quality coverage of the media, lively and authoritative. In "A New Regime at the *Times*," 10-20, on the retirement of Abe Rosenthal, "one disgruntled reporter last year programmed his home computer so that when he logged in, it told him how many more days were left until Rosenthal's 65th birthday." Timely with "AIDS and the Right to Know," 8-18, a piece about listing AIDS as the cause of death in an obituary. "The Two Faces of Breslin," 5-12, a good, deep story revealing that the winner of the Pulitzer Prize doesn't play by the same ethical rules as the rest of us. Best of year, cover story "The Struggle for the Soul of CBS News," 9-15, (with Bill Powell) describing the chaos of restructuring CBS. Interviewed Bill Moyers, one of best quotes of the year: "Pretty soon, tax policy had to compete with stories about three-legged sheep, and the three-legged sheep won."

Apple, R.W., Jr.
The New York Times. (★ ★ ½)

The Washington bureau's ace political reporter from 1969-76, "Johnny" Apple spent the next decade in London, returning to his old beat as 1986 opened. Apple produced some nice material during the year, but the 10 years away took the edge off his political reporting and at mid-year he was given a broader portfolio where he could pick his spots. We liked "Red Carpet for a Rebel," 2-7, an early spot on the PR firm of Black, Manafort & Stone, boosting Jonas Savimbi for a 600K fee. His wrapup of "The Political Summit," 5-7, from Tokyo caught the group dynamic of the economic summit. An Iowa report, 4-1, on how the Democratic hoped-for farm revolt wasn't shaping up was an early sign of his rustiness, not bad, but not great. A Sunday magazine piece on Mario Cuomo, 9-14, was just so-so. An early review article on the Challenger disaster stuck with us, "The Need to Cross That Last Frontier," 2-2, that understood the shuttle is a space Conastoga of the pioneers. His best: "Risks for the Democrats," 11-27, on the party's introspection on how to play the Iranian-Contra crisis.

Archibald, George
The Washington Times. (★ ★)

National news correspondent. Able to handle controversial material adroitly, the British-born Archibald scored in '86 with the Michael Deaver amorality play, getting his teeth into the story early and shaking until *The New York Times* and *Washington Post* were drawn into it. A two-part series, 4-10,11, (with Lucy Keyser) was the best effort on covering the Deaver revelations at that point.

The biggest, most important newsbeat of the saga was his front-pager headline piece of 4-24, revealing that Deaver continued to receive President Reagan's daily schedule as a courtesy, enabling him to trade on that inside material with megabuck clients. Also well handled, a delicate story on columnist Joe Sobran, "Sobran and Jewish Critics Trade Charges," 6-9, on alleged anti-Semitic comments.

Barrett, Lawrence
Time. (★)

National political correspondent. Most often seen buried in a double byline on major pieces, he occasionally shows up alone in a sidebar. One such effort was "Liberalist and Populist Tugs," 10-6: "Reagan has reminded the entire electorate that politicians can take strong stands and succeed. Whatever they think of his policies, voters clearly admire that quality and continue to look for it in candidates." He was the first to see, in September, that Paul Laxalt's ardor for a presidential run in '88 had cooled. And his idea that the Southern regional primary "Super Tuesday" will only make New Hampshire that much more important struck us as right.

Bethell, Tom
The American Spectator. (★ ★ ½)

TAS's Washington columnist, also appearing regularly in *National Review* and *The Washington Times*. British-born Bethell was an early supply-side devotee whose advocacy showed instead of the analytical framework. He advanced in '86 by hewing to the framework. His *TAS* "Capitol Ideas" is wide-ranging and never trivial, usually off the beaten political track. "King David's Royal Family," September, dispelling some myths about AIDS after visiting a nun's home for AIDS patients in Greenwich Village. "Seoul Searching," October, observations on the economies of Northeast Asia, after a five-country tour. One of his best ever, "Searching For the Next Marcos," 4-25, *NR*, on State Department/AID negligence on Third World growth problems.

Blumenthal, Sidney
The Washington Post. (★ ★ ★)

A talented young liberal hired by Ben Bradlee to keep watch on the conservatives, Blumenthal is loathed, even hated by those he watches, probably because he has X-ray vision and a sharp knife that draws blood. He sliced the Kirkpatrick doctrine as Marcos tumbled in "An Ideology That Didn't Match Reality." Democrats "Capitalize on Fear of Meese," 6-9, was a clever front-pager on fundraising. Also shrewd observations on the nitpicking among the intellectualoids in "Norman Podhoretz and the Right Stuff," 5-18. He's against the grain with "Forget Centrist Forces — Watch Kennedy Forces," 2-9, on how liberals, not centrists, will benefit from Teddy dropout (a piece even his critics admired). His best: "Once Upon a Time in America," 1-13, *The New Republic*, wrapping up Ferraro/Zaccaro in a sulfuric review of Gerry's book, stunning, a stake in the heart; she was not heard from again. "Candidates Stray From Reagan Line," 11-1, catches GOP candidates promising government activism. Yes, he makes mistakes, but a critic acknowledges "he's possibly the best analyst of things not visible to the ordinary eye who is currently covering politics."

Boyd, Gerald M.
The New York Times. (★)

Second banana to Bernard Weinraub on the White House beat, covering the Veep, utility infielding, general bread-and-butter stuff that never surprises, but that's the job description. We see his byline daily and noted favorably a report on a Reagan Saturday radio address, 2-2, pointing in the direction of a campaign to protect his military budget. We'll expect a splash from him when he moves up the ladder.

Brandt, Thomas
The Washington Times. (★)

"Wirth, Kramer Fight It Out at Ideological Gulch," 10-14, strictly meat and potatoes: "The winner may be the man who can best paint his opponent a political monotone and himself in the bright colors of rationality." And, "Mr. Wirth appears not as defensive as the Kramer camp about allegations of extremism." At least no political tilt.

Brownstein, Ronald
National Journal. (★ ★ ★)

Political/White House correspondent, departing in '87 to write a book. Formerly finance and banking reporter on the *NJ* staff, he's been covering the White House and national politics since 1983, turning out reports so thorough, comprehensive that we detect other reporters cribbing from him. Very strong in '86 with fresh information and solid treatment in his profiles on Sen. Joseph Biden, 2-22, almost a basic reference work, and Jesse Jackson, 3-22. "Moving Up," 3-1, an early look at the consequences of the new southern regional primary. A serious and competent dip into demographics, "In the Mainstream," 3-1, reporting the baby bust generation is more conservative on a wide range of issues than the boom generation. Thorough on the rush for fundraising by the potential 1988 candidates, "The Money Hunt," 6-7. Cautious, thoughtful analysis in "Winning in Michigan," 6-21, finding less there than meets the eye after the first round. A super piece, catching critically important changes on the margin, "J-O-B-S," 7-26. Broad, forward-looking perspective in the analytic "Keeping One Eye on 1988," 9-27, and tight, essential wrap-up reporting in both "End of the Road," 11-8, and "The Big Sweep," 11-8, the only reporter to see a GOP "block" in the 9 biggest states in future redistricting.

Chaze, William
U.S. News & World Report. (★)

A senior editor for special reports, Chaze concentrates on global political issues. Usually producing light, airy pieces, Chaze's best writing was evident in "Now for the End Game," 9-22, a comprehensive cover story on the Daniloff case.

Cohen, Richard E.
National Journal. (★ ★)

Congressional reporter. Thorough reporting in the *NJ* tradition, and usually insightful analysis. "Filling a Void," 2-1, timely on the policy debate within the Dem Leadership Council over the liberal heritage and new directions. Attentive to the fundraising efforts of the '86 congressional candidates, keeping abreast of who's ahead and the consequences for the races, 2-15 and 2-22. "Limited Impact," 2-22, analyzing the Scalia decision on Gramm-Rudman could have had a broader scope. An early "Wright Out Front," 3-1, reported the race for House Speakership is probably locked up. Cohen worked the Democratic side a little harder this year, to good effect: "The Best Offense," 3-22, on its defensive politics as a strategy for protecting its House majority; "A Healthy Race," 6-21, projecting how the contest for Senate Democratic leadership may help the party. But "Dole's High-Risk Game," 9-6, examined how a Democratic victory could bring his leadership into question and "A Subsurface Change," 9-20, offered a broad view of the two-party system's future heading into the South's Senate elections. "Back in Charge," 11-8, another fine perspective on how the Democrats plan to approach national problems.

Deigh, Robb
Insight. (★)

General assignment on the range of political, foreign, military stories that can be pulled together in Washington, clear and concise but nothing startling so far. "In OPEC's Pricing Strategy What Goes Down Must Go Up," 10-13, is an adequate update, but surface stuff. "The Tough Judge Who Rules America's Phone Companies," 9-15, a good sidebar to the cover story, but could have been tighter.

Dentzer, Susan
Newsweek. (NR)

Unfortunately, not enough bylined material to justify a rating, but, from what little we've seen, she's worth reading. We just wish they gave her more to do. One piece we appreciated: "A Cure for Job Stress," 6-2.

MediaGuide

Dewar, Helen
The Washington Post. (★)

Capitol Hill. An ideological liberal who lets it show in her reporting, which reduces its value. But she can do political reporting. Yes, there's heavy breathing as she posits a Democratic takeover of the Senate, but she does make the case, as in "Cranston Out-Distancing Foes," 3-17 from L.A., good detail on internal problems preventing GOP from capitalizing on Alan's "vulnerability." We liked "Senate Democrats Still Traumatized," etc., 7-14, on the "shock" of losing control in 1980, and prospects for 1988. An able "South Could Rise Again if Democrats Win the Senate," 7-22, points out region would capture half the key committee chairmanships. But here comes a favorite source of wisdom, Norman Ornstein of the American Enterprise Institute in her pre-election entry on the Senate races "Vast Changes Improbable If Democrats Regain Control," 11-2: "A difference, but not a day-and-night difference," he says. Boilerplate.

Diamond, Edwin
New York. (★ ★)

One of the best of the media writers, who, along with political columnist Michael Kramer, is the reason we take the magazine. His vantage point is still a little too close to the foxhole, but there's always plenty to learn at that level. We'll remember '86 as the year he peered at Time Inc., most intently, with " 'People Lite'?" 1-6, a fast start in reporting on the company's photo Edsel, *Picture Week*, the "magazine for people who find too much to read in *People*." A takeout, "Trouble in Paradise," 2-17, on the barnacle-encrusted Eden, is too long, given our payoff as readers, but he makes his points, among them: "The reading hasn't been all that good for the magazines Time Inc. is publishing either." His best we saw in '86 was "Circus of the Stars," 2-3, on NBC's "The McLaughlin Group," the only TV talk show we *always* watch, live or taped on our trusty VCR. Diamond is the only media writer who came close to understanding the genius of the show, which President Reagan has called "a political version of *Animal House*." Up sights!

Diamond, Stuart
The New York Times. (★ ★)

New York. Business reporter. Although we cite *The Wall Street Journal* for early coverage of Chernobyl, Diamond's science reporting and analysis dominated after the first days of May through the rest of the year. Among several pieces we noted at the time: "U.S. Experts Say Chernobyl's Design Made Workers' Risk-Taking Worse," 8-18, "careless low level technicians" not sufficient as an explanation for the disaster; "Moscow Now Sees Chernobyl's Peril Lasting For Years," 8-22, the Soviets readjust their estimates, 6,500 deaths by cancer now seen possible; "Design Flaws, Known to Moscow, Called Major

Factor at Chernobyl," 8-26, but the diaster stemmed from defects warned about nine years ago — and that still exist at other plants; "Reactor Fallout Said to Match Past World Total," 9-23, but "50% more cesium"!

Dickenson, James R.
The Washington Post. (★)

A veteran pinchhitter on the political beat when he's not doing editing chores, he can rise above the flock. Of several scattered pieces we saw during the year, two were noted: "Holding Uncle Sam Accountable," 2-5, an interview with the comptroller general re Gramm-Rudman, very well done. A pre-election op-ed column on "The Drop-Off Voters," 10-31, was prescient is seeing light turnout now favors the Democrats after decades of Republicans praying for rain. We remember Dickenson as one of the great sportswriters of the late 1960s, who got bored and switched to politics.

Diegmueller, Karen
Insight. (★ ½)

A seasoned reporter who has been given big assignments and impresses with assiduous fact-gathering and presentation. A cover on "The Truth About Divorce," 10-13, covers close to 5,000 words and we read every one, the best collection of stats, trends and sociology we've seen in a periodical of general circulation. Best line from a counselor: "A lot of couples wait until they're dead on arrival before they get help." A survey of Argentina's headaches, 5-25, is shallow, though, over her head.

Dillin, John
The Christian Science Monitor. (★)

A political correspondent we always check out, Dillin was exasperating in 1986. Sometimes a nugget, as in "Michigan GOP Cranks Up for '88," 6-6, clearing up the confused delegate process, reporting that Rev. Robinson's "people" were never even told his name when signing up as his delegates. "Bid By Jesse Jackson in '88 Could Skew Result of South's Superprimary," 4-18, was a nice mix of reporting and analysis, a reading on how the megaprimary cooked up by Dixie Dems could play right into Jesse's hands. But, he was too inconsistent in '86, alternating between fast-paced, insightful reporting and numb pedestrianism. His lead in "Reagan Makes Himself Issue in the Election," 11-3: "Here's the outlook. The stakes are high: control of the U.S. Senate. The race is close: Republicans and Democrats appear to have equal prospects of capturing the Senate majority. The importance to the White House is tremendous: President Reagan could face two very difficult years on Capitol Hill if the Democrats take over the Senate." ZZZZZZ.

MediaGuide

Dionne, E.J., Jr.
The New York Times. (★ ★ ★ ½)

Washington bureau national political correspondent. Only 34, with the potential of a young Reston, he was pulled back at mid-year from Rome — where he earned the best part of his ★ ★ ★ ½ — to take the lead on the '86 congressional elections. He has scope, range, daring and great balance. Best from Rome: "Pope Urges Philippine Peace," 2-17, a reminder of the Pope's 1981 warning to Philippine church on liberation theology; a tight, professional report on Father Curran's liberal views on sexuality under fire, 3-16; "Vatican Seeks Struggle by Poor to End Injustice," 4-6, balancing liberation theology and capitalism; a marvelous feature on the "Jet-Age Pope" who still believes in "angels, devils and indulgences," 7-18, distinctively Dionne. On the political beat: "Election '86: Uncertainty on Issues Clouds Races," 8-31, and "Assessing What Voters Said Before They Say It," 9-15, lift routine ham-and-egg stories into rich omelets with simple flourishes. A GOP pro is quoted: "The most worrisome thing in looking at the way Republicans are running the country right now is their lack of aggressiveness...To the extent that (they) allow the Democrats to be seen as slightly folksier versions of themselves, we lose." And they did. An excellent post-election wrap-up leads the Sunday news review, 11-9.

Donohoe, Cathryn
The Washington Times. (★ ★ ★)

Among the best political feature writers in the national press. "Cautious Mikulski Campaigns," 10-23, crisp, compelling political writing, quoting former GOP foe of Maryland's Rep. Mikulski: "I thought I was going to win the election...But when they go into the booth, they vote for her. I have never been able to understand it." Super profiles on two journalists, R.E. Tyrrell, Jr., 12-2-85, and Jack Germond, 4-21. One of the best political profiles of the year "Cuomo: Is Democratic Prospect a 'Terrible Tease'," 9-11, gets inside Mario like we've not seen before, frothy, informative fun: "Holding up his arms to pantomime President Reagan's famous 'want-ad' remarks, Mr. Cuomo is withering: 'What he's really saying is, "Look, you can't take care of all those poor people. A lot of them deserve to be poor...Hey, look, it's not for me to do your thing. It's for you to do your thing. And if you fail, you fail." 'OK. That's a very popular point of view with the people who aren't failing'."

Drew, Elizabeth
The New Yorker. (★ ★ ½)

Her "Letter From Washington" column appears sporadically, not even once a month, but it's about as good as anything that appears in the weekly magazine. We've gotten more comfortable with her work in the last two years, after years of irritation at the self-importance that gave it false notes. She's reined in her opinions a bit and began to work hard at pure reporting, to good effect. Her review of the House passage of the tax-reform bill, 1-6, was useful and an accurate chronology. On 6-16, she skips through the Senate Finance Committee and tax reform, David Stockman's book ("His tone is hyperbolic, and his style is somewhat brattish"), and SALT II ("The President's decision...set off a mighty roar"). As in 1985, her most important work was in covering the arms-control debate, partly because so few journalists seem willing to do pure reporting in this area. Her excellent letter of 7-28 was thoroughly informative, with a good eye for quotes: "A high State Department official said to me recently, 'The Pentagon was supposed to be to the right of us and the ACDA to the left of us, but with ACDA over there with the Pentagon, it's much more difficult for us'." One of the 10 best of '86.

Edsall, Thomas B.
The Washington Post. (★ ★ ★)

A benchful of political reporters at the *Post*, but Edsall is one we always watch. He keeps an eye on that "mother's milk" of politics, money, better than all the competition, as with "Bush's PAC Outpacing Foes," 2-5, showing the Veep's $ power. "Is the FEC Undermining Campaign Law?" 10-22, packed with new information on FEC decisions widening latitude of fundraising laws. A portside view of "Bush Plans to Conquer Right By Dividing It," 2-9, is early in spotting this development; he also got an early bead on Pat Robertson and the evangelicals and wound up in a cul de sac covering them. A shrewd "Whites Learn Minority Politics," 11-2, on whites leveraging in black communities as blacks once had to do. One of the rare big insights of '86: "Massachusetts: A Model for Democrats," 10-5, seeing unusual income-class crossover. A socialist who never, ever lets his political bias show. He's a dark horse to get the big assignment in '88.

Fineman, Howard
Newsweek. (★)

We struggle with Fineman, seeing promise and expecting he'll stop wobbling one of these days. But his ego keeps jumping in before the talent we think is there, snotty "I know it all" little political pieces appear with too much regularity. He was blamed for his "Jack Kemp Stalls Out" report of 9-22, so late that Kemp was climbing in conventional wisdom when the column appeared, but it was the editors, we found, reaching for a piece he'd written lots earlier when it was true. We're not giving up yet. "But if Elected I Might Serve," 7-28, and "God and GOP in Michigan," 8-4, came through.

MediaGuide

Fleming, Stewart
Financial Times. (★ ½)

Washington. An uneven performance in '86, but a quizzical vantage point often turns up new angles. We liked "The Fed Restrained by Fear of a Free-Falling Dollar," 1-3, a nice account. But in "Pragmatist Widens Fed's Scope for Argument," 5-14, new Fed appointee H. Robert Heller (the choice of supply-siders) is really a "pragmatist," while Gov. Wayne Angell is an "individualist" and Gov. Manuel Johnson, though a "confessed supply-sider...is too deep a thinker to be the narrow ideologue." Hmmm. In "This Time a Voice from the Shadows," 10-4, the nonexistent supply-siders are trying to "pack" the Fed with more clones: "It is ironic that just as Mr. Reagan's voodoo economics is being written off as a failure...The Reaganauts are wetting their lips in anticipation of seeing a supply-side loyalist on the board to press the case for even lower interest rates." This is two weeks after Johnson and Angell said they thought interest rates should *not* be lowered, due to rising commodity prices. A good catch of Barber Conable, 9-2, saying the World Bank can't sell Reaganomics to the Third World. "Baker Warns Further Pressures on Currencies," 6-4, on Treasury's gyrations, looks good in retrospect. At his breezy best, 7-12, in a Wall Street thinkpiece: "The failure of the U.S. economy to expand more rapidly caught most economists on the hop."

Gailey, Phil
The New York Times. (★ ★ ½)

Burned up the track in the first half of 1986, and it looked like he would become the premier political reporter of the major dailies. Then a slump. What went wrong? Maybe shoving him to the back of the bus when E.J. Dionne, Jr. came aboard. But this guy is talented. "Bush Stands By Attack on Cuomo," 2-7, has all the nuances just right on the Veep's tanglefoot. A 2-15 interview with Cuomo is impressive, relying on Cuomo quotes, Gailey standing aside. One of best Sunday Mag political pieces, "From Biden to Babbitt to Nunn," 5-19, reveals weakness of Democrat second-string "centrists." A nifty piece, 6-19, on how the abortion issue knits Catholics and fundamentalist Protestants into the GOP fabric. "Bush and 1988: Like a Game of Blackjack," 8-20, a tasty roundup on Geo., the man to beat. Best, because of timing: "Bush and Kemp in the Early Hall of Mirrors," 6-6, displaying his finely honed sense for the right questions. Somebody should hire this slugger.

Geyer, Georgie Anne
The Washington Times, Universal Press Syndicate. (★ ★ ½)

Geyer globetrotted in '86, reporting material we didn't see elsewhere. In "Vying for India's Favors," 2-11, she finds Soviet influence at every level there, but new openings for the U.S. as Rajiv jettisons hot house economic models. Sultan Qaboos, is the key player in the Gulf's shifting relationship of forces, and she shows why in an interview, "Oman's Inimical Neighbors Accept the Sultan's Terms," 2-27. Few and far between, accounts of what Turkish Cypriots want, she fills the hole with "Visit to a Cypriot Country That Doesn't Exist," 3-27. Sudden impoverishment following huge and transformational wealth, as all over the Middle East unemployed "workers" are now going home, "Middle East on the Move," 7-7: "The danger, is not so much Islamic fundamentalism of the type that killed Anwar Sadat, but a kind of existential emptiness that could easily lead to anarchy." A lapse here and there: handwringing about traditional Catholic thinking and teaching on family planning, redeemed by straight reporting of the Pontiff's message on the destruction of personality and culture, "The Pope's Key Concerns in Colombia," 7-10; "El Salvador's Courage," 10-17, on reform of agriculture and taxes as sources of stability there doesn't make the case.

Greenhouse, Linda
The New York Times. (★ ½)
Washington bureau. Senate beat, she has a good glove and accurate arm who handled everything hit at her in 1986. Sensitive coverage of the Judge Harry Claiborne Senate impeachment trial impressed us greatly, 9-24, for example. In assessing Senate prospects for Contra aid brightening, 6-27, she picks up the theme, "What if Reagan is right?" and important thought among politicians that others missed.

Hallow, Ralph Z.
The Washington Times. (★ ½)

Plucked from the budget beat where he did well in '85 to cover politics in '86, the change of altitude was too much for him. His output was average (great + awful divided by 2), with a good eye for the offbeat, but too quick to lurch into print without careful reporting. Schooled in monetary economics, his "Reagan Asks Talks to Reform Currency," 2-7, was excellent on State of the Union, pre-political beat. "Pollsters Say Protectionism May Backfire on Democrats," 5-26, and "DuPont Proposes Drug Testing For Teens," 9-17, also very well done. But when it came to straight political news, he was not in the ballpark. Editors?

Hoffman, David
The Washington Post. (★ ½)

A bright, pleasant young backup reporter at the White House to his mentor Lou Cannon. We chided Hoffman last year for picking up bad habits from Cannon, unattributed quotes at critical points, obvious buttering of sources. We thought we saw improvement in 1986, although only after a joint byline with Cannon on an interview with the President, "Reagan Optimistic on Euromissile Pact," 2-11, which seemed sophomoric, a blown opportunity. An

"Outlook" lead, "Spin Control: The Dizziness Following Reykjavik," 11-12, a reprise on Reagan the movie-actor President, seemed petty. Hoffman's most impressive effort of '86, the lengthy "Bush: Loyal Soldier Maneuvers in Private," 10-28, which was razor sharp in catching the Vice President as an Establishment figure who really is the Yin to Reagan's Yang; for a liberal, surprisingly sensitive to nuance and conservative shadings.

Hume, Ellen
The Wall Street Journal. (½★)

You sometimes see her on PBS television's "Washington Week in Review," but don't expect much under her byline. We've poured over our notes and find the biggest impression she made on us in '86 was with "YMCA New Elite Clubs Tax Abuse," 3-31, which seems to imply that unless a gymnasium is smelly, it can't be working class, and shouldn't get a tax break, even if YMCA.

Kamen, Al
The Washington Post. (★½)

Justice/Supreme Court beat, steady and reliable on the bread-and-butter stuff. Capable of unusual angles that keep us attentive to his byline, especially on SCOTUS politics. "Time Running Out for Reagan to Reshape Court," 1-22, was very early, sharp analysis that clicked and may even have helped move up the Burger/Rehnquist switch. "Court Avoids Prayer Controversy," 3-26, is another we noted for its clarity, solid court roundup.

Kirschten, Dick
National Journal. (★★)

Author of the "White House Notebook," a well-read column on Capitol Hill. He provided one of the best profiles on the relatively unknown successor to McFarlane at NSC, Vice Adm. Poindexter, 1-25, and sparkled with insights as to why the Vice President wasn't looking presidential: "Poor George Bush. Nothing makes a guy look less presidential than to have his handlers argue among themselves whether's he's being handled correctly," 2-15. His column is always peppered with quotes from identified officials and their remarks add insights into the subject or about the individual. It's something that keeps him ahead of his competition, and it's thoroughly refreshing to not see "some say" or "a high-level source stated" appear. He can misjudge at times, as in his lead to "Building Bridges," 11-8, calling the results of the 1986 elections a consequence of sending a lame-duck president out on the campaign trail.

Klose, Kevin
The Washington Post. (★★)

Chicago. Klose warrants a special merit badge for being the only reporter to take seriously the Lyndon LaRouche phenomenon in the Illinois Democratic primary: "Ultraright Victories Scrutinized," 3-26, the best spot analysis, saw the appeal to Joe Sixpack; "LaRouche Followers Gained in Black Wards," 3-26, probes a bit deeper. In the wake of the Daniloff matter, Klose, former Moscow bureau chief, tells how it was, "Living By Moscow's Rules," 9-7, in an impressive "Outlook" feature.

Kramer, Michael
New York. (★★½)

The best read political reporter on the New York/Washington shuttle (where his magazine is *gratis*), and always worth the time. Alternates between national politics and New York State, NYC and Israel politics and has a healthy respect for issues and ideas as well as political horseraces. "How Reagan Does It," 5-9, departs from the liberal line that RR's success is largely luck and acting ability. The secret: "When it comes to *action*, Reagan has generally respected Hans Morgenthau's definition of prudence as 'the adaption of morality to circumstances'." He misfired after Reykjavik, first deciding Gorby had won a great PR coup, the second half of the article subtracting from that idea as Reagan's poll numbers rolled in. His best of 1986: "Reagan Crosses the Line of Bluff," 4-7, exceptional analysis on the Gulf of Sidra maneuvers, anticipating Tripoli.

Lemann, Nicholas
The Atlantic. (★★)

An issue-oriented reporter who can write the long, thoughtful, offbeat piece that gets talked about. He surprised us showing up in the *NY Times* special business tab with "New Tycoons Reshape Politics," 6-9, about the involvement of a new class of younger Wall Streeters in the political world. His blockbuster in the July *Atlantic*, widely read and reprinted, revived discussion about the self-sustaining culture of the black ghetto and what to do about it, "The Origins of the Underclass:" "Everything that has happened to lower-class blacks over the decades, every new twist, from segregation to the migration north to the civil rights movement, seems to have separated them from society even more — separated them from whites, from the South, from middle-class black life, and finally even from uplifting preachment. They are immigrants who not only have not assimilated in the new land but may have even become more insular there."

Mackenzie, Richard
Insight. (★ ★ ½)

Senior writer. An outstanding gem in the collection of talent over at *Insight*. There's a range to subjects he covers, not all restricted to foreign reporting. He's particularly rewarding on the Middle East, as in his Iran-Iraq features, 3-31 and 4-21; Pakistan, 5-12, and Jordan, 5-17 and 6-22. All year we followed all the press on Iraq, but Mackenzie's three-part cover story, 9-22, out of Baghdad, was the definitive work on that country. First, the impact on the people and economy — 100,000 combat deaths. Then "How Not to Wage a War: Iraq Does It By the Book," and the third part on the Iraqi secret police, "A State of Pervasive Control." One of the 10 best foreign dispatches of '86.

Magnuson, Ed
Time. (★ ½)

Senior writer, assigned mostly to political stories. Original, interesting pieces, occasionally tackling subject matter not found elsewhere: "Weekend Warriors No More," 9-8, for example, about the changing of the national guard (with Jonathan Beaty and Bruce Van Voorst). Articulate and well-spoken, he's always worth a read.

Mansfield, Stephanie
The Washington Post. (★ ★ ★ ★)

Style section. The most entertaining journalist in America, her byline a magnet for us, whether we're interested in her subject or not. She grabbed us first with, "Steamy Sex! Shop Talk! Judith Krantz!" 5-20, an absolutely delightful newspaper pastiche, a conscious parody of her predecessor, Sally Quinn. The lead into J. Krantz: "She is a tiny woman, her hair bleached the precise color of Giorgio perfume, her skin as smooth as Pratesi sheets, the layer of terra-cotta makeup barely disguising the keenly etched lines around her gray-green eyes which shimmer like Baccarat at the bottom of a Bel Air hot tub. She is too thin. And too rich." Then catch: "The Rise and Gall of Roger Stone," 6-16, on the political skulduggerer, priceless; "Tennessee Cashes In," 9-15, on Miss America Kellye Cash, breathless; and "And Now, Heeeeeeere's Oprah!" 11-2, on the talkshow's Ms. Winfrey, relentless. Wow!!

Martin, Richard
Insight. (★ ★ ★ ½)

One of editor Oberfeld's whiz kids, not yet 30 and slamming four-bagger cover stories with ease, running around the world for many, but staying at home for domestic scores, too. "All in All a Tough Act to Follow," 10-13, handles the Peres/Shamir switch with aplomb. A three-part cover story on Nicaraguan refugees, "Telling the Tale of Mass Exodus," 4-28, sparkles with on-the-ground people interviews. "Turmoil in the Temple of Labor," 3-24, another three-parter on Israel, with unusual angles, even fair depth on economic analysis, which is all too rare on Israel stories anywhere. At home, a cover on the problems of the professional sports industry, "Playing the Pros: An Iffy Business," 8-25, held our attention although we resisted the topic at first. A real find with a full career ahead.

Mashek, John
U.S. News & World Report. (★)

Chief political correspondent, a 25-year veteran of the political beat whose batteries ran down sometime in the '70s. Rarely a fresh angle, but great attention to scorecard details that keep his numerous reports seeming fair, non-ideological, non-partisan, etc., but without juice. Typical: "A Scrambled Deck for '88," a light 7-14 cover story describing the potential White House wild cards.

Mathews, Jay
The Washington Post. (★ ★)

West Coast. More than just a regional flycatcher, Mathews can handle a wide range of subjects and we usually finish what we start of his material, spot news, features or opinion, because there's no padding, unusual at the *Post*. Good anecdotes and quotes carry an 11-14 interview with David Jacobsen, the released hostage: "I will never go to a zoo again because I would let all the animals free." He looks at California's Prop. 5, limiting liability, but with Haywood motorcyclists and Joan Claybrook livening it up, 4-4. His "Outlook" essay on "A Renegade China Watcher and a Rigged Academy," 5-18, is the very best account we've seen of the Steven Mosher/Stanford/China forced abortion story, done very carefully, credibly. Exceptional on "Initiative Seeks to Make English the Civil Tongue," 10-11, on California's Prop. 63, the most balanced, thorough account we saw.

Mayer, Jane
The Wall Street Journal. (★ ★ ½)

One of the Washington bureau's talented liberals, with a solid 1985 and an even better 1986, covering media events and some political events. An eye-catching front page feature on "The Era of the Geezer" in politics, 7-31, as Reagan's age makes it chic to be on the campaign trail, the focus on North Carolina Democrat Terry Sanford, 67, who does wind up geezing to victory. Her best and most controversial effort: "Pundit George Will is a Media Super Star," 5-7, a razor-fine sketch that peels the pundit's thin skin, throwing in his 1976 cutting remarks of candidate Reagan just in case Nancy — George's lunch partner lately — hadn't seem them. Will fired off a letter to the *Journal* accusing Mayer of errors galore, but she wins a split decision on points.

MediaGuide 255

McLeod, Don
Insight. (★ ½)

A veteran newsman with a long stretch at Associated Press, enjoying himself apparently as a senior writer at the magazine, doing politics and business material with equal competence. He pitched in on the Paul Laxalt cover with "A State of Sinful Contradiction," 8-4, that focused on the problems any Nevada politician would have in running for national office, the best summary we've seen. His three-part cover story on "The Politics of World Trade," 6-30, is rather sophisticated, including a history of U.S. protectionism, Smoot-Hawley of 1929-30, and a separate piece on the beginnings, the tariff of 1828. Ambitious and carried off.

O'Leary, Jeremiah
The Washington Times. (★)

White House correspondent. The oldest deadline daily reporter in Washington, almost 45 years of it with the old *Washington Star*. His byline is frequently paired with the newcomers on the block. Okay on basics, but he sometimes leaves unasked the questions that ought not to be. "Reagan, Poindexter Work Well Together," 1-24, was good reporting on Don Regan giving the new NSC director free access to the President; but at the time we really wanted to know if that meant NSC had been "tamed." He shows he can use his sources to get out ahead, as in "NSC Shifts Foretell Row Over View of Soviets," 7-7. A longer commentary with some analysis, "When Baby's Cradle Fell," 2-27; he recalls when he was in Haiti in the midst of 1963 abortive coup against Papa Doc. Papa survived because he was vicious, unlike his Baby. A scoop, "Carlucci Heads List of NSC Candidates," 12-1.

Ostling, Richard
Time. (★ ★)

Sorry, all other religion writers, but Ostling is where we go to church. Covering not only *THE* Church, but all sorts of groups, sects, saints, cults and whatnot, often to an intriguing level that whets the spiritual appetite as in "The Second Founder of the Faith," 9-29, about the life and times of St. Augustine. Keeps up on Catholic, "John Paul's Cleanup Campaign," 10-13, and fundamentalist issues, "It's Good Enough for Them," 6-23, about the new Southern Baptist president; "Summons to the 'Unknowns'," 7-28, describing Billy Graham's new evangelical training school, and the unusual: "A Sinister Search for 'Identity'," 10-20, is a chilling piece about the use of religion to further white racist aims.

Pear, Robert
The New York Times. (★★½)

A Washington bureau veteran since 1979, we looked carefully at Pear in '85 and found him fastidious and interested in new ideas. He gravitates to health issues, but really seems to be able to handle anything they throw at him, and we've become comfortable with his byline. A report on U.S. official disagreements on Philippine/Marcos fraud is a revelation, 2-12, and Pear plays it straight. Then an enterprising Sunday front-pager, 5-4, on tensions between state courts and the federal bench over individual rights. "A Tenfold Increase in AIDS Deaths Seen by 1991," 6-13, rattled us with its thoroughness. And here he is, by gosh, with "Persistence of Bill Bradley is Paying Off," 5-9, on tax reform, very early recognition with a piece that moved along, nothing fancy, but moved along. We noted a dozen other Pear stories in this vein.

Platt, Adam
Insight. (★★★)

Another of the whizkids at *Insight*, not yet 30 and producing exciting copy out of the Pacific Rim, and wherever. His "Booming Asia at the Crossroads," 5-12, a four-part series was terrific, the timing so right and the material compelling: Hong Kong, Singapore, South Korea, Taiwan, plus an interview w/Richard Holbrook. No flash in the pan, Platt came back again and again in 1986 with great, confident material: "People's Army Marks Time While the Economy Regroups," 6-2, and "In the Orient: Prosperity Ignites Democracy," 5-12. And a gaudy, provocative two-part cover story, "New Cultural Sun Rises in Japan," 11-3, a good case that the center of gravity in fashion and style is moving toward Tokyo.

Prewett, Virginia
Freelance. (NR)

Central America correspondent. We only see a few items a year from her, but they're always superb. Her best in '86: her report on the legacy of land reform in El Salvador, appearing in *Human Events*, was the year's best anywhere on policies that feed civil war in that country.

Randolph, Eleanor
The Washington Post. (★★)

The print media reporter at the *Post* and a good one. She could have taken the rest of 1986 off after her three-part series on the *NY Times*: "The Rich and Troubled Times (As Executive Editor Abe Rosenthal Approaches Retirement Age, Tremors Shake 'The Newspaper of Record')," 1-7; "Abe Rosenthal Letting Go," 1-8; "Grasping For the Keys to the Kingdom," 1-9. *"The New York Times* today is a nervous institution preparing for what may be one of the most difficult periods in its 134-year history — the retirement of Executive Editor Abraham Michael Rosenthal....Once the waiting is over, the change at the top of the *Times* will be more than a mere switch in corporate personnel. It will be the end of a brilliant, lucrative and tumultuous era — two decades in which one of the world's most powerful institutions has been dominated by one of journalism's most distinctive and controversial men.''

Remnick, David
The Washington Post. (★ ½)

Sunday magazine staff. A promising young writer who kept up with the "Style" section heavies until moving to the mag. "Where the Elite Meet to Read," 2-9, is an okay trip to the *Economist*, but a bit overblown. Better with "The Voice of a Natural," 3-20, a Bernard Malamud remembrance, and "Geoffrey Wolff and the Chilling Inspiration," 3-22, with the snippy remark: "His beard is very white. This may mean he is very sage." A cover story on Alger Hiss, 10-12, keeps you reading with this: "He stumbles sometimes over roots and curbs he cannot see. His breath is wheezy and short. His eyes are blue as cornflowers, but they have failed him in old age, giving him only the cloudy curve of the headstones, the weary bending of the trees in the wind. 'As you can tell,' says Alger Hiss, 'I'm a very old man'.''

Roberts, Steven V.
The New York Times. (★ ½)

Steady yeomanlike political reporter. A standout with a 2-7 piece reporting on Rep. Stephen Solarz investigation of Marcos, questioning Solarz's use of political power. Solid and objective on Democratic budget hearings in Chicago, 2-16. Best of '86, a Sunday magazine feature, "Politicking Goes High-Tech," 11-2, on TV "Spot Wars" in the Missouri U.S. Senate race; a slow start almost kept us from the fast finish, however.

Rogers, David
The Wall Street Journal. (★ ½)

A hustling political reporter whose byline rode dozens of datelines in 1986, doing congressional matchups, with a glint now and then of a bigger landscape. A front page leader, "Dole's Leadership Role In Senate Helps Shape His Bid for Presidency," 8-15, important in seeing Dole forcing himself into a new attitude if he's serious about '88: "A complex man, he is foremost a survivor. His slashing wit, which hurt him in the 1976 campaign, is more tempered these days, but his humor is self-deprecating only when he is in fact in control." Another up front, "North Carolina Vote Could Indicate Future of Two-Party South," 10-30, strains to put a big spin on the Sanford-Broyhill Senate race, but we get little sense of the small picture as Rogers reports the lack of a burning issue.

No mention of Democrat Sanford backing Reagan on SDI, or Republican Broyhill peddling protectionism. Not much of his output stuck to the ribs in '86, but the talent is there.

Saikowski, Charlotte
The Christian Science Monitor. (½ ★)

A Beltway beat reporter — and it shows. Rising above it a bit, with an inspired "Reagan Losing Steam? Never! Says Buchanan," 6-30, but the timely interview with Pat wasn't worked hard enough. "Bush Mixes Confidence and Caution," 6-9, wafer thin and stale — Bush pleads 11th commandment. "An Energetic Reagan Stumps for Senate Seats," 10-29, reports mounting public fears about the still-gargantuan budget and trade deficits and possible recession next year, but did she really mean in the heartland or in DC? "Reagan Will Have Tougher Time Shaping His Legacy," 11-6: "The day of major initiatives from the Oval Office is over in any case. The President has had few major legislative victories since 1982." Also covering defense/national security issues. "Whether to Stick with SALT II," 4-2, a cursory sketch of internal debate, the selection of what was reported suggesting she knows which way she'd vote. "Summit Collapse Tests Reagan's Leadership," 10-14, reports gloom in Washington because of no "arms understanding." And "The Post-Reykjavik Blues," 10-24, still gloomy, because Reagan won't compromise on SDI, the arms control "impasse."

Shipler, David K.
The New York Times. (★ ★)

State Department. His "The Routes to the Summit," 4-23, a report jam-packed with information, quotes from G. Arbatov and Gorbachev on linking the summit to the international situation, covered the terrain, giving us what we needed to know at the time. A bang-up job with "Missionaries for Democracy: U.S. Aid for Global Pluralism," 6-1, on the National Endowment for Democracy, well-organized, balanced and detailed. In "Principle and Pragmatism in Foreign Policy," 11-9, an early article on the Administration's Iran policy, we found Shipler's reporting cautious, without much to say, but admirably keeping his cool. A former foreign correspondent covering the Middle East, Shipler authored *Arab and Jew — Wounded Spirits in a Promised Land* in 1986.

Shribman, David
The Wall Street Journal. (★ ★)

A heavy hitter competing with David Rogers for the Political Bigfoot role in 1988. Always a "good read" on politics and politicians in '86, although he mostly sees what's ahead of him. As in an early look at Gary Hart, "Democratic Puzzle," 1-3, trying to catch the quicksilver, or a nice piece on Pete DuPont, first GOP presidential candidate, 4-2, where there's no deep look at why the effort, what the plan. A former *NY Times*man, he first wowed us with a 5-1-85

MediaGuide

front-pager on tensions between House and Senate Republicans, double bylined with Rogers. But maybe Rogers provided the bigger spin in that, we wonder, after seeing no over-arching material in '86. Still, he's grand at the lower plateau. Best we saw, "Mario Cuomo Emerges As a Major New Voice in Democratic Circles," 9-4, a great lead that captures a piece of Mario: "The governor of New York is speaking to the corps of newly hired teachers here, talking about how his administration increased state aid and teachers' salaries. But before long, Mario Cuomo is reminiscing about the perfume his teachers wore at P.S. 50 and recalling the man who taught shop and imposed discipline at P.S. 142."

Sperling, Godfrey, Jr.
The Christian Science Monitor. (★ ½)

Senior Washington correspondent. A Beltway institution, with his Wednesday VIP breakfasts. He swam against the conventional current that often overwhelms other inside veterans. Early, "Reagan's Goals," 1-28, has the President "confounding the critics who were certain he'd be a lame duck by this time" but who "will be a formidable force right up to the very end." One of his best, "Jesse Jackson and the Morality Issue," 4-22: "Jackson may well find his 'family values' issue unique and...appealing...Reagan and the Republican party should no longer enjoy the political edge of holding a monopoly on [the]...issue." And " 'I'm Fond of Ron'," 8-19, a reprise on the failure of lame-duck scenarios to take hold: "His influence is continuing long after critics have said it was beginning to fade....What really irks many of these critics is Reagan's continuous optimism." With all his standing, though, he never makes waves.

Taylor, Paul
The Washington Post. (★ ★ ½)

A semi-secure hold on the national political correspondent's slot, Taylor had many fine individual pieces in 1986, but last year we were "guessing he'll be a (★ ★ ★) after the '86 elections, at least," and he wasn't. His reportage on individual races was cheeky and knowing, but there wasn't any clues from him on what joined together these separate elections. Other than their being separate pieces on the same chessboard, he left us wondering if he's too small-picture oriented for the top political job at the *Post*. A Senator Biden profile, though, "Scolding on the Stump," 3-3, was excellent, with critics saying one does not get to White House on self-flagellation alone. He has Democrats tired of being the Contras on national defense, trying to remold as the "Party of Lean Hawks," 3-26. His August reports out of the muddy Michigan pre-presidential soundings seemed muddy. Better with his Cuomo profile, 9-26. Best of the year, "The Pennsylvania Exception," 8-25: "[Pa.'s] political realignment is both one-of-a-kind and upside-down and has been for a quarter century. During that stretch, Keystone Democrats have established a record of election-day futility second to none — and done so with their feet planted on some of the most Democratic sod in the country." But he needs to climb higher to see deeper for (★ ★ ★).

Taylor, Stuart, Jr.
The New York Times. (★★)

Supreme Court reporter. One of the best on this beat. He's clear and focused on essentials in his coverage, and analytically adept. In "Ruling on Budget-Balancing Law: A Bittersweet Victory for the President," 2-8, he was the first to unambiguously credit the Meese/Reagan constitutional arguments for the Federal Court ruling that struck down key provisions of Gramm-Rudman — an analytical scoop. There's no confusing spin tacked on to his reports, as in "High Court Bans Layoff Method Favoring Blacks," 5-20, on the affirmative action case of Jackson, Michigan teachers.

Tolchin, Martin
The New York Times. (★★)

A veteran *Times*man who has always played it straight on the political beat, accurate, reliable, still enthusiastic, best at investigative stuff, weak on analytics. A wry sense of humor pokes through now and then and he's capable of glossy writing. He spent much of the year bird-dogging the Mike Deaver/Sleaze story and came up with Deaver's Korean connections. "Committees Prepare Negative Tactics in House Races," 10-28, was one of the better efforts in the campaign homestretch: "Mr. Gaylord, asked if the Republicans would send out negative mailings in the campaign's final days, replied: 'I hope so. They will expose the Democratic members for what they are'."

Tyler, Patrick E.
The Washington Post. (★★½)

The *Post* beat the competition hands down in '86 on coverage of the Pelton espionage trial, Tyler the best of the team on that national security story. His "Super-Secret Work Revealed," 5-28, (with Bob Woodward), was the blockbuster of that series of reports, spelling out what Pelton had revealed to the Soviets in "one of the worst intelligence losses suffered by the United States in recent history." Follow-up reports (co-authored with Susan Schmidt) were unmatched in filling out the Pelton story. In the *Post* series "Angola: Two Faces of War," his "The Rebels," 7-28, covered the ground on UNITA's state within a state, where "a thriving mini-economy within a battered national one" exists. Also notable "Rebel Success Turns on South African Aid," 7-30, reporting from UNITA territory on Savimbi's logistical and strategic problems.

Weinraub, Bernard
The New York Times. (★★½)

White House. A solid, competent professional, as we observed in the *'86 MG*, but a bit better than that in the last year, showing greater depth. We liked "Test of a Presidency," 3-15, relating RR's push for Contra aid to his early anti-Red experience. The most balanced piece of the season on "What They're Saying

MediaGuide 261

About Michael Deaver," 5-16, suggesting a garden-variety amorality. "The Speech That Launched 1,000 Critics," 7-28, displays superb reporting and again, balance, on background to RR's South Africa address. A Sunday magazine cover story on "The Reagan Legacy," 6-22, doesn't quite make it in trying to explain RR's popularity. His 1986 will be remembered most for his big "pooper-scoop," his interview with White House chief-of-staff Donald Regan, "The Shovel Brigade," 11-16: "Some of us are like a shovel brigade that follow a parade down Main Street cleaning up."

Wermiel, Stephen
The Wall Street Journal. (★ ½)

Supreme Court reporter, above average in analytical ability, suggesting possible implications flowing from decisions or personnel that seem authoritative. "Changes on High Court Likely to Increase Conservatives' Clout," 6-18, is clear and concise analysis of the story and background of SCOTUS proposed composition. Early in '86, a provocative report on the Scalia Fifth Circuit decision on Gramm-Rudman, "Ruling is Seen Reaching Beyond Budget To Affect the Debate Over U.S. Agencies," 2-10, seeing it may "fuel the attack by some Reagan administration officials on the independence of a variety of regulatory agencies, from the Federal Reserve Board to the Federal Trade Commission." An important piece that we'll long remember, as the situation still exists and Scalia is on the High Court — which Wermiel mentions as a possibility in his piece.

West, Diana
The Washington Times. Insight. (★)

A young up-and-comer who can blossom with close editing. Caught our attention early with snappy newsfeature accounts of the New York PEN confab, 1-16,17. "Presidential Point Man for Contras," 4-10, a nice try at a profile of State Department's Elliot Abrams. "Battling Chavez Fights for Senate," 10-22, covers a lot of material, but it's too slow, too long. An *Insight* cover story on Paul Laxalt, "High Promise in a Low Profile," is quite good, crisp, but only after an almost endless lead that fools around with photographs of the two pals, Ron and Paul: "It is all right there in the picture, just as it is in hundreds of other pictures hung in hundreds of other offices, the president with one of hundreds of other political figures. But here is the difference. This photograph hangs in the Senate office of Nevada Republican Paul Laxalt. And in his case the thousand words the picture calls to mind are true." And that is the THIRD graph. Editors!!!

SOCIAL/POLITICAL COMMENTATORS

Baker, Russell
The New York Times. (★ ½)

The *Times*' gentle in-house humorist has strained to be funny in recent years. He's a good old boy worth a look, even with the occasional sourpuss, if only for the easy, nostalgic tone. Like an old, worn pair of jeans, he's too comfortable and familiar to abandon. In one of his funniest columns in years, "Maybe Just Desserts," 11-29, he describes the improbability but definite possibility of one rumor floating around the Iranian arms deal: "what about the cake Robert McFarlane, the former White House foreign-policy wizard, took to Teheran on a plane loaded with munitions? Did the President bake that cake? Was it a peace offering for the Ayatollah Khomeini? Sweets for the sweet from the Great Satan?....Trivial you say? It wouldn't be trivial if the President baked this cake, would it? In that event, my friend, you would be quick to demand to know, "what else did the President bake, and when did he bake it?"

Beichman, Arnold
The Washington Times. (★)

A devotee of "the leopard never changes its spots" school of analysis, Beichman is rigorously alert to any penetrations of Soviet disinformation in western media accounts. A relentless watchdog on this, he blasted both *The Wall Street Journal*, 7-21, and CBC, 10-15, for indulging a pro-left ethos. Timely with his interventions on policy issues, as in "An Earlier Warning on SDI," 10-16, penetrating in his assembly of critical details, as in "South Africa's Future Agonies," 10-22. Generally fresh insight in each commentary, but also an inherent predictability that may limit his effectiveness, suggesting he's ideologically hidebound, as in "Inside Czarist Russia in 1839," 7-7, (the evil empire never changes), or "So Why Did Stalin Happen?" 2-11, a historical retrospect that reaffirmed all "reform" as mere tactical readjustments for the preservation of Soviet totalitarianism. But who knows? Maybe he's right.

Brookhiser, Richard
National Review. (★ ½)

Managing Editor. He spends most of his time putting out *National Review*, where he's in line to succeed WFB. Sometimes trivial, as in "Two Curtain Calls," 6-6, thin stuff about an identity between Sweden's Palme and Haiti's Duvalier. He's better with efforts that aren't spun off as hurriedly. When he thinks through on a subject, he can be impressive with a strategic focus that's rich and informing: "Rescuing the Military," 2-14, a wide-ranging examination and critique of the parties and conceptions involved in military reform efforts. A conservative thinker with some originality, he can be analytically sharp. His best, "Pat Robertson Seeks Lower Office," 8-29, identifying what is permanent and will remain from this still new force in GOP politics, while catching its passing aspect as well: "The Robertson phenomenon is one form of a more general trend in the conservative movement: the pre-Jack fling...like bachelors looking up old flames as the wedding approaches, conservatives' eyes rove."

Buckley, William F.
Universal Press Syndicate. (★)

Editor of *National Review*, his editorials still worth a look, though he's gone flat in recent years, the cutting edge dulled. But '86 showed some bounce. "The Bush Business," 2-25, was a timely intervention into the fuss over Bush's "conservatism" and the end of any institutional advantage for securing the presidential nomination. He can still evoke a "Did you see what Buckley wrote?" stir, as in "Looking Out for Number Two," 3-21, a proposal to tattoo AIDS victims, or with his rumination on what he'd do if he were a South African black. A look at the hold on the Labour Party exerted by the UK's fire-in-the-belly Trotskyists, "Beware the British Militants," 9-23. Best we saw, "Marcos: Reflections," 3-7, acutely perceptive: "There is nothing, curiously, more denigrated in the modern world than the dictator who does not quite have the stomach to use all the force necessary to stay in power....Marcos was deposed, because, at the margin, he was soft."

Carter, Hodding III
The Wall Street Journal. (★)

Op-ed Columnist. A spear-chucker for the liberals, who occasionally makes a piercing point. His columns in '86, however, were disappointing. Though aggressive on the attack, his efforts on behalf of the liberal agenda were easily deflected. Too much scatter-shot venting without solid penetration. "Will the U.S. Try to Put Aquino on a Leash," 2-27, foamed and frothed about Reagan's embrace of the Philippine "tyrant," with nothing new being said. "A Have and Have-Not America," 7-24, looking at statistical "social dynamite" in the structure of society, concludes: "too few have far too much (12% of all American households control 38% of all our personal wealth) and too many have far too little." "Take PBS Off Its Strict Federal Diet," 9-25, was an intriguing headline, but public television's problem, he advised, is a gutlessness in the face of White House hostility.

Chamberlain, John
King Features Syndicate. (★ ★)

Into his 80s but still has gathered no moss. Trenchant, focused, and alert, zipping off columns with seeming ease, the grand old man is still razor-sharp. We see him in *The Washington Times*, using his grasp of history and economics to produce insightful examinations of foreign and domestic policies: "Patiently

Setting a Trap," 6-11, takes a whack at congressional libs who act as self-annointed Secretaries of State in dealing with the Sandinistas; "Safe Conduct to 2010," 7-1, a rich geo-political sweep of SDI's strategic impact several years out. "Using Detente to Smash Containment," 5-7, a typically tough critique, scoping the misfiring of U.S. policies toward communists from FDR's Grand Design to the era of detente: "Congress doesn't know any more about running the nation's foreign policy than George Steinbrenner knows about running the New York Yankees. The Big Brains on the House Side of Capitol Hill are that incompetent."

Cockburn, Alexander
The Nation. (★ ★ ★)

Our favorite Marxist, Cockburn appears monthly in a *Wall Street Journal* op-ed column, his most important forum, where he regularly infuriates the readers. A shameless leftist from the U.K., fortyish, son of a noted British intellectual and communist, he is straightforward, always passionate, a gifted writer with a devilish sense of humor, often armed with fresh arguments and insights. He was the first to notice the Democrats laying off Reagan in the fall elections, "Mainstream Democrats Swept Along With the Current," 10-23, and lashes the liberals for their wimpishness: "Often the only way you can tell one candidate from another is a certain craven edge to the Democrat's voice."

Cohen, Richard
The Washington Post. (★ ★ ★ ½)

The best of the *Post's* "liberal" columnists, Cohen's '86 may have been his finest. His new Sunday magazine column, "Critic at Large," which made a splash in the magazine's maiden edition, 9-7, by infuriating some of D.C.'s black citizenry with "Closing the Door on Crime," is consistently engaging, playful. His twice-a-week op-ed column took on a muscularity in '86 that made us forget an earlier whine, replacing knee-jerk with punchy commentary. We liked "It's Time to Pull the Plug on Marcos," 2-11, with Marcos promising "a water buffalo in every pot," and "He Lucked Out Again," 2-28, on Reagan and the Philippines: "Never play cards with a man named 'Doc'." "Keep That Bench Warm," 7-1, drips with sarcasm on Daniel Manion, the Reagan appeals court appointee. "Overblown Epidemic," 9-12, makes pungent arguments on the media hype on drugs and threat to civil liberties. "Linda Chavez, Playing With Mud," 11-2, flags the Maryland GOP Senate candidate for nasty innuendos; Cohen is also quick to jump on liberals who play below the belt. His "Soft-Core Hypocrisy," 3-25, was among his weakest (Wm. F. Buckley has written for *Penthouse*!) Best: "An Israel Example," 4-16, on how El-Al Airlines keeps terror-free by relentless security measures.

MediaGuide 265

D'Souza, Dinesh
Policy Review. (★ ★ ★)

Managing Editor. A young new writer of conservative bent, D'Souza is fresh and invigorating, tough but never strident. A former editor of *The Darmouth Review*, a training ground for new talent. His "Whose Pawns Are the Bishops" is a classic, an '85 treatment of the subject that no one bested in '86. Broad in scope, incisive with critical detail, he was stellar again in '86 with "Feminism's New Agenda" (Winter), "Shanty Raids at Dartmouth" (Spring), "TV News: The Politics of Social Climbing"(Summer), "The Liberal Censorship" (Fall). Analytically penetrating: "N.Y. Plays Itself" (*Vanity Fair*, 1-86), matching Cuomo and Kemp as contenders for '88; focused, to the point, with something new to say, as in "LaRouche Panics the Democratic Party" (*LA Times*, 3-30). "Pat Robertson's World" (*The American Spectator*, 11-86), one of the year's best on the return of fundamentalists to the political arena: "Probe establishment GOP types and at first they cite the kooky fundamentalist beliefs; but then their faces grow dark and they mutter: Abortion, School Prayer, Pornography."

Evans, Harold
U.S.News & World Report. (★ ½)

Alternating editorial column duties with Editor-in-Chief Zuckerman until he left to become a consultant for Conde-Nast, Evans was always readable, but breezy and noncommittal in his columns. A two-sided editorial just isn't forceful in its arguments. Two of his best were "Cradle to Grave Injustice," 7-28, on U.S. policy towards South Africa, and "Whose English Language," 8-25, in defense of Americanisms.

Fallows, James
The Atlantic. (★ ½)

Washington Editor. Adding East Asia to his beat in '86, Fallows mixed reports from Tokyo with coverage of the national scene. Perhaps the new assignment helped account for his marginal slip this year. "The Spend-Up," 7-86, stood out as a confused and confusing traipse through the issue of defense-cost growth and readiness problems. What drives up weapons prices? A hodge-podge of "perhaps this, perhaps that" to support a novel assertion: "Whatever the combination, the result was clear: Americans could make more money producing weapons than doing practically anything else, such as competing with the Japanese." His Japan reports were mixed. "Letter From Tokyo," 8-86, was stale and puerile on the reason behind U.S. problems in competing with Japan (they work harder than we do). "The Japanese Are Different From You And Me," 9-86, far better, with sufficient insight and development of peculiarly Japanese cultural practices and beliefs to make it orginal, worthwhile.

Fields, Suzanne
The Washington Times. (★ ★ ★)

The leading voice of anti-feminism in the press corps, an ex-liberal, daughter of a D.C. bookmaker, piquantly witty, Barbara Stanwyck-ish. Fields somehow stays consistently entertaining, finding unusual topics to celebrate the differences of the sexes. "What She Never Understood," 4-17, a wry remembrance of Simone de Beauvoir. In "How Could They Have Known It Was Rape?" 5-22, she's wonderfully angry as campus cops overlook a murder-rape thinking it was just innocent fornication they observed. Among her best: "The Pride is Back: Male in America" (*Insight*, 6-16), she kicks sand at the 98-pound Mr. Sensitive Male: "only a man can compare kissing with getting to first base catching a glimpse of forbidden lace with making it to second, the first touch of female flesh with rounding third, or lovemaking to a home run. (Men score, women count the ways.)" On the other side of the coin, Ms. Fields was the first to take note of the infamous Harvard-Yale study on marriage and professional women ("She Who Hesitates...," 2-27), that later spawned several magazine cover stories.

Fossedal, Gregory
Copley News Service. (★ ★ ★)

A brainy, unguided missile, the Star Wars expert in the news media. At 28, still a boy wonder, the original conservative Dartmouth college editor, Foss was too hot to handle at *The Wall Street Journal* with his advocacy of the Strategic Defense Initiative. Now cooling down in Palo Alto with a stream of columns appearing in *The Washington Times* as well as the Copley papers. His "Danger Ahead for SDI," 8-4, lapped the field in seeing the implications of Reagan's July letter to Gorbachev that unfolded at Reykjavik. An unconventional "Hooray for 'Divided Alliance'" (*San Diego Union*, 6-13), points out NATO allies always oppose Reagan action until he acts. "The KGB's Reaganalysis," 4-16, is stark on how the most anti-Red President of all may come away with an empty bag. "But What Does He Want Us to Do?," 10-31, chides George Will on SDI for being "virtually mute" when it counts. Powerful stuff in "A Morality Test for South Africa Opposition," (*NY Times* op-ed, 2-4), urging Bishop Tutu to apply a democracy standard and shun support of the ANC, Qaddafi and Nicaragua's Ortega. One of "his generation's most promising journalists," according to *The Washington Post*, he can't do it from Palo Alto, however. Come East, young man!

Garment, Suzanne
The Wall Street Journal. (★ ★)

"Capital Chronicle" Columnist. Sometimes we just don't want to wade through her column and instead move directly to the middle of it. There we find thoughtful analysis or fresh information we never expected given the heavy and

MediaGuide 267

tedious introduction, as for example, "Packard Plan: Will Anyone Carry It Out?" 2-28. Much better, her 3-7 column, biting on the "capacity for gratuitous self-mortification" that confuses and saps our Mideast policy. But too much initial gumming in "Start Treating U.S. Intelligence as Vital Business," 4-18, weakened the effectiveness of an otherwise superior effort. "Gramm-Rudman: A Hushed Stage for the Drama," 4-25, ended with a promising analytic perspective, but reading the paragraphs back upward, the column strayed further and further from any reward. Yet, she is thoughtful and seriously analytical, alert to what's left unaddressed by others, as for example, "South Africa Becomes a Part of U.S. Politics," 7-25. A little less of an academic flavor would move her up a notch.

Goodman, Ellen
The Boston Globe. Washington Post Writers Group. (★ ½)

Occasionally insightful commentary buoyed by a subtle humor. Unfortunately, she sometimes ends up out of her league, as in "Protecting the Young Star Warriors Who Can't Promise Protection," 1-30, which seemed to be a empty conglomeration of other people's (William Broad and "a *Washington Monthly* writer") efforts in describing SDI researchers. Better on social issues, "Denying Diversity," 11-11, on religion in the classroom and textbooks, and "Not in Front of the Children," 2-25, on TV's role in the stripping away of childhood innocence: "In the electronic age, the parent is less of a guide and more of a fellow traveler. We don't slowly expose our children to the world in a series of monitored field trips anymore. We don't control the flow of information into their lives. It comes through a garrulous and permanent guest who doesn't respond to the command, 'Shh, the children.'"

Greenberg, Paul
Freelance Syndicate. (★ ★)

The editorial page editor of *The Pine Bluff* [Ark] *Commercial*, his syndicated columns, often in *The Washington Times*, are always well-written, lively and usually provocative. Wide-ranging on issues from national security to profound questions of culture, re-examining and testing old assumptions with an instinct for insight and depth, as in "Cultural Exchanges That Aren't," 6-7. At the time we saw it, his "Waldheim File," 4-4, was the best organized indictment of Kurt we'd seen. The best we saw, though, "Without Borges," 6-25, a powerfully moving testimony to that historian and poet of the soul who used his blindness as a mirror for inner illumination. Best when examining questions of character, but insightful rather than simply moralizing.

Greenfield, Meg
Newsweek. (★ ½)

The *Post*'s neoliberal (or sometimes neoconservative) editorial page editor, Greenfield writes occasional columns and shares the back page of *Newsweek* with George Will (neoroyalist). Very bright and travels around a lot, so we always take a look, but too often dull stuff, as in "Police State Surprise," 10-8, thinking out loud about China on her autumn Asian tour. Then there's the nugget, later in the same tour, "Cory Aquino's Secret Weapon," 10-20: "It lies in remaining her improbable self, in some strange combination of staring down and shaming her enemies and her doubters." Better at moralizing, often wryly humorous, as in "Why Nothing is Wrong Anymore," 7-28.

Grenier, Richard
The Washington Times. (★ ★ ★ ★)

The star columnist of the *Times*, the "Point Man," after the platoon leader who "walks point" to detect land mines. Grenier — a foreign correspondent, film critic, novelist — was 52 when he wrote his first column at Editor de Borchgrave's invitation and it was magic. Imagine Harpo Marx graduating from the U.S. Naval Academy, taking graduate work at Harvard and the Institut d'Etudes Politiques in Paris, spending half his journalistic career in France, London and Madrid, taking a turn at *The New York Times* before his first rocket/columns for the *WT*!! The fellow can write profoundly serious 1,200-word columns (the normal column length is 750) on the fate of western civilization, honking his horn with pretty girls popping up around every turn. Catch "If 'Evita' Could Be a Hit, Just Think of 'Imelda!'," 9-19, not only hilarious, but analytically sound on the Philippines. Grenier's "Meet You in the Ladies Room at the Peking Railroad Station," 9-8, a classic. Globetrotting, he writes the best straight piece we've seen on the year's Chilean controversy, "Who Knows What's Good For Chileans," (London *Telegraph*, 9-14). Best line, 4-2, on *The Washington Post's* Mary McGrory: "Reading Miss McGrory is an acquired taste. Like drinking sulfuric acid, one might say." Wonderful.

Johnson, Haynes
The Washington Post. (½ ★)

Once a liberal voice with some resonance and range, he's become flat and limited over the years. "Tilting the Budget," 2-5, hits the Administration for soaking up capital and weakening U.S. ability to compete with its defense budget, an old whine in a new bottle. "An Attack of Unseemly Rhetoric," 4-23, after the Libya strike, criticizes the swaggering, a tsk-tsk pecking and clucking without any bite. In "Tomorrow? Who Cares?," 10-1, he's probably repeating something he overheard at a Democratic cocktail party: "Our problem isthe fact that we are increasing consumption at a high rate but increasing investment in production at a more modest rate...To repay our increased debt, we must lower the standard of living in the future." The same with "The Reagan Restorative," 1-12, a sort of snake oil compliment: "one of the marvels of our time, Ronald Reagan" whose brand of personal leadership qualities "ought to be patented as a national treasure."

Kilpatrick, James J.
Universal Press Syndicate. (★)

Kilpo is still quick on defense, swatting the liberals over Nicaragua, South Africa, or domestic social policies. But he's made the same arguments for so many years the fizz is gone. "It's Obvious Why We Must Help the Contras," 4-4, was informed argument, but without punch. "U.S. History Repeats Itself in South Africa," 6-30, has no cutting edge. He fights the old battles, even when they're new ones, and that's been a debilitating limitation for him in '86. More meritorious, "A Meditation for Independence Day," (*National Review*, 7-4) this normally hard-to-please conservative observes: "There will be time enough, tomorrow and tomorrow and tomorrow, to dwell upon the bad news that those of us in the news business must report. Now and then, like Burke's silent cattle in the shadow of the oak, we should let the presence of good news rise above the grasshopper's importunate chink."

Kinsley, Michael
The New Republic. (★ ★ ★ ★)

Editor and TRB columnist, the most important of today's liberal, young (35) journalists. A complex 512K mind with 20 megabytes of memory, Kinsley produces razor-sharp analytics without sources and maybe without using the telephone. Out of Oxford economics, Harvard law, and Nader's Raiders, his lofty standards of political discourse and behavior are applied to both parties with such exactitude, along with a rather dry charm, that he's practically a national asset. "Incredible Dr. Hammer," 1-20, a gem in taking the pants off Oxy's Armand. "Podhoretz is Wrong," 3-20, slams Norman for (yipes) McCarthyism for writing that "in a conflict where the only choice is between communists and anti-communists, anyone who refuses to help the anti-communists is agreeing to help the communists." He displays his grasp of economics in "Kemp's Budget Plan Falls About 90 Yards Short," 5-15, a serious parry. Less serious: "Yucks in the Yuckiness of the Porn Report," 7-17, deriding those trying to wrestle with a monstrous problem, a problem of his loftiness. In "We Wuz Robbed," 6-9, he bites into the Democratic Leadership Council and finds, yuk, mush: "Politics is not a game of capture-the-flag. If all the important things Democrats would like to say are already being said by Republicans, it's hard to see why stealing them back is worth the trouble." On the whole, incandescent.

Krauthammer, Charles
The New Republic. (★ ★)

As combative as ever, sparring with liberals and conservatives alike. Vigorous in efforts to trim flab from the neoliberal agenda, he spent a good part of '86 hammering away at neo-isolationist threats to U.S. foreign policy, as in "Interventionism: An Exchange," 4-28. In "Rebuttal," 3-31, he clashed with Kinsley over aid to the anti-Sandinistas, and upbraided the House Armed Services Committee Chairman for shortsightedness in "Aspin Fights The Has-Beens," 8-5. Krauthammer brings a new dimension of serious standards to the foreign and defense policy debates within the Democratic Party, but comes down so often on the side of Reagan, as in "Why Reagan Nixed SALT," 6-24, that he persuades liberals he's really a neocon with a neolib disguise. But he scorches the Administration when he sees retreat or vague strategic unclarity, sounding alarms as with "In Pursuit of the End of Days," 10-21: "The impasse over SDI was not the Reykjavik surprise. The new news is the offensive cuts offered by both sides. They amount to a revolution in the postwar world. A hair-raising revolution."

Kristol, Irving
The Wall Street Journal. (★ ★ ★)

A most complex mind can produce the most lucid prose, NYU's Professor Kristol has demonstrated in his monthly op-ed column since 1973. The genuine and original "neoconservative" leading a movement away from liberalism, Kristol may be the most influential intellectual of the era, adding in his twin quarterlies, *The Public Interest* and *The National Interest*, and his "godfathering" of the supply-side economic revival. In "Three Economic Notes for 1986," 1-9, he goes to great trouble to explain to professional economists, which he is not, that the dollar has not weakened; the yen has gotten stronger. ("This may sound like sophistry, but it's not.") In "Why a Debate Over Contra Aid?," 4-11, he approaches excruciating persuasiveness. His best, we think: "Schools Can Do This Much," 9-8, about as delicious as social commentary can get: "Even in the rather chaotic American society of today, such a consensus exists among the overwhelming majority of American parents. They would like to see their children neat rather than slovenly, polite rather than rude, respectful rather than insolent, inclined toward self-restraint rather than self-indulgence, aware that they have duties and obligations as well as rights. That is not too much to ask."

Lambro, Donald
United Feature Syndicate. (★ ★)

"A one-man search-and-destroy mission against government waste," as *The Washington Post* called him, Lambro is unmatched on that front. His waste-fraud-mismanagement reports are the best of the genre, solid with fact, detail, and perspective. Two outstanding examples in '86: "Health-care Abuses That Cost $2 Billion" (*The Washington Times*, 6-11), and "One for the Scalpel—Budgetary Malpractice In Health Research," (*Policy Review*, Spring #86). "Spare-Parts Progress Report," (*The Washington Times*, 7-17) probably the clearest picture on the Packard Commission Report by anyone for the year. New from him in '86, a few forays into the battle of ideas and GOP politics, "GOP Hedges on TV Campaign Blitz," 10-16, and "For GOP, This May Be Year of Governorships," 10-17, both okay.

Lapham, Lewis
Harper's. (½ ★)

Editor. Occasionally there's evidence of his former skill with sardonic wit, but more often than not, it's mere manipulative technique now, all wordsmithing. Lapham kept swinging, but connected with little in '86. What he thinks clever has become tedious, as in "Uptown," 10-86, with the following advice to Democrats in search of grander designs: "Why not wrap the poor? Bundle them up in denominations of 500 or 1,000 and sell them to wealthy collectors looking for a reason to set a trend. If not enough collectors can be found, the bundled poor could be donated to museums and classified as tax deductions....Safely and attractively wraped, they might serve as ornaments in the nation's office plazas and hotel lobbies." Similarly one-dimensional, "Nuclear Etiquette," 5-86, "Pictures at an Exhibition," 3-86.

Lerner, Max
New York Post. (★ ★)

We've been reading Max (now 85) since the early '50s, and still don't notice much slowing of his river of ideas and analysis. We pick up his column when it appears in *The Washington Times*, as it does frequently. His best of '86, "A Vision With Consequences," 10-20, on Reagan astride the forces of history with SDI: "He may have stumbled on a burden and vision equal to the travail of the presidency....shifting the discourse of deterrence from a rivalry in destructive technology to a rivalry in defensive technology. By that fact he is also shifting the center of moral gravity between the two superpowers. Once the pivot of deterrence shifts, then inevitably — resist it who may — the moral perspectives shift with it. The world increasingly has to judge the ethos of each camp by its actions on the central issue of deterrence. Even the Soviet leaders are straining to show that it is they and not their American rivals who care about steep reductions in destructive weapons. With every month and year they will also have to contend that they care about developing defensive weapons systems."

Lofton, John
The Washington Times. (★★½)

If hardline conservatives have to prep for Mary McGrory's column by drinking sulfuric acid, lefthanders had better wrestle fire-eating dragons before tackling Lofton. We noted last year that his born-again evangelism was intruding on his journalism, but there was no doubt 1986 was a strong reporting year for him. The heart of his best work is in catching liberal virtucrats at their own game and pulling their wings off. Good research on "Maybe He Should Try Abracadabra," 4-11, hits Rep. Michael Barnes disingenuousness on the Contadora process. "Dodd's Self-Fulfilling Prophecies," 4-4, quotes Senator Dodd over 10 years in opposing aid to Vietnam, Angola, Central America. He is wonderfully outraged, 5-28, on learning Phil Donahue took Vladimir Posner, the Kremlin's official U.S. talk-show guest, to a $262 dinner. He nails Sen. Metzenbaum for moralizing on Mike Deaver, reminding us of Metz's $250K "finder's fee," 5-7. A remembrance of Jimmy Cagney, 4-2, reminds us that Lofton can be a good writer when he isn't smoking, as he is in "Courting Media Disaster," 5-5, a great taped interview with Supreme Court reporter Lyle Denniston, who suggests rape and murder may be protected by the 1st amendment.

Masty, S.J.
The Washington Times. (★★)

A thirtyish, bearded columnist with a diabolical sense of humor, Masty appears now and then after being cut from the regular staff by some humorless editor. "The Secret Life of Albert Einstein," 4-8, was up with the funniest sketches of the newspaper year, a sendup on TV's biographical focus on the sex lives of great men. "A Midnight Visitation From Beyond the Grave," 4-10, has the ghost of Jefferson visiting George Bush: "'OK, if inflation came back, would you consider wage and price controls?' (asks TJ). 'Golly heck, no,no,no,' shrieked the veep, flapping his pajama sleeves like somebody's auntie." With encouragement, the next S.J. Perelman, but he may bag it for law school or some such.

McCarthy, Colman
The Washington Post. (★)

He still gushes and oozes with the mushiest of mushy liberalism, but nobody's heart bleeds as eloquently as his. He can be incredibly naive as in an interview with a retired "labor organizer" who recounted his 1928 experience in Nicaragua: "I was taking part in rapes, burning huts, cutting off genitals....while we were in the Marines we were taught not to have a conscience," 3-19. Unabashedly solicitious with "feeling states," as in "A Last Talk With a Condemned Man," 1-13, (hours before James Terry Roach was to be electrocuted): "Instead of talking about his legal case...we discussed his life and values. I told him...I had heard from a number of readers who expressed gladness that he was being executedI wanted to learn Roach's feelings.'' On the fringes of society, into the depths of those suffering unnoticed — the homeless, the condemned, "misfits" and the disturbed, the solitary witnesses of conscience — McCarthy services it all. And somebody should.

McGrory, Mary
The Washington Post. (★ ★ ½)

Mother McGrory, an uncommon scold, wields a sulfurous pen on behalf of liberal causes and political liberals, often an influence on liberal thought. We thought she slipped a bit from a stellar '85, not as *au courant*, or absorbing. But not by much. In "The Parallel That Counts," 3-18, she has Jonas Savimbi taking hostages that the Angola contras mutilate; tough stuff. She throws a bone to Paul Laxalt, "a Reagan non-threatening western personality," 3-6, and offers a charming, offbeat "A Lonely American in Verona," 9-21, watching Aida from the bleachers. Our favorite was "Hornswoggling the Press," 10-7, on the Administration/Libya disinformation story: "Comparing people (Qadafi) who get on the President's nerves to Adolf Hitler is something that the Secretary of State does rather casually. He did it in the case of Nicaragua's Daniel Ortega. It pleases the boss, elevates the pest to a world menace, and justifies any sordid means to an end.''

Novak, Michael
National Review, The Washington Times. (★ ½)

Author of the "Tomorrow and Tomorrow" column in *National Review*, Novak produces informed observations and analyses of the problems and perspectives of the pontiff and his Church. Conceptually well-focused and organized, he never slips into the insufficient and flawed, but all too common, "traditionalist vs. progressive" framework; "Post-Synod Elation," 1-31, and "The Curran Crisis," 4-26, both are examples of his deftness with the subject. It's his strong suit, yet he was sparse here for '86, both in *National Review* and his syndicated columns. Some ventures into other areas turned out better this year than previously. "Applying the Pincers," (*The Washington Times*, 3-3) a description in broad terms of Soviet's global strategy, was one such, and "Growing Middle Incomes," 8-15, another.

Podhoretz, Norman
News America Syndicate. (★)

The editor of *Commentary*, his fire-breathing produces better magazines than columns. Perceptive, incisive on a variety of subjects, and always singularly focused and hard as nails. Nothing he approaches is treated with anything less than life-and-death urgency; a neoconservative, he was just as certain of his views when he was a socialist. "Jackson's Orphans and the Contras," (*New York Post*, 2-25) castigates old Democratic friends — those politically orphaned by the death of Scoop Jackson — for saying things are getting better and the reflexive "blame America first" is waning. "Call Communism By Its Real Name," 3-11, a "no mercy" bashing of opponents of anti-Sandinista aid, who screamed "red-baiter" and "McCarthyite" when told their opposition was a siding with communism. "A Day in the Decline of America," 3-25, links the passage of NY's gay rights bill with defeat of "contra" aid as two events some future Gibbon will note. In "Europe's 'Decadence' Perils NATO," 4-22, he chews up U.S. allies for their irresolute, sappy will, and criticizes Irving Kristol's "global unilateralism." He's never trivial in his treatment of a subject, almost always proceeding from its implications for western civilization. The stridency in his voice grates at times.

Rabinowitz, Dorothy
News America Syndicate. (★)

A neoconservative media critic who takes on the networks, slamming them for substituting moralizing for news. But we can only take so much of this. In "TV's Sermonettes in Prime Time," *New York Post*, 4-11, she took on the medium for passing off twaddle as drama, ripping apart the made-for-tv movies that are advanced with resounding testimonials to their ground-breaking importance and transcendental meaningfulness. A watchdog for assaults on traditional values, she's relentless in exposing the networks when they cross the line and replace individual responsibility with "society" as the culprit for every social disorder: "Misguided Sense of Protection," (*The Washington Times*, 7-14) lambasts TV's "news analysis" that inadequate funding is responsible for public health problems like AIDS or for the occurrence of those disturbed who go amok in public and kill. At her best in "Teaching Bill Cosby About Comedy," 3-21, a defense of new comedic dimensions against the preachments of social improvements.

Raspberry, William
The Washington Post. (★ ★ ½)

Around for a long time with mildly interesting coverage of the local D.C. scene, Raspberry moved out aggressively in '86, challenging the old consensus on social issues with honed insight and critical evidence for a fresh new approach. Two of his best: "The Vanishing Black Family," 1-26, going beyond conventional solutions of more money and compassion to focus on rebuilding the collapsed value system in black ghettos, and "Studying Success," 3-12, empirical data on how to make public-private housing partnerships work. On foreign affairs, he's often informative where others are lax, as on South Africa, 6-6, honestly revealing the wealth redistributionist perspectives of the Rev. Boesak. His best for the year, "Would Elections Really Help Haiti?," 2-5, was one of the sharpest analyses of the U.S. foreign policy's "Achilles' heel," that lapped the field with its singular insight: "The fascinating thing is that for all of our ostensible concern for Third World peasants and our deep-dyed opposition to leftist political systems, we make virtually no effort to export the American economic system."

Rosenblatt, Roger
Time. (★ ½)

Senior writer doubling as one of *Time*'s premier essayists. A tough way to make a living, though, with a weekly deadline on thoughtful, poetic observations on the human condition. Sometimes it works, and he has his fans. In "Poetry and Politics," 10-13, he explores the connection, however tenuous, between the political and the poetic. Later, in "The Too Personal Presidency," 11-24, Reagan is scrutinized for his handling of the public and the Iranian arms dealings. His best, "The Freedom of the Damned," 10-6, about the cost of indulgence, reacting to the murder of Jennifer Levin in New York City: "Between parent and child there is no monster like silence. It grows even faster than children, filling first a heart, then a house, then history....The freedom they are given too often is the freedom of the damned, with which they may strangle themselves late on a summer night, in a city, in a park, where they have gone to be alone." But why in the world, as he asked himself repeatedly, did his editors send him to Reykjavik?

Rowan, Carl
News America Syndicate. (½ ★)

So predictable in '86, that he was tiresome, without anything fresh or new to say. Slight variations on the same droning theme — Reagan: "Scorns Government's Historic Role," 2-21; "Plays a Cynical Game with Poverty," 2-7; "Ignorance Is His Bliss;" "Plays Chamberlain to Botha's Hitler," 7-30 — all one-dimensional huffing and puffing. He was tough with white liberals in "Just More Slander of the Black Family," 2-11, but still too bound by old lib establishment thinking to be more than conventional knee-jerk on the issue. On the edge of becoming an automatic skip, '86 showed no signs of a turnaround.

Samuelson, Robert
Newsweek. (★ ★ ½)

Occasionally quirky, eccentric economic subject matter gradually giving way to more social commentary with economic overtones, at which he is better. "The Consumer Hit Parade," 10-6, or ten things that shook the world and the way it works, a good example. "Goodbye to the Age of Steel," 11-3, explains all this to *Newsweek*'s broad audience. "The Discovery of Money," puts good old-fashioned American greed into perspective. "The Super Bowl of Scandal," 12-1, excellent at putting Boesky into perspective while lecturing on the value of hostile takeovers. At his worst when he tries to address a narrower, professional audience, often wasting its time by confessing ignorance at length, such as "The Interest Rate Mystery," 3-12: "What happened? No one really knows...Interest rates remain a subject of immense confusion and mystery...But our ignorance is unsettling. In the end, lower interest rates may be a delayed reaction to lower inflation. But who knows?"

Schmertz, Herb
The Washington Times via *Heritage Features Syndicate.* (★ ½)

Mobil Oil's switch-hitting superflack, the media critic with the easiest swing, bashing lefties and righties with equal glee in a way that doesn't break the skin. In "The T.S. Report," 6-29, he catches "reknowned humorist" Russell Baker desperately "sitting on the razor's edge" looking for a topic and coming up with the Duke of Windsor's twice-a-day shave. His best column ever, "Down Sally's Alley," 9-15, a sendup of Sally Quinn's first novel *Regrets Only*: "Since this is an important review, the Reviewer — like every single character in every single clothed appearance in *Regrets Only* — has dressed properly for its composition. He wears hand-cobbled English shoes of softly burnished cordovan. For his trousers he has chosen — because this is a book about Washington and by a woman — a soft creamy wool flannel in a muted gray that echoes the half-tones of photographs printed in the "Style" section of *The Washington Post*, where Sal was once *the* Style reporter."

Seligman, Daniel
Fortune. (★ ★ ★)

A horseplaying, card-sharping neoconservative who writes the "Keeping Up" column with the help of Nexus. On the 10th anniversary of the column, 12-8-86, the editors acknowledged that "Keeping Up" consistently generates more mail than any of the other features except the Fortune 500 directories. In fact, for years Seligman has been the only reliable pole holding up the magazine's tent, watchdogging the media, puncturing the pomposity of the elites, defending the unjustly maligned, all done with gentlemanly restraint and wit. He growls at *The New York Times*, 1-20, for wanting to tax frequent flyer awards. A favorite was an item wondering why *The Times* and other papers so frequently quote the oil-price opinions of Daniel Yergin, whose 1982 book predicted a continuing 2% annual rise in the real, non-inflated oil price to the year 2000. He remembers stuff like that. Then he researches *The Times* files on South Africa and finds an uncommon aversion to mentioning the African National Congress's domination by communists. In his 12-8 anniversary column, he confesses to all the errors he's made in ten years that he can identify, "The Wrongs of the Decade," and finds only five, not one more than a mouthful of crow.

MediaGuide

Sobran, Joseph
Universal Press Syndicate. (★)

A senior editor of *National Review* who takes on left-liberal verities from the perspective of the "Old Right" set. Bashing "collectivist" schemes — affirmative action, 7-8, rent control, 7-24, Planned Parenthood, 10-14, — his syndicated columns are still a little too much of tired conservative opinion. Much better, with some fresh insight and observation, his efforts in *National Review*, "Unpacking the Court", 4-11. "The Politics of Aids," 5-23, how a public health issue has been distorted into a civil liberties issue, was his best, critical and hard, yet with decided compassion displayed.

Tyrrell, R. Emmett, Jr.
The Washington Post. (★ ½)

The wunderkind founder and editor of *The American Spectator* monthly, now in his 40s and ensconced in Alexandria, Va., after 15 years or so in Bloomington, Ind. Tyrrell's syndicated column needs more substance to support his Menckenesque prose; it isn't as much fun seeing him kick liberals as it was when they were alive. A fine effort, for example, with "Reagan: Too Much the Loner," 10-19, on RR trying to do it all himself, which "undoubtedly allows him greater political freedom, but it weakens his capacity to define the present and prefigure the future." He's best when he works his *Spectator* column, "The Continuing Crisis." His May column was his best in years, with the funniest line we saw in the American press in '86: "Many a lonely Englishman's prospects for conjugal felicity were improved when the European Court of Justice ruled that guards at Heathrow Airport can no longer bar inflatable sex dolls from England. Had the ruling been made years ago, *The New Republic*'s Mr. Henry Fairlie might never have had to leave England."

Wade, Lawrence
The Washington Times. (★ ★)

The best distinctly black columnist in '85, Wade lost ground in 1986 by weaker reporting, frothier writing, and a distracting tendency to use the first person singular in every column. A Qaddafi column, "Sometimes Big Guys Have to Fight Back," 4-2, uses a personal anecdote to make a point, so does "The Gender Trap," 4-4, on sex discrimination. The ultimate is in "Why IRA's Should Be Spared," 5-9, because "that is Larry Wade's ideal world." Better with "Overlooking His Own Fettered Feet," 5-5, cutting Hodding Carter's linkage of bigotry and black poverty, then "Black on Black Racism," 9-15, zapping John Conyers and Coleman Young on the Lucas race for Michigan governor. Best with "Gotta Have Heart," 11-7, a sharp post-election comment on GOP blowing Senate because they didn't court the black vote.

Will, George
The Washington Post, Newsweek. (★ ½)

Another rather disappointing year. Will is called upon to write so many thoughtful books and pieces and say so many thoughtful things on TV and the lecture circuit that he no longer has time to think. His shorter *Post* columns are better than the *Newsweek* essays because he has less space for what he has to say. He observes and cheers Rep. Gephardt embracing modern mercantilism, 2-16, but misses the political motive. There's a barely plausible scenario in "Prime Time for Bob Dole," 5-18, if the Veep falters, but really just a gratuity to Dole; similarly, "Kemp's Game Plan May Work," 3-26. "A Dismal Campaign in California," 11-2, is spirited on the Senate race, but unenlightening in any respect. Better with "Judicial Kerosene," 2-2, giving the doomed Calif. Chief Justice Rose Bird her due, for a "kind of crazy bravery." He's best, unhappily, when he's mean. "George Bush: The Sound of a Lapdog," 1-30: "The unpleasant sound Bush is emitting as he traipses from one conservative gathering to another is a thin, tinny 'arf' — the sound of a lapdog. He is panting along Mondale's path to the presidency."

Zuckerman, Mortimer
U.S.News & World Report. (★)

Chairman and Editor-In-Chief. He shared editorial page responsibilities with his now-departed editorial director Harold Evans. Occasionally hard-hitting material, particularly when the issue is close to his heart, as in the Daniloff drama, U.S.-Soviet relations or terrorism; as in "The Daniloff Dilemmas, 10-3; "Why This Summit Was A Success, 10-27; and "Playing the Terrorist's Game," 6-9. But his best was "End of an Era," 2-25, a very clear overview of the Philippine electoral crisis that was far superior to much of the other press's efforts there. Interestingly, Zuckerman, a real estate tycoon as well as publisher, turned out to be one of the better reporters on the Manila scene during that period.

BIOGRAPHICS

Abelson, Alan. *Barron's.* Editor. B. 1925, NYC. CCNY, 1946, BS-English/Chemistry; U. of IA, 1947, MA-Creative writing. Freelance NYC, to 1949. *New York Journal-American* copyboy, metro reporter, financial desk to 1956. *Barron's,* reporter to 1965; Managing Editor, 1966; "Up & Down Wall Street" columnist, current, 1981; Editor, current. Also current, NBC-TV "News at Sunrise" business commentator.

Adams, James Ring. *Forbes.* Senior Editor. B. 1944, Edgewood, MD. Yale, 1966, BA; Cornell, 1984, PhD-Government. *Yale Daily News,* staff member, Managing Editor. Freelance articles. *The Wall Street Journal,* editorial writer, 1972-82. Manhattan Institute, research asst., to 1983. *The Wall Street Journal,* Editorial Board member, 1972-86. *Forbes,* Senior Editor, current, 1986. Author *Secrets of the Tax Revolt,* 1984.

Adams, Nathan Miller. *Reader's Digest.* Senior Editor. B. 1934, NYC. Colby College, 1958, Art. US Air Force, 1960-63. *New York Journal-American,* "Logbook of Crime" columnist, feature writer, to 1965. Time, Inc., stringer, London, to 1968. *Sunday Times,* London, 1967. *Reader's Digest,* Senior Editor, special assignments, Europe-Middle East, current, 1968. Author *The Fifth Horseman,* 1967 (Literary Guild Selection).

Alm, Richard. *U.S. News & World Report.* Associate Editor. FL State U.; U. of KS, MA-Journalism; AZ State U., Economics. *Arizona Republic. Dallas Morning News. U.S. News & World Report,* Associate Editor, economy & trade, current, 1983. TX Headliner Award for Special Reporting, 1982.

Almond, Peter J. *The Washington Times.* London Correspondent. B. 1946, Northampton, UK. Neiman Fellow, Harvard, 1981. *Northern Echo* (Darlington, UK), 1964. *Yorkshire Evening Press,* to 1969. *Cleveland Press,* reporter, to 1979; investigative, to 1982. *The Washington Times,* State Dept. correspondent, to 1985; London correspondent, current, 1985. Heywood Broun Award (Newspaper Guild), 1979; Thomas L. Stokes Award, 1979; Charles Stewart Mott Award, 1976; Northeast OH Press Club, First Place Business Reporting, 1982; OH UPI First Place, Series, 1982.

Alter, Jonathan. *Newsweek.* Associate Editor. B. 1957, Chicago, IL. Harvard, 1979, History. Freelance, Washington, to 1981. *The Washington Monthly,* editor, writer, to 1983. *Newsweek,* Associate Editor/News Media Writer, current, 1983.

Anderson, Jack. United Feature Syndicate. Columnist. B. 1922, Long Beach, CA. Studied U. of UT, 1940-41; Georgetown, 1947-48; George Washington U., 1948. US Merchant Marine, 1944-45; US Army, 1946-47. *Salt Lake Tribune,* reporter, 1939-41. Missionary, Church Jesus Christ of Latter Day Saints, to 1944. *Deseret News,* war correspondent, 1945. *Washington Merry-Go-Round,* reporter, from 1947; partner, from 1965; owner, from 1969. *Parade,* Washington Editor, 1954-68; Washington Bureau Chief, from 1968. United Feature Syndicate, columnist, current. Author & co-author 12 books. Pulitzer Prize for National Reporting, 1972.

Andrews, Fred. *The New York Times.* Business & Financial Editor. B. 1938, Roanoke, VA. Duke, 1960, BA-Political Science, *magna cum laude;* Princeton, 1965, MA-Politics. *The Richmond News-Leader,* intern-reporter, summers 1958, '60. Union Carbide, copywriter, 1962. Fair Campaign Practices Committee, Inc., NY, reseach associate; director of research, to 1965. U. of MD, Far East Division, Taiwan, instructor, 1966. *The New York Times*/Time-Life News Service, correspondent, Taiwan, to 1968. *The Wall Street Journal,* reporter, "Tax Report" columnist, to

1976. *The New York Times,* reporter; "Taxes and Accounting" columnist; "Management" columnist; deputy editor, 1977 to 1985; Business and Financial Editor, current, 1985. Author *Tax Tips and Dodges; More Tax Tips and Dodges; Old Hundred Names: Pictures of the People of Taiwan:* co-editor *The Equity Funding Papers: The Anatomy of a Fraud.*

Andrews, Walter E. Jr. *The Washington Times.* Pentagon Correspondent. B. 1933, Elizabeth, NJ. St. Peter's College, 1955, Chemistry. Reuters, Washington, to 1980. Bell Labs Public Relations, to 1982. *Army Times,* to 1983. *The Washington Times,* Pentagon correspondent, current.

Apple, R.W. *The New York Times.* Chief Washington Correspondent. B. 1934, Akron, OH. Columbia, 1961, History, *magna cum laude. The Wall Street Journal,* staff reporter, to 1961. US Army, to 1959. NBC News, TV writer & correspondent, to 1963. *The New York Times,* metro staff, to 1965, 1968; Saigon Bureau Chief, to 1968; chief Africa correspondent, to 1969; national political correspondent, Washington; London Bureau Chief, 1976 to 1985; chief Washington correspondent, current, 1985.

Archibald, George. *The Washington Times.* Reporter. B. 1944 Newmarket, Suffolk, UK. Old Dominion U., 1967, BA-Political Science/History. *The Arizona Republic* editorial writer/columnist to 1973. Various administrative jobs, Capitol Hill to 1982. *The Washington Times,* national news correspondent, current, 1982 (first reporter hired).

Armbrister, Trevor. *Reader's Digest.* Senior Editor, Washington Bureau. B. 1933, Norwalk, CT. Washington & Lee U., 1956, English. *Trailways Magazine,* Editor, 1958-61. *The Saturday Evening Post,* Asst Editor, to 1962; Contributing Editor, to 1965; Washington Bureau Chief, to 1969. Freelance, to 1976. *Reader's Digest,* Roving Editor, to 1979; Senior Editor, Washington bureau, current, 1979. Author *A Matter Of Accountability,* 1970; *Act of Vengeance,* 1975: co-author *O Congress* (with Don Riegel), 1972; *A Time to Heal: The Memoirs of Gerald R. Ford* (with former President Ford, 1977-79).

Armstrong, Larry. *BusinessWeek.* Tokyo Bureau Manager. Northwestern, BA-Chemistry, MSJ. *Medical World News,* editorial trainee, 1970. *Electronics* magazine, Washington correspondent, to 1972; Dallas Bureau Chief, 1972; Chicago Bureau Manager, to 1978. *BusinessWeek,* Chicago correspondent, to 1984; Tokyo Bureau Manager, current, 1984.

Arnold, Robert. *BusinessWeek.* Senior Editor. U. of MO, BA, MA-Journalism. *The Wall Street Journal. The Washington Post. BusinessWeek,* Staff Editor, labor dept., 1978, Editor, 1979-85; Senior Editor, information processing, industries, defense, labor, current, 1985.

Asman, David. *The Wall Street Journal.* Editor of the "Americas" Column & Co-Editor of the *Manager's Journal.* B. 1954, Hollis, NY. Marlboro College (VT), 1977, BA-Anthropology; Grad work-Northwestern. *Prospect,* Editor to 1980: *Manhattan Report on Economic Policy* to 1982: Freelance to 1983: *The Wall Street Journal,* Editor, "Americas" Column, current, 1983. Co-editor *The Wall Street Journal on Management: The Best of Manager's Journal.*

Attanasio, Paul. *The Washington Post.* Chief Movie Critic. B. NY. Harvard, BA; Harvard Law, JD. Freelance writer, to 1984. *The Washington Post,* intern, "Style" section, 1984; chief movie critic, current, 1984. Also current, *The Movie Show,* HBO/Cinemax.

Auerbach, Stuart. *The Washington Post.* Financial Correspondent. B. 1934, NYC. Williams College, 1957, BA-Political Science. *The Berkshire Eagle* (Pittsfield, MA), reporter, Suburban Bureau Chief, to 1960. *The Miami Herald,* reporter; columnist, to 1966. *The Washington Post,* reporter, to 1969; national medical/science reporter, campaign political correspondent, Latin America assignment, to 1976; Middle East correspondent, Beirut, to 1977; legal affairs correspondent, columnist, to 1979; South Asia correspondent, New Delhi, to 1982; financial correspondent, current, 1982.

Baig, Edward C. *FORTUNE.* Reporter/Researcher. B. NY. York College, BA-Political Science; Adelphi U., MBA. *FORTUNE,* cable desk; reporter, researcher, current, 1980.

Baker, Russell Wayne. *The New York Times.* Columnist. B. 1925, Loudon County, VA. Johns Hopkins U., 1947, BA-English Literature. US Navy, to 1945. *The Sun* (Baltimore, MD), reporter; London bureau member; White House correspondent, to 1954. *The New York Times,* Washington bureau member, to 1962; columnist, Editorial Page "Observer", current, 1962. Author 9 books, most recently *So This Is Depravity,* 1980; *Growing Up,* 1982; *The Rescue of Miss Yashell and Other Pipe Dreams,* 1983. Frank Sullivan Memorial Award, 1976; George Polk Award for Commentary, 1979; Pulitzer Prize for Distinguished Commentary, 1979; Pulitzer Prize for Biography, 1983.

Baldacchino, Joseph F. Jr. *Human Events.* Associate Editor. B. 1948, Detroit, MI. Mt. St. Mary's College (MD), 1970, BA-History, *magna cum laude;* Catholic U. of America, 1983, MA-Political Theory. Cambridge (MD) *Dorchester News* to 1972. *Human Events,* Asst Editor, to 1972; Associate Editor, current, 1975. Author *Economics and the Moral Order,* 1985.

Baldwin, William. *Forbes.* Senior Editor. Harvard, 1973, AB-Linguistics. *News Journal* (Wilmington, DE). *Forbes,* reporter; Houston Bureau Chief; Senior Editor, current, 1980.

Balmaseda, Liz. *Newsweek.* Central American Bureau Chief. B. 1959, Cuba. Florida International U., 1981, Communications Technology. WINZ News Radio (Miami), reporter to 1979. *The Miami Herald,* city desk reporter, to 1985. *Newsweek,* Central America Bureau Chief, current, 1985. Ernie Pyle Award; Second Place, Scripps Howard, 1985, Feature Writing.

Bandow, Douglas. Copley News Service. Columnist. B. 1957, Washington, DC. Florida State U., 1976, BS-Economics; Stanford Law, 1979, JD. Reagan for President Committee, Senior Policy Analyst, to 1980. Office of the President-Elect, Senior Policy Analyst, to 1981. Special Asst to the President for Policy Development, to 1982. *Inquiry Magazine,* Editor, to 1984. Copley News Service, columnist, current, 1983. Cato Institute, Senior Fellow, current, 1984. Editor *U.S. Aid To The Developing World: A Free Market Agenda,* 1985. Freedoms Foundation Citation for Journalistic Activities, 1979.

Banks, Howard. *Forbes.* Washington Bureau Chief & "What's Ahead for Business" Columnist. B. 1938, Hatfield, Hertfordshire, UK. De Havilland Aeronautical Technical School. Aerospace industry & various trade & technical papers, to 1970. *The Economist,* Industrial Editor; "Business Britain" Editor; West Coast correspondent, to 1982. *Forbes,* Washington Bureau Chief, "What's Ahead for Business" columnist, current.

Barnes, Fred. *The New Republic.* Senior Editor. B. 1943, West Point, NY. U. of VA, 1965, BA-History. Neiman Fellow, Harvard, 1977-78. *The Charlotte News & Courier,* reporter, to 1967. *The Washington Star,* reporter, Supreme Court reporter, White House correspondent, to 1979. *The Sun* (Baltimore, MD), national political reporter, to 1985. *The New Republic,* Senior Editor, current, 1985.

Barone, Michael. *The Washington Post.* Editorial Page Staff Member. B. 1944, Highland Park, MI. Harvard, 1966, AB-History; Yale, 1969, LLB. Law clerk to Judge Wade H. McCree at the US Court of Appeals, to 1971. Peter D. Hart Research Associates, Vice-President, to 1982. *The Washington Post,* Editorial Page staff member, current, 1982. Co-author of *The Almanac of American Politics* (1972, current).

Barron, John. *Reader's Digest.* Senior Editor. B. 1930, Wichita Falls, TX. U. of MO, 1951, BA-Journalism, 1952, MA. US Navy, to 1957, to rank of Lieutenant. *The Washington Star,* to 1965. *Reader's Digest,* from 1965, currently Senior Editor, 1986. Author *KGB: The Secret Work of Soviet Secret Agents,* 1974; *MIG Pilot,* 1980; *KGB Today,* 1983: co-author *Murder of a Gentle Land,* 1978. George Polk Memorial Award, 1964; Raymond Clapper Award for Distinguished Washington Correspondence, 1964; Washington Newspaper Guild Front Page Award & Grand Award, both 1964; Sir James Goldsmith International Award, 1985.

Bartholomew, Douglas. *The American Spectator.* Chief Saloon Correspondent. B. 1949, Cleveland, OH. Northwestern, 1971, BA-Journalism. *Peru Daily Tribune* (IN), reporter, to 1971. *The News Herald* (OH), reporter, to 1973. Educational Testing Service, Editor, to 1977. Bank of America, Editor, to 1984. Freelance journalist, to 1986. *The American Spectator,* Chief Saloon Correspondent, current, 1980. First Prize, Enterprise Reporting, AP, 1972.

Barmash, Isadore. *The New York Times.* "Business Day" Reporter. B. 1921, Philadelphia, PA. Charles Morris Price School, 1941, Journalism. *Home Furnishings Daily,* Editor-in-Chief. *Woman's Wear Daily,* Managing Editor. Fairchild Publications, reporter, Bureau Chief, editorial copy chief. *The New York Herald Tribune,* financial/business feature writer, to 1965. *The New York Times,* "Business Day" reporter, current, 1965.

Bartlett, Sarah. *BusinessWeek.* Money & Banking Editor. B. 1955, Buffalo, NY. U. of Sussex (UK), 1977, BA-Political Science, 1979, MPhil-Development Studies. *FORTUNE,* reporter, to 1983. *BusinessWeek,* International Money Editor to 1983; Money and Banking Editor, current, 1986. Co-recipient Overseas Press Club Award for Best Magazine Reporting Overseas, 1985.

Bartley, Robert L. *The Wall Street Journal.* Editor & Vice President. B. 1937, Marshall, MN. IA State U., BSJ; U. of WI, MS-Political Science. *Grinnell Herald-Register* (IA), reporter, 1959-60. US Army, to 1960. *Iowa State Daily,* Editor-in-Chief. *The Wall Street Journal,* staff reporter, 1962-64; Editorial Page staff member, to 1972; Editor, Editorial Page, to 1979; Editor, current, 1979. Overseas Press Club Citation for Excellence, 1977; Gerald Loeb Award for Editorials on international monetary problems, 1979; Pulitzer Prize for Editorial Writing, 1980.

Bayles, Martha. *The Wall Street Journal.* TV Critic. B. 1948, Boston, MA. Harvard-Radcliffe, 1970, BA-Art History. *The Wall Street Journal,* TV critic, current, 1984. Also current, freelance work, various publications.

Behar, Richard. *Forbes.* Staff Writer. B. 1960, NYC. NYU, 1982, Journalism/History. *The New York Times,* stringer/researcher, education desk, to 1982; writer for *New York Times Selective Guide to Colleges,* 1982. *Forbes,* staff writer, investigative business reporting, current, 1982.

Belcher, Mary. *The Washington Times.* White House Reporter. B. 1951, Columbus, OH. U. of CO, 1981, Journalism. *Education Daily,* Congressional reporter, 1982-84. *The Washington Times,* White House reporter, current, 1984.

Belkin, Lisa. *The New York Times.* Business Reporter. B. 1960, NYC. Princeton, 1982, Politics. *The New York Times,* clerk, to 1984; consumer reporter, to 1985; business reporter, current, 1985.

Belsie, Laurent. *The Christian Science Monitor.* Staff Writer, Chicago. B. 1959, Paris, France. Northwestern, 1980, Journalism. Reuters, intern, 1978. *Jackson Citizen-Patriot* (MI), intern, 1979. *The Christian Science Monitor,* various editing posts, 1981-83; staff writer, Chicago bureau, current, 1983.

MediaGuide

Benjamin, Evelyn. *FORTUNE.* Deputy Chief of Research. Bennington College, Economics. Time, Inc., 1957-60. *FORTUNE,* research associate, to 1970; Associate Editor; Deputy Chief of Research, current, responsible for compilation of *FORTUNE's* directories.

Bennett, Amanda. *The Wall Street Journal.* Reporter. Harvard, 1975, AB-English literature. *The Wall Street Journal,* reporter, Toronto, to 1978; Detroit bureau, to 1982; Washington bureau, to 1983; Peking bureau, to 1985; management reporter, NY, current, 1985.

Bennett, Ralph Kinney. *Reader's Digest.* Senior Editor. B. 1941, Latrobe, PA. Allegheny College, 1963, English. *The Greenburg Tribune-Review* (PA), part-time reporter, 1960-63. *The New Haven Register,* staff writer, to 1964. *The Philadelphia Inquirer,* staff writer, to 1966. *The National Observer,* staff writer, to 1968. *Reader's Digest,* Associate Editor, Washington bureau, to 1976; Senior Editor, Washington, current, 1976.

Bennett, Robert A. *The New York Times.* "Business Day" Reporter. B. 1941, Newark, NJ. Studied U. of Chicago. *The American Banker,* reporter, 1962 to 1973. Econocast Services, founder & CEO, to 1979. *The New York Times,* banking reporter, to 1985; "Business Day" reporter, current, 1985.

Berg, Eric. *The New York Times.* "Business Day" Reporter. B. 1958, NY. U. of PA, 1980, Economics; Stanford, MBA. *Chicago Tribune, Cleveland Plain Dealer,* reporter, to 1980. *Dallas Times Herald,* business & financial reporter, to 1982. *The New York Times,* "Business Day" reporter, current, 1984.

Bering-Jensen, Henrik. *Insight.* Writer. B. 1951, Copenhagen, Denmark. Oxford, MA-English Literature. Stanford, International Fellow, 1981-82. Reviewer for Danish newspapers, 1977-85 (some appeared in American publications). *Insight,* writer, current, 1985.

Bernstein, Peter W. *U.S. News & World Report.* Managing Editor, Business, Personal Finance, Horizons & Special Projects. Fellow, *Pretoria News,* South Africa. *New York Daily News. FORTUNE,* Washington Editor. *U.S. News & World Report,* Managing Editor, business, 1985-86; Managing Editor, business, personal finance, Horizons sections & special projects. Editor *Arthur Young Tax Guide.*

Bernstein, Richard. *The New York Times.* Paris Bureau Chief. B. 1944, NYC. U. of CT, 1962-66; Harvard, MA, 1970. *TIME,* staff writer, 1973 to 1976; Hong Kong correspondent, to 1978; State Dept. correspondent, to 1980; Peking Bureau Chief, to 1982. *The New York Times,* metro reporter, to 1983; UN correspondent, to 1984; foreign correspodent, Paris, to 1986; Paris Bureau Chief, current, 1986. Author *From The Center of the Earth: The Search for the Truth About China,* 1982.

Bethell, Tom. *The American Spectator,* Washington Correspondent. *National Review,* Contributing Editor. B. London. Oxford, 1962, Philosophy & Psychology. Freelance *The American Spectator,* Contributing Editor & Washington correspondent, current. *National Review,* Contributing Editor, current. Also current, freelance. Honorable mention, Gerald Loeb Award; First Prize, John Hancock Award; First Prize, Amos Tuck Award, all 1980.

Bianco, Anthony. *BusinessWeek.* Senior Writer. B. 1953, Oceanside, CA. U. of MN, 1976, BA-Humanities. *Minneapolis Tribune,* reporter, 1976. *Willamette Week* (Portland, OR), business writer, 1978-80. *BusinessWeek,* correspondent, San Francisco, to 1982; NY bureau; senior writer, current. Amos Tuck Media Award, 1979.

Bird, Kai. *The Nation.* Columnist. B. 1951, Eugene, OR. Carleton College, 1973, BA-History; Northwestern, 1975, MS-Journalism. Thomas J. Watson Fellow, 1973-74; Alicia Patterson Fellow, 1984; John Simon Guggenheim Fellow, 1985; German Marshall Fellow, 1986-87. Freelance, Far

East, to 1976. *Newsweek International,* Associate Editor, to 1977. *The Nation,* Associate Editor, to 1982; "Capitol Letter" columnist, current, 1982.

Bishop, Jerry E. *The Wall Street Journal.* Staff Reporter. B. Dalhart, TX. U. of TX, 1952, BA-Journalism. *The Wall Street Journal,* copyreader, 1955-57; reporter, NY, to 1959; reporter, Washington, to 1960; reporter, NY, current, 1960, science & medicine.

Blake, George. *The Cincinnati Enquirer.* Editor & Vice President. B. 1945, Chicago, IL. Wheeling College, 1967, Economics. *Joliet Herald News,* reporter, Copy Editor, to 1973. *Times-Union* (Rochester, NY), Copy Editor, 1973. *Pacific Daily News* (Guam), Managing Editor, to 1976. Gannett News Service, Washington reporter, 1977. *Fort Myers News-Press,* Executive Editor, to 1980. *The Cincinnati Enquirer,* Editor & Vice President, current, 1980.

Bleiberg, Robert M. *Barron's.* Editorial Director & Publisher. B. 1924, Brooklyn, NY. Columbia, 1943, BA-Economics; NYU, 1950, MBA. *Barron's,* Associate Editor, to 1954; Editor, to 1981; Editor & Publisher, to 1982; Editorial Director & Publisher, current, 1982. Dow Jones & Co., Inc., Vice-President, Magazine Group, current, 1980. NYU GBA Alumni Achievement Award, 1981; NY Financial Writers Association's Elliot V. Bell Award for Significant Long-term Contribution to Financial Journalism, 1985.

Block, Alex Ben. *Forbes.* Associate Editor. B. 1946, Syracuse, NY. Ithaca College, 1968, BA-Business Administration. *Forbes,* reporter, to 1970. *The Miami News,* Entertainment Editor, movie critic, to 1976. *The Detroit News,* columnist, to 1979. *Los Angeles Herald Examiner,* Asst City Editor; Business/Entertainment columnist, to 1984. *Forbes,* Associate Editor, West Coast bureau, entertainment industry, current, 1984. San Fernando Valley Press Club Best Spot News Story, 1982; LA Press Club Best Entertainment Story, 1984; Silver Angel Awards, 1983, '84; Hearst Awards, 1981, '82, '83, '84.

Blumenthal, Sidney. *The Washington Post.* Political Reporter. B. 1948, Chicago, IL. Brandeis, 1969. *The New Republic,* national political correspondent, to 1985. *The Washington Post,* political reporter, current, 1985. Author *The Permanent Campaign* 1980; 2nd Ed., 1983: *The Rise of the Counter-Establishment,* 1986.

Blundell, William. *The Wall Street Journal.* National Correspondent. B. 1934, NJ. Syracuse, 1956, BS-Psychology; grad work, Journalism, U. of KS, 1961. *The Wall Street Journal,* Dallas reporter, to 1964; NY reporter, to 1965; "Page One" rewrite man, to 1968; LA Bureau Chief, to 1978; national correspondent, current, 1986 (editing duties added 1986). Author *Storytelling Step by Step: A Guide to Better Feature Writing,* 1986. Scripps-Howard Foundation Award for Public Service, 1974; American Society of Newspaper Editors Award for Best Non-deadline Feature Writing, 1982: co-winner Meyer Berger Award for Distinguished Metropolitan Reporting, 1966.

Bonafede, Dom. *National Journal.* Special Contributing Editor. B. 1933, Buffalo, NY. Rutgers, 1953, English, Journalism. Neiman Fellow, Harvard, 1959-60. *Havana Herald,* reporter, Asst Editor, 1953. *Miami News,* reporter, to 1957. *The Miami Herald,* chief Latin America correspondent, to 1963. *New York Herald Tribune,* Washington correspondent, to 1966. *Newsweek,* Washington correspondent, chief Latin American correspondent, to 1969. *National Journal,* White House correspondent, to 1979; Chief political correspondent, to 1984; special contributing editor, current, 1984. *Washington Journalism Review,* senior writer, 1978-82. *The Washingtonian,* Contributing Editor, current, 1974. American U., Asst Professor, Journalism, current, 1985. Contributor *Reporting The News,* 1965; *The Presidency Reappraised,* 1977; *Studying The Presidency,* 1983. Overseas Press Club Citation for coverage of Cuba & Caribbean, 1960; NY Reporters Association Award for series on Congressional ethics, 1965; Raymond Clapper Runner-up Award for same series, 1965.

MediaGuide

Borger, Gloria. *U.S. News & World Report.* Assistant Managing Editor, Special Reports, National Affairs. Colgate U. *The Washington Star,* MD & Washington political reporter, 1975-78. *Newsweek,* political & Capitol Hill reporter, to 1986. *U.S. News & World Report,* Asst Managing Editor, special reports, national affairs, current, 1986.

Boroweic, Andrew. *The Washington Times.* Chief Roving Foreign Correspondent. B. 1928, Poland. Alliance College, 1951, BA-Social Science; Columbia, 1952, MSJ. AP, re-write man, reporter, foreign correspondent, chief of various bureaus, to 1966. *The Washington Star,* roving foreign correspondent, to 1975. Carnegie Endowment, senior associate, to 1977. Freelance writer, to 1981. *Chicago, Sun-Times,* foreign correspondent (Middle East, Europe, Africa), to 1984. *The Washington Times,* chief roving foreign correspondent, current, 1984. Author *The Mediterranean Feud,* 1983; *Yugoslavia After Tito,* 1977. Overseas Press Club Best Reporting from Abroad Award, 1963, Citation same category, 1965; First Prize Front Page Awards, Washington-Baltimore Guild, 1971.

Bourne, Eric. *The Christian Science Monitor.* Special Correspondent. B. UK. Degree in History & English Literature. British Press Association, Foreign Editor. *News Chronicle,* foreign room. Reuters, War correspondent (WW II); chief correspondent, Germany, to 1947. *Sunday Times,* to 1950. *The Christian Science Monitor,* special correspondent, current (originally based in Belgrade, now in Vienna), 1950.

Bovard, James. Freelance Writer. B. 1956, Ames, IA. Attended Virginia Tech, General Arts & Sciences. Policy studies for the Cato Institute & Heritage Foundation. *The Wall Street Journal,* frequent contributor, current. Also current, *The New York Times, The New Republic, The Detroit News,* contributor.

Boyer, Peter. *The New York Times.* Culture News Reporter. U. of MS, 1973; USC, 1976, Journalism. AP, reporter; columnist, Los Angeles, to 1981. *Los Angeles Times,* entertainment industry reporter, to 1984; Atlanta Bureau Chief, 1984. NPR, media critic, to 1985. CBS News, media critic, 1985. *The New York Times,* culture news reporter, current, 1985.

Bradlee, Benjamin Crowninshield. *The Washington Post.* Executive Editor. B. 1921, Boston. MA. Harvard, 1943, AB. US Naval Reserve, to 1945. *Sunday News* (Manchester), reporter, to 1946. *The Washington Post,* reporter, to 1951; press attache, Paris embassy, to 1953. *Newsweek,* European correspondent, to 1957; reporter, Washington Bureau, to 1961; Senior Editor, Bureau Chief, to 1965. *The Washington Post,* Managing Editor, to 1968; Vice-President, Executive Editor, current, 1968. Author *That Special Grace,* 1964; *Conversations With Kennedy,* 1975.

Brandt, Thomas D. *The Washington Times.* National Political Writer. B. 1945, Pittsburgh, PA. Georgetown, 1980, Master of Liberal Studies. US Army, Editor, correspondent, 1968-70. *Coral Gables Times Guide* (FL), city hall reporter, 1970. *The Miami News,* Asst City Editor, political writer, to 1975. *The Fort Lauderdale News* (FL), chief news feature writer, 1975. *Miami Magazine,* political columnist, to 1976. US House of Representatives, legislative staff work, to 1982. *The Washington Times,* Capitol Hill Bureau Chief, to 1986; national political writer, current, 1986. US Army, Editor, Best Unit Newspaper, 1970; Best Feature Story, FL Society of Newspaper Editors, 1970.

Bray, Nicholas. *The Wall Street Journal*/Europe. Paris Bureau Chief. Magdalen College, Oxford, Languages; SOAS, London, Social Anthropology. Reuters, chief correspondent, Belgium, Luxembourg, covering NATO/Common Market, 1972-82. *The Wall Street Journal*/Europe, Paris correspondent, to 1984; Paris Bureau Chief, current, 1984.

Bray, Thomas J. *The Detroit News.* Editorial Page Editor. B. 1941, NYC. Princeton, 1963, History. *San Antonio Evening News,* to 1964. US Army Reserves, 1/64-7/64. *The Wall Street Journal,* reporter, national news desk, bureau chief, Associate Editor-Editorial Page, to 1983. *The Detroit News,* Editorial Page Editor, current, 1983.

Breslin, Jimmy. *New York Daily News.* Columnist. B. 1929, Jamaica, NY. Studied at Long Island U., 1947-50. Syndicated columnist, current. *New York Daily News,* columnist, current. Author 6 books, including *Table Money,* 1983: co-author *Forty-four Caliber,* 1978. Sigma Delta Chi Award for National Reporting, 1964; Meyer Berger Award for Local Reporting, 1964; NY Reporters Association Award for Reporting, 1964; Pulitzer Prize for Commentary, 1986.

Brimelow, Peter. *Barron's.* Contributing Editor. B. 1947, UK. U. of Sussex, 1970, BA-History/Economics; Stanford, 1972, MBA-Finance/Economics. Richardson Securities of Canada, investment analyst, to 1973. *Financial Post,* Asst Editor, to 1976; columnist, Contributing Editor, to 1980. *MacLean's Magazine* (Canada), Business Editor, to 1978. *The Wall Street Journal,* guest editorial writer, 1980. *Toronto Sun* Syndicate, columnist, to 1982. *Barron's,* Associate Editor, to 1983; Contributing Editor, current, 1984. *FORTUNE,* Associate Editor, to 1984. *Chief Executive Magazine,* Contributing Editor, current, 1984. Author of *The Wall Street Gurus,* 1986; *The Frozen Crisis: Canada and the Canadian Question Revisited,* 1986.

Brinkley, Joel. *The New York Times.* Washington Bureau Reporter. B. 1952, Washington, DC. U. of NC, 1975. AP, reporter, 1975. *Richmond News-Leader,* reporter, to 1978. *The Courier-Journal* (KY), reporter; editor, to 1983. *The New York Times,* reporter, Washington, current, 1983. Pulitzer Prize in International Reporting, 1980.

Brittan, Samuel. *Financial Times.* Principal Economic Commentator & Assistant Editor. B. 1933, London, UK. Jesus College, Cambridge, Economics. *Financial Times,* various posts, to 1961. *The Observer,* Economics Editor, to 1964. Department of Economic Affairs, advisor, 1965. *Financial Times,* principal economic commentator, current, 1966; Asst Editor, current, 1978. Author 9 books, including *Jobs, Pay, Unions and the Ownership of Capital,* 1984. Nuffield College, research fellow, 1973-74; visiting fellow, to 1982. Chicago Law, visiting Professor, 1978. Senior Wincott Award for Financial Journalists, 1971; George Orwell Prize for Political Journalism, 1981.

Broad, William. *The New York Times.* Science Reporter. B. 1951, Milwaukee, WI. Webster College (St. Louis, MO), 1973; U. of WI, 1977, MA. U. of WI, Madison, University Industry Research Program, reporter, to 1978; concurrently, teaching asst, History of Science Dept., research assistant, Anesthesiology Dept., to 1978. *Science,* reporter, to 1982. *The New York Times,* science reporter, current, 1983. Science-in-Society Journalism Award, National Association of Science Writers, 1981.

Brock, David. *Insight.* Writer. B. 1962. U. of CA, Berkeley, 1985, History. *The Wall Street Journal,* intern, summer 1985. *Insight,* writer, current, 1986.

Broder, David S. *The Washington Post.* Reporter & Columnist. B. 1929, Chicago Heights, IL. U. of Chicago, 1947, BA-Political Science, MA, 1951. *The Pantagraph* (Bloomington, IL), reporter, 1953-55. *Congressional Quarterly,* reporter, to 1960. *The Washington Star,* reporter, to 1965. *The New York Times,* Washington bureau reporter, to 1966. *The Washington Post,* reporter & columnist, current, 1966. Pulitzer Prize, 1973.

Brody, Michael. *FORTUNE.* Associate Editor. Harvard, 1970, *magna cum laude;* London School of Economics, MS-Economics. *Investor's Chronicle* (UK), Economics Editor. *Barron's,* Senior Editor. *FORTUNE,* associate editor, current, 1984.

Bronson, Gail. *Forbes.* Senior Editor. B. 1951, Washington, DC. Emory U., 1973, BA-Political Science, *magna cum laude. The Wall Street Journal,* intern, summer, 1973; reporter, 1974-81. *Money,* staff writer, 1982. *U.S. News & World Report,* Associate Editor, to 1985. *Forbes,* Senior Editor, current, 1985.

Brooke, James B. *The New York Times.* Metro Reporter. B. 1955, NYC. Yale, 1977, BA-Latin American Studies. *The Berkshire Eagle,* freelancer/reporter, to 1978. *The Washington Star,* reporter, 1980. Stringer, Brazil, various publications, to 1981. *The Miami Herald,* South America correspondent, to 1984. *The New York Times,* metro reporter, current, 1984.

Brookes, Warren. *The Detroit News.* Columnist. B. 1929, Summit, NJ. Harvard, 1952, BA-Economics. *Boston Herald,* political economic columnist, to 1985. Heritage Features Syndicate, "The Economy in Mind" columnist, current, 1985. Hearst Features Syndicate, columnist, current, 1985. *The Detroit News,* columnist, current, 1985. Author *Economy In Mind,* 1982. Two 1st place USIC Editorial Awards, 1978, '79; one 2nd Place, 1980.

Brookhiser, Richard. *National Review.* Managing Editor. B. 1955, Rochester, NY. Yale, 1977, English. *National Review,* Associate, to 1979; Senior Editor, to 1985; Managing Editor, current, 1985. Author *The Outside Story: How Democrats and Republicans Reelected Reagan,* 1986.

Brophy, Beth. *U.S. News & World Report.* Associate Editor. William Smith College (Geneva, NY); Northwestern, 1978, MSJ. CBS News. Capitol Publications. Medill News Service. Freelance. *Forbes,* government & public policy reporter, 1979-82. *USA TODAY,* business writer & columnist, to 1985. *U.S. News & World Report,* Associate Editor, specializing personal finance & the workplace, current, 1985. Author *Everything College Didn't Teach You About Money: Money Management for the Young Professional.*

Brown, Peter. Scripps-Howard News Service. White House & Political Reporter. B. 1949, NYC. Syracuse, 1972, BS-Broadcast Journalism; 1974, MS-Newspapers. Neiman Fellow, Harvard, 1981-82. UPI, Albany & Boston bureau reporter, to 1976; State Capitol Bureau Chief, Hartford, CT, to 1978; New England Political Editor, to 1979; political reporter, Washington, to 1980; health & human services reporter, 1981; Congress reporter, 1982. Scripps-Howard News Service, White House & political reporter, current, 1982.

Brownstein, Ronald. *National Journal.* Political & White House Correspondent. B. 1958, NYC. SUNY, Binghamton, 1979, English Literature. Freelance writer, current. *National Journal,* finance/banking reporter, from 1983; currently political & White House correspondent.

Brownstein, Vivian. *FORTUNE.* Economist & Associate Editor. George Washington U.; studied NYU. Board of Governors, Federal Reserve System, Economist. Commisssion on Money and Credit of the Committee for Economic Development, Economist. *FORTUNE,* 1960-68; Economist & Associate Editor, current, 1976.

Broyles, William Jr. *U.S. News & World Report.* Contributing Editor. Rice U., BA; Oxford, MA. US Marines; Bronze Star. *Texas Monthly,* founding Editor, 1972; Editor, to 1982. *California,* Editor-in-Chief, 1980-82. *Newsweek,* Editor-in-Chief, to 1984. Freelance. *U.S. News & World Report,* Contributing Editor, current, 1986, bi-monthly essayist. Author *Brothers in Arms: A Journey from War to Peace,* 1986.

Buchanan, Edna. *The Miami Herald.* Crime Reporter. B. 1940, Paterson, NJ. *The Miami Beach Daily Sun,* reporter, 1965-70. *The Miami Herald,* reporter, to 1971; criminal courts reporter, to 1972; police reporter, current, 1972. Author *Carr: Five Years of Rape and Murder,* 1979. Paul

Hansell Award for Distinguished Journalism, FL Society of Newspaper Editors, 1979-80; Green Eye Shade Award for Deadline Reporting, Sigma Delta Chi, 1982; Pulitzer Prize for General Reporting, 1986.

Buchwald, Art. *Los Angeles Times* Syndicate. Columnist. B. 1925, Mt. Vernon, NY. USC. *The New York Herald Tribune,* columnist. *Los Angeles Times* Syndicate, columnist, current. Author *A Gift from the Boys,* 1958 (novel): *Paris After Dark,* 1950; *Art Buchwald's Secret List of Paris,* 1961 (Paris Guidebooks): 20 collections of writings & columns, most recently *You Can Fool All of the People All of the Time,* 1985: *Irving's Delight,* 1975; *The Bollo Caper,* 1983 (children's stories). Pulitzer Prize for Outstanding Commentary, 1982.

Buckley, William F. Jr. *National Review.* Founder, President & Editor. B. 1925, NYC. Studied U. of Mexico, 1943; Yale, 1950, BA-Political Science, Economics & History. *Yale Daily News,* chairman. US Army 1944-46. Yale, asst instructor, Spanish, 1947-51. *American Mercury.* associate editor, to 1955. Freelance writing, current, 1955. *National Review,* founder, 1955; Editor, current. National Review, Inc., President, current. Universal Press Syndicate, "On the Right" columnist, current, 1962. "Firing Line" host, PBS, current, 1966. US Information Agency, Advisory Commission on Information member, 1969-72. Public member, US delegation, 28th General Assembly of the UN, 1973. Author 23 books, including *Right Reason,* 1985; *High Jinx,* 1986: co-author *McCarthy and His Enemies* (with L. Brent Bozell), 1954. Best Columnist of the Year Award, 1967; USC's Distinguished Achievement Award in Journalism, 1968; Fellow of the Society of Professional Journalists, Sigma Delta Chi, 1976; Bellarmine Medal, 1977; NYU's Creative Leadership Award, 1981; Union League's Lincoln Literary Award, 1985.

Burns, Jimmy. *Financial Times.* Foreign Desk Page Editor, Latin America. B. 1953, Madrid, Spain. Stonyhurst College, University College (UK), BA-Latin American Studies; London School of Economics, MA-Politics. BBC Television, scriptwriter, 1975-77. Yorkshire Television, researcher, 1975-77. *Catholic Herald,* reporter, 1975-77. *The Christian Science Monitor,* Lisbon correspondent, to 1980; Buenos Aires correspondent, 1982-86. *Financial Times,* Lisbon correspondent, to 1980; International Desk Editor, to 1982; Buenos Aires correspondent, to 1986; Foreign Desk Page Editor, Latin America, current, 1986.

Burns, John. *The New York Times.* B. 1944, Nottingham, UK. McGill U., Quebec; Harvard, 1980-81, Russian; Cambridge, 1984, Chinese. *The Ottowa Citizen. The Toronto Globe and Mail,* general assignment, to 1969; parliamentary correspondent, to 1971; China correspondent, to 1975. *The New York Times,* metro reporter, 1975; South Africa correspondent, to 1981; Moscow Bureau Chief, to 1984; Peking Bureau Chief, expelled 1986. Co-recipient George Polk Memorial Award for Foreign Correspondence, 1979.

Butler, Steven B. *Financial Times.* Southeast Asia Correspondent. B. 1951, Berlin, NH. Sarah Lawrence College, 1973, BA; Columbia, 1980, PhD-Political Science; field research, China, 1980; post-doctoral research, U. of MI, 1980-81, Center for Chinese Studies; fellowship, Institute of Current World Affairs for South Korea, 1983-86. Cornell, Asst Professor, Government, to 1982. National Public Radio, consultant for special series on China and Japan, summer 1983. *The Christian Science Monitor,* contributor, to 1986. *Financial Times,* Seoul correspondent, to 1986; Southeast Asia correspondent, current, 1986.

Buxton, James. *Financial Times.* Scotland Correspondent. B. 1947, Norfolk, UK. Cambridge, MA-History. *Evening Echo* (Hemel, Hempstead), reporter, 1969-72. *Financial Times,* London staff, to 1974; Foreign desk, to 1977; Middle East correspondent, to 1980; Rome correspondent, to 1986; Scotland correspondent, current, 1986.

Byrne, John A. *BusinessWeek.* Management Department Editor. William Patterson College (NJ), 1975, BA-Political Science. *Forbes,* Washington correspondent, staff member; Associate Editor, 1981-84. *BusinessWeek,* Management Dept. Editor, current, 1984. Author *The Headhunters,* 1986.

Byron, Christopher. *Forbes.* Assistant Managing Editor. Yale; Columbia Law School. Citicorp Capitol Markets Training Program, 1984. *TIME,* foreign correspondent, London, Bonn; editor, NY, to 1983. Time, Inc., Senior Editor, TV Cable Week, 1983. *Forbes,* Assistant Managing Editor, overseeing law, technology, & *Forbes* annual survey of industry, current, 1985. Author *The Fanciest Dive,* 1984.

Cahan, Vicky. *BusinessWeek.* Washington Correspondent. Syracuse, BA. Bureau of National Affairs, Senior Editor, 1973-79. *BusinessWeek,* Washington correspondent, occupational safety & health, to 1986; Washington correspondent, financial regulation, current, 1986.

Canby, Vincent. *The New York Times.* Senior Film Critic. B. 1924, Chicago. Dartmouth, 1947, BA-English. *The Chicago Journal of Commerce,* general reporter/asst to the Drama Editor, to 1950. Public relations, 1951. *Motion Picture Herald,* reporter, to 1959. *Variety,* motion picture reporter & critic, to 1965. *The New York Times,* cultural news reporter, to 1969; senior film critic, current, 1969. Author *Unnatural Scenery,* 1979; *Living Quarters,* 1975; 3 plays: "After All," "End of the War," "The Old Flag."

Cannon, Lou. *The Washington Post.* White House Correspondent. B. NYC. Attended U. of NV, San Francisco State College. *Contra Costa Times* (Walnut Creek, CA), editorial. *San Jose Mercury News,* editor, reporter. Ridder Newspapers, Washington correspondent. *The Washington Post,* political reporter, 1972-77; LA bureau staff, to 1980; White House reporter, current, 1980. Author *Ronnie and Jessie: A Political Odyssey,* 1969; *The McCloskey Challenge,* 1972; *Reporting: An Inside View,* 1977; *Reagan,* 1982. American Political Science Association Award for Distinguished Reporting of Public Affairs, 1969.

Carey, Peter Kevin. *San Jose Mercury News.* Investigative Reporter/Special Projects. B. 1940, San Francisco, CA. U. of CA, Berkeley, 1964, Economics; Stanford, Professional Journalism Fellow, 1983-84. *San Francisco Examiner,* reporter, 1964. *Livermore Independent* (CA), editor, reporter, to 1967. *San Jose Mercury News,* currently investigative reporter/special projects, 1967. CA-NV AP "Mark Twain" Award, 1983; 2 San Francisco Press Club Awards, 1984; Investigative Reporters & Editors "Torchlight" Award, 1986; George Polk Award for International Reporting, 1986; Pulitzer Prize for International Reporting, 1986.

Carter, Craig C. *FORTUNE.* Washington Reporter/Researcher. B. Kansas City, MO. Columbia, *magna cum laude,* Phi Beta Kappa. *Chain Store Age Magazine,* reporter, to 1982. *FORTUNE,* reporter/researcher, from 1982; currently reporter/researcher, Washington.

Carter, Hodding III. *The Wall Street Journal.* Op-Ed Columnist. B. 1935, New Orleans, LA. Princeton, 1957. Neiman Fellow, Harvard, 1965-66. *Delta Democrat Times* (Greenville, MS), reporter, to 1962; Managing Editor, to 1966; Editor/Associate Publisher, to 1977. Asst Secretary of State/Spokesman for Pres. Carter, to 1980. *The Wall Street Journal,* Op-Ed Columnist, current, 1981. Also current, "Capitol Journal," PBS, Editor-in-Chief/Chief correspondent; "This Week with David Brinkley," ABC, discussion panelist. Author *The South Also Rises.* 4 Emmy awards 1983, 1984; National Sigma Delta Chi Award for Editorial Writing 1961; Edward R. Murrow Award, Overseas Press Club, 1983.

Catto, Henry E. Jr. *Washington Journalism Review.* Contributing Editor. B. 1930, Dallas, TX. Williams College, 1952, BA-American History. Insurance, real estate, personal investing, to 1969. Deputy US Representative to the Organization of American States, to 1971. US Ambassador to

El Salvador, to 1973. Chief of Protocol for the White House & State Dept. US Permanent Representative, European Office of the UN, to 1977 (rank of Ambassador, 1976-77). Washington Communications Corporation, (publishes *Washington Journalism Review),* founder & chairman, 1979, current. Asst Secretary of Defense for Public Affairs, 1981-83. H & C Communications, vice-chairman, current. Also current, monthly columnist, *San Antonio Light;* Contributing Editor, *Washington Journalism Review;* frequent commentator, "All Things Considered," NPR.

Cave, Ray. *TIME.* Corporate Editor. St. John's College, 1949, BA. *The Sun* (Baltimore, MD), Asst City Editor, reporter, 1952-59. *Sports Illustrated,* staff writer, to 1962; Senior Editor, to 1970; Asst Managing Editor, to 1974; Executive Editor, to 1975, 1976-77. Time, Inc., acting editorial director, 1975. *TIME,* Managing Editor; Corporate Editor, current.

Chakravarty, Subrata Narayan. *Forbes.* Senior Editor. B. 1947, Calcutta, India. Yale, 1969, AB-Intensive Political Science; Harvard, 1971, MBA. Harvard Graduate School of Business Administration, research asst, 1971-72. *Forbes,* reporter, to 1974; staff writer, to 1976. Goodyear India Ltd., New Delhi, India, Manager, Corporate Planning, to 1979. *Forbes,* Associate Editor, to 1984; Senior Editor, current, 1984.

Chamberlain, John. King Features Syndicate. Columnist. B. 1903, New Haven, CN. Yale, 1925, History. Advertising writer, 1925. *The New York Times,* reporter, to 1929; daily book columnist, 1933-36; contributing daily book columnist, 1941-44. Sunday *New York Times Book Review,* Asst Editor, 1928-33. *FORTUNE,* staff writer, 1936-41. *Harper's,* Book Editor, 1939-47. Columbia, Journalism Lecturer, 1934-35; Associate Professor, 1941-44. New School of Social Research, Lecturer, 1935. Columbia Summer School, Lecturer, 1937. *LIFE,* staff writer, 1944-50. *The Freeman,* Editor, to 1952. *Barron's,* staff writer, to 1960. *The Wall Street Journal,* staff writer, to 1960. Troy (AL) School of Journalism, Dean, 1972-77. King Features Syndicate, "These Days" Columnist, current, 1961. Author 6 books, including *A Life With the Printed Word,* 1982.

Chapman, Stephen. *Chicago Tribune.* Columnist. B. 1954, Brady, TX. Harvard, 1976, History. Freelance writer, to 1978. *The New Republic,* staff writer, Associate Editor, to 1981. *Chicago Tribune,* columnist (syndicated since 1982), current, 1981.

Chavez, Lydia. *The New York Times.* Metro Reporter. U. of CA, Berkeley, 1974, BA-Comparative Literature; *Universite de France,* Montpellier, 1975; Columbia, 1977, MSJ. Contributor *The Albequerque Times,* 1977; *TIME,* to 1980; *New York,* to 1980. *Los Angeles Times,* energy & financial news reporter, to 1983. *The New York Times,* stringer, "Long Island Weekly" section, to 1980; San Salvador correspondent, 1983-84; foreign correspondent, Buenos Aires, to 1986; metro reporter, current, 1986.

Cheshire, William P. *The Washington Times.* Editorial Page Editor. B. 1931, Durham, NC. U. of NC, 1958, BA-Journalism. *The Richmond News Leader* (VA), reporter/Chief of Statehouse staff, to 1961. *The Canton Enterprise* (NC), Associate Editor, to 1963. *The Evening Post* (Charleston, SC), Associate Editor, to 1968. *The State,* Associate Editor, to 1972. Helms for Senate Committee, Director of Communications, 1972. Capitol Broadcasting Company (Raleigh, NC), Editorial Director, to 1975. *The Greensboro Record* (NC), Editorial Page Editor, to 1978. *The Charleston Daily Mail,* Editor-in-Chief, to 1984. *The Washington Times,* Editor, Editorial Page, current, 1984. George Washington Honor Medal, 1975; Council for the Defense of Freedom Award, 1978.

Chira, Susan. *The New York Times.* Tokyo Correspondent. B. NYC. Harvard, 1980, History & East Asian Studies, *summa cum laude, Phi Beta Kappa;* Inter-University Center for Japanese Language Studies (Tokyo); Middlebury College, Japanese. *The Harvard Crimson,* reporter; Editor; President to 1980. *The New York Times,* metro trainee, to 1982; reporter, to 1984; Tokyo correspondent, current, 1984.

Christian, Shirley. *The New York Times.* Buenos Aires Bureau Chief. B. 1938, Windsor, MO. Pittsburgh State U. (KS), 1960, Language & Literature; OH State U., 1966, MA. AP, UN correspondent, Foreign News Editor (NY), Bureau Chief, Santiago, Chile, to 1979. *The Miami Herald,* Central American correspondent, to 1984. *The New York Times,* Washington bureau, to 1986; Buenos Aires Bureau Chief, current, 1986. Pulitzer Prize for International Reporting, 1981; George Polk Award for International Reporting under Perilous Circumstances, 1981; Maria Moors Cabot Award, 1985.

Claiborne, William L. *The Washington Post.* Southern Africa Correspondent. B. 1936, NYC. Hobart College, 1960, English. *Democrat & Chronicle* (Rochester, NY), reporter, to 1966. *The Suffolk Sun,* city editor, to 1969. *The Washington Post,* night city editor, to 1970; metro reporter, to 1972; national reporter, to 1974; New York correspondent, to 1977; Jerusalem correspondent, to 1982; New Delhi correspondent, to 1985; Jerusalem correspondent, to 1986; Southern Africa correspondent (based in Johannesburg), current, 1986.

Clark, Evert. *BusinessWeek.* Senior Staff Writer, Science Policy. U. of NC. *The Durham Morning Herald* (NC), reporter, Asst City Editor, Aviation Editor, Feature Editor. *Newsweek,* science correspondent, Watergate reporter. *The New York Times,* science correspondent. *Aviation Week & Space Technology,* Space Technology Editor, Washington Bureau Chief. *BusinessWeek,* Technology News Editor; senior staff writer, science policy, current. Co-author *Contrabandista!.*

Clark, Lindley H. Jr. *The Wall Street Journal.* Economic News Editor. B. Indianapolis, IN. Earlham College (Richmond, IN), 1948, BA; U. of Chicago, 1949, MA. *The Wall Street Journal,* Copy Editor, 1949; reporter, rewriter, 1951-56; "Page One" Editor, to 1961; Editorial Writer, to 1965; Associate Editor, to 1972; Economic News Editor, current, 1972; "Outlook" column writer, current; "Speaking of Business" columnist, current. Author *The Secret Tax,* 1976.

Clark, Timothy B. *National Journal.* Financial Reporter. B. 1942, Washington, DC. Harvard, 1963, History. *Congressional Quarterly,* writer, Editor, to 1969. *Empire State Report,* founder & publisher, to 1977. *National Journal,* co-founder, 1969, to 1974; financial reporter, current, 1978.

Clift, Eleanor. *Los Angeles Times.* White House Correspondent. B. 1940, Brooklyn, NY. Hofstra College, Hunter College, no degree, Philosophy, English. *Newsweek,* researcher, New York, to 1965; office manager, Atlanta, to 1972; Atlanta bureau correspondent, to 1976; White House correspondent, to 1985; News Editor & Deputy Bureau Chief, 1985. *Los Angeles Times,* White House correspondent, current, 1985.

Clifton, Tony. *Newsweek.* London Bureau Chief. B. 1937, Melbourne, Australia. *Benalla Standard,* 1956-59. *The Herald* (Melbourne, Australia), to 1960. *Stratford Express* (UK), to 1963. *Daily Mail* (UK), to 1965. *Sunday Times* (UK), to 1970. *Newsweek,* Hong Kong correspondent, to 1975; Beirut correspondent, to 1978; London Bureau Chief, current. Author *God Cried.* Co-winner 3 Overseas Press Club awards.

Cody, Edward. *The Washington Post.* Mexico Correspondent. B. 1943, Portland, OR. Gonzaga U., 1965; U. of Paris Law, 1966-67; Columbia, 1968, Journalism. *The Charlotte Observer* (NC), reporter, to 1969. AP, editor, to 1973; correspondent, to 1978. *The Washington Post,* editor, to 1979; Cairo correspondent, to 1980; Paris correspondent, 1981; Beirut correspondent, to 1982; Miami (for Central America/Caribbean) correspondent, to 1986; Mexico correspondent, current, 1986. Overseas Press Club, Best Daily Newspaper or Wire Service Reporting from Abroad, 1976.

Cohen, Richard. *The Washington Post.* Columnist. B. 1941, NYC. NYU, 1967, Sociology; Columbia, 1968, MSJ. UPI, NY bureau, 1967-68; education & MD legislative correspondent, to 1976. *The Washington Post & The Washington Post* Writers Group, columnist, current, 1976. Freelance, current. Co-author (with Jules Witcover) *A Heartbeat Away—The Investigation and Resignation of Spiro T. Agnew.*

Cohen, Richard E. *National Journal.* Congressional Reporter. B. 1948, Northampton, MA. Brown, 1969, AB-History; Georgetown Law, 1972, JD. Legislative aide to Senator Edward W. Brooke, 1969-72. *National Journal,* legal & regulatory issues reporter, to 1977; Congressional reporter, current, 1977. Author *Congressional Leadership: Seeking A New Role,* 1980.

Cohen, Roger. *The Wall Street Journal*/Europe. Rome Bureau Chief. Oxford, 1977, History & French. Reuters, London correspondent, to 1983. *The Wall Street Journal*/Europe, Rome Bureau Chief, current, 1983.

Cohen, Stephen F. *The Nation.* "Sovieticus" Columnist. B. 1938, Indianapolis, IN. IN U., 1960, BA, 1962, MA; Columbia, 1969, PhD. Princeton, Professor, Soviet Relations & History, current, 1968. *The Nation,* columnist "Sovieticus", current, 1982. Newspaper Guild Page One Award for Column-writing, 1985.

Cole, Robert. *The New York Times.* Financial & Business News Reporter. B. 1925, Woonsocket, RI. U. of TX, Austin, 1947, Journalism; Carson-Newman College (TN); Cornell. *The Mexico City Herald,* reporter, to 1950. *The New York Journal of Commerce,* Foreign Editor, to 1962. *The New York Times,* Financial Copy Desk Editor; "Personal Finance" columnist, to 1974; NYSE reporter, to 1976; Financial & Business News reporter, current, 1976. Award from U. of MO, 1971; Gerald Loeb Award, 1985.

Comarow, Avery. *U.S. News & World Report.* Assistant Managing Editor, Horizons. U. of MD. *Money,* staff writer & Washington correspondent, 1972-79. *Consumer Reports,* Washington Editor, to 1982. *Science '86,* Senior Editor, to 1985; Asst Managing Editor, to 1986. *U.S. News & World Report,* Asst Managing Editor, Horizons, current, 1986.

Comstock, Robert. *The Record.* Executive Editor. B. 1927, NYC. Rutgers, 1952. *New Jersey News,* 1953. *The Record* (Bergen, NJ), reporter, Political Editor, News Editor, editorial writer, from 1953; Executive Editor, current. NJ State Director of Public Information, 1975-77.

Conine, Ernest. *Los Angeles Times.* Editorial Writer & Columnist. B. 1925, Dallas, TX. Southern Methodist U., 1948, Journalism. UPI, Dallas, to 1951. US Army, Psychological Warfare Division, to 1952. *Dallas Times Herald,* Washington correspondent, to 1955. *BusinessWeek,* Washington bureau, to 1959; Moscow bureau, to 1961; Boston bureau, to 1963. *Los Angeles Times,* Vienna bureau, Eastern Europe, to 1964; editorial writer & columnist, current, 1964.

Cook, James. *Forbes.* Executive Editor. B. 1926, Schenectady, NY. Bowdoin College, 1947, AB; Columbia, 1948, AM. Yankton College, instructor, to 1949. OH U., instructor, to 1952. *Popular Publications,* Editor, to 1955. *Forbes,* Executive Editor, current, 1955.

Coone, Tim. *Financial Times.* Buenos Aires Correspondent. B. 1952, Aberdeen, MD. Newcastle U. (UK), 1978, BS-Agricultural Economics. Freelance, current, 1978. *Financial Times,* stringer, 1982-86; Buenos Aires correspondent, current, 1986.

Corrigan, Richard. *National Journal.* Staff Correspondent. B. 1937, Glenridge, NJ. U. of FL, 1959, Journalism. *St. Petersburg Times,* to 1960. *The Washington Post,* 1962-69. *National Journal,* staff correspondent, business, labor, science & technology, current, 1969. President's Commission for a National Agenda for the '80's, staff member, 1980.

Corry, John. *The New York Times.* Cultural Reporter & Critic. B. 1933, NY. Hope College, 1954, Philosophy. Neiman Fellow, Harvard, 1965. *The New York Times,* sports dept., National News Editor/reporter, to 1968. *Harper's,* writer, to 1971. *The New York Times,* metro reporter; columnist; cultural reporter & critic, current, 1971. Author, *TV News and the Dominant Culture,* 1986.

Covault, Craig P. *Aviation Space & Space Technology.* Senior Space Editor. B. 1949, Dayton, OH. Bowling Green State U., 1971, BSJ. *Urbana Citizen* (IL), staff writer, to 1972. *Aviation Week & Space Technology,* Senior Space Editor, current, 1972. Freelance work, current. Ball Memorial Trophy, Aviation/Space Writers Association, 1982; National Space Club's Writing Award, 1984, '85; Jesse Neal Award, 1985.

Cowell, Alan. *The New York Times.* Johannesburg Bureau Chief. B. 1947, Manchester, England. St. Edmund Hall, Oxford, School of Modern Languages, 1968, BA. Reuters, foreign correspondent, to 1974; correspondent, Ankara, to 1981. *The New York Times,* foreign correspondent, Nairobi, Kenya, to 1983; Johannesburg Bureau Chief, current, 1983.

Crock, Stan. *BusinessWeek.* News Editor, Washington Bureau. Columbia, BA-Political Science, JD-Law; Northwestern, MSJ. *The Palm Beach Post* (FL), reporter. AP, reporter. *The Wall Street Journal,* regulatory agency reporter. *BusinessWeek,* Regulatory News Editor (McGraw-Hill World News), 1983; News Editor, Washington bureau, current.

Crossette, Barbara. *The New York Times.* Bangkok Bureau Chief. B. 1939, Philadelphia, PA. Muhlenburg College, 1963, BA; U. of CO, 1965, MA; U. of London, Institute of Historical Research, research work, 1965. *The Teacher* (UK), Production Editor. *Philadelphia Bulletin,* Copy Editor, to 1970. *The Birmingham Post,* (UK), Features Editor, political & general features writer, to 1973. *The New York Times,* foreign desk, to 1977; Editor "Westchester Weekly" section, 1977; Asst Metro Editor, 1977; Asst News Editor, to 1979; Weekend News Editor, to 1981; foreign affairs reporter, Washington, to 1982; Asst Foreign Editor, to 1983; Deputy Foreign Editor, to 1984; Bangkok Bureau Chief, current, 1984. Columbia, member adjuct faculty, Journalism, current, 1975. Fulbright Teaching Fellow, 1980. Editor *America's Wonderful Little Hotels and Inns,* published annually.

Crozier, Brian. *National Review.* Columnist & Contributing Editor. B. 1918, Kuridala, Queensland, Australia. U. of London, Trinity College of Music, 1935-36. Music/art critic, (UK), to 1939. Reporter, provincial newspapers, UK, to 1941. Aeronautics inspector, to 1943. Reuters (UK), to 1944. *News Chronicle,* (UK), foreign sub-editor, to 1948. *Sydney Morning Herald* (Australia), sub-editor & staff writer, to 1951. Reuter-Australian AP, day editor, to 1952; foreign correspondent, Southeast Asia, 1952. *The New York Times,* stringer, to 1953. *Straits Times,* features editor, Singapore, to 1953. *The Economist's Foreign Report,* Editor, leader writer/correspondent, to 1964. BBC Overseas Services, commentator, 1954-65. Forum World Services (UK), Chairman, to 1974. Institute for the Study of Conflict (UK), Director & Co-founder, 1970-79. *Now!,* columnist, 1980-82. *The Times,* columnist, to 1983. *National Review,* columnist, Contributing Editor, current, 1978. Author 15 books, including *The Andropov Deception,* 1986: co-author *This War Called Peace,* 1984; *Socialism: The Grand Delusion,* 1986.

Crudele, John T. *The New York Times.* Financial Reporter. B. 1953, Brooklyn, NY. Syracuse, 1974; NYU, 1979, MA. *Sports Illustrated,* reporter, to 1975. *Electronic News,* reporter,to 1979. Reuters, financial reporter, to 1985. *The New York Times,* financial reporter, current, 1985.

Cunningham, Miles. *Insight.* Writer. B. 1930, Rapid City, SD. U. of TN, 1955, Journalism. USMC Air Station, base newspaper, to 1957. *Times-Union* (Rochester, NY), political reporter, to 1963. Gannett News Service, Albany & Trenton politics reporter, to 1965. *Philadelphia Bulletin,* politics reporter, to 1982. Congressional staff member, to 1983. *The Washington Times,* national, foreign

& copy desks, to 1985. *Insight,* writer, current, 1985. PA Press Assocation Award for Investigative Series, 2nd Place, 1972.

Curran, John J. *FORTUNE.* Associate Editor. Bard College, 1975, BA-Languages & Literature. Freelance, to 1977. *Wall Street Transcript,* weekly stock option columnist, to 1978. *FORTUNE,* reporter/researcher; Associate Editor, current.

Daniloff, Nicholas. *U.S. News & World Report.* Diplomatic Correspondent. B. 1934, Paris, France. Harvard, 1956, BA; Oxford, 1959, BA, 1965, MA. UPI, foreign correspondent, to 1965; State Dept. correspondent, 1966-80. *The Washington Post,* Foreign Editor, to 1966. *U.S. News & World Report,* Moscow correspondent, 1981-9/86; diplomatic correspondent, current, 1986.

Danguilan-Vitug, Marites. *The Christian Science Monitor.* Philippine Correspondent. B. 1955, Solano, Nueva Vizcaya, Philippines. U. of the Philippines, 1975, AB-Broadcast Communications; MA-Communications. Neiman Fellow, Harvard, 1986-87. Freelance, to 1978. *World Paper,* contributor, 1986. *The Christian Science Monitor,* correspondent, to 1986. *Business Day* (Philippines), reporter, current, 1979. *Newsday,* correspondent, current, 1984.

Day, Anthony. *Los Angeles Times.* Editorial Page Editor. B. 1933, Miami, FL. Harvard, 1955, AB, *cum laude.* Neiman Fellow, 1966-67. *Philadelphia Bulletin,* reporter, 1957-60; Washington bureau, to 1969; Washington Bureau Chief, 1969. *Los Angeles Times,* Chief Editorial Writer, to 1971; Editorial Page Editor, current, 1971.

de Borchgrave, Arnaud. *The Washington Times,* Editor-in-Chief. *Insight,* Editor-in-Chief. B. 1926, Brussels, Belgium. British Royal Navy, to 1946. Independent News Service, freelance reporter, to 1947. UPI, telex operator, correspondent, to 1948; Brussels Bureau Chief, to 1950. *Newsweek,* Paris Bureau Chief, European correspondent, to 1954; Deputy Foreign Editor, to 1955; Foreign Editor, 1955; Senior Editor, to 1959; chief European correspondent, to 1961; Foreign Editor & Managing Editor-International Editions, to 1963; chief roving foreign correspondent, to 1980. Center for Strategic & International Studies, Senior Associate, to 1985. *The Washington Times,* Editor-in-Chief, current, 1985. *Insight,* Editor-in-Chief, current, 1985. Co-author (with Robert Moss) *The Spike,* 1980; *Monimbo,* 1983. Two Best Magazine Reporting from Abroad Awards, 3 Newspaper Guild of NY Page One Awards, Best Magazine Interpretations of Foreign Affairs Award, George Washington Medal of Honor for Excellence in Published Works.

Deigh, Robert. *Insight.* Reporter. B. 1952, Casablanca, Morocco. VA Commonwealth U., 1977, BSJ. American U., 1983, MS-Public Relations. US Army, reporter, photographer, Central America, 1974-75. *The Virginia Gazette,* political reporter, 1977-80. *Foreign Agriculture Magazine,* writer, Foreign Agricultural Service, US Dept. of Agriculture, to 1985. *Insight,* reporter, politics & business, current, 1985. Two 1st Place VA Press Association Awards for Investigative Reporting, 1978.

DeMuth, Christopher. *The American Spectator.* Contributing Editor. B. Kenilworth, IL. Harvard, 1968, AB; U. of Chicago Law, 1973, JD. Staff Asst to the President, to 1970. Sidney & Austin, Chicago, Attorney, to 1976. Consolidated Rail Corporation, Philadelphia, Associate General Counsel, to 1977. Harvard, Director of Faculty Project on Regulation, Lecturer, to 1981. Presidential Task Force on Regulatory Relief, Executive Director, to 1983. Office of Information & Regulatory Affairs, OMB, Administrator, to 1984. Freelance, current, 1971. *Regulation,* Editor & Publisher, current. *The American Spectator,* Contributing Editor, current.

Denby, David. *New York.* Film Critic. B. 1943, NYC. Columbia, 1965, BA-English. *The Atlantic,* film critic, to 1973. *The Boston Phoenix,* film critic, to 1978. *New York,* current, film critic, 1978.

MediaGuide 295

Denton, Herbert H. *The Washington Post.* Canada Correspondent. B. 1943, Muncie, IN. Harvard, 1965, BA-History, *cum laude. The Washington Post,* metro staff, 1968-73; Suburban Editor, to 1976; City Editor, to 1980; national staff, to 1982; Beirut correspondent, to 1984; Canada correspondent, current, 1985.

Dentzer, Susan. *Newsweek.* Business News Writer. B. 1955, Philadelphia, PA. Dartmouth, 1977, BA-English literature. *The Southamptom Press and Chronicle-News,* reporter, to 1978. *Wall Street Transcript,* Editor/columnist, 1979. *Newsweek,* reporter/researcher, to 1981; business news writer, current, 1981. Co-recepient 2nd Place University Award in Media, Lincoln U. of MO, 1984.

De Onis, Juan. *Los Angeles Times.* Rio de Janeiro Bureau Chief. B. 1927, NYC. BA-Economics, 1948; Williams College, MA; Columbia, 1952, MSJ. *Worchester Telegram* (MA), reporter, 1952. UPI, reporter, to 1957. *The New York Times,* correspondent, UN, Washington, Latin America, Middle East, to 1981. *Newsweek International,* columnist, to 1983. *International Herald Tribune,* Latin America correspondent, 1981-83. *Los Angeles Times,* Rio de Janeiro Bureau Chief, current, 1983. Overseas Press Club Ed Stout Award; Maria Moors Cabot Award.

de Silva, Mervyn. *Financial Times & Newsweek.* Stringer. B. 1929, Colombo, Sri Lanka. Royal College Colombo, English. *Daily News,* Colombo, Parliamentary reporter, columnist, 1953-60; Editor, 1970. *Ceylon Observer,* Parliamentary Editor, to 1967; Deputy Editor, to 1970. BBC, stringer, current. *Associated Newspapers of Ceylon,* Editor-in-Chief, 1971-76. *Times of Ceylon,* Editor-in-Chief, to 1978. *Financial Times,* stringer, current, 1973. *Newsweek,* stringer, current, 1976. *Lanka Guardian,* Editor-in-Chief, Editor & Publisher, current, 1978. *Island,* columnist, current.

Desmond, Edward W. *TIME.* Staff Writer. B. 1958, Seattle, WA. Amherst College, 1980, BA-English; Fletcher School of Law & Diplomacy, 1982, MA. Freelance, to 1984. *TIME,* reporter/researcher, to 1985; staff writer, current, 1985.

Diamond, Edwin. *New York.* Media Columnist. B. 1925, Chicago, IL. U. of Chicago, 1949, BA-Political Science, MA, PhD. *Newsweek,* Senior Editor, to 1970; commentator, to 1977. Washington TV commentator, to 1977. *New York Daily News,* Deputy Editor, to 1980. *Adweek,* Editorial Director, to 1984. MIT, faculty member, to 1984. *New York,* Contributing Editor, to 1977; media columnist, current, 1985. NYU, faculty member, current, 1984. Founder/originator News Study Group. Co-author (with Bruce Mazlish) *Jimmy Carter,* 1980. Page One Newspaper Guild Awards from Chicago, Washington.

Diaz, Tom. *The Washington Times.* Assistant Managing Editor. B. 1940, Ft. Olgethorpe, GA. U. of FL, 1963, BA-Political Science; Georgetown Law, 1972, JD; Law Journal. US Depts. of Commerce & Defense, various staff jobs, 1963-72. Law practice, to 1982. *Federal Times,* columnist, weekly freelance, 1980-82. *The Washington Times,* "Barely Civil" columnist, Supreme Court correspondent, to 1985; national security reporter, to 1986; Asst National News Editor, 1986; Asst Managing Editor, current, 1986.

Dickenson, James R. *The Washington Post.* Political Correspondent. B. 1931, McDonald, KS. San Diego State U., 1953, BA-History; U. of IA, 1959, MA-Journalism. US Marines, 1953-57. *Huntington Park Daily Signal* (CA), 1959-60. UPI, San Francisco, 1960. *The National Observer,* national political correspondent, 1962-74. *The Washington Star,* national political correspondent, National Editor, political columnist, to 1981. *The Washington Post,* Asst National Editor, politics, to 1984; political correspondent, current, 1984.

Diegmueller, Karen. *Insight.* Writer. B. 1950, Cincinnati, OH. U. of Cincinnati, 1977, BA-Political Science, *summa cum laude;* U. of WI, 1979, MA-Journalism. *Boone County Recorder* (Burlington,

KY), reporter, 1980. *The Daily Journal* (Kankakee, IL), reporter, to 1981. *The Home News* (New Brunswick, NJ), reporter, County Bureau Chief, statehouse reporter, to 1985. *Insight,* writer, current, 1985. Co-author *Effective Feature Writing,* 1982. Second Place for Editorial Writing, KY Press Assocation, 1980.

Diehl, Jackson. *The Washington Post.* Eastern Europe Correspondent. B. 1956, San Antonio, TX. Yale, 1978, English. *The Washington Post,* metro reporter, to 1981; foreign desk, 1981; South America correspondent, to 1985; Eastern Europe correspondent, Warsaw, current, 1985. Inter-American Press Association Award, 1984.

Dierdorff, John A. *BusinessWeek.* Managing Editor. B. 1928, Chicago, IL. Yale, 1949, English. *Yakima Morning Herald* (WA), staff writer, 1950-52. *The Oregonian* (Portland, OR), staff writer, to 1956. *BusinessWeek,* Copy Editor, to 1960; Asst Editor, to 1961; Asst Managing Editor, to 1969; Senior Editor, to 1976; Asst Managing Editor, to 1977; Managing Editor, current, 1977.

Dionne, Eugene J. *The New York Times.* Political Correspondent. B. 1952, Boston, MA. Harvard, 1973, BA; Oxford, Rhodes scholar, Political Sociology, 1982, PhD. *The New York Times,* consultant, Sunday magazine, 1975-77; polling operations asst, 1976; reporter, to 1978; reporter, Albany, NY, to 1979; national desk reporter, to 1981; Albany Bureau Chief, to 1983; foreign correspondent, to 1984; Rome Bureau Chief, to 1986; political correspondent, Washington, current, 1986.

Dobbs, Michael. *The Washington Post.* Paris Correspondent. B. 1950, Belfast, UK. U. of York (UK), 1972, Economics. Reuters correspondent, to 1975. Freelance, Africa, 1976. *The Washington Post,* special correspondent, Yugoslavia, to 1980; Eastern Europe correspondent, to 1982; Paris correspondent, current, 1983. Co-author *Poland, Solidarity, Walesa.* Nicholas Tomalin Award, London *Sunday Times,* 1975; Citation for Excellence, Overseas Press Club, 1981.

Doder, Dusko. *The Washington Post.* National Reporter. B. 1937, Yugoslavia. Washington U. (MO), 1962, Philosophy/Political Science; Columbia, 1964, MSJ, 1965, MA. Wilson Fellow, 1976-77, 1985-86. AP, correspondent, to 1968. UPI, Moscow correspondent, to 1970. *The Washington Post,* Asst Foreign Editor, to 1972; State Dept. correspondent, to 1973; foreign correspondent, to 1976. Moscow correspondent, 1978, 1980; Canada correspondent, to 1980; Asst Foreign Editor, to 1981. Moscow Bureau Chief, to 1985; national reporter, current, 1986. Author *The Yugoslavs,* 1978; *Shadows & Whispers,* 1986. Overseas Press Club Citation for Excellence, 1983; Weintal Prize, Diplomatic Reporting, 1984.

Donohoe, Cathryn. *The Washington Times.* Reporter. B. Bronx, NY. Middlebury College, 1958, BA-American Literature, *cum laude;* Columbia, Russian Literature; American U., Journalism. Radio Liberty, research and policy advisor. Freelance writer. *The Washington Times,* feature reporter, current, 1985. Co-recipient American Society of Magazine Editors' National Magazine Award for Public Service, 1985.

Donne, Michael. *Financial Times.* Aerospace Correspondent. B. 1928, London, UK. U. of London, Birbeck College. *Financial News of London,* 1945-46. Military, to 1948. *Financial Times,* since 1946; aerospace correspondent, current, 1953; defense correspondent, 1956-83; broadcasting correspondent, 1961-75. Frequent TV/radio broadcaster on aerospace & defense, also current. Author *Leader of the Skies,* 1981; *Per Ardua Ad Astra,* 1984. Appointed Officer of the Order of the British Empire, 1986, in the Queen's Birthday Honors.

Dorfman, Dan. *New York.* "The Bottom Line" Columnist. B. 1931, Brooklyn, NY. *Fairchild Publications,* to 1964. *Herald Tribune,* to 1965. *World Journal Tribune,* to 1967. *The Wall Street Journal,* to 1973. *Wall Street Letter,* to 1974. *Esquire* magazine, to 1979. *Chicago Tribune* Syndicate, to 1984. *New York,* to 1976; "The Bottom Line" columnist, current, 1984. News America Syndicate, columnist, current, 1984. Also current, CNN "Moneyline" columnist.

MediaGuide

Dougherty, Philip. *The New York Times.* "Advertising News" Columnist. B. 1923, Bronx, NY. Attended Columbia. US Military Police, 1942-46. *The New York Times,* copyboy, 1942; clerk, to 1950; society news staff, to 1963; news staff, to 1966; "Advertising News" columnist, current, 1966. Also current, "Advertising News" daily 3-minute radio commentary, WQXR, NYC.

Dowd, Ann Reilly. *FORTUNE.* Associate Editor. Smith College; Northwestern, MSJ. Press secretary, Congressman Larry Pressler (R-SD). *Dun's Business Monthly,* Senior Editor, to 1983. *FORTUNE,* Associate Editor, Washington, current, 1983.

Dowd, Maureen. *The New York Times.* Washington Bureau Reporter. B. 1952, Washington, DC. Catholic U., 1973, English Literature. *The Washington Star,* editorial asst, sports columnist, metro reporter, feature writer, to 1981. *TIME,* correspondent, writer, to 1983. *The New York Times,* metro reporter, to 1986; Washington bureau reporter, current, 1986.

Dowling, Robert J. *BusinessWeek.* Senior Editor. Villanova U. *The Sun* (Baltimore, MD), business/financial reporter. *American Banker,* banking & monetary affairs correspondent, to 1978. McGraw-Hill World News, correspondent, to 1980. *BusinessWeek,* Brussels Bureau Chief, to 1983; Senior Editor, international coverage, current, 1983.

Downie, Leonard Jr. *The Washington Post.* Managing Editor. B. 1942. OH State U., BA & MA-Journalism & Political Science. Alicia Patterson Foundation Fellow, 1971-72. *The Washington Post,* intern, summer 1964; investigative reporter, to 1971, 1973-74; Asst Managing Editor, metro news, to 1979; London correspondent, to 1982; National Editor, to 1984; Managing Editor, current, 1984. Author *Justice Denied,* 1971; *Mortgage on America,* 1974; *The New Muckrakers,* 1976. Two Washington-Baltimore Newspaper Guild Front Page Awards; American Bar Association Gavel Award for Legal Reporting; John Hancock Award for Business & Financial Writing.

Drogin, Bob. *Los Angeles Times.* National Correspondent. B. 1952, Jersey City, NJ. Oberlin, 1973, BA-Asian Studies; Columbia, 1976, MSJ. *Lorain Journal,* police reporter, 1973. UNICEF associate, Indonesia, to 1975. Freelance reporter/photographer, NY, Paris, 1976. *The Charlotte Observer* (NC), police, investigative/projects, to 1980. UNICEF officer, Thai/Cambodian border, 1980. *Philadelphia Inquirer,* reporter, to 1983. *Los Angeles Times,* national correspondent, NY, current, 1983. NC Press Association Award for Investigative Reporting, 1978, & Spot Reporting, 1979: co-recipient Pulitzer Prize for Meritorious Public Service, 1981; Robert F. Kennedy Journalism Award, Grand Prize & First Place, 1981; George Polk Award for Regional Reporting, 1981; Roy F. Howard Public Service Award, 1981; Villers Foundation Media Award, 1985.

D'Souza, Dinesh. *Policy Review.* Managing Editor. B. 1961, Bombay, India. Dartmouth, 1983, BA-English Literature, *Phi Beta Kappa. The Dartmouth Review,* Editor, to 1983. *Prospect,* Editor, 1984. Freelance, current, 1985. *Policy Review,* Managing Editor, current, 1985. Author *Falwell: Before The Millenium,* 1984. First Place, In-depth Reporting, Society of Professional Journalists, 1982.

DuBois, Peter C. *Barron's.* Foreign Editor. Princeton, 1952-56, English. RCA Records, staff writer. Union Carbide, technical writer. *The Journal of Commerce,* reporter. *BusinessWeek,* 1964-65. *Barron's,* 1960-64; 1965-67. Securities analyst/salesman, to 1973. *Barron's,* Associate Editor, to 1982; creator, "International Trader" column, 1978; Foreign Editor, current, 1982.

Duncan, Richard. *TIME.* Assistant Managing Editor. B. 1935, Cincinnati, OH. Dartmouth, 1957, BA-English; Columbia, International Fellow, 1961, MSJ. Pulitzer Traveling Fellow, 1962. AP, to 1962. *TIME,* correspondent, to 1966; Caribbean Bureau Chief, to 1968; Ottawa Bureau Chief, to 1970; Washington News Editor, to 1972; Western Regional Bureau Chief, to 1975; Deputy Chief of Correspondents, to 1978; Chief of Correspondents, to 1986; Asst Managing Editor, current, 1986.

Dunn, Donald. *BusinessWeek.* "Personal Business" Editor. U. of MO, Journalism. *Sales Management,* Asst Managing Editor. *Television Magazine,* Managing Editor, Editorial Director, to 1967. *BusinessWeek,* Contributing Editor, to 1977; Media and Advertising Department Editor, to 1980; "Personal Business" Editor, current, 1980. Author *The Making of 'No, No, Nanette',* 1972; *Ponzi, The Boston Swindler,* 1975; *Ripoff: The Corruption that Plagues America,* 1979; several books and lyrics for off-off-Broadway musicals: co-author (with Thomas F.X. Smith) *The Powerticians of New Jersey.*

Easterbrook, Gregg. *The Atlantic.* National Correspondent. *Newsweek.* Contributing Editor. B. 1953, Buffalo, NY. CO College, 1976, Political Science. *Washington Monthly*, editor, to 1981. *The Atlantic*, National correspondent, current, 1981. Two Investigative Reporters & Editors Awards 1980, '82; John Hancock Award for Business Writing, 1980; Livingston Award for National Reporting, 1986.

Eaton, William J. *Los Angeles Times.* Moscow Bureau. B. 1930, Chicago. Northwestern, 1951, BSJ, 1952, MSJ. City News Bureau, Chicago, to 1953. UPI, to 1966. *Chicago Daily News*, to 1977. Knight-Ridder Newspapers, to 1978. *Los Angeles Times*, since 1978, currently Moscow bureau. Pulitzer Prize for International Reporting, 1970.

Echikson, William. *The Christian Science Monitor.* Foreign Correspondent. B. 1959, NYC. Yale, 1981, History. *Yale Daily News*, reporter, to 1980; News Editor, to 1981. *Newsday*, reporter. *Newsweek*, stringer (Europe). *The Christian Science Monitor*, stringer; Foreign correspondent, current.

Edsall, Thomas. *The Washington Post.* Political Reporter. B. 1941, Cambridge, MA. Boston U., 1966, Political Science. *Providence Journal* (RI). *The Evening Sun & The Morning Sun* (Baltimore, MD). *The Washington Post*, political reporter, current, 1981. Freelance, also current. Author *The Politics of Inequality*, 1984. Washington-Baltimore Guild Grand Prize, 1982.

Ehrbar, Aloysius. *FORTUNE.* Member, Board of Editors. Northwestern, BSJ, MSJ; U. of Rochester, MBA. City News Bureau, Chicago, reporter, editor. *Democrat and Chronicle* (Rochester, NY), reporter, financial editor. *FORTUNE*, Associate Editor, to 1978; Board of Editors member, current, 1978. John Hancock Award for Excellence in Business and Financial Writing; INGAA-U. of MO Award for Business Writing.

Elliott, John. *Financial Times.* South Asia Correspondent. B. 1939, UK. Christ's Hospital, UK. Building & architectural magazines, to 1966. *Financial Times*, to 1968; labor correspondent, to 1971; Labor Editor, to 1976; Management Editor, to 1978; Industrial Editor, to 1983; South Asia correspondent, New Delhi, current, 1983. Author *Conflict or Co-operation—The Growth of Industrial Democracy*, 1978. British Institute of Management Journalist and Author of the Year Awards, 1977, '79, '83.

Ellison, Katherine E. *San Jose Mercury News.* National Correspondent. B. 1957, Minneapolis, MN. Stanford, 1979, International Relations. *Los Angeles Times*, intern, 1978. *The Washington Post*, intern, 1979. *Newsweek*, intern, 1980. *San Jose Mercury News*, since 1980; national correspondent, current. Overseas Press Club Fellow, 1979; Investigative Reporters & Editors Award, 1986; George Polk Award, 1986; Pulitzer Prize for International Reporting, 1986.

Emery, Glenn D. *Insight.* General Editor/News. B. 1954, Akron, OH. U. of VT, Math. *The Washington Times*, reporter, 1982-85. *Insight*, writer, 1985; General Editor/news, current, 1986.

England, Robert. *Insight.* Business Writer. B. 1944, York, SC. Duke, 1967, English. *Hartford Times*, reporter, to 1969. *Washington Magazine*, editor, to 1976. *Delaware Valley Business Magazine*, editor, to 1978. *Metro Newark*, editor, to 1985. *Oil & Gas Technology*, editor, to 1985. *Insight*, business writer, current, 1985.

Evans, Harold. Conde-Nast Publications. Consultant. B. 1928, Manchester, UK. Durham U. (UK), 1952, Economics; U. of Chicago, Stanford, MA. Ashton-under-Lyne Group (Lancashire, UK), reporter, 1944. *Manchester Evening News* (UK), sub-editor, editorial/political writer, to 1956; Asst Editor, to 1961. *Manchester Guardian* (UK), reporter. *The Northern Echo*, Editor, to 1966. *The Sunday Times* (UK), chief asst to the Editor, 1966; Managing Editor, to 1967; Editor, to 1981. *The Times of London*, Editor, 1981. *U.S. News & World Report*, Editorial Director/writer, to 1986. Conde-Nast Publications, consultant, current, 1986. Author 8 books including *Good Times, Bad Times*: co-author *Suffer The Children; We Learned to Ski*. European Gold Medal of Institute of Journalists; International Editor of the Year (1976), World Press Review.

Evans, Katherine Winton. *Washington Journalism Review*. Editor. B. 1925, Spokane, WA. Vassar, 1946, American Civilization. *Minneapolis Times*, editorial writer, to 1948. Capitol Hill staff, Senator Hubert Humphrey & Senator Paul Douglas, to 1953. *New York Herald Tribune*, Washington columnist, "Women's Page," 1961-62. Freelance, to 1980. *Washington Journalism Review*, Managing Editor, to 1982; Editor, current, 1982.

Evans, Medford Stanton. *Human Events*. Contributing Editor. B. 1934, Kingsville, TX. Yale, 1955, BA; grad work, NYU, 1955. *Freeman*, Assistant Editor, 1955. *National Review*, editorial staff, to 1956; Associate Editor, 1960-68. *The Indianapolis News*, Chief Editorial Writer, 1959-60. *Human Events*, Managing Editor, 1956-59; Contributing Editor, current, 1968. Author of several books, including *Assassination of Joe McCarthy*, 1970. Freedoms Foundation Award for Editorial Writing, 1959, '60, '65, '66; National Headliners Club Award for Outstanding Editorial Pages, 1960.

Evans, Rowland Jr. News America Syndicate. "Inside Report" Columnist (with Robert Novak). B. 1921, White Marsh, PA. Attended Yale. US Marines. *Philadelphia Bulletin*. AP, Washington Bureau member, to 1953; Senate reporter, to 1955. *New York Herald Tribune*, assorted national magazines, to 1962. News America Syndicate, "Inside Report" columnist (with Robert Novak), current, 1963. *Evans-Novak Political Report* (bi-weekly newsletter), co-author (with Robert Novak), current. *Evans-Novak Tax Report* (bi-weekly newsletter), co-author (with Robert Novak), current. *Reader's Digest*, roving editor (with Robert Novak), current (4 articles per year). Freelance work, current. Also current, co-host (with Robert Novak) "Evans & Novak" and "Insiders," CNN. Frequent appearances "Meet the Press," NBC; "Nightline," ABC. Co-author (with Robert Novak) *Lyndon B. Johnson: The Exercise of Power*, 1966; *Nixon in the White House: The Frustration of Power*, 1971; *The Reagan Revolution*, 1981.

Fallows, James. *The Atlantic*. Washington Editor. B. 1949, Philadelphia, PA. Harvard, 1970, BA, *magna cum laude*; diploma, Economic Development, Oxford, Rhodes scholar, 1972. *Washington Monthly*, staff editor, to 1974. Freelance writer, to 1976. *Texas Monthly*, Associate Editor, to 1976. Chief speechwriter for President Carter, to 1979. *The Atlantic*, Washington Editor, current, 1979 (reporting from Asia 1986-88; US-Japan Leadership Fellow). Author *National Defense*, 1981.

Fanning, Katharine. *The Christian Science Monitor*. Editor. B. 1927, Chicago, IL. Smith College, 1949, English literature. *Anchorage Daily News*, Editor/Publisher, to 1983. *The Christian Science Monitor*, Editor, current, 1983. *Anchorage Daily News* won 1976 Pulitzer Prize Gold Medal for Public Service under editorship. Elijah Parish Lovejoy Award, 1979; Pulitzer Prize Board member, 1982-83.

Farnsworth, Clyde. *The New York Times.* Financial Reporter. B. 1931, OH. Yale, 1952, BA-English. UPI, to 1959. *New York Herald Tribune*, to 1962. *The New York Times*, financial reporter, current, 1962. Author *Out of This Nettle*, 1971; *No Money Down*, 1962. Overseas Press Club and Sigma Delta Chi Awards for Foreign Correspondence, 1968.

Ferguson, Tim. *The Wall Street Journal.* Editorial Features Editor. B. 1955, Santa Ana, CA. Stanford, 1977, BA-Economics. *Orange County Register* (CA), reporter; asst metro editor; Editorial Page Editor, to 1983. *The Wall Street Journal*, Editorial Features Editor, current, 1983. Gerald Loeb Award for Business & Financial Journalism, 1980.

Field, Alan. *Forbes.* Southwest Bureau Manager. B. 1944, NYC. Brandeis, 1965, BA-History; Columbia, 1967, MA-International Affairs; Institute of International Studies, Geneva, Switzerland, 1969. *Newsweek*, reporter, to 1976; Tokyo Bureau correspondent, to 1979. *BusinessWeek*, Tokyo Bureau correspondent, to 1982; Mexico City Bureau Chief, to 1984. *Forbes*, Southwest Bureau Manager, current, 1984. Overseas Press Club Award for Best Magazine Reporting from Abroad, 1985.

Fields, Suzanne. *The Washington Times.* Columnist. B. 1936, Washington, DC. George Washington U., 1957, BA-English literature; 1964, MA; Catholic U. of America, 1970, PhD. *World Week Magazine*, staff writer, 1957. Freelance, from 1965. *Innovations* Magazine (for mental-health professionals), editor, from 1971. *Vogue*, columnist, 1980-81. *The Washington Times*, columnist, current, 1984. Author *Like Father, Like Daughter*, 1983.

Fineman, Mark. *Los Angeles Times.* Manila Bureau Chief. B. 1952, Chicago, IL. Syracuse, 1974, BA-Journalism/Philosophy. *Chicago Sun-Times*, staff writer, to 1978. *Allentown Call-Chronicle*, staff writer, to 1980. *Philadelphia Inquirer*, Asia correspondent, to 1986. *Los Angeles Times*, Manila Bureau Chief, current, 1986. Amos Tuck Award, 2nd prize, 1979; Amos Tuck Award, 1st prize, 1980; Overseas Press Club Citation for Excellence, 1985; George Polk Award, 1985.

Fink, Donald E. Jr. *Aviation Week & Space Technology.* Editor-in-Chief. B. 1935, Flint, MI. U. of MN, 1957, Technical Journalism. US Air Force, 1958-61. *Cedar Rapids Gazette* (IA), police & aviation reporter, to 1962. *Aviation Week & Space Technology*, engineering editor, NY, to 1963; space technology editor, to 1966; Asst European Editor, Geneva, to 1969; Paris Bureau Chief, to 1972; Management Editor, LA, to 1975; LA Bureau Chief, to 1978; Asst Managing Editor, NY, to 1981; Managing Editor, technical, to 1985; Editor-in-Chief, current, 1985. Also current, *Commercial Space*, 1985.

Finn, Ed. *Forbes.* Senior Editor. B. 1954, Whitisville, MA. Tufts, 1976, BA-English/Political Science; Columbia, 1983, MA-International Banking & Finance. *Blackstone Valley Tribune*, Asst Managing Editor, to 1977. *Southbridge Evening News* (MA), Managing Editor, to 1979. *The Wall Street Journal*, International Editor, to 1984; reporter, Dallas, to 1986. *Forbes*, Senior Editor, International Business, Banking & Finance, current, 1986.

Flanigan, Bill. *Forbes.* Senior Editor. B. 1940. Brooklyn College, 1962, BA-English. *Bayonet* (US Army newspaper, Korea), Editor, to 1964. *Electrical World*, writer, reporter, editor, to 1968. *BusinessWeek*, editor/writer personal business features, to 1976. *New York*, "Your Own Business" columnist, to 1978. *Esquire*, personal financial columnist, to 1979. *The Wall Street Journal*, "Your Money Matters" columnist, to 1980. *Forbes*, Senior Editor, current, 1980; originator "Personal Affairs" & "Careers" sections. CNN guest commentator, "Moneyline," 1985. Current, WABC radio host, "Bill Flanigan Show" (weekly money call-in program). Author 4 books, most recently *The Takers*, 1984.

Flanigan, James. *Los Angeles Times.* Business Columnist. B. 1936, NYC. Manhattan College, 1961, History, English. *New York Herald-Tribune,* copy, editorial asst, Paris edition correspondent, desk editor, finance & business reporter, to 1966. *Forbes,* Bureau Chief: Washington, LA, London, Houston; Asst Managing Editor, to 1980, 1981-82, 1984-85. *Los Angeles Times,* business columnist, 1980, 1983-84, NY, current, 1986.

Fleming, Thomas J. *Chronicles: A Magazine of American Culture.* Editor. B. 1945, Superior, WI. Charleston College, 1967, BA; U. of NC, 1973, PhD. College Professor (Classics, etc.): UNC, Miami U. of Ohio, Charleston College, Shaw U. *The Southern Partisan,* founding editor, 1979-83. *Chronicles,* Managing Editor, current, 1984. Freelance, current.

Flint, Jerry. *Forbes.* National Editor. B. 1931, Detroit, MI. Wayne U., 1953, Journalism. *The Wall Street Journal,* reporter, to 1967. *The New York Times,* Detroit Bureau Chief; asst to National Editor, Business Editor; labor writer, to 1979. *Forbes,* Washington Bureau Chief; Asst Managing Editor; National Editor, current, 1979. Author *The Dream Machine.*

Fly, Richard. *BusinessWeek.* Washington Correspondent. U. of TX, Austin. *The Houston Chronicle,* legislative reporter, 1975-80. *The Dallas Times-Herald,* White House reporter, to 1985. *BusinessWeek,* Washington correspondent, White House & national politics, current, 1986.

Foldessy, Edward P. *The Wall Street Journal.* Special Writer. B. NY. Iona College (New Rochelle, NY), 1963, BS-Physics. *The Wall Street Journal,* asst, national news desk, "What's News," to 1964; news asst, "Bond Markets"/"Financial Business" columns, to 1966; reporter; special writer, current; "Credit Markets" columnist, current, 1980.

Forbes, Malcolm S., Jr. *Forbes.* Deputy Editor-in-Chief & Editorial Writer. B. 1947, Morristown, NJ. Princeton, 1970, BA-History. *Business Today,* (Princeton business quarterly), founder. Forbes, Inc., Director, 1971; Vice-President/Secretary, 1973; President & Chief Executive Officer, current, 1980. *Forbes,* Associate Editor, to 1978; Senior Editor, to 1982, Deputy Editor-in-Chief & writer, current, 1982. Author *Fact & Comment,* 1974; "Some Call It Greed," 1977 (documentary). Four Crystal Owls (only multiple recipient in the 45 year history of the U.S. Steel award).

Forbes, Malcolm S., Sr. *Forbes.* Chairman & Editor-in-Chief. B. 1919, NYC. Princeton, 1941, AB. *Fairfield Times* (Lancaster, OH), Owner, Publisher, 1941. *Lancaster Tribune,* founder, 1942. US Army, to 1945; Bronze Star, Purple Heart. *Forbes,* Associate Publisher, to 1954; Publisher & Editor-in-Chief, current, 1957. NJ Senator, 1952-58. Forbes Inc., President, to 1964; Chairman, current, 1980. 60 Fifth Avenue Corp., Chairman of the Board, current; Forbes Trinchera Inc., President, current.

Forsyth, Randall W. *Barron's.* "Capital Markets" Editor, "Current Yield" Columnist. B. 1952, NYC. NYU, 1975, Economics, grad work-Economics & Finance. *Barron's,* Asst Editor, to 1976. Merrill Lynch Market Letter, staff writer, to 1980. Dow Jones "Capital Market" Report, reporter, to 1983. *Barron's,* "Capital Markets" Editor, "Current Yield" Columnist, current, 1983.

Fossedal, Gregory A. Copley News Service, Columnist. *Harper's & The American Spectator,* Contributing Editor. B. 1959. Dartmouth, 1981, BA-English Literature, *summa cum laude,* Phi Beta Kappa; U. of WI, Marxist Sociological Thought, 1977. *The Daily Dartmouth,* Editor-in-Chief, 1979-80. *The Dartmouth Review,* founder & Editor, to 1981. *Dallas Morning News,* editorial columnist, to 1982. *Charleston Daily Mail* (NC), editorial writer, spring 1982. *The Washington Times,* editorial page writer, to 1983. *The San Diego Union* (CA), editorial page writer, 1983. *The Wall Street Journal,* editorial page writer, to 1986. Hoover Institute, Stanford, Media Fellow, current, 1986. *Harper's,* Contributing Editor, current, 1986. *The American Spectator,* Contributing Editor, current, 1986. Ernest M. Hopkins Institute, Dartmouth, member, Board of Directors, current, 1986. Copley News Service, columnist, current, 1986. Co-author (with Terry Dolan) *Ronald Reagan: A President Succeeds*, 1983; (with Daniel O. Graham) *A Defense That Defends: Blocking Nuclear Attack*, 1984.

Frailey, Fred William. *U.S. News & World Report.* Assistant Managing Editor & "Business Briefing" Columnist. B. 1944, Arkansas City, KS. U. of KS, 1966, Journalism. *Daily Kansan*, Managing Editor, 1966. *Sun-Times* (Chicago, IL), suburban reporter, Labor Editor, to 1971. *U.S. News & World Report*, Chicago Bureau Chief, to 1974, labor writer, Washington, to 1978; transportation writer, to 1979; Graphics Editor; Asst Managing Editor & "Business Briefing" columnist, current. Author 2 books.

Francis, David R. *The Christian Science Monitor.* Canadian Correspondent & "Global Markets" Columnist. B. Newmarket, Ontario. Carleton U. (Ottawa), BJ, BA. *Winnepeg Free Press*, 1954-55. *Victoria Colonist*, to 1957. *Financial Post* (Toronto), to 1960. *The Christian Science Monitor*, business & financial correspondent, NY, to 1968; business correspondent, Washington, to 1972; Bonn correspondent, to 1974; business & financial editor, to 1983; "Global Markets" columnist, current; Canadian correspondent, current, 1986. New England Education Writer's Award, 1961; Gerald Loeb Award, 1967, '75.

Frank, Allan Dodds. *Forbes.* Associate Editor. B. 1947, Pittsburgh, PA. Colgate, 1969, AB-History; Columbia, MSJ; Yale, 1981, MS-Law. *Anchorage Daily News* (AK), reporter, Juneau Bureau Chief, Sports Editor, 1970-73. *The Washington Star*, national staff writer, to 1981. *Forbes*, Washington correspondent, to 1985; Associate Editor, current, 1985. 1st Prize Award, Alaska Press Club; Washington-Baltimore Newspaper Guild Front Page Award, 1976.

Frank, Richard S. *National Journal.* Editor. B. 1931, Paterson, NJ. Syracuse, 1953, BA; U. of Chicago, 1956, MA. *Evening Record* (Bergen, NJ), local gov't. reporter, to 1957. *Evening Sun* (Baltimore, MD), state & local gov't./politics, to 1964. Administrative Asst to the Mayor of Baltimore, to 1965. *Philadelphia Bulletin*, state legislature, Congress, White House, to 1971. *National Journal*, legal affairs, economics, trade, to 1976; Editor, current, 1976.

Frankel, Glenn. *The Washington Post.* Israel Correspondent. B. 1949, NYC. Columbia, 1971, History. Professional Journalism Fellow, Stanford, 1982-83. *Richmond Mercury*, staff writer, to 1975. *The Record*, (Bergen, NJ), staff writer, to 1979. *The Washington Post*, staff writer, to 1982; Southern Africa correspondent, to 1986; Israel correspondent, current, 1986.

Frankel, Max. *The New York Times.* Executive Editor. B. 1930, Gera, Germany. Columbia, 1952, AB; 1953, MA-Political Science. *The Columbia Daily Spectator*, Editor-in-Chief. US Army, 1953-55. *The New York Times* Columbia correspondent, to 1953; staff, NY, to 1956; foreign correspondent, Austria, to 1957; Moscow correspondent, to 1960; UN correspondent, 1961; Washington correspondent, to 1963; diplomatic correspondent, to 1966; White House correspondent, to 1968; chief Washington correspondent & head of Washington Bureau, to 1972; Sunday Editor, to 1976; Editorial Page Editor, to 1986; Executive Editor, current, 1986. Overseas Press Club Award for Foreign Reporting, 1965; George Polk Memorial Award for Foreign Affairs, 1970; Pulitzer Prize for International Reporting, 1973.

Franklin, William B. *BusinessWeek.* "Business Outlook" Editor. Denver U.; Columbia, MA. *BusinessWeek*, 1950-63; "Business Outlook" Editor, current, 1965. Bureau of National Affairs & Conference Board, 1963-65. *The Economist*, special correspondent. Also current, Financial News Network, commentator. Former president, NY Association of Business Economists.

MediaGuide 303

Frazier, Steve. *The Wall Street Journal.* Reporter. U. of KS, 1978, BSJ. *Daily Kansan* (U. of KS), reporter, editorial director, editor. *The Miami Herald, The Wichita Eagle and Beacon, The Topeka State Journal, The Abilene Reflector-Chronicle,* intern, 1977-78. *The Wall Street Journal,* reporter, Dallas, to 1981; reporter, LA, to 1984; Mexico City Bureau Chief, to 1986; reporter, Houston, current, 1986.

Freedman, Jonathan. *The Tribune* (San Diego, CA), Editorial Writer. Copley News Service, Columnist. B. 1950, Rochester, MN. Columbia, 1972, Literature, *Phi Beta Kappa, cum laude.* Cornell Woolrich Writing Fellowship, 1973. AP, reporter, Sao Paulo & Rio de Janeiro, to 1975. Freelance writer, 1979-80. *The Tribune* (San Diego, CA), editorial writer, current, 1981. Copley News Service, columnist, current, 1986. US-Japan Journalists Exchange Program, 1985. Author *The Man Who'd Bounce The World,* 1979. Two-time Distinguished Service Award, National Society of Professional Journalists, 1985; Special Citation for Editorials, Columbia, 1985; Distinguished Writing Award, American Society of Newspaper Editors, 1986.

Friedman, Thomas L. *The New York Times.* Jerusalem Bureau Chief. B. 1953, Minneapolis, MN. Brandeis, 1975, BA-Middle East Studies; St. Antony's College, Oxford, 1978, MPhil. UPI, London/Beirut correspondent, to 1981. *The New York Times,* business reporter, to 1982; Beirut Bureau Chief, to 1984; Jerusalem Bureau Chief, current, 1984. Overseas Press Club Award for Business Reporting Abroad, 1980. George Polk Award for International Reporting, 1983. Livingston Award for Young Journalists, 1983; Pulitzer Prize for International Reporting, 1982.

Fritz, Sara. *Los Angeles Times.* Congressional Reporter. B. 1944, Pittsburgh, PA. Denison U., 1966, Writing. *The Pittsburgh Press,* copy desk, 1966. UPI, Harrisburg PA Bureau Chief, to 1973; Washington Weekend Editor, to 1975; national labor reporter, to 1978. *U.S. News & World Report,* labor reporter, to 1980; chief White House correspondent, to 1983. *Los Angeles Times,* Congressional reporter, current, 1983. Permanent judge, Sidney Hillman Awards. Executive Committee, Reporter's Committee for Freedom of the Press.

Fromm, Joseph. *U.S. News & World Report.* Contributing Editor. B. 1920, South Bend, IN. U. of Chicago, Northwestern. *Mishawaka Enterprise* (IN), reporter, to 1935. *South Bend News-Times,* reporter, to 1936. *South Bend Tribune,* reporter, to 1937. *Southtown Economist* (Chicago), reporter, to 1939. UPI, radio news writer, to 1940. AP, chief of radio news bureau, to 1941. *Chicago Sun* (Air edition), managing editor, to 1942. *U.S. News & World Report,* foreign correspondent & Senior Editor, to 1974; Deputy Editor, Asst Editor, to 1985; Contributing Editor, current, 1985. Also current, Chairman, US Committee, International Institute for Strategic Studies.

Fuerbringer, Jonathan. *The New York Times.* National Economics Correspondent. B. 1945, NYC. Harvard, 1967, BA-American History; Columbia, 1968, MSJ. *The Boston Globe,* copy editor; reporter; state house reporter; financial reporter. *The Washington Star,* reporter, national economics correspondent, to 1981. *The New York Times,* national economics correspondent, current, 1981.

Fung, Vigor. *The Asian Wall Street Journal.* Staff Reporter. Chinese U. of Hong Kong, Journalism; Hong Kong U., MS-Political Science. *The South China Morning Post* (Hong Kong), intern. *The Asian Wall Street Journal,* staff reporter, current, 1980.

Gailey, Philip Lane. *The New York Times.* Washington Reporter. B. 1944, Homer, GA. U. of GA, 1966, Journalism. *The Atlanta Constitution,* reporter, to 1973; *The Miami Herald,* Washington correspondent, to 1978. *The Washington Star,* to 1982. *The New York Times,* Washington reporter, current, 1982.

Gannon, James P. *The Des Moines Register.* Editor. B. 1939, Minneapolis, MN. Marquette U., 1961, Journalism. *The Wall Street Journal,* reporter, Chicago, to 1966; labor reporter, Washington, to 1969; Pittsburgh Bureau Chief, to 1971; White House correspondent, to 1972; Treasury, Fed, & economic policy correspondent, to 1976; national political correspondent, to 1978. *The Des Moines Register*, Executive Editor, to 1982; Editor, current, 1982.

Garcia, Beatrice E. *The Wall Street Journal*. Reporter, "Abreast of the Market" Columnist. Fairleigh Dickenson U. (Teaneck, NJ), 1978, English. *Shopper's Newspaper* (Fair Lawn, NJ), reporter, 1977. Chase Manhattan Bank, NYC, public relations associate, 1978. Munifacts News Wire, NY, reporter, 1980. *The Wall Street Journal*, Capitol Markets reporter, current, 1982; "Abreast of the Market" columnist, current, 1985.

Gardner, David. *Financial Times*. Mexico & Central America Correspondent. B. 1952, Brussels, Belgium. St. John's, Oxford, 1975, BA-English Literature. Freelance journalist, Spain, to 1979. *Financial Times*, London, to 1983; Mexico & Central America correspondent, current, 1984.

Garment, Suzanne. *The Wall Street Journal*. Associate Editor, Editorial Page, "Capitol Comment" Columnist. B. Buffalo, NY. Radcliffe, 1967, BA; U. of Sussex (UK), 1968, MA; Harvard, 1973, PhD. Harvard, lecturer; John F. Kennedy Institute of Politics, research fellow. Yale, Asst Professor, Political Science, to 1978. Special asst to the US Permanent Representative to the UN, 1975. *The Wall Street Journal*, editorial writer, to 1979; Associate Editor, editorial page, current, 1979; "Capitol Comment" columnist, current, 1981. Author *Decision to Prosecute: Organization and Public Policy in the Antitrust Division*, 1977; co-author (with Daniel P. Moynihan) *A Dangerous Place*, 1978. Honorable Mention for series of columns on Cuba, Inter American Press Association, 1986.

Gelb, Arthur. *The New York Times*. Managing Editor. B. NYC. NYU, 1948. *The New York Times*, from 1944, copyboy, reporter, asst drama critic, to 1962; Chief Cultural Correspondent, to 1967; Metro Editor, to 1976; Asst Managing Editor, to 1977; Deputy Managing Editor, to 1986; Managing Editor, current, 1986. Co-author (with Barbara Gelb) *O'Neill* (biography of Eugene O'Neill).

Gelb, Leslie. *The New York Times*. Deputy Editor, Editorial Page. B. 1937, New Rochelle, NY. Tufts, BA-Government & Philosophy; Harvard, 1961, MA, 1964, PhD. Wesleyan, Asst Professor, to 1966. Executive Asst, Senator Jacob Javits, to 1967. Department of Defense, Director of Policy Planning & Arms Control, International Security Affairs/Director Pentagon Papers project, to 1969. Brookings Institution, Senior Fellow, to 1973. Dept. of State, Asst Secretary of State (Director, Bureau of Politico-Military Affairs), 1977-1979. Carnegie Endowment for International Peace, Senior Associate, Security and Arms Control, to 1981. *The New York Times*, diplomatic correspondent, to 1977; national security correspondent, 1981-86; Deputy Editor, Editorial Page, current, 1986. Also current, commentator for *The New York Times* "Washington Report", syndicated. TV work: Senior Consultant, producer, "Crisis Game", ABC (Winner Emmy, DuPont, Hood Awards), 1983; Senior Editor, "45/85", ABC, 1985; Panelist, "Capitol Journal", educational TV. Co-author *The Irony of Vietnam: The System Worked*, 1980; *Our Own Worst Enemy: The Unmaking of American Foreign Policy*, 1984; *Star Wars*, in progress. Pulitzer Prize for Explanatory Journalism, 1985.

Gergen, David R. *U.S. News & World Report*. Editor. B. 1942, Durham, NC. Yale; Harvard Law, 1967. *Los Angeles Times* Syndicate, columnist. American Enterprise Institute, resident fellow. White House staff, most recently Communications Director, 1981-83. John F. Kennedy Fellow, Harvard, 1984. *U.S. News & World Report*, contributing columnist, 1985; Managing Editor, to 1986; Editor, current, 1986.

German, William. *San Francisco Chronicle*. Executive Editor. B. 1919, Brooklyn, NY. Brooklyn College, 1939, Political Science/English; Columbia, 1940, MSJ. Neiman Fellow, Harvard, 1949-50. *San Francisco Chronicle*, copyboy, reporter, Asst Foreign Editor, copy desk chief, to 1943; News Editor, Executive Foreign Editor, to 1977; Editor, *Chronicle* Foreign Service; Managing Editor, to 1982; Executive Editor, current, 1982.

MediaGuide

Gertz, William David. *The Washington Times.* National Security Correspondent. B. 1952, Glen Cove, NY. Attended Washington College, English Literature, & George Washington U., Journalism. *New York News World*, Washington correspondent, 1979-80; State Dept. correspondent, to 1981. Paragon House Publishers, NY, book editor, to 1983. *New York City Tribune*, Washington correspondent, to 1984. *The Washington Times*, national security correspondent, current, 1985.

Gest, Kathryn Waters. *Congressional Quarterly.* Managing Editor. B. 1947, Boston, MA. Northwestern, 1969, BS; Columbia, 1970, MS. *The Patriot Ledger* (Quincy, MA), reporter, 1968. Voice of America, writer, Europe Desk (in Washington), 1969. *St. Louis Globe-Democrat*, reporter, to 1977. *TIME*, St. Louis correspondent, 1975-77. *The Christian Science Monitor*, St. Louis correspondent, 1976-77. *Congressional Quarterly*, reporter, Washington, to 1978; News Editor, to 1980; Asst Managing Editor, to 1983; Managing Editor, current, 1983. Award for Investigative Reporting, Inland Daily Press Club, 1977.

Geyelin, Philip. *The Washington Post* Writers Group. Foreign Affairs Columnist. B. Devon, PA. Yale, 1944, English Literature. *The Wall Street Journal*, Washington Bureau, 1947-56; Paris/London correspondent, covering Europe/Middle East, to 1960; diplomatic correspondent, to 1967. *The Washington Post*, Editorial Page Editor, to 1979. *The Washington Post* Writers Group, foreign affairs columnist, current, 1980.

Gillette, Robert. *Los Angeles Times.* Warsaw Bureau Chief. B. 1943, Rochester, NY. U. of CA, Berkeley, 1966, BA-Geology/Physical Sciences. Nieman Fellow, Harvard, 1975-76. *The Blade* (Toledo, OH), science writer, to 1968. *San Francisco Examiner*, science writer, to 1971. *Science*, "News and Comment" section reporter, to 1976. *Los Angeles Times*, science writer, to 1980; Moscow Bureau Chief, to 1984; Warsaw Bureau Chief, current, 1984. Co-winner (both with Robert Rawitch) LA Press Club Award, Best Print News Story not under Deadline, 1979; Clarence Darrow Foundation Award, 1979.

Gilliam, Dorothy. *The Washington Post.* Columnist, "Metro" Section. B. Memphis, TN. Lincoln U., BA; Columbia, MSJ. Tuskegee Institute (AL), Associate Director of Information. *Jet*, Associate Editor. WTTG-TV, Washington, "Panorama" special reporter. *The Washington Post*, reporter, from 1961; Asst Editor, "Style" section; columnist, "Metro" section, current. Author *Paul Robeson, All American*, 1976. Anne O'Hare McCormick Award, NY Newspaper Women's Club; "Journalist of the Year" & "Achievement in Journalism" Awards, Capital Press Club (awarded different years); Unity Award in Journalism, Lincoln U.; Columbia Alumni of the Year Award.

Gilmore, Kenneth O. *Reader's Digest.* Editor-in-Chief. B. 1930, Providence, RI. Brown, 1953. *Reader's Digest*, Washington staff member, 1957-68; Washington Editor, to 1973; Asst Managing Editor, to 1975; Managing Editor, to 1982; Executive Editor, Vice-President, The Reader's Digest Association, Inc.; member, Board of Directors & Executive Committee, current, 1984; Editor-in-Chief, current.

Girardet, Edward R. *The Christian Science Monitor.* Foreign Correspondent. B. 1951, White Plains, NY. Clifton College (Bristol, UK); U. of Nottingham; Free U. in West Berlin, 1973, German Literature. Journalists in Europe Fellow, 1977. English teacher, Paris. UPI, reporter, 1974-76. NBC, radio correspondent, Geneva, to 1979. Freelance writer/radio reporter, Paris, to 1977; 1978-79; Afganistan & Pakistan, 1979. *The Christian Science Monitor*, foreign correspondent, 1979; London-based foreign correspondent, current, 1986. Also current, producer/reporter of US & European TV documentaries. Author *Afganistan: The Soviet War* (Overseas Press Club Citation, 1985). Sigma Delta Chi Award for Foreign Reporting, 1980.

Gladwell, Malcolm. *Insight*, Writer. *The American Spectator*, Contributor. B. 1963, Hampshire, UK. Trinity College, U. of Toronto, 1984, History. Ethics & Public Policy Center, Asst Editor,

1985. *The American Spectator*, Asst Managing Editor, 1984-85; contributor, current, 1986. *Insight*, writer, current, 1986.

Glasgall, William. *BusinessWeek*. International Money Editor. Boston U. Walter Bagehot Fellow in Business & Economic Journalism, Columbia. AP, energy reporter. *BusinessWeek*, energy editor, 1981-86; International Money Editor, current, 1986.

Glassman, James K. *The New Republic*; Contributing Editor, Business Columnist. *The Washingtonian*, Financial Editor. B. 1947, Washington, DC. Harvard, 1969, Government. *Boston Herald-Traveler*, reporter, to 1970. *Provincetown Advocate* (MA), Editor & Publisher, to 1972. *Figaro* (New Orleans), Editor & Publisher, to 1978. *The Washingtonian*, Executive Editor, to 1981. *The New Republic*, Publisher, to 1984. *U.S. News & World Report*, Executive Vice-President, to 1986. *The Atlantic*, President, to 1986. *The New Republic*, Contributing Editor & business columnist, current. *The Washingtonian*, Financial Editor, current.

Goodman, Ellen Holtz. *The Boston Globe*. Feature Writer & Columnist. *The Washington Post* Writers Group, Columnist. B. 1941, Newton, MA. Radcliffe, 1963, BA, *cum laude*. Neiman Fellow, Harvard, 1974. *Newsweek*, researcher/reporter, to 1965. *Detroit Free Press*, feature writer, to 1967. *The Boston Globe*, feature writer, columnist, current, 1967. *The Washington Post* Writers Group, columnist, current, 1976. Author *Close to Home*, 1979; *Turning Points*, 1979; *At Large*, 1981. New England Press Association Columnist of the Year Award, 1975, & Newspaper Woman of the Year Award, 1978; Pulitzer Prize for Commentary, 1980; American Society Newspaper Editors Prize for Column Writing, 1980.

Graham, Bradley. *The Washington Post*. Buenos Aires Bureau Chief. B. 1952, Chicago, IL. Yale, MA, 1974; Stanford, 1978, MBA. *Yale Daily News*, Managing Editor, to 1974. *St. Petersburg Times*, intern, summers 1972, '73. *The Trenton Times*, city & statehouse reporter, to 1976. *The Washington Post*, intern, summers 1974, '77; business writer, to 1979; Bonn Bureau Chief, to 1982; Warsaw Bureau Chief, to 1985; Buenos Aires Bureau Chief, current, 1985. American Society of Newspaper Editors Award for Deadline Writing, 1986.

Graham, Donald Edward. *The Washington Post*. Publisher. B. 1945, Baltimore, MD. Harvard, 1966, BA. US Army, to 1968. *The Washington Post*, from 1971; Asst Managing Editor, Sports, 1974-75; Asst General Manager, to 1976; Executive Vice-President & General Manager, to 1979; Publisher, 1979, current.

Graham, Katharine. The Washington Post Company. Chairman & Chief Executive Officer. B. 1917, NYC. Vassar, U. of Chicago, 1938. *San Francisco News*, reporter. *The Washington Post*, editorial/circulation depts, to 1969; Publisher, to 1979. The Washington Post Company, President, to 1973; Chairman & Chief Executive Officer, current, 1973.

Greeley, Brendan M. Jr. *Aviation Week & Space Technology*. Military Editor. B. 1939, Ft. Riley, KS. US Military Academy, 1961, Engineering. US Marines, Naval Aviator, designated 1963; flew A4 Series aircraft thru 21 yrs with USMC; Commander, Marine Attack Squadron 223. *Aviation Week & Space Technology*, Military Editor, current.

Greenberg, Paul. Freelance Syndicate, Columnist. *Pine Bluff Commercial* (AR), Editorial Page Editor. B. 1937, Shreveport, LA. U. of MO, 1958, BA-Journalism; 1959, MA-History; Columbia, grad work-American History, 1960-62. US Army, to 1960; discharged Captain, 1967. *Pine Bluff Commercial* (AR), Editorial Page Editor, to 1966; current, 1967. *Chicago Daily News*, editorial writer, 1966-67. Freelance Syndicate, columnist, current, 1971. Grenville Clark Memorial Award, First Place, 1964; National Newspaper Association Editorial Award, First Place, 1968; Pulitzer Prize for Editorial Writing, 1969; American Society of Newspaper Editors Distinguished Writing Award, Commentary, 1981; Walker Stone Award, Scripps Howard News Service, First Place, 1986.

MediaGuide 307

Greene, Bob. *Chicago Tribune*, Columnist. *Esquire*, Contributing Editor & "American Beat" Columnist. B. 1947, Columbus, OH. Northwestern, 1969, BSJ. *Sun-Times* (Chicago, IL), reporter, to 1971; columnist, to 1978. *Chicago Tribune*, columnist (syndicated through Tribune Media Services), current, 1978. *Esquire*, Contributing Editor, "American Beat" columnist, current, 1980. Also current, ABC News "Nightline," contributing correspondent. Author 8 books: *Cheeseburgers: The Best of Bob Greene*. National Headliner Award; Peter Lisafor Award for Exemplary Journalism.

Greene, Richard. *Forbes*. Contributing Editor. B. 1947, West Haven, CT. Northwestern, 1977, BSJ. *Forbes*, reporter/researcher, to 1979; reporter, to 1981; staff writer, to 1982; Associate Editor, to 1984; Contributing Editor, current, 1984. Also current, freelance journalist, 1984. Champion Media Awards for Economic Understanding, 1978.

Greenfield, Meg. *The Washington Post*, Editorial Page Editor. *Newsweek*, Columnist. B. 1930, Seattle, WA. Smith, 1952, BA, *summa cum laude*; Fulbright Scholar, Newnham College, Cambridge, to 1953. *Reporter* magazine, to 1965; Washington Editor, to 1968. *The Washington Post*, editorial writer, to 1970; Deputy Editorial Page Editor, to 1979; Editorial Page Editor, current, 1979. *Newsweek*, columnist, current, 1974. Pulitzer Prize for Editorial Writing, 1978.

Greenhouse, Linda. *The New York Times*. Supreme Court Reporter. B. 1947, NYC. Radcliffe, BA-Government, *magna cum laude*; Yale Law, 1978, MS-Law, Ford Foundation Fellow. *The New York Times*, clerk to James Reston, 1968; reporter, to 1970; Westchester County correspondent, to 1973; night rewrite staff, 1973; Albany correspondent, to 1976; Albany Bureau Chief, to 1978; Supreme Court reporter, Washington, current, 1978.

Greenhouse, Steven. *The New York Times*. Financial Correspondent, Chicago. B. Long Island, NY. Wesleyan U., 1973; Columbia, 1975, Economics Reporting; NYU, 1982, JD, valedictorian. *The Chelsea Clinton News* (NYC), reporter. *The Westsider* (NYC), reporter. *The Reocrd* (Bergen, NJ), labor & economics reporter, 1976. Law clerk, US District Court Judge Robert L. Carter, 1982-83. *The New York Times*, copyboy, 1973; reporter, 1983-84, financial correspondent, Chicago, current, 1984.

Gregory, William. *Aviation Week & Space Technology*. Northeast US Senior Editor. B. 1924, Kansas City, MO. Creighton U. (Omaha, NE), 1947, BSJ. US Naval Reserves, 1942-46. *Clinton Herald* (IA), reporter, to 1950. *Kansas City Times*, reporter, copy editor, to 1956. *Aviation Week & Space Technology*, from 1956; Managing Editor, 1958-72; Executive Editor, to 1979; Editor-in-Chief; Northeast US Senior Editor, current. Robert S. Ball Award, Aviation and Space Writers Association, 1975.

Grenier, Richard. *The Washington Times*, "Point Man" Columnist. *The American Spectator*, Senior Editor. B. 1933, Cambridge, MA. US Naval Academy, Engineering. *Agence France Presse*, 1962, Paris. *Financial Times*, Paris, to 1969. Group W. Broadcasting, Paris, 1968-70. *Commentary*. *The New York Times*. *The American Spectator*, Senior Editor. *The Washington Times*, "Point Man" columnist, current. Freelance work, current. Author *Yes and Back Again*, 1967; *The Marrakesh One-Two*, 1983; *The Gandhi Nobody Knows*, 1983.

Griffiths, David. *BusinessWeek*. Washington Correspondent. U. of VA, BA; U. of MO, MSJ. US Army. *The Kansas City Star*, reporter, 1973-77. *Aviation Week & Space Technology*, reporter, to 1981. *Defense Week*, reporter, to 1983. *BusinessWeek*, national security/defense reporter, Washington, current, 1983.

Grover, Ronald. *BusinessWeek*. Los Angeles Correspondent. George Washington U., BA-Political Science, MBA; Columbia, MSJ. *The Washington Star*, reporter, to 1979. McGraw-Hill World News, energy correspondent, Washington, to 1982. *BusinessWeek*, economic & political correspondent, Washington, to 1986; LA correspondent, current, 1986.

Guillermoprieto, Alma. *Newsweek.* Rio de Janeiro Bureau Chief. B. 1949, Mexico City. Alicia Patterson Foundation Fellow, 1985. *The Guardian* (UK), Central America stringer, 1978-82. *Latin America Newsletters* (UK), Central America stringer, 1978-82. *The Washington Post*, Central America stringer, 1978-82; staff reporter, to 1985. *Newsweek*, Rio de Janeiro Bureau Chief, current, 1986.

Gupte, Pranay. Freelance Writer. B. 1948, Bombay, India. U. of Bombay; Brandeis, 1970, BA-Political Science/Economics; Columbia, 1971, MSJ. *The New York Times*, news clerk, business/national desks, summer 1968, '69, '70; personal asst to A.M. Rosenthal, to 1973; metro reporter, 1973, '78; suburban correspondent, to 1976; UN correspondent, 1977, '79; foreign correspondent, Africa & Middle East, to 1982. *International Herald Tribune*, editorial page columnist, current, 1982. Freelance writer, current, 1982. Author *Vengence: India After The Assassination of Indira Gandhi*, 1986; *The Crowded Earth: People and the Politics of Population*, 1984; *Egypt A Population Study*, 1981. Publisher's Award for series in *The New York Times*, 1977. UN Travel Fellowship, 1982, '85. Best Columnist, Internationl Newspaper, Population Institute, 1984; Award for Highest Accomplishment in Journalism, National Federation of Asian Indian Organizations, 1986.

Guskind, Robert S. *National Journal.* Contributing Editor. B. 1958, Passaic, NJ. Georgetown, 1980, BA-Government, *magna cum laude*, *Phi Beta Kappa*. WGTB-FM, news director, 1976-79. Freelance writer, current, 1980. *The Washington Post* Writers Group, "The Neal Peirce Column," associate, current, 1980. *National Journal*, contributor, 1982-84; Contributing Editor, current, 1984.

Gwertzman, Bernard M. *The New York Times.* Washington Diplomatic Correspondent. B. 1935, NYC. Harvard, 1957, BA, 1960, MA-Soviet Affairs. *The Evening Star*, diplomatic correspondent, to 1968. *The New York Times*, State Dept. correspondent, to 1969; Moscow Bureau Chief, to 1971; Washington diplomatic correspondent, current, 1971. Co-author *Fulbright: The Dissenter*. Front Page Award, Washington Newspaper Guild, 1966; Edward Weintal Award for Distinguished Diplomatic Reporting, 1984.

Haberman, Clyde. *The New York Times.* Tokyo Bureau Chief. B. 1945, Bronx, NY. CCNY, 1966, BA. *The New York Times*, campus stringer, to 1966. *The New York Post*, reporter, to 1976. *The New York Times*, editor, "Week in Review" section, to 1978; reporter, to 1983; Tokyo Bureau Chief, current, 1983.

Hadar, Mary. *The Washington Post.* Assistant Managing Editor, "Style" section. B. Brooklyn, NY. U. of PA, BA; Columbia MSJ. *The Sun* (Baltimore, MD). *The Jerusalem Post*, Foreign Editor. *The Washington Post*, copy editor, "Style" section, 1977-79; night editor, "Style" section, to 1981; Deputy Editor, "Style" section, to 1983; Asst Managing Editor, "Style" section, current, 1983.

Hall, Alan. *BusinessWeek.* Senior Editor. Cornell, BSJ. *Plastics World*, bureau chief. *Modern Plastics*, Associate Editor. *Chemical Week*, News Editor, to 1979. *BusinessWeek*, research editor, to 1985; Associate Editor, Science & Technology, to 1986; Senior Editor, Science & Technology Section, current, 1986. Author *The Wildfood Trailguide; Wood Finishing and Refinishing.* AAAS/Westinghouse Award for Science Journalism; Deadline Club Award for Science Writing, NYC Chapter Society of Professional Journalists/Sigma Delta Chi.

Hall, David. *The Denver Post.* Senior Vice-President & Editor. B. 1943, Lebanon, TN. U. of TN, 1965, BSJ; 1966, MA-Economics. *Nashville Tennessean*, part-time reporter, to 1964. *Chicago Daily News*, financial reporter, Asst Financial Editor, Middle East correspondent, editorial writer, chief editorial writer, Asst Managing Editor, to 1978. *St. Paul Pioneer Press and Dispatch*, Managing Editor, to 1982; Executive Editor, to 1984. *The Denver Post*, Editor & Vice-President, to 1986; Editor & Senior Vice-President, current, 1986.

MediaGuide 309

Hall, William. *Financial Times.* NY Correspondent. B. 1946, Birkenhead, UK. Cambridge, 1965-68, Economics. *The Banker,* asst editor, 1971-75. *Financial Times,* "LEX" column, to 1979; shipping correspondent, to 1981; banking correspondent, to 1983; NY correspondent, current, 1983.

Halloran, Richard. *The New York Times.* Military Affairs/Defense Correspondent. B. 1930, Washington, DC. Dartmouth, 1951, BA; U. of MI, 1957, MA-East Asian Studies; Ford Foundation Fellow, Advanced International Reporting, Columbia, 1964-65. *BusinessWeek,* staff writer; Asst Foreign Editor; Far East Bureau Chief, to 1964. *The Washington Post,* Northeast Asia correspondent; Asian specialist; economic correspondent, to 1969. *The New York Times,* reporter; diplomatic correspondent, to 1972; Tokyo Bureau Chief, to 1976; reporter, Washington, to 1979; military affairs/defense correspondent, current, 1979. Author *Japan: Images and Realities; Conflict and Compromise: The Dynamics of Foreign Policy.*

Hallow, Ralph Z. *The Washington Times.* Political Writer. B. 1938, Pittsburgh, PA. U. of Pittsburgh, 1960, AB, grad work-Law & History, U. of MO, Journalism. Northwestern, Ford Foundation Fellow. *The Pittsburgh Press* (PA), Night City Editor, to 1969. *The Pittsburgh Post-Gazette* (PA), Editorial Board member, to 1977. *Chicago Tribune,* Editorial Board, to 1982. *The Washington Times,* editorial writer, 1982; Deputy Editorial Page Editor, to 1984; financial writer, to 1985; political writer, current, 1985.

Hamill, Pete (William Peter). *The Village Voice.* Contributor. B. 1935, Brooklyn, NY. Studied Pratt Institute, 1952, & Mexico City College, 1956-57. US Naval Reserves, 1952-54. Commercial artist, to 1960. *The New York Post,* reporter, columnist, to 1974. *The Saturday Evening Post,* Contributing Editor, 1963-64. *New York Daily News,* columnist, 1965-67, 1969-79. *The Village Voice,* contributor, current, 1974. Meyer Berger Award, Columbia, 1962; Newspaper Reporters Association Award, 1962.

Harden, Blaine. *The Washington Post.* Africa Correspondent. B. 1952, Moses Lake, WA. Gonzaga U. (Spokane, WA), 1974, BA-Philosophy & Political Science; Syracuse, 1976, MA-Journalism. *The Trenton Times* (NJ), reporter, to 1977. *The Washington Post,* metro reporter, to 1980; Sunday magazine reporter, to 1982; metro reporter, to 1983; Africa correspondent, current, 1984. *The Washingtonian,* senior writer, 1983-84. Livingston Award for Young Journalists, 1986.

Hargreaves, Ian. *Financial Times.* Features Editor. B. 1951, Lancashire, UK. Queen's College, Cambridge, English Literature. *Keighley News,* reporter, 1973-74. *Telegraph and Argus* (Bradford, UK), reporter; feature writer, to 1976. *Financial Times,* labor reporter; transport correspondent; NY correspondent; social policy editor; resources editor; Features Editor, current.

Harries, Owen. *The National Interest.* Editor. B. Wales, UK. U. of Wales, 1950, Political Science; Oxford, 1952. U. of Sydney, Australia, faculty member, to 1965. U. of New South Wales, Australia, faculty member, to 1975. Senior Advisor to Australian Foreign Minister, to 1977; Head of Policy Planning, Dept. of Foreign Affairs, to 1979; Senior Advisor to Prime Minister Malcolm Fraser, to 1981; Australian Ambassador, UNESCO, Paris, to 1983. Heritage Foundation Fellow, to 1984. *The National Interest,* Editor, current, 1985. Also current, freelance work. Editor *Liberty and Politics.*

Harwood, Richard. *The Washington Post.* Deputy Managing Editor. Vanderbilt U. Neiman Fellow, Harvard, 1955. Carnegie Fellow in Journalism, Columbia, 1965. *The Courier-Journal* (Louisville, KY). *The Times* (Trenton, NJ), Evening & Sunday editions, Editor, 1974-76. *The Washington Post,* national politics & public affairs reporter; Vietnam correspondent; National Editor; Asst Managing Editor for national news, 1966-74; Deputy Managing Editor, current, 1976.

Hayes, Thomas C. *The New York Times.* Western Economic Correspondent. B. 1950, Cincinnati, OH. Northwestern, 1973, BSJ; grad work at U. of MA, Amherst, & Xavier U. Walter Bagehot Fellow in Business & Economic Journalism, Columbia, 1978-79. *The Cincinnati Post*, sports reporter, summers 1968-70. *The Cincinnati Enquirer*, business reporter, to 1978. *The New York Times*, "Business Day" reporter, to 1981; Western economic correspondent, current, 1981.

Hector, Gary. *FORTUNE.* Associate Editor. Columbia, MSJ; NYU, MBA-Finance. *San Jose Mercury News*, reporter. *American Banker*, reporter. *FORTUNE*, freelance writer, to 1982; Associate Editor, Menlo Park, CA, current, 1982. Gerald Loeb Award for Distinguished Business & Financial Journalism, 1981.

Helmore, Kristin. *The Christian Science Monitor.* Reporter. *The Christian Science Monitor*, reporter, current. Overseas Press Club Madeline Dane Ross Award.

Hempstone, Smith. The Hempstone Syndicate. "Our Times" Columnist. B. 1929, Washington, DC. U. of the South, (Sewanee, TN), 1950, BA-History. Neiman Fellow, Harvard, 1964. *Louisville Times*, reporter, 1954. *National Geographic*, writer, 1955. *The Washington Star*, reporter, 1956; foreign correspondent, 1966 to 1969; Associate Editor, to 1975. Institute of Current World Affairs, fellow, to 1960. *Chicago Daily News*, foreign correspondent, to 1963; 1965. *The Washington Times*, Executive Editor, to 1983; Editor-in-Chief, to 1985. The Hempstone Syndicate, "Our Times" columnist, to 1981; current, 1986. Author *In The Midst of Lions*, 1968; *A Tract of Time*, 1966; *Rebels, Mercenaries, and Dividends*, 1962; *Africa, Angry Young Giant*, 1961. Overseas Press Club, 1961 & Sigma Delta Chi, Foreign Correspondence, 1961, '68.

Henderson, C. Nell. *The Washington Post.* Business Writer. B. 1959, TX. Harvard, 1980, BA-Government, *cum laude*; London School of Economics, 1983, Economics. City News Service, LA, CA, reporter, 1981. *Evening Outlook* (Santa Monica, CA), reporter, to 1982. *Los Angeles Times*, suburban reporter, 1983-84. *The Washington Post*, business writer, current, 1984.

Hendrickson, Paul. *The Washington Post.* On Leave. B. 1944, Fresno, CA. Seminary; St. Louis U., AB-English; Penn State, MA. Alicia Patterson Foundation Fellow, 1979-80; Lyndhurst Foundation Fellow, 1985-88. *Holiday Magazine*, 1971-72. *Detroit Free Press*, to 1974. *National Observer*, to 1977. *The Washington Post*, current, 1977 (on leave, 1986). Author *Seminary: A Search*, 1983. Penney-Missouri Best Single Story, 1985.

Herman, R. Thomas. *The Wall Street Journal.* Reporter. B. NY. Yale, 1968, BA. *Yale Daily News*, reporter, political editor. *The Wall Street Journal*, intern, Washington, summer 1967; NY staff, to 1969; Atlanta bureau, to 1974; NY bureau, to 1976; Hong Kong (*The Asian Wall Street Journal*) reporter, to 1977; reporter, NY, current, 1980; co-author "Credit Markets" column, current, 1980.

Hersh, Seymour. *The Atlantic.* Contributing Editor. B. 1937, Chicago, IL. U. of Chicago, 1958, BA-History. City News Bureau, police reporter, to 1960. UPI, correspondent, Pierre, SD, 1962-63. AP, Chicago/Washington correspondent, to 1967. Press secretary to Eugene McCarthy of MN (NH primary), 1968. *The New York Times*, Washington staff, 1972-75, 1979; NY staff, to 1978. *The Atlantic*, national correspondent, from 1983; currently Contributing Editor. Author *Chemical and Biological Warfare: America's Hidden Arsenal*, 1968; *My Lai 4: A Report on the Massacre and its Aftermath*, 1970; *The Army's Secret Investigation of the Massacre of My Lai 4*, 1972; *The Price of Power: Kissinger in the Nixon White House*, 1983 (National Book Critics Circle Award winner for non-fiction); *"The Target Is Destroyed": What Really Happened to Flight 007 and What America Knew About It*, 1986. Worth Bingham Prize, 1970; Sigma Delta Chi Distinguished Service Award, 1970, '81; Pulitzer Prize for International Reporting, 1970; George Polk Memorial Award, 1970, '73, '75, '81; Scripps-Howard Public Service Award, 1973; Sidney Hillman Award, 1974; John Peter Zenger Freedom of the Press Award, 1975; Drew Pearson Prize.

MediaGuide

Hershey, Robert D. Jr. *The New York Times.* Washington Bureau Reporter. B. 1939, Berlin, Germany. Gettysburg College, 1961, BA-Philosophy; NYU, American Civilization program. *The New York Times,* copyboy, 1962; news clerk, 1963; news assistant, to 1966; financial dept. copy desk, to 1967; financial news reporter, to 1973; Asst Editor, deputy editor of the Sunday financial news section, to 1975; SEC & banking regulation reporter, to 1977; London business & economics correspondent, to 1980; Washington reporter, current, 1980.

Hertzberg, Hendrik. *The New Republic,* Contributing Editor. *TK Enterprises* (projected opinion magazine), Partner. B. 1943, NYC. Harvard, 1965, Government. US National Student Association, editorial director, to 1966. *Newsweek,* San Francisco correspondent, to 1967. US Navy, to 1969. *The New Yorker,* staff writer, to 1977. White House staff, chief speechwriter, to 1981. Harvard Institute of Politics, fellow, to 1986. *The New Republic,* Editor, to 1985; Contributing Editor, current, 1985. *TK Enterprises,* current, 1986.

Hetzer, Barbara. *FORTUNE.* Reporter/Researcher. B. Brooklyn, NY. Queens College, 1984, BA. *Woman's Day,* editorial assistant. *Cuisine,* editorial asst. *FORTUNE,* reporter/researcher, current, 1985; reporter, *FORTUNE 500,* 1986.

Hiatt, Fred. *The Washington Post.* East Asia Correspondent. B. 1955, Washington, DC. Harvard, 1977, BA-History. *Atlanta Journal,* City Hall reporter, 1979-80. *The Washington Star,* VA reporter, 1981. *The Washington Post,* VA reporter, to 1983; Pentagon reporter, to 1986; associate, US-Japan program, Harvard, 1986-87; scheduled, Tokyo, East Asia correspondent, 1987.

Hicks, Jonathan P. *The New York Times.* Business & Financial News Staff. B. 1955, St. Louis, MO. U. of MO, 1979, BA-Political Science; U. of CA, Berkeley, fellowship for minority journalists, 1980. *The Arizona Daily Star,* reporter, to 1982. *The Plain Dealer* (Cleveland, OH), business reporter, to 1985. *The New York Times,* business & financial reporter, current, 1986.

Hildreth, James. *U.S. News & World Report.* Associate Editor. W VA U. US Marines. UPI. Newhouse Newspapers, to 1981. *U.S. News & World Report,* White House correspondent; Associate Editor, Congress, current.

Himmelfarb, Joel. *Human Events.* Associate Editor. B. 1959, Baltimore, MD. U. of MD, 1982, BA-Political Assignment. *Human Events,* Associate Editor, current, 1982; "Conservative Forum" writer, current, 1982; writer, current, 1982.

Hitchens, Christopher. *The Nation.* Washington Columnist. B. 1949, Portsmouth, Hampshire, UK. Balliol College, Oxford, 1970, Philosophy, Politics & Economics. London *Times* Higher Education Supplement, social science correspondent; Insight team (Sunday *Times*); *Times* Literary Supplement, American columnist, current. *Weekend World,* London Weekend TV, Researcher/reporter. *The Daily Express,* foreign correspondent. *New Statesman,* staff writer & Foreign Editor. *The Spectator* (UK), Washington columnist, current. *The Nation,* Washington columnist, current.

Hoagland, Jim. *The Washington Post.* Associate Editor & Chief Foreign Correspondent. B. 1940, Rock Hill, SC. U. of SC, 1961, Journalism. Ford Foundation Fellow, Columbia, International Affairs, 1968-69. *The New York Times International Edition,* copy editor, Paris, 1964-66. *The Washington Post,* metro reporter, to 1968; Africa correspondent, 1969-72; Middle East correspondent, to 1975; Paris correspondent, to 1977; National Affairs reporter, to 1979; Foreign Editor, to 1981; Asst Managing Editor, Foreign News, to 1986; Associate Editor & Chief Foreign correspondent, Paris, current, 1986. Author *South Africa: Civilizations in Conflict,* 1972. Pulitzer Prize for International Reporting, 1971; Bob Considine Award, Overseas Press Club, International Reporting, 1977.

Hoffman, Ellen. *National Journal.* Contributing Editor. B. 1943, NY. U. of MN, 1964, BA-European History; Georgetown, 1966, MA. *The Washington Post*, reporter, to 1971. US Senate Subcommittee on Children & Youth, Staff member/Director, to 1977. The Children's Defense Fund, Director of Governmental Affairs, to 1983. Freelance, current, 1983. Self-syndicated column, "The Resourceful Traveler," current, 1983. Also current, Contributing Editor, *National Journal.*

Hoge, Warren. *The New York Times.* Foreign Editor. B. 1941, NYC. Yale, 1963, BA-English; George Washington U., Literature/Political Science. US Army Reserves, 1964. *The Washington Star*, police & courts reporter, to 1966. *The New York Post*, Washington correspondent, to 1970; Night City Editor, City Editor, Metro Editor, to 1976. *The New York Times*, metro reporter, 1976; Asst Metro Editor, Deputy Metro Editor, to 1979; Rio de Janeiro Bureau Chief, to 1983; Foreign Editor, current, 1983.

Hollie, Pamela G. *The New York Times.* "Business Day" Reporter. B. 1948, Topeka, KS. Washburn U., 1970, BA; Columbia, 1971, MSJ. *Washburn Review*, Editor-in-Chief. Gannett Fellowship, U. of HI, 1976-77. *The Wall Street Journal*, reporter, 1969-75. *The Honolulu Advertiser*, special correspondent, Micronesia, to 1976. *The New York Times*, national business correspondent, LA, 1978-81; foreign correspondent, Manila, to 1983; "Business Day" reporter, current, 1983.

Holman, Michael. *Financial Times.* Africa Editor. B. 1945, Penzance, UK. University College of Rhodesia, 1967, BA-English; U. of Edinburgh, 1971, MS-Politics. Freelance, Salisbury, Rhodesia (now Harare, Zimbabwe), 1973-77. *The Financial Mail*, Rhodesia editor, Johannesburg, South Africa, 1975-77. *Financial Times*, Africa correspondent, Lusaka, Zambia, to 1984; Africa Editor (based in London), current, 1984.

Holmes, John P. III. *Insight.* Science & Space Writer. B. 1955, Dalhart, TX. TX Tech U., 1977, Journalism. *The Corpus Christi Caller-Times* (TX), reporter, to 1978. *The Lubbock Avalanche-Journal* (TX), reporter, Regional Editor, to 1980. Press Secretary, US Representative Kent Hance (D-TX), to 1982. *The Washington Times*, "Capital Life" writer, to 1984; Space, science & national news reporter, to 1985. *Insight*, science & space writer, current, 1985. *Texas Business Magazine*, Washington correspondent, current, 1982. *Home Team Sports* magazine, Editor, current, 1985. H.L. Mencken Award for Investigative Journalism (for work at *The Washington Times*), 1985.

Holusha, John. *The New York Times.* Detroit Bureau Chief. Newark College of Engineering, 1965, BS-Chemical Engineering; grad work, George Washington U., 1976-78, Economics. Walter Bagehot Fellow, Columbia, 1975-76. *The Daily Record* (Morristown, NJ), reporter. *The Advance* (Dover, NJ), reporter. *The Star Ledger* (Newark, NJ), reporter, Asst City Editor, Night City Editor, to 1970. *The Washington Star*, reporter, Asst National Editor, Asst Financial Editor, to 1979. *The New York Times*, asst to the Financial Editor, to 1981; Editor, 1980 National & International Economic Surveys; Detroit Bureau Chief, current, 1982.

Holzman, David C. *Insight.* Writer. B. 1953, Cambridge, MA. U. of CA, Berkeley, 1975, Zoology. Center for Science in the Public Interest, researcher/writer, to 1977. *People & Energy*, staff writer, to 1978; Editor, to 1980. Freelance writer, science, technology & medicine, to 1986. *Insight*, medical writer, current, 1986.

Hornik, Richard. *TIME.* Peking Bureau Chief. B. 1948, NYC. Brown, 1970, Political Science. *National Journal*, researcher, to 1972. National Commission on Productivity, Writer/Editor, to 1974. *Eastwest Markets*, Contributing Editor, 1975; Associate Editor, to 1978. *TIME*, Washington energy & economics correspondent, to 1980; Eastern Europe Bureau Chief, to 1983; Boston Bureau Chief, to 1984; Peking Bureau Chief, current, 1985.

MediaGuide

Horowitz, Rose. *The Journal of Commerce.* Foreign Trade Reporter. B. 1960, NYC. Queens College (NY), 1982, BA-English, *magna cum laude*; Columbia, 1984, MA-International Affairs. AP, Pittsburgh, PA; Charleston, WVA, 1984. *The Journal of Commerce*, foreign trade reporter, current, 1985.

Houck, James I. *The Sun* (Baltimore, MD). Managing Editor. B. 1941, Bakersfield, CA. U. of CA, Berkeley, Journalism. *Bakersfield Californian*, reporter & Editor, 1960-62. *Daily Californian*, UCB, Managing Editor, 1963. *San Francisco Examiner*, Copy Editor, Telegraph Editor, News Editor, to 1981. *Dallas Morning News*, Sunday editor, Associate Managing Editor, 1971-72. *The Sun*, Managing Editor, current, 1982.

House, Karen Elliot. *The Wall Street Journal.* Foreign Editor. B. Matador, TX. U. of TX, Austin, 1970, Journalism. *Daily Texan*, Managing Editor. *Newsweek*, stringer, to 1970. *Dallas News*, education reporter; political reporter, to 1974. *The Wall Street Journal*, regulatory agencies, energy, environment & agriculture reporter, to 1978; diplomatic correspondent, to 1983; Asst Foreign Editor, to 1984; Foreign Editor, current, 1984. Institute of American Politics, Harvard, fall 1982. Edward Weintal Award, 1980; Edwin M. Hood Award for Excellence in Diplomatic Reporting, 1982; USC's Journalism Alumni Association's Distinguished Achievement Award, 1983; Overseas Press Club's Bob Considine Award for Best Daily Newspaper Interpretation of Foreign Affairs, 1984; Pulitzer Prize for Distinguished Reporting on International Affairs, 1984; U. of Tx, Outstanding Young Alumna, 1986.

Housego, David. *Financial Times.* Paris Bureau Chief. B. 1940, Horsham, UK. Oxford, Politics, Philosophy, Economics. *Times Educational Supplement*, reporter, 1964-67. *Times*, sub-editor, to 1968, reporter, Teheran, to 1975. *The Economist*, reporter, Teheran, to 1975; Energy & Middle East writer, to 1976. *Financial Times*, reporter, Teheran, to 1975; Asia correspondent, 1976-81; Paris Bureau Chief, current, 1981.

Huffman, Diana. *National Journal.* Managing Editor. B. 1949, Louisville, KY. Northwestern, 1971, BA-Political Science; Columbia, 1972, MSJ; Georgetown Law, 1977, JD. WNET-TV, NYC, producer/reporter, to 1973. *Sentinel* (Montgomery Cty., MD), News Editor, to 1976. WJLA-TV, Washington, Asst Assignment Editor, 1976. Senate Judiciary Subcommittee on Administrative Practice & Procedure, counsel, to 1978. *Legal Times*, Asst Editor/reporter, to 1980; Editor, to 1983. *National Journal*, Managing Editor, current, 1983.

Hughes, John. *Los Angeles Times* Syndicate. Columnist. B. 1930, Neath, South Wales. Neiman Fellow, Harvard, 1961-62. *The Christian Science Monitor*, Africa correspondent, to 1961; Asst Overseas News Editor, to 1964; Far East correspondent, to 1970; Managing Editor, 1970; Editor, to 1976; Editor/manager, to 1979. Hughes Newspaper Co., founder/President, to 1981, 1985. USIA, Associate Director, 1981. Voice of America, Director, 1982. Asst Secretary of State for Public Affairs/State Dept. Spokesman, to 1985. *Los Angeles Times* Syndicate, columnist, current. Also current, TV commentator. Sigma Delta Chi Yankee Quill Award, 1977; Overseas Press Club Award for Best Daily Reporting from Abroad, 1971; Pulitzer Prize for International Reporting, 1967.

Ibrahim, Youssef M. *The Wall Street Journal.* Energy Editor. B. Cairo, Eqypt. American U., Cairo, 1968, BA; Columbia, 1970, MA-Journalism. *The New York Times*, foreign correspondent, to 1981. *Mideast Markets*, Associate Editor. *The Wall Street Journal*, Energy Editor, current, 1981. Overseas Press Club Citation, 1986.

Ignatius, David. *The Washington Post.* Associate Editor, "Outlook." B. 1950, Cambridge, MA. Harvard, to 1973; King's College, Cambridge, 1975, Economics. *Washington Monthly*, Editor, to 1976. *The Wall Street Journal*, steel correspondent, to 1978; Justice Dept. & CIA correspondent, to 1979; Senate correspondent, to 1980; Middle East correspondent, to 1983; diplomatic correspondent, to 1985. *The Washington Post*, Associate Editor, "Outlook," current, 1985. Edward Weintal Prize Diplomatic Reporting, 1985.

Ingrassia, Lawrence. *The Wall Street Journal.* Boston Bureau Chief. B. Laurel, MS. U. of IL, Champaign-Urbana, 1974, BS-Communications. *Chicago Sun-Times*, reporter, to 1978. *The Wall Street Journal*, reporter, to 1979; first reporter, Minneapolis, to 1983; News Editor, London, 1983; Deputy Bureau Chief, London, to 1986; Boston Bureau Chief, current, 1986.

Ingrassia, Paul J. *The Wall Street Journal.* Detroit Bureau Chief. B. 1950, Laurel, MS. U. of IL, 1972, BSJ; U. of WI, 1973, MA. Lindsay-Schaub Newspapers, editorial writer, to 1976. *The Wall Street Journal*, reporter, Chicago, to 1980; News Editor, Chicago, to 1981; Cleveland Bureau Chief, to 1985; Detroit Bureau Chief, current, 1985.

Insolia, Anthony. *Newsday.* Editor & Senior Vice President. B. 1926, Tuckahoe, NY. NYU, 1949, Journalism. *Yonkers Daily Times*, reporter, 1949. Park Row News Service (NYC), reporter, to 1951. *Stamford Advocate* (CT), reporter, to 1955. *Newsday*, reporter, to 1959; copy editor, to 1960; Morning City Editor, to 1966; News Director, to 1969; Day Managing Editor, to 1970; Managing Editor, to 1978; Executive Editor, 1978; Editor & Vice President, to 1982; Editor & Senior Vice President, current, 1982.

Irwin, Victoria. *The Christian Science Monitor.* NY Bureau Chief & Reporter. B. 1954, Seattle, WA. Principia College, 1975, BA-Sociology; Columbia, 1978, MSJ. *The Gresham Outlook* (OR), reporter, 1976-77. *The Christian Science Monitor*, copy clerk, Living Page writer, National News Desk Editor, 1978-83; reporter, NY, current, 1983; NY Bureau Chief, current.

Isgro, Anna Cifelli. *FORTUNE.* Associate Editor, Washington. Fairleigh Dickenson U. (NJ); Columbia, MA-International Affairs. UN Public Information Office. Population Institute, research director. *FORTUNE*, reporter/researcher; Associate Editor, Washington, current.

Iyer, Pico. *TIME.* "World Affairs" Writer. B. 1957, Oxford, UK. Oxford, 1978, BA-English Language/Literature, 1982, MA; Harvard, 1980, AM. *Santa Barbara News and Review*, profile writer, 1980. *The Movies*, contributor, 1983. Freelance, current, 1977. *TIME*, "World Affairs" writer, reviewer, current, 1982.

Jackson, Brooks D. *The Wall Street Journal.* Washington Bureau Reporter. B. 1941, Seattle, WA. Northwestern, 1964, BS; Syracuse, 1967, MS. AP, reporter, NYC & Washington, to 1980. *The Wall Street Journal*, reporter, Washington bureau, current, 1980. AP Reporting Performance Award, 1974, First Runner-up, 1976; Raymond Clapper Award for Washington Reporting, 1974; John Hancock Award for Business & Financial Reporting, 1978.

Jackson, Robert D. *Los Angeles Times.* Investigative Reporter. B. 1935, St. Louis, MO. St. Louis U., 1956, AB, 1960, MA-Political Science. Fulbright Fellow, U. of Copenhagen, 1961-62. *St. Louis Globe-Democrat*, city desk staff, 1956-65. *Los Angeles Times*, city desk staff, to 1967; Washington-based investigative reporter, current, 1967. Sigma Delta Chi National Reporting Award, 1970.

Jameson, Sam. *Los Angeles Times.* Tokyo Bureau Chief. B. 1936, Pittsburg, PA. Northwestern, 1958, BSJ, 1959, MSJ. US Army, *Pacific Stars & Stripes*, Tokyo, 1960-62. *Chicago Tribune*, Chicago, 1959-60; Tokyo Bureau Chief, 1963-71. *Los Angeles Times*, Tokyo Bureau Chief, current, 1971. Loeb Award.

MediaGuide 315

Janensch, Paul. *The Courier-Journal* & *The Louisville Times.* Executive Editor. B. 1938, Chicago, IL. Georgetown, 1960, BA-Philosophy; Columbia, 1964, MSJ. City News Bureau, Chicago, to 1962. UPI, radio newswire writer, to 1963. *Pollution Abstracts, Inc.*, publisher, to 1975. *Philadelphia Daily News*, Managing Editor, to 1976. *The Courier-Journal*, reporter, City Editor, Washington bureau, to 1968; Managing Editor, to 1979. *The Louisville Times*, Managing Editor, to 1978. *The Courier-Journal* & *The Louisville Times*, Executive Editor, current, 1979.

Janssen, Richard F. *BusinessWeek.* Senior Editor. B. 1933, St. Louis, MO. Washington U. (MO), 1954, Political Science. US Army, to 1956. *The Wall Street Journal*, reporter, Chicago, to 1963; Washington bureau, economics correspondent, "Outlook" columnist, to 1972; London correspondent, European Bureau Chief, to 1978; financial/economic reporter, editor, NY, to 1981. *BusinessWeek*, Senior Editor, finance & personal business, current, 1981.

Javetski, William. *BusinessWeek.* State Department Correspondent. Hunter College; U. of CA, Berkeley, MA. USC Journalism School, teacher, Business Journalism. *The Merced Sun-Star* (CA), reporter. *The San Jose Mercury News*, writer. *The Berkeley Gazette*, reporter. *BusinessWeek*, LA correspondent; Toronto correspondent, to 1983; Toronto Bureau Chief, to 1986; State Dept. correspondent, current, 1986.

Jenkins, Loren. *The Washington Post.* Rome Bureau Chief. B. New Orleans, LA. U. of CO, 1961, Political Science. Peace Corps, Freetown, Sierra Leone, to 1963. *Daily Item* (Port Chester, NY), reporter, to 1965. UPI, newsman, NYC, to 1966; correspondent, London, Paris, Madrid, to 1969. *Newsweek*, special correspondent, Madrid, to 1970; correspondent, Beirut Bureau Chief, to 1972; Bureau Chief, Hong Kong & Saigon, to 1975; Rome Bureau Chief, to 1980. *The Washington Post*, special correspondent, Madrid, 1969-70; special roving correspondent, Rome, 1980-85; Rome Bureau Chief, current, 1985. Overseas Press Club Award for Best Newsmagazine Foreign Reporting, 1976; Pulitzer Prize for Foreign Reporting, 1983.

Jensen, Holger. *The Washington Times.* Foreign Editor. B. 1944, Shanghai, China. U. of Cape Town (South Africa), English Literature & Political Science. AP, foreign correspondent, to 1976. *Newsweek*, correspondent; Hong Kong Bureau Chief; Southern Africa Bureau Chief, to 1983. *The Washington Times*, Foreign Editor, current, 1986. APME Photo Award of the Year, 1972; Overseas Press Club Foreign Reporting from Abroad, 1974.

Johnson, Haynes. *The Washington Post.* National Affairs Columnist. B. NYC. U. of MO, BSJ; U. of WI, Madison, MA-American History. Two-time Ferris Professor of Journalism, Princeton. *New Journal* (Wilmington, DE), reporter, 1956-57. *The Washington Star*, city reporter; Copy Editor; Night City Editor; national reporter, to 1969. *The Washington Post*, national reporter; Asst Managing Editor; national affairs columnist, current. Author 4 books, most recently *In The Absence of Power: Governing America*, 1980: co-author 4 books, most recently *Lyndon*, 1973: editor *The Fall of a President*, 1974. Pulitzer Prize for Reporting, 1966; Sigma Delta Chi Award for General Reporting.

Jonas, Norman. *BusinessWeek.* Economics Editor. CCNY, *magna cum laude, Phi Beta Kappa*. Reporter business/economic/financial issues for *The Wall Street Journal, The New York Journal-American, The New York Times*. McGraw-Hill World News, senior economic correspondent, Washington. *BusinessWeek*, senior economic correspondent, Washington; senior writer, to 1985; Economics Editor, current, 1985.

Kael, Pauline. *The New Yorker.* Film Critic. B. 1919, Sonoma County, CA. U. of CA, Berkeley, 1940, Philosophy. Freelance, current. *The New Yorker*, film critic, current, 1968. Author 9 books, most recently *State of the Art*, 1985: contributed "Raising Kane" in *The Citizen Kane Book*, 1971. George Polk Award for Criticism, 1970; Front Page Awards for Best Magazine Column, 1974, & Distinguished Journalism, 1983.

Kaiser, Robert G. *The Washington Post*. Assistant Managing Editor/National News. B. Washington, DC. Yale; London School of Economics, MS; Columbia, Certificate, International Reporting. Duke, teaching fellow, 1974-75. *The Washington Post*, intern, summer 1963; London correspondent, part-time, 1964-66; city reporter, to 1969; Saigon correspondent, to 1971; Moscow correspondent, to 1974; national news reporter, 1975-82; Associate Editor, Editor "Outlook," to 1985; Asst Managing Editor/national news, current, 1985. Co-author 4 books.

Kamm, Henry. *The New York Times*. Athens Bureau Chief. B. 1925, Breslau, Germany. US Army, 1943-46. NYU, 1949, BA, *Phi Beta Kappa*. *The New York Times*, editorial index dept. member, Copy Editor, to 1960; Asst News Editor, *The Times International Edition*, Paris, to 1964; foreign correspondent, to 1967; Moscow Bureau Chief, to 1969; Asia correspondent, to 1971; roving correspondent, to 1982; Rome Bureau Chief, to 1984; Athens Bureau Chief, current, 1984. George Polk Memorial Award for Foreign Reporting, 1969; Pulitzer Prize for International Reporting, 1978: co-winner Sigma Delta Chi Distinguished Service Award for Outstanding Foreign Correspondence, 1968.

Kann, Peter Robert. *The Wall Street Journal*. Associate Publisher; Executive Vice-President, Dow Jones; President, International & Magazine Groups. B. Princeton, NJ. Harvard, 1964, BA-Government. *Harvard Crimson*, political editor, member editorial board. *The Wall Street Journal*, intern, summer, 1963; Pittsburgh bureau, to 1966; LA bureau, 1966; reporter, Vietnam, to 1968; roving Asian correspondent, Hong Kong, to 1976; first publisher & editor of *The Asian Wall Street Journal*, to 1979; Dow Jones corporate representative, Asia, to 1979; asst to the Chairman & Chief Executive, 1979; Associate Publisher, current, 1979; Vice-president, Dow Jones, member Management Committee, to 1985; Executive Vice-president, Dow Jones, current, 1985; President, International & Magazine groups, current, 1985. Pulitzer Prize for Distinguished Reporting on International Affairs, 1972.

Kaplan, Roger. *Reader's Digest*. Associate Editor. B. 1946, Neuilly, France. U. of Chicago, 1970, Literature & History, 1974, MA. Freelance, to 1984. *Commentary*, to 1986. *The American Spectator*, to 1986. *The Detroit News*, editorial writer, Op-ed Editor, to 1986. *The New York Post*, editorial writer, Op-ed Editor, to 1986. *Reader's Digest*, Associate Editor, current, 1986. UPI MI Newspapers Editorial Writing, 2nd Place, 1985.

Karmin, Monroe W. *U.S. News & World Report*. Senior Editor. B. 1929, Mineola, NY. U. of IL, 1950, Journalism; Columbia, 1953, MSJ. *The Wall Street Journal*, Washington bureau, to 1974. House Banking Committee Member, to 1976. *Chicago Daily News*, Washington bureau, 1977. Knight-Ridder Newspapers, Washington bureau, to 1981. *U.S. News & World Report*, Senior Editor, economics, current, 1981. Co-winner Pulitzer Prize for National Reporting, 1967; Sigma Delta Chi Distinguished Service Award, 1966.

Kaufman, Michael. *The New York Times*. Warsaw Bureau Chief. B. 1938, Paris, France. CCNY, 1959, BA. *The New York Times*, copyboy, clerk, news asst, caption writer, radio script writer; metro staff, to 1975; foreign correspondent, Nairobi, to 1979; foreign correspondent, New Delhi, to 1982; Ottawa Bureau Chief, to 1984; Warsaw Bureau Chief, current, 1984. Author *In Their Own Good Time; Rooftops and Alleys: Adventures with a City Kid*. George Polk Memorial Award for International Reporting, 1979.

Kaus, Mickey. *The New Republic*. West Coast Correspondent. B. 1951, Santa Monica, CA. Harvard, 1973, Social Studies. *Washington Monthly*, Editor, 1978-80. *American Lawyer*, Senior Editor, to 1982. *Harper's*, Politics Editor, to 1983. Speechwriter, Senator Ernest F. Hollings, to 1984. *The New Republic*, West Coast correspondent, current, 1985. Freelance, also current.

Kaylor, Robert. *U.S. News & World Report*. Associate Editor. *U.S. News & World Report*, Sinapore Bureau Chief, to 1986; Associate Editor, defense, current, 1986.

Kelley, Wayne P. Jr. *Congressional Quarterly.* Publisher. B. 1933, Rochester, NY. Vanderbilt, 1955, BA. US Army, to 1957. Neiman Fellow, Harvard, 1963-64. *The Augusta Chronicle* (GA), city editor, reporter, 1960-65. *The Journal* (Atlanta, GA), Washington correspondent, reporter, to 1969. *Congressional Quarterly,* Associate Editor, to 1972; Managing Editor, to 1974; Executive Editor, to 1980; Publisher, current, 1980; Executive Vice-President, current, 1984.

Kempster, Norman. *Los Angeles Times.* State Department Correspondent. B. 1936, Sacramento, CA. CA State U., Sacramento, 1957, Language Arts. Professional Journalism Fellowship, Stanford, 1967-68; Jos Alex Memorial lecturer, Harvard, 1983, honorary Nieman fellow. UPI, Sacramento, to 1961; Olympia, WA, Bureau Chief, to 1966; Deputy Bureau Chief, to 1968; Washington bureau (economics, White House correspondent), to 1973. *The Washington Star,* White House correspondent, to 1976. *Los Angeles Times,* Pentagon correspondent, to 1981; Jerusalem Bureau Chief, to 1984; State Dept. correspondent, current, 1984.

Kestin, Hesh. *Forbes.* European Correspondent. B. 1943, NYC. *New York Herald Tribune. Paterson* (NJ) *Call. Newsday. True* Magazine, Articles Editor. *Jerusalem Post,* Bureau Chief. *Newsview* (Tel Aviv), Editor-in-Chief. *Middle East Times* (Nicosia, Cyprus), Israel correspondent. *Present Tense,* contributing editor. *Forbes,* European correspondent, current.

Kifner, John. *The New York Times.* Cairo Bureau Chief. B. 1941, Cornwall-on-Hudson, NY. Williams College, 1963, BA. Neiman Fellow, Harvard, 1971-72. *The New York Times,* metro staff; national correspondent, 1969-78; covered Iranian revolution, 1979; Beirut Bureau Chief, to 1982; Warsaw Bureau Chief, to 1984; Beirut Bureau Chief, to 1985; Cairo Bureau Chief, current, 1985. Sidney Hillman Award for Reporting, 1971; Page One Award, NY Newspaper Guild, 1971, 1973; Award for Race Relations Reporting, Columbia, 1973; George Polk Memorial Award for Foreign Reporting, 1979.

Kilborn, Peter T. *The New York Times.* Economics Correspondent. B. 1939, Providence, RI. Trinity College, 1961, BA-English; Columbia 1962, MSJ-Economics. Providence *Journal-Bulletin,* reporter, to 1963. McGraw-Hill World News & *BusinessWeek,* Paris correspondent, to 1968. *BusinessWeek,* staff writer, asst tech editor, to 1971; LA Bureau Chief, to 1973; Companies Editor, to 1974. *Newsweek,* Senior Editor, to 1978. *The New York Times,* financial reporter, to 1975, 1978; London economics correspondent, to 1977; Sunday Business Section Editor, to 1982; Economics Editor, Washington, to 1983; economics correspondent, Washington, current, 1983.

Kilpatrick, James Jackson. Universal Press Syndicate. Columnist. B. 1920, Oklahoma City, OK. U. of MO, 1941, BJ-History. *Richmond* (VA) *News Leader,* reporter, to 1949; Editor, to 1966. *Washington Star* Syndicate, columnist, to 1981. Universal Press Syndicate, columnist, current, 1981. William Allen White Award, U. of KS; Medal of Honor for Distinguished Service to Journalism from his *alma mater.*

Kincaid, Cliff. *Human Events.* Associate Editor & "Focus on Media" Columnist. B. 1954, Kansas City, MO. U. of Toledo, Journalism. Accuracy in Media, former Asst to Chairman of the Board; radio commentary writer, commentator, current. *Human Events,* Associate Editor, current; "Focus on the Media" columnist, current. Also current, "Crossfire," CNN, occasional co-host.

Kinnane-Roelofsma, Derk. *Insight.* Senior Writer. B. 1932, NYC. Columbia, 1955, BA-Humanities; Trinity College, Dublin, 1955-56; Tulane (New Orleans, LA), Teaching Fellow, 1960, MA. U. of Baghdad, Iraq, 1960-61. Freelance (London, Paris, Dublin), 1961-63. Reuters, European Editor, 1964; correspondent, 1965. *Agence France-Presse,* Editor, English Language Service, 1966, 1970. *The Irish Times* (Dublin), Paris correspondent, 1966-67. Societe Jegu, Account Executive for client US Dept. of Commerce, 1968. *Kayhan International* (Tehran, Iran), Editor, to 1971. BBC, stringer, 1970-71. *UNESCO Features* (Paris), Asst Editor, to 1980; Editor-in-Chief, to 1985. *Insight,* senior writer, current, 1985.

Kinsley, Michael. *The New Republic.* Editor & "TRB from Washington" Columnist. B. 1951, Detroit, MI. Harvard; Magdalen College; Oxford; Harvard Law. *Washington Monthly*, Managing Editor, to 1975. *Harper's*, Editor, to 1983. *The New Republic*, Managing Editor, to 1976; Editor, to 1979, current, 1983; columnist "TRB from Washington", current, 1983.

Kinzer, Stephen. *The New York Times.* Managua Bureau Chief. B. 1951, NYC. NYU, 1969; Boston U., 1973, MA. Administrative Asst to Governor Michael S. Dukakis (MA), 1975. Boston U., adjunct professor, Journalism, to 1979. *The Boston Phoenix*, columnist, to 1979. *The Boston Globe*, reporter, to 1982. *The New York Times*, metro reporter, 1983; Managua Bureau Chief, current, 1984. Freelance articles. Author *Bitter Fruit*, 1982.

Kirkland, Richard I. Jr. *FORTUNE.* Board of Editors Member & European Correspondent, London. Birmingham-Southern College, BA-English, *summa cum laude, Phi Beta Kappa*; Duke, AB-English, MA; NYU "Careers in Business" accelerated MBA program. *FORTUNE*, reporter/researcher, to 1981; Associate Editor, Washington, to 1985; Board of Editors member, European correspondent, London, current, 1985.

Kirkpatrick, Jeane. *Los Angeles Times* Syndicate. Columnist. B. 1926, Duncan, OK. Stephens College, 1946, AA-Political Science; Barnard, 1948, AB; Columbia, 1950, MA, 1967, PhD; grad work (French gov't. Fellow), *U. Paris Institute de Science Politique*, 1952-53. Dept. of State, Research analyst, 1951-53. George Washington U., research associate, to 1956. Georgetown, Associate Professor, Political Science, 1967-73; Professor, to 1978; Thomas and Dorothy Leavey U., Georgetown, Professor, current, 1978 (on leave 1981-85). American Enterprise Institute for Public Policy Research, Senior Fellow, since 1977 (on leave 1981-85). Member cabinet, US permanent representative to the UN, 1981-85. *Los Angeles Times* Syndicate, columnist, current. Contributor to various journals, current. Author 9 books, including *The Reagan Phenomenon*, 1982. Presidential Medal of Freedom, 1985.

Kleiman, Robert. *The New York Times.* Editorial Board Member. B. NYC. U. of MI, 1939, *Phi Beta Kappa*. *The Washington Post*, reporter, to 1941. *The New York Journal of Commerce*, White House correspondent, to 1943. Voice of America, White House correspondent, 1942. OWI Psychological Warfare Teams, Chief, 1943. *U.S. News & World Report*, associate editor, to 1948; Central European Editor, Germany Bureau Chief, to 1951; Paris Bureau Chief, to 1962. CBS, commentator, Paris, to 1963. *The New York Times*, member Editorial Board, current, 1963 (on leave of absence, 1986). Author *Atlantic Crisis-American Diplomacy Confronts a Resurgent Europe*, 1964.

Klein, Edward. *The New York Times.* Editor, *The New York Times Magazine*. B. 1936, Yonkers, NY. Columbia, 1960, BS, 1961, MSJ. *New York World-Telegram*, reporter, to 1960. *The Sun*, reporter, to 1960. *The Japan Times*, reporter, editor, to 1962. UPI, Tokyo correspondent, to 1965. *Newsweek*, Associate Editor, to 1969; Foreign Editor, to 1975; Asst Managing Editor, to 1977. *The New York Times*, Editor of *The New York Times Magazine*, current, 1977. Author *The Parachutists*, 1981; co-author (with Richard Z. Chesnoff & Robert Littell) *If Israel Lost the War*, 1969.

Klott, Gary. *The New York Times.* Business & Financial Reporter. B. 1949, Chicago, IL. U. of IL, 1971, Economics. UPI, national business & economic correspondent, to 1984. *The New York Times*, business & financial reporter, current, 1984. Author *The New York Times Complete Guide To Personal Investing*, 1987.

Knickerbocker, Brad. *The Christian Science Monitor.* National News Editor. B. 1942, MI. Hobart College, 1964, English. US Naval Aviator, to 1970. *Democrat and Chronicle* (Rochester, NY), reporter, to 1972. *The Christian Science Monitor*, Boston City Hall reporter, to 1975; editorial writer, to 1976; San Francisco correspondent, to 1981; Washington Bureau Manager and Pentagon correspondent, to 1985; National News Editor, current, 1985.

Knowlton, Christopher. *FORTUNE.* Reporter/Researcher. Harvard, BA-English & American Literature, *cum laude.* Freelance writer, to 1985. *FORTUNE,* reporter/researcher, current, 1985. Author *The Real World,* 1984.

Knue, Paul F. *The Cincinnati Post.* Editor. B. 1947, Lawrenceburg, IN. Murray State U., 1969, Journalism & English. *The Evansville* (IN) *Courier,* reporter/copy editor, to 1970. *The Fort Wayne Journal-Gazette,* copy editor, 1970. *The Evansville Press,* Managing Editor, to 1979. *The Kentucky Post,* Editor, to 1983. *The Cincinnati Post,* copy editor, night news editor, weekend co-editor, to 1975; Editor, current, 1983.

Kondracke, Morton. *The New Republic.* Senior Editor. Dartmouth, 1960. Nieman Fellow, Harvard, 1973-74. *Chicago Sun-Times,* 1963-68; Washington bureau, to 1973; White House correspondent, to 1977. National Public Radio, "All Things Considered" & "Communique" commentator, 1979-82. WRC-AM, talk show host, 1981-83. United Feature Syndicate, columnist, 1983-85. *The New Republic,* Executive Editor, 1978-85; Senior Editor, current, 1986. *Newsweek,* Washington Bureau Chief, 1985-86. "The McLaughlin Group," commentator, current.

Koretz, Gene. *BusinessWeek.* "Economic Diary" Editor. B. 1931, NYC. U. of OK, BA-English Literature & Educational Psychology; U. of CT, MA; Columbia, MA. U. of CT, Robert College (Istanbul, Turkey), IN U., CCNY, English & Psychology teacher. Columbia Graduate School of Journalism, teacher, Economic Journalism. *International Economic Letter,* Citibank, editor/writer. *NEWSWEEK,* editor/writer. *BusinessWeek,* "Economic Diary" editor/writer, current.

Koselka, Rita. *Forbes.* Reporter. B. 1961, Adrian, MI. U. of Notre Dame, 1982, History/Modern Languages. Rotary Scholar, France, 1984. First Boston Corp., analyst, 1983. *Forbes,* reporter, current, 1985.

Kosner, Edward. *New York.* Editor & Publisher. B. 1937, NYC. CCNY, 1958, BA-English/History. *The New York Post,* rewriteman, Asst City Editor, to 1963. *Newsweek,* "National Affairs" writer, to 1967; General Editor, to 1969; National Affairs Editor, to 1972; Asst Managing Editor, to 1972; Managing Editor, to 1975; Editor, to 1979. *New York,* Editor, to 1986; Editor & Publisher, current, 1986. Member, Executive Committee, American Society of Magazine Editors, 1977-86; President, 1984-86. Robert F. Kennedy Journalism Award, 1971; American Bar Association Silver Gavel Award, 1971.

Kosterlitz, Julie. *National Journal.* Staff Correspondent. B. 1955, Chicago, IL. U. of CA, Santa Cruz, 1979, History. *Williamette Week* (Portland, OR), business reporter, to 1980. *Common Cause* magazine, to 1985. *National Journal,* staff correspondent, health/income security, current, 1985. *Washington Monthly* Journalism Award, 1983.

Koten, John F. *The Wall Street Journal.* Reporter, Chicago. B. Killeen, TX. Carleton College (Northfield, MN). AP-Dow Jones, 1977. *The Wall Street Journal,* Atlanta bureau reporter, to 1980; Detroit bureau reporter, to 1984; Second Front's Marketing columnist, 1984; Chicago bureau reporter, current, 1984.

Kovach, Bill. *The New York Times.* Washington Bureau Chief. B. 1932, Greenville, TN. East TN State U., 1959, BS. *Johnson City* (TN) *Press-Chronicle,* reporter, to 1961. *The Nashville Tennessean,* reporter, to 1968. *The New York Times,* reporter, to 1969; Albany (NY) Bureau Chief, to 1970; New England Bureau Chief, to 1971; urban affairs reporter, Washington, to 1974; News Editor, Washington, to 1976; Deputy National Editor & Project Editor, to 1979; Washington Bureau Chief, current, 1979. Author *The Battle of Nashville,* 1964; contributor *Assignment America,* 1974.

Kraar, Louis. *FORTUNE.* Board of Editors Member. U. of NC, History. Edward R. Murrow Fellow, 1968-69. *The Wall Street Journal,* Pentagon correspondent. *TIME,* foreign correspondent, Asia. *FORTUNE,* Far East correspondent, Singapore; Board of Editors member, Hong Kong, current.

Kramer, Barry. *The Wall Street Journal.* Foreign Features Editor & Special Writer. Rutgers, 1962, BA-Biological Sciences & Journalism; Columbia, 1963, MA-Journalism. WRSU, newsman, to 1962. *The New York Herald-Tribune,* campus correspondent, to 1962. AP, newsman, Newark, NJ, to 1964; AP-wire editor, NY, 1965-67; Saigon correspondent, to 1968; World Service desk, 1969. US Army, 1964-65; 1969. *The Wall Street Journal,* reporter, NY, to 1976; Asia correspondent, to 1981; Foreign Features Editor, special writer, current, 1981.

Kramer, Hilton. *The New Criterion.* Editor. B. 1928, Gloucester, MA. Syracuse, 1950, English & Philosophy. *Arts Magazine,* Managing Editor, Editor, 1954-61. *The Nation,* art critic, to 1963. *The New Leader,* art critic & Associate Editor, to 1965. *The New York Times,* Art News Editor, to 1973; Chief Art Critic, to 1982. *The New Criterion,* Editor, current, 1982. Also current, columnist for *Frankfurter Allgemeine Zeitung,* 1986; freelance book critic for *The Wall Street Journal,* 1985; frequent broadcaster on "State of the Arts," CBC, Toronto, 1985. Author *The Age of the Avant-Garde,* 1973; *The Revenge of the Philistines.*

Kramer, Joel R. *Minneapolis Star and Tribune.* Executive Editor. B. 1948, Brooklyn, NY. Harvard, 1969, BA-History & Science. *The Harvard Crimson,* Editor. *Science,* reporter, to 1970. Freelance writer, to 1972. *Newsday* (Long Island, NY), various positions to Asst Managing Editor, to 1980. *Buffalo Courier-Express,* Executive Editor, to 1982. *Minneapolis Star and Tribune,* Executive Editor, current, 1983. Shared 1973 Pulitzer Prize for Public Service, awarded to *Newsday* for "The Heroin Trail."

Kramer, Michael. *New York.* Political Editor. B. 1945, NYC. Amherst, 1967, Political Science; Columbia Law, 1970. *New York,* city political columnist, to 1976; Political Editor, current, 1979. *MORE,* Editor & Publisher, 1976-78. Berkeley Books, Publisher, 1978. Co-author *The Ethnic Factor,* 1972; *"I Never Wanted To be Vice-President of Anything"* (political biography of Nelson Rockefeller), 1976. Overseas Press Club Award for Reporting from Central America, 1982.

Kraus, Albert L. *The Journal of Commerce.* Editor. B. 1920, NYC. Queens College (NY), 1941, BA-History; Columbia, 1942, Journalism. Nieman Fellow, Harvard, 1954-55. *Journal-Bulletin* (Providence, RI), business & financial reporter, to 1956. *The New York Times,* business, financial, banking; asst to Financial Editor; Asst Financial Editor, to 1972. *Bond Buyer,* Senior Vice-President, to 1978. *The Journal of Commerce,* Editorial Director; Editor, current.

Krauthammer, Charles. *The New Republic,* Senior Editor. *The Washington Post* Writers Group, Columnist. B. 1950, NYC. McGill U., 1970; Balliol College, Oxford, 1971, Political Science, Economics; Harvard Med, 1975. MA General Hospital, Resident, Psychiatry, to 1977; Chief Resident, Psychiatric Consultation Services, to 1978. Dept. of HEW, Director Division of Science Alcohol, Drug Abuse & Mental Health Administration, to 1980. Speechwriter, Vice-President Walter Mondale, to 1981. *TIME,* essayist, current, 1983. *The New Republic,* Senior Editor, current, 1981. *The Washington Post* Writers Group, columnist, current, 1985.

Kristol, Irving. *The Public Interest.* Co-editor. B. 1920, NYC. CCNY, 1940. US Army, to 1946. *Commentary,* Managing Editor, to 1952. *Encounter,* co-founder, Co-editor, to 1958. *The Reporter,* Editor, to 1960. Basic Books, Inc., NY, Executive Vice-President to 1969. *The Public Interest,* Co-editor, current, 1965. NYU faculty member, current, 1969; Professor of Social Thought, Graduate School of Business Administration, current, 1979. American Enterprise Institute, Senior Fellow, current. Author *On the Democratic Idea in America,* 1972; *Two Cheers for Capitalism,* 1978; *Reflections of a Neoconservative,* 1983.

Kronholz, June. *The Wall Street Journal.* Hong Kong Bureau Chief. B. Pittsburg, PA. OH U., 1969, BS; National Endowment for the Humanities, Professional Journalism Fellow, U. of MI, 1974-75. *The Miami Herald*, intern, 1968; reporter, to 1974. *The Wall Street Journal*, reporter, Dallas, to 1979; London bureau reporter, to 1983; Boston Bureau Chief, to 1985; Hong Kong Bureau Chief, current, 1985.

Kucewicz, William. *The Wall Street Journal.* Editorial Writer & Editorial Board Member. B. Yonkers, NY. NYU, Economics, politics. NYU student newspaper, Editor-in-Chief. *The Public Interest*, Asst Editor, 1975-76. AP-Dow Jones, copyreader, 1975; reporter, London, to 1979. *The Wall Street Journal*, editorial writer, current, 1979; Editorial Board member, current, 1985. Citation for Excellence, Overseas Press Club, 1981.

Kurtz, Howard. *The Washington Post.* Justice Department Reporter. B. 1953, Brooklyn, NY. SUNY, Buffalo, 1974, English. *The Record* (Bergen, NJ), reporter, 1975-76. Columnist Jack Anderson, reporter, to 1978. *The Washington Star*, reporter, to 1981. *The Washington Post*, Justice Dept. reporter, current, 1981. Freelance, current. Washington-Baltimore Newspaper Guild Front Page Awards, 1981, 1985; DC-MD Press Association Award, 1st Prize, 1982.

Kuttner, Robert. *The New Republic.* Economics Correspondent. B. 1943, NYC. Oberlin, 1965, Government. *The Village Voice*, Washington Editor, to 1973. *The Washington Post*, national writer, to 1975. US Senate Banking Committee, Investigator, to 1978. *Working Papers*, Editor-in-Chief, to 1982. *Boston Globe*, columnist, current, 1984. *BusinessWeek*, columnist, current, 1985. *The New Republic*, economic correspondent, current, 1982. Author *The Economic Illusion*, 1984; *Revolt of the Haves*, 1980. Guggenheim Fellow, 1986-87.

Kwitny, Jonathan. *The Wall Street Journal.* Feature Writer. B. 1943, Indianapolis, IN. U. of MO, BJ; NYU, MA-History. *The Indianapolis Star*, reporter. *News Tribune* (Perth Amboy, NJ), reporter. *The New York Post*, reporter. *The Wall Street Journal*, feature writer, current, 1971. Freelance, current. Author 5 books including *Endless Enemies: The Making of an Unfriendly World*, 1985 (Pulitzer Prize nomination for general nonfiction). Honor Medal for Career Achievement, U. of MO School of Journalism, 1982.

Laderman, Jeffrey M. *BusinessWeek.* Markets & Investments Editor. Rutgers; Columbia, MA-Journalism. Staff writer, local NJ newspapers. *The Detroit News*, reporter, writer, to 1982. *BusinessWeek*, Markets & Investments Staff Editor, to 1985; Markets & Investments Editor, current, 1985.

Laitin, Joseph. *The Washington Post.* Ombudsman. B. Brooklyn, NY. Deputy Press Secretary to President Johnson; Asst to the Director, Office of Management & Budget, Johnson & Nixon Administrations; Asst Secretary of Defense for Public Affairs, Asst Administrator of the Federal Aviation Administration, Ford Administration; Asst Secretary of the Treasury for Public Affairs, Carter Administration. UPI, Reuters, correspondent. Writer & producer of documentaries for all 3 networks. Freelance writer, current. Government Relations Consultant, current. Washington Advisory Board member of Hill & Knowlton, current. *The Washington Post*, Ombudsman, current, 1986. Defense Dept. Medal for Distinguished Public Service, 1975, upon being fired with Secretary of Defense James Schlesinger by President Ford.

Lambro, Donald. United Press Syndicate. Washington Columnist. B. Wellesley, MA. Boston U., Journalism. *The Boston Traveler*, reporter, to 1968. UPI, CT state legislature; Washington correspondent. United Press Syndicate, Washington columnist, current. Also current, radio commentator, AP Radio network & Mutual Broadcasting System. Author *Washington-City of Scandals; Fat City: How Washington Wastes Your Taxes:* "Star Spangled Spenders" (PBS program).

Landro, Laura. *The Wall Street Journal.* Reporter. OH U., 1976, BSJ. McGraw-Hill World News, London, to 1977. McGraw-Hill Energy Newsletter Group, Asst Editor, to 1978. *BusinessWeek*, Staff Editor, to 1981. *The Wall Street Journal*, reporter, NY, covering entertainment, cable & publishing. Gerald Loeb Award for Deadline Reporting, 1986.

Lawrence, David Jr. *Detroit Free Press.* Publisher & Chairman. B. 1942, NYC. U. of FL, 1963, Journalism; Harvard Advanced Management Program, 1983. *St. Petersburg Times*, reporter, Copy Editor, Telegraph Editor, News Editor, to 1967. *The Washington Post*, Asst News Editor, News Editor, "Style" section, to 1969. *The Palm Beach Post*, Managing Editor, to 1971. *Philadelphia Daily News*, Asst to the Editor, Managing Editor, to 1975. *Charlotte Observer*, Executive Editor, Editor, to 1978. *Detroit Free Press*, Executive Editor, to 1985; Publisher and Chairman, current, 1985. Human Rights Award, Institute of Human Relations of the American Jewish Committee, 1986.

Lawrence, John F. *Los Angeles Times.* Assistant Managing Editor, Economic Affairs. Oberlin, 1956, BA. *Cleveland Plain Dealer*, correspondent, to 1956. *Economist* (UK), correspondent, to 1972. *The Wall Street Journal*, reporter, to 1961; Philadelphia Bureau Chief, to 1963; Pittsburg Bureau Chief, to 1965; Asst Managing Editor, Pacific Coast Edition, to 1968. *Los Angeles Times*, Financial Editor, to 1972; Washington Bureau Chief, to 1975; Asst Managing Editor, current, 1975. Loeb Achievement Award, John Hancock Award, both 1971.

Lawrence, Steve. *Forbes.* Senior Editor. B. 1942, NYC. U. of CA, 1964, BA-Philosophy; Northwestern, 1966, MSJ. *New York Daily News*, special projects, Asst Business Editor. *Dallas Times-Herald*, Executive Business Editor. *The New York Times*, Enterprise Editor, "Business Day," to 1984. Time, Inc., Senior Editor, Magazine Development, to 1986. *Forbes*, Senior Editor, current, 1986.

Lee, Susan. *Forbes.* Senior Editor & "The Big Portfolios: Money & Investments" Columnist. Sarah Lawrence, 1965, BA; Columbia, 1969, MA, 1975, PhD. John Jay Fellow, Columbia, 1972; President's Fellow, 1974. Columbia, adjunct Asst Professor, Economics Dept., to 1980. *FORTUNE*, Associate Editor, to 1981. *The Wall Street Journal*, Editorial Board member, to 1983. *BusinessWeek*, Senior Writer, columnist, to 1984. *Forbes*, Senior Editor, "The Big Portfolios: Money & Investments" columnist, current, 1984. Also current, ABC-TV, "Good Morning America" commentator. Author 3 books, including *Susan Lee's ABZ's of Economics*, 1986: co-author *A New Economic View of American History*, 1979. NCFE Award, Editorial Writing, 1982.

Leinster, Colin. *FORTUNE.* Associate Editor. Polytechnic of North London, Journalism. Newspaper reporter, London. *LIFE*, Vietnam correspondent. Freelance journalist, 1974-84. *FORTUNE*, Associate Editor, current, 1984.

Lelyveld, Joseph. *The New York Times.* London Bureau Chief. B. 1937, Cincinnati, OH. Harvard, 1958, BA-English History & Literature, *summa cum laude*, 1959, MA-American History; Columbia 1960, MSJ; Fulbright grant, 1960-61, Burma. *The New York Times*, copyboy, to 1963; financial writer, 1963; metro staff, to 1965; foreign correspondent, Africa, to 1967; India Bureau Chief, to 1969; reporter, NY, to 1972; Hong Kong Bureau Chief, 1973-74; Washington reporter, columnist, to 1977; deputy foreign editor, to 1980; South African correspondent, to 1983; staff writer, 1984; London Bureau Chief, current, 1985. Author *Move Your Shadow* (Pulitzer Prize, 1986). Page One Award; George Polk Memorial Award; Byline Award.

Lemann, Nicholas. *The Atlantic.* National Correspondent. B. 1954, New Orleans, LA. Harvard, 1976, American History & Literature. *The Washington Monthly*, Managing Editor, to 1978. *Texas Monthly*, Associate Editor, to 1979; Executive Editor, 1981-83. *The Washington Post*, reporter, to 1981. *The Atlantic*, national correspondent, current, 1983. Freelance, current.

MediaGuide

LeMoyne, James. *The New York Times.* San Salvador Bureau Chief. B. 1951, Heidelberg, Germany. Harvard, 1975, Social Studies; Balliol College, Harvard, 1977, BA-Philosophy & Political Theory; London School of Economics, 1979, MA-20th Century European Diplomatic History. *The Washington Post,* stringer, London, to 1981. *Newsweek,* stringer, London, to 1981; Associate Editor, Central American reporter, to 1983. *The New York Times,* metro reporter, to 1984; San Salvador Bureau Chief, current, 1984. Co-winner NY Newspaper Guild Page One Award, 1982.

Lerner, Max. *The New York Post,* Columnist. *Los Angeles Times* Syndicate, Columnist. B. 1902, Minsk, Russia. Yale, 1923, AB-Government; Washington U., 1925, AM; Robert Brookings Graduate School of Economics & Government, 1927, PhD. *Encyclopedia of Social Sciences,* Editor, Managing Editor, to 1932. Sarah Lawrence College, Social Science Faculty member, to 1935. Wellesley Summer Institiute, Faculty Chairman, 1933-35. National Emergency Council, Director, Consumers Division, 1934. Harvard, Government Dept. lecturer, to 1936; Visiting Professor, 1939-41. *The Nation,* Editor, to 1938. Williams College, Political Science Professor, 1938-43. *PM,* NYC, editorial director, to 1948. *The New York Star,* columnist, to 1949. Brandeis, American Civilization Professor, to 1973 (Dean of the Graduate School, 1954-56); Professor Emeritus, current, 1974. *The New York Post,* columnist, current, 1949. *Los Angeles Times* Syndicate, columnist, current, 1949. US International U. (San Diego, CA), Distinguished Professor of Human Behavior, current, 1975. U. of Notre Dame, Professor, American Studies, 1982-84. Author 14 books, most recent including *Ted and the Kennedy Legend,* 1980. Ford Foundation Grant, 1963-64.

Lescaze, Lee. *The Wall Street Journal.* Assistant Foreign Editor. Harvard, 1960, BA-General Studies. *The Washington Post,* copyboy, 1963; reporter, to 1967; Vietnam correspondent, to 1970; Hong Kong correspondent, to 1973; Foreign Editor, to 1975; National Editor, to 1977; NY Bureau Chief, to 1980; White House correspondent, to 1982; Asst Managing Editor, "Style" section, to 1983. *The Wall Street Journal,* editing & writing, 1983; NY News Editor, 1984; Assistant Foreign Editor, current, 1984.

Lewis, Anthony. *The New York Times.* "Abroad at Home" Columnist. B. 1927, NYC. Harvard, 1948. Neiman fellow, Harvard, 1956-57. *The New York Times,* Sunday dept., to 1952. *The Washington Daily News,* reporter, to 1955. *The New York Times,* Supreme Court reporter, to 1965; London Bureau Chief, to 1972; "Abroad at Home" columnist, current. Harvard Law, lecturer. Author *Gideon's Trumpet; Portrait of A Decade.* Pulitzer Prize, 1955, '63; Elijah Parish Lovejoy Award, 1983.

Lewis, Ephraim A. *BusinessWeek.* Senior Editor. Attended U. of PA, NYU; graduated Brooklyn College. *BusinessWeek,* Assistant Marketing Editor, 1962-67; Minneapolis Bureau Manager, 1967; Marketing Editor, to 1969; Associate Editor, to 1976; Senior correspondent, McGraw-Hill World News, 1976; Senior Editor, current, 1976, government, energy, books, sports business, *BusinessWeek* Top 1000, other scoreboards. Responsible for *BusinessWeek*'s personal business supplement & *BusinessWeek*/Harris polls.

Lewis, Flora. *The New York Times.* "Foreign Affairs" Columnist. B. LA, CA. UCLA, 1941, BA-Political Science; Columbia, 1942, MSJ. *Los Angeles Times,* reporter, 1941. AP, to 1946. Freelance, to 1956. McGraw Hill, Editor, 1955. *The Washington Post,* Bureau Chief (Bonn, London, Washington, NY), to 1966. *Newsday,* syndicated columnist, to 1972. *The New York Times,* Paris Bureau Chief, to 1976; European diplomatic correspondent/Bureau Chief, to 1980; "Foreign Affairs" columnist, current, 1980. Author *One of Our H-Bombs Is Missing,* 1967; *Red Pawn,* 1964; *Case History of Hope,* 1958. Fourth Estate Award, National Press Club, 1985; Matrix Award for Newspapers, NY Women in Communications, 1985; French Legion of Honor, 1981; Award for Distinguished Diplomatic Reporting, Georgetown School of Foreign Affairs, 1978; Columbia Journalism's School's 50th Anniversary Award, 1977; Aspen Institute's Award for Journalistic Excellence, 1977.

Lewis, Paul M. *The New York Times*, European Economic Correspondent. B. 1937, London. Balliol College, Oxford, 1959-61. *Financial Times*, Common Market correspondent, to 1967; Paris correspondent, to 1971; Washington Bureau Chief, to 1976. *The New York Times*, economic correspondent, current, 1977.

Levin, Doron P. *The Wall Street Journal.* Automotive & General Assignment Reporter. B. 1950, Haifa, Israel. Cornell, 1972, History; Columbia, 1977, MSJ. *St. Petersburg Times*, police, business, reporter, 1977-80. *The Wall Street Journal*, automotive & general assignment reporter, current, 1981.

Lindsey, Robert H. *The New York Times.* West Coast Operations Director. B. 1935, Glendale, CA. San Jose State College, 1956. *The San Jose Mercury News*, reporter, to 1968. *The New York Times*, transportation news dept., NY, to 1975; Western economic correspondent, to 1977; Los Angeles Bureau Chief, to 1985; West Coast Operations Director, current, 1985. Author *The Falcon and the Snowman: A True Story of Friendship and Espionage*, 1979 (Edgar Allen Poe Award winner, 1980); *The Flight of the Falcon*, 1983: co-author *Reagan: The Man, the Presidency*, 1980.

Lipsky, Seth. *The Wall Street Journal*/Europe. Editorial Page Editor/Editorial Director, International Editions. B. NYC. Harvard, 1968, BA-English Literature. *Anniston Star* (AL), reporter, to 1969. US Army, 1969-70; *Army Digest* magazine, Pentagon reporter; *Pacific Stars and Stripes*, Vietnam combat reporter. *Far Eastern Economic Review*, Asst Editor, 1974-75. *The Wall Street Journal*, staff reporter, Detroit, to 1974; Asia correspondent, to 1976; founding staff reporter, *The Asian Wall Street Journal*, to 1978; Managing Editor *The Asian Wall Street Journal*, to 1980; Associate Editor, Editorial Page, NY, to 1982; Foreign Editor, to 1984; Senior Editor, 1984; Editorial Page Editor, *The Wall Street Journal*/Europe, current; Editorial Director, International Editions, current, 1986.

Loeb, Marshall. *FORTUNE.* Managing Editor. B. 1929, Chicago, IL. U. of MO, 1950, BJ; grad work, U. of Goettingen, W. Germany, 1951-52. *Garfield News* and *Austinite* (Chicago), reporter, 1944-45. *Garfieldian (Austin News)*, reporter, columnist, to 1947. *Columbia Missourian*, reporter, to 1950. *Garfieldian*, reporter, columnist, to 1951. UPI, staff correspondent, Frankfurt, Germany, to 1954. *St. Louis Globe-Democrat*, reporter, to 1956. *TIME*, Contributing Editor, to 1961; Associate Editor, to 1965; Senior Editor, to 1980; Economics Editor/columnist, to 1980. *Money*, to 1986. *FORTUNE*, Managing Editor, current, 1986. Also current, commentator CBS Radio Network, ABC-TV Money Tips. Associate Fellow, Yale; Berkeley College, current, 1977. Author *Marshall Loeb's Money Guide*, 1983; co-author *Plunging Into Politics* (with William Safire), 1962. Sherman Fairchild Foundation Honorable Mention, 1962; INGAA Award, U. of MO, 1966; Gerald M. Loeb Award, 1974; John Hancock Award, 1974; Citation Media Awards for Economic Understanding, 1978; Sigma Delta Chi of NY Citation, 1979. Dallas Press Club Award, 1978; Freedoms Foundation Award, 1978; Champion Media Award, 1981.

Lohr, Steve. *The New York Times.* London Economic Correspondent. Colgate U., 1974; Columbia, MSJ. *Binghamton Press*, business & financial reporter. Gannett News Service, business & financial reporter. Freelance work. *The New York Times*, Copy Editor, financial desk, reporter, to 1981; foreign correspondent, Tokyo, to 1984; Manila Bureau Chief, to 1985; economic correspondent, London, current, 1985.

Loomis, Carol Junge. *FORTUNE.* Board of Editors Member. U. of MO, Journalism. Maytag Co., Editor, house organ, to 1954. *FORTUNE*, research associate, to 1958; Associate Editor, asst to the Chief of Research, to 1968; Board of Editors member, current, 1968. Gerald Loeb Award; John Hancock Award; Newspaper Guild of NY Page One Award.

MediaGuide

Looney, Ralph. *Rocky Mountain News.* Editor. B. 1924, Lexington, KY. U. of KY, 1948, BA. *Lexington Herald* (KY), office boy, to 1942. *Lexington Leader* (KY), sports writer, proofreader, 1943; reporter/photographer, to 1950; reporter, to 1953. *Albuquerque Tribune*, reporter, 1955. *St. Louis Globe-Democrat*, reporter, 1955; copyreader; Chief Copy Editor, to 1956. *Albuquerque Tribune*, City Editor, to 1968; Asst Managing Editor, to 1973; Editor, to 1980. *Rocky Mountain News* (Denver, CO), Editor, current, 1980. Freelance work. Author *Haunted Highways, The Ghost Towns of New Mexico*, 1969. Robert F. Kennedy Journalism Award, 1970; George Washington Honor Medal, Freedoms Foundation, Editorial Writing, 1969; NM Medal of Merit, 1968; 19 E.H. Shaffer 1st Place Awards, NM Press Association, 1965-80.

Lopez, Laura. *TIME.* Managua Correspondent. B. 1957, Inglewood, CA. CA State U., Chico, 1979, Information & Communication Science. *TIME*, stringer/Mexico City office manager, to 1983; writer, world section, 1984; correspondent, NY, to 1985; correspondent, Managua, current, 1985.

Ma, Christopher Yi-Wen. *U.S. News & World Report.* Deputy Managing Editor. Harvard, 1972; Boalt Hall School of Law, U. of CA. Michael Clark Rockefeller Traveling Fellow, People's Republic of China; Churchill Fellow, International Relations, Princeton. FCC, legal staff member. *Newsweek*, Washington correspondent, to 1984; *Newsweek Access*, Senior Editor, to 1985. *U.S. News & World Report*, Asst Managing Editor, business, to 1986; Deputy Managing Editor, current, 1986. Co-author *Teleshock: How to Survive the Breakup of Ma Bell.*

Machalaba, Daniel. *The Wall Street Journal.* Reporter. B. NYC. NYU, 1971, BA/MA-English. *The Evening News* (Patterson, NJ), reporter, 1972. Fairchild Publications, NYC, reporter, to 1976; Managing Editor, Fairchild's textile staff, *Daily News Record*, 1976. *The Wall Street Journal*, reporter, Philadelphia bureau, to 1979; publishing industry reporter, NY, to 1983; transportation industry reporter, NY, current, 1983.

Mackenzie, Richard. *Insight.* Senior Writer. B. 1946, Brisbane, Australia. El Centro, Dallas, 1974, Journalism & Criminal Science. Australian newspapers & TV, 1965-70. Mirror Newspapers (Toronto, Canada), Copy Editor & Layout Editor, to 1971. *Dallas Times Herald*, reporter, feature writer, to 1976. Freelance writer, to 1981. *Sydney Morning Herald* (Australia), NY bureau, North American Syn. Manager, to 1985. *Insight*, senior writer, current, 1985.

Madison, Christopher. *National Journal.* Foreign Policy Reporter. B. 1951, Brooklyn, NY. Northwestern, 1973, BA-English, 1974, MSJ. *Independent Register* (Libertyville, IL), reporter, to 1975. McGraw-Hill, Washington energy reporter, to 1978. *Legal Times*, Washington energy & environment reporter, to 1980. *National Journal*, energy reporter, to 1981; trade reporter, to 1984; foreign policy reporter, current, 1984.

Magnet, Myron. *FORTUNE.* Board of Editors Member. Columbia, BA, PhD; Cambridge, MA. Middlebury College (VT), teacher. Columbia, teacher, English & Political Theory. *FORTUNE*, freelance, 1980-82; Associate Editor, to 1983; Board of Editors member, current, 1983.

Magnuson, Ed. *TIME.* Writer. B. St. Cloud, MN. U. of MN, 1950, Journalism. *Minneapolis Tribune*, reporter; Asst City Editor, to 1960. *TIME* magazine, correspondent, to 1961; writer, current, 1961. 100+ *TIME* cover stories, 21 on Watergate.

Malabre, Alfred Leopold. *The Wall Street Journal.* News Editor. B. 1931, NYC. Yale, 1952, BA. Poynter Fellow, 1976. *Hartford Courant*, copy editor, to 1958. *The Wall Street Journal*, reporter, Bonn Bureau Chief, Economics Editor, News Editor, & "Outlook" columnist, 1958-69; News Editor, current, 1969. Author *Understanding The Economy: For People Who Can't Understand Economics*, 1976; *America's Dilemma: Jobs Vs. Prices*, 1978; *Investing for Profit in the '80's*, 1982.

Mallin, Jay. *The Washington Times.* Reporter. B. 1959, Havana, Cuba. U. of FL, English, grad work in Electrical Engineering. Freelance, current. *The Washington Times,* Copy Editor, 1984; African correspondent, to 1985; Asst Foreign Editor, to 1986; metro reporter, current, 1986.

Mann, James. *Los Angeles Times.* Peking Bureau Chief. B. 1946, Albany, NY. Harvard, 1968, AB-Social Relations; U. of PA, nondegree program in International Economics & History of the Middle East, 1975. *Journal-Courier* (New Haven, CT), staff writer, to 1969. *The Washington Post,* staff writer, to 1972. *Philadelphia Inquirer,* reporter, to 1975. *The Sun* (Baltimore, MD), Supreme Court/Justice reporter, to 1978. *Los Angeles Times,* Supreme Court reporter, Washington, to 1984; Peking Bureau Chief, current, 1984. First Place Award for Humor for a *Post* Column, Washington-Baltimore Newspaper Guild, 1970; his Watergate articles among those for which *Post* won Pulitzer Prize for Public Service, 1972.

Mann, Paul. *Aviation Week & Space Technology.* Senior Congressional Editor. B. Canandaigua, NY. US Congress, staff member, 1977-80. *Military Science and Technology,* Washington Editor, 1980. *Military Electronics,* Washington Editor, 1980. *Aviation Week & Space Technology,* Senior Congressional Editor, current.

Manning, Robert A. *U.S. News & World Report.* Diplomatic Correspondent. B. 1949, Bronx, NY. State U. of CA, History, Anthropology. Freelance writer, policy analyst, current, 1972. *Africa* magazine, US correspondent, 1979-84. *Far Eastern Economic Review,* Washington correspondent, 1980-85. *U.S. News & World Report,* diplomatic correspondent, current. Radio contributor NPR, BBC, CBC. PBS documentaries "Behind the Lines," 1981; "The Death of Henry Liu," 1985.

Mansfield, Stephanie. *The Washington Post.* Reporter, "Style" section. B. 1950, Philadelphia, PA. Trinity College (Washington, DC), 1972, BA-English. *Daily Mail* (London), to 1974. *Daily Telegraph* (London), to 1976. *The Washington Post,* "Food" section, to 1978; metro reporter, to 1981; reporter, "Style" section, current, 1981.

Marcial, Gene G. *BusinessWeek.* "Inside Wall Street" Editor. Santo Tomas U. (Manila, Philippines); NYU, MA-Political Science; currently at NYU Law. *The Elyria Chronicle-Telegram* (OH), writer. *The Hong Kong Standard,* writer. *The Wall Street Journal,* stock market writer, to 1981. *BusinessWeek,* "Inside Wall Street" Editor, current, 1981.

Markham, James. *The New York Times.* Bonn Bureau Chief. B. 1943, Washington, DC. Princeton, 1965, European History; Rhodes Scholar, Balliol College, Oxford, 1967. *TIME,* 1966. AP, to 1970. *The New York Times,* NY, 1973; Saigon Bureau Chief, to 1975; Beirut Bureau Chief, to 1976; Madrid Bureau Chief, to 1982; Bonn Bureau Chief, current, 1982.

Marquand, Robert. *The Christian Science Monitor.* Education Writer. B. 1957, FL. Principia College, 1980, English, Religion-Philosophy. *The Christian Science Monitor,* editorial asst, Literary & Fine Arts Page, 1982; Poetry Editor, to 1984; education writer, current, 1985. Benjamin Fine Journalism Award, 1986.

Marsh, David. *Financial Times.* Bonn Correspondent. B. 1952, Shoreham, UK. Queen's College, Oxford, BA-Chemistry. Reuters, London, Frankfurt, Brussels, Bonn, 1974-78. *Financial Times,* economics staff member, to 1982; staff correspondent, Paris, to 1986; Bonn correspondent, current, 1986.

Marshall, Tyler. *Los Angeles Times.* London Bureau. B. 1941, Detroit. MI. Stanford, 1967, Political Science. *Sacramento Bee,* 1964-65. UPI, San Francisco, 1968. McGraw-Hill World News, San Francisco, to 1971; Bonn, to 1974; London, to 1979. *Los Angeles Times,* New Delhi, to 1983; Bonn, to 1985; London, current, 1985.

Martin, Everett. *The Wall Street Journal.* Senior Special Writer. B. IL. IN U., 1949, Journalism. City News Bureau, Chicago. *Elkhart Truth* (IN). Insurance salesman, to 1953. *The Christian Science Monitor*, copyboy; New England News Editor; Detroit Bureau Chief. *The Wall Street Journal*, industries reporter. *TIME*, business writer. *Newsweek*, Deputy Foreign Editor, to 1965; Hong Kong Bureau Chief, 1965; Saigon Bureau Chief, to 1968; Hong Kong correspondent, to 1970. Fletcher School of Law & Diplomacy, journalist-in-residence, 1970. *The Wall Street Journal*, South American correspondent, to 1982; Senior Special Writer, to 1986; retired March 1986. Recipient Overseas Press Club Award for Allende coup coverage, 1973; Maria Moors Cabot Prize for South American coverage, 1983.

Martin, Jurek. *Financial Times.* Foreign Editor & Assistant Editor. B. 1942, UK. Hertford College, Oxford, 1963, Modern History. Sabbatical, U. of SC, 1981-82. *Financial Times*, foreign desk, 1966-68; Washington correspondent, to 1970; NY Bureau Chief, to 1972; Foreign News Editor, London, to 1975; Washington Bureau Chief, to 1981; Tokyo Bureau Chief, 1982-86; Foreign Editor & Asst Editor, current, 1986. David Holden Award, British Press Awards, Best Resident Foreign Correspondent, 1984.

Martin, Richard. *Insight.* Writer. B. 1958, Jackson, MS. Yale, 1980, Literature. *Arkansas Times*, Associate Editor, to 1983. *Globescan*, Contributing Editor, 1984. *Insight*, writer, current, 1985.

Martin, Richard. *The Wall Street Journal.* Chicago Bureau Chief. B. 1939, Salt Lake City, UT. U. of Denver, 1961, BA-History. *The Mountaineer* (Fort Carson, CO, US Army), reporter, photographer, editor, to 1963. *The Wall Street Journal*, staff reporter, Dallas, 1961, 1964; staff reporter, Detroit, 1965; staff reporter, various editing assignments, NYC, to 1972; Asst NY Bureau Chief, 1972; Boston Bureau Chief, to 1976; Cleveland Bureau Chief, to 1977; Chicago Bureau Chief, current, 1977.

Mashek, John W. *U.S. News & World Report.* National Political Correspondent. B. 1931, Sioux Falls, SD. U. of MN, 1953, Journalism & Political Science. *Dallas Morning News*, federal beat, courthouse, state & local politics, 1955-60; Washington bureau, to 1964. *U.S. News & World Report*, Houston bureau, to 1970; Congressional correspondent, to 1974; White House correspondent, to 1978; national political correspondent, current, 1978.

Mason, Todd. *BusinessWeek.* Dallas Bureau Manager. U. of WI, BA. *The Marshfield News Herald* (WI), reporter. *The Midland Daily News* (MI), reporter. *The Miami News*, business writer, to 1978. *The Fort Lauderdale News*, Business Editor, to 1982. *BusinessWeek*, stringer/correspondent, Ft. Lauderdale, FL, 1980-82; Dallas Bureau Manager, current, 1982.

Mathews, Jay. *The Washington Post.* Los Angeles Bureau Chief. B. 1945, Long Beach, CA. Harvard, 1967, Government, 1971, MA-East Asian Studies. AP, intern, NY, 1966. US Army, to 1969. *The Washington Star*, intern, 1970. *The Washington Post*, metro reporter, to 1975; Asst Foreign Editor, to 1976; Hong Kong Bureau Chief, to 1979; Peking Bureau Chief, to 1980; LA Bureau Chief, current, 1981. Co-Author (with Linda Mathews), *One Billion: A China Chronicle*, 1983. National Education Reporting Award, 1983; National Semi-finalist, pending finalist selection, Journalist in Space Program.

Matusow, Barbara. *Washington Journalism Review.* Senior Editor. B. 1938, Philadelphia, PA. PA State U., 1960, French. NBC-WRC-TV, Washington, trainee, associate producer, 1968. CBS News, NY, radio writer, producer, 1970. WNBC-TV, NY, tv-writer, producer, 1971. WRC-TV, Washington, producer, 1973, WJLA-TV, Washington, producer, 1976. Freelance writer, 1978-85. *Washington Journalism Review*, Senior Editor, current, 1986. Author *The Evening Stars: The Making of the Network News Anchor*, 1983.

May, Clifford. *The New York Times.* Domestic Correspondent. B. 1951, NYC. Sarah Lawrence, 1973, BA-Russian; Columbia, 1975, MSJ, 1975, MA-International Affairs. *The Record* (Bergen, NJ), reporter, 1975. *Newsweek*, Associate Editor, to 1977. Hearst Newspapers, roving foreign correspondent, to 1978. *Geo Magazine*, Senior Editor, to 1980. *The New York Times*, Science Editor, Sunday Magazine, to 1983; Africa correspondent, to 1985; domestic correspondent, current, 1985.

May, Todd Jr. *FORTUNE.* Chief Economist & Board of Editors Member. Northwestern. Econometric Institute, Economic Analyst, Department Head, to 1952. Union Carbide, Associate Economist, Economist, 1960-69. Economic Advisory Board member, US Secretary of Commerce, 1967-68. *FORTUNE*, Associate Editor, 1952-60; Associate Economist, 1969; Board of Editors, current, 1972; Chief Economist, current, 1980.

Maynes, Charles William. *Foreign Policy.* Editor. B. 1938, Huron, SD. Harvard, 1960, History; Rhodes Scholar, 1960. Foreign Service Officer, UN, Laos, USSR, 1962-70. Legislative asst, Congress, to 1972. Carnegie Endowment for International Peace, Secretary, to 1977. Asst Secretary of State for International Organizations, to 1980. *Foreign Policy*, Editor, current, 1980. Also current, Syndication Sales, columnist, 1985. Olive Branch Award, Outstanding Magazine Coverage of the Nuclear Arms Race, 1983.

McCartney, Robert J. *The Washington Post.* Central European Bureau Chief. B. 1953, Evanston, IL. Amherst College, 1975, American Studies, *magna cum laude*. *The Wall Street Journal*, staff reporter, Boston, to 1976. *The International Daily News*, Business Editor, Rome, Italy, to 1978. AP-Dow Jones News Service, staff correspondent, Rome, Italy, to 1980. AP, staff correspondent, Rome, Italy, to 1982. *The Washington Post*, Asst Foreign Editor, Washington, to 1983; Mexico City/Central America Bureau Chief, to 1986; Central European Bureau Chief, Bonn, West Germany, current, 1986.

McCaslin, John. *The Washington Times.* Justice Department Correspondent. B. 1957, Alexandria, VA. Old Dominion U., 1980, Speech Communications/Journalism. KOFI radio (Kalispell, MT), News Director, to 1982. KJJR-KBBZ/FM (Kalispell, MT), News Director, to 1984. UPI, correspondent, to 1984. *The Washington Times*, White House correspondent, to 1985; Justice Dept. correspondent, current, 1985.

McCoy, Charles. *The Wall Street Journal.* Reporter, Chicago. U. of TX, Austin, 1982; *Facultad de Filosofia Y Letras*, Spain, Spanish. *San Antonio Light*, reporting intern, summer 1981, '82. *Daily Texan*, sports reporter, 1982. *The Wall Street Journal*, Dallas bureau reporter, to 1985; banking reporter, Chicago bureau, current, 1985.

McCrary, Daniel D. *BusinessWeek.* Senior Editor. MI State U. *The Wall Street Journal*, reporter, to 1960. McGraw-Hill World News, Washington bureau reporter, to 1964; Asst London Bureau Chief, to 1968; Asst News Editor, Washington, to 1972. *BusinessWeek*, General Editor, to 1976; Associate Editor, to 1981; Senior Editor, late-breaking news coverage, current, 1981.

McGough, Robert. *Forbes.* Reporter. B. 1956, Wichita, KS. Rice U., 1978, BA-English. Bookstore Manager, Houston, to 1979. *The Ridgefield Press* (CT), reporter, to 1980. *The Redding Pilot* (CT), Editor, to 1981. *Forbes*, reporter/researcher, to 1984; reporter, current, 1984.

McGrory, Mary. *The Washington Post*, Columnist. Universal Press Syndicate, Columnist. B. Boston, MA. Emmanuel College (Boston). *The Boston Herald*, 1947. *The Washington Star*, book reviewer, to 1954; national commentator, columnist, to 1981. Universal Press Syndicate, columnist, current, 1960. *The Washington Post*, columnist, current, 1981. Pulitzer Prize for Commentary, 1975; George Polk Memorial Award, 1963; Elijah Parish Lovejoy Fellow, 1985, Colby College.

McGurn, William. *The Wall Street Journal*/Europe. Editorial Features Editor. B. 1958, Oceanside, CA. U. of Notre Dame, 1980, BA-Philosophy; Boston U., 1981, MSJ. *The American Spectator*, Asst Managing Editor, to 1983. *This World*, Managing Editor, to 1984. *The Wall Street Journal*/Europe, Editorial Features Editor, current, 1984.

McLaughlin, John. *National Review.* Washington Editor. Boston College, 1951, BA, 1952, MA-Philosophy, 1961, MA-English; Stanford, 1963, studied communications; Columbia, 1967, PhD-Communications. Fairfield U. (CT), Director of Communcations & educator, 1960-63. *America* Magazine, Associate Editor, 1967-70. ABC-TV, NYC, consultant, 1969. US Senate candidate, 1970. Special asst to the President, Washington, to 1974. McLaughlin & Co., Communications Consultants, President, to 1979. "The McLaughlin Group," moderator, aired PBS, NBC & USIA, current. "John McLaughlin's One on One," host/producer, Washington, current. NPR, NBC Radio Network, commentator, current. *National Review*, Washington Editor, current. Excellence in Journalism Award, Catholic Press Association, 1970.

McLeod, Don. *Insight.* Senior Writer. B. 1936, Memphis, TN. Memphis State, 1958, BA-Sociology, 1963, MA-History. AP, Memphis, to 1967; Nashville, to 1969; Washington, to 1983. *The Washington Times*, reporter, to 1984; National Editor, to 1985. *Insight*, Senior Writer, current, 1985.

McWilliams, Rita. *The Washington Times.* National Desk Reporter. B. 1959, Washington, DC. Washington College (Chestertown, MD), 1980, BA-Political Science; Boston U., 1981, MA-Journalism. Cambridge (MD) *Banner*, reporter, to 1983. *The Daily Progress* (Charlottesville, VA), reporter, to 1984. *The Washington Times*, regional reporter, to 1986; national desk reporter, current, 1986.

Meacham, James. *The Economist.* Military Editor. B. 1930, Portsmouth. U. of MO, 1952, BSJ; George Washington U., MS-International Affairs; US Naval War College, 1967. US Navy, Line Officer, to 1973. *The Economist*, Military Editor, current, 1974. Also current, contributor, *Arab Defence Journal*.

Meier, Barry. *The Wall Street Journal.* Reporter. Attended Syracuse, 1969-73; U. of NM, 1975-76. Eclipse Press (NY), Associate Editor, 1978-80. *Chemical Week*, environment editor, 1983-84. *The Wall Street Journal*, reporter, NY, current, 1984.

Meisels, Andrew. *The Washington Times & The New York Daily News.* Israel-based Correspondent. B. 1933, Budapest, Hungary. CCNY, 1955, English. AP, NJ/NY, newsman, to 1963. ABC News, Israel correspondent, to 1982. Satellite News Channel, Israel correspondent, to 1983. *The New York Daily News*, Israel-based correspondent, current, 1985. *The Washington Times*, Israel-based correspondent, current, 1985. Overseas Press Club Award, Best Radio Spot News Reporting from Abroad, 1974. Author *Son of a Star; Six Other Days*: contributor *Lightning Out of Israel*.

Melloan, George. *The Wall Street Journal.* Deputy Editor, Editorial Page. B. Greenwood, IN. Butler U. (IN), BSJ. *The Wall Street Journal*, copyreader, 1952; reporter; "Page One" editing staff member; Editor, "Business" column; Atlanta & Cleveland Bureau Manager; foreign correspondent, London bureau, to 1970; Editorial writer, current, 1970; Deputy Editor, Editorial Page, current, 1973. Co-author (with Joan Melloan) *The Carter Economy*, 1978. Gerald Loeb Award for Distinguished Business & Financial Journalism in Commentary, 1982; Inter-American Press Association Daily Gleaner Award, 1983.

Meriwether, Heath. *The Miami Herald.* Executive Editor. B. 1944, Columbia, MO. U. of MO, 1966, BA-Journalism & History; Harvard, 1967, MA-Teaching. *Columbia Daily Tribune*, sports writer, to 1970. *The Miami Herald*, reporter, 1970; education writer, 1971; Broward City Editor,

1972; Palm Beach Editor, to 1975; City Desk Assignments Editor, to 1977; Executive City Editor, to 1979; Asst Managing Editor, News, to 1981; Managing Editor, to 1981; Executive Editor, current, 1983. *Herald* received 2 Pulitzer Prizes under editorship, 1986.

Mervosh, Edward. *U.S. News & World Report.* Senior Economic Editor & "Economic Outlook" Columnist. Washington & Jefferson College, BA; Columbia, MA. *BusinessWeek*, Economics Editor, to 1985. *U.S. News & World Report*, Senior Economics Editor, "Economic Outlook" columnist, current, 1985. Also current, weekly program host on FNN. Co-author *The Decline of America.*

Merwin, John. *Forbes.* Senior Editor. Trinity U. (San Antonio, TX), BA-Journalism; U. of TX, MA-Survey Research; studied Southern Methodist U., Business, Law, & Government. *Dallas Morning News*, city reporter, 1971. KERA-TV, Dallas, reporter, documentary film producer, to 1974. *D Magazine*, co-founder. *Forbes*, Associate Editor, West Coast bureau, to 1980; West Coast Bureau Chief, to 1983; Senior Editor, current, 1983.

Methvin, Eugene Hilburn. *Reader's Digest.* Senior Editor. B. 1934, Vienna, GA. U. of GA, 1955, BA-Journalism, *cum laude*. *The Vienna News* (GA), 1950-51. *Constitution* (Atlanta, GA), reporter, 1952. US Air Force, 1955-58. *Washington Daily News*, reporter, to 1960. *Reader's Digest*, Washington editorial office from 1960, staff writer, Associate Editor; Senior Editor, current. Author *The Riot Makers, The Technology of Social Demolition*, 1970; *The Rise of Radicalism, The Social Psychology of Messianic Extremism*, 1973. Sigma Delta Chi Society of Professional Journalists National Award for Public Service in Magazine Reporting, 1965.

Meyer, Cord. News America Syndicate. Foreign Affairs Columnist. B. 1920. Yale, 1942, BA, *summa cum laude*; Harvard, Society of Fellows, 1946-47, 1949-51. US Marines, 1942-45, ret. Captain; Bronze Star, Purple Heart, Presidential Unit Citation. Special asst to Harold Stassen as member US Delegation to Founding Conference of UN, 1945. United World Federalists, President, 1947-49. CIA, 1951-67; Asst Deputy Director for Plans, to 1973; Chief of Station, London, to 1976 (3 Times awarded Distinguished Intelligence Medal). News America Syndicate, national columnist, current, 1978. Georgetown, lecturer, 1982-85. Author *Waves of Darkness*, 1946 (O. Henry Prize winner); *Peace or Anarchy*, 1947; *Facing Reality*, 1980. Special Weintal Award for Foreign Affairs Column, 1986.

Meyerson, Adam. *Policy Review.* Editor. B. 1953, Philadelphia, PA. Yale, 1974, History/Arts & Letters. *The American Spectator*, Managing Editor, to 1977. *The Wall Street Journal*, editorial writer, to 1983. *Policy Review*, Editor, current, 1983. Co-editor (with David Asman) *The Wall Street Journal on Management: The Best of Manager's Journal.*

Michaels, James Walker. *Forbes.* Editor. B. 1921, Buffalo, NY. Harvard, 1943, Economics, *cum laude*. Served in India & Burma, WWII. State Dept. UPI, New Delhi Bureau Manager. *Buffalo Evening News*. *Forbes*, 1954-57; Managing Editor, to 1961; Editor, current, 1961.

Miller, Judith. *The New York Times.* Paris Correspondent. B. 1948, NYC. Barnard College, 1969, BA-Economics; Center for European Studies, U. of Brussels; Princeton, 1972, MA. NPR, foreign affairs, national security specialist. *The Progressive*, Washington correspondent, to 1977. Freelance work. *The New York Times*, Washington bureau reporter, to 1983; Cairo Bureau Chief, to 1985; Paris correspondent, current, 1985.

Miller, Matt. *The Asian Wall Street Journal.* Reporter. Macalester College (St. Paul, MN), BA-Asian Studies; U. of the Philippines. *Asia Travel Trade Magazine*, deputy editor. Freelance photographer/journalist. *The Asian Wall Street Journal*, reporter, Hong Kong, 1981-85; reporter, New Delhi, current, 1985. Journalist of the Year, Hong Kong Newspaper Society, 1984.

MediaGuide 331

Miller, Norman C. *The Los Angeles Times.* National Editor. B. 1934, Pittsburgh, PA. PA State U., 1956, Journalism. *The Wall Street Journal*, reporter, to 1964; Detroit Bureau Chief, to 1966; Congressional correspondent/political writer, to 1973; Washington Bureau Chief, to 1983. *The Los Angeles Times*, National Editor, current, 1983. Pulitzer Prize, 1964; George Polk Award, 1964.

Minard, Lawrence. *Forbes.* Assistant Managing Editor. B. 1949, Seattle, WA. Trinity College, 1972, Economics. *Forbes*, reporter, 1974; staff writer, 1976; special economic correspondent, Japan, to 1978; European Bureau Manager, to 1983; West Coast & Pacific Bureau Manager, to 1985; Asst Managing Editor, current, 1985. Co-winner Gerald Loeb Award for Distinguished Financial Reporting with David L. Warsh (economic columnist for *The Boston Globe*), 1976.

Mintz, Morton. *The Washington Post.* Reporter. B. 1922, Ann Arbor, MI. U. of MI, 1943, Economics. Nieman Fellow, Harvard, 1963. *St. Louis Star Times*, 1946-50. *St. Louis Globe-Democrat*, to 1958. *The Washington Post*, from 1958; currently reporter, consumer issues. Heywood Broun Award, 1963; Raymond Clapper Award, 1963; George Polk Award, 1963; Washington Newspaper Guild Public Service Award, 1963; Sidney Hillman Award, 1972; A.J. Liebling Award, 1974; Worth Bingham Award, 1977; Columbia Journalism, 1983; Washington-Baltimore Newspaper Guild Public Service Award, 1977, '86 & Grand Award, 1986.

Mohr, Charles. *The New York Times.* Washington Bureau Staff. B. 1929, Loup City, NE. U. of NE, 1951, History/Journalism. *The Lincoln Star*, to 1951. UPI, Chicago, to 1953. *TIME*, to 1963. *The New York Times*, Presidential campaign, 1964, '76; White House correspondent, to 1965, '77; Vietnam Bureau Chief, to 1966; Southeast Asia correspondent, to 1970; Africa correspondent, to 1975; Washington bureau staff member, current, 1978.

Molotsky, Irvin D. *The New York Times.* Consumer & Cultural Affairs Reporter, Washington. B. 1938, Camden, NJ. Temple, 1960, BS. *The Trentonian* (NJ), reporter, Editor. *Newsday* (LI, NY), Editor, Nassau office; Editor, Suffolk office. *The New York Times*, Copy Editor, metro desk; Editor, "Long Island Weekly" section; Asst Metro Editor; Asst Family/Style Editor; Long Island Bureau Chief, 1967-79; Washington bureau reporter; night editor; consumer news & cultural affairs reporter, Washington, current. SUNY at Stony Brook, NYU, Brooklyn College, American U., C.W. Post College, teacher.

Montalbano, William D. *Los Angeles Times.* Buenos Aires Bureau Chief. B. 1940, NY. Rutgers, 1960, BA-English; Columbia, 1962, MSJ. *Star Ledger* (Newark, NJ), reporter, to 1962. *Patriot-Ledger* (Quincy, MA), reporter-editor, to 1963. *Buenos Aires Herald*, reporter-editor, to 1965. UPI, Cables Desk, NY, to 1967. *The Miami Herald*, Latin America correspondent, senior correspondent, projects editor, founding Peking Bureau Chief, Chief of Correspondents, to 1983. *Los Angeles Times*, founding El Salvador Bureau Chief, to 1984; Buenos Aires Bureau Chief, current, covering all South America except Brazil, 1984. Co-author 3 books. Cabot Prize, Ernie Pyle, Overseas Press Club.

Morley, Jefferson. *The New Republic.* Associate Editor. B. 1958, NYC. Yale, 1980, History. *Worthington Globe* (MN), reporter, summer 1978. *Minneapolis Tribune*, reporter, summer 1979. *The Washington Post*, reporter, summer, 1981. *Foreign Policy*, editorial asst, 1981. Asst to Bruce Cameron, human rights lobbyist, to 1982. *Harper's*, Asst Editor, 1983. *The New Republic*, Associate Editor, current, 1983.

Morrison, David. *National Journal.* National Security Correspondent. B. 1953, Minneapolis, MN. Columbia, 1978, History, 1982, MSJ. Center for Defense Information, Senior Research Analyst, to 1985. Freelance, current, 1980. *National Journal*, national security correspondent, current, 1985.

Morrison, Mark. *BusinessWeek.* Senior Editor. U. of TX. *The Houston Post*, reporter, to 1974. *BusinessWeek*, correspondent, Houston, to 1978; Chicago Bureau Manager; Senior Editor, current, coverage corporate strategies, management, marketing, people.

Mosher, Lawrence. *National Journal.* Contributing Editor. B. 1929, LA, CA. Stanford, 1951, History, Journalism. *The Record* (Bergen, NJ), reporter, 1958-59. *New York World-Telegram & The Sun*, reporter, to 1962. Copley News Service, foreign correspondent, Hong Kong, Beirut, to 1967. *The National Observer*, reporter, to 1977. Georgetown, Center for Contemporary Arab Studies, writer-in-residence, to 1979. *National Journal*, staff writer; Contributing Editor, current, 1979. *The Water Reporter* (newsletter), Publisher & Editor, current, 1984. Co-author *America's Wild and Scenic Rivers*, 1983; *Bordering on Trouble: Resources and Politics in the Americas*, 1986. Copley Ring of Truth Award for Best Foreign Reporting, 1965; National Wildlife Federation Communicator of the Year Award, 1982.

Mufson, Steve. *The Wall Street Journal.* Reporter. B. NYC. Yale, 1980, BA. *Yale Daily News*, Editor-in-Chief. *Steady Work* (Yale periodical), Co-editor, co-founder. *The Wall Street Journal*, intern, summer 1979; NY reporter, 1980-84; reporter, London bureau, to 1986.

Mullin, Dennis. *U.S. News & World Report.* White House Correspondent. Edward R. Murrow Fellow, 1985-86. *U.S. News & World Report*, Middle East Bureau Chief, 1974-79; Diplomatic correspondent, to 1985; White House correspondent, current, 1986.

Munro, Ross H. *TIME.* South Asia Bureau Chief. B. 1941, Vancouver, Canada. U. of British Columbia, 1965, BA-Political Science; Stanford, grad work. *The Globe & Mail* (Toronto, Canada), various beats & bureaus, 1967-71; Washington Bureau Chief, to 1975; Peking Bureau Chief, to 1977. *TIME*, Pacific/Asia economic correspondent, to 1980; Hong Kong Bureau Chief, to 1982; national security correspondent, Washington, to 1985; South Asia Bureau Chief, current, 1985.

Murdoch, Keith Rupert. *The New York Post.* Publisher. B. 1931, Melbourne, Australia. Worchester College, Oxford, England, 1953, MA. News American Publishing Inc., Chairman: *The New York Post, New York Magazine, Village Voice*, current, 1977; NAPI: *The Star, San Antonio Express and News,* current, 1974; NAPI: *Boston Herald, Chicago Sun-Times*, 1983. News International Ltd. Group, Chairman, London, current. News Ltd. Group & Associated Companies, Chief Executive Managing Director, Australia, current, 1983.

Mydans, Seth. *The New York Times.* Manila Bureau Chief. B. 1946. Harvard, 1968. *The Boston Globe*, copy editor, 1971-73. AP, correspondent, Moscow, Bangkok, London, Boston, NY, to 1981. *Newsweek*, correspondent, Moscow, Bangkok, London, to 1983. *The New York Times*, metro reporter, to 1984; Moscow correspondent, to 1985; Manila Bureau Chief, current, 1985.

Naj, Amal K. *The Wall Street Journal.* Auto Industry Reporter, Detroit. B. 1951, Madras, India. Wilson College, Bombay, 1971, BS, The Queen's U., Belfast, 1975, Economics. *The Wall Street Journal*, 1978; auto industry reporter, Detroit, current, 1983.

Nagorski, Andrew. *Newsweek.* Bonn Bureau Chief. B. 1947, Edinburgh, Scotland. Amherst College, 1969, Phi Beta Kappa. *Newsweek*, writer/Associate Editor/General Editor, to 1978 (*Newsweek International*); Asian Editor (International Edition)/Hong Kong Bureau Chief, to 1980; Moscow Bureau Chief, to 1982 (expelled); Rome Bureau Chief, to 1985; Bonn Bureau Chief, current, 1985. Freelance, current. Author *Reluctant Farewell: An American Reporter's Candid Look Inside The Soviet Union*, 1985; contributor *Africa and the United States*, 1978. Co-winner (with Peter Younghusband) Overseas Press Club Award, 1974.

Nasar, Sylvia. *FORTUNE.* Associate Editor. Antioch College, BA-Literature; NYU, MA-Economics. Institute for Economic Analysis, NYU, asst research scientist. Scientists' Institute for Public Information, Director of Energy Programs. Control Data Corporation, Senior Economist. *FORTUNE,* Associate Editor, current, 1983. Co-author (with Wassily Leontief, James Koo, Ira Sohn) *The Future of Nonfuel Minerals in the U.S. and World Economy,* 1983.

Navasky, Victor Saul. *The Nation.* Editor. B. 1932, NYC. Swarthmore College, 1954, AB, *Phi Beta Kappa*; Yale, 1959, LLB. US Army, 1954-56. Special asst to Governor G. Mennen Williams, MI, 1959-60. *Monocle Magazine,* Editor & Publisher, to 1965. *The New York Times Magazine,* Editor, 1970-72. Guggenheim Fellow, 1974-75. Russell Sage Foundation Visiting Professor, to 1976. Ferris Professor of Journalism, Princeton, to 1977. *The Nation,* Editor, current, 1978. Author *Kennedy Justice,* 1971; *Naming Names,* 1980 (American Book Award winner, 1981).

Neher, Jacques. Freelance Business & Economics Writer. B. 1953, Cleveland, OH. U. of FL, 1975, BSJ & Latin American Studies. *Tampa Times,* City Hall & Courts reporter, to 1977. *Rubber & Plastics News,* Managing Editor, to 1978. *Advertising Age,* reporter, to 1981. *Crain's Cleveland Business,* Editor, to 1985. Freelance work, current, appearing *Chicago Tribune, The Journal of Commerce.* Jesse Neale Award, 1981; Sigma Delta Chi/Cleveland Press Club, First Place Editorial Writing, 1984.

Neikirk, William R. *Chicago Tribune.* Washington Economics Correspondent. B. 1938, Irvine, KY. U. of KY, 1960, BA-Journalism. *The Kernal* (U. of KY), Editor, 1959-60. *Lexington Herald* (KY), Asst State Editor, 1960. AP, 1961-70; economic reporter, to 1974; Chief Economics Correspondent, 1974. *Chicago Tribune,* economics correspondent, Washington, to 1977; White House correspondent, 1977; Washington economics correspondent, to 1983; Washington Bureau News Editor, to 1984; Washington economics correspondent, current, 1984. Co-author *The Work Revolution,* 1983. *Chicago Tribune* Edward Scott Beck Award, 1975; U. of MO Business Writing Award, 1978, '79. John Hancock Business Writing Award, 1978, '79; Gerald Loeb Business Writing Award, 1978; Peter Lisagor Award, 1978, '84; Champion Media Award for Business Writing, 1979;.

Neilan, Edward. *The Washington Times.* Northeast Asia Correspondent. B. 1932, Torrance, CA. USC, 1954, BA-Journalism/Political Science; U. of London, Institute for International Education Scholarship, grad work, summer 1956. *The Daily Trojan,* USC, Managing Editor, to 1954. *Evening Star-News* (Culver City, CA), sports editor, reporter, 1950-54; City Editor, reporter, to 1957. Consultant, Ministry of Information, Republic of Korea, to 1960. *The Christian Science Monitor,* Tokyo correspondent, 1959-60 (contract). Copley News Service, Tokyo correspondent, 1959-60; Southeast Asia Bureau Chief, 1962-70; diplomatic correspondent, Washington, Deputy Bureau Chief, to 1976. *The Asia Mail,* "American Perspectives on Asia and the Pacific," Editor-founder, to 1983. The Alexandria Gazette Corporation, President, Editor & Publisher; columnist; CEO for *The Alexandria Gazette, Springfield Independent, Burke Herald, Fairfax Tribune,* 1978-82. *The Washington Times,* Asst Foreign Editor, 1982-83; Foreign Editor, to 1986; Northeast Asia correspondent, current, 1986. Co-author (with Charles M. Smith) *The Future of the China Market: Prospects for Sino-American Trade,* 1974. Overseas Press Club Citation for Excellence, 1974; UPI Journalist of the Year in Virginia Award, 1982 (for work as Editor & columnist for *The Alexandria Gazette*).

Nelson, Anne. Freelance Writer. *Los Angeles Times,* Contributor. B. 1954, Fort Sill, OK. Yale, 1976, American Studies. *The New Yorker,* editorial staff, to 1977. Freelance writer/photographer, to 1983. *Maclean's Magazine* (Canada), Central America correspondent, 1980-83. Canadian Broadcasting Corporation, associate producer, NY bureau, "The Journal," to 1984. Independent writer & consultant, current, specializing in Latin America, 1984. Contributor to *Los Angeles Times* "Opinion" section, current, 1984. Author *Murder Under Two Flags,* 1986.

Nelson, John H. (Jack). *Los Angeles Times.* Washington Bureau Chief. B. 1929, Talladega, AL. GA State U., Economics; Harvard, Politics, History, Public Administration. Nieman Fellow, Harvard. *Daily Herald* (Biloxi, MS), reporter, to 1949. *Constitution* (Atlanta, GA), staff writer, to 1965. *Los Angeles Times,* Atlanta Bureau Chief, to 1970; investigative reporter, Washington, to 1975; Washington Bureau Chief, current, 1975. "Washington Week in Review", PBS, current, frequent appearances. Author *Captive Voices-High School Journalism In America*: co-author *The FBI and the Berrigans; Censors and the Schools; The Orangeburg Massacre.* Drew Pearson Award for Investigative Reporting, 1975; Pulitzer Prize, 1960.

Newport John Paul Jr. *FORTUNE.* Reporter/researcher. B. Fort Worth, TX. Harvard, *cum laude. Fort Worth Star-Telegram,* reporter, to 1982. *FORTUNE,* reporter/researcher, current, 1982. John Hancock Award for Business & Financial Journalism, 1981.

Newton, Maxwell. *The New York Post.* Financial & Economic Columnist. *The Australian Financial Review,* Founding Editor (only national financial daily). *The Australian,* Founding Editor (only national daily). Financial & economic columnist, current, appearing in *The New York Post, Sun-Times* (Chicago, IL), *Boston Herald, The Times* (London, UK) & 4 Australian papers. Author *The Fed.*

Nielsen, John. *FORTUNE.* Associate Editor. B. Highland Park, IL. US Naval Academy, Annapolis. *Newsweek,* General Editor. *TIME,* Associate Editor. *FORTUNE,* Associate Editor, current, 1984.

Novak, Michael. *National Review.* "Tomorrow & Tomorrow" Columnist. B. 1933, Johnstown, PA. Stonehill College, 1956, AB; Harvard, 1965, MA; Gregorian U. (Rome); Catholic U. Harvard, teaching fellow. Stanford, Asst Prof of Humanities, to 1968. SUNY at Old Westbury, Professor, to 1973. Rockefeller Foundation, Humanities Program, to 1976. Syracuse, Ledden-Watson Distinguished Professor of Religion, 1976. Co-founder, *Catholicism in Crisis/This World.* American Enterprise Institute, Resident Scholar, current, 1978. Freelance, current. Syndicated Columnist, "Illusions & Realities," current. *National Review,* columnist, "Tomorrow & Tomorrow," current. Author 13 books, including *Will It Liberate: Questions about Liberation Theology,* 1986: co-author *Toward the Future: Catholic Social Thought and the U.S. Economy* (with the Lay commission on Catholic Social Teaching and U.S. Economy). 1984; *A Book of Elements* (with Karen Laub-Novak), 1972. George Washington Honor Medal, Freedoms Foundation, 1984; Award of Excellence, Religion in Media, 8th annual Angel Awards, 1985; 1st US member Argentina National Academy of Sciences, Morals & Politics, 1985.

Novak, Robert D. News America Syndicate. "Inside Report" Columnist (with Rowland Evans). B. 1931, Joliet, IL. U. of IL, 1952. *Champaign-Urbana Courier,* reporter, 1952. US Army, to 1954. AP, Omaha, NE; Lincoln, NE; statehouse/political reporter, Indianapolis, IN, to 1957; Capitol Hill reporter, Washington, to 1958. *The Wall Street Journal,* Senate correspondent & political reporter, to 1961; Chief Congressional Correspondent, to 1963. News America Syndicate, "Inside Report" columnist (with Rowland Evans), current, 1963. *Evans-Novak Political Report,* bi-weekly newsletter co-author (with Rowland Evans), current. *Evans-Novak Tax Report,* bi-weekly newsletter co-author (with Rowland Evans). *Reader's Digest,* roving editor (with Rowland Evans), current (4 articles/year). Freelance work. Also current, "Evans & Novak" & "Insiders" co-host, with Rowland Evans, CNN. Frequent guest "Crossfire," CNN; "Meet the Press," NBC. Member "McLaughlin Group," NBC. Author *The Agony of the GOP,* 1965; co-author with Rowland Evans *Lyndon B. Johnson: The Exercise of Power,* 1966; *Nixon in the White House: The Frustration of Power,* 1971; *The Reagan Revolution,* 1981.

Nulty, Peter. *FORTUNE.* Associate Editor. Wesleyan U.; Columbia, MA-International Affairs. *Middle East Monitor,* Editor. *Middle East Journal,* Asst Editor. *FORTUNE,* reporter/researcher; Associate Editor, current.

Oakes, John B. *The New York Times.* Senior Editor. B. 1913, Elkins Park, PA. Princeton, 1934, AB, valedictorian, *Phi Beta Kappa*; U. of Dijon, France, 1935; Rhodes Scholar, Queen's College, Oxford, AB, AM, 1936. *State Gazette*, reporter. *Trenton Times*, NJ, reporter, to 1937. *The Washington Post*, reporter, special feature writer, to 1941. US Army, to 1946, from private to lieutenant-colonel; Bronze Star (US), member of Order of Empire (UK), *Croix de Guerre* (France). *The New York Times*, sunday department, 1946; Editor of "Review of the Week," to 1949; Editorial Board member, to 1961; Editor, Editorial Page, to 1977; Senior Editor, 1977; now retired. Special grant from Carnegie Corporation for study and travel, 1959; Collegiate School Award of Honor, 1963; Columbia-Catherwood Award, 1960; George Polk Memorial Award, 1966; Thomas Jefferson Award of Unitarian Universalist District of NY, 1968; Silurian Society Award; Woodrow Wilson Award, 1970.

Oberdorfer, Don. *The Washington Post.* National News Staff Member. B. Atlanta, GA. Princeton, BA-International Affairs. Ferris Professor of Journalism, Princeton, 1977. *The Charlotte Observer*, Washington correspondent; local reporter. *The Saturday Evening Post*, Associate Editor. Knight newspapers, national correspondent. *The Washington Post*, White House & diplomatic affairs correspondent, 1968-72; Tokyo correspondent, to 1975; national news staff member, current, 1977. Author *Tet!*, 1971.

Oberfeld, Kirk E. *Insight.* Managing Editor. B. 1945, Orange, NJ. Kalamazoo College (MI), 1967, BA-Political Science; OH State U., 1971, MA-Journalism. UPI, writer, summers 1970, '71. *Battle Creek Enquirer and News* (MI), Editorial Page Editor, to 1973; City Editor, to 1975. *Philadelphia Bulletin*, NJ News Editor, to 1976; "Focus" (features) Editor, to 1977; Director of News Technology, to 1978. *The Washington Star*, Principal Asst Metro Editor, to 1980; Principal Asst Features Editor, to 1981. *The Washington Times*, Deputy Features Editor, to 1983; Asst Managing Editor, to 1985; National Edition Editor, 1985. *Insight*, Managing Editor, current, 1985. National design awards.

Oka, Takashi. *The Christian Science Monitor.* Japan Correspondent. B. Japan. Harvard, grad work; Fellow, Institute of Current World Affairs, 1964-66. *The New York Times*, Tokyo News Bureau Head, 1968-71. Worked to set up Japanese edition of *Newsweek*, 1986. *The Christian Science Monitor*, copyboy, summer 1950; foreign correspondent, to 1964; opened Peking bureau, 1979; Chief Far Eastern Correspondent; Japan correspondent, current, 1986.

O'Brien, Conor Cruise. *The Atlantic.* Contributing Editor. Trinity College (Dublin), PhD-History. Irish Foreign Office, Asst Secretary-General & Deputy Chief, Irish delegation to the UN. Personal representative, UN Secretary-General Dag Hammarskjold, the Congo, 1961. U. of Ghana, vice-chancellor. NYU, Albert Schweitzer Professor of Humanities. *The Atlantic*, Contributing Editor, current. Author many books, including *The Siege: Zionism and Israel*, 1986.

O'Leary, Jeremiah. *The Washington Times.* White House Correspondent. B. 1919, Washington, DC. George Washington U., 1941, English. *The Washington Star*, City Hall & State Dept. reporter, nearly 45 years; Asst City Editor; Latin America; White House, to 1981. National Security Council, asst to William P. Clark, to 1982. *The Washington Times*, White House correspondent, current, to 1982. Oldest deadline daily paper reporter in Washington. Maria Moors Cabot Gold Medal, 1980; First Prize, National Reporting, Washington Newspaper Guild, 1963, Kennedy assassination coverage.

O'Leary, Timothy. *The Washington Times.* South America Correspondent. B. 1956, Alexandria, VA. George Washington U., 1980, BA-English Literature; Columbia, 1982, MSJ. *The Washington Star*, editorial asst, to 1981. *The Times-Picayune/States-Item* (New Orleans, LA), reporter, to 1983. *The Washington Times*, reporter, to 1984; South America correspondent, current, 1984.

Ostling, Richard. *TIME.* Writer. B. 1940, Endicott, NY. U. of MI, 1962, AB; Northwestern, 1963, MSJ; George Washington U., 1970, MA-Religion. *Morning News & Evening Journal* (Wilmington, DE), copyreader, reporter, to 1965. *Christianity Today,* Asst News Editor; News Editor, to 1969. *TIME,* staff correspondent, to 1974; writer & Associate Editor, current, 1975. Also current, "Report on Religion," syndicated weekly CBS radio, 1979.

O'Sullivan, John. *The Times* of London. Associate Editor. B. 1942, Liverpool, UK. London U., 1965, BA-Classics; Harvard, 1983, Fellow, Institute of Politics. Irish radio/TV, London correspondent, to 1972. London *Daily Telegraph,* "Parliamentary Sketch" Writer/Editorial Writer, to 1977; Asst Editor, to 1979; Chief Asst Editor, to 1984, columnist, to 1986. *Policy Review,* Editor, to 1983. *The New York Post,* Editorial Page Editor, to 1986. *The American Spectator,* columnist, to 1986. *The Times* of London, columnist, to 1986; Associate Editor, current, 1986.

Ottaway, David. *The Washington Post.* Diplomatic & National Security Correspondent. B. 1939, New York. Harvard, 1962, History; Columbia, 1972, Ph.D.-Political Science. UPI, Paris/Algiers correspondent, to 1963. *TIME/The New York Times,* Algeria correspondent, to 1966. Africa correspondent, to 1979; Cairo Bureau Chief/Middle East correspondent, to 1985. *The Washington Post,* diplomatic & national security correspondent, current, 1985. Co-author (with Marina Ottaway) *Afrocommunism,* 1981; *Ethiopia: Empire in Revolution,* 1978; *Algeria: The Politics of Socialist Revolution,* 1968. Two Overseas Press Club awards.

Parker, Maynard. *Newsweek.* Editor. B. 1940, LA, CA. Stanford, 1962, AB-History; Columbia, 1963, MSJ. *LIFE,* NYC, reporter, to 1964; Hong Kong correspondent, to 1967. *Newsweek,* Hong Kong correspondent, to 1969; Saigon Bureau Chief, to 1970; Hong Kong Bureau Chief, to 1973; Managing Editor, *Newsweek International,* to 1975; Senior Editor, National Affairs *Newsweek,* to 1977; Asst Managing Editor, to 1980; Executive Editor, to 1982; Editor, current, 1982.

Parks, Michael. *Los Angeles Times.* Southern Africa Correspondent. B. 1943, Detroit, MI. U. of Windsor (Windsor, Canada), 1965, Classics. *Detroit News,* reporter, to 1965. *TIME,* Time-Life News Service correspondent, to 1966. *The Suffolk Sun* (Long Island, NY), Asst City Editor, to 1968. *The Sun* (Baltimore, MD), political reporter, 1970; Southeast Asia correspondent, to 1972; Moscow correspondent, to 1975; Middle East correspondent, to 1978; Peking correspondent, to 1980. *Los Angeles Times,* Peking correspondent, to 1984; Southern Africa correspondent, current, 1984.

Patterson, Jack. *BusinessWeek.* Editorial Page Editor. Emory U. (GA); grad work, Columbia. *BusinessWeek,* Asst Marketing Editor, 1955-59; Atlanta Bureau Manager, to 1966; Cities Editor, to 1973; Associate Editor; Senior Writer; Editor, Books Dept.; Editorial Page Editor, current.

Pear, Robert. *The New York Times.* Washington Bureau Reporter. B. 1949, Washington. Harvard, 1971, BA-English, History & Literature, *magna cum laude, Phi Beta Kappa*; Henry Prize Fellow, Balliol College, Oxford, 1973; Master of Philosophy; Columbia, 1974, MSJ. Pulitzer Traveling Fellow, Henry Woodward Sackett Prize. *The Washington Star,* Harvard correspondent, to 1971; summer intern; reporter, 1974-79; Bureau Chief, to 1979. *The New York Times,* reporter, Washington bureau, current, 1979.

Pearlstine, Norman. *The Wall Street Journal.* Managing Editor & Vice-President. Haverford College (PA), 1964; U. of PA Law, 1967. *The Wall Street Journal,* reporter, to 1973; Toyko Bureau Chief, to 1976; Managing Editor, *The Asian Wall Street Journal,* to 1978. *Forbes,* Executive Editor, to 1980. *The Wall Street Journal,* National News Editor, to 1982; Editor & Publisher-*The Wall Journal*/Europe, to 1983; Managing Editor, *The Wall Street Journal,* NY, current, 1983; Vice-President, current, 1983.

MediaGuide

Peirce, Neal R. *National Journal.* Co-founder & Contributing Editor. B. 1932, Philadelphia, PA. Princeton, 1954, History, *Phi Beta Kappa. Congressional Quarterly*, Political Editor, to 1969. NBC News, consultant/commentator, national elections, to 1966. CBS News, consultant/commentator, national elections, to 1976. *The Washington Post* Writer's Group, columnist, current, 1975. *National Journal*, co-founder, 1969; Contributing Editor, current. Co-author book series on US states & regions.

Peretz, Martin. *The New Republic.* Editor-in-Chief. B. 1939, NYC. Brandeis, 1959, BA; Harvard, 1965, MA, 1966, PhD; Bard College, 1982, PhD-Hebrew Literature. Woodrow Wilson Fellow, 1959-61. Harvard instructor, 1965-68; Asst Professor, to 1972; Social Studies lecturer, current, 1972. *The New Republic*, Editorial Board Chairman, 1974-75; Editor-in-Chief, current, 1975. U. of MO School of Journalism Medal of Excellence, 1982.

Perry, James. *The Wall Street Journal.* Politics & Features, London. B. 1927, Elmira, NY. Trinity, 1950, English. *Leatherneck Magazine*, 1946. *Hartford Times*, reporter, 1950-52. *Philadelphia Bulletin*, general/rewrite, to 1962. *National Observer*, politics, to 1977. *The Wall Street Journal*, politics, Washington, to 1985; politics, London, current, to 1987; returning to DC to cover the '88 election, June, 1987.

Peters, Charles. *The Washington Monthly.* Editor-in-Chief. B. 1926, Charleston, WVA. Columbia, 1949, Humanities. Poynter Fellow, Yale, 1980. *The Washington Monthly*, Editor-in-Chief, current, 1969. Columbia Journalism Award, 1978.

Pfaff, William W. III. *Los Angeles Times* Syndicate, Political Columnist. *The International Herald Tribune*, Political Columnist. *The New Yorker*, Contributor. B. 1928, Council Bluffs, IA. U. of Notre Dame, 1949, Philosophy of Literature. Rockefeller Grant, International Studies, Columbia's Russian Institute. Infantry, Special Forces Unit, American Army, Korea. *The Commonweal*, editor, 1949-55. Free Europe Organizations & Publications, Director of Research & Publications. Hudson Institute, member, current, 1961. Hudson Research Europe, Ltd., Deputy Director, 1971-78. U. of CA, Regents Lecturer. *Los Angeles Times* Syndicate, political columnist, current. *The International Herald Tribune*, political columnist, current. *The New Yorker*, contributor ("Reflections" Column), current, 1971. Author *Condemned to Freedom*, 1971: co-author (with Edmund Stillman) *The New Politics*, 1961; *The Politics of Hysteria*, 1964; *Power and Impotence*, 1966.

Phalon, Richard. *Forbes.* Contributing Editor. *New York Herald Tribune*, financial writer, 1954-64. *The New York Times*, metro reporter, to 1971; financial writer, to 1980. *Forbes*, from 1980; reported from Japan, 1983-84; opened Pacific bureau, Tokyo, 1985; Contributing Editor, current. Co-recipient NY Newspaper Guild Award, Investigative Journalism; NY Newspaper Reporters Association Award, Investigative Journalism.

Phillips, Kevin. *Los Angeles Times & The Christian Science Monitor.* Contributing Columnist. B. 1940, NYC. Colgate U., 1961, AB, *magna cum laude, Phi Beta Kappa*; U. of Edinburgh, First Class Certificate in Economics; Harvard Law, 1964, JD. Administrative asst to Rep. Paul A. Fino, to 1968. Nixon for President Committee, asst to the Campaign Manager & chief political/voting analyst, 1968. Special asst to the US Attorney General, to 1970. King Features Syndicate, columnist, to 1983. American Political Research Corporation, President, current. *The American Political Report*, Editor & Publisher, current. *Business and Public Affairs Fortnightly*, Editor & Publisher, current. CBS Spectrum & NPR, commentator, current. *Los Angeles Times*, contributing columnist, current. *The Christian Science Monitor*, contributing columnist, current. Author 5 books, including *Staying on Top: The Business Case for A National Industrial Strategy*, 1984.

Pike, Otis G. Newhouse News Service. Columnist. B. 1921, Riverhead, NY. Princeton, 1943, Politics & History; Columbia Law, 1948. US Congressman, from 1961-1979. *Newsday*, Columnist, to 1981. Newhouse News Service, columnist, current, 1981.

Pinkerton, Stewart. *The Wall Street Journal.* Deputy Managing Editor. B. 1942, Minneapolis, MN. Princeton, 1964, AB-English; NY Law School, 1982, JD. *The Wall Street Journal*, news asst, to 1965; Regional Copy Editor, to 1966; reporter, to 1971; "Page One" rewrite, NY, 1971; Managing Editor, Dow Jones Canada, to 1975; Asst NY Bureau Manager, 1975; NY Bureau Manager, to 1983; Asst Managing Editor, to 1985; Deputy Managing Editor, current, 1985.

Platt, Adam. *Insight.* Writer. B. 1958, Washington, DC. Georgetown School of Foreign Service, 1981, Humanities in International Affairs; Columbia School of Journalism, 1984. Business International-Asia Pacific, editorial asst, China desk, to 1983. *Insight*, writer, current, 1985.

Platt, Gordon. *The Journal of Commerce.* Financial Editor. B. 1949, Danbury, CT. Syracuse, 1971, Journalism & Psychology, Newhouse Scholarship, 1967-71. *The Daily Bond Buyer/The Money Manager*/Munifacts News Wire, Associate Editor, to 1980. *The Journal of Commerce*, Asst Managing Editor, to 1986; Financial Editor, current, 1986. Gannett Award, 1971.

Podhoretz, John. *The Washington Times*, "Critic-at-Large" Columnist. *Insight*, Executive Editor. B. 1961, NYC. U. of Chicago, 1982, Political Science. *The American Spectator*, movie critic, to 1982; to 1985. *TIME*, reporter/researcher, to 1984. *The Washington Times*, Features Editor, to 1985; "Critic at Large" columnist, current, 1984. *Insight*, Executive Editor, current, 1985.

Podhoretz, Norman. *Commentary*, Editor. News America Syndicate, Columnist. B. 1930, Brooklyn, NY. Columbia, 1950; Cambridge, 1953, English. *Commentary*, Editor, current, 1960. Freelance contributor, current. News America Syndicate, columnist, current, 1985. Author *Doings and Undoings: The Fifties and After in American Writing*, 1964; *Making It*, 1968; *Breaking Ranks: A Political Memoir*, 1979; *The Present Danger*, 1980; *Why We Were In Vietnam*, 1982; *The Bloody Crossroads: Where Literature and Politics Meet*, 1986.

Pond, Elizabeth. *The Christian Science Monitor.* European Correspondent. Principia College, BA-International Relations; Harvard, MA-Soviet Union Regional Studies. Alicia Patterson Fellow, 1969-70; National Endowment for the Humanities Fellow, U. of MI. *The Christian Science Monitor*, sub-editor (overseas news), to 1967; Saigon correspondent, 1967, 1969; Tokyo correspondent, to 1974; Moscow correspondent, to 1976; European correspondent, current, 1977. *From the Yaroslavsky Station*, 1981 (rev., 1984, 1985): co-author *Der Gefesselte Riese* 1981; *Indochina in Conflict* (Joseph J. Zasloff & Alan E. Goodman), 1972. UCLA Dumont Citation, 1969; Overseas Press Club Citation, 1982.

Powell, Sally. *BusinessWeek.* Senior Editor. B. Budapest, Hungary. *Theatre Arts* magazine, Managing Editor. *Brooklyn Eagle*, Editor, Entertainment Page. *World Telegram*, Copy Editor. *Electronics* magazine, Chief Copy Editor; Associate Managing Editor, to 1970. *BusinessWeek*, creator, book review section, 1970; first woman named Senior Editor, 1980, current, marketing, legal affairs, media, advertising, corporate woman, social issues, & transportation.

Powers, Charles T. *Los Angeles Times.* Nairobi Bureau Chief (on leave). B. 1943, Neosho, MO. KS State U., 1966, BA-Journalism & English. Nieman Fellow, Harvard, 1986-87. *Kansas State Collegian*, Editor, reporter, 1962-66. *The Kansas City Star*, intern, summers 1962, '63, '64; reporter, 1966-69. *Los Angeles Times*, staff writer, to 1971; staff writer, "West Magazine," to 1972; staff writer, "View" section, to 1975; staff writer, NYC, to 1980; Nairobi Bureau Chief, to 1986; currently on leave. *Times* Editorial Award, 1973, '75 (co-winner, 1982).

Prewett, Virginia. Freelance writer. B. Gordonsville, TN. Cumberlain U., NYU. *Chicago Sun-Times* Syndicate. *Washington Daily News*, roving correspondent in Latin America. *The Washington Post*, columnist. *The Washington Times*, columnist, to 1983. *Human Events*, contributor, to 1986. *The*

MediaGuide 339

Wall Street Journal, contributor, to 1986. *The Hemisphere Hotline* (intelligence reports), Editor & Publisher, current, 1970. Also current, freelance writer. Author 3 books. Maria Moors Cabot Medal; Citation, Center for Latin American Studies, U. of FL at Gainesville; Ed Stout Citation, Overseas Press Club.

Prina, L. Edgar. Copley News Service. Senior Correspondent. B. 1917, West New York, NJ. Syracuse, 1938, AB-Political Science & Journalism, 1940, MA-Political Science. *Evening News* (Hornell, NY), Telegraph Ed/editorial writer, to 1941. *The New York Star*, Copy Editor, Asst Night City Editor, to 1948; Washington correspondent, to 1950. *The Evening Star* (Washington), national staff reporter, editorial writer, to 1966. Copley News Service, military affairs correspondent & editor, to 1977; Bureau Chief, to 1984; senior correspondent, specializing national security, current, 1985. Freelance, current. Washington Newspaper Guild Award for Best General News Story; 7 Copley Ring of Truth Awards for Enterprise, Spot News & Interpretive Articles.

Prokesh, Steven. *The New York Times*. "Business Day" Reporter. B. 1953, Geneva, NY. Yale, 1975. UPI, staff writer, to 1978. *BusinessWeek*, Pittsburgh correspondent, to 1980; Cleveland Bureau Chief, to 1982; Management Editor, to 1985. *The New York Times*, "Business Day" reporter, current, 1985.

Pruden, Wesley. *The Washington Times*. Managing Editor & "Pruden on Politics" Columnist. B. 1935, Jackson, MS. Little Rock (AR) Junior College, 1955, History. *Arkansas Gazette* (Little Rock, AR), staff writer, 1952-56. *The Commercial Appeal*, staff writer. US Air Force, 1957. *The National Observer*, staff writer, from 1963, (Vietnam, 1965-68, 1971; Middle East, 1969; London, 1970). Freelance, from 1976. *The Washington Times*, Managing Editor, "Pruden on Politics" columnist, current, 1985.

Putka, Gary. *The Wall Street Journal*. Reporter, London. OH U., 1977, Journalism. *Journal Herald* (Dayton, OH), intern, summer 1975. AP, correspondent/intern, Israel, 1975-76. *Securities Week*, reporter/chief editor, 1977. *BusinessWeek*, reporter/editor, 1980. *The Wall Street Journal*, senior special writer, "Heard on the Market" (NY Markets section), to 1984; reporter, London, current, 1984.

Quinn, Jane Bryant. *Newsweek*, Contributing Editor. *The Washington Post* Writers Group, Financial Columnist. B. 1939, Niagara Falls, NY. Middlebury College, 1960, BA, *magna cum laude*, Phi Beta Kappa. *Insider's Newsletter*, Associate Editor, 1962-65; Co-editor, 1966-67. Cowles Book Co., Senior Editor, 1968. *Business Week Letter*, Editor-in-Chief, to 1973; General Manager, to 1974. *The Washington Post* Writers Group, columnist, current, 1974. *Women's Day Magazine*, contributor, financial columnist, current, 1974. NBC News & Information Service, contributor, 1976-77. WCBS-TV, NYC, business correspondent, 1979; CBS-TV News, current, 1980. *Newsweek*, Contributing Editor, current, 1978. Author *Everyone's Money Book*, 1979; 2nd ed., 1980. John Hancock Award for Excellence in Business & Financial Journalism, 1975; Janus Award for Excellence in TV reporting, 1980; National Press Club Award for Consumer Journalism, 1980, 1982, 1983; Matrix Award, 1983; National Headliner Award for Consistently Outstanding Magazine Feature Column, 1986.

Quinn, John Collins. *USA TODAY*. Editor. B. 1925. Providence College, 1945, AB; Columbia, 1946, MSJ. *The Journal-Bulletin* (Providence, RI), copyboy, reporter, Asst City Editor, Washington correspondent, Asst Managing Editor, Day Managing Editor, 1943-66. Gannett Co., Inc., current, 1966: *Democrat and Chronicle* & *Times Union* (Rochester, NY), Executive Editor, to 1971; Gannett News Service, General Manager, 1967-80; Vice-President, parent company, 1971-75; Senior Vice-President, News & Information, to 1980; Senior Vice-President Chief News Executive, parent company, 1980-83; President, current, 1980; Gannett Co., Executive Vice-President, current; *USA TODAY*, Editor, current, 1983. Editor of the Year Award, National Press Foundation, 1986.

Quinn-Judge, Paul. *The Christian Science Monitor.* Moscow Correspondent. B. 1949, London, UK. Cambridge, 1968-70, Slavonic languages. American Friends Service Committee, aid worker, 1981. Freelance, Southeast Asia, 1981. *Far Eastern Economic Review,* Indochina correspondent, to 1986. *The Christian Science Monitor,* special correspondent, Southeast Asia, 1984; Moscow correspondent, current, 1984.

Quint, Michael. *The New York Times.* "Business Day" Reporter. Antioch College, 1973, BA. *American Banking Daily,* to 1980. *The New York Times,* "Business Day" reporter, current, 1980.

Rachid, Rosalind Kilkenny. *The Journal of Commerce.* Staff Reporter, International Trade (Acting Editor Foreign Trade Dept.). B. 1951, Georgetown, Guyana. CCNY, 1971, BA-French; U. of Madrid, 1971, Certificate in Spanish Language and Literature; NYU, 1985, MA-Journalism. English/French instructor, Uganda, 1973-74. English instructor, Zaire, to 1980. Bear Stearns & Co., Accounts Executive Asst, 1982-85. *Carib News,* freelance reporter, 1982-85. *The Journal of Commerce,* staff reporter, international trade, current, 1985; acting editor, Foreign Trade Dept., current.

Raines, Howell. *The New York Times.* Deputy Editor, Washington Bureau. B. 1943, Birmingham, AL. Birmingham-Southern College, 1964, BA; U. of AL, 1973, MA-English. *The Birmingham Post-Herald,* to 1965. WBRC-TV, Birmingham, to 1968. *The Tuscaloosa News* (AL), to 1970. *The Birmingham News,* reporter, 1971. *Constitution* (Atlanta, GA), Political Editor. *The St. Petersburg Times* (FL), Political Editor, to 1978. *The New York Times,* national correspondent, Atlanta, 1978; chief Atlanta correspondent, to 1982; White House correspondent, to 1985; Deputy Editor, Washington Bureau, current, 1985. Author *Whiskey Man,* 1977; *My Soul Is Rested,* 1977; contributor, *Campaign Money,* 1976.

Raspberry, William J. *The Washington Post & The Washington Post* Writers Group. Urban Affairs Columnist. B. Okolona, MS. Indiana Central College, BA-History. US Army, 1960-62. *Indianapolis Recorder* (IN), reporter-photographer-editor, 1956-60. *The Washington Post,* variety of positions; currently urban affairs columnist. Capitol Press Club Journalist of the Year Award, 1965.

Rauch, Jonathan C. *National Journal.* Staff Correspondent. B. 1960, Phoenix, AZ. Yale, 1982, History. *Winston-Salem Journal. National Journal,* staff correspondent, current.

Redburn, Tom. *Los Angeles Times.* Washington Bureau Reporter. B. 1950, LA, CA. Pomona College, 1972, Sociology/History. *Washington Monthly,* editor-writer, 1974-75. *Environmental Action,* editor-writer, to 1976. *Washington Newsworks,* reporter, 1976. *Los Angeles Times,* business staff, to 1984; Washington bureau reporter, current, 1984. Gerald Loeb Award, 1979; Greater LA Press Club Best Business Story, 1982.

Reed, Fred. *The Washington Times.* Columnist. B. 1945, Bluefield, WVA. Hampden-Sydney College, 1970, History. *The Free Lance-Star* (Fredericksburg, VA), stringer, Israel, 1973. *Army Times,* stringer/staffer, Vietnam, to 1976. Freelance, to 1981. *Federal Times,* columnist, 1978-81. *Soldier of Fortune* magazine, staff writer, 1980-81. *Washingtonian* magazine, staff writer, 1981. *The Washington Times,* military, science & op-ed columnist, current, 1982.

Reed, Julia Evans. *U.S. News & World Report.* Associate Editor. American U., 1984, BA-Political Science. *Newsweek,* Washington bureau staff. *Florida Kiplinger Letter,* reporter, 1984-86. *The Orlando Sentinel,* business reporter, 1984-86. *U.S. News & World Report,* Associate Editor, business, current, 1986.

Reston, James. *The New York Times.* "Washington" Columnist, Consultant. Cincinnati Reds traveling secretary, to 1934. AP, sportswriter, to 1937; writer, London, to 1939. *The New York*

Times, London, to 1945; national correspondent, Washington; diplomatic correspondent, to 1953; Washington Bureau Chief, correspondent, to 1964; Associate Editor, to 1968; Executive Editor in charge of News & Sunday Depts., to 1969; Vice President, 1969-74; member, Board of Directors, 1973; "Washington" columnist, current; consultant, current. Also current, owner *The Vineyard Gazette* (Edgartown, MA), 1968. Pulitzer Prize, 1945; Pulitzer Prize for Distinguished Reporting, 1957.

Revzin, Philip. *The Wall Street Journal.* Paris Bureau Chief. B. Chicago, IL. Stanford, BA-English; Columbia, MA-English. *The Wall Street Journal*, intern, summer 1972; Cleveland bureau reporter, 1974-77; London bureau reporter, to 1980; Asst NY Bureau Chief, to 1983; London Bureau Chief, to 1986; senior correspondent, Paris, 1986; Paris Bureau Chief, current, 1986. Overseas Press Club Citation for Best Business News Reporting from Abroad, 1978.

Richman, Louis S. *FORTUNE.* Associate Editor, Frankfurt, West Germany. Dickenson College (Carlisle, PA), BA-History; Brandeis, MA-Modern & Contemporary History; MIT's Sloan School, MA-Management (Editor, *Sloan Management Review*). Brandeis, History teacher. Hamilton College, History teacher. US Emergency Glass Company (Boston, MA), controller. Arlington, MA, Chamber of Commerce, Executive Director. Arlington, MA, Redevelopment Board member. *FORTUNE*, reporter, 1981; Associate Editor, current, 1982; established first *FORTUNE* editorial office in Frankfurt, West Germany.

Ricklefs, Roger. *The Wall Street Journal.* National Correspondent. B. San Rafael, CA. Harvard, 1961, AB. *The Wall Street Journal*, reporter, NY, 1964-66; reporter, London, to 1970; "Page One" rewrite staff, special writer, NY, to 1972; reporter, page-one features, to 1982; Asst Editor, "Second Front", to 1983; Paris Bureau Chief, to 1986; national correspondent, current, 1986.

Riding, Alan. *The New York Times.* Rio de Janeiro Bureau Chief. B. 1943, Rio de Janeiro, Brazil. Bristol U., England, 1964, Economics; Gray's Inn, London, Law, 1964-66. BBC, 1966. Reuters, London, NY, Buenos Aires, to 1971. Freelance for *The New York Times*, *The Financial Times*, *The Economist*, to 1978. *The New York Times*, Mexico City Bureau Chief, to 1984; Rio de Janeiro Bureau Chief, current, 1984. Overseas Press Club Citation for Excellence, 1973; Maria Moors Cabot Prize for coverage of Mexico & Central America, 1980.

Riemer, Blanca. *BusinessWeek.* Washington Correspondent. B. Lima, Peru. Sorbonne, Paris, France, 1966, Diploma in Literature; *Institut d'Etudes Politiques*, Paris, 1968, Diploma of International Relations. Walter Bagehot Fellowship Program in Economic and Business Journalism, participant, Columbia, 1983. *Agence France-Presse*, financial reporter, Paris; economics correspondent, NY; economics correspondent, Washington. McGraw-Hill World News, correspondent, Bogota, Columbia, to 1983. *BusinessWeek*, Washington correspondent covering monetary policy & international finance, Washington, current.

Robbins, William H. *The New York Times.* Kansas City Bureau Chief. B. 1924, Lumberton, NC. Wake Forest College, 1948, BA; MA, 1949. Wake Forest College, English instructor, to 1950. *The Wilmington Star* (NC), reporter. *The Richmond Times-Dispatch* (VA), reporter. *The Sun* (Baltimore, MD), reporter. *Motor Magazine*, Managing Editor, 1957-58. *The New York Times*, copy editor, business news dept.; national copy desk; Asst Real Estate Editor, to 1969; Asst News Editor, agriculture reporter, Washington bureau; business reporter, Chicago, to 1980; Philadelphia Bureau Chief, to 1985; Kansas City Bureau Chief, current, 1985. Author *The American Food Scandal*, 1973.

Roberts, Steven V. *The New York Times.* Chief Congressional Correspondent. B. 1943, Bayonne, NJ. Harvard, 1964, Government, *magna cum laude*. *The Harvard Crimson*, Editor. *The New York Times*, research asst to James Reston, to 1965; city staff reporter, to 1968; covered national political issues, 1968 campaign; LA Bureau Chief, to 1974; Athens Bureau Chief, to 1977; Washington bureau reporter, to 1980; Congressional correspondent, to 1984; chief Congressional correspondent, current, 1984. Freelance, current. Elected to membership, Standing Committee of Correspondents, 1984. Author *Eureka*, 1974.

Robinson, Anthony Edward. *Financial Times.* Johannesburg Correspondent. B. 1942, Grimsby, Lincolnshire, UK. London School of Economics, BS-Economics. Reuters, London, Brussels, Milan, 1967-71. *Financial Times,* Rome correspondent, to 1976; London, 1977; East Europe correspondent, to 1982; Moscow correspondent, to 1983; Johannesburg correspondent, current, 1984.

Rogers, Ed. *The Washington Times.* National News Reporter. B. 1917, Ashburn, GA. U. of GA, 1938, ABJ; Woodrow Wilson School of Law, 1957, LLB. *The Atlanta Georgian,* to 1938. Insurance claims adjuster, to 1941. *The Nashville Banner,* 1941. US Naval Reserve, to 1946. UPI, reporter/desk, Florida, Atlanta, Washington, to 1982. *The Washington Times,* national news reporter, current, 1982.

Rogers, Michael. *FORTUNE.* Reporter/Researcher. B. NYC. Haverford College, BA; Northwestern, MSJ. *The Ledger* (Lakeland, FL), reporter, to 1983. *FORTUNE,* reporter/researcher, current, 1983.

Ropelewski, Robert R. *Aviation Week & Space Technology.* B. 1942, Erie, PA. PA State U., 1965, Engineering, Journalism. *Aviation Week & Space Technology,* Engineering Editor, LA, 1972; Paris Bureau Chief to 1978; European Editor, 1978; LA Bureau Chief to 1984; Senior Military Editor, Washington, to 1985; Washington Bureau Chief, current, 1985. Writing Award, Aviation/Space Writers Association, 1976 for series entitled, "Both Sides of the Suez".

Rosenbaum, David E. *The New York Times.* Washington Bureau Correspondent. B. 1942, Miami, FL. Dartmouth, 1963, AB; Columbia, 1965, MSJ. Borden Graduate Award, Pulitzer Traveling fellowship. *The St. Petersburg Times,* to 1966. *Ilford Recorder* (UK), 1966. *Congressional Quarterly,* to 1968. *The New York Times,* reporter, editor, Washington, to 1981; Enterprise Editor, NY, to 1984; correspondent specializing taxes, economic & domestic policy issues, Washington, current, 1984.

Rosenblatt, Robert A. *Los Angeles Times.* Washington Correspondent. B. 1943, NYC. CCNY, 1964, BA-Economics; Columbia, 1966, MSJ. *Broadcasting Magazine,* reporter, to 1965. *The Charlotte Observer* (NC), reporter, 1966-69. *Los Angeles Times,* financial news reporter, to 1976; Washington correspondent, specializing issues involving aging & the elderly, current, 1976. Gerald Loeb Financial Journalism Award, 1978.

Rosenfeld, Stephen. *The Washington Post.* Deputy Editorial Page Editor & Columnist. B. 1932, Pittsfield, MA. Harvard, 1953, BA-European History & Literature. US Marine, 1953-55. *The Berkshire Eagle,* to 1957. Columbia's Russian Institute, to 1959. *The Washington Post,* city staff, to 1962; editorial writer, to 1964, 1966-82; Moscow correspondent, 1964-65; Deputy Editorial Page Editor, current, 1982; columnist, current. Author *The Time of Their Dying,* 1977: co-author (with Barbara Rosenfeld) *Return from Red Square,* 1967.

Rosenthal, Abraham Michael. *The New York Times.* Associate Editor & Op-Ed Columnist. B. 1922, Sault Ste. Marie, Ontario, Canada. CCNY, 1944, BS-Social Science. *The New York Times,* UN correspondent, to 1954; based in India, to 1958; Warsaw, to 1959; Geneva, to 1961; Tokyo, to 1963; Metro Editor, NY, to 1966; Asst Managing Editor, to 1968; Associate Managing Editor, to 1969; Managing Editor, to 1977; Executive Editor, to 1986; Associate Editor & Op-Ed columnist, current, 1986. Author *38 Witnesses*: co-author *One More Victim; The Night The Lights Went Out; The Pope's Visit to the U.S..* Overseas Press Club Citation for work in India, 1956, & for work in India & Poland, 1959; Pulitzer Prize for International Reporting, 1960; Number One Award, 1960; George Polk Memorial Award, 1960, 1965; Page One Award, NY Newspaper Guild, 1960.

MediaGuide

Rosenthal, Jack. *The New York Times.* Editorial Page Editor. B. 1935, Tel Aviv. Harvard, 1956, AB-History. *The Harvard Crimson,* Executive Editor. *The Oregonian* (Portland, OR), reporter, editor. Press officer, State Dept. & Justice Dept., 1966-69. *The New York Times,* Washington bureau reporter, to 1973, *The New York Times Magazine,* asst Sunday Editor; editorial writer; Deputy Editor of the Editorial Page, to 1986; Editorial Page Editor, current, 1986. Pulitzer Prize for Editorial Writing, 1982.

Rosett, Claudia. *The Asian Wall Street Journal.* Editorial Page Editor. B. 1955, New Haven, CT. Yale, 1976, Intensive English. Freelance, Chile, South America, 1981-82; New York, to 1984. *Policy Review,* 1984. *The Wall Street Journal,* Book Editor, editorial section, to 1986. *The Asian Wall Street Journal,* Editorial Page Editor, current, 1986.

Rosewicz, Barbara. *The Wall Street Journal.* Middle East Correspondent. U. of KS, 1978, BA-Journalism. UPI, reporter, Dallas; reporter (Topeka, KS); Topeka Bureau Chief, to 1981; Supreme Court reporter; Congressional reporter, to 1984. *The Wall Street Journal,* NY bureau, to 1985; Middle East correspondent, Cairo, current, 1985.

Rotbart, Dean. *The Wall Street Journal.* News Editor. Northwestern, 1979; Columbia, 1980, MSJ. *Binghamton Evening Press,* intern, summer, 1978. *The Wall Street Journal,* intern, summer, 1979; reporter, Dallas, Denver, Cleveland, to 1984; one of 3 "Heard on the Street" columnists, to 1986; News Editor, current, 1986. 19th Annual John Hancock Award for Excellence in Business & Financial Journalism; NY State Publishers' Award for Excellence in Governmental Reporting, 1978.

Rothstein, Edward. *The New Republic.* Music Critic. B. 1953, Brooklyn, NY. Yale, 1973, Intensive Mathematics; Brandeis, 1974, coursework for MA in Mathematics; Columbia, 1978; MA-English Literature; U. of Chicago, 1978-80, Humanities Fellow, Committee on Social Thought (residency completed for PhD). *The New York Times,* music critic, to 1984. *The New Republic,* music critic, current, 1984. Freelance work, current, 1976. Also current, Senior Editor, *The Free Press,* Macmillan, Inc. Bennett Prize in Comparative Literature, Columbia, 1978; Publisher's Award, *The New York Times,* 1981.

Rowe, James L. Jr. *The Washington Post.* Domestic/International Finance/Economics Correspondent. B. 1948, Chicago, IL. Catholic U. of America, 1969, AB-Economics; U. of WI, 1969-70, grad work Economics, Soviet Studies. *The Washington Post,* domestic economic affairs reporter, to 1978; NY financial correspondent, to 1981; domestic & international finance & economics specializing in US banking & Latin American economics, current, 1982.

Rowe, Sandra Mims. *The Virginian-Pilot & The Ledger-Star.* Executive Editor. B. 1948, Charlotte, NC. East Carolina U., 1970, English. *The Ledger-Star,* reporter, to 1976; Asst City Editor, to 1977; "Daily Break" Editor, to 1978; Asst Managing Editor, to 1980; Managing Editor, to 1982. *The Virginian-Pilot & The Ledger-Star,* Managing Editor, to 1984; Executive Editor, current, 1984.

Rowen, Hobart. *The Washington Post.* Economics Editor & Columnist. B. 1918, Burlington, VT. CCNY, 1938, BSS Honors, Government & Sociology. *New York Journal of Commerce,* reporter, to 1942. *Newsweek,* Washington correspondent, "Business Trends" Editor, 1944-65. *The Washington Post,* Financial Editor, to 1969; Asst Managing Editor, to 1975; Economics Editor & columnist, current, 1975. *The Washington Post* Writer's Group, columnist, current, 1975. Also current, panelist, "Washington Week in Review," PBS. Author *The Free Enterprisers: Kennedy, Johnson and the Business Establishment,* 1964: co-author *Bad Times and Beyond,* 1974; *The Fall of the President,* 1974. Sigma Delta Chi Distinguished Service Award, 1960; John Hancock Distinguished Service Award, 1966; Gerald Loeb Award for Business News Reporting, 1977; Journalist of the Year, National Economic Association, 1984; *Washington Journalism Review,* Best in the Business, 1985.

Royko, Mike. *Chicago Tribune.* Columnist. B. 1935, Chicago, IL. Wright Junior College, 1951-52. US Air Force, to 1956. Chicago Northside Newspapers, reporter, 1956. Chicago City News Bureau, reporter, Asst City Editor, to 1959. *Chicago Daily News,* columnist, to 1978; Associate Editor, 1977-78. *Chicago Sun-Times,* columnist, to 1984. *Chicago Tribune,* columnist, current, 1984. Author *Up Against It,* 1967; *I May Be Wrong But I Doubt It,* 1968; *Boss - Richard J. Daley of Chicago,* 1971; *Slats Grobnik and Other Friends,* 1973. Heywood Broun Award, 1968; Pulitzer Prize for Commentary, 1972; U. of MO School of Journalism Medal for Service, 1979; named to Chicago Press Club Journalism Hall of Fame, 1980.

Royster, Vermont. *The Wall Street Journal.* Public Affairs Columnist. B. 1914, Raleigh, NC. U. of NC, 1935, Classical Languages (Latin & Greek). *The Wall Street Journal,* Washington correspondent to 1940; Chief Washington Correspondent to 1950; Associate Editor to 1958; Editor, to 1971; Public Affairs Columnist, to 1986, retired 1986. Author *My Own, My Country's Time,* 1983; *A Pride of Prejudices,* 1967; *Journey Through the Soviet Union,* 1962; *The Essential Royster* (selected by Edmund Fuller), 1985. Two Pulitzer Prizes, 1953, '84; Fourth Estate Award, National Press Club, Washington, 1984; Medal for Distinguished Service in Journalism, Sigma Delta Chi, 1958; Presidential Medal of Freedom, 1986.

Ruby, Michael. *U.S. News & World Report.* Executive Editor. U. of MO, BSJ. Neiman Fellow, Harvard, 1974-75. *BusinessWeek,* correspondent, acting Bureau Chief, Chicago, writer, NY, 1966-71. *Newsweek,* business writer, to 1978; Senior Editor, business, to 1981; National Affairs Editor, to 1982; Managing Editor, international editions, to 1983; Chief of Correspondents; Asst Managing Editor, to 1986. *U.S. News & World Report,* Executive Editor, current, 1986.

Rudnitsky, Howard. *Forbes.* Senior Editor. CCNY, Baruch School, 1959, BBS. Moody's Investor Services. *Forbes,* Statistical Dept. Head, 1961-69; staff writer; Associate Editor, to 1978; Senior Editor, current, 1978. Co-winner (with Allan Sloan) Loeb Award, 1985.

Rukeyser, William Simon. Formerly of *FORTUNE.* B. 1939, NYC. Princeton, 1961, AB; Christ's College, Cambridge, 1962-63. *The Wall Street Journal,* copyreader, 1961-62; staff reporter, Europe, 1963-67. *FORTUNE,* Associate Editor, to 1971; member, Board of Editors, to 1972. *Money,* Managing Editor, to 1980. *FORTUNE,* Managing Editor, to 1986.

Rule, Sheila. *The New York Times.* Nairobi Bureau Chief. B. 1950, St. Louis, MO. U. of MO at Columbia, 1972, Journalism. *St. Louis Post-Dispatch,* reporter, to 1977. *The New York Times,* metro reporter, to 1984; temporary assignment, Nairobi, to 1985; Nairobi Bureau Chief, current, 1985. Meyer Berger Award, 1985.

Rusher, William Allen. *National Review.* Publisher. B. 1923, Chicago, IL. Princeton, 1943, AB; Harvard, 1948, JD. US Army Air Force, 1943-46. Shearman & Sterling & Wright, NYC, associate, 1948-56. NY Senate Finance Committee, special counsel, 1955. US Senate, Internal Security Subcommittee, associate counsel, 1956-57. *National Review,* Publisher, current, 1957; Director, Vice-president, National Review, Inc., current. Universal Press Syndicate, columnist, 1973-82. Newspaper Enterprise Association, "The Conservative Advocate" columnist, current, 1982. Author *Special Counsel,* 1968; *The Making of the New Majority Party,* 1975; *How to Win Arguments,* 1981; *The Rise of the Right,* 1984: co-author (with Mark Hatfield and Arlie Schardt) *Amnesty?,* 1973.

Ryskind, Allan H. *Human Events.* Capitol Hill Editor. B. 1934, NY. Pomona College, 1956, BA-Political Science; UCLA, 1959, MA. City News Service, Los Angeles, summer 1959. *Human Events,* Asst Editor, to 1967; Capitol Hill Editor, current, 1967; also co-owner. Author *Hubert* (biography of Hubert Humphrey), 1968.

Safire, William. *The New York Times.* Columnist. B. 1929, NYC. Attended Syracuse, 1947-49. *New York Herald Tribune* Syndicate, reporter, to 1951. WNBC-WNBT, Europe & Middle East correspondent, to 1951. US Army correspondent, to 1954. WNBC, NYC, radio & tv producer, to 1955. Tex McCrary Inc., Vice-president, to 1960. Safire Public Relations, Inc., President, to 1968. Special asst to President Nixon, to 1973. *The New York Times*, "Essay" columnist, current, 1973; "On Language" columnist, (*The New York Times Magazine)*, current, 1979. Author 8 books, including *I Stand Corrected*, 1984: co-author *Plunging Into Politics* (with Marshall Loeb), 1964; *What's The Good Word?* (with Leonard Safir), 1982. Pulitzer Prize for Distinguished Commentary, 1978.

Salamon, Julie. *The Wall Street Journal.* Film Critic, Leisure & Arts Page. B. Seaman, OH. Tufts, 1975, BA; NYU, 1978, JD. *Tufts Observer*, Editor. *The Pittsburgh Press*, intern, 1976. *The New York Times*, freelance reporter, 1978. *The Wall Street Journal*, intern, summer 1977; reporter, 1978-83; film critic, Leisure & Arts Page, current, 1983. "Front Page" Award for Criticism, NY Newswomen's Club, 1985.

Salpukas, Agis. *The New York Times.* Transportation Reporter. B. 1939, Kaunas, Lithuania. Long Island U., 1962, History & German; Columbia, 1965, MA. *The New York Times*, Suffolk Cty LI reporter, to 1970; reporter, Detroit bureau, to 1973; Detroit Bureau Chief, to 1976; "Business Day" reporter, to 1981; Transportation, airlines, trucking & railroads reporter, current, 1981. Sigma Delta Chi award.

Sanger, David E. *The New York Times.* Technology Reporter. B. 1960, White Plains, NY. Harvard, 1982, Government. *The New York Times*, college stringer, to 1982; news clerk, to 1983; technology reporter, current, 1983.

Sanoff, Alvin P. *U.S. News & World Report.* Social Trends Senior Editor. B. 1941, NYC. Harvard, 1963, Sociology. NEH Fellow, U. of MI, 1974-75. *The Sun* (Baltimore, MD), reporter, editorial writing, 1967-71. *Dayton Journal Herald* (OH), Editorial Page Editor, to 1977. *U.S. News & World Report*, Associate Editor; Senior Editor, social trends, current. OH AP Award for Best Editorial Writing, 1974.

Saporito, Bill. *FORTUNE.* Associate Editor. B. Harrison, NJ. Bucknell, BA-American Studies; Syracuse, MA-Journalism. *New York Daily News*, 1978. *Chain Store Age Supermarkets* Magazine, Senior Editor. Freelance writer, 1982-84. *FORTUNE*, Associate Editor, current, 1984; established editorial office, Pittsburgh, PA.

Scharff, Edward E. *Institutional Investor.* Senior Editor. B. 1946, St. Louis, MO. Princeton, 1968, English. *The Washington Star*, covered Capitol Hill; Washington & VA local politics; sociological & demographic trends; business, 1970-78. *Money*, covered personal finance, to 1980. *TIME*, "Economy & Business" section, to 1982. *Institutional Investor*, Senior Editor, current, 1983. Author *Worldly Power, The Making of The Wall Street Journal*, 1986. Washington-Baltimore Newspaper Guild Front Page Award, 1974; nominee, Pulitzer Prize, 1974.

Schiebla, Shirley Hobbs. *Barron's.* Washington Editor. B. Newport News, VA. William & Mary, U. of NC, BA. *The Wall Street Journal*, Washington correspondent. Founded/ran own Washington news bureau. *Financial Times*, correspondent. *The Richmond News Leader*, correspondent. *Daily Press* (Newport News, VA), correspondent. *Barron's*, part-time writer, 1958-62; Associate Editor, to 1967; Washington Editor, current, 1967. Author *Poverty Is Where the Money Is*, 1968.

Schiffren, Lisa. *The Detroit News.* Editorial Writer. B. 1959, NYC. Bryn Mawr, 1982, AB-History. *The Washington Times*, reporter, 1984. *The Detroit News*, editorial writer, current, 1984. 2nd Place MI UPI Editorial Award, 1985; 1st Place MI AP Editorial Award, 1985; 1st Place UPI Editorial Award, 1986; 1st Place Detroit Press Club Foundation Editorial Award, 1986.

Schmemann, Serge. *The New York Times.* Moscow Bureau Chief. B. 1945, France. Harvard, 1967, BA-English; Columbia, 1971, MA-Slavic Studies. AP, to 1980. *The New York Times*, metro staff member, to 1981; Moscow correspondent, to 1984; Moscow Bureau Chief, current, 1984.

Schmertz, Herbert. Heritage Features Syndicate. "For the Record" Columnist. B. 1930, Yonkers, NY. Union College, 1952, AB; Columbia, 1955, LLB. American Arbitration Association, member. Federal Mediation & Conciliation Service, general counsel, asst to the Director, to 1966. Mobil Oil Corporation, currently Director & Vice-president. Heritage Features Syndicate, "For the Record" columnist, current. Author *Good-bye to the Low Profile:* co-author *Takeover.*

Schnanche, Don A. *Los Angeles Times.* Rome Bureau Chief. B. 1926, New Brunswick, NJ. U. of GA, 1949, Journalism. *Marietta Daily Journal* (GA), reporter, City Editor, to 1950. International News Service, Southern correspondent, to 1950; war correspondent, Korea, to 1952. Reuters-AAP, Tokyo, 1952. *Sports Illustrated*, founding staff & staff writer, 1953-54. *LIFE*, NY reporter, 1953; Asst Editor, Military Affairs, 1955-57; Washington correspondent, Military & Space, to 1960. *Saturday Evening Post*, Washington Bureau Chief & Contributing Editor, to 1963; Executive Editor, Managing Editor, to 1964. *Holiday* Magazine, Editor-in-Chief, to 1967. Communicaid, Inc., President, to 1968. Freelance writer, 1967-76. *Los Angeles Times*, Cairo Bureau Chief, to 1982; Rome Bureau Chief, current, 1982. Author *Man High*, 1959; *Mister Pop*, 1970; *Panther Paradox*, 1970.

Schneider, Keith. *The New York Times.* Washington Bureau Reporter. B. 1956, White Plains, NY. Haverford College, 1978. Freelance writer, to 1979. *Wilkes-Barre Times Leader* (PA), reporter, 1979. *The News and Courier* (SC), reporter, to 1981. Two independent news services, Editor, to 1985. *The New York Times*, reporter, Washington bureau, current, 1985. George Polk Award for Investigative Reporting, 1984.

Schulz, William. *Reader's Digest.* Washington Editor/Bureau Chief. B. 1939, NYC. Antioch College, 1961, Political Science. Fulton Lewis Jr. King Features Syndicated Column, ghostwriter, to 1966. *Reader's Digest*, Associate Editor, to 1971; Senior Editor, to 1973; Washington Editor/Bureau Chief, current, 1973.

Schumacher, Edward. *The New York Times.* Madrid Bureau Chief. B. 1946, Barranquilla, Colombia. Vanderbilt, 1968, BA; Tufts, Fletcher School of Law & Diplomacy, 1973, MA. US Army, to 1971. *The Quincy Patriot Ledger* (MA), reporter, 1971-74, 1975-77. Fulbright Fellow, Japan, 1974. *The Philadelphia Inquirer*, reporter, to 1979. *The New York Times*, metro reporter, 1979; Buenos Aires Bureau Chief, to 1984; Madrid Bureau Chief, current, 1984.

Sciolino, Elaine. *The New York Times.* UN Bureau Chief. B. 1948, Buffalo, NY. Canisius College (Buffalo, NY), 1970; NYU, 1971, MA-History. *Newsweek*, reporter; Paris correspondent, to 1980; Rome Bureau Chief, to 1982; roving international correspondent, 1983-84. Edward R. Murrow Press Fellow, 1982-83. *The New York Times*, metro reporter, to 1985; UN Bureau Chief, current, 1985. Page One Award, 1978; Religious Public Relations Council Merit Award, 1979; Overseas Press Club Citation for Magazine Reporting from Abroad, 1983: co-winner National Headliners Award for Outstanding Coverage of a Major News Event, 1981.

Seib, Gerald F. *The Wall Street Journal.* Middle East Correspondent. U. of KS, 1978, BSJ. *Daily Kansan*, Editor, fall 1977. Sears Foundation Congressional intern, office of US Representative Gillis Long (LA), spring 1978. *The Wall Street Journal*, Dallas bureau intern, summer 1977; Dallas bureau reporter, 1978-80; Washington bureau Pentagon/State Dept. reporter, to 1984; Middle East correspondent, current, 1984.

MediaGuide 347

Seiler, John. *The Washington Times.* Editorial Page Writer. B. 1955, Detroit, MI. Hillsdale College, 1977, Political Economy. *Colorado Springs Gazette-Telegraph* (CO), reporter, to 1978. US Army, to 1982. *University Bookman*, Asst Editor, 1982. *Conservative Digest*, Asst Editor, to 1983. *The American Sentinel* newsletter, Editor, to 1985; Asst Editor, 1986. *The Washington Times*, Editorial Page writer, current, 1986. Freelance work, current.

Seligman, Daniel. *FORTUNE.* Associate Managing Editor. B. 1924, NYC. Rutgers; NYU, AB. *The New Leader*, 1946; labor columnist, 1949-50. *The American Mercury*, Asst Editor, 1946-50. *FORTUNE*, Associate Editor, to 1959; Board of Editors member, to 1966; Asst Managing Editor, to 1969. Time, Inc., Senior Staff Editor, 1969. *FORTUNE*, Executive Editor, to 1977; Associate Managing Editor, current, 1977; "Keeping Up" columnist, also current.

Sellers, Patricia. *FORTUNE.* Reporter/Researcher. U. of Charlottesville (VA), BA-English, *Phi Beta Kappa. Washington Business Journal*, staff writer, to 1984. *FORTUNE*, reporter/researcher, current, 1984.

Sellers, Valita. *The Wall Street Journal.* News Assistant, Philadelphia. *The Wall Street Journal*, news asst, NY, 1984-85; news asst, Philadelphia, to 5/86.

Semple, Robert B. Jr. *The New York Times.* Editor of the Op-Ed Page. B. 1936, St. Louis, MO. Yale, 1959; Berkeley, 1961, MA-History. *The New York Times*, reporter, political reporter, White House correspondent, Washington, to 1973; Deputy National Editor, to 1975; London Bureau Chief, to 1977; Foreign Editor, to 1982; Editor, Op-Ed Page, current, 1982. Also current, appearances on NBC-TV "Meet the Press."

Seneker, Harold. *Forbes.* Senior Editor. B. Philadelphia, PA. PA State U. 1967, BA-Biology. Value Line analyst, to 1970. Trade papers, to 1976. *Forbes*, Senior Editor, current. Developer, Forbes 400.

Shabecoff, Philip. *The New York Times.* Washington Bureau Reporter. B. 1934, Bronx, NY. Hunter College, BA; U. of Chicago, MA. *The New York Times*, newsroom stenographer, 1959-60; news asst, business & financial dept., to 1962; foreign trade reporter, to 1964; foreign correspondent, West Germany, to 1968; foreign correspondent, Tokyo, to 1970; Washington bureau reporter, current, 1970, environmental news/issues. Contributor *The Presidency Reappraised; American Government.*

Shapiro, Robert J. *U.S. News & World Report.* Associate Editor, "Tomorrow" Columnist. B. 1950, Baltimore, MD. U. of Chicago, 1970, AB-Committee on the Analysis of Ideas & Study of Method, high honors; London School of Economics, 1972, MS-Political Theory; Harvard, 1980, MA, PhD-Political Theory, Government. Institute of Policy Studies, Fellow, 1972-73. Harvard, Fellow, 1975-77. National Bureau of Economic Research, Fellow, 1980-81. Legislative aide to Senator Daniel P. Moynihan, to 1983; Legislative Director to Mr. Moynihan, to 1985. *U.S. News & World Report*, Associate Editor, current, 1986; "Tomorrow" columnist, current, 1986.

Shapiro, Walter. *Newsweek.* General Editor/National Affairs Writer. B. 1947, NYC. U. of MI, 1970, BA-History; 1971, grad work, European History. *Congressional Quarterly*, reporter, to 1970. *Washington Monthly*, Editor, to 1976; Contributing Editor, current, 1976. Special asst/press secretary to Secretary of Labor Ray Marshall, to 1978. Speechwriter to President Carter, 1979. *The Washington Post*, staff writer for the Sunday magazine, to 1983. *Newsweek*, General Editor/national affairs writer, current, 1983.

Shaw, Desmond. *The Weekly.* Washington Bureau Chief & Columnist. B. 1939, Boston, MA. Boston College, 1960, Journalism. *Boston Gazette*, reporter to 1965; Washington bureau, to 1968. *The Weekly*, correspondent, Saigon bureau, to 1971; Washington bureau to 1980; Chief, political section (NY), to 1985; Washington Bureau Chief & columnist, current, 1985.

Shaw, Terri. *The Washington Post.* Foreign Correspondent. B. 1940, Washington, DC. Antioch College, 1963, BA; Columbia, 1965, MSJ. *Buffalo Courier-Express*, to 1964. AP, to 1970. Freelance work, South America, 1966-67. *The Washington Post*, foreign correspondent, current, 1970.

Sheils, Merrill. *U.S. News & World Report.* Writer/Editor. Smith College. *Newsweek*, religion researcher, religion & education writer, to 1975; Education Editor, to 1977; business writer, Business Editor, to 1983; National Affairs Editor, to 1985; developer, *Newsweek's* redesign, to 1986. *U.S. News & World Report*, writer, editor, current, 1987.

Shepard, Stephen B. *BusinessWeek.* Editor-in-Chief. CCNY, 1961; Columbia, 1964, MS. Columbia Graduate School of Journalism, adjunct professor, 1970-75; Founder/Director, Walter Bagehot Fellowship Program in Economics & Business Journalism. *Newsweek*, Senior Editor, National Affairs, to 1980. *Saturday Review*, Editor, to 1982. *BusinessWeek*, Editor, 1965-76; Executive Editor, 1982-84; Editor-in-Chief, current, 1984. Freelance articles. National Magazine Award; Sigma Delta Chi Headliners Award; U. of MO Award.

Shenon, Philip. *The New York Times.* Washington Bureau Reporter. B. 1959. Brown, 1981, English, *magna cum laude*. *The Brown Daily Herald*, Editor-in-Chief, President. *The New York Times*, James Reston's clerk, to 1982; copyboy, financial desk, to 1983; metro reporter, to 1985; reporter, Washington bureau, current, 1985.

Sherman, Stratford P. *FORTUNE.* Associate Editor. Harvard, *cum laude*. *Harvard Lampoon*, writer. Taught in the Netherlands Antilles. William Morrow Co., editorial asst, to 1977. *FORTUNE*, reporter/researcher, to 1982; Associate Editor, current, 1982.

Shields, Mark. *The Washington Post.* Columnist. B. 1937, Weymouth, MA. U. of Notre Dame, 1959, Philosophy/History. Government asst, various positions. *The Washington Post*, editorial writer, 1979-81; columnist, current, 1979. Mutual Radio Network, 5 times/week commentary, 1984. CBS-TV, on-air analyst, 1984 Republican & Democratic conventions, campaign & election night. WMAL radio, ABC Washington, 5 times/week commentary, to 1986. Author *On the Campaign Trail*, 1985. Washington Dateline Award for Local Journalism, Sigma Delta Chi, 1985.

Shiner, Josette S. *The Washington Times*, Deputy Managing Editor. B. 1954, Orange, NJ. U. of CO, 1976, Communications. *The New York News World*, National Desk Editor, 1976; Washington bureau, 1977. *The Washington Times*, Features Editor, 1982; Asst Managing Editor, 1985; Deputy Managing Editor, current, 1985. National Press Club's Vivian Award & Meritorious Service Recognition, 1981; U. of GA Atrium Award, 1984.

Shogan, Robert. *Los Angeles Times.* National Political Correspondent. B. 1930, NYC. Syracuse, 1951, Journalism-American Studies. *Detroit Free Press*, 1956-59; *Miami News* Telegraph Editor to 1961; *The Wall Street Journal*, Asst Editor to 1965; Peace Corps, evaluation officer, 1966; *Newsweek* correspondent to 1972. *Los Angeles Times*, national political correspondent, current, 1973. Author *None of the Above*, 1982; *Promises to Keep*, 1977; *A Question of Judgement*, 1972: co-author (with Tom Craig) *Detroit Race Riot*. MI AP Sweepstakes, 1st Place Feature Writing, 1958.

Shribman, David. *The Wall Street Journal.* National Political Reporter. Dartmouth, 1976, AB-History; Cambridge, graduate fellow, to 1977. *Buffalo Evening News*, metro reporter, to 1979; Washington bureau reporter, to 1980. *The Washington Star*, reporter. *The New York Times*, feature writer; Congressional correspondent; national politics reporter, to 1984. *The Wall Street Journal*, national political reporter, Washington, current, 1984.

Sidey, Hugh. *TIME.* Washington Contributing Editor. B. 1927, Greenfield, IA. IA State U., 1950, BS. US Army, 1945-46. *Adair City Free Press* (IA), reporter, 1950. *The Nonpariel* (Council Bluffs, IA), reporter, to 1951. *Omaha World-Herald*, reporter, to 1955. *LIFE Magazine*, correspondent, to 1958. *TIME*, correspondent, to 1966; columnist, to 1969; chief, to 1978; Washington Contributing Editor, current, 1978. Author *John F. Kennedy, President,* 1963; *A Very Personal Presidency, Lyndon Johnson in the White House,* 1966; *These United States,* 1975; *Portrait of a President,* 1975.

Sieff, Martin. *The Washington Times.* Assistant Foreign Desk Editor/Soviet & Middle East Affairs Editor. B. 1950, Belfast, Northern Ireland. Exeter College, Oxford, Modern History; London School of Economics, grad work. *Jerusalem Post*, researcher, Middle East affairs analyst, to 1979. *Belfast Telegraph*, Copy Editor, Production Editor, to 1984. *Belfast Newsletter*, Copy Editor, Foreign News Editor, to 1985. *The Washington Times*, Asst Foreign Desk Editor, Soviet & Middle East Affairs Editor, current, 1986.

Silk, Leonard. *The New York Times.* Economics Columnist. B. 1918, Philadelphia, PA. U. of WI, 1940, AB; Duke, 1947, PhD, *Phi Beta Kappa*. Senior Fellow, Brookings Institution, 1969-70. Poytner Fellow, Yale, 1974-75. Duke, Economics instructor, 1941-42. US Army Air Forces, to 1945. U. of ME, Economics instructor, to 1948. Simmons College, Asst Professor, Economics, to 1950. US Mission to NATO, Asst Economic Commissioner, 1952-54. *BusinessWeek*, Economics Editor, to 1964; Senior Editor, 1959-66; Vice-chairman & Economist, to 1967; Editorial Page Editor & Chairman of the Editorial Board, to 1969. *The New York Times*, Editorial Board member, to 1976; Economics columnist, "The Economic Scene," current, 1976. Author 11 books, most recently *Economics in the Real World,* 1985: co-author *The World of Economics* (with Professor Phillip Saunders), 1969; *A Primer on Business Forecasting* (with Louise M. Curley), 1970, 1973; *The American Establishment* (with Mark Silk), 1980; *Reagan: The Man, the President* (with Hedrick Smith *et al.*), 1981. Loeb Award for Distinguished Business & Financial Journalism, 1961, '66, '67, '71, '72; Gerald Loeb Memorial Award, 1977; Overseas Press Club Citation for Foreign Economic Reporting, 1967; Overseas Press Club Bache Award for Best Business Reporting from Abroad, 1972; Elliot V. Bell Award, 1983.

Simison, Robert L. *The Wall Street Journal*/Europe. "Page One" Editor. B. Waukon, IA. U. of KS, 1974, BSJ. *The Wall Street Journal*, reporter, Dallas, to 1978; reporter, Detroit, to 1984; special writer, Dallas, to 1985; Dallas Deputy Bureau Chief, to 1986; *The Wall Street Journal*/Europe, "Page One" Editor, current, 1986.

Simonds, John E. *Honolulu Star-Bulletin.* Executive Editor. B. 1935, Boston, MA. Bowdoin College (Brunswick, ME), 1957, English. *Daily Tribune* (Seymour, IN), reporter, to 1958. UPI, reporter, to 1960. *The Journal* (Providence, RI), reporter; Asst City Editor, to 1965. *Washington Evening Star*, reporter; Asst City Editor, to 1966. Gannett News Service, correspondent (Washington), to 1975. *Honolulu Star-Bulletin*, Managing Editor, to 1980; Executive Editor, current, 1980.

Simons, Lewis M. *San Jose Mercury News*/Knight-Ridder Newspapers. Tokyo Bureau Chief. B. 1939, Paterson, NJ. NYU, 1962, English Literature; Columbia, 1964, MSJ. US Marines, 1962-64. AP, Denver correspondent, to 1967; Saigon correspondent, to 1968; Malaysia/Singapore Bureau Chief, to 1970. *The Washington Post*, New Delhi Bureau Chief, to 1975; Bangkok Bureau Chief, to 1978; metro staff, to 1982. *San Jose Mercury News*/Knight-Ridder Newspapers, Tokyo Bureau Chief, current, 1982. Edward R. Murrow Fellow, Council on Foreign Relations. American Newspaper Guild Investigative Reporting Award, 1981; American Newspaper Guild Grand Prize, 1981; Overseas Press Club Citation, 1983; Investigative Reporters & Editors Grand Prize, 1986; George Polk Award, International Reporting, 1986; Pulitzer Prize in International Reporting, 1986.

Simpson, Christopher. *The Washington Times.* Capitol Hill Bureau Chief. B. 1955, Anderson, SC. Clemson, 1977, History & Psychology; grad work, U. of SC, Journalism, 1979-80. *The Greensboro Record* (NC), police reporter, 1979-80. *The Newport News Daily Press* (VA), state government/political reporter, to 1985. *The Washington Times*, Congressional reporter & political writer, to 1986; Capitol Hill Bureau Chief, current, 1986.

Sitomer, Curtis J. *The Christian Science Monitor.* Senior Correspondent & "Justice" Columnist. B. 1932, NYC. Principia College, 1955, Political Science. *The Christian Science Monitor*, 1965; West Coast Bureau Chief, 1971-76; American News Editor, to 1982; Special Sections Editor, to 1983; senior correspondent, current, 1983; "Justice" columnist, current, 1983 (column syndicated weekly). National Headliner Award for Special Column of the Year, 1986.

Skrzycki, Cindy. *U.S. News & World Report.* Associate Editor. American U., MA-Journalism & Public Affairs. *Buffalo Evening News*, reporter. Fairchild Publications, reporter. *Fort Worth Star-Telegram*, reporter. *U.S. News & World Report*, business writer, from 1983; Associate Editor, current.

Sloan, Allan. *Forbes.* Senior Editor. Brooklyn College, 1966, BA-English; Columbia, 1967, MSJ. *Detroit Free Press*, business writer, 1972-79. *Forbes*, staff writer & Associate Editor, to 1981. *Money*, staff writer, to 1984. *Forbes*, Senior Editor, current, 1984. Author *Three Plus One Equals Billions: The Bendix-Marietta War*, 1983. Gerald Loeb Award, 1975; co-winner (with Howard Rudnitsky) Loeb Award, 1985.

Slutsker, Gary. *Forbes.* Associate Editor. B. 1955, NYC. Middlebury College, 1977, AB-Political Science, Honors; Columbia, 1978, MSJ. *Electronic News*, reporter, to 1980. *Venture Magazine*, Associate Editor, to 1982; Senior Editor, to 1984. *Forbes*, staff writer, to 1985; Associate Editor, current, 1985. Edit "Faces Behind the Figures" section.

Smith, Geoffrey N. *Financial World.* Executive Editor. B. 1939, Cleveland, OH. Princeton, 1961, AB; NYU, 1970, MBA. US Army. Prentice-Hall, Harcourt Brace, Manuscript Editor, 1964. *Forbes*, staff writer, 1966-70; Asst Managing Editor, to 1976; European Bureau Chief, to 1978; Special Operations Editor, creator "Up & Comers" column, 1979, "The Numbers Game" column, 1980, & "Taxing Matters," to 1986. *Financial World*, Executive Editor, current, 1986. Author *Sweat Equity*, 1986.

Smith, Hedrick. *The New York Times.* Chief Washington Correspondent. B. 1933, Kilmacolm, Scotland. Williams College, 1955, American History & Literature; Fulbright Scholar, Balliol College, Oxford, Political Science. Nieman Fellow, Harvard, 1969. US Air Force, to 1959. UPI, to 1962. *The New York Times*, Washington correspondent; foreign correspondent, Saigon, Paris, Cairo; Moscow Bureau Chief, 1971-74; Deputy National Editor, to 1976; Washington Bureau Chief, to 1979; chief Washington correspondent, to 1985; leave of absence, 1986. Author *The Russians* (Overseas Press Club Book Award): co-author *Reagan: The Man, The President* (with Leonard Silk *et al.*), 1981. Pulitzer Prize for coverage of Soviet Union, 1974: co-winner 1972 Pulitzer Prize (Pentagon Papers series).

Smith, Lee. *FORTUNE.* Board of Editors Member. Yale. NYC Dept. of Consumer Affairs, Director of Research. *Black Enterprise*, Managing Editor. *Newsweek*, Associate Editor. *FORTUNE*, associate editor; Board of Editors, Tokyo (*FORTUNE* International); Board of Editors member, Washington, current.

Smith, Stephen. *Newsweek.* Executive Editor. B. 1949, NYC. U. of PA, 1971, BA-History. *Daily Hampshire Gazette*, City Hall reporter, political writer, to 1973. *Albany Times-Union*, special assignment reporter, to 1974. *Philadelphia Inquirer*, reporter, to 1975; Deputy Regional Editor, to 1976. *The Boston Globe*, Asst Business Editor, 1976; roving New England reporter, 1977; Asst Metro Editor, to 1978. *Horizon* magazine, Senior Editor, 1978. *TIME*, staff writer, to 1980; Senior Editor, 1981; "Nation" Editor, to 1985; acting Asst Managing Editor, to 1986. *Newsweek*, Executive Editor, current, 1986. Ernie Pyle Memorial Award, 1977.

Solomon, Burt. *National Journal.* Staff Correspondent. B. 1948, Baltimore, MD. Harvard, 1970, Social Studies. *Texas Observer*, freelance reporter, 1971-72. *The Danvers Times* (MA), reporter, to 1973. *The Real Paper* (Cambridge, MA), reporter, to 1975. *The Energy Daily*, Editor, to 1985. *National Journal*, staff correspondent, current.

Spaeth, Anthony P. *The Asian Wall Street Journal.* Reporter, Manila. Williams College (MA), 1977. *The Asian Wall Street Journal*, reporter, to 1984; reporter, Manila, current, 1984.

Stabler, Charles N. *The Wall Street Journal.* Assistant Managing Editor. B. 1925, Trenton, NJ. Swarthmore College, 1950, Economics. *Times-Dispatch* (Richmond, VA), reporter, to 1952. *The Wall Street Journal*, reporter, to 1955; established Southeastern bureau, 1955; Managing Editor, Pacific Coast edition, to 1964; Dow Jones Books, Director, to 1966; News Editor, *The Wall Street Journal* NY, Banking & Finance Editor, to 1981; Asst Managing Editor, current, 1981. Loeb Award, 1967.

Stanfield, Rochelle L. *National Journal.* Staff Correspondent. B. 1940, Chicago, IL. Northwestern, 1962, BSJ, 1963, MSJ. The Council of State Governments, to 1966. Voice of America, news writer, 1966. National Governors' Association, to 1970. US Advisory Commission on Intergovernmental Relations, information officer. US Conference of Mayors, to 1976. *National Journal*, staff correspondent, current, 1976.

Stark, Andrew. *The American Spectator.* Contributor. B. 1956, Vancouver, Canada. U. of British Columbia, 1978, BA-Political Science; The London School of Economics, 1979, MS-Economics; Harvard, 1985, PhD-Government. *The American Spectator*, Asst Managing Editor, 1980-81; Cambridge Editor, to 1985; Contributor, current, 1985. Harvard, Teaching Fellow, Dept of Government, 1981-82. Policy advisor to Prime Minister Brian Mulroney of Canada, current, 1985.

Steiger, Paul E. *The Wall Street Journal.* Deputy Managing Editor. Yale, 1964, BA-Economics. *The Wall Street Journal*, staff reporter, San Francisco, 1966-68. *Los Angeles Times*, staff writer, to 1971; economic correspondent, Washington, to 1978; Business Editor, LA, to 1983. *The Wall Street Journal*, Asst Managing Editor, to 1985; Deputy Managing Editor, current, 1985. Co-author *The 70's Crash*. 3 Gerald Loeb Awards, 2 John Hancock Awards for Economic and Business Coverage.

Stein, Benjamin J. *The American Spectator.* Contributing Editor. *The Los Angeles Herald-Examiner*, Columnist. B. 1944, Washington, DC. Columbia, 1966, BA-Economics; Yale Law, 1970, valedictorian. Speechwriter to President Nixon. *The Wall Street Journal*, columnist and editorial writer, 1974-76; freelance contributor, current. *The New York Times*, *The Washington Post*, op-ed page writer, current. *The Los Angeles Herald-Examiner*, columnist, current. *The American Spectator*, Contributing Editor, current, 1972. Author 8 books, most recently *HER ONLY SIN*, 1986: co-author (with Herbert Stein) *On The Brink*, 1977; *Moneypower*, 1979. Freedoms Foundation Outstanding Essay Award, 1979.

Stephens, Philip Francis. *Financial Times.* Economics Correspondent. B. 1953, London. Worcester College, Oxford, 1971-74, Modern History. Fulbright Fellow, Economic Journalism at *Los Angeles Times*, 1986. Europa publications, Asst Editor, to 1976. *Commerce International*, writer; Editor, to 1979. Reuters, London correspondent; Brussels correspondent, to 1983. *Financial Times*, economics writer, 1978-83; economics correspondent, current, 1985.

Sterba, James P. *The Wall Street Journal.* Assistant Foreign Editor. B. 1943, Detroit, MI. MI State U., 1966, BA-Journalism. *The Evening Star*, Washington reporter, to 1967. *The New York Times*, asst to James Reston, to 1968; reporter, 1968; war correspondent, Saigon, to 1970; Bureau Chief, Jakarta, Indonesia/roving Asian correspondent, to 1973; Denver Bureau Chief, to 1975; Bureau Chief, Houston, TX, to 1977; economic development correspondent, 1978; Hong Kong Bureau Chief, to 1980; Peking Bureau Chief, 1981; Science writer, 1982. *The Wall Street Journal*, reporter and editor for the foreign desk, 1982; Asst Foreign Editor & special writer, current, 1983. Distinguished Alumni Award, MI State, 1970.

Stern, Richard L. *Forbes.* Senior Editor. B. 1941, NYC. Adelphi U., Psychology. AP, National Editor, 1970-74. *Securities Week*, editor, to 1976. *Institutional Investor*, "Wall Street Letter" Managing Editor, to 1979. *New York Daily News*, business columnist, to 1980. *Forbes*, Senior Editor, current, 1980. 1984 Loeb Award.

Sterngold, James. *The New York Times.* "Business Day" Reporter. B. 1954, Detroit, MI. Columbia, 1980, MSJ. Time-Life Books, freelance writer, 1978-80. AP-Dow Jones Newswire, Hong Kong bureau founder/correspondent, to 1984. *The New York Times*, "Business Day" reporter, current, 1984.

Stevens, Charles W. *The Wall Street Journal.* B. 1955, Cleveland, OH. Syracuse, 1977, Newspaper. *The Miami Herald*, 1977-78. *The Wall Street Journal*, Boston bureau, 1980; Detroit bureau, 1983; New York bureau, current, 1983.

Stockton, William. *The New York Times.* Mexico Bureau Chief. B. 1944, Raton, NM. NM Institute of Mining & Techology, 1966, BS-Chemistry. Nieman Fellow, Harvard, 1972-73. AP, 1968-75. Physicians Radio Network, Executive Editor, to 1979. *The New York Times*, Director, science news & Editor, "Science Times," to 1982; asst to the Executive Editor, A.M. Rosenthal, to 1985; Mexico Bureau Chief, current, 1985. Author *Final Approach*, 1977; *Altered Destinies*, 1979: co-author *Spaceliner* (with John Noble Wilford), 1981.

Stokes, Bruce. *National Journal.* International Economics Correspondent. B. 1948, Butler, PA. Georgetown, 1970, BSFS-International Affairs; Johns Hopkins, 1975, MA. Worldwatch Institute, Senior Researcher, to 1982. NPR, Producer, 1983. *National Journal*, international economics correspondent, current, 1984.

Strobel, Warren Paul. *The Washington Times.* National Desk Reporter. B. 1962, Camp Zama, Japan. U. of MO, at Columbia, 1984, Journalism. *Maneater*, U. of MO, Editor, 1983. *Missourian* (Columbia, MO), state capitol bureau, spring 1984; city hall reporter, fall 1984. *The Washington Times*, intern, metro desk, summer 1984; metro reporter, to 1986; national desk reporter, current, 1986.

Stroud, Joe H. *Detroit Free Press.* Editor. B. 1936, AR. Hendrix College, BA-History & Political Science; Tulane, MA-History. Various newspapers in Pine Bluff & Little Rock, AR., reporter/editorial writer. *Winston-Salem Journal & The Sentinel*, Editor, Editorial Pages. *Detroit Free Press*, Associate Editor, to 1973; Editor, current, 1973. William Allen White Awards for Editorial Excellence (1973, '76, '77, '79, '80); Overseas Press Club Citation for Reporting Excellence, 1974; Paul Tobenkin Memorial Award, 1976.

Struck, Myron. *The Washington Times.* Reporter/Assistant National Editor. B. 1953, NYC. Miami-Dade Community College, 1971-73; FL International U., 1973-75. *The Good Times*, newspaper, FL International U., founder, 1975. *The Miami Herald*, Sunday Features staff writer, editor, 1974-75. Press asst to Michael Abrams, Chairman, Dade County (FL) Democratic Party, 1975. *Roll Call, The Newspaper of Capitol Hill*, reporter, News Editor, to 1976, 1979. Press secretary to

MediaGuide

Representative Phillip Burton (D-CA), 1977-79. States News Service, reporter, desk editor, to 1981. *The Washington Post*, reporter, "Federal Report" page, to 1985. *The Washington Times*, reporter, Asst National Editor, political coordinator for '86 elections, current, 1985.

Sturm, Paul W. Jr. *BusinessWeek*. Assistant Managing Editor. Oberlin; Columbia, MSJ; Georgetown Law Center, JD. *Newsweek International*, writer. ESPN, "Business Times" editor. *Forbes*, various posts in London, Washington, LA; Managing Editor. *BusinessWeek*, Asst Managing Editor, current, 1985. Supervises annual issue of *BusinessWeek* "Top 1000."

Sullivan, Allanna. *The Wall Street Journal*. Reporter, NY. Queen's College (NY), 1971, BA-English; Columbia, 1977, MSJ. *Boating* magazine, to 1975. *The Record* (Bergen, NJ), Copy Editor, 1977. *Nucleonics Week* (McGraw-Hill publications), Wire Editor, to 1978. *Coal Age* magazine, Asst Editor, Associate Editor, to 1982. AP-Dow Jones, reporter, to 1984. *The Wall Street Journal*, reporter, current, 1984.

Sullivan, John Fox. *National Journal*. President & Publisher. B. 1943, Philadelphia. Yale, 1966, American Studies; Columbia, 1968. *Newsweek*, to 1975. *National Journal*, President & Publisher, current, 1975.

Summers, Colonel Harry G. Jr. *U.S. News & World Report*. Senior Military Correspondent. B. 1932, Covington, KY. U. of MD, 1957, BS-Military Science; US Army Command & General Staff College, 1968, MS-Military Arts & Science; Army War College, 1981. Military career: infantry squad leader, Korea; battalion & corps operations officer, Vietnam; negotiator with North Vietnam on POW/MIA issues; negotiator, terms of US withdrawl from Hanoi; General MacArthur Chair of Military Research, Army War College, 1947-85. Freelance work for *Kansas City Star, Kansas City Times*, 1968-75; other publications, current, 1980. *U.S. News & World Report*, senior military correspondent, current, 1985. Lecturer on Military Strategy & Military-Media Relations, current. Author *On Strategy: A Critical Analysis of the Vietnam War*, 1982 (Furness Award, OH State U.); "Vietnam War Almanac," (*Facts on File*), 1985.

Szulc, Tad. Freelance Writer. B. 1926, Warsaw, Poland. U. of Brazil, 1946, History. UPI, UN correspondent, 1949-53. *The New York Times*, correspondent, Washington, Latin American, Spain & Portugal, Eastern Europe, to 1973. Freelance writer, contributor *Los Angeles Times, Foreign Policy, The New York Times Magazine*. Author 15 books including *Illusion of Peace*, 1978; *Fidel: A Critical Portrait*, 1986. Maria Moors Cabot Gold Medal, Hemispheric Reporting, Columbia, 1959; Overseas Press Club Best Book on Foreign Affairs (*Illusion of Peace*), 1978; Knight of the Cross of the *Legion d'Honneur* (France), 1984.

Tagaza, Emilia. *Financial Times*. Canberra Correspondent. B. 1953, Manila, Philippines. U. of the Philippines, 1975, AB-Mass Communication & Broadcast Communication. *Asian Business Magazine*, Asst Editor, Features Editor, to 1978. *Asia Banking Magazine*, Manila correspondent, 1982-85; Canberra correspondent, current, 1985. *The Christian Science Monitor*, Manila correspondent, 1983-85. *Financial Times*, freelance correspondent, Manila, to 1985; Canberra correspondent, current, 1985.

Tagliabue, John. *The New York Times*. Economics Correspondent, Bonn. B. 1942, NJ. St. Peter's College; Catholic U. (Milan); U. of Bonn (West Germany). *The Sun* (Baltimore, MD), Bonn Bureau correspondent, to 1980. *The New York Times*, economics correspondent, Bonn, current, 1980.

Talbott, Strobe. *TIME*. Diplomatic Correspondent. B. 1946, Dayton, OH. Yale, 1968, BA; Oxford, Rhodes Scholar, 1971, MA. *TIME*, Eastern European correspondent, to 1973; State Dept. correspondent, to 1975; White House correspondent, to 1977; diplomatic correspondent, current, 1977. Author *Endgame: The Inside Story of SALT II*, 1979; *Deadly Gambits*. Edward Weintal Prize for Distinguished Diplomatic Reporting, 1980; Overseas Press Club Award, 1983.

Tamayo, Juan O. *The Miami Herald.* Middle East Correspondent. B. 1948, Guantanamo, Cuba. Marquette U., 1971, Journalism. UPI, Hartford, CT Bureau, to 1976; Foreign Desk, NY, to 1979; Mexico City Bureau, News Director for Central America, to 1982. *The Miami Herald*, Latin American Desk, to 1986; Middle East correspondent, Jerusalem, current, 1986.

Tanzer, Andrew. *Forbes.* Tokyo Bureau Chief. B. 1957, Washington, DC. Wesleyan U., 1979, BA-East Asian Studies, *magna cum laude*; Columbia, 1980, MSJ (Overseas Press Club Fellow). *Far Eastern Economic Review* (Hong Kong), Taiwan reporter, to 1983; Hong Kong reporter, to 1984. *Forbes*, LA bureau staff writer, to 1985; Tokyo Bureau Chief, current, 1985.

Taubman, Philip. *The New York Times.* Moscow Bureau Reporter. B. 1948, New York, NY. Stanford, 1970, Modern European History. *Time*, Boston bureau, 1970-73; staff writer, NY, 1976; Washington bureau, 1977. *Esquire*, Roving Editor, 1979. *The New York Times*, Washington bureau, 1985; Moscow bureau reporter, current, 1985. Polk Award for National Reporting, 1982; Polk Award for Foreign Policy Reporting, 1984.

Taylor, Frederick. *The Wall Street Journal.* Executive Editor. B. Portland, OR. U. of OR, Eugene, 1950, BS. *The Oregonian*, stringer, to 1950; sports writer, 1952-54. *Astoria Budget* (OR), to 1952. US Air Force, 1955-57. *The Wall Street Journal*, copyreader, NY, 1955, 1957; reporter; "Page One" rewriteman; Detroit Bureau Chief, 1959-64; Washington "Labor Letter" originator/columnist (with John Grimes), to 1966; Pentagon correspondent, to 1968; Asst Managing Editor, West Coast operations, San Francisco, to 1970; Managing Editor, to 1977; Executive Editor, to 1986; retired 1986 to run weekly newspaper in Oregon.

Taylor, Paul. *The Washington Post.* Reporter. B. 1949, NYC. Yale, 1970, BA-American Studies. *Winston-Salem Sentinel*, reporter, to 1973. *Philadelphia Inquirer*, reporter & columnist, to 1981. *The Washington Post*, reporter, current, 1981.

Taylor, Stuart Jr. *The New York Times.* Washington Bureau Reporter. Princeton, 1970, *Phi Beta Kappa*; Harvard Law, 1977, first in class, acting officer *Harvard Law Review*; Frederick Sheldon Traveling Fellow, Harvard, 1977-78. *The Sun/The Evening Sun* (Baltimore, MD), reporter, to 1974. Wilmer, Cutler & Pickering, Washington, attorney, to 1980. *The New York Times*, Washington reporter, specializing in legal affairs, current, 1980.

Taylor, Walter. *U.S. News & World Report.* Singapore Bureau Chief. *U.S. News & World Report*, Asia correspondent, covering Tokyo & Peking, to 1986; Singapore Bureau Chief, current, 1986.

Temko, Edward James (Ned). *The Christian Science Monitor.* South Africa Correspondent. Williams College, 1974, Political Science, *magna cum laude*. AP, reporter, 1976. UPI, Brussels correspondent, to 1977; Beirut correspondent, to 1979. *The Christian Science Monitor*, Middle East correspondent, to 1981; Moscow Bureau Chief, to 1983; Middle East correspondent, to 1985; South Africa correspondent, Johannesburg, current, 1985.

Terry, Edith. *BusinessWeek.* Acting Toronto Bureau Chief. B. 1952, Montgomery, AL. Yale, 1974, BA-Asian History; Stanford, 1976, MA-East Asian Studies. Philippine Agency for National Minorities, researcher, to 1972. Library of Congress, Editor of the Chinese section, to 1977. *The China Business Review*, Associate Editor, to 1980. *BusinessWeek*, staff editor, to 1983; Toronto correspondent, to 1986; Acting Bureau Chief, current, 1986. Author *The China Traders*, 1986; *The Executive Guide To China*, 1984.

Thatcher, Gary L. *The Christian Science Monitor.* Diplomatic Correspondent. B. 1949, Beaumont, TX. C.W. Post College, Long Island U., 1972, BA-Communications, *summa cum laude*. WDAM-TV (Hattiesburg, MS), reporter, to 1973. WAPI-TV (Birmingham, AL), reporter, to 1974. *The*

Christian Science Monitor, staff writer, to 1976; Atlanta correspondent, to 1978; Africa correspondent (based in Johannesburg), to 1981; National Editor, to 1983; Moscow correspondent, to 1986; diplomatic correspondent, current, 1986. Leelanau Center for Education, Glen Arbor, MI, lecturer, 1982, '83, '86. Clarion Award, Women in Communication, 1979; Certificate of Merit, American Bar Association, 1979.

Thomas, Evan. *Newsweek.* Washington Bureau Chief. Harvard, 1973; U. of VA Law, 1977. *TIME*, legal affairs reporter, to 1979; Supreme Court & Justice Dept. correspondent, to 1981; Congressional correspondent, to 1983; "Nation" section writer, Associate Editor, to 1986. *Newsweek*, Washington Bureau Chief, current, 1986.

Thomas, Rich. *Newsweek.* Chief Economic Correspondent. B. 1931, Detroit, MI. U. of MI, 1952, BA-English Literature; grad work, U. of Frankfurt, West Germany, 1955, & U. of MI, 1956-57. US Army, 1952-55. U. of MI, Teaching Fellow, 1957. UPI, correspondent, Detroit, to 1959. McGraw-Hill, Public Affairs, to 1960. *The New York Post*, Financial Editor, to 1962. *Newsweek*, writer/editor, NY, to 1970; Chief Economic Correspondent, Washington, current, 1970. Gerald M. Loeb Award, 1970.

Thurow, Roger. *The Wall Street Journal.* Reporter, London. B. Elgin, IL. U. of IA, 1979, BA-Journalism/Political Science. *Daily Iowan*, to 1977. *The Wall Street Journal*, intern, summer 1979; Dallas bureau reporter, 1980-81; Houston bureau, to 1982; Bonn bureau reporter (principal East-West reporter), to 1986; London bureau to report on South Africa, current, 1986.

Tinsley, Jack B. *Fort Worth Star-Telegram.* Vice President & Executive Editor. B. 1934, Angelina County, TX. Sam Houston State U., 1958, Speech & Journalism. *Fort Worth Star-Telegram*, reporter, education writer, Sunday editor, Asst Managing Editor, Asst to Editor, to 1975; Executive Editor, current, 1975. Newspaper won 2 Pulitzer Prizes (Spot News Photography, 1981; Meritorious Public Service, 1985) under editorship.

Tolchin, Martin. *The New York Times.* Washington Bureau Reporter. B. 1928, NYC. ID State College, U. of UT; New York Law School, 1951. US Army, to 1953. Law clerk, NYC, to 1954. *The New York Times*, reporter, NY, to 1970; City Hall Bureau Chief, to 1973; Washington bureau reporter, current, 1973: White House correspondent, 1978-79; regional reporter; currently covering Congress. Co-author (with Susan Tolchin) *To the Victor: Political Patronage from the Clubhouse to the White House; Clout: Womanpower & Politics.* The Women's Press Club, NY Reporters Association, One Hundred Year Association, NY Newspaper Guild, & Citizen's Budget Commission, 1966.

Tomlinson, Kenneth Y. *Reader's Digest.* Executive Editor. B. 1944, Grayson County, VA. Randolph-Macon College, BA. *Richmond Times-Dispatch*, reporter, 1965-68. National Voluntary Service Advisory Commission, 1981-83. Voice of America, Director, 1982-84. *Reader's Digest*, correspondent, Senior Editor, 1968-82 (Paris-based European Editor, 1977-78); Managing Editor, 1984-85; Executive Editor, current, 1985.

Tonelson, Alan. *Foreign Policy.* Associate Editor. B. 1953, Flushing, NY. Princeton, 1970, History. *The Inter Dependent* (UN Association), Associate Editor, to 1979. *The Wilson Quarterly* (Woodrow Wilson International Center for Scholars), Associate Editor, to 1981. *Foreign Policy* (Carnegie Endowment for International Peace), Associate Editor, current, 1983. Also current, freelance writing, 1982.

Toth, Robert C. *Los Angeles Times.* Washington Bureau Staff Writer. B. 1928, Blakely, PA. Washington U., 1952, BS-Chemical Engineering; Columbia, 1955, MSJ. Nieman Fellow, Harvard, 1960-61; Pulitzer Traveling Scholar, 1955. US Marines, 1946-48; US Army, 1952-53. *Rubber World*,

Associate Editor, 1953-54. *The Journal* (Providence, RI), reporter, 1955-57. *New York Herald Tribune*, staff writer, NY, to 1960; staff writer, Washington, to 1962. *The New York Times*, staff science writer, Washington, to 1963. *Los Angeles Times*, staff writer, Washington, science & Supreme Court, to 1965; London Bureau Chief, to 1970; State Dept. correspondent, to 1972; White House correspondent, to 1974; Moscow Bureau Chief, to 1977; science writer, Washington, to 1979; staff writer, Washington, national security affairs, current, 1979. Sigma Delta Chi Award, Foreign Correspondence, 1978; Overseas Press Club Award for Foreign Correspondence, 1978; George Polk Award for Foreign Correspondence, 1978: co-winner *Times* Editorial Award, 1985; Edward Weintal Prize for Diplomatic Reporting, 1986.

Trachtenberg, Jeffrey. *Forbes*. Staff Writer & "Faces"/"Marketing" Editor. B. 1950, Mineola, NY. Franklin & Marshall College, 1972, BA-Literature. *Socio-Economic Publications*, labor reporter, 1974-77. *Lebhar-Friedman Publications*, business writer, to 1979. *Women's Wear Daily*, business reporter & 7th Ave. reporter, Hollywood feature writer, 1978-84. *Forbes*, staff writer, "Faces" Editor, "Marketing" Editor, current, 1984.

Tracy, Eleanor Johnson. *FORTUNE*. Associate Editor. Wheaton College; studied at Brown, Johns Hopkins, Columbia & NYU. *The Journal-Bulletin* (Providence, RI), feature writer, reporter. *The Sun* (Baltimore, MD), feature writer, reporter. *San Francisco Chronicle*, feature writer, reporter. Time, Inc., researcher, 1956. *TIME*, acting head researcher, 1956-57. *FORTUNE*, research associate, from 1957; Associate Editor, current.

Treaster, Joseph B. *The New York Times*. Caribbean Bureau Chief. B. 1941. U. of Miami, 1963, Journalism. *The Miami Herald*, reporter, to 1963. US Army newspapers, reporter, Vietnam, to 1965. *The New York Times*, reporter, to 1984; Caribbean Bureau Chief, current, 1984. Occasional magazine freelance work. Co-author *Inside Report on the Hostage Crisis: No Hiding Place*. 3 Overseas Press Club Awards, 2 Page One Awards & Inter-American Press Association Award.

Trewitt, Henry. *U.S. News & World Report*. Deputy Managing Editor, Foreign Affairs. Neiman Fellow, Harvard. *Santa Fe New Mexican*, 1949-51. *Chattanooga Times*, 1951-56. *The Sun* (Baltimore, MD), 1957-61; Bonn bureau correspondent, to 1966. *Newsweek*, diplomatic & White House correspondent, to 1974. *The Sun*, diplomatic correspondent, to 1985. *U.S. News & World Report*, Deputy Managing Editor, Foreign Affairs, current, 1985. Author *McNamara: His Ordeal in the Pentagon*. Weintal Award, Diplomatic Correspondence, 1982.

Trimble, Jeff. *U.S. News & News Report*. Moscow Bureau Chief. *U.S. News & World Report*, Rome Bureau Chief, to 1986; Moscow Bureau Chief, current, 1986.

Truell, Peter. *The Wall Street Journal*/Europe. London Reporter. Marlborough College (UK), 1973, Arts & Sciences; Pembroke College, Cambridge, 1977, MA-Modern History, specializing in economics & business history; St. Anthony's College, Oxford, 1979, MPhil. *Librarie Du Liban* (Beirut, Lebanon), Asst Editor, Dictionary dept., 1979. Orion Bank Ltd., London, junior executive, 1980. *Economist Financial Report*, London, Managing Editor, to 1982. *Middle East Economic Digest*, Deputy Editor, 1982. *The Wall Street Journal*/Europe, reporter, London, current, 1982.

Tucker, William. *The American Spectator*, New York Correspondent. B. 1942, Orange, NJ. Amherst College, 1964, BA-English/Economics. *Rockland Journal-News*, reporter, to 1973. *The Record* (Bergen, NJ), reporter, to 1975. *Rockland County Times*, writer-editor, to 1976. *Harper's*, Contributing Editor, to 1982; current, 1983. *The American Spectator*, NY correspondent, current. Freelance writer, current, 1976. Author *Vigilante-The Backlash Against Crime in America*, 1985; *Progress and Privilege: America in the Age of Environmentalism*, 1982. Gerald Loeb Awards (1 Honorable Mention in 1977), 1978, '80; Amos Tuck Award, 1980; John Hancock Award for Business Writing, 1977.

Tumulty, Karen. *Los Angeles Times.* Washington Bureau Staff Writer. B. 1955, San Antonio, TX. U. of TX, Austin, 1977, BJ, high honors; Harvard, 1981, MBA. *Daily Texan* (U TX newspaper), staff member. Long News Service, part-time reporter, 1976-77. *San Antonio Light*, intern, summer 1976; Business Editor, reporter, to 1979. *Los Angeles Times*, intern, summer 1980; energy writer, to 1983; Washington bureau staff writer, current, 1983.

Tuohy, William. *Los Angeles Times.* Bonn Bureau Chief. B. 1926, Chicago, IL. Northwestern, 1951, English. *San Francisco Chronicle*, copyboy, reporter, Night City Editor, to 1959. *Newsweek*, back-of-book writer, Associate Editor, Asst National Editor, national political correspondent, 1964; Saigon Bureau Chief, 1965. *Los Angeles Times*, Saigon Bureau Chief, to 1968; Beirut Bureau Chief, to 1971; Rome Bureau Chief, to 1977; London, to 1985; Bonn Bureau Chief, current, 1985. Headliners Award, 1965; Pulitzer Prize, 1969; Overseas Press Club, 1969.

Tyler, Patrick E. *The Washington Post.* Middle East Correspondent. B. 1951, St. Louis, MO. U. of SC, 1974, Journalism. *The Hampton County Guardian* (SC), Editor, 1974. *The Allandale County Citizen* (SC), Editor, 1974. *Charlotte News* (NC), reporter, 1975. *The St. Petersburg Times*, police/courts reporter, to 1978. *Congressional Quarterly*, 1978. PBS, WCET (Cincinati, OH), host, "Congressional Outlook" documentary series, 1978. *The Washington Post*, metro, investigative, foreign staffs, to 1986; Middle East correspondent, current, fall 1986.

Tyrrell, R. Emmett Jr. *The American Spectator.* Founder/Editor. B. 1943, Chicago, IL. Indiana U., 1965, BA-History, 1967, MA. *The American Spectator* (originally called *The Alternative*), founder, 1967; Editor, current, 1967. Also current, "Public Nuisances" columnist, King Features Syndicate, Inc.

Ungeheuer, Frederick. *TIME.* Senior Correspondent. B. 1932, Frankfurt-am-Main, Germany. Harvard, 1956, Government (Theory). Reuters Ltd., correspondent, to 1963. TIME-LIFE News Service, correspondent, West Africa Bureau Chief, to 1969. *Harper's*, Contributing Editor, to 1971. *Eastwest Markets/Mideast Markets*, Editor, to 1977. *TIME*, UN Bureau Chief, to 1973; European economic correspondent, to 1980; financial correspondent, to 1982; senior correspondent, current, 1982.

Urquhart, John D. Dow Jones-Canada. Ottawa Bureau Chief. U. of Toronto, Liberal Arts. Reuters, Editor, London, 1960-63. *International Herald Tribune*, reporter, Paris, to 1967. AP-Dow Jones, reporter, London, to 1972. Dow Jones, reporter, to 1976. Dow Jones-Canada, Bureau Chief, Ottawa, current, 1976.

Uttal, Bro. *FORTUNE.* Board of Editors Member. Harvard, *magna cum laude*; Harvard, MBA. Educational Management Associates, Inc., consultant. *The Phoenix* (Cambridge, MA), columnist. *Boston After Dark*, columnist. *FORTUNE*, reporter/researcher, to 1982; Board of Editors, current, 1982, based in Menlo Park, CA.

VanSlambrouck, Paul. *The Christian Science Monitor.* International News Editor. B. 1950, Teaneck, NJ. U. of CA, Santa Barbara, 1972, Anthropology. *San Francisco Business Magazine*, writer/photographer, to 1975; Associate Editor, to 1976. *The Christian Science Monitor*, New England news reporter, to 1977; Asst Editor, Business Page, to 1979; magazine writer, Boston, 1979; domestic correspondent, to 1981; foreign correspondent, Johannesburg, to 1985; International News Editor, current, 1985.

Vartan, Vartanig G. *The New York Times.* "Market Place" Columnist. B. Pasadena, CA. Yale. UPI, 1957-62. *The New York Herald Tribune*, 1957-62. *The Christian Science Monitor*, columnist, 1957-62. *The New York Times*, from 1963; "Market Place" columnist, current. Author *50 Wall Street; The Dinosaur Fund*.

Vickery, Hugh. *The Washington Times.* Business Reporter. B. 1957, Yokuska, Japan. Hamilton College (Clinton, NY), 1980, Government. *National Geographic,* freelance feature writer, to 1983. *Washington Business Review,* reporter, to 1981. *Association Management* magazine, Associate Editor, to 1983. *The Washington Times,* business reporter, current, 1983.

Von Kuehnelt-Leddihn, Erik Ritter. *National Review* European Correspondent. Freelance. B. 1909, Tobelbad, Austria. U. of Budapest, Doctor of Economics & Politcal Science. *The Spectator,* London. Georgetown, teacher, 1937. St. Peter's College, (NJ) Department Head, History & Sociology. Fordham, Japanese instructor, 1942-43. Chestnut Hill College, (PA) faculty member, to 1947. Freelance, current. *National Review,* European correspondent, current. Most recent publications *Die falsch gestellten Weichen. Der Rote Faden 1789-1984,* 1985; *Gleichheit oder Freheit?,* 1985; *Leftism (From de Sade and Marx to Hitler and Pol Pot),* (revised edition of *Leftism-From Sade and Marx to Hitler and Marcuse,* 1974), in progress.

Wade, Lawrence. *The Washington Times.* Columnist. B. 1948, Cleveland, OH. OH State U., 1977, Journalism. *The Wall Street Journal,* reporter, 1977. *The Miami Herald,* reporter, 1978. *The Journal Herald* (Dayton, OH), editorial writer, columnist, reporter, 1980. *The Orlando Sentinel* (FL), editorial writer, 1982. US Commission on Civil Rights, Spokesman, Director of Press & Communications, 1984. *The Washington Times,* columnist, current.

Walczak, Lee. *BusinessWeek.* Washington Bureau Manager. U. of MD; U. of MO, MA-Journalism. McGraw-Hill World News, health, transportation reporter, Washington. *BusinessWeek,* NY; White House correspondent; Editor, "Washington Outlook;" Political News Editor; Washington Bureau Manager, current, 1985.

Walsh, Edward. *The Washington Post.* National Staff Reporter. B. 1942, Chicago, IL. College of St. Thomas (St. Paul, MN), 1963, BA-Political Science/Journalism. Congressional Fellow, American Political Science Association, 1970-71. Nieman Fellow, Harvard, 1981-82. *The Catholic Messenger* (Davenport, IA), reporter/Asst Editor, 1965-67. *Houston Chronicle,* staff reporter, to 1970. *The Washington Post,* metro reporter, 1971-75; White House correspondent, to 1981; Jerusalem correspondent, to 1985; national staff reporter, current, 1985. Merriman Smith Memorial Award, White House Correspondents Association, 1979.

Walsh, Kenneth. *U.S. News & World Report.* White House Correspondent. *U.S. News & World Report,* Congressional correspondent, to 1986; White House correspondent, current, 1986.

Walsh, Mary Williams. *The Wall Street Journal.* Mexico Bureau Chief. B. Wausau, WI. U. of WI, 1979, BA-French & English. Walter Bagehot Fellow, Columbia, 1982, 1983. Western Publishing, editorial asst, 1978. *The Progressive,* Associate Editor, 1979. *The Wall Street Journal,* Philadelphia bureau staff reporter, 1982-85; Mexico Bureau Chief, current, 1985.

Wattenberg, Ben. United Features Syndicate. Columnist. B. 1933, NYC. Hobart College, 1955, BA. US Air Force, to 1958. Asst to President Johnson, Washington, 1966-68. Business consultant, Washington, to 1979. Aide to Vice-President Humphrey, 1970. Campaign adviser to Senator Henry Jackson, 1972, 1976. Mary Washington College, Eminent Scholar, Professor at Large, 1973-74. Presidential Advisory Board on Ambassadorial Appointments, member, to 1980. US International U., Distinguished Visiting Professor, 1978, 1979. International Broadcasting, Vice-Chairman of the Board, 1981. Democracy Program, Vice-Chairman of the Board, to 1983. Coalition for a Democratic Majority, co-founder, Chairman, current, 1972. Reading Is Fundamental, Board of Directors, current, 1977. Hudson Institute, trustee, current, 1976. American Enterprise Institute, Senior Fellow, current, 1977. United Features Syndicate, columnist, current, 1977. *Public Opinion,* Co-editor, current, 1977. Author *The Real Majority,* 1970; *The Real America,* 1974; *The Good News Is The Bad News Is Wrong,* 1984: co-author 3 books.

Weberman, Ben. *Forbes.* Economics Editor. B. 1923, NYC. CCNY, 1943, BS-Mathematics; NYU, 1955, MBA. International Statistical Bureau, Associate Economist, 1946-51. *The Journal of Commerce,* financial writer, to 1954; Financial Editor, to 1956. *New York Herald Tribune,* Bond Market columnist, to 1961; Financial Editor, to 1964; American Banker, Financial Editor, to 1975. *Forbes,* Economics Editor, current, 1976. Also current, Publisher & Editor, *Reporting on Governments* (weekly bond & money market newsletter). Author *Interest Rate Futures, Profits and Pitfalls,* 1979.

Weinraub, Bernard. *The New York Times.* Washington Bureau Reporter. B. 1937, NYC. CCNY, BA. US Army. *The New York Times,* copyboy, 1961; news clerk; news asst, UN Bureau; reporter, 1963-67; foreign correspondent, to 1968; metro staff, to 1970; London correspondent, to 1973, 1975-77; India correspondent, to 1975; Washington bureau reporter, current, 1977. Newspaper Guild Award.

Weisberg, Jacob. Freelance Writer. B. 1964, Chicago, IL. Yale, BA-Humanities to be conferred 1987. City News Bureau of Chicago, reporter, 1985. *The New Republic,* political reporter-researcher, to 1986. Freelance writer, New Haven, CT, current, 1986. John Hersey Prize for Journalism, Yale, 1985.

Weisman, Steven. *The New York Times.* New Delhi Bureau Chief. B. 1946, LA, CA. Yale, 1968, BA. *The New York Times,* metro reporter, 1970-74; specialized politics & city's financial crisis, to 1976; Albany bureau reporter, 1976; City Hall Bureau Chief, to 1978; Albany Bureau Chief, 1978; Washington bureau reporter, to 1979; White House correspondent, to 1981; senior White House correspondent, to 1985; New Delhi Bureau Chief, current, 1985. Silurian Society Award, 1975.

Wellborn, Stanley N. *U.S. News & World Report.* Senior Editor. B. 1944, San Diego, CA. Washburn U., 1966, English. Washington Journalism Center Fellow, 1969; Ford Foundation Fellow in Education Writing, 1976. *Topeka Capitol-Journal* (KS), 1962-66. Peace Corps member, Ghana, 1967-69. *Congressional Quarterly,* legislative & political writer, 1969-72. *U.S. News & World Report,* science, medicine, education, politics from 1972, currently Senior Editor. Contributor *Dollar Politics.* Distinguished Achievement Award, Education Writers Association, 1982; Space Pioneer Award for Challenger coverage, L5 Society, 1986.

Welling, Kathryn M. *Barron's.* Managing Editor. B. 1952, Fort Wayne, IN. Northwestern, 1974, Journalism, Urban Affairs. Dow Jones News Retrieval Service, copy reader, 1974. AP-Dow Jones, copy reader, 1975. *The Wall Street Journal,* copy editor, 1976. *Barron's,* Associate Editor, to 1982; asst to the Editor, to 1983; Managing Editor, current, 1983.

West, Diana. *The Washington Times.* Features Writer. B. 1961, LA, CA. Yale, 1983, English. *The Public Interest,* Asst Editor, to 1984. *The Washington Times,* feature writer, current, 1985.

West, Woody. *Insight.* Associate Editor. B. 1934, Montana. St. John's College, American U., 1961, History. *Lincoln Star* (NE), reporter, 1961. *Omaha World-Herald,* copy editor, to 1962. *The Washington Star,* Asst National Editor, Asst City Editor, reporter, to 1980; editorial writer, 1975-81. *The Milwaukee Journal,* editorial writer, Washington, to 1982. *The Washington Times,* editorial writer, 1983. *Insight,* Managing Editor, to 1986; Associate Editor, current, 1986.

White, George. *Detroit Free Press,* Columnist & Business Reporter. Freelance. B. 1953, Detroit, MI. MI State U., 1975, BA-History & Journalism; 1981, MA-African History. *Minneapolis Tribune,* urban environment, Native American affairs, investigative assignments, to 1979. *U.S. News & World Report,* regional correspondent, midwest, to 1984. *Detroit Free Press,* columnist & business reporter, current 1984. Freelance, current (*The Christian Science Monitor, Los Angeles Times*).

Whitney, Craig R. *The New York Times.* Assistant Managing Editor. B. 1943, Milford, MA. Harvard, 1965, BA, *magna cum laude. The Worcester Telegram* (MA), reporter, 1963-65. US Navy, to 1969. *The New York Times*, asst to James Reston, Washington, to 1966; metro news staff, 1969-1971; Saigon Bureau Chief, to 1973; Bonn Bureau Chief, to 1977; Moscow correspondent, to 1980; Deputy Foreign Editor, to 1982; Foreign Editor, to 1983; Asst Managing Editor, current, 1983.

Wicker, Thomas Grey. *The New York Times.* Political Columnist. B. 1926, Hamlet, NC. U. of NC, 1948. Nieman fellow, Harvard, 1957-58. *Sandhill Citizen* (Aberdeen, NC), Editor. *The Daily Robesonia* (Lumberton, NC), Sports & Telegraph Editor. NC State Board of Public Welfare, Information Director. *The Winston-Salem Journal*, Copy Editor; Sports Editor, 1954-44; Editor, Sunday feature section, to 1957; editorial writer; city hall reporter, to 1959. US Naval Reserves, 1952-54. *The Tennessean* (Nashville, TN), Associate Editor, to 1960. *The New York Times*, Washington bureau reporter; White House correspondent, to 1964; Washington Bureau Chief, to 1966; "In the Nation" columnist, current, 1966. Author *Kennedy Without Tears*, 1964; *JFK & LBJ: The Influence of Personality Upon Politics*, 1968; *A Time to Die*, 1975; *On Press*, 1978. John Peter Zenger Award for Freedom of the Press, U. of AZ, 1984.

Wiegner, Kathleen K. *Forbes.* West Coast Bureau Manager. B. 1938, Milwaukee, WI. U. of WI, 1960, BS-English/Journalism, 1962, MA-English/Comparative Literature, 1967, PhD-English/Comparative Literature. U. of WI, instructor, to 1967; Asst Professor, to 1974. *Forbes*, reporter-researcher, to 1975; reporter, to 1978; staff writer, to 1979; Associate Editor, to 1984; Senior Editor, to 1985; West Coast Bureau Manager, current, 1985.

Wiggins, Philip. *The New York Times.* "Business Day" Reporter. B. 1942, East Orange, NJ. Rutgers. WINS News Radio, writer. *New Issue Outlook*, asst to the Publisher; writer. *The New York Times*, copy reader; news asst; "Business Day" reporter, current. Author *Unorganized Violence.*

Wildstrom, Stephen H. *BusinessWeek.* Senior News Editor. U. of MI, *Phi Beta Kappa*. AP, staff member, Detroit, 1969-72. *BusinessWeek*, correspondent, Detroit, to 1974; correspondent, Washington (McGraw-Hill World News), to 1977; economic correspondent, to 1985; Senior News Editor, Washington, current, 1985.

Wilford, John Noble. *The New York Times.* Science Reporter. B. 1933. U. of TN, 1955, BSJ, *magna cum laude*; Syracuse, MS-Political Science. Ford Foundation Fellow, Columbia. *The Wall Street Journal*, reporter. US Army, Counter Intelligence Corps, 1957-59. *TIME*, Contributing Editor, to 1965; science section writer, 1965. *The New York Times*, reporter, science dept., to 1973; Asst National News Editor, to 1974; Science Director, to 1979; science reporter, current, 1979. Author *We Reach the Moon*, 1969; *The Mapmakers*, 1981: co-author (with William Stockton) *Spaceliner*, 1981; *The New York Times Guide to the Return of Halley's Comet*, 1985. G.M. Loeb Award Achievement Award, 1972; National Space Club's Press Award, 1974; American Association for the Advancement of Science/Westinghouse Science Writing Award, 1983; Pulitzer Prize for National Reporting, Science Writing, 1984.

Will, George. *Newsweek*, Contributing Editor. *The Washington Post* Writers Group, Political Columnist. B. 1941, Champaign, IL. Attended Trinity College, Oxford; Princeton. Teacher, Politics, MI State U., U. of IL, U. of Toronto. Congressional aide, Senator Allot of Colorado, to 1972. *National Review*, Washington Editor, 1972. *The Washington Post* Writers Group, columnist, current, 1972. *Newsweek*, columnist, current. Also current, television commentary, ABC. Author *The Pursuit of Happiness and Other Sobering Thoughts*, 1979; *The Pursuit of Virtue and Other Tory Notions*, 1982; *Statecraft as Soulcraft: What Government Does*, 1982. Pulitzer Prize for Commentary, 1977.

Williams, Dan. *Los Angeles Times.* Mexico City Bureau Chief. B. 1949, Pittsburgh, PA. Yale, 1971, BA-Political Science; Defense Language Institute, Cantonese. US Army, 1971-74. *The Miami News,* business writer, 1977-79. *The Miami Herald,* Latin American community reporter, Miami city-government reporter, Peking Bureau Chief, Jerusalem Bureau Chief, to 1983. *Los Angeles Times,* San Salvador Bureau Chief, to 1985; Mexico City Bureau Chief, current, 1985.

Williams, Nick B. Jr. *Los Angeles Times.* Southeast Asia Bureau Chief. B. 1937, Santa Monica, CA. Claremont Men's College (CA), 1959, Business Administration. *San Diego Union,* metro reporter, Sunday desk, to 1964. *Chicago Sun-Times,* metro, financial & Sunday desks, to 1967. *Los Angeles Times,* Copy Editor, Metro News Editor, to 1972; Asst National Editor, to 1976; Asst & Deputy Foreign Editor, to 1985; Southeast Asia Bureau Chief, Bangkok, current, 1985.

Williams, Winston. *The New York Times.* Business/Financial Reporter. Brown; Columbia, 1973, BA, 1974, MSJ. *BusinessWeek,* correspondent, to 1975; Pittsburgh Bureau Chief, to 1977. *The New York Times,* business/financial reporter, current. 1977.

Willoughby, Jack. *Forbes.* Staff Writer. Carleton College (Ottawa, Canada), 1977, BA-Journalism. Walter Bagehot Fellow, Columbia, 1983-84. *Globe & Mail* (Canada's only daily), business writer, 1977-83. *Forbes,* staff writer, current, 1984. National Business Writing Award, Investigative Journalism (for work at *Globe & Mail*).

Wilson, George C. *The Washington Post.* National Staff Member. B. Orange, NJ. Attended Georgia Tech; Bucknell; *Alliance Francais* (Paris, France). *The Washington Post,* staff member since 1966; Pentagon reporter; Vietnam correspondent; national staff member, covering military affairs, current. Co-author (with F. Carl Schumacher Jr.) *Bridge of No Return: The Ordeal of the U.S.S. Pueblo.* Mark Watson Memorial Award for Distinguished Military News Coverage, 1970.

Winder, David. *The Christian Science Monitor.* London Correspondent. B. South Africa. Fellowship at Columbia Graduate School of Journalism. *The Natal Witness* (South Africa). *The Christian Science Monitor,* Boston, NY, LA Bureaus, 1965-70; UN correspondent, to 1973; London Bureau, to 1978; Asst International News Editor, to 1983; roving Third World correspondent, to 1984; London correspondent, current, 1984. Population Action Council's Award, 1983.

Wines, Michael. *Los Angeles Times.* Washington Economic Correspondent. B. 1951, Louisville, KY. U. of KY, 1973, BA-Political Science/Journalism; Columbia, 1974, MSJ. *Lexington Herald* (KY), reporter, 1974. *The Louisville Times* (KY), reporter, to 1981. *National Journal,* Washington reporter, regulatory affairs, to 1984. *Los Angeles Times,* Washington economic correspondent, current, 1984.

Winter, Thomas Swanson. *Human Events.* Editor & Co-owner. B. 1937, Teaneck, NJ. Harvard, 1959, BA-Government, 1961, MBA. *Human Events,* Asst Editor, to 1964; Editor, current, 1964.

Witcher, S. Karene, *The Wall Street Journal.* Reporter. B. Monroe, GA. Davidson College (NC), 1975, BA-English; U. of Montpellier, France; U. of MO, 1977, MSJ. *The Asian Wall Street Journal,* reporter, Hong Kong, to 1979; reporter, Singapore, to 1982; *The Wall Street Journal,* reporter, NY, current, 1982.

Wolman, Clive R. *Financial Times.* Financial Services Correspondent. B. 1956, Sheffield, England. Oxford, Philosophy, Politics & Economics, First Class Honors. *Reading Evening Post,* reporter, 1978-80. *Jerusalem Post,* sub-editor; economic & industry ministry correspondent, to 1981. *Financial Times,* company comments writer, to 1983; personal finance editor, to 1985; financial services correspondent, current, 1985.

Wolman, William. *BusinessWeek.* Editor. B. Canada. McGill U. (Montreal); Stanford, PhD-Economics. Citibank, Vice-President in charge of economic publications, 1969-71. Argus Research, economic trends forecaster, to 1974. ESPN, "Business Times," Executive Editor, 1983. *BusinessWeek*, economics staff, 1960-65; Economics Editor, to 1969; Senior Editor, Economics department, 1974-79; Deputy Editor, to 1983; Editor, current, 1984. Also current, bi-weekly commentator, "Nightly Business Report," PBS. Author *The Beat Inflation Strategy; The Decline of U.S. Power.* U. of MO Journalism Award, 1978; National Magazine Award, 1981; Deadline Club Award, 1981; John Hancock Award, 1981; Champion-Tuck Award, 1984.

Woodward, Bob. *The Washington Post.* Assistant Managing Editor/Investigative. B. Geneva, IL. Yale, BA-English & History. US Navy, communications officer. *Montgomery County Sentinel* (MD), investigative reporter, to 1971. *The Washington Post*, investigative reporter; Asst Managing Editor/investigative, current. Co-author (with Carl Bernstein) *All The President's Men*, 1974, *The Final Days*, 1976; (with Scott Armstrong) *The Brethren*, 1979. Pulitzer Prize with Carl Bernstein for Watergate coverage, 1973; Drew Pearson Foundation Award; Heywood Broun Award; George Polk Memorial Award; Sigma Delta Chi Award.

Worsthorne, Peregrine. *Sunday Telegraph.* Editor. B. 1923, Chelsea, London, UK. Peterhouse, Cambridge; Magdalen College, Oxford, History. *The Times*, Washington correspondent, to 1952; Leader writer, to 1955. *Daily Telegraph*, Leader writer, 1955. *Sunday Telegraph*, Asst Editor, to 1986; Editor, current, 1986.

Woutat, Donald. *Los Angeles Times.* Energy Writer. B. 1944, Grand Forks, ND. U. of ND, 1969, English. *Daily News-Miner* (Fairbanks, AK), reporter, to 1970. *Minneapolis Star*, reporter, to 1974. *News Journal* (Wilmington, DE), police, Asst City Editor, to 1976. AP, reporter, to 1979. *Detroit Free Press*, auto writer, to 1981. *The Wall Street Journal*, Detroit bureau, 1984. *Los Angeles Times*, Detroit Bureau Chief, to 1984; high technology writer, to 1986; energy writer, current, 1986.

Wright, Michael. *National Journal.* Executive Editor. B. 1942, Fort Benning, GA. U. of AL, 1964. US Navy, to 1968. *Constitution* (Atlanta, GA), city hall reporter, editorial writer, federal courts reporter, to 1970. *U.S. News & World Report*, regional correspondent (Atlanta), Congressional correspondent, to 1976; White House reporter, to 1978. *The New York Times*, Editor, Sunday "Week in Review", to 1986. *National Journal*, Executive Editor, current, 1986.

Wysocki, Bernard B. Jr. *The Wall Street Journal.* Tokyo Bureau Chief. B. Waterloo, IA. Dartmouth, 1971, AB-Liberal Arts. *Amherst Record* (MA), reporter, 1972. *Daily Hampshire Gazette* (Northampton, MA), 1973. *Albany Times-Union* (NY), business & economics reporter, to 1975. *The Wall Street Journal*, reporter, Cleveland, to 1978; reporter, Chicago, to 1979; Philadelphia Bureau Chief, to 1982; News Editor, NY, to 1983; NY News Editor, to 1985; Tokyo Bureau Chief, current, 1985.

Yardley, Jonathan. *The Washington Post.* Book Critic. B. Pittsburgh, PA. U. of NC, BA-English. Neiman Fellow, Harvard. *The New York Times. Greensboro Daily News* (NC). *The Miami Herald. The Washington Star*, book critic, to 1981. Freelance, current. *The Washington Post*, book critic, current, 1981. Author *Ring: A Biography of Ring Lardner.* Pulitzer Prize for Distinguished Criticism, 1981.

Yoder, Edwin. *The Washington Post* Writers Group. Columnist. B. 1934, Greensboro, NC. U. of NC, 1956, BA; Oxford, 1958. *Charlotte News*, editorial writer, to 1961. *Greensboro Daily News*, editorial writer, to 1964; Associate Editor, to 1975. U. of NC, Asst Professor, history, 1964-65. *The Washington Star*, Editorial Page Editor, to 1981. *The Washington Post* Writers Group, columnist, current, 1981. NC Press Association Award for Editorial Writing, 1958, 1961, 1966; Walker Stone Award, Scripps-Howard Foundation, 1978; Pulitzer Prize for Editorial Writing, 1979.

MediaGuide

Young, Leah R. *The Journal of Commerce.* Reporter/Washington Insurance Editor. B. 1942, Brooklyn, NY. George Washington U., 1964, AB-Political Science; Columbia, 1965, MA-Journalism. UPI, foreign desk, to 1966. *Baltimore News-American*, magazine writer, to 1966. Ghost writer for Senator Harrison Williams, 1966. *The Journal of Commerce*, reporter, Washington Insurance Editor specializing in insurance, law & banking issues, current, 1966.

Younghusband, Peter. *The Washington Times.* Special Correspondent, South Africa. B. 1931, Cape Town, South Africa. Educated in South Africa. *Northern Echo* (Darlington, England), reporter, 1958. Reuters, London, desk rewriter, 1959. *Cape Times* (Cape Town), reporter, 1960. *Drum Magazine* (Johannesburg), feature writer, 1961. *London Daily Mail*, foreign correspondent (Africa, Middle East, Far East), to 1970; Washington Bureau Chief/White House correspondent, 1970. *Newsweek*, special correspondent, South Africa, to 1986. *The Washington Times*, special correspondent, South Africa, current, 1986. Co-winner (with Andrew Nagorski) Overseas Press Club Award, 1974.

Zalaznick, Sheldon. *Forbes.* Managing Editor. B. 1928, NYC, University College, NYU, 1948, BA-English Literature; Columbia Teachers College, 1950, MA. High school English teacher, NYC, to 1952. *Newsweek*, copyboy, clip desk, researcher, sports, editor, to 1956. Public Relations, NYC, to 1959. *Forbes*, Associate Editor, Senior Editor, to 1963. *New York Herald Tribune*, Founding Editor, "New York" (the Sunday magazine), Sunday Editor, to 1966. General Learning Corp., staff writer. *FORTUNE*, Associate Editor, to 1969; NY Editorial Director, to 1976. *Forbes*, Managing Editor, current, 1976.

Zaslow, Jeffrey. *The Wall Street Journal.* Staff Reporter, Chicago. B. 1958, Philadelphia, PA. Carnegie-Mellon U., 1980, Creative Writing. *The Orlando Sentinel* (FL), feature writer, to 1983. *The Wall Street Journal*, commodity reporter, features, Chicago, current, 1983.

Zonana, Victor F. *Los Angeles Times.* San Francisco Bureau Founder, Financial Reporter. B. 1954, NYC. Dartmouth, 1975, AB-Economics, *summa cum laude, Phi Beta Kappa. The Wall Street Journal*, staff reporter, Philadelphia, San Francisco, to 1985. *Los Angeles Times*, opened first financial bureau, San Francisco, covering Northern California business & economics, current, 1985. Honorable Mention, Pannell Ken Forster Financial Writing Award, 1986.

Zucker, Seymour. *BusinessWeek.* Senior Editor, Economic News. Brooklyn College; New School for Social Research, PhD-Economics. Port Authority of NY & NJ, economist. NBC Planning Department, staff economist. *BusinessWeek*, Economics Editor, 1974-80; Senior Editor, Economic News (economics, Wall Street, markets & investments), current, 1980.

Zuckerman, Mortimer B. *U.S. News & World Report*, Chairman & Editor-in-Chief. *The Atlantic*, Chairman. B. 1937, Canada. McGill U. (Montreal), 1957, Economics & Political Theory, 1961, Law; U. of PA, 1961, MBA; Harvard, 1962, Master of Law. Boston Properties (real estate development firm), Chairman/Founder, current, 1970. *The Atlantic*, Chairman, current, 1980. *U.S. News & World Report*, Chairman, Editor-in-Chief & editorial writer, current, 1984.

INDEX

A

Abelson, Alan, 84, 85, 117
Alexander, Charles, 106
Almond, Peter, 164
Alter, Jonathan, 105, 241
Anders, George, 117
Anderson, Harry, 24, 105
Andrews, Fred, 63
Andrews, Walter, 220
Apple, R.W. Jr., 11, 29, 31, 38, 64, 75, 78, 241
Archibald, George, 241
Armbruster, William, 164
Asman, David, 73, 164
Auerbach, Stuart, 117
Axebank, Albert, 165

B

Bailey, Jeff, 115, 118
Baker, Russell, 63, 262
Balmaseda, Liz, 165
Bangsberg, P.T., 99, 115, 165
Banks, Howard, 118
Barnard, Bruce, 118
Barnathan, Joyce, 105, 165
Barnes, Fred, 33, 38, 81, 103, 114, 231
Barnes, John, 166
Barone, Michael, 231
Barrett, Lawrence I., 242
Barringer, Felicity, 21, 67, 166
Barry, John M., 118
Bartlett, Sarah, 119
Bartley, Robert L., 73, 111
Baum, Julian, 115, 166
Beatty, Jack, 83
Beaty, Jonathan, 253
Beeston, Richard, 33
Behar, Richard, 119
Behr, Peter, 80, 119
Beichman, Arnold, 262

Bennett, Amanda, 120
Bennett, Robert A., 63, 115, 120
Berg, Eric, 63, 120
Berger, Joan, 121, 134
Bering-Jensen, Henrik, 114, 167
Bernstein, Richard, 68, 167
Berquist, Robert, 66
Berry, John, 121
Berthelsen, John, 76, 115, 168, 204
Bethell, Tom, 102, 242
Betts, Paul, 168
Bianco, Anthony, 36, 37, 85, 86, 114, 121
Birnbaum, Jeffrey, 27, 122, 146
Bishop, Jerry, 21, 35
Bladen, Ashby, 122
Bleiberg, Robert, 84, 122
Blumenthal, Sidney, 11, 38, 40, 79, 115, 242
Blustein, Paul, 123
Boffey, Phil M., 19, 20, 33, 35, 154
Bohlen, Celestine, 21, 28, 80, 168
Borger, Gloria, 104
Bornstein, Paul, 123, 157
Boroweic, Andrew, 115, 169
Borrell, John, 29
Bourne, Eric, 169
Boustany, Nora, 169
Boyd, Gerald M., 243
Bradlee, Ben, 9, 77, 79, 80, 242
Brandt, Thomas, 243
Branigan, William, 24, 80, 170
Breen, Tom, 170
Bridges, Tyler, 170
Brimelow, Peter, 123
Brinkley, Joel, 18, 23, 220, 224
Brittan, Samuel, 88, 123
Broad, William J., 19, 33, 220, 267
Broder, David, 38, 75, 78, 231

Brokaw, Tom, 44
Brooke, James B., 171
Brookes, Warren, 27, 114, 124
Brookhiser, Richard, 102, 262
Brownstein, Ronald, 38, 101, 115, 243
Broyles, William Jr., 232
Bruce, James, 171
Buchan, David, 171
Buckley, Priscilla, 102
Buckley, William F. Jr., 50, 78, 81, 102, 263
Bulkeley, William, 124
Burgess, John, 24, 80, 171
Burns, John F., 66, 67, 114, 172, 184, 213
Burton, Sandra, 108
Buss, Dale, 125
Butler, Steven B., 39, 172
Bylinsky, Gene, 125

C

Calame, Barney, 21, 75
Cannon, Lou, 31, 77, 228, 232, 250
Carley, William M., 15, 71, 125
Carr, Jonathon, 172
Carrington, Tim, 29, 34, 221
Carroll, Doug, 109
Carter, Hodding III, 263
Chamberlain, John, 263
Chavez, Lydia, 173
Chaze, William, 244
Cheshire, William, 111
Chesnoff, Richard Z., 173
Chipello, Christopher J., 173
Chira, Susan, 65, 67, 115, 173, 187
Christian, Shirley, 68, 115, 174
Cieply, Michael, 126
Claiborne, William, 174, 213
Clark, Lindley H. Jr., 16, 126, 145
Clark, Timothy, 101, 126

Clift, Eleanor, 104
Clines, Francis X., 174
Cockburn, Alexander, 40, 115, 264
Cockburn, Patrick, 175
Codevilla, Angelo M., 32, 87
Cody, Edward, 80, 175
Coffey, Shelby III, 13
Cohen, Richard, 41, 78, 79, 114, 231, 264
Cohen, Richard E., 244
Cohen, Roger, 176
Cohen, Sam, 176
Cole, Robert J., 126
Cook, James, 127
Coone, Tim, 176
Cooper, James C., 127
Corddry, Charles, 221
Cornwell, Rupert, 177
Corry, John, 44, 45
Couvalt, Craig, 20
Cowell, Alan, 22, 177
Cox, James, 109
Cronkite, Walter, 42
Crossette, Barbara, 69, 177
Crozier, Brian, 233
Cruz, Arturo Jr., 87
Cullen, Robert B., 91
Cullison, A.E., 27, 99, 115, 178
Curtius, Mary, 178
Cushman, John H. Jr., 33, 221

D

D'Anastasio, Mark, 76
D'Souza, Dinesh, 115, 265
Danguilan-Vitug, Marites, 179
Daniloff, Nicholas, 13, 79, 110, 179
Davidson, Ian, 222
De Borchgrave, Arnaud, 9, 111, 112
De Onis, Juan, 179
De Silva, Mervyn, 179
DeYoung, Karen, 180
Debes, Cheryl, 127

MediaGuide

Deibel, Terry L., 92
Deigh, Robb, 244
Dentzer, Susan, 244
Devory, Anne, 77
Dewar, Helen, 245
Diamond, Edwin, 245
Diamond, Stuart, 21, 245
Dickenson, James R., 246
Dickey, Christopher, 29, 30, 180
Diegmueller, Karen, 246
Diehl, Jackson, 180
Dillin, John, 246
Dionne, E.J. Jr., 35, 64, 68, 78, 114, 214, 247, 249
Doan, Michael, 179
Dobbs, Michael, 80, 115, 181
Doder, Dusko, 79
Donahue, Phil, 59
Donaldson, Sam, 58
Done, Kevin, 181
Donnelly, Richard A., 84
Donohoe, Cathryn, 38, 115, 247
Dowd, Anne Reilly, 127
Downie, Leonard Jr., 77
Drew, Elizabeth, 32, 38, 247
Drozdiak, William, 181
Duffy, Michael, 107
Dunn, Donald H., 128

E

Easterbrook, Gregg, 105
Echikson, William, 115, 182
Edsall, Thomas B., 39, 78, 115, 248
Ehrbar, Aloysius, 128
Einfrank, Aaron, 115, 182
Elfin, Mel, 104
Elliott, John, 182
England, Robert, 128
Engleberg, Steven, 222
Evans, Harold, 265, 278
Evans, Rowland, 16, 25, 27, 39, 78, 114, 136, 233

F

Fabrikant, Geraldine, 128
Fallows, James, 265
Farnsworth, Clyde, 129
Ferguson, Andrew, 81
Fialka, John, 21, 222
Fields, Suzanne, 36, 115, 266
Fineman, Howard, 248
Fineman, Mark, 25, 183
Fink, Donald, 20, 83, 223
Fisher, Anne B., 129
Fitzgerald, Mary, 183
Fleming, Stewart, 249
Flint, Jerry, 90, 115, 129
Fly, Richard, 130
Foldessy, Edward P., 130
Fontaine, Roger, 223
Forbes, Malcolm S. Jr., 4, 89, 130
Forbes, Malcolm S. Sr., 89
Forbes, Mary Lou, 111
Ford, Peter, 183
Forsyth, Randall, 84, 115, 130
Fossedal, Gregory, 33, 41, 81, 115, 266
Fox, Steve, 98
Francis, David R., 131
Frank, Allan Dodds, 131
Frank, Reuven, 47, 53
Frank, Richard S., 101
Frankel, Glenn, 184
Frankel, Max, 8, 9, 62-64, 66, 69
Franklin, William B., 132
Friedman, Thomas L., 68, 115, 184
Fuerbringer, Jonathan, 27, 132
Fung, Vigor, 76, 115, 184

G

Gailey, Phil, 249
Gall, Norman, 132
Gardner, David, 185
Gargan, Edward A., 67, 185
Garment, Suzanne, 266

Garvin, Glenn, 185
Gelb, Arthur, 20, 65
Gelb, Leslie H., 25, 63, 223, 225
Gelman, Eric, 133
Gergen, David, 12, 13, 109, 110
Germani, Carla, 186
Germond, Jack, 16, 233
Gerstenzang, James, 224
Gerth, Jeff, 18, 23, 220, 224
Gertz, William, 224
Getler, Michael, 77, 80
Getschow, George, 36
Geyer, Georgie Anne, 249
Giersch, Herbert, 88
Giradet, Edward, 186
Gladwell, Malcolm, 81, 133
Glassman, James K., 103, 115, 133
Gleckman, Howard, 26, 86, 133
Golden, Soma, 63
Goodman, Ellen, 267
Gordon, Michael, 29, 224
Goshko, John, 25
Graglia, Lino, 87
Graham, Bradley, 80, 186
Graham, Donald, 9, 77
Graham, Katharine, 9, 106, 112
Graham, Robert, 187
Graulich, David, 17, 18
Gray, Pat Bellew, 134
Greenberg, Nikki Finke, 105
Greenberg, Paul, 267
Greenberger, Robert, 31, 225
Greenfield, Meg, 78, 268
Greenhouse, Linda, 250
Greenhouse, Steven, 134
Gregory, William, 83, 223, 225
Grenier, Richard, 36, 112, 114, 268
Grossman, Lawrence, 60
Grunwald, Henry Anatole, 106, 108
Gupte, Pranay, 187
Gwertzman, Bernard, 21, 31, 114, 226

H

Haberman, Clyde, 67, 187, 207
Hall, Trish, 134
Hall, William, 135
Halloran, Richard, 226
Hallow, Ralph Z., 250
Hamilton, Joan O'C., 86, 135
Hampton, William J., 86, 135
Harden, Blaine, 80, 115, 188
Harries, Owen, 100
Harris, Anthony, 135
Harsch, Joseph, 234
Hartman, David, 90
Hector, Gary, 136
Hempstone, Smith, 234
Henderson, David, 102
Herman, Tom, 130, 136
Hershey, Robert D. Jr., 136
Hertzberg, Daniel, 136
Hertzberg, Hendrik, 136, 158
Hiatt, Fred, 226
Hieronymous, William, 39, 137
Hijazi, Ishan, 188
Himmelfarb, Joel, 97
Hitchens, Christopher, 234
Hoffman, David, 11, 31, 39, 250
Hoge, Warren, 66
Holusha, John, 137
Homan, Richard, 188
Honan, William, 66
Horowitz, Rose A., 137
House, Karen Elliott, 31, 227
Housego, David, 189
Huey, John, 137
Hughes, John, 235
Hughes, Thomas L., 92
Hume, Ellen, 251
Hunt, Albert, 73-75
Hyland, William G., 91

I

Ibrahim, Youssef, 75, 138
Ignatius, David, 79

MediaGuide 369

Irish, Jeffrey S., 36
Iyer, Pico, 189

J

Jacoby, Tamar, 91
James, Canute, 189
Jameson, Sam, 189
Jenkins, Loren, 190
Jenkins, Simon, 23
Jennings, Peter, 43, 44
Johnson, Haynes, 268
Jonas, Norman, 142
Jones, Clayton, 190

K

Kadlec, Daniel, 109
Kaiser, Robert G., 79, 91
Kaletsky, Anatole, 28, 138
Kamen, Al, 251
Kamm, Henry, 190
Kann, Peter R., 17, 18, 72
Karmin, Monroe, 138
Kates, Anne, 109
Kaufman, Michael T., 67, 191
Kaus, Mickey, 103
Kaylor, Robert, 191
Kempe, Frederick, 21, 25, 29, 34, 227, 229
Kemble, Penn, 87
Kestin, Hesh, 39, 139, 221
Kifner, John, 68, 191
Kilborn, Peter T., 10, 26, 27, 114, 139, 217
Kilgore, Bernard, 14, 15, 19, 97
Kilpatrick, James J., 78, 269
Kinsley, Michael, 10, 41, 95, 103, 114, 269
Kinzer, Stephen, 192
Kirkland, Richard I. Jr., 139
Kirkpatrick, Jeane J., 78, 86
Kirschten, Dick, 251
Klein, Edward, 65
Klose, Kevin, 252

Klott, Gary, 140
Kneale, Dennis, 140
Knight, Robin, 192
Koepp, Stephen, 140
Kondracke, Morton, 12, 103, 104, 235
Koretz, Gene, 140
Koselka, Rita, 141
Koten, John, 141
Kovach, William, 64
Kraar, Louis, 141
Kraft, Joseph, 9-11
Kramer, Michael, 29, 252
Kraus, Al, 99
Krauss, Clifford, 192
Krauthammer, Charles, 78, 100, 103, 270
Kristof, Nicholas D., 63, 115, 193
Kristol, Irving, 5, 41, 100, 115, 270, 274
Kronholz, June, 17, 25, 193
Kummer, Corby, 82
Kuttner, Robert, 27, 103
Kwitny, Jonathan, 37

L

Labich, Kenneth, 142
Laderman, Jeffrey M., 142
Lambro, Donald, 270
Lapham, Lewis, 95, 271
Lawrence, Richard, 142
Layne, Christopher, 92
Lee, Gary, 80, 193
Lee, Susan, 37, 90, 115, 142, 143
Lelyveld, Joseph, 66, 68, 194
Lemann, Nicholas, 252
LeMoyne, James, 194
Lenehan, Michael, 82
Lerner, Max, 32, 41, 271
Levin, Doron P., 143
Lewis, Anthony, 41, 63, 111, 114, 195, 235
Lewis, Flora, 63, 194
Lewis, I.A., 25

Lewis, Paul, 143
Liu, Melinda, 195
Loeb, Marshall, 13, 14, 89, 94
Lofton, John, 272
Lohr, Steve, 195
Long, William, 195
Loomis, Carol J., 143
Lopez, Laura, 196
Louis, Arthur M., 144
Luce, Henry, 13, 93

M

MacDougall, Colina, 196
MacLeod, Scott, 196
Mackenzie, Richard, 39, 253
Magnet, Myron, 144
Magnuson, Ed, 253
Mailer, Norman, 50
Main, Jeremy, 144
Malabre, Alfred L., 145
Mandelbaum, Michael, 91, 92
Mann, Jim, 196
Manning, Richard, 197
Mansfield, Stephanie, 36, 114, 253
Mapes, Glenn, 72
Markham, James, 197
Marsh, David, 197
Martin, Jurek, 27, 67, 88, 115, 197
Martin, Richard, 40, 114, 253
Mashek, John, 254
Masty, S.J., 272
Mathews, Jay, 254
Matusow, Barbara, 12
Mayer, Jane, 31, 254
Maynes, Charles William, 90, 93
McCarthy, Colman, 272
McCartney, Robert J., 198
McGinley, Laurie, 16, 20, 74
McGrory, Mary, 268, 272, 273
McGurn, William, 27
McLaughlin, John, 102, 236
McLeod, Don, 255
McManus, Doyle, 183

Meisels, Andrew, 198
Melcher, Richard A., 145
Merry, Robert, 75
Mervosh, Edward, 110, 146
Meyer, Cord, 236
Meyerson, Adam, 73
Michaels, James W., 89, 90
Miller, Arthur, 55
Miller, Judith, 29, 30, 64, 198
Miller, Matt, 76, 199
Mitchell, Cynthia F., 146
Moffett, Matt, 146
Mohr, Charles, 29, 33
Montalbano, William D., 199
Moore, Geoffrey, 99
Morgan, Jeremy, 200
Morrison, David, 227
Moyers, Bill, 57
Mufson, Steve, 23
Mullarky, Karen, 106
Mullin, Sue, 185
Muravchick, Joshua, 91
Murphy, Cullen, 82
Murray, Alan, 146
Murray, Charles, 81
Murrow, Edward R., 59
Mydans, Seth, 25, 68, 200

N

Nasar, Sylvia, 147
Nash, Nathaniel C., 147
Neilan, Ed, 200
Nenneman, Richard A., 147
Newton, Maxwell, 147
Nordland, Rod, 105, 201
Norman, James R., 86, 115, 148
Norman, Peter, 148
Norris, Floyd, 84
Norton, Christopher, 201
Novak, Michael, 273
Novak, Robert, 16, 25, 27, 39, 78, 103, 114, 136, 233
Nye, Joseph H., 91

MediaGuide

O

O'Boyle, Thomas C., 201
O'Brien, Conor Cruise, 82, 201
O'Leary, Jeremiah, 255
O'Leary, Timothy, 202
O'Neil, William J., 98
O'Reilly, Brian, 148
O'Rourke, P.J., 82
Oberfeld, Kirk, 7, 8
Omang, Joanne, 77
Oram, Roderick, 135
Orme, William, 27, 99, 202
Ostling, Richard, 255
Otnes, Fred, 82
Ottaway, David, 28
Otten, Alan, 15
Owen, Geoffrey, 88

P, Q

Parks, Michael, 202
Pear, Robert, 256
Pearlstine, Norman, 21, 70, 75
Peck, Seymour, 66
Pelikan, Jeri, 82
Pennar, Karen, 149
Peretz, Martin, 103
Perry, James, 203
Petre, Peter, 37, 115, 149
Phillips, Warren H., 70, 72
Pincus, Walter, 31, 33, 228
Pine, Art, 149
Pipes, Richard, 41, 87
Platt, Adam, 8, 40, 115, 256
Platt, Gordon, 149
Pleszczynski, Wladyslaw, 81
Podhoretz, Norman, 78, 86, 87, 103, 273
Pollack, Andrew, 63, 150
Pond, Elizabeth, 203
Potts, Mark, 80
Pouschine, Tatiana, 143
Powell, Bill, 105, 150, 241
Powers, Charles, 203
Prewett, Virginia, 256
Prokesch, Steven, 63, 114, 150
Pruden, Wesley, 236
Puddington, Arch, 81
Pura, Raphael, 76, 168, 204
Quinn, Jane Bryant, 150
Quinn, John C., 109
Quinn-Judge, Paul, 24, 115, 204
Quint, Michael, 130, 151

R

Rabinowitz, Dorothy, 274
Raines, Howell Jr., 64
Randal, Jonathan, 204
Randolph, Eleanor, 9, 256
Rapoport, Carla, 67, 88, 114, 205
Rasky, Susan, 151
Raspberry, William, 41, 79, 274
Rather, Dan, 43, 44, 52
Rauch, Jonathan, 27
Redburn, Tom, 151
Reed, Julia, 152
Reeves, Richard, 237
Reich, Robert, 64
Reinhold, Robert, 152
Reischauer, Edwin O., 65
Remnick, David, 257
Rensberger, Boyce, 19, 20
Reston, James, 9-11, 63, 237
Revzin, Philip, 205
Rich, Frank, 66
Richards, Bill, 221
Richburg, Keith, 206
Ricklefs, Roger, 75, 206
Riding, Alan, 69, 206
Riemer, Blanca, 27, 86, 115, 152
Riley, Barry, 152
Riley, Karen, 153
Robbins, Carla Anne, 153
Robbins, William, 257
Roberts, Steven V., 257
Robinson, Anthony, 22, 40, 88, 114, 207, 215
Rogers, David, 73, 257, 258

Rohter, Larry, 66, 208
Rosenbaum, David, 26, 37, 114, 140, 153
Rosenblatt, Roger, 275
Rosenfeld, Stephen F., 78, 237
Rosenthal, A.M., 8-11, 53, 62-66, 217, 241, 256
Rosenthal, Jack, 63
Rosewicz, Barbara, 75
Ross, Michael, 208
Rowan, Carl, 275
Rowan, Roy, 153
Rowen, Hobart, 10, 27, 115, 154, 217
Royster, Vermont, 14, 237
Rublin, Lauren R., 154
Ruby, Michael, 12, 13, 110
Rukeyser, William S., 13, 14, 94
Rule, Sheila, 208
Rupert, James, 40, 80, 114, 209
Rusher, William, 102
Russell, George, 108
Rutherford, Malcolm, 238
Ryan, Leo, 209
Ryskind, Allan, 96

S

Safer, Morley, 48
Safire, William, 30, 63, 238
Sagan, Carl, 91
Saikowski, Charlotte, 258
Samuelson, Robert, 275
Sanger, David E., 19, 36, 63, 114, 140, 154
Sapulkis, Agis, 154
Scarf, Margie, 82
Scherschel, Patricia, 155
Schmemann, Serge, 21, 66, 67, 115, 209
Schmertz, Herb, 276
Schneider, Stephen, 91
Schumacher, Edward, 29, 91, 210
Schwartz, Maralee, 78
Sciolino, Elaine, 228

Seabury, Jane, 155
Seib, Gerald, 17, 40, 75, 114, 210
Seligman, Daniel, 115, 276
Sellers, Valita, 36
Serrill, Michael, 210
Shenon, Philip, 228
Shepard, Stephen B., 85, 86
Sherman, Stratford, P., 115, 155
Sherrid, Pamela, 155
Sherwell, Chris, 211
Shields, Mark, 115, 239
Shipler, David, 28, 29, 258
Shribman, David, 75, 258
Sidey, Hugh, 239
Sieff, Martin, 115, 211
Silk, Leonard, 10, 156
Simon, Bernard, 211
Sindayen, Nelly, 108
Singer, Max, 87
Sloan, Allan, 37, 115, 156
Smith, Geoffrey, 156
Smith, Stephen, 12, 104
Smith, Richard M., 104
Smith, Wayne S., 92
Smith, William, 212
Sobran, Joseph, 104, 277
Southerland, Daniel, 252
Spaeth, Anthony, 17, 25, 40, 76, 212
Sparks, Allister, 22, 80, 213
Sperling, Godfrey Jr., 259
Sterba, James P., 213
Stern, Linda, 157
Stern, Richard, 157
Stevens, Charles W., 157
Stewart, James B., 28, 114, 158, 205
Stewart, William, 108
Stockton, William, 213
Stoppard, Tom, 49
Strobel, Warren, 33
Sullivan, John Fox, 101
Sullivan, Michael, 219
Sulzberger, Arthur Ochs, 9

MediaGuide 373

Summers, Col. H.G., 229
Suro, Roberto, 68, 214
Suzman, Helen, 22, 65
Swardson, Anne, 158
Symonds, William C., 37, 86, 158

T

Taber, George M., 106
Tagliabue, John, 159
Talbott, Strobe, 91, 107, 229
Tamayo, Juan, 214
Tanner, James B., 159
Taubman, Philip, 66, 214
Taylor, Paul, 11, 78, 225, 259
Taylor, Robert, 21
Taylor, Stuart Jr., 260
Taylor, Walter, 215
Temko, Edward (Ned), 22, 114, 215
Tenorio, Vyvyan, 215
Terry, Edith, 159
Thomas, Evan, 12, 105
Thomas, Rich, 27, 105, 115, 159
Thomas, Richard B., 106
Thompson, Starley, 91
Thomson, Robert, 215
Thurow, Roger, 216
Ticer, Scott, 160
Tolchin, Martin, 260
Tonelson, Alan, 92
Trachtenberg, Jeffrey A., 160
Treaster, Joseph, 216
Truell, Peter, 75, 115, 217
Tucker, Robert, 100
Tyler, Patrick, 260
Tyrrell, R. Emmett Jr., 78, 81, 82, 277

U

Urquhart, John, 160
Uttal, Bro, 160

V

Valery, Nicholas, 37, 114, 161
Van Atta, Dale, 95
Van Voorst, Bruce, 107, 253
Vigilante, Richard, 102
Vinocur, John, 9
Vise, David, 80, 161

W

Wade, Lawrence, 277
Walbert, Laura R., 156
Walcott, John, 17, 34, 74, 104, 229
Waldholz, Michael, 21, 35
Wallace, Mike, 59
Walsh, Mary Williams, 28, 75, 115, 163, 217
Wass, Murray, 103
Watson, Ripley Jr., 161
Wattenberg, Ben, 48
Weinraub, Bernard, 28, 33, 260
Weisman, Stephen, 68, 217
Welles, Chris, 161
Wermiel, Stephen, 27, 261
West, Diana, 261
West, Paul, 103
Weymouth, Lally, 112
Whitley, Andrew, 218
Whitney, Craig, 64, 66
Whitworth, William, 83
Wicker, Tom, 63, 240
Wildstrom, Stephen, 162
Wilkenson, Ray, 105
Will, George, 78, 268, 278
Williams, Dan B., 218
Williams, Winston, 38, 63, 162
Willoughby, Jack, 162
Winter, Thomas, 96, 97
Witcher, S. Karene, 15, 28, 163, 217
Witcover, Jules, 16, 233

Wolman, Clive, 163
Wolman, William, 85
Woodward, Bob, 30, 31, 230, 260
Worthy, Ford S., 163
Wysocki, Bernard Jr., 219

Y

Yoder, Edwin, 240
Younghusband, Peter, 22, 219

Z

Zuckerman, Mortimer, 13, 110, 278, 265

1986 POLYCONOMICS PAPERS ON THE WORLD POLITICAL ECONOMY

- ☐ "Gramm-Rudman: Trivia Pursuit," Jan. 24, 1986. $2
- ☐ "For Awhile, Clear Sailing," Feb. 3. $2
- ☐ "No More Recessions: A Scenario," Feb. 24. $2
- ☐ "The Philippine Election & Constitutional Crisis," Feb. 24. $3
- ☐ "At the Fed: All's Well That End's Well," Mar. 31. $2
- ☐ "The 'Cost of Capital' and Packwood's Bill," Apr. 1. $2
- ☐ "What the Global Bull Market is Trying to Tell Us," Apr. 23. $2
- ☐ "The Tokyo Summit: A Good Bet," Apr. 30. $2
- ☐ "Tax Reform: The Final Round," May 27. $2
- ☐ "May: A Great Month for JBIII," June 2. $2
- ☐ "The Case for Lower Interest Rates," June 19. $2
- ☐ "The World Economy Holds Us Back," July 21. $2
- ☐ "Deflation, Deficits and Debt: Separating Cause and Effect," July 31. $2
- ☐ "The Falling Interest Rate on Gold," Aug. 19. $2
- ☐ "A Trip to Northeast Asia," Sept. 9. $3
- ☐ "Temporary Setback to Monetary Reform," Sept. 30. $2
- ☐ "Reagan's Homestretch: Money and Star Wars," Oct. 10. $2
- ☐ "The Urgency of European Tax Reform," Oct. 22. $2
- ☐ "Three Myths for the New Year: Low Wages, Uncompetitive Manufacturing and Excess Debt," Dec. 16. $3
- ☐ "The Outlook for 1987," Jan. 6, 1987. $3
- ☐ "The 1986 MediaGuide," $9.95
- ☐ "The Way the World Works," by Jude Wanniski, 345 pp. $9.95

MediaGuide
Polyconomics, Inc.
86 Maple Avenue
Morristown, NJ 07960

Please send me copies of the material checked above.

Signature _____

Name _____
(Please Print)

Address _____

City _____ State _____ Zip Code _____